Great Speeches by Great Lawyers.

A COLLECTION

OF

ARGUMENTS AND SPEECHES

BEFORE COURTS AND JURIES.

BY EMINENT LAWYERS.

WITH

INTRODUCTORY NOTES, ANALYSES, ETC.

BY

WILLIAM L. SNYDER,
OF THE NEW YORK BAR.

Fred B. Rothman & Co.
LITTLETON, COLORADO
1981

Library of Congress Cataloging in Publication Data

Great speeches by great lawyers.

   Reprint. Originally published: New York : Baker,
Voorhis, 1881.
   Includes index.
   1. Forensic orations. 2. American orations.
3. English orations. I. Snyder, William Lamartine,
1848-1916.
K181.G73   1981   347'.075   81-13812
ISBN 0-8377-1118-5   342.775   AACR2

Great Speeches by Great Lawyers.

A COLLECTION

OF

ARGUMENTS AND SPEECHES

BEFORE COURTS AND JURIES.

BY EMINENT LAWYERS.

WITH

INTRODUCTORY NOTES, ANALYSES, ETC.

BY

WILLIAM L. SNYDER,

OF THE NEW YORK BAR.

NEW YORK:
BAKER, VOORHIS & CO., PUBLISHERS,
66 NASSAU STREET.
1881.

PREFACE.

THE object and design of this work is to preserve some of the best efforts of eminent lawyers, selecting those which have justly been regarded as models of legal reasoning and forensic power. The task is an exceedingly difficult one, in view of the fact that some of the most distinguished advocates have left but few traces of their intellectual labor. Their fame is often traditional; the recollections of their great efforts and high achievements fade in the near generations. The memory of the eloquence of Ogden Hoffman and David Graham lingers in the minds of a few living men, and in another decade will have been forgotten. What remains of the forensic utterances of Dexter and Otis; of John Adams, Joseph Hopkinson, Jared Ingersoll, Sargeant S. Prentiss, Robert Goodale Harper, Luther Martin, Edward D. Baker, Rufus Choate even, and a hundred others, whose names are familiar, who have graced the profession with their genius and learning? Whatever remains—in memoirs, in fugitive pamphlets, in reports of trials, or wherever found—it is our purpose to gather and preserve.

With this view, and believing that a collection of legal speeches and arguments, embracing topics upon various branches of the law, would be instructive and valuable, especially to the younger members of the profession, the publishers began many years ago to collect materials for this work. The original intention was to divide it into subjects corresponding with the main divisions of jurisprudence, and to illustrate each by the arguments and opinions of distinguished advocates and jurists. It was, however, found impracticable to pursue this plan, and it was finally determined to select the best efforts of eminent lawyers in this country and Great Britain and arrange them conveniently, with an analysis of each, and a full index to indicate the points of chief importance to the practitioner and student.

Much valuable information can be acquired from arguments upon which learned counsel have spent weeks and months of thought and labor, revealing, in some instances, the results of a lifetime of study and research—information of incalculable practical value to lawyers in the active practice of their profession. Great profit will also be derived from studying the plan which successful advocates have pursued in presenting a cause to the court or jury ; and the manner in which they have arranged and woven their materials, so as to persuade the will, excite the sympathies, or convince the judgment.

Care has been taken to give the speeches or arguments in full, omitting only detailed statements of evidence of no general interest, whenever such omission could be made without disturbing the plan and harmony of the argument.

The original purpose of the publishers was to make the work so full and complete, that they might with propriety call it a "Cyclopedia of Legal Eloquence, Argument, and Opinion." But whether they will be able to succeed in so ambitious an undertaking must depend upon the favor with which this volume is received. If it meets with the approval and support of the profession and the public, two additional volumes will be produced, which it is believed will be sufficient to properly present the design of the work. It is hoped that the book may be useful as a work of reference as well as a standard collection of legal eloquence.

On behalf of the publishers and myself, I cordially thank those gentlemen who have given access to their libraries and manuscripts during the preparation of this work, and for the kindly interest they have manifested in its success.

WILLIAM L. SNYDER.

New York, March, 1881.

CONTENTS.

APPENDIX.

INTRODUCTION.

THE history of human experience has shown that the individuals who have exerted the most potent influences in the world were those who possessed, in the most eminent degree, the supreme power of eloquence. The men who could *persuade* others have held, among civilized nations the highest places in the State, and gathered the honors and rewards which belong to an exalted station. The power which an orator possesses, touches the feelings and passions of the human heart, controls the will, and convinces the judgment. The proper solution, therefore, of the most important issues which have arisen, with respect to the fortunes of nations and of individuals, are the result of its exercise. According to the magnitude and consequence of the cause which he advocates, so will be the scope and extent of the advocate's power. This truth is embodied in the trite saying that "the pen is mightier than the sword." The pen indicates the powers of reason, the resources of the mind and intellect; the sword signifies physical force, and military authority. The former represents the object to be accomplished; the latter, the means of accomplishing that object and conducting it to a successful consummation.

Wars and revolutions are the agencies by which popular rights are established. Every great war, since time began, has contributed to some extent, either directly or indirectly, to the advancement and welfare of the commonwealth of man. The sword is the instrument by which revolution is accomplished; it is the means to an end. But it is the voice of the orator echoing the protest of the masses against vice and oppression, against bad government and bad laws, which arouses popular sentiment, puts armies in motion, and makes revolution possible. As men advance from the shadows of barbarism into the light of civilization; as savages become citizens, and, in the highest sense, reasonable creatures, they are influenced by reason and appeals to judgment, rather than by passion and a challenge to arms. Consequently, as the world grows older, it grows better, for the ballot is gradually usurping the functions of the bayonet, and what was at one time accomplished by the sword, is now more perfectly accomplished by the exercise of the suffrage. But the power behind the ballot is identical with the power behind the bayonet. The force of eloquence which incites men to fight, is the same force which influences them to vote.

Hence, it follows that the most distinguished names in history are those of the world's orators, rather than its generals. Many of the latter are associated with memories of splendid empire, arbitrary power, military despotism; the former with whatever charters, whatever laws, whatever institutions or customs exist to-day, by which the greatest measure of liberty is secured to the citizen, and the dearest and commonest rights guaranteed to the subject. The two most famous orators of antiquity were the greatest of advocates, and both were martyrs in the cause of popular government and universal citizenship. Their names will endure to the end of time; their influence will be felt to the remotest generation.

The truth of these general observations as to the influence of eloquence, none will deny. It will not be necessary, therefore, to pursue this branch of the subject further, by any attempt to illustrate it with examples from history. It will, doubtless, be conceded, that, in its most comprehensive sense, eloquence is the greatest power which it is possible to exercise upon the affairs of men.

The two important inquiries, then, which naturally suggest themselves in considering this topic are, can this power be acquired? and, if so, how can it be acquired? The lives of the great orators—some of the most distinguished of whom have been men of untiring energy and application—demonstrate that a man of fair talent and ability may, by dint of perseverance and study, become an accomplished speaker and successful advocate.

It is true he cannot expect to command that superb eloquence which springs from a mind originally endowed with the attributes of genius—wit, humor, poetic fancy, a dramatic emotional nature. There is, indeed, a kind of ideal eloquence, a superior display of intellectual power, accompanied by a sort of magnetism which thrills and excites, or charms and entrances—called forth suddenly, when affairs of public or individual concern have reached a climax—which is born of genius, and is the fruit of inspiration. It is defined perfectly by Mr. Webster, when he says: " True eloquence, indeed, does not consist in speech. It cannot be brought from far. Labor and learning may toil for it, but they will toil in vain.

Words and phrases may be marshalled in every way, but they cannot compass it. It must exist in the man, in the subject, and in the occasion. Affected passion, intense expression, the pomp of declamation, all may aspire to it; they cannot reach it. It comes, if it comes at all, like the outbreaking of a fountain from the earth, or the bursting forth of volcanic fires, with spontaneous, original, native force. The graces taught in the schools, the costly ornaments and studied contrivances of speech, shock and disgust men, when their own lives, and the fate of their wives, their children, and their country, hang on the decision of the hour. Then words have lost their power, rhetoric is vain, and all elaborate oratory contemptible. Even genius itself then feels rebuked and subdued, as in the presence of higher qualities. Then patriotism is eloquent; then self-devotion is eloquent. The clear conception, outrunning the deductions of logic; the high purpose, the firm resolve, the dauntless spirit, speaking on the tongue, beaming from the eye, informing every feature, and urging the whole man onward—right onward to his object—this, this is eloquence; or, rather, it is greater and higher than all eloquence—it is action, noble, sublime, godlike action!"

It is true, that, to be an ideal orator, one must possess the best faculties and rarest gifts which it is possible for nature to bestow; elements not taught in books, and which cannot be acquired. The profession of the advocate embraces a science, universal in its application, " which," in the elegant language of Sir William Blackstone, " distinguishes the criterions of right and wrong; which teaches to establish the one, and prevent, punish, and redress the other; which employs in its theory the noblest faculties of the soul, and exerts in its practice the cardinal virtues of the heart; a science which is universal in its extent, accommodated to each individual, yet comprehending the whole community." In the exercise of his powers, therefore, the orator and advocate will be called upon to touch the feelings, passions, and sympathies, and appeal to every impulse within the circle of human experience. To reach the ideal standard, an orator must be many-sided, and combine within himself every great mental quality—a vigorous understanding and tenacious memory, wit, judgment, imagination, a knowledge of human nature, enthusiasm, self-possession, dramatic power, moral courage, a strong will, and native energy. He should possess, also, certain physical gifts—a clear voice, and sturdy frame. To become a great jury lawyer, many of the characteristics named are essential, especially the power to read human nature. But it is indeed seldom that all these rare qualifications are bestowed upon a single individual. In a majority of instances, men who have possessed but few of these gifts, have risen to the highest walks of the profession. A man of genius, who possesses industry, and the will, never fails to be great, in accordance with the measure of his opportunities. Genius and industry, united, accomplish all things ; genius divorced from industry, seldom accomplishes anything.

Yet it is possible for a man of vigorous mind and strong will to become an impressive and convincing speaker, and even to achieve distinction and acquire fame as an advocate, without being an ideal orator; for, at the forum, knowledge is a commanding and controlling power, and in its most practical sense, knowledge is not a gift; it comes not by inspiration or intuition—it must be acquired. In this view of the subject, eloquence may safely be said to be an art which may be attained by any person possessing fair talent and ability, who may choose to devote sufficient time and labor for its acquisition.

The first requisite in order to become an advocate, is to get a practical, thorough knowledge of the subjects which he will be called upon to discuss. To a certain point, there is no difference in the line of preparation and study to be pursued, whether the orator is training for the senate or the forum ; whether it is desired to excel in parliamentary or forensic eloquence ; as an advocate or a statesman. Both must possess in the main the same kind of knowledge, since it is the purpose of both—and the object of eloquence always is—to persuade and convince. The uses, also, to which this common knowledge is put are often analogous; and the questions which each are called upon to discuss in their several departments, frequently grow out of the same general principles of equity and public policy. The popular representative has his country and his constituents for his clients, while the advocate has confided to his trust the interests of an individual. The duty of the former is to frame laws ; the duty of the latter to maintain them, punish infractions and violations thereof, secure to the citizen their benefit and protection, and prevent deprivation of life, liberty or property without due process of law.

Certain kinds of information and particular branches of study, relating mainly to constitutional and philosophical history, are essential, whether the field of labor is the senate or the forum. But the advocate, in order to excel in his profession, must master, in addition, the elementary and fundamental principles upon which the great body of the common law rests ; and these, though comparatively few, require years of application to thoroughly acquire, since they constitute the groundwork and foundation of all legal science. This technical knowledge may, for convenience, be classified as follows : (1) the law of crimes, or criminal jurisprudence ; (2) the system of equity jurisprudence, akin to, and founded upon the law of ethics and moral philosophy ; (3) the principles regulating the law of contracts; (4) the philosophy of the law as to liability and damages for injuries, independent of contracts, growing out of the negligence and carelessness of individuals—willful and malicious acts whereby another is injured in his good name, health, reputation, or property rights—designated as the law of torts; (5) the principles and history of the law of real property. In addition to these, a thorough acquaintance with the law of evidence is absolutely essential. The advocate must be able to bring out all the facts which are to be woven into his appeal to the jury. The testimony must be elicited in a skillful manner, and frequently the truth must be developed from the lips of hostile and unwilling witnesses.

He should, in addition, possess information upon general subjects. The fine arts, polite literature, poetry, music, painting, and sculpture, should be studied and made to contribute to the common stock of knowledge. An advocate will find occasion to use all he knows in a variety of ways. The minds of men are as varied as the tints in the clouds, and if the advocate is familiar with the subject, a fair knowledge of human nature will indicate what to say upon a particular branch of the discussion, in order to remove prejudices and inspire confidence. From a mind filled with classic imagery and poetic pictures, drop, almost unconsciously, tropes and metaphors which fix the thought, rivet the attention, and lend a pleasing charm to the speaker's style. Examples of the modest and effective use of metaphor will be found in many of the arguments and speeches in this volume. In this respect the style of Mr. Prentiss may be studied with profit.

In order, then, to become a great advocate, industry and perseverance are essential. No one about entering upon the duties of his profession should fall into the error that he can depend upon genius alone and succeed. The lawyer that leans only upon genius, in this day and age, leans upon a slender reed ; for without application and industry it is impossible even for one possessing a delicate fancy, a fervid imagination, and fluency of speech, to excel as an orator and an advocate. As well might he attempt to pierce its disc by shooting feathers at the sun. His very fluency might lead him into blunders which would render his position ridiculous. He must acquire knowledge, and a perusal of these pages will show how much it is necessary for him to acquire.

There are many instances in which a rich vocabulary, in itself extraordinary, has been improved by cultivation, and developed to a very remarkable degree. But after all "knowledge is power." Back of the vocabulary there must be knowledge. Genius must have materials to work upon ; and knowledge can only be acquired by laborious study and close application. The old maxim holds good in this respect, that there is no excellence without great labor. The degree and excellence of professional success are commensurate with the industry and diligence of the individual. The triumphs of the forum are the reward and result of unceasing application. Contemplation of the difficulties mastered and overcome by those who figure in history as men of genius, inspires wonder and admiration.

The Athenian, universally regarded as the first and greatest advocate and orator who has lived, had to overcome an impediment in his speech, an obstacle which lay at the threshold of his ambition ; one which would have discouraged and disheartened ordinary men, since it was an infirmity which forbade the very use of language and the power of articulation. He was laughed down ; in his first attempts he stammered, hesitated, and failed. But he persevered until he attained the summit of human excellence. The secret of the power of the Roman orator was arduous devotion to study, and Middleton says that " his industry was incredible, beyond the example or even conception of our days." Sheridan failed in his maiden speech in Parliament, and was advised by Woodfall to keep to his line as a dramatist ; but the advice was met with the vehement declaration, " It is in me, and it shall come out of me." But Sheridan, bright and gifted as he was, only succeeded by careful and elaborate preparation and study. Fox, " the most brilliant and accomplished debater the world ever knew," only became such by degrees, through toil and difficulty. Lord Mansfield studied eloquence all his life, and often practiced his manner and gestures before a glass. Lord Sommers went to the front in a five-minute speech at the trial of the Seven Bishops, but in that successful effort was condensed all the learning on the subject—the fruits of a lifetime of professional study.   Curran, who stood next to Erskine as a jury lawyer, was known at school as "Stuttering Jack."   When Disraeli was laughed down, and his scream of disappointment, " the time will come when you *shall* hear me," could scarcely be heard above the derisive laughter his failure had provoked, who dreamed that his talent, energy, and perseverance would one day make him Prime Minister of the British Empire, wearing the title of Earl of Beaconsfield.   William Pinkney let out the secret in open court once, when he told the judges that his opinion on the question in controversy had not been hastily formed since the commencement of the trial; " it is," he said, " the result of a deliberate examination of all the authorities, of a thorough investigation of the law in all its forms, made at leisure, and under a deep sense of a fearful responsibility to my client."   Yet no man ever sought, with more care and ingenuity, to convey the impression that he never studied, than William Pinkney.   Rufus Choate was a great worker.   He labored incessantly, and, like Henry Clay, practiced elocution daily, it is said, for a period of more than forty years.

Other examples, almost without number, could be given.   We might enumerate the names of famous men who have attracted the world's attention at the forum and in the senate, and the stories of their lives would be all alike in this, that toil and application are the price of success ; and that eloquence, after all, in its practical sense, is an art, which may be acquired by any person possessing fair talent and ability who may choose to devote sufficient time and labor for its acquisition.

If there are any exceptions to this rule they are rare indeed. Where is there an example of an advocate or an orator who was carried to the summit of earthly ambition through the sheer force of his genius?   There is one great name, which is perhaps regarded as within the exception—the famous orator of Virginia, and powerful advocate of the American Revolution—Patrick Henry.   A perusal of his argument, however, in Jones *v.* Walker, given in this work, will go far to prove that even this wonderful man is within the rule, not the exception.   If we can trust his biographer, he was good for nothing but an orator.   The idea of ever making a successful merchant of him provokes a smile, while to the acquaintances of his early manhood the mere proposition that he might perhaps become an advocate and an orator would have occasioned even greater surprise. He was indeed a child of Nature. He despised the school room, and, when opportunity offered, would wander off, with rod and gun, among the woods and hills. He loved Nature—the clouds, the forest, all that makes the landscape. The supposition that he would ever become a distinguished advocate, and the greatest orator of his age, exerting an influence against the British king equal to that of John Adams, would have been regarded by his friends as an extravagant chimera. He did not commence the study of law until after he was married and settled, and had thrice failed in mercantile and agricultural pursuits. But the fact remains that his mind was stored with knowledge which could be acquired only by study and application; and his argument upon the right to confiscate "British debts," is entirely inconsistent with the theory that he was indifferent as to professional learning and acquirements.

The secret, then, of this wonderful art, which has exerted such an influence, and is so universally desired, consists in two simple propositions—knowing what to say, and how to say it. Knowledge of the subjects to be discussed is the first requisite; an acquaintance with practical rules of rhetoric, is the second. The latter study is necessary, and its importance should not be underrated ; but the student might read all the works that have been written upon it from Aristotle to Whately, and from Whately to the present time, and yet fail in his purpose. Hume comes nearest the truth when he says that eloquence can only be taught by *examples*. These are spread before the reader in the following pages, and among them will be found some of the best models in the range of legal eloquence. A study of them will show, in every instance, that clear statement is an essential feature, accompanied by an exposition of elementary principles applied to the facts—the whole modestly and gracefully adorned with the beauties of rhetoric.

W. L. S.

ARGUMENTS AND SPEECHES

BEFORE COURTS AND JURIES.

ARGUMENT OF PATRICK HENRY,

On the Right of a State, during the Revolution, to Confiscate British Debts.

[Jones *v.* Walker, 2 Paine.]

AT A CIRCUIT COURT OF THE UNITED STATES, HELD AT RICHMOND, VA., NOVEMBER TERM, 1791.

Analysis of Mr. Henry's Argument.

1. Debts a subject of forfeiture in common war.
2. Hostile nations have the right to remit to its citizens debts due the enemy.
3. Extent to which a sovereign, in time of war, is justified in confiscating debts.
4. Grotius and Vattel on the subject of confiscation.
5. Effect of the revolution on British debts. Greatness of America.
6. The law of custom only binding on nations adopting it.
7. The law of custom prevailing in Europe not binding in America.
8. America an independent nation long prior to 1783.
9. The acts of confiscation warranted by necessity.
10. Distinction between common war and revolution.
11. Picture of the horrors of the American revolution.
12. England, by withdrawing her protection, destroyed title in all property.
13. The issuing of paper money by the colonies compelled by necessity.
14. Contracts dissolved without the consent of the king of Great Britain.
15. Consequences which would have resulted had England conquered America.
16. In a state of nature, municipal rights and obligations are dissolved.
17. Debts, like other property, subject to forfeiture.
18. Effect of the payment of paper currency to the loan office.
19. Application of the law of salvage.
20. Defendant's debt did not exist when the treaty of peace was signed.
21. Plaintiff must show full compliance with the treaty.
22. Power of interpretation of treaties in the courts.
23. A chose in action a subject of forfeiture.

The argument of Mr. Henry in the great case of "The British Debts," is regarded by his biographer as presenting the most distinguished display of the professional talents of the famous Virginia orator and patriot. The controversy involved the honor of his native commonwealth, and the question as to limitations of her sovereign power was brought before the court for review. When Virginia became an independent State, owing no longer allegiance to the mother country, could she exercise the absolute power which inheres in every sovereignty, and confiscate the debts of her enemies, or was the treaty made between the United States and Great Britain, at the close of the revolution, declaring that there should not be any lawful impediment in the collection of British debts, the supreme law? The case arose upon the following facts:

Dr. Thomas Walker, in the county of Albemarle, in the colony of Virginia, prior to the American revolution, on the 11th day of May, 1772, executed, under his hand and seal, a bond to the mercantile house of Farrell & Jones, British subjects, for £2,903, 15s. 8d. sterling. After the close of the revolution, in 1791, William Jones, as surviving partner of the firm of Farrell & Jones, brought suit in the United States Circuit Court, at Richmond, Va., to recover the amount due on the bond. A brief synopsis of the pleadings will enable the reader to thoroughly comprehend the questions discussed.

There were five pleas interposed to the declaration, as follows : (1) First, payment, upon which issue was joined. (2) Second, that an act of the legislature passed during the revolution, October 20, 1777, made it lawful for a citizen of the commonwealth, owing money to a subject of Great Britain, to pay the same, or any part thereof, from time to time, into the loan office of the State, and take a certificate for the same in the name of the creditor, which receipt should *discharge* him from so much of the debt; and exhibiting a certificate for $7,173 (£2,151, 18s.) in bar of so much of plaintiff's demand. (3) Third, that the debt had escheated to the State, under an act of Assembly, passed May 3d, 1779, declaring "that all the property, real and personal, within the commonwealth, belonging at that time to any British subject, should be deemed to be vested in the commonwealth;" and further, that a demand for its recovery was barred by the act of May 6th, 1782, declaring " that no demand whatsoever, originally due to a subject of Great Britain, should be recoverable in any court of this commonwealth." (4) Fourth, that the king of Great Britain and his subjects were still alien enemies, and that the state of war still continued, on the ground of the several direct violations of the definite treaty of peace, which follows : 1. In continuing to carry off the negroes in his possession, the property of American citizens, and refusing to deliver them, or permit the owners to take them, according to the express stipulations of that treaty; 2. In the forcible retention of the forts Niagara and Detroit, and the adjacent territory; 3. In supplying the Indians, who were at war with the United States, with arms and ammunition, furnished within the territories of the United States, to wit, at the forts Detroit and Niagara, and at other forts and stations forcibly held by the troops and armies of the king within the United States; and in purchasing from the Indians, within the territories aforesaid, the plunder taken by them in war from the United States, and the persons of American citizens made prisoners; which several infractions, the plea contends, had abolished the treaty of peace and placed Great Britain and the United States in a state of war ; and that hence the plaintiff, being an alien enemy, had no right to sue in the courts of the United States. (5) Fifth, that the debt was extinguished and annulled by a dissolution of the British government in this country, on the 4th of July, 1776.

The plaintiff replied to the second plea, insisting on the treaty of peace of 1783, whereby it was stipulated that creditors on either side should meet with no lawful impediment to the recovery of *bona fide* debts theretofore contracted, and also the Constitution of the United States declaring treaties then made, or which should thereafter be made, to be the supreme law of the land, anything in the Constitution or laws of any State to the contrary notwithstanding. The defendant rejoined, that the treaty had been annulled by violations of it on the part of Great Britain; and, further, that the debt was not within the treaty, inasmuch as it had been discharged (or at least £2,151, 8s. of it) by payment to the loan office of the State of Virginia. Plaintiff demurred to the rejoinder, and to the third, fourth and fifth pleas, which brought the following questions squarely before the court. First.—Was the debt annulled by the dissolution of the government which existed when the debt was contracted ? Second.—When Virginia became a sovereign State, on the 4th of July, 1776, had she the power and authority to confiscate British debts and sequestrate British property ? Third.—Was the debt revived by the treaty of peace of 1783 between the United States and Great Britain, whereby it was stipulated that creditors on either side should meet with no lawful impediment in the recovery of all *bona fide* debts previously contracted? Fourth.—Could a British subject derive benefit under a treaty which had been violated on several distinct occasions by the British king ?

Mr. Henry discussed these issues with eminent learning, skill and ingenuity, and in a manner so eloquent as to give it rank among the great legal arguments, and one which, in some respects, has not been surpassed at the judicial forum. He established first the proposition, that since debts were property subject to confiscation in common wars, arising upon the slightest imaginary pretexts, or invoked through selfishness solely for conquest and empire, *a fortiori* were they subject to forfeiture in a revolution " commenced in attainder, perfidy and confiscation." That when Virginia became an independent State by virtue of Jefferson's immortal declaration, she was immediately clothed with power to exercise the right of eminent domain, and to take to herself the debts of her enemies; and having exercised this right, the debt was discharged and extinguished, and beyond the purview of the treaty of peace, and could not, therefore, be revived thereby. That, even if the treaty could operate upon the debt, no British subject could take advantage of it, because the British government had violated its terms, and thereby annulled its provisions. It was a great argument, and attracted wide-spread attention. Mr. Henry occupied three days in its delivery, and Mr. Wirt says, that during that time the court-room was crowded to its utmost capacity, and that there could not be got together a quorum of the legislature then in session at Richmond. Legislators, Senators, ladies of fashion, everybody crowded to the court-room to listen to the stirring eloquence of one of the greatest of living orators.

The case was argued twice: in 1791 before Judges Johnson and Blair of the Supreme Court, and Griffin, judge of the district, and again, in 1793, before Judges Jay, Iredell, and the same district judge. The case was decided against Mr. Henry, in favor of the English creditor. (2 Paine's C. Ct. Rep. p. 688.) The argument given here was made upon the first hearing, and is taken from Mr. Wirt's life of Patrick Henry. That gentleman tells us that it is from Mr. Robertson's stenographic notes, from which an imperfect analysis was made, though the report, he says, may unquestionably be relied on, so far as it professes to state the principles of law and the substance of the argument; but, as a sample of eloquence it is subject to all the objections urged to the printed debates of the Virginia Convention.

The following eminent gentlemen took part in the argument: for the plaintiff, Mr. Ronald, Mr. Baker, Mr. Wickham, and Mr. Starke ; for the defendant, Mr. Henry, Mr. Marshall (afterwards Chief Justice of the United States), Mr. Alexander Campbell, and Mr. Innis, the attorney-general of Virginia. Mr. Henry said :

MAY IT PLEASE YOUR HONORS:—I stand here to support, according to my power, that side of the question which respects the American debtor. I beg leave to beseech the patience of this honorable court, because the subject is very great and important, and because I have not only the greatness of the subject to consider, but those numerous observations which have come from the opposing counsel to answer. Thus, therefore, the matter proper for my discussion is unavoidably accumulated. Sir, there is a circumstance in this case that is more to be deplored than that which I have just mentioned, and that is this: those animosities which the injustice of the British nation hath produced, and which I had well hoped would never again be the subject of discussion, are necessarily brought forth. The conduct of that nation which bore so hard upon us in the late contest, becomes once more the subject of investigation. I know, sir, how well it becomes a liberal man and a Christian to forget and to forgive. As individuals professing a holy religion, it is our bounden duty to forgive injuries done us as individuals. But when to the character of Christian you add the character of a patriot, you are in a different situation. Our mild and holy system of religion inculcates an admirable maxim of forbearance. If your enemy smite one cheek, turn the other to him. But you must stop there. You cannot apply this to your country. As members of a social community, this maxim does not apply to you. When you consider injuries done to your country, your political duty tells you of vengeance. Forgive as a private man, but never forgive public injuries. Observations of this nature are exceedingly unpleasant, but it is my duty to use them.

1. DEBTS A SUBJECT OF FORFEITURE IN COMMON WAR.

The first point which I shall endeavor to establish will be, that debts in common wars become subject to forfeiture; and if forfeited in common wars, much more must they be so in a revolution war, as the late contest was. In considering this subject, it will be necessary to define what a debt is. I mean by it an engagement or promise by one man to pay another for a valuable consideration an adequate price. By a contract thus made for a valuable consideration, there arises what, in the law phrase, is called a *lien* on the body and goods of the promisor or debtor. This interest, which the creditor becomes entitled to in the goods and body of his debtor, is such as may be taken from the creditor, if he be found the subject of a hostile country. This position is supported by the following authorities:

Here Mr. Henry cited copious extracts from Grotius and Vattel, which seemed to support his position. He then proceeded :

This authority decides, in a most clear and satisfactory manner, that, as a nation, we had powers as extensive and unlimited as any nation on earth. This great writer, after stating the equality and independence of nations, and who are and who are not enemies, does away the distinction between corporeal and incorporeal rights, and declares that war gives the same right over the debts as over the other goods of an enemy. He illustrates his doctrine by the instance of Alexander's remitting to the Thessalians a debt due by them to the Theban commonwealth. This is a case in point; for supposing the subjects of Alexander had been indebted to the Thebans, might he not have remitted the debts due by them to that people, as well as the debts due them by his allies, the Thessalians ? Let me not be told that he was entitled to the goods of the Thebans because he had conquered them. If he could remit a debt due by those whose claim of friendship was so inferior, those who were only attached to him by the feeble ties of contingent and temporary alliance; if his Macedonians, his immediate and natural subjects, were indebted to the Thebans, could he not have remitted their debts ?

2. Hostile nations have the right to remit to its citizens debts due the enemy.

This author states, in clear, unequivocal terms, by fair inference and unavoidable deduction, that when two nations are at war, either nation has a right, according to the laws of nature and nations, to remit to its own citizens debts which they may owe to the enemy. If this point wanted further elucidation, it is pointedly proved by the authority which I first quoted from Grotius, that it is an inseparable concomitant of sovereign power, that debts and contracts similar to those which existed in America at the time the war with Great Britain broke out, may, in virtue of the eminent domain or right, be cancelled and destroyed. "A king has a greater right in the goods of his subjects for the public advantage than the proprietors themselves. And when the exigency of the State requires a supply, every man is more obliged to contribute toward it than to satisfy his creditors. The sovereign may discharge a debtor

from the obligation of paying, either for a certain time or forever."
What language can be more expressive than this? Can the mind
of man conceive anything more comprehensive? Rights are of
two sorts: private and inferior, or eminent and superior, such as the
community hold over the persons and estates of its members for
the common benefit. The latter is paramount to the former. A
king or chief of a nation has a greater right, than the owner himself, over any property in the nation. The individual who owns
private property cannot dispose of it, contrary to the will of his sovereign, to injure the public. This author is known to be no advocate for tyranny, yet he mentions that a king has a superior power
over the property in his nation, and that, by virtue thereof, he may
discharge his subjects forever from debts which they owe to an
enemy.

3. EXTENT TO WHICH A SOVEREIGN, IN TIME OF WAR, IS JUSTI-
FIED IN CONFISCATING DEBTS.

The instance which our author derives from the Roman history
affords a striking instance of the length to which the necessities
and exigencies of a nation will warrant it to go. It was a juncture
critical to the Roman affairs. But their situation was not more
critical or dangerous than ours at the time these debts were confiscated. It was after the total defeat and dreadful slaughter at
Cannæ, when the State was in the most imminent danger. Our
situation in the late war was equally perilous. Every consideration
must give way to the public safety. That admirable Roman maxim,
salus populi suprema lex, governed that people in every emergency.
It is a maxim that ought to govern every community. It was not
peculiar to the Roman people. The impression came from the
same source from which we derive our existence. Self-preservation, that great dictate implanted in us by nature, must regulate
our conduct; we must have a power to act according to our necessities, and it remains for human judgment to decide what are the
proper occasions for the exercise of this power. Call to your recollection our situation during the late arduous contest. Was it
not necessary in our day of trial to go to the last iota of human
right? The Romans fought for their altars and household gods.
By these terms they meant everything dear and valuable to men.
Was not our stake as important as theirs? But many other nations
engage in the most bloody wars for the most trivial and frivolous

causes. If other nations who carried on wars for the mere point of honor, or a punctilio of gallantry, were warranted in the exercise of this power, were not we who fought for everything most inestimable and valuable to mankind, justified in using it? Our finances were in a more distressing situation than theirs at this awful period of our existence. Our war was in opposition to the most grievous oppression; we resisted, and our resistance was approved and blessed by heaven. The most illustrious men who have considered human affairs, when they have revolved human rights and considered how far a nation is warranted to act in cases of emergency, declare that the only ingredient essential to the rectitude and validity of its measures is, that they be for the public good. I need hardly observe that the confiscation of these debts was for the public good.

4. Grotius and Vattel on the subject of confiscation.

Those who decided it were constitutionally enabled to determine it. Grotius shows that you have not only power over the goods of your enemies, but, according to the exigency of affairs, you may seize the property of your citizens.

After reading a passage from Grotius to sustain this proposition, he continued:

I read these authorities to prove that the property of an enemy is liable to forfeiture, and that debts are as much the subject of hostile contests as tangible property. And Vattel, p. 484, as before mentioned, pointedly enumerates rights and debts among such property of the enemy as is liable to confiscation. To this last author I must frequently resort in the course of my argument. I put great confidence in him from the weight of his authority, for he is universally respected by all the wise and enlightened of mankind, being no less celebrated for his great judgment and knowledge than for his universal philanthropy. One of his first principles of the law of nations is, a perfect equality of rights among nations; that each nation ought to be left in the peaceable enjoyment of that liberty it has derived from nature. I refer your honors to his preliminary discourse from 6th to the 12th page; and as it will greatly elucidate the subject and tend to prove the position I have attempted to support, I will read sections 17, 18, 19 and 20 of this discourse.

Here Mr. Henry read the sections referred to. He then continued:

5. EFFECT OF THE REVOLUTION ON BRITISH DEBTS.—GREATNESS OF AMERICA.

When the war commenced, these things, called British debts, lost their quality of external obligation and became matters of internal obligation, because the creditors had no right of constraint over the debtors. They were before the war matters of perfect external obligation, accompanied by a right of constraint; but the war having taken away this right of constraint over the debtors, they were changed into an internal obligation binding the conscience only. For it will not surely be denied that the creditor lost the right of constraint over his debtor.

From the authority of this respectable author, therefore, from the clearest principles of the laws of nature and nations, these debts became subject to forfeiture or remission. Those authors state, in language as emphatic and nervous as the human mind can conceive or the human tongue can utter, that independent nations have the power of confiscating the property of their enemies; and so had this gallant nation. America, being a sovereign and complete nation in all its forms and departments, possessed all the rights of the most powerful and ancient nations. Respecting the power of legislation, it was a nation complete and without human control. Respecting public justice, it was a nation blessed by heaven, with the experience of past times; not like those nations whose crude systems of jurisprudence originated in the ages of barbarity and ignorance of human rights. America was a sovereign nation when her sons stepped forth to resist the unjust hand of oppression and declared themselves independent. The consent of Great Britain was not necessary (as the gentlemen on the other side urge) to create us a nation. Yes, sir, we were a nation long before the monarch of that little island in the Atlantic ocean gave his puny assent to it. America was long before that time a great and gallant nation. In the estimation of other nations we were so; the beneficent hand of heaven enabled her to triumph and secured to her the most sacred rights mortals can enjoy. When these illustrious authors, these friends to human nature, these kind instructors of human errors and frailties [1] contemplate the obligations and corresponding rights of nations, and define the internal right which is without constraint and not binding, do they not understand such rights as these which the British creditors now claim?

[1] In the second argument, he eulogized the writers on the laws of nations, as "benevolent spirits who held up the torch of science to a benighted world."

Here this man tells us what conscience says ought to be done, and what is compulsory. These British debts must come within the grasp of human power, like all other human things. They ceased to have that external quality, and fell into that mass of power which belonged to our legislature by the law of nations.

6. THE LAW OF CUSTOM ONLY BINDING ON NATIONS ADOPTING IT.

But we are told that, admitting this to be true in the fullest latitude, yet the customary law of Europe is against the exercise of this power of confiscation of debts, in support of which position they rely on what is added by Vattel, p. 484. Let us examine what he says: "The sovereign has naturally the same right over what his subjects may be indebted to enemies; therefore he may confiscate debts of this nature if the term of payment happen in the time of war, or at least he may prohibit his subjects from paying while the war lasts. But at present, in regard to the advantage and safety of commerce, all the sovereigns of Europe have departed from this rigor. And as this custom has generally been received, he who should act contrary to it would injure the public faith; for strangers trusted his subjects only from a firm persuasion that the general custom would be observed." Excellent man! and excellent sentiments! The principle cannot be denied to be good; but when you apply it to the case before the court, does it warrant their conclusions? The author says, that although a nation has a right to confiscate debts due by its people to an enemy, yet at present the custom of Europe is contrary. It is not enough for this author to tell us that this custom is contrary to the right. He admits the right. Let us see whether this custom has existence here. Vattel, having spoken of the necessary law of nations, which is immutable, and the obligations whereof are indispensable, thus proceeds to distinguish the several other kinds of natural law in the same preliminary discourse:

"Certain maxims and customs consecrated by long use, and observed by nations between each other as a kind of law, form this customary law of nations, or the custom of nations. This law is founded on a tacit consent, or, if you will, on a tacit convention of the nations that observe it, with respect to each other. Whence it appears that it is only binding to those nations that have adopted it, and that is not universal, any more than conventional laws. It must be here also observed of this customary law, that the particulars relating to it do not belong to a systematic treatise on the law of nations, but that we ought to confine ourselves to the giving a general theory of it, that is, to the rules which here ought to be

observed, as well with respect to its effects as in relation to the
matter itself; and in this last respect these rules will serve to distinguish the lawful and innocent customs from those that are unjust and illegal !

"When a custom is generally established, either between all the
polite nations in the world, or only between those of a certain continent, as of Europe for example, or those who have a more frequent correspondence; if that custom is in its own nature indifferent, and, much more, if it be a wise and useful one, it ought to be
obligatory on all those nations who are considered as having given
their consent to it. And they are bound to observe it, with respect
to each other, while they have not expressly declared that they will
not adhere to it. But if that custom contains anything unjust or
illegal, it is of no force, and every nation is under an obligation to
abandon it, nothing being able to oblige or permit a nation to violate a natural law.

"These three kinds of the law of nations, voluntary, conventional and customary, together, compose the positive law of nations;
for they all proceed from the volition of nations: the voluntary
law from their presumed consent, the conventional law from an
express consent, and the customary law from a tacit consent; and
as there can be no other manner of deducing any law from the will
of nations, there are only these three kinds of the positive law of
nations." [1]

This excellent author, after having stated the voluntary law of
nations to be the result of the equality of nations, and the conventional law to be particular compacts or treaties, binding only on
the contracting parties, declares that the customary law of nations
is only binding to those nations that have adopted it; that it is a
particular and not a universal law; that it applies only to distinct
nations. The case of Alexander and the Thebans is founded on
the general law of nations, applicable to nations at war. It is
enough for me, then, to show that America, being at war, was entitled to the privilege of national law.

7. THE LAW OF CUSTOM PREVAILING IN EUROPE NOT BINDING
IN AMERICA.

But, says Vattel, the present state of European refinement controls the general law, of which he had been before speaking. We
know that the customary law of nations can only bind those who
are parties to the custom. In the year 1776, when America announced her will to be free, or in the year 1777, when the law concerning British debts passed, was there a customary law of America

[1] Vattel, pp. 11 and 12.

to this effect ?   Or were the customary laws of Europe binding on America ?   Were we a party to any such customary law ?   Was there anything in our Constitution or laws which tied up our hands ?   No, sir.   To make this customary law obligatory, the assent of all the parties to be bound by it is necessary.   There must be an interchange of it.   It is not for one nation or community to say to another, you are bound by this law, because our kingdom approves of it.   It must not only be reciprocal in its advantages and principles, but it must have been reciprocal in its exercise.   Virginia could not, therefore, be bound by it.   Let us see whether it could be a hard case on the British creditors that this customary law of nations did not apply in their favor.   Were these debts contracted from a persuasion of its observance ?   Did the creditors trust to this customary law of nations ?   No, sir; they trusted to what they thought as firm, the statute and common law of England.   Victorious and successful as their nation had lately been, when they, in their pride and inconsiderate self-confidence, stretched out the hand of oppression, their subjects placed no reliance on the customs of particular nations.   They put confidence in those barriers of right which were derived from their own nation.   Their reliance was, that the tribunals established in this country, under the same royal authority as in England, would do them justice.   If we were not willing, they possessed the power of compelling us to do them justice.

These debts having, therefore, not been contracted from any reliance on the customary law of nations, were they contracted from a regard "to the rights of commerce?" from a view of promoting the commerce of those little things called colonies?   This regard could not have been the ground they were contracted on, for their conduct evinced that they wished to take the right of commerce from us.   What other ingredient remains to show the operation of this custom in their favor ?   The book speaks of strangers trusting subjects of a different nation, from a reliance on the observance of the customary law.   The fact here was, that fellow subjects trusted us on the footing just stated; trusting to the existing compulsory process of law, not relying on a passive inert custom.   A fearful, plodding, sagacious trader would not rely on so flimsy, so uncertain a dependence.   Something similar to what he thought positive satisfaction he relied on.   Were we not subject to the same king ?   The cases are then at variance.   He states the custom to exist for the advantage of commerce, and that a departure from it would injure the public faith. Public faith is in this case out of the question. The public faith was not pledged; it could not, therefore, be injured. I have already read to your honors from the 11th page of the preliminary discourse of Vattel, "that the customary law of nations is only binding on those who have adopted it, and that it is not universal any more than conventional law." It is evident, we could not be bound by any convention or treaty to which we, ourselves, were not a party; and from this authority it is equally obvious that we could not be bound by any customary law to which we were not parties.

8. AMERICA AN INDEPENDENT NATION LONG PRIOR TO 1783.

I think, therefore, with great submission to the court, that the right for which I contended, that is, that in common wars between independent nations either of the contending parties has a right to confiscate or remit debts due by its people to the enemy, is not shaken by the customary law of nations, as far as it regards us, because the custom could not affect us. But, gentlemen, say we were not completely independent till the year 1783! To take them on their own ground, their arguments will fail them. There is a customary law which will operate pretty strongly on our side of the question. What were the inducements of the debtor? On what did the American debtor rely? Sir, he relied for protection on that system of common and statute law on which the creditors depended. Was he deceived in that reliance? That he was most miserably deceived, I believe will not admit of a doubt. The customary law of nations will only apply to distinct nations mutually consenting thereto. When tyranny attempted to rivet her chains upon us, and we boldly broke them asunder, we were remitted to that amplitude of freedom which the beneficent hand of nature gave us. We were not bound by fetters which are of benefit to one party, while they are destructive to the other. Would it be proper that we should be bound and they unrestrained? Vattel, book the 3d, ch. 8, sec. 137, says, that "the lawful end gives a true right only to those means which are necessary for obtaining such end. Whatever exceeds this is censured by the laws of nature as faulty, and will be condemned at the tribunal of conscience. Hence it is that the right to such or such acts of hostility varies according to their circumstances. What is just and perfectly innocent in a war, in one particular situation, is not always so in another. Right goes hand in hand with necessity and the exigency of the case, but never exceeds it." This, sir, is the first dictate of nature and the practice of nations; and if your misfortunes and distresses should be sad and dreadful, you are let loose from those common restraints which may be proper on common occasions, in order to preserve the great rights of human nature.

9. The acts of confiscation warranted by necessity.

This is laid down by that great writer in clear and unequivocal terms. If, then, sir, it be certain, from a recurrence to facts, that it was necessary for America to seize on British property, this book warrants the legislature of this State in passing those confiscating and prohibitory laws. I need only refer to your recollection for our pressing situation during the late contest, and happy am I that this all-important question comes on before the heads of those who were actors in the great scene are laid in the dust. An uninformed posterity would be unacquainted with the awful necessity which impelled us on. If the means were within reach, we were warranted by the laws of nature and nations to use them. The fact was, that we were attacked by one of the most formidable nations under heaven; a nation that carried terror and dread with its thunder to both hemispheres. Our united property enabled us to look in the face that mighty people. Dared we to have gone in opposition to them bound hand and foot? Would we have dared to resist them fettered? for we should have been fettered if we had been deprived of so considerable a part of our little stock of national resources. In that most critical and dangerous emergency, our all was but a little thing. Had we a treasury, an exchequer? Had we commerce? Had we any revenue? Had we anything from which a nation could draw wealth? No, sir. Our credit became the scorn of our foes. However, the efforts of certain patriotic characters (there were not a few of them, thank heaven,) gave us credit among our own people. But we had not a farthing to spare. We were obliged to go on a most grievous anticipation, the weight of which we feel at this day. Recur to our actual situation and the means we had of defending ourselves. The actual situation of America is described here, where this author says, "that right goes hand in hand with necessity." The necessity being great and dreadful, you are warranted to lay hold of every atom of money within your reach, especially if it be the money of your enemies. It is prudent and necessary to strengthen yourselves and weaken your enemies. Vattel, book 3d, ch. 8, sec. 138, says: "The business of a just war being to suppress violence and injustice, it gives a right to compel, by force, him who is deaf to the voice of justice. It gives a right of doing against the enemy whatever is necessary for weakening him, for disabling him from making any further resistance in support of his injustice; and the most effectual, the most proper methods may be chosen, provided they have nothing odious, be not unlawful in themselves, or exploded by the law of nature." Here let me pause for a moment, and ask whether it be odious in itself, or exploded by the law of nature, to seize those debts?

No, because the money was taken from the very offenders. We fought for the great, unalienable, hereditary rights of human nature. An unwarrantable attack was made upon us; an attack, not only not congenial with motherly or parental tenderness, but incompatible with the principles of humanity or civilization. Our defense, then, was a necessary one. What says Vattel, book 3d, ch. 8, sec. 136: " The end of a just war is to revenge or prevent injury; that is, to procure by force the justice which cannot otherwise be obtained; to compel an unjust person to repair an injury already done, or to give securities against any wrong threatened by him. On a declaration of war, therefore, this nation has a right of doing against the enemy whatever is necessary to this justifiable end of bringing him to reason and obtaining justice and security from him." We have taken nothing in this necessary defense, but from the very offenders—those who unjustly attacked us; for we had a right of considering every individual of the British nation as an enemy. This I prove by the same great writer, p. 519, sec. 139, of the same book: " An enemy attacking me unjustly gives an undoubted right of repelling his violence; and he who opposes me in arms, when I demand only my right, becomes himself the real aggressor by his unjust resistance. He is the first author of the violence, and obliges me to make use of force for securing myself against the wrongs intended me either in my person or possessions; for if the effects of this force proceed so far as to take away his life, he owes the misfortune to himself, for if, by sparing him, I should submit to the injury, the good would soon become the prey of the wicked. Hence the right of killing enemies in a just war is derived; when their resistance cannot be suppressed, when they are not to be reduced by milder methods, there is a right of taking away their life. Under the name of enemies, as we have already shown, are comprehended not only the first author of the war, but

likewise all who join him and fight for his cause." Thus I think
the first part of my position confirmed and unshaken: that, in common wars, a nation not restrained by the customary law of nations,
has a right to confiscate debts.

10. DISTINCTION BETWEEN COMMON WAR AND REVOLUTION.

From this I will go on to the other branch of my position: that
if, in common wars, debts be liable to forfeiture, *a fortiori*, must
they be so in a revolution war. Let me contrast the late war with
wars in common. According to those people called kings, wars in
common are systematic and produced for trifles, for not conform-
ing to imaginary honors, because you have not lowered your flag
before him at sea; or for a supposed affront to the person of an
ambassador. Nations are set by the ears, and the most horrid devastations are brought on mankind for the most frivolous causes.
If then, when small matters are in contest, debts be forfeitable,
what must have accrued to us as engaged in the late revolution
war—a war commenced in attainder, perfidy and confiscation? If
we take with us this great principle of Vattel, that right goes in
hand with necessity, and consider the peculiar situation of the
American people, we will find reason more than sufficient to give
us a right of confiscating those debts.

The most striking peculiarity attended the American war. In
the first of it we were stripped of every municipal right. Rights
and obligations are correspondent, co-extensive and inseparable;
they must exist together or not at all. We were, therefore, when
stripped of all our municipal rights, clear of every municipal obligation, burden, and onerous engagement. If, then, the obligation
be gone, what is become of the correspondent right? They are
mutually gone. The case of sovereign and independent nations at
war is far different, because there private right is respected and
domestic *asylum* held sacred. Was it the case in our war? No,
sir; daggers were planted in your chambers, and mischief, death
and destruction might meet you at your fireside.

11. PICTURE OF THE HORRORS OF THE AMERICAN REVOLUTION.

There is an essential variance between the late war and common
wars. In common wars children are not obliged to fight against
their fathers, nor brothers against brothers, nor kindred against
kindred. Our men were compelled, contrary to the most sacred
ties of humanity, to shed the blood of their dearest connexions.

In common wars, contending parties respect municipal rights, and leave, even to those they invade, the means of paying debts and complying with obligations; they touch not private property. For example, when a British army lands in France, they plunder nothing; they pay for what they have, and respect the tribunals of justice, unless they have a mind to be called a savage nation. Were we thus treated? Were we permitted to exercise industry and to collect debts by which we might be enabled to pay British creditors? Had we a power to pursue commerce? No, sir. What became of our agriculture? Our inhabitants were mercilessly and brutally plundered, and our enemies professed to maintain their army by those means only. Our slaves carried away, our crops burnt, a cruel war carried on against our agriculture—disability to pay debts produced by pillage and devastation, contrary to every principle of national law. From that series of plenty in which we had been accustomed to live and to revel, we were plunged into every species of human calamity: our lives attacked, charge of rebels fixed upon us, confiscation and attainder denounced against the whole continent, and he that was called king of England sat judge upon our case. He pronounced his judgment; not like those to whom poetic fancy has given existence; not like him who sits in the infernal regions and dooms to the Stygian lake those spirits who deserve it, because he spares the innocent and sends some to the fields of Elysium; not like him who sat in ancient imperial Rome and wished the people had but one neck, that he might at one blow strike off their heads and spare himself the trouble of carnage and massacre, because one city would have satisfied his vengeance; not like any of his fellow-men!—for nothing would satiate his sanguinary ferocity but the indiscriminate destruction of the whole continent, involving the innocent with the guilty. Yes; he sat in judgment with his coadjutors, and pronounced proscription, attainder and forfeiture against men, women, and even children at the breast! Is not this description pointedly true in all its parts? And who were his coadjutors and executioners in this strange court of judicature? Like the fiends of poetic imagination—Hessians, Indians and Negroes were his coadjutors and executioners. Is there anything in this sad detail of offenses which is unfounded? anything not enforced by the act of parliament against America? We were thereby driven out of their protection and branded by the epithet "rebels!" The term rebel may not now appear in all its train of horrid consequences. We know that when a person is called rebel by that government, his goods and life are forfeited, and his very blood pronounced to be corrupted, and the severity of the punishment entailed on his posterity. To whom may we apply for the verity of this? The jurisprudence and history of that nation prove that, when they speak of rebels, nothing but blood will satisfy them. Is there nothing hideous in this part of the portrait? It is unparalleled in the annals of mankind. Though I have respect for individuals of that nation, my duty constrains me to speak thus.

When we contemplate this mode of warfare, and the sentiments of the writers on natural law on this subject, we are justified in saying that, in this revolution war, we had a right to consider British debts as subject to confiscation, and to seize the property of those who originated that war. As to the injuries done to agriculture, they appear in a diminutive view when compared to the injuries and indignities offered to persons and mansions of abode. Sir, from your seat you might have seen instances of the most grievous hostility: not only private property wantonly pillaged, but men, women and children dragged publicly from their habitations, and indiscriminately devoted to destruction. The rights of humanity were sacrificed! We were then deprived not only of the benefits of municipal, but natural law. If there shall grow out of these considerations a palpable disability to pay those debts, I ask if the claim be just? For that disability was produced by those excesses, by those very men who come on us now for payment. Here give me leave to say that they sold us a bad title in whatever they sold us, in real as well as in personal property.

12. England, by withdrawing her protection, destroyed title in all property.

Describe the nature of a debt: it is an engagement or promise to pay, but it must be for a valuable consideration. If this be clear, was not the title to whatever property they sold us, bad in every sense of the word when the war followed? What can add value to property? Force. Notwithstanding the equity and fairness of the debt when incurred, if the security of the property received was afterward destroyed, the title has proved defective. Suppose millions were contracted for and received, those millions give you no advantage without force to protect them. This necessary protection is withdrawn by the very men who were bound to afford it, and who now demand payment. Neither lands, slaves,

2

nor other property, are worth a shilling without protecting force.
This title was destroyed, when the act of parliament, putting us out
of their protection, passed against America. I say, sir, the title
was destroyed by the very offenders who come here now and demand payment. Justice and equity cancel the obligation as to the
price that was to be given for it, because the tenure is destroyed
and the effects purchased have no value. Such a claim is unsupported by the plainest notions of right and wrong. For this long
catalogue of offenses committed against the citizens of America,
every individual of the British nation is accountable. How are
you to be compensated for those depredations on persons and
property ? Are you to go to the kingdom of England to find the
very individual who did you the outrage, and demand satisfaction
of him ? To tell you of such a remedy as this, is adding insult to
injury. Every individual is chargeable with national offenses.

Mr. Henry cited Vattel to maintain this proposition. He then proceeded :

These observations of Vattel amount to this: that a king or
conductor of a nation is considered as a moral person, by means
of whom the nation acquires or loses its rights, and subjects itself
to penalties. The individuals, and the nation which they compose,
are one. I will, therefore, take it for granted, that whatever violences and excesses were committed on this continent, are chargeable to the plaintiff in this very action. Recollect our distressed
situation. We had no exchequer, no finances, no army, no navy,
no common means of defense. Our necessity—dire necessity—
compelled us to throw aside those rules which respect private property, and to make impresses on our own citizens to support the
war. Right and necessity being co-extensive, we were compelled
to exert a right the most eminent over the whole community. The
salus populi demanded what we did. If we had a right to disregard the legal fences drawn round the property of our citizens, had
we not a greater right to take British property ?

13. THE ISSUING OF PAPER MONEY BY THE COLONIES COMPELLED
BY NECESSITY.

Another peculiarity contributes to aid our defense. The want
of an exchequer obliged us to emit paper money, and compel our
citizens to receive it for gold. In the ears of some men this sounds
harshly. But they are young men, who do not know and feel the
irresistible necessity that urged us. Would your armies have been

raised, clothed, maintained or kept together without paper money? Without it, the war would have stood still, resistance to tyranny would have stopped, and despotism, with all its horrid train of appurtenances, must have depressed your country. We compelled the people to receive it in payment of all debts; we induced and invited them (if we did not compel them) to put it into the treasury as a complete discharge from their debts. Sir, I trust I shall not live to see the day when the public councils of America will give ground to say that this was a State trick, contrived to delude and defraud the citizens. What must it be ostensibly, when, by the compact of your nation, they had publicly bound and pledged themselves that it was and should be money, if afterward, in the course of human events, when temptations present themselves, they shall declare that it is not money? Sir, the honest planter is unskilled in political tricks and deceptions. His interest ought never to be sacrificed. The law is his guide; the law compelled him to receive it, and his countrymen would have branded him with the name of enemy if he had refused it. The laws of the country are as sacred as the imaginary sanctity of British debts. Sir, national engagements ought to be held sacred; the public violation of this solemn engagement will destroy all confidence in the government If you depart from the national compact one iota, you give a dangerous precedent which may imperceptibly and gradually introduce the most destructive encroachment on human rights.

I will beg leave here to dissent from the position of the gentlemen on the other side, which denied that we were a people till our enemies were pleased to say we were so. That we were a people. and had a right to do everything which a great and a royal, nay, an imperial people could do, is clear and indisputable. Though under the humble appearance of republicanism, our government and national existence, when examined, are as solid as a rock, not resting on the mere fraud and oppression of rulers, nor the credulity nor barbarous ignorance of the people, but founded on the consent and conviction of enlightened human nature. That we had every right that completely independent nations can have, will be satisfactorily proved to your honors by again referring to Vattel.

Here Mr. Henry read a passage from Vattel, the effect of which is, that during a civil war the parties acknowledging no common judge on earth are to be considered as two distinct people, and to govern themselves in the conduct of the war by the general laws of nations. He then proceeded:

Here then, sir, is proof abundant, that, before the acknowledgment of American independence by Great Britain, we had a right
to be considered as a nation, because on earth we had no common
superior to give a decision of the dispute between us and our sovereign.   After declaring ourselves a sovereign people, we had every
right a nation can claim as an independent community.   But the
gentlemen on the other side greatly rely upon this principle, that a
contract cannot be dissolved without the consent of all the contracting parties; the inference is, that the consent of the king of Great
Britain was necessary to the dissolution of the government.
Tyranny has too often and too successfully riveted his chains to
warrant a belief that a tyrant will ever voluntarily release his subjects from the governmental compact.   Rather might it be expected
that the last iota of human misery would be borne, and the oppression would descend from father to son, to the latest period of
earthly existence.   The despotism of our sovereign ought to be
considered as an implied consent, on his part, to dissolve the compact between us; and he and his subjects must be considered as
one—there can be no distinction; for, in any other view, his consent could not have been obtained without force.   There is such a
thing, indeed, as tyranny from free choice.   Sweden, not long ago,
surrendered its liberties in one day, as Denmark had done formerly; so that this branch of the human family is cut off from every
possible enjoyment of human rights.   But the right to resist oppression is not denied.   The gentleman's doctrine cannot, therefore, apply to national communities.

14. Contracts dissolved without the consent of the king of Great Britain.

If any additional force was wanting to confirm what I advance,
it would be derived from the treaty of peace, which further proves
that we were entitled to all the privileges of independent nations.
The consent of all the people of Europe said we were free.   Our
former master withheld his consent till a few unlucky events compelled him.   And when he gave his *fiat*, it gave us, by relation back
to the time of the declaration of independence, all the rights and
privileges of a completely sovereign nation; our independence was
acknowledged by him previous to the completion of the treaty of
peace.   It was not a condition of the treaty, but was acknowledged, by his own overture, preparatory to it.   View the consequences of their fatal doctrine.   There would not only have been

long arrears of debts to pay, but a long catalogue of crimes to be punished.   If the ultimate acknowledgment of our independence by Great Britain had not relation back to the time of the declaration of independence, all the intermediate acts of legislation would be void, and every decision and act, consequent thereon, would be null.   But, sir, we were a complete nation on every principle, according to the authorities I have already read, in addition to which I will refer your honors to Vattel, book 4th, ch. 7, sec. 88, to show we were entitled to the benefits of national law, and to use all the resources of the community: " From the equality of all nations really sovereign and independent, it is a principle of the voluntary law of nations, that no nation can control another in its internal municipal legislation."   If we consider the business of confiscation according to the immemorial usages of Great Britain, we will find that the law and practice of that country support my position.   In the wars which respect revolutions, which have taken place in that island—life, fortune, goods, debts, and everything else were confiscated.   The *crimen læsæ majestatis*, as it is called, involved everything.   Every possible punishment has been inflicted on suffering humanity that it could endure, by the party which had the superiority in those wars, over the defeated party which was charged with rebellion.

15. Consequences which would have resulted had England conquered America.

What would have been the consequences, sir, if we had been conquered ?   Were we not fighting against that majesty ?   Would the justice of our opposition have been considered ?   The most horrid forfeitures, confiscations and attainders would have been pronounced against us.   Consider their history, from the time of William the First till this day.   Were not his Normans gratified with the confiscation of the richest estates in England ?   Read the excessive cruelties, attainders and confiscations of that reign.   England depopulated, its inhabitants stripped of the dearest privileges of humanity, degraded with the most ignominious badges of bondage, and totally deprived of the power of resistance to usurpation and tyranny.   This inability continued to the time of Henry the Eighth.   In his reign, the business of confiscation and attainder made considerable havoc.   After his reign, some stop was put to that effusion of blood which preceded and happened under it. Recollect the sad and lamentable effects of the York and Lan-

castrian wars. Remember the rancorous hatred and inveterate de-
testations of contending factions, the distinction of white and red
roses. To come a little lower: what happened in that island in the
rebellions of 1715 and 1745? If we had been conquered, would
not our men have shared the fate of the people of Ireland? A
great part of that island was confiscated, though the Irish people
thought themselves engaged in a laudable cause. What confiscation and punishments were inflicted in Scotland? The plains of
Culloden, and the neighboring gibbets, will show you. I thank
heaven that the spirit of liberty, under the protection of the Almighty, saved us from experiencing so hard a destiny. But had we
been subdued, would not every right have been wrested from us?
What right would have been saved? Would debts have been
saved? Would it not be absurd to save debts while they should
burn, hang and destroy?

Before we can decide with precision, we are to consider the
dangers we should have been exposed to had we been subdued.
After presenting to your view this true picture of what would have
been our situation, had we been subjugated; surely a correspondent
right will be found, growing out of the law of nations, in our favor.
Had our subjugation been effected, and we pleaded for pardon—
represented that we defended the most valuable rights of human
nature, and thought they were wrong—would our petition have
availed? I feel myself impelled, from what has passed, to ask
this question. I would not wish to have lived to see the sad scenes
we should have experienced. Needy avarice and savage cruelty
would have had full scope. Hungry Germans, blood-thirsty Indians, and nations of another color would have been let loose upon
us. The sad effects of such warfare have had their full influence
on a number of our fellow-citizens. Sir, if you had seen the sad
scenes which I have known; if you had seen the simple but tranquil
felicity of helpless and unoffending women and children, in little
log-huts on the frontiers, disturbed and destroyed by the sad effects
of British warfare and Indian butchery, your soul would have been
struck with horror! Even those helpless women and children were
the objects of the most shocking barbarity.

Give me leave again to recur to Vattel, p. 9: "Nations being
free, independent and equal, and having a right to judge according
to the dictates of conscience, of what is to be done in order to fulfill its duties; the effect of all this is the producing, at least ex-
ternally and among men, a perfect equality of rights between na-

tions in the administration of their affairs, and the pursuit of their pretensions, without regard to the intrinsic justice of their conduct, of which others have no right to form a definite judgment, so that, what is permitted in one, is also permitted in the other; and they ought to be considered in human society as having an equal right." If it be allowed to the British nation to put to death, to forfeit and confiscate debts and everything else, may we not (having an equal right) confiscate—not life, for we never desire it—but that which is the common object of confiscation: property, goods, and debts, which strengthen ourselves and weaken our enemies? I trust that this short recapitulation of events shows that, if there ever was in the history of man a case requiring the full use of all human means, it was our case in the late contest; and we were, therefore, warranted to confiscate the British debts.

16. IN A STATE OF NATURE, MUNICIPAL RIGHTS AND OBLIGATIONS ARE DISSOLVED.

I beg leave to add that these debts are lost on another principle. By the dissolution of the British government, America went into a state of nature; on the dissolution of that of which we had been members, there being no government antecedent, we went necessarily into a state of nature. To prove this, I need only refer to the declaration of independence, pronounced on the fourth day of July, 1776, and our State Constitution. It recites many instances of misrule by the king of England; it asserts the right and expediency of dissolving the British government and going into a state of nature, or, in other words, to establish a new government. The right of dissolving it and forming a new system, had preceded the fourth day of July, 1776. A recapitulation of the events of the tyrannical acts of government would demonstrate a right to dissolve it. But I may go farther and even say, that the act of parliament which declared us out of the king's protection dissolved it. For what is government? It is an express or implied compact between the rulers and ruled, stipulating reciprocal protection and obedience. That protection was withdrawn, solemnly withdrawn from us. Of consequence, obedience ceased to be due. Our municipal rights were taken away by one blow. Municipal obligations and government were also taken away by the same blow. Well, then, there being no antecedent government, we returned into a state of nature. Unless we did so, our new compact of government could only be a usurpation. In a state of nature, there is no legal lien in the person or property of any one. If you are not clear of every antecedent engagement, what is the legality or strength of the present Constitution of government? If any antecedent engagements are to bind, how far are they to reach? You had no right to form a new government, if the old system existed; and if it did not exist, you were necessarily and inevitably in a state of nature. In my humble opinion, by giving validity to such claims, you destroy the very idea of the right to form a new government. Vattel calls government the totality of persons, estates, and effects, formed by every individual of the new society, and that totality represented by the governing power. How can the totality exist while an antecedent right exists elsewhere? See Grotius, p. 4, which I have already read, and note 29; because the design and good of civil society necessarily require that the natural and acquired rights of each member should admit of limitations several ways, and, to a certain degree, by the authority of him or them in whose hands the sovereign authority is lodged. When we formed a new government, did there exist any authority that limited our rights? How can the totality exist, if any other person or persons have an existing claim upon you? It appears to me that that equality which is involved in a state of nature cannot exist while such claim exists. The court will recollect what I have already read out of Vattel, in the sections 15 and 18. The equality here ascribed to independent nations is equally ascribed to men in a state of nature. A moral society of persons cannot exist without this absolute equality. The existence of individuals in a state of nature depends in like manner upon, and is inseparable from such equality.

Rights, as before mentioned, Vattel, pp. 8 and 9, are divided into internal and external; of external rights he makes the distinction of perfect and imperfect. I beseech your honors to fix this distinction in your minds. The perfect external right only is accompanied with the right of constraint. The imperfect right loses that quality and leaves it to the party to comply or not to comply with it. When the former government was dissolved, the American people became indebted to nobody. You either owe everything or nothing; and every contract and engagement must be done away, if any. In a state of nature you are free and equal. But how are you free, if another have a lien on your body? Where is your freedom or your equality with that person who has the right of constraining you? This right of constraint implies a complete authority over you, but not, however, to enslave you. This constraint is always adequate to the right or obligation.   Where can you find the possibility of this equality which nature gives her sons, if we admit an existing right of constraint?   If it be a fact that on the dissolution of the government we did enter into a state of nature (and that we did, I humbly judge cannot be denied, as at that time no government existed at all), it destroys all claim to one farthing. This will be found to be true, as well upon the ground of equity and good conscience as in law, when it is considered, that when we went into a state of nature, the means of paying debts were taken away from us by them; because, so far as they had power over us, they prevented us from getting money to pay debts.   They inter-dicted us from the pursuit of profitable commerce; from getting gold and silver, the only things they would take; they unjustly drove us to this extremity.   By the concession of the worthy gen-tleman, their attack upon us was unjust.

17. DEBTS, LIKE OTHER PROPERTY, SUBJECT TO FORFEITURE.

But, then, debts are not subject to confiscation, say gentlemen, because there were no inquests, no office found for the common-wealth.   Has a debt an ear-mark?   Is it tangible or visible?   Has it any discriminating quality?   Unless tangible or visible, how is it to be ascertained or distinguished?   What does an inquest mean? A solemn inquiry by a jury, by ocular examination, with other proofs.   If an inquest of office were to be had of land, a jury could tell the lines and boundaries of it, because they may be distin-guished from others, and its identity may thereby be ascertained. If a horse be the object of inquiry, he can be easily distinguished from any other horse.   In like manner every other article of visible property may be subject to inquests; but such a thing as an inquest of a debt never existed, as far as my legal knowledge extends. What are to be the consequences if this proceeding be requisite? You must set up a court of inquisition, summon the whole nation, and ask every man how much do you owe?   This would be pro-ductive of endless confusion, perplexity and expense, without the desired effect.   The laws of war and of nations require no more than that the sovereign power should openly signify its will that the debts be forfeited.   There is no particular forensic form neces-sary.   The question here is not whether this confiscation be tra-versed in all the forms of municipal regulations.   There is a ques-tion between Great Britain and America similar to that between Alexander and the Thebans.   Has the sovereign signified his pleasure that debts be remitted? A sign is completely sufficient, if it be understood by the people. There is a necessity of thus speaking the legislative will, that the other party may know it and retaliate; for what is allowed to one, is to both parties. This was different from the nature of a solemn war. War is lawful or unlawful, according to the manner of conducting it. In the prosecution of a lawful solemn war, it is necessary that you do not depart from certain rules of moderation, honor and humanity, but act according to the usual practice of belligerent powers. Did the mother-country conduct the war against us in this manner? We did openly say, we mean to confiscate your debts, and modify them, because they have lost their perfect external quality; they are imperfect; we claim that right, as a sovereign people, over that species of your property. Sir, it was not done in a corner. It was understood by our enemies. They had a right to retaliate on any species of our property they could find. The right of retaliation, or just retortion, for equivalent damage on any part of an enemy's property, is permitted to every nation. What right has the British nation (for if the nation have not the right, none of its people have) to demand a breach of faith in the American government to its citizens?

18. Effect of the payment of paper currency to the loan office.

I have already mentioned the engagement of the government with its citizens respecting the paper money. If you take it, it shall be money. Shall it be judged now not to be money? Shall this compact be broken for the sake of the British nation? No, sir; the language of national law is otherwise. Sir, the laws of confiscation and paper money made together one system, connected and sanctioned by the legislature, on which depended once the fate of our country, and on which depend now the happiness, the ease and comfort of thousands of your fellow-citizens. Will it not be a breach of the compact with your people, to say that the money is not to keep up its original standard in the quality given it by law? What were the effects of this system? What would have been the effects, had your citizens been apprised that British debts must be paid? Would they have taken the money? Would they have deposited the money in the loan office, if they had been warned by law that they must deposit it subject to the future regulations of peace; that it should not release them from their creditors? However right it may appear now to decry the paper money, it would have been fatal then; for America might have perished without the aid and effect of that medium. Your citizens, trusting to this compact, submitted to a number of things almost intolerable—impressments and violences on their property; it encouraged them to exert themselves in defense of their property against the enemy during the war. If the debt in the declaration mentioned be recovered, the compact is subverted as respecting the paper money. And this subversion is to take effect for the interest of those men whom, by all laws human and divine, we were obliged to consider as enemies; men who were obliged to comply with the regulations and requisitions of their king; and our people will have been laboring, not for themselves, but for the benefit of the British subject.

19. APPLICATION OF THE LAW OF SALVAGE.

When a vessel is in danger in a storm, those who abide on board of her, and encounter the dangers of the sea to save her, are allowed some little compensation for salvage, for their fidelity and gallantry in endeavoring to prevent her loss; while those who abandon her are entitled to nothing. But, in opposition to this wise and politic principle, we who have withstood the storms and dangers, receive no compensation; but those who left the political ship and joined those on the other side of the water who wished to sink her, and who caused her to fight eight long years for her preservation, shall come in at last and get their full share of this vessel, and yet will have been exonerated from every charge. For whom, then, were the people of America engaged in war? Not for themselves, I am sure; the property that they saved will not be for themselves, but for those whom they had a right to call enemies. I am not willing to ascribe to the meanest American the love of money, or desire of eluding the payment of his debts, as the motive of engaging in the war. No, sir; he had nobler and better views. But he thinks himself well entitled to those debts, from the laws and usages of nations, as a compensation for the injuries he has sustained. There is a sad drawback on this property saved. A national debt for seventeen years, considerable taxes which were profusely laid during the war on lands and slaves; and, since the peace, we have been loaded with a heavy taxation. I know that I advocate this cause on a very advantageous ground when I speak of the right of salvage. The cargo on board the wrecked vessel belongs to the British, it will have been saved for them; but the salvage is due to us only. If you take it on the ground of interest, you may hold as a pledge, you may retain for salvage. If you take it on the scale of the common law, or of national law, you may oppose damages to debts, retain the debts, to retribute and compensate for the injuries they have done you. I have not got over and I trust established the first point; that is, that debts in common wars are subject to forfeiture, and much more so in a revolution war like the American was.

Here Mr. Henry proceeded to argue that a debt once forfeited is gone for ever, unless revived by treaty. He discussed the rules by which treaties are to be construed, and contended that they could confer no benefit unless mutually observed in good faith; that the stipulations of a treaty are in the nature of a condition precedent, and that a breach on either side dissolves the covenant. He then showed in what respects the treaty had been violated by England, and that these violations were admitted by the demurrer. Next he argued that a British subject could claim no advantage from a treaty annulled by the sovereign, because the individual was bound by the acts of the sovereign. He continued:

Here are two moral persons, Great Britain and America, making a contract. The plaintiff claims and the defendant defends under and through them; and if either nation or moral person has no right to benefits from such a contract, individuals claiming under them can have none. The plaintiff then claims under his nation, but if that nation have committed perfidy respecting the observance of the compact, no right can be carried therefrom to the plaintiff. It puts him back in the same situation he was in before the treaty.

Here Mr. Henry cited Vattel to sustain his position. To consider a treaty void as to all the individuals of a nation collectively, while each individual of that nation might separately enforce it, was a paradoxical absurdity. He then claimed that the treaty, even if in force, could not operate on plaintiff's claim since it was discharged by payment into the loan office, before the treaty was made. He continued:

20. DEFENDANT'S DEBT DID NOT EXIST WHEN THE TREATY OF PEACE WAS SIGNED.

To derive a benefit from the treaty, the plaintiff must demand a *bona fide* debt; that is, a debt *bona fide* due. The word debt implies that the thing is due; for if it be not due, how can it be a debt? To give to these words, "all debts heretofore contracted," a strictly literal sense, would be to authorize a renewed demand for debts which had been actually paid off to the creditor; for these were certainly within the words of the treaty, being debts heretofore contracted. To avoid this absurd and dishonest consequence, you must look at the intention of the thing; and the intention certainly was to embrace those cases where there had not been a legal payment. I ask why a payment made in gold and silver is a legal payment? Because the coin of those metals is made current by the laws of this country. If paper be made current by the same authority, why should not a payment in it be equally valid? The British subject cannot demand payment, because I confront his demand with a receipt. Why will a receipt discharge in any instance? Because it is founded on the laws of the country. A receipt given in consequence of a payment in coin, is a legal discharge, only because the laws of the country make it so. I ask, then, why a receipt given in consequence of a payment into the treasury be not of equal validity, since it has precisely the same foundation? It is expressly constituted a discharge by a legislature having competent authority. This debt, therefore, having been legally paid by the contractor, was not due from him at the time of making the treaty, and therefore is not within the intention of that instrument. But, say the gentlemen on the other side, the one payment has the consent of the creditor, and the other has not; he who paid coin has the creditor's consent to the discharge, but he who paid money into the treasury wants it. Have we not satisfied this honorable court that the governing power had a right to put itself in the place of the British subjects? Having had an unquestionable right to confiscate, sequester or modify those debts as they pleased, they had an equally indubitable right to substitute themselves in the stead of the plaintiff, otherwise those authorities have been quoted in vain.

Here Mr. Henry argued that the contract was governed by the *lex loci contractus*, and having been discharged under a valid law of the place where it was made, there was no subsisting debt when the treaty was made. He then discussed the right of the court to take cognizance of the violation of the treaty, on the ground that the facts being admitted by the pleadings, it must declare the law arising on the facts. He continued:

21. PLAINTIFF MUST SHOW FULL COMPLIANCE WITH THE TREATY.

The existence or non-existence of the treaty was a legal inference from the facts agreed, which the court alone were competent to decide. The plaintiff himself had forced this question on the

court, by relying in his replication on the treaty, as restoring his
right to recover this debt.   He sets up his right under this instrument expressly, and then questions the jurisdiction of the court to
decide upon the instrument!   The treaty, *quoad hoc*, is the covenant
of the parties in this suit; the question presented by the pleadings
is, whether the plaintiff who, by that covenant, has taken upon
himself the performance of a precedent condition, can claim any
benefit under it, until he shall show that this precedent condition
has been performed.   On this question the gentleman's argument
is, that the court have no power to decide on the construction of
the covenant, which he himself has brought before them; that they
have nothing to do with the dependence or independence of the
stipulations, or the reciprocal rights of the parties, to claim under
the covenant without showing a previous performance on their respective parts!   On the contrary, I insist that, under the Constitution of the United States, the question belongs peculiarly and exclusively to the judicial department; that by the Constitution it
was expressly provided that the judicial power should extend to
all cases arising under treaties; that the law of treaties embraces
the whole extent of natural and national law; that the Constitution,
therefore, by referring all cases arising under treaties to the judiciary, has of necessity invested them with the power of appealing to
that code of laws by which alone the construction, the operation,
the efficacy, the legal existence or non-existence of treaties must
be tested; and by this code we are told, in the most emphatic
terms, that he who violates one article of a treaty releases the
other party from the performance of any part of it; that the reference of all cases arising under treaties to the judicial department,
carries with it every power near or remote, direct or collateral,
which is essential to a fair and just decision of those cases; that
in every such case the very first question is, is there a treaty or
not?—not whether there has been a treaty, but whether there is an
existing, obligatory, operative treaty.   To decide this question, the
court must bring the facts to the standard of the laws of nations;
and by this standard it had been shown that, in the case at bar,
there existed no treaty from which a British subject could claim
any benefit.   If the judicial department has not the power of deciding this question, there was no department in the American
government which possesses it.   The State governments have
nothing to do with it; Congress cannot touch the subject; they
may, indeed, declare war for a violation; but a nation is not to be

forced to this extremity on every occasion.   There are other modes
of redress, short of a declaration of war, to which nations have a
right to resort; and one of them, as I have shown, was the power
of withholding from the perfidious violator of a treaty those benefits which he claimed under it.   Now, Congress cannot by a law
declare a treaty void; it is not among those grants of power which
the Constitution makes to them; they cannot, therefore, meddle
with the subject in any other way than by a declaration of war;
neither can the President and Senate touch it.   They can make
treaties; but the Constitution gives them no power to expound a
treaty, much less to declare it void; they can only unite with the
House of Representatives in punishing an infraction by a declaration of war.   To the judiciary alone, then, belongs this pacific
power of withholding legal benefits claimed under a treaty, because
of the *mala fides* of the party claiming them.

22. POWER OF INTERPRETATION OF TREATIES IN THE COURTS.

Now, what will be the situation of this country, compared with
that of Great Britain, if you deny this power to the judiciary?   If
you have not observed the treaty with good faith, and go to England, claiming any benefit under the treaty, there is a power there,
called royal prerogative, which will tell you: No; go home and act
honestly, and you shall have your rights under the treaty.   Your
breach of faith will not drive them to a declaration of war; there
is a power there which obtains redress by withholding your rights,
until you act with good faith; but where is the reciprocal and corresponding power in our government, if it be not in the judiciary?
It is nowhere; we have no redress short of a declaration of war.
Is this one of the precious fruits of the adoption of the federal
Constitution, to bind us hand and foot with the fetters of technicality, and leave us no way of bursting them asunder, but by a declaration of war and the effusion of human blood!   It was never
intended.   The wisdom and virtue which framed the Constitution
could never have intended to place the country in this humiliating
and awful predicament.   Give to this power of deciding on treaties,
which is delegated to the federal judiciary, a liberal construction;
give them all the incidental powers necessary to carry it into effect;
open to them the whole region of natural and national law, which
furnishes the only rule of expounding those national compacts
called treaties, and your government is unmutilated, its measure of
power is full up to the exigencies of the nation, and you treat on

equal terms. But upon the opposite construction, much better would it be that America should have no treaties at all, than that, having them, she should want those means of enforcement and redress which all other nations possess.

Mr. Henry then ridiculed the argument of the plaintiff, that under the law of nations only estates of an alien enemy were liable to confiscation, and that mere *choses* in action, owing to their incorporeal and intangible nature, could not be confiscated. He continued:

23. A CHOSE IN ACTION A SUBJECT OF FORFEITURE.

But a chose in action is not liable to forfeiture. Why? Because it is too terrible to be done. There is such a thing as straining at a gnat and swallowing a camel. Things much more terrible have been done; things from which our nature, where it has any pretensions to be pure and correct, must recoil with horror. Show me those laws which forfeit your life, attaint your blood, and beggar your wife and children. Those sanguinary and inhuman laws, to which everything valuable must yield, are to be found in the code of that people under whom the plaintiff now claims. Is it so terrible to confiscate debts, when they forfeit life and corrupt the very source of your blood? Though every other thing dear to humanity is forfeitable, yet debts, it seems, must be spared! Debts are too sacred to be touched! It is a mercantile idea that worships mammon instead of God. A chose in action shall pass; it is without your reach. What authority can they adduce in support of such conclusive pre-eminence for debts? No political or human institution has placed them above other things. If debt be the most sacred of earthly obligations, I am uninformed from whence it has derived that eminence. The principle is to be found in the day-books, journals and ledgers of merchants, not in the writings or reasonings of the wise and well-informed—the enlightened instructors of mankind. Can any gentleman show me any instance where the life or property of a gentleman or plebeian in England is forfeited, and yet his debts spared? The State can claim debts due to one guilty of high treason. Are they not subject to confiscation? I concur in that sound principle, that good faith is essential to the happiness of mankind; that its want stops all human intercourse and renders us miserable. This principle is permanent and universal. Look to what point of the compass you will, you will find it pervading all nations. Who does not set down its sacred influence as the only thing that comforts human life? Does the plaintiff claim through good faith ? How does he derive his claim ? Through perfidy; through a polluted channel. Everything of that kind would have come better from our side of the question than from theirs.

But the gentleman [1] has observed, that neither the declaration of the legislature, by the act of 1779, that the British subjects had become aliens, and their property vested in the commonwealth, nor any other act passed on the subject, could divest the debts out of the British creditors. It cannot be done without the solemnity of an inquiry by a jury. The debt of A. or B. cannot be given to C., without this solemnity. Is the little legality of forms which are necessary when you speak of estates and titles, requisite on such mighty occasions as these ? When the fate of a nation is concerned, you are to speak the language of nature. When your very existence is at stake, are you to speak the technical language of books, and to be confined to the limited rules of technical criticism ? to those tricks and quirks, those little twists and twirls of low chicanery and sophistry, which are so beneficial to professional men ? Alexander said, in the style of that mighty man, to the Thessalian: "You are free from the Thebans," and the debts they owed them were thereby remitted. Every other sovereign has the same right to use the same natural, manly and laconic language; not when he is victorious only, but in every situation, if he be in a state of hostility with other nations. The acts use not the language of technicality, they speak not of releases, discharges and acquittances; but they speak the legislative will, in simple speech, to the human understanding—a style better suited to the purpose than the turgid and pompous phraseology of many great writers.

[1] Mr. Ronald.

PUBLIC OPINION INVARIABLY AGAINST THE PRISONER.

JAMES T. BRADY.

My learned friend, the District Attorney,[1] and myself, do not exactly agree in our notions about men and human nature. He said that I "spoke rather like a cynic than a philosopher," when I declared that man would much more readily believe evil of his neighbor than good. I retain my opinion. There is an instinct in every human being that relates to the purpose for which the Almighty seems to\have designed him,—a roving hunter,—"to live as the hunter liveth, and to die as the hunter dieth." No race of mankind is ever satisfied with the place in which it first achieved prosperity. However large, rich and fertile the domain possessed, we are ever eager to push out, even in the midst of our luxuries and enjoyments, and seek new theatres for physical and intellectual effort. When we look back upon history, we find that civilization has forced its path over the ruins of empires; and there is not a single fallen column, there is not a smouldering cornice, nor a piece of stone round which the weeds cluster in desolate places where at one period luxury, refinement, and art may have existed, which was not in its overthrow a necessary foothold for that prog-ress which, we think, has advanced us to a position so enviable in these latter days. We are a restless, roving race of hunters; and the very mo-ment you give the common multitude an object to pursue, the instinct of the chase naturally tends to superiority over judgment and humanity. When any thing flieth from mankind they all pursue; let it turn with the courage of a rat, and the multitude are likely to fall back. The instinct of our race is developed in the administration of the law. When a man is charged with what is termed a "great crime," did you ever know the news-papers to suggest that he might possibly be innocent? Is that because editors are destitute of humanity? No, but entirely because of this in-stinct. If you go into a court of justice you will find that in almost every extraordinary case, the instincts of the multitude are with the State. When the prosecution are in want of testimony, any man who, far off in Texas, knows a fact that can assist the People, will communicate it to the district attorney; but if you were charged with crime, accused, though innocent— arrested, and brought to trial, men who were present, and saw the deed committed by another, would often rather suffer you to die guiltless on the scaffold, than come forward and confess that they were at the scene of the occurrence, if that might expose them to shame or even to trouble.—
[From his argument in defense of Huntington, charged with forgery, December 29, 1856.]

[1] Mr. A. Oakey Hall.

ARGUMENT OF WILLIAM PINKNEY,

On the Law of Constructive Treason, in the Defense of John Hodges.

[U. S. *v.* Hodges, 2 Wheeler's Cr. Cas. 477.]

AT A CIRCUIT COURT OF THE UNITED STATES, HELD AT BALTIMORE, MD., MAY TERM, 1815.

Analysis of Mr. Pinkney's Argument.

ADDRESS TO THE COURT.	ADDRESS TO THE JURY.
1. The jury, judges of both the law and the facts.	8. Conduct of the court and the prosecution.
2. Criminal intent the essence of every offense.	9. Law of treason defined.—Opinion of the court not law.
3. Illustrations of the rule.	
4. Adhering to the enemy and levying war.	10. Motives of the prisoner laudable, not criminal.
5. The unmistakable intention of the prisoner.	
6. Crime proceeds always from a wicked heart.	11. Arraignment of the doctrine of constructive treason.
7. The circumstances of the surrender.	12. Practical results of doctrine announced by the court.

The dual argument of Mr. Pinkney to the court and jury, forms part of an episode in juridical history, which has no parallel since Thomas Erskine, at the trial of the Dean of St. Asaph, withstood with respect and firmness what he regarded, on the part of the court, as an encroachment upon the province of the jury and the constitutional and legal rights of his client. The conduct of the latter resulted in the passage of Lord Camden's Act, which practically secured the liberty of the press and the freedom of speech; the conduct of the former abolished forever the idea that such an offense as " constructive treason " could possibly exist under our system. The history and circumstances surrounding the accusation and arrest of John Hodges were part of the *res gestæ* of the unfortunate engagement at Bladensburg and the burning of the city of Washington, by the British, under General Ross, in the summer of 1814, in all of which Mr. Pinkney bore a conspicuous part in defending his home and country. On their way to Washington, the English sailed up the Chesapeake into the Patuxent river, and landed at Benedict. Thence they passed through Upper Marlborough to Bladensburg, where a battle was fought with the Americans, in which Mr. Pinkney, at the head of his gallant brigade of Baltimore riflemen, received a serious wound. Four British stragglers, who had fallen behind the main army, were taken prisoners by some of the inhabitants of Marlborough. When General

Ross discovered the fact, he demanded the return of the men from the Marlborough authorities, and accompanied his demand with a threat, that if they were
not surrendered before 12 o'clock that night, he would lay the town in ashes,
and hold as hostages the wives and children of the inhabitants. It seems that
the prisoners had been sent to the American camp some miles distant, and to
save the town John Hodges and his brother hastened thither, and besought General Bowie, who had charge of the captives, to deliver them, that they might be
restored to the enemy, at the same time informing him that the safety of the
town depended upon their immediate return. The General, aware of the danger which would result from a longer detention, and being himself powerless to
avert the threatened destruction, reluctantly gave the prisoners to Hodges, who
surrendered them to the enemy. For this act he was indicted for treason, and
tried before Hon. Justices Duvall, Bland and Houston, in the United States Circuit Court held at Baltimore, in May, 1815. Elias Glenn, Esq., appeared for
the government; U. S. Heath, J. E. Hall, and William Pinkney appeared for the
prisoner.

The crime of treason is thus defined by the Constitution: " Treason against
the United States shall consist only in levying war against them, or in adhering
to their enemies, giving them aid and comfort." [1] By an act of Congress, approved April 30, 1790, it is declared, that " if any person or persons owing allegiance to the United States of America, shall levy war against them, or shall adhere to their enemies, giving them aid and comfort, within the United States or
elsewhere, and shall be thereof convicted on confession in open court, or on the
testimony of two witnesses to the same overt act of treason, whereof he or they
shall stand indicted, such person or persons shall be adjudged guilty of treason
against the United States, and shall suffer death." Under this act it was claimed
that the delivery of the prisoners by Hodges to the enemy was adhering to them,
and giving them aid and comfort, and was treason against the United States.

Such an attempt to deprive a good citizen of his life under the forms of law,
perhaps cannot be found in the history of American jurisprudence, and it would
seem almost incredible that in the tribunals of a popular government, an effort
should be made to revive judicial murder under the guise of constructive treason.
To claim that the delivery to the enemy of four prisoners, compelled by a barbarous and inhuman threat, involving the ruin of an entire community, was deliberate treason, and that such surrender, under such circumstances, could be
construed into a *willful* intention to furnish "aid and comfort" to the enemy,
seems absurd. Nevertheless, such a claim was not only made by counsel for the
government, but was sustained by the court.

When the trial came on it was proven by the prosecution, that the prisoner
had intentionally surrendered the captives to the British. Mr. Pinkney then, on
behalf of the accused, read an address from the grand jury to the President of
the United States, in which the jurors expressed their respect for the motives of
Hodges, and prayed that a *nolle prosequi* should be entered. At this stage of the
trial counsel for the government asked the court to direct the jury, that the crime
of treason had been established. That the case presented but two inquiries : (1)
Did the accused deliver the prisoners? (2) Did he intend to do so? These acts

---

[1] Const. Art. 3, § 5.

having been proven, it was claimed they involved the intention, and that the crime of treason had been made out. Having prayed for the instruction of the court, the judges said they would hear counsel. Mr. Pinkney then addressed the court as follows:

MAY IT PLEASE YOUR HONORS:—There is no law in this prayer, for it excludes that which is the essence of the offense—intention; and if it was otherwise, the court has no right to instruct the jury as if this were a civil case. No instance has occurred in modern times of an attempt to bind the jury in such a case by the opinion of the court. What remedy is there for the party if you err? We may appeal to a higher tribunal, it is true; but what is the consequence? The man is hanged and your judgment is reversed.

I. THE JURY, JUDGES OF BOTH THE LAW AND THE FACTS.

In England, did their courts interfere in this mode in the celebrated cases of Hardy, and Horne Tooke and others? No, it would not have been endured. The best security for the rights of individuals is to be found in the trial by jury. But the excellence of this institution consists in its exclusive power. The jury are here judges of law and fact,[1] and are responsible only to God, to the prisoner, and to their own consciences. After the case is closed you may indeed advise the jury, if they ask it, or if you think proper to do so without being asked by them. But to interrupt the progress of the trial in the way proposed would be monstrous. Suppose the court to give the direction, I shall not submit to it as the prisoner's counsel. I will, on the contrary, tell the jury that it is not law. It is my right to do so, and in a case of blood I dare not forego the exercise of it. I trust I shall not be placed in a predicament which will thus set my duty to a man whose life is in my charge against my respect for this tribunal. I pray your honors to suffer this cause to go on in the customary and legal manner.

In reply to Mr. Pinkney the court said, they were bound to declare the law whenever they were called upon in civil and criminal cases, and requested to hear from counsel for the prosecution. Mr. Glenn commented upon the authorities to

---

[1] Hon. Benj. R. Curtis, in U. S. v. Morris (1 Curtis' C. Ct. R. 23), held that under the Constitution and laws of the United States the jury are not the judges of the law in a trial. They are to take the law from the court, and apply it to the facts in evidence, and then frame their general verdict of guilty or not guilty. In Morris' case, the questions of law related to the constitutionality of an act of Congress. To the general rule laid down by Judge Curtis, however, there seem to be two exceptions, namely, in trials for treason and libel.

support his position, and cited 1 East's C. L. p. 70; Vigol's Case, 2 Dall. p. 346; Cranbourne's Case, Salk. p. 633.

MR. PINKNEY.—Nothing but an utter confusion of ideas could have introduced a doubt upon the subject. The gentleman's prayer excluded all idea of criminal intention; or it relied upon the influence of criminal motive, as a necessary corollary from the naked facts charged, as the overt acts in the indictment.

2. Criminal intent the essence of every offense.

It may be affirmed as an universal proposition, that criminal intention is the essence of every species of crime. All indictments commence with an assertion of corrupt motives; and in indictments for treason, the overt acts laid are to show the manner in which the wicked intention is carried into execution. In the speeches of Lord Erskine, to whom the world is so largely indebted for a correct knowledge of the principles of civil liberty and the law of treason, you will find him perpetually contending, and contending with effect, that although the crown had proved the facts charged, it had not shown the evil design, the corrupt purpose, without which the facts are nothing.

Here Mr. Pinkney referred to and read part of Mr. Erskine's remarks in the case of Lord George Gordon. In that case it was proved that the prisoner incited the acts which produced the consequences complained of, yet he was acquitted, because he was not the enemy of the king, nor the friend of any man who was his enemy. He then continued:

3. Illustrations of the rule.

Take the case of a man who, in time of war, is charged with the defense of an important fortress or castle, which he surrenders to an incompetent force. What more effectual means could he have adopted to aid the enemy than the delivery of this fortress? The books will tell you, that if he was bribed to this desertion of his duty; if he did it with a view to benefit the enemy; he is guilty of treason. But if pusillanimity was the cause, or if it arose from a false calculation of his own means, or the force of the enemy, he is not a traitor. You may banish him with ignomy from the ranks which he has disgraced, or try him by martial law as a coward or a fool; but he has committed no treason.

Suppose a powerful force to invade the country, to which resistance is hopeless. They levy contributions; they do not proclaim that they will hang me if I neglect to comply with this order; but

they threaten plunder and desolation.   I know they have the power
to execute that threat, and I comply accordingly.   Now the paying
of money, or the furnishing of provisions, is an assistance; it is
"giving aid and comfort" much more effectually than the delivery
of a few prisoners or a deserter.   Yet no man will call this treason,
because there is no evidence of hostility to the interests of the
country.   The authorities say it is not treason.

In Stone's case,[1] the indictment charged as an overt act of adherence to the enemy, that the prisoner conspired, with others, to
collect intelligence, within England and Ireland, of the disposition
of the king's subjects, in case of an invasion of either country, and
to communicate such intelligence to the enemy.   The tendency of
parts of the correspondence, which was given in evidence, was to
advise the enemy against an invasion of England, by representing
the improbability of its being attended with any success, from the
general disposition of the people.

Now it was scarcely possible that such a correspondence could
have been opened and maintained with other than corrupt motives.
Yet the counsel were allowed to argue that the letters were transmitted with a good intent, in order to avert the danger of so great
a calamity as an invasion, and the court said, the jury were to judge
from all the circumstances, whether the intelligence had been sent
with that view.

4. ADHERING TO THE ENEMY AND LEVYING WAR.

My client is charged, as Stone was charged, with being an adherent; and like him is entitled to be sheltered by his motives from
the imputation of treason.   The district attorney confounds the indictment which you are now trying with an indictment for levying
war.   I admit that it has been decided, that if a man becomes an
integral part of the enemy's force, and acts with it, he necessarily
levies war and is guilty of treason, unless it appears that he did so
pro terrore mortis.   The law will suffer no other exculpation of such
conduct; it will excuse it upon no other motive.   But will the gentlemen refer us to some authority which declares, that if a man,
without joining the enemy so as to levy war, does, upon virtuous or
even pardonable inducements (having no reference to the promotion
of the enemy's views), that which happens or is calculated to be
advantageous to the enemy, he is therefore a traitor?   What is an

[1] I East's C. L. p. 79.

adherent ?   Can he be anything less than a willing partisan, a corrupt auxiliary of the enemy ?   Such, at least, is the natural and
ordinary import of the word; and you cannot strain it beyond that
import by the refinements of construction, to the prejudice of the
accused, without reviving the ferocious and appalling doctrine of
constructive treason, which once made England bleed at every pore,
and stained the palace and the cottage with judicial murder.   The
protecting spirit of the Constitution, and of the statute which acts
upon it, as well as humanity and justice, would be outraged by such
a course.

5. THE UNMISTAKABLE INTENTION OF THE PRISONER.

Unlike the conduct of Stone, the conduct of Hodges presents
nothing ambiguous to the most zealous scrutiny.   His honorable
feelings and intentions are acknowledged by all; he was urged by
the solicitation of those whom he respected; he was led by a generous sympathy for the situation of one who is deservedly dear to
all who know him; he was actuated by an apprehension, by no
means unreasonable, for the quiet and safety of the affrighted
women and helpless children of the neighborhood, and for the security of the persons and property of the whole district.   The
treason of adherence cannot be committed by one whose heart is
warm with all the honorable feelings of the man and the patriot.
" Overt acts undoubtedly do discover the man's intentions; but I
conceive they are not to be considered merely as evidence, but as
the means made use of to effect the purposes of the heart." [1]

6. CRIME PROCEEDS ALWAYS FROM A WICKED HEART.

This is the master key which lets you into the whole secret of
this title of the criminal law.   Sir Walter Tyrrel, who, in shooting
at a deer killed the king, could not be convicted of treason.   The
killing was *per infortunium*.   So, where a person *non compos* slays
another designedly, still he is innocent, because there is no malignity in his heart.   So in every homicide, it is felonious, justifiable or
excusable, according to the purpose with which the act was perpetrated.   It is murder where it is done through malice; manslaughter,
if without malice; where it is done through misfortune, or in self
defense, it is excusable, and it is justifiable when done in advancement of public justice, in obedience to the laws.   If the heart be

---

[1] Foster, p. 203.

uncontaminated by corrupt intentions, the man is innocent, for it is motive that qualifies actions. As it will be with God so it is with the man: the latent intention of the heart must be searched.

7. THE CIRCUMSTANCES OF THE SURRENDER.

Look at the *locus in quo*—the scene where the plot of this treason is laid. A hostile force, but the day before, had traversed the country in all the pride of victory. The *jus belli* was lord of the ascendant. The army, if such a force may deserve the name, which had been relied upon for the defense of the capitol, had been broken up and dissipated to every quarter of the compass. The country was menaced by an enemy with whom, to adopt the language of Cæsar, it was easier to do than to say. If I were addressing the jury I might appeal to their love of country. I might remind them that they are administering law for posterity as well as for us. But I am addressing a tribunal where these considerations have their full weight, and I expect with confidence that the court will vindicate the doctrines which I have had the honor to advance.

DUVALL, C. J.—The court would have been better satisfied if the whole case had been gone through in the usual way; but as the district attorney had prayed an opinion on the law, the court will give their opinion.

Here the court made the following decision: 1st. Hodges is accused of adhering to the enemy, and the overt act laid consists in the delivery of certain prisoners; and I am of opinion that the overt act laid in the indictment and proved by the witnesses, is high treason against the United States. 2d. When the act itself amounts to treason, it involves the intention, and such was the character of this act. No threat of destruction of property will excuse or justify such an act: nothing but a threat of life, and that likely to be put into execution. 3d. The jury are not bound to conform to this opinion, because they have a right, in all criminal cases, to decide on the law and the facts.

HOUSTON, J.—I do not entirely agree with the chief justice in any except the last remark.

MR. PINKNEY (rising and addressing the jury).—The opinion which the chief justice has just delivered is not, and I thank God for it, the law of the land. If you have the slightest doubt on the subject, I will undertake to remove it, to show you that the cases have been misconceived, and that the conclusions drawn from them are erroneous.

8. Conduct of the court and the prosecution.

No man can feel for the learned judge who has just given you his instruction, a reverence and affection more sincere than I do. But reverence and affection for him shall not stand in the way of the great duty which I owe to a fellow citizen who relies on me to shield his innocence from the charge of guilt, and his life from an attainder for treason. I had hoped that, since his motives were admitted on all hands to be entitled to praise, since the grand jury had associated with their indictment a certificate of the purity of his views, and a solemn recommendation that the prosecution should be abandoned, he would at least have been left by the district attorney, and the court, to obtain from you, as he could, a deliverance from the danger that encompassed him. In that hope I have been disappointed. As if the salvation of the State depended upon the conviction of this unfortunate man, whose situation, one would think, an inquisitor might deplore, the district attorney has gone out of his way to bring down vengeance upon him; and one of the court has told you that he is a traitor, and that you ought to find him so.

In a case where justice might be expected to be softened into clemency, and even to connive at acquittal, where every generous sentiment must take part with the accused, and law might be thought to fear the reproach of tyranny, if it should succeed in crushing him; in such a case the established order of trial is deserted, a pernicious novelty is introduced, the court is called upon to mix itself in your deliberations, to mutilate the defense of the prisoner's counsel, to harden your consciences against the solicitations of an enlightened mercy, and to sacrifice the prisoner to gloomy and exterminating principles, which would render the noble and beneficent system of law, for which we are distinguished, a hideous spectacle of cruelty and oppression. For the sake of the country to which I belong, as well as of my client, I will not only protest before you against these principles, but will examine and speak of them with freedom, restrained only by the decorum which this place requires.

9. Law of treason defined.—Opinion of the court not law.

In my argument to the court, I showed that if it be done treacherously it is treason; but that if the commander act from any motive not corrupt, no indictment can touch him.   If the fort be as impregnable as Gibraltar, and be garrisoned with 50,000 men, and it is surrendered to a force of half that number, from motives of fear, the commander cannot be punished as a traitor.   What can be more strong to show that upon an indictment for adherence, the law looks into the heart, and adapts its penalties accordingly ?   Has that authority been answered ?

In the case of Stone, which was parallel with the point, the court said expressly, if the heart be pure it matters not how incorrect the conduct.   So the counsel argued, and Stone was acquitted. Has any answer been given to that authority ?   Has any been even attempted ?

This indictment charges Hodges with having done certain things wickedly, maliciously, and traitorously.   Must not the United States prove what they allege ?   When the law allows even words to be given in evidence as explanatory of intention to exculpate, it admits that exculpation may be made out by proof of innocent motives; that overt acts alone do not furnish a criterion; that concomitant facts, illustrative of the state of the heart, must not be neglected.

A military force levies contributions.   If you pay them for the purpose of saving the country from farther mischief, although there be no fear or danger of death, the law says this is not treason.   By the doctrine of the chief justice, however, it is treason, and consequently his doctrine is unsound.

10. MOTIVES OF THE PRISONER LAUDABLE, NOT CRIMINAL.

On this occasion, the enemy were in complete power in the district where the transactions occurred which are complained of in the indictment.   They were unawed by the thing which we called an army, for it had fled in every direction.   They were omnipotent. The law of war prevailed, and every other law was silent.   The domestic code was suspended.   They menaced pillage and conflagration; and, after they had wantonly destroyed edifices which all civilized warfare had hitherto respected, was it to be believed that they would spare a petty village which had renewed hostilities before the seal of its capitulation was dry ?   There was menace— power to execute—probability—nay, certainty, that it would be executed.

How, then, can you find a wicked and traitorous motive in the breast of my client ?   There is not only the absence of any wicked

motive, but there is the visible presence of those which are laudable : an attachment to Dr. Beanes, anxiety for the defenseless
people about him, a desire to preserve the country from the afflictions which hung over it. In conduct so characterized, so produced, we discover the operations of an excellent heart upon a
mind which virtuous inducements could betray into error, but what
way we can distort it into treason I have not yet been able distinctly to learn.

11. ARRAIGNMENT OF THE DOCTRINE OF CONSTRUCTIVE TREASON.

The conduct is in itself treasonable, says the chief justice. It
necessarily imports the wicked intention charged by the indictment. The construction makes it treason, because it aids and comforts the enemy.

These are strong and comprehensive positions; but they have
not been proved; and they cannot be proved until we relapse into
the gulf of constructive treason, from which our ancestors in another country have long since escaped.

Gracious God ! In the nineteenth century to *talk* of constructive treason ! Is it possible that in this favored land—this last
asylum of liberty—blest with all that can render a nation happy at
home and respected abroad—this should be law? No. I stand up
as a man to rescue my country from this reproach. I say there is
no color for this slander upon our jurisprudence. Had I thought
otherwise I should have asked for mercy, not for law. I would
have sent my client to the feet of the president, not have brought
him, with bold defiance, to confront his accusers, and demand your
verdict. He could have had a *nolle prosequi*. I confirmed him in
his resolution not to ask it, by telling him that he was safe without
it. Under these circumstances I may claim some respect for my
opinion. My opportunities for forming a judgment upon this subject, I am compelled to say, by the strange turn which this cause
has taken, are superior to those of the chief justice. I say nothing
of the knowledge which long study and extensive practice enabled
me to bring to the consideration of the case. I rely upon this; my
opinion has not been hastily formed since the commencement of
the trial. It is the result of a deliberate examination of all the authorities, of a thorough investigation of the law of treason in all its
forms, made at leisure and under a deep sense of a fearful responsibility of my client. It depends upon me whether he should submit
himself to your justice, or use with the chief magistrate the inter-

cession of the grand jury, which could not have failed to have been successful. You are charged with his life and honor, because I assured him that the law was a pledge for the security of both. I declared to him that I would stake my own life upon the safety of his; and I declare to you now, that you have as much power to shed the blood of the advocate as to harm the client whom he defends.

If the mere naked fact of delivery constitute the crime of treason, why not hang the man who goes under a flag of truce to return or exchange prisoners? According to the doctrine of the chief justice, this man is equally guilty with him who stands at the bar, if you are forbidden to examine his mind, but are commanded by the law to look only to his acts. I ask you to consider this in the spirit of Stone's case. That doctrine, I pledge myself, goes through every nerve and artery of the law.

12. PRACTICAL RESULTS OF DOCTRINE ANNOUNCED BY THE COURT.

If the doctrine of the chief justice be the law of the land, every man concerned in the deeds of blood that were acted during our recent war, was a murderer.

Our gallant soldiers who had repulsed the hostile step whenever it trod upon our shores; our gallant tars who unfurled our flag, acquired for us a name and rank upon the ocean which will not soon be obliterated—these are all liable to be arraigned at this bar. These men have carried dismay and death into the ranks of the foe; blood calls for blood. You dare not inquire into the causes which produced the circumstances; which attended the motives; which prompted the deeds of carnage. The act you are told by the chief justice, and such is the reasoning of the attorney general, involves the intent.

Gentlemen! this desolating doctrine would sweep us from the face of the earth. Even when we deserved to be crowned with laurels we should be stretched on a gibbet. I tremble for my children, for my country, when I reflect upon the consequences of these detestable tenets which reduces indiscretion and wickedness to the same level. Which of you is there that in some unguarded moment may not, with honest motives, be imprudent? Which of you can hope to pass through life without the imputation of crime, if your motives may be separated from your conduct, and guilt

may be fastened upon your actions, although the heart be innocent ?

Gentlemen ! so solemnly, so deeply, so religiously do I feel impressed with this principle, that I know not how to leave the case
with you, although at the present moment it strikes my mind in so
clear a light that I know not how to make it more clear.

If this damnable prosecution should prevail, it would be the
duty of the district attorney instantly to arraign Gen. Bowie, one
of the witnesses in this case, than whom a purer patriot never
lived. Nay, half Prince George's county would come within its
baleful influence.

Yet such is the law the chief justice recommends to you. His
associate does not concur with him. In this conflict of opinion I
should be entitled to your verdict, but I rest the case upon more
exalted grounds. I call upon you as honorable men, as you are
just, as you value your liberties, as you prize your Constitution, to
say—and to say it promptly—that my client is not guilty.

The jury, without hesitating a moment, rendered a verdict of not guilty.

ARGUMENT OF WILLIAM WIRT,

IN THE CASE OF GIBBONS V. OGDEN.

[9 Wheat. 1.]

IN THE SUPREME COURT OF THE UNITED STATES, FEBRUARY TERM, 1824.

CONSTITUTIONAL LAW.—The power to regulate commerce is vested exclusively in Congress, and embraces navigation within the limits of every State. This power, when exercised, is supreme, and State laws repugnant thereto are void.

ANALYSIS OF MR. WIRT'S ARGUMENT.

1. Of the powers vested in Congress, and the rules of construction applicable thereto.

2. Exclusive and concurrent powers tested and distinguished.

3. The power of a State may be taken away by implication.—Repugnancy and occasional interference distinguished.

4. Why the power to promote the progress of science was vested exclusively in Congress.

5. The grant from its nature exclusive, not concurrent.

6. The power, even if concurrent, is repugnant to the laws of Congress.

7. The term "possessors," as used in the State statute, an evasion.

8. Nature and character of the patent laws.

9. The laws of New York conflict with the power of Congress to regulate commerce.

10. Distinction as to quarantine and police regulations.

11. The coasting trade protected by the laws of Congress.

12. Peroration.—Reply to Mr. Emmett.

" The Steamboat Case from New York," as it was familiarly termed while pending in the courts, involves one of the most interesting and important discussions to be met with in the annals of American jurisprudence. It is interesting, because it is associated with the greatest, certainly the most useful invention in the history of civilization—an achievement of scientific skill which will secure the fame of Robert Fulton throughout all coming time. It is important, because its effect was to nullify and sweep out of existence the laws of a sovereign State, which secured to its citizens privileges of the most vital importance and of incalculable value, after those statutes had been declared valid by the highest judicial authority in the State—a tribunal composed of some of the most learned and distinguished jurists of the age. The magnitude of the questions presented will appear upon a recital of the facts.

[47]

Thomas Gibbons, a citizen of Elizabethtown, in the State of New Jersey, was the owner of two boats named, respectively, the "Stoudinger" and the "Bellona," which were propelled by steam and used to transport passengers between the city of New York and Elizabethtown. These vessels were duly enrolled and licensed under an act of Congress passed February 18th, 1793 (L. U. S. vol. 1, p. 332, chap. 8), entitled "An Act for enrolling and licensing ships and vessels to be employed in the coasting trade and fisheries, and for regulating the same." Aaron Ogden filed his bill in Chancery and obtained an injunction restraining Gibbons from running or navigating his boats, upon the ground that the Legislature of the State of New York had granted to Robert R. Livingston and Robert Fulton, the original inventors of the use of steam as a motive power, the exclusive right and privilege to navigate the waters of New York State with boats moved by steam or fire, and that Livingston and Fulton had granted and assigned to him (Ogden) these rights and privileges. Gibbons filed his answer and asked that the injunction be dissolved, among other reasons, because the law of New York purporting to create and establish an exclusive right to navigate the waters of the State were repugnant to the Constitution of the United States, which conferred upon Congress alone the power to regulate commerce, and to promote the progress of science and the useful arts. That, by virtue of the license obtained by him, pursuant to the act of Congress passed February 18th, 1793, he acquired the right to employ his boats in the coasting trade, to navigate between parts of the same State, or of different States, and this right, he claimed, could not be interfered with or restricted by the law of any particular State. After an elaborate argument and upon due deliberation, the Chancellor denied the motion and made the injunction perpetual. From this decision an appeal was taken to the highest tribunal in the State, where the judgment of the lower court was affirmed. The appeal was carried to the Supreme Court of the United States, where it was argued by Mr. Webster and Attorney-General Wirt on the part of the appellant, and by Mr. Oakley and Mr. Thomas Addis Emmett for the respondent, and resulted in a reversal of the judgment and a dissolution of the injunction. The controversy has been regarded as one of the ablest and most brilliant intellectual contests which had taken place before the Supreme Court up to that time.

The effect of the laws here sought to be annulled was felt throughout the Union, in every State bordering upon the ocean or navigable waters, and, while the litigation was pending, was productive of hostile legislation which brought the neighboring States of Connecticut and New Jersey upon the verge of civil war with their sister commonwealth, the great Empire State. By the laws of New York no person could navigate the waters within its jurisdiction without a license from Livingston and Fulton, upon penalty of forfeiture of the vessel. By the laws of Connecticut no one having such a license was allowed to enter her waters; while in New Jersey it was enacted, that if any of her citizens should be restrained or hindered from using steam vessels plying between her ports and those of New York, such person might bring an action for damages in New Jersey, and recover treble costs against the party who had thus interfered under the laws of New York. Upon the theory that each State was an independent sovereignty, these acts of retortion and reprisal must eventually have resulted in civil war. The importance of the litigation, therefore, cannot

be overestimated.   A tribunal clothed with the power to pass upon such momentous questions as were here presented, has never before existed in the world.   No
wonder that Edward Everett was most profoundly impressed when he entered the
portals of the Supreme Court and contemplated the moral grandeur of such a body.
" From it," he said, in his elegant way, "from it the voice of equity and justice
has gone forth to the most powerful States of the Union, administering the law
between citizens of independent States, settling dangerous controversies, adjusting disputed boundaries, annulling unconstitutional laws, reversing erroneous
decisions, and, with a few mild words of judicial wisdom, disposing of questions
a hundredfold more important than those which, within the past year, from the
plains of Holstein, have shaken the pillars of Continental Europe and all but
brought a million of men into deadly conflict with each other."

No person, however, appreciated more keenly than Mr. Wirt himself, the significance of the occasion and the great intellectual display about to take place.
Shortly before the argument he wrote to his friend, Judge Carr, urging him
to be present on the occasion.   "Emmett and Oakley," he writes, " on one
side, Webster and myself on the other.   Come down and hear it.   Emmett's
whole soul is in the cause, and he will stretch all his powers.   Oakley is said to
be one of the first logicians of the age; as much a Phocion as Emmett is a
Themistocles, and Webster is as ambitious as Cæsar.   He will not be outdone
by any man, if it is within the compass of his power to avoid it.   It will be a
combat worth witnessing.   I have the last speech, and have yet to study the
cause; but I know the facts, and have only to weave the argument.   Now, if you
will come down, you will kill two birds with one stone.   We will first feast you,
and then cure you and send you home a well man.   Don't make light of this
proposition, and put me off with 'I wish it was in my power.'   It is in your
power.   You have only to will it, and it is done; and that you ought to will it,
heaven and earth know.   If you do not, you will be quite as much to blame as
the man who kills himself with strong drink.   In point of morality there will be
no difference between you.   You cannot make a *sound* distinction between the
two cases to save your life.   So do the thing that is right, and give us none of
your ' *clish maclaver*,' as Burns says."

It has been too often said of the great American orator, that he was a mere
declaimer, but possessed no great merits as a lawyer.   This assertion is not borne
out by the facts.   His argument in the present case is an example of clear, well
constructed reasoning, and conclusive as an argument.   The peroration in reply
to Mr. Emmett is a fine specimen of the finished style of this charming and accomplished rhetorician, and has often been quoted as a model of graceful declamation.   In closing the argument on the part of the appellant, Mr. Wirt said:

MAY IT PLEASE YOUR HONORS:—On the part of the appellant,
I trust I shall be able to demonstrate that the laws of the State of
New York are unconstitutional and void: (1st.) Because they are
in conflict with powers exclusively vested in Congress, which powers
Congress has fully exercised by laws now subsisting and in full
force.   (2d.) Because, if the powers be concurrent, the legislation
of the State is in conflict with that of Congress, and is, therefore,
void.   4

The powers with which the laws of New York conflict, are the power " to promote the progress of science and the useful arts by securing, for a limited time, to authors and inventors the exclusive right to their respective writings and inventions," and the power " to regulate commerce with foreign nations and among the several States." If these powers were exclusive in Congress, and it had exercised them by subsisting laws; and if the laws of New York interfere with the laws of Congress, by obstructing, impeding, retarding, burdening, or in any other manner controlling their operation, the laws of New York are void, and the judgment of the State court, founded on the assumption of their validity, must be reversed.

1. OF THE POWERS VESTED IN CONGRESS, AND THE RULES OF CONSTRUCTION APPLICABLE THERETO.

In discussing this question, the general principles assumed as postulates on the other side may be, for the most part, admitted. Thus it may be admitted, that by force of the declaration of independence each State became sovereign; that they were, then, independent of each other, and foreign to each other; that, by virtue of their separate sovereignty, they had, each, full power to levy war, to make peace, to establish and regulate commerce, to encourage the arts, and generally to perform all other acts of sovereignty. I shall also concede that the government of the United States is one of delegated powers, and that it is one of enumerated powers, as contended for by the counsel for the respondent. Yet they admitted that there were implied powers, and have given a different rule for the construction of the two classes of powers, which was, that " the express powers are to be construed *strictly*, the implied powers *liberally*." The implied powers, I presume, however, are only those which are necessary and proper to carry the powers expressly given into effect. They are the means to an end. This clause had not been generally regarded as in fact giving any new powers. Congress would have had them without the express declaration. The clause was inserted only *ex abundanti cautela*. With this explanation I shall concede that the Constitution of the United States is one of delegated and enumerated powers; and that all powers not delegated by the Constitution to the national government, nor prohibited by it to the States, are reserved to the States respectively, or to the people.

The peculiar rule of construction demanded for those powers

may also be conceded. But the express powers are to be strictly construed; the implied powers are to be construed liberally. By this it is understood to be meant, that Congress can do no more than they are *expressly* authorized to do; though the means of doing it are left to their discretion, under no other limit than that they shall be necessary and proper to the end.

On the other hand, the counsel for the respondent themselves admitted that Congress, nevertheless, has some exclusive powers; and, in conformity with the decisions of the court, they admit that those exclusive powers exist under three heads: (1.) When the power is given to Congress in express terms of exclusion. (2.) When a power is given to Congress, and a like power is expressly prohibited to the States. (3.) Where a power given to Congress is of such a nature that the exercise of the same power by the States would be repugnant.

With regard to the degree of repugnancy, it was insisted that the repugnancy must be manifest, necessary, unavoidable, total and direct. Certainly, if the powers be repugnant at all, they must be so with all these qualifications. If Congress, in the lawful exercise of its power, says that a thing shall be done, and the State says it shall not; or, which is the same thing, if Congress says that a thing shall be done on certain terms, and the State says it shall not be done except on certain other terms, the repugnancy has all the epithets which can be lavished upon it, and the State law must be void for this repugnancy.

2. Exclusive and concurrent powers tested and distinguished.

A new test for the application of this third head of exclusive power has been proposed. The respondent has said that "no power can be exclusive from its own nature, except where it formed no part of State authority previous to the Constitution, but was first created by the Constitution itself." But why were these national powers thus created by the Constitution? Because they look to the whole United States as their theatre of action. And are not all the powers given to Congress of the same character? Under the power to regulate commerce, the commerce to be regulated is that *of the United States* with foreign nations, among the several States, and with the Indian tribes. No State had any previous power of regulating these. The same thing might be affirmed of all the other powers enumerated in the Constitution. They were all created by the Constitution, because they are to be wielded by the whole Union over the whole Union, which no State could previously do. If any one power, created by the Constitution, may be exclusive for that reason, then all may be exclusive, because all are originally created. If, on the other hand, we are to consider the powers enumerated in the Constitution, not with reference to the greater arm that wields them and the more extended territory over which they operate, but merely in reference to the nature of the particular power in itself considered, then, according to this new test, all the powers given to Congress are *concurrent*, because there is no one power given to it which, considered in this light, might not have been previously exercised by the States within their respective sovereignties.

But this argument proves too much; for it has been conceded that some of the powers are exclusive from their nature; whereas, if the argument were true, none of them could be exclusive. On this argument the entire class or head of exclusive powers, arising from the nature of the power, must be abolished. But this court has repeatedly determined that there is such a class of exclusive powers. The power of establishing a uniform rule of naturalization is one of the instances. Its exclusive character is rested on the constitutional requisition that the rule established under it should be uniform.[1]

But the objection is urged that this would have been a concurrent power, but for the auxiliary provision in the Constitution that a citizen of one State shall be entitled to all the privileges of a citizen in every other State. We answer, that it is not so determined by the court in the case cited, and that the commentators on the Constitution place it exclusively on the nature of the power as described in the grant.[2]

So, also, the power of establishing *uniform* laws on the subject of bankruptcies, is clearly an exclusive power from its nature. The court has, indeed, determined, that until Congress thought fit to exercise the power, the States might pass local bankrupt laws, provided they did not impair the obligation of contracts; but that, as soon as Congress legislate on the subject, the power of the States is at an end.[3]

---

[1] Chirac *v.* Chirac, 2 Wheat. R. 269.
[2] The Federalist, No. 42.
[3] Sturges *v.* Crowninshield, 4 Wheat. R. 122.

3. THE POWER OF A STATE MAY BE TAKEN AWAY BY IMPLICA-
TION.—REPUGNANCY AND OCCASIONAL INTER-
FERENCE DISTINGUISHED.

But it has been said that this doctrine takes away State power by implication, which is contrary to the principles of interpretation laid down by the commentators on the Constitution. It was not the opinion of the authors of the *Federalist*, that a State power could not be alienated by implication. Their doctrine was, that it might be alienated by implication, provided the implication be inevitable; and that it is inevitable wherever a direct and palpable repugnancy exists. The distinction between repugnancy and occasional interference is manifest. The occasional interference alluded to in the *Federalist*, and admitted by this court in its adjudications, is not a repugnancy between the powers themselves; it is a mere incidental interference in the operation of powers harmonious in themselves. The case put was of a tax laid by Congress and a tax laid by the State upon the same subject, *e. g.*, on a tract of land, The taxes operate upon, and are to be satisfied out of the same subject. It might be inconvenient to the proprietor to pay both taxes. In an extreme case, the subject might be inadequate to the satisfaction of both. Then the tax laid by the paramount authority must be first satisfied. Still this incidental interference in their operation is not an inherent repugnance in the nature of the powers themselves.

It has also been said, that to constitute the power an exclusive one in Congress, the repugnancy must be such that the State can pass no law on the subject which will not be repugnant to the power given to Congress.

This requires qualification before it can be admitted. Some subjects are, in their nature, extremely multifarious and complex. The same subject may consist of a great variety of branches, each extending itself into remote, minute and infinite ramifications. One branch alone of such a subject might be given exclusively to Congress (and the power is exclusive only so far as it is granted), yet on other branches of the same subject the States may act, without interfering with the power exclusively granted to Congress. Commerce is such a subject. It is so complex, multifarious and indefinite, that it would be extremely difficult, if not impracticable, to make a digest of all the operations which belong to it. One or more branches of this subject might be given exclusively to Con-

gress; the others may be left open to the States. They may, therefore, legislate on commerce, though they cannot touch that branch
which is given exclusively to Congress.

So Congress has the power to promote the progress of science
and the useful arts, but only in one mode, viz., by securing, for a
limited time, to authors and inventors the exclusive right to their
respective writings and discoveries. This might be an exclusive
power, and was contended to be so. Yet there are a thousand other
modes in which the progress of science and the useful arts may be
promoted, as by establishing and endowing literary and philosophical societies, and many others which might be mentioned. Hence,
notwithstanding this particular exclusive grant to Congress of one
mode of promoting the progress of science and the useful arts, the
States may rightfully make many enactments on the general subject, without any repugnance with the peculiar grant to Congress.

4. WHY THE POWER TO PROMOTE THE PROGRESS OF SCIENCE WAS
VESTED EXCLUSIVELY IN CONGRESS.

But, to come now to the question whether these State laws be repugnant to this grant of power, we must first inquire why it was
conferred on Congress. Why was it thought a matter of sufficient
importance to confer this power upon the national government?
The answer to this question will be found in the history of the
country, in the nature of our institutions, and the great national
objects which the Constitution had in view. The country was in
its infancy; its population was small, its territory immense; it had
recently thrown off its bondage by the war of the revolution, and
was left exhausted and poor—poor in everything but virtue and the
love of country. It was still dependent on the arts of Europe for
all the comforts and almost all the necessaries of life. We had
hardly any manufactures, science or literature of our own. Our
statesmen saw the great destiny which was before the nation, but
they saw also the necessity of exciting the energies of the people,
of invoking the genius of invention, and of creating and diffusing
the lights of science. These were objects in which the whole nation was concerned, and were, therefore, naturally and properly
confided to the national government. The States, indeed, might
have exercised their inherent power of legislating on this subject;
but their sphere of action was comparatively small; their regulations would naturally have been various and conflicting. Discouragement and discontent would have arisen in some States from

the superior privileges conferred on the works of genius in others; contests would have ensued among them on the point of the originality of invention; and laws of retortion and reprisal would have followed. All these difficulties would be avoided by giving the power to Congress, and giving it exclusively of the States. If it were wisely exerted by Congress, there could be no necessity for a concurrent exercise of the power by the States.

5. The grant from its nature exclusive, not concurrent.

The terms of the grant are: "Congress shall have power to promote the progress of science and the useful arts, by securing, for a limited time, to authors and inventors the *exclusive* right to their respective writings and discoveries." This exclusive right is to be co-extensive with the territory of the Union. The laws to be made for securing it must be uniform, and must extend throughout the country. The exclusive nature of every power is to be tested by the character of the acts which Congress is to pass. This is the case with the naturalization laws. The exclusiveness of the power to establish them resulted from their character of uniformity. So here, the exclusiveness results from the character of the right which they are to confer. It is to be exclusive. It is not, indeed, said that Congress shall have the exclusive power, but it is said that they shall have power to do a certain act, which, when done, shall be exclusive in its operation. The power to do such an act must be an exclusive power. It can, in the nature of things, be performed only by a single hand. Is not the power of one sovereign to confer *exclusive* rights on a given subject, within a certain territory, inconsistent with a power in another independent sovereign, to confer *exclusive* rights on the same subject, in the same territory? Do not the powers clash? The right to be conferred by Congress is to exclude all other rights on the subject in the United States; New York being one of those States. The right to be conferred by New York is to exclude all other rights on the subject within the State of New York. That one right may exclude another is perfectly intelligible; but that two rights should reciprocally exclude each other, and yet both continue to subsist in perfect harmony, is inconceivable. Can a concurrent power exist, if, from the very nature of its action, it must take away, or render nugatory, the power given to Congress? Supposing the power to be concurrent, Congress may secure the right for one period of

time, and the respective States for another. Congress may secure
it for the whole Union, and each State may secure it to a different
claimant for its own territory. Congress possesses the power of
granting an exclusive right to authors and inventors within the
United States. New York claims the power to grant such exclusive right within that State. An author or inventor in that State
may take a grant for a period of time far longer than that allowed
by the act of Congress. He may take a similar grant from every
other State in the Union; and thus this pretended concurrent
power supersedes, abrogates and annuls the power of Congress.
What would become of the power of Congress after the whole
sphere of its action was taken away by this concurrent power of
the States? Who would apply to the power of Congress for a patent
or a copyright, while the States held up higher privileges? This
concurrent legislation would degenerate into advertisements for
custom. These powers would be in the market, and the highest
bidder would take all. Are not powers repugnant, when one may
take from the other the whole territory on which alone it can act?
Is not the repugnance such as to annihilate the power of Congress
as completely as if the whole Union was itself annihilated?

Something has been said of Congress repealing the laws of the
State, wherever they should conflict with those of the Union. But
where is this power of repeal? There is no such head of power in
the Constitution. Congress can act only by positive legislation on
any subject, and this it has done in the present instance. But this
action would be in vain, if another authority can act on the same
subject. If this concurrent power would defeat the power of Congress, by withdrawing from it the whole territory on which it is to
act, it would also defeat it by giving a monopoly of all the elements
with which invention is to work. This has been done by these
laws as to fire and steam. Why should it not be done equally with
all the other elements, such as gravitation, magnetism, galvanism,
electricity, and others? What is to consecrate these agents of
nature, and secure them from State monopoly, more than fire or
steam? If not, then is the power of Congress subject to be defeated by this concurrent power, first by a monopoly of all the territory on which it can act, and then by a monopoly of all the elements and natural agents on which invention can be exerted. Still,
it will be said that there is no direct repugnance between these
powers, and that the power of Congress may still act. But on what
can it act? The territory is gone, and all the powers of invention

are appropriated.   There is no difference whatever between a direct enactment that the law of Congress shall have no operation in New York, and enactments which render that operation impossible.   If, then, this process of reasoning be correct, the inevitable conclusion from it is, that a power in the States to grant *exclusive* patents is utterly inconsistent with the power given to the national government to grant such exclusive patents; and hence, that the power given to Congress is one which is exclusive from its nature.

6. The power, even if concurrent, is repugnant to the laws of Congress.

But suppose, for the sake of the argument, that the States have this concurrent power, yet it cannot be denied, that if the legislation of the State be repugnant to the laws of Congress, that of the State is void, so far as the repugnance exists.   In the present case the repugnance is manifest.   The law of Congress declares, that all inventors of useful improvements throughout the United States, shall be entitled to the exclusive right in their discoveries for fourteen years *only*.   The law of New York declares, that this inventor shall be entitled to the exclusive use of his discovery for thirty years, and as much longer as the State shall permit.   The law of Congress, by limiting the exclusive right to fourteen years, in effect declares, that after the expiration of that time the discovery shall be the common right of the whole people of the United States. The law of New York declares that it shall not, after fourteen years, be the exclusive right of the people of the United States, but that it shall be the exclusive right of this inventor for thirty years, and for so much longer as she, in her sovereign will and pleasure, may permit.   If this be not repugnance, direct and palpable, we must have a new vocabulary for the definition of the word.

But it was said, that the appellant had no patent under the United States, and, therefore, could not raise the question.   To this I answer, it was not necessary that he should have a patent. The question as to the validity of the law of New York is raised whenever a right is asserted under that law and is resisted by the party against whom it is asserted; and that validity is to be tested, not by comparing the law of New York with a patent, but by comparing it with the Constitution and laws of the United States.

It was also said, that there could be no repugnance, because it was admitted that wherever a patent from the United States appears, the patent obtained under the State law must yield to it; that the patent under the State is valid only until the patent from the paramount power appears; and that the rights derived from the different sovereigns must be found practically to clash before the law of New York was to give way for repugnancy. This is an insidious argument, and fraught with all the dangers which have been enumerated. For if the New York patentee be the inventor, the law of New York is absolute, and however unconstitutional it may be, there is no power of resistance. Besides, the argument is incorrect. To illustrate this, suppose a grant from Virginia, within the military reservation of Ohio, after she had ceded the whole territory to the United States; would the party in possession, even if a mere intruder, be bound to show a grant from the United States before he could resist the unlawful grant of Virginia? But there the plaintiff would be claiming under a State which had previously ceded away the power to make such grants, which is precisely the case here, so that there need be no repugnance arising from patents. If a repugnance exist between the laws of New York and the Constitution and laws of the United States, any citizen of the United States has a right to act as if the law of New York were a nullity; and the question of its nullity and validity arises wherever an attempt is made to enforce it.

7. The term "possessors," as used in the State statute, an evasion.

But it was argued that the power of Congress is limited to inventors, and that the power to encourage by patents the introduction of foreign discoveries, stands clear of this constitutional grant. If it were necessary, this doctrine might be questioned. The statute of the 21st James I, c. 3, uses the same word with the Constitution, "inventors;" and the decisions upon the construction of this statute might be referred to, in order to show that it has been considered as embracing discoveries imported from abroad.[1] But, even acceding to this doctrine, I may ask whether the question now before the court has anything to do with an art, machine or improvement imported from abroad? The privilege here granted by the State is to an American citizen who claims to be the inventor. The privilege is the reward of invention, not of importation, and this it is which brings it in conflict with the act of Congress. It is true, the law does not call him the inventor; it calls him merely the "possessor." But can the Constitution and laws of the United States be evaded in this manner? If he was not the inventor, why

[1] 17 Vin. 211.

this unjust tax which has been levied upon our admiration and gratitude? When the validity of a law is challenged for a fraudulent evasion of the rights of others, you are not bound by its own averments, but may resort to proof *aliunde* to establish the facts. The word *possessor* is a new and unusual word to apply to such a case, and marks a studious effort to conceal the truth. He was, of necessity, either the inventor or the importer. If he was the *importer*, there is no conceivable reason why he should be called by any other than that name. The Legislature of New York, in its act in behalf of Fitch, passed before the adoption of the Constitution, had no difficulty in applying the natural and appropriate name to him. But when the final law was passed in favor of Livingston and Fulton, in 1798, the Constitution of the United States, which cedes this power to Congress, had been adopted, and the laws by which that power is executed had been passed. This Constitution and these laws used the term *inventors*. But the privilege was too short. The State of New York offered better terms. The only difficulty was to give them effect without encroaching upon that power which had been constitutionally exercised by Congress. It would not do to call them *inventors*, and the device was adopted of calling him merely the *possessor*, which was a manifest evasion of the law of Congress.

8. NATURE AND CHARACTER OF THE PATENT LAWS.

But it was contended that the patent laws of the United States give no right; they only secure a pre-existing right at common law. What, then, do these statutes accomplish? If they do nothing more than give the inventor a chattel interest in his invention, and a remedy for its violation, he had these at common law. And if they only give him a mere right to use his invention in the States, with their permission, he had that before. The case of Millar *v.* Taylor proves the right to have been perfect at common law. The time of enjoyment was far greater. Thompson's Seasons had been published forty years when that action was brought. If the patent and copyright laws were merely intended to secure an exclusive right throughout the United States, and are, in fact, a limitation on the common law right (as was contended by the respondent's counsel), when this right has been thus secured throughout the United States, and a limitation constitutionally put upon it by Congress, can a State interfere with this regulation? The limitation is not for the advantages of the inventor, but of society at large, which is

to take the benefit of the invention after the period of limitation
has expired. The patentee pays a duty on his patent, which is an
effective source of revenue to the United States. It is virtually a
contract between each patentee and the people of the United
States, by which the time of exclusive and secure enjoyment is limited, and then the benefit of the discovery results to the public. A
State cannot, by its local laws, defeat this resulting interest of the
whole Union.

But it was said, that a State might prohibit the use of a patented
machine if it be noxious to the health of its citizens, or of an immoral or impious book, the copyright of which had been secured.
The answer to all such arguments was, that it will be time enough
to consider such questions when they arise. The constitutional power
of Congress is to patent *useful* discoveries. The patent authorizes
the patentee to *use* his invention, and it is the use which is secured.
When a discovery is deemed *useful* by the national government,
and a patent shall issue authorizing the patentee to use it throughout the United States, and the patentee shall be obstructed by a
State in the exercise of this right, on the ground that the discovery
is useless and dangerous, it will be time enough to consider the
power of the States to defeat the exercise of the right on this
ground. But this is not the question before the court. It might
be admitted that a State has authority to prohibit the use of a patented machine on that ground, or of a book, the copyright of which
had been secured, on the ground of its impiety or immorality. But
the laws which are now in judgment were not passed upon any
such ground. The question raised by them is, can the States ob-
struct the operation of an act of Congress by taking the power
from the national legislature into their own hands? Can they prohibit the publication of an immoral book, licensed by Congress, on
the pretext of its immorality, and then give an exclusive right to
publish the same book themselves? Can they prohibit the use of
an invention on the ground of its noxiousness, and then authorize
the exclusive use of the same invention by their own law?

But there is no pretext of noxiousness here. The authority to
enact these laws is taken up under a totally distinct head of State
power. It is the sovereign power to grant exclusive privileges and
create monopolies, the Constitution and laws of the United States
to the contrary notwithstanding. This is the real power under
which these laws are defended; and it may perplex, although it
cannot enlighten the discussion, to confound it with another and a

distinct head of State power.   If then the power of securing to
authors and inventors the use of their writings and discoveries be
exclusively vested in Congress, the acts of New York are void, because they are founded on the exercise of the same power by the
State.   And if the power be concurrent, these acts are still void,
because they interfere with the legislation of Congress on the same
subject.

9. The laws of New York conflict with the power of Congress to regulate commerce.

These laws were also void, because they interfere with the power
given to Congress, to regulate commerce with foreign nations and
among the several States.   This nullity of the State laws will be
supported, first, upon the ground of the power being exclusive in
Congress; and, secondly, that, if concurrent, these laws directly interfered with those of Congress on the same subject.

That this power is exclusive is manifest from the fact that the
commerce to be regulated is that of the United States; the government by which it is to be regulated is also that of the United
States; and the subject itself is one undivided subject.   It is an
entire, regular and uniform system which is to be carried into effect,
and will not admit of the participation and interference of another
hand.   Does not regulation, *ex vi termini*, imply harmony and uniformity of action ?   If this must be admitted to be the natural and
proper force of the term, let us suppose that the additional term,
uniform, had been introduced into the Constitution, so as to provide that Congress should have power to make uniform regulations
of commerce throughout the United States.   Then, according to
the adjudications on the power of establishing a uniform rule of
naturalization, and uniform laws of bankruptcy, throughout the
United States, this power would unquestionably have been exclusive in Congress.   But *regulation* of that commerce which pervades
the Union, necessarily implies *uniformity*, and the same result,
therefore, follows as if the word had been inserted.

10. Distinction as to quarantine and police regulations.

With regard to the quarantine laws, and other regulations of
police respecting the public health in the several States, they do
not partake of the character of regulations of the commerce of the
United States.   It has been said that these local regulations were
recognized by Congress, which had made them a part of its own

system of commerce. But this recognition would have been superfluous, if they could have stood without it on the basis of State
sovereignty; and so far as their adoption by Congress can be considered as affecting the question, the manner and purpose of the
recognition operates the other way. It will be found that, by
the commercial regulations which Congress has made, a general
system is adopted, which, if executed in every instance, shall carry
ships and vessels into all the ports of the several States, their local
quarantine laws to the contrary notwithstanding. An express regulation is, therefore, introduced, requiring the collectors of the customs to conform the execution of their official duties, under the
navigation and revenue laws, with the quarantine laws of the respective States. Without such a provision, the local health laws
must give way to the supremacy of the navigation and revenue laws
of the Union.

A serious objection to the exclusive nature of this power of
regulating commerce is supposed to arise from the express prohibitions on the States, contained in the 10th section of the 1st article
of the Constitution. It has been considered that these prohibitions
imply that, as to everything not prohibited, the power of the State
was meant to be reserved, and the authority of the authors of the
Federalist was cited in support of this interpretation. But another
commentator of hardly less imposing authority, and writing, not as
a polemic for the purpose of vindicating the Constitution against
popular objections, but for the mere purpose of didactic instruction as a professor, with this section before him, and with a strong
leaning towards State pretensions, considers the power to regulate
commerce as an exclusive power.[1] But the difference between them
is rather in appearance than in reality. It does not appear that
the author of that number of the *Federalist* did himself consider
these police regulations as, properly speaking, regulations of the
commerce of the Union. But the objectors to the Constitution
had presented them as such, and his argument in substance is, that
if they are, the Constitution does not affect them. The other
commentator did not consider them as regulations of the commerce
of the United States; for if he did, he could not admit them, as he
did, to be left in the States, and yet hold the opinion that the
power to regulate commerce was exclusively vested in Congress.
But may not a reason for these prohibitions be found, in the recent
experience of the country, very different from that which has here-

[1] Tucker's Blackstone, Pt. I, Appx. 180.

tofore been assigned for them. The acts prohibited were precisely those which the States had been passing, and which mainly led to the adoption of the Constitution. The section might have been inserted *ex abundanti cautela*. Or the convention might have regarded the previous clause, which grants the power to regulate commerce as exclusive throughout the whole subject; and this section might have been inserted to qualify its exclusive character, so far as to permit the States to do the things mentioned, under the superintendence and with the consent of Congress. If either or both of these motives combined for inserting the clause, the inference which had been drawn from it against the exclusive power of Congress to regulate commerce, would appear to be wholly unwarranted.

But if these police regulations of the States are to be considered as a part of the immense mass of commercial powers, is not the subject susceptible of division, and may not some portions of it be exclusively vested in Congress? It was viewing the subject in this light that induced my learned associate[1] to assume the position which has been misconceived on the other side. This proposition was, not that all the commercial powers are exclusive, but that, those powers being separated, there are some which are exclusive in their nature; and among them is that power which concerns navigation, and which prescribes the vehicles in which commerce shall be carried on.

It is, however, immaterial, so far as this case was concerned, whether the power of Congress to regulate commerce be exclusive or concurrent. Supposing it to be concurrent, it could not be denied that where Congress has legislated concerning a subject on which it is authorized to act, all State legislation which interferes with it is absolutely void.

II. The Coasting Trade Protected by the Laws of Congress.

It is not denied that Congress has power to regulate the coasting trade. It is not denied that Congress has regulated it. If the vessel now in question was sailing under the authority of these regulations, and has been arrested by a law of New York forbidding her sailing, the State law must, of necessity, be void. The coasting trade did, indeed, exist before the Constitution was adopted; I might safely admit that it existed by the *jus commune* of nations;

[1] Mr. Webster.

that it existed by an imperfect right; and that the States might
prohibit or permit it at their pleasure, imposing upon it any regulations they thought fit, within the limits of their respective territorial
jurisdictions.   But those regulations were as various as the States,
continually conflicting, and the source of perpetual discord and
confusion.   In this condition the Constitution found the coasting
trade.   It was not a thing which required to be created, for it already existed.   But it was a thing which demanded regulation, and
the power of regulating it was given to Congress.   They acted
upon it as an existing subject, and regulated it in an uniform manner
throughout the Union.   After this regulation it was no longer an
imperfect right, subject to the future control of the States.   It became a perfect right, protected by the laws of Congress, with
which the States had no authority to interfere.   It was for the very
purpose of putting an end to this interference, that the power was
given to Congress; and if they still have a right to act upon the
subject, the power was given in vain.   To say that Congress shall
regulate it, and yet to say that the States shall alter these regulations at pleasure, or disregard them altogether, would be to say, in
the same breath, that Congress shall regulate it and shall not regulate it; to give the power with one hand, and to take it back with
the other.   By the acts for regulating the coasting trade, Congress
has defined what shall be required to authorize a vessel to trade
from port to port; and in this definition not one word is said as to
whether it is to be moved by sails or by fire; whether it carries
passengers or merchandise.   The license gives the authority to sail,
without any of those qualifications.

That the regulation of commerce and navigation includes the
authority of regulating passenger vessels as well as others, would
appear from the most approved definitions of the term *commerce*.
It always implies intercommunication and intercourse.   This is the
sense in which the Constitution uses it; and the great national object was to regulate the terms on which intercourse between foreigners and this country, and between the different States of the Union,
should be carried on.   If freight be the test of commerce, this vessel was earning freight; for what is freight but the compensation
paid for the use of a ship?   The compensation for the carrying of
passengers may be insured as freight.   The whole subject is regulated by the general commercial law; and Congress has superadded
special regulations applicable to vessels employed in transporting
passengers from Europe.   In none of the acts regulating the navi-

gation of the country, whether employed in the foreign or coasting trade, has any allusion been made to the kind of vehicles employed, further than the general description of ships or vessels, nor to the means or agents by which they were propelled.

12. Peroration.—Reply to Mr. Emmett.

In conclusion, I observe that my learned friend (Mr. Emmett) has eloquently personified the State of New York, casting her eyes over the ocean, witnessing everywhere this triumph of her genius, and exclaiming, in the language of Æneas:

> " Quæ regio in terris, nostri non plena laboris?"

Sir, it was not in the moment of triumph, nor with feelings of triumph, that Æneas uttered that exclamation.[1] It was when, with his faithful Achates by his side, he was surveying the works of art with which the palace of Carthage was adorned, and his attention had been caught by a representation of the battles of Troy. There he saw the sons of Atreus and Priam, and the fierce Achilles. The whole extent of his misfortunes—the loss and desolation of his friends, the fall of his beloved country—rush upon his recollection.

> " Constitit, et *lachrymans;* Quis jam locus, inquit, Achate,
> 　Quæ regio in terris, nostri non plena laboris? "

Sir, the passage may, hereafter, have a closer application to the cause than my eloquent and classical friend intended. For, if the state of things which has already commenced, is to go on; if the spirit of hostility which already exists in three of our States, is to catch by contagion and spread among the rest, as, from the progress of the human passions and the unavoidable conflict of interest, it will too surely do, what are we to expect? Civil wars have often arisen from far inferior causes, and have desolated some of the fairest provinces of the earth. History is full of the afflicting narratives of such wars, from causes far inferior; and it will continue to be her mournful office to record them till time shall be no more. It is a momentous decision which this court is called on to

---

[1] To those who are familiar with the speech of Mr. Emmett, as reported in Wheaton, this explanation is due. It was corrected after the argument, and the portion of it to which Mr. Wirt's reply refers, now reads : " And conscious of the value of her own good works, she may *turn the mournful exclamation of Æneas into an expression of triumph, and* exultingly ask ' Quæ regio in terris,' " &c. The words in *italics* were interpolated after the speech was made, and their introduction takes away the chief point of the reply.

make.   Here are three States almost on the eve of war.   It is the high province of this court to interpose its benign and mediatorial influence.   The framers of our admirable Constitution would have deserved the wreath of immortality which they have acquired, had they done nothing else than to establish this guardian tribunal to harmonize the jarring elements in our system.   But, sir, if you do not interpose your friendly hand and extirpate the seeds of anarchy which New York has sown, you *will* have civil war.   The war of legislation, which has already commenced, will, according to its usual course, become a war of blows.   Your country will be shaken with civil strife.   Your republican institutions will perish in the conflict.   Your Constitution will fall.   The last hope of nations will be gone.   And what will be the effect upon the rest of the world ?   Look abroad at the scenes which are now passing on our globe, and judge of that effect.   The friends of free government throughout the earth, who have been heretofore animated by our example, and have held it up before them as their polar star, to guide them through the stormy seas of revolution, will witness our fall *with dismay and despair*.   The arm that is everywhere lifted in the cause of liberty, will drop, unnerved, by the warrior's side.   Despotism will have its day of triumph, and will accomplish the purpose at which it too certainly aims.   It will cover the earth with the mantle of mourning.   Then, sir, when New York shall look upon this scene of ruin, if she have the generous feelings which I believe her to have, it will not be with her head aloft, in the pride of conscious triumph—"her rapt soul sitting in her eyes;" no, sir, no ; dejected, with shame and confusion—drooping under the weight of her sorrow, with a voice suffocated with despair, *well* may *she then* exclaim:

" Quis jam locus,
Quæ regio in terris, nostri non plena laboris ! "

ARGUMENT OF DANIEL WEBSTER

IN THE CASE OF OGDEN V. SAUNDERS.

[12 Wheat. 213.]

IN THE SUPREME COURT OF THE UNITED STATES, JANUARY TERM, 1827.

CONSTITUTIONAL LAW.—A certificate of discharge under a State insolvent law is no bar to an action brought by a citizen of another State, in the Courts of the United States, or of any other State than that where the discharge was obtained.

ANALYSIS OF MR. WEBSTER'S ARGUMENT.

1. Bankrupt laws can be established only by national authority.
2. Obligation of contracts considered.
3. The duty of performing a contract rests upon universal law. — Illustration of the principle.
4. A statute which diminishes or lessens an obligation, impairs it.

5. The law acts upon a contract only when it is broken, but forms no part of the contract itself.
6. Object and purpose of the constitutional prohibition.
7. Grants of powers to Congress and prohibitions to the States considered.

The argument of Mr. Webster in the case of Ogden v. Saunders—though not so famous as his splendid effort in behalf of his *alma mater* (4 Wheat. 518), which made his reputation as the foremost constitutional lawyer in America; nor so well known as his exhaustive and learned exposition of the law of charitable uses in the Girard Will Case (2 How. 127), nor so elaborate as the speech delivered on the trial of John Francis Knapp, charged with aiding and abetting in the murder of Joseph White, which was pronounced by so competent an author-ity as Rufus Choate, as a more difficult and higher effort of mind than that more famous "Oration for the Crown,"—is, perhaps, equal to any of his great discussions as a specimen of perfect reasoning and clear statement. The ques-tions presented are of the utmost importance to the commercial world, and the manner in which they are discussed indicate the power and force of his under-standing—not inferior to that possessed by any man who has ever worn the robes of his noble and honorable profession—and worthy of the first lawyer and the first statesman of his age. The propositions advanced are demonstrated with mathematical accuracy, by a chain of argument leading inevitably to the con-clusions reached. The facts upon which the case arose are as follows :

Ogden had been discharged from his debts, under an insolvent law of the State of New York, known as the Three-Fourths Act, and was afterwards sued by Saunders, a citizen of Kentucky, in the United States Court for the District of Louisiana, on a bill of exchange drawn by Jordan, at Lexington, Kentucky, which had been accepted by Ogden prior to his insolvency, and protested for non-payment. The debtor, among other defenses, pleaded his discharge under the New York Statute as a bar to the action. Judgment was rendered in favor of the plaintiff, upon a special verdict. An appeal was taken to the Supreme Court of the United States, which was finally argued at the January Term, 1827, by Mr. Webster and Mr. Wheaton for the creditor (the respondent and defendant in error); and the Attorney-General, Mr. Livingston, Mr. D. B. Ogden, Mr. Jones, and Mr. Sampson, for the debtor (the appellant and plaintiff in error).

On behalf of the creditor it was claimed, that the statute of a State, discharging a debtor without full payment, was a law impairing the obligation of a contract, and in violation of the Constitution of the United States, being within the prohibition declaring that no State shall pass any law impairing the obligation of contracts; and the act being void, Ogden's discharge under it was no bar to plaintiff's action. The debtor, on the other hand, contended that the contract sued upon derived its obligation from the law under which it was made. That since the obligation was created by the law in force at its date, it could be modified and determined by it; and hence that such law could not impair the obligation, since no obligation could arise under the law, which was inconsistent with the law itself. That, accordingly, a contract made in a State of which the parties were citizens, was subject to a State bankrupt law existing at the date of the contract. The propositions advanced by the debtor were attacked by Mr. Webster on two grounds: (1) He denied that a contract, ordinarily, derives binding force from the particular laws of a State ; (2) That an insolvent law impaired the obligation of a contract, and the power to pass such a law was denied to the State by the federal Constitution, by which the power to pass bankrupt laws was vested exclusively in Congress, and such power could be exercised only by national authority.

Under the first proposition he asserted that all human obligations sprang from the universal law which recognizes everywhere a moral duty on the part of every individual to perform what he undertakes. That the laws of a State simply provide a remedy for enforcing an obligation already existing, and can operate upon the contract only when it is broken. He illustrated this by showing that a contract made in an uncivilized country or remote territory, where no civil government or formal statutory provisions existed, could be enforced in any tribunal here having jurisdiction of the parties; which could not be, if it were true that the contract depended for its existence upon some positive law prevailing in the place where the contract was made. Under his second proposition he showed that a bankrupt law deprived the creditor of a remedy, but did not extinguish the debt; that so long as the remedy was not denied by Congress, the creditor could enforce his claim in the federal courts; and the plea that the remedy had been denied in the State court, contrary to the organic law of the land, was no bar, and no answer, in the federal tribunal, which would recognize only a discharge under a national bankrupt law.

This selection, it is true, presents no room for rhetorical display, but the argument itself is great. When all the counsel had addressed the court, Mr. Webster closed the case for the creditor (the respondent and defendant in error) as follows :

MAY IT PLEASE THE COURT:—The question arising in this case is not more important, nor so important even, in its bearing on individual cases of private right, as in its character of a public political question. The Constitution was intended to accomplish a great political object. Its design was not so much to prevent injustice or injury in one case, or in successive single cases, as it was to make general salutary provisions, which, in their operation, should give security to all contracts, stability to credit, uniformity among all the States in those things which materially concern the foreign commerce of the country, and their own credit, trade, and intercourse with each other. The real question is, therefore, a much broader one than has been argued. It is this: Whether the Constitution has not, for general political purposes, ordained that bankrupt laws should be established only by national authority? We contend that such was the intention of the Constitution; an intention, as we think, plainly manifested in several of its provisions.

I. BANKRUPT LAWS CAN BE ESTABLISHED ONLY BY NATIONAL AUTHORITY.

The act of New York, under which this question arises, provides that a debtor may be discharged from all his debts, upon assigning his property to trustees for the use of his creditors. When applied to the discharge of debts contracted before the date of the law, this court has decided that the act is invalid.[1] The act itself makes no distinction between past and future debts, but provides for the discharge of both in the same manner. In the case, then, of a debt already existing, it is admitted that the act does impair the obligation of contracts. We wish the full extent of this decision to be well considered. It is not merely that the legislature of the State cannot interfere by law, in the particular case of A. or B., to injure or impair rights which have become vested under contracts; but it is, that they have no power by general law to regulate the manner in which all debtors may be discharged from subsisting contracts; in other words, they cannot pass general bankrupt laws to be applied *in præsenti*. Now, it is not contended that such laws are unjust, and ought not to be passed by any legislature. It is not said that they are unwise or impolitic. On the contrary, we know the general practice to be, that, when bankrupt laws are established, they make no distinction between present and future debts. While all agree that special acts, made for individual cases, are unjust, all admit that a general law, made for all cases, may be both just and

[1] Sturges *v.* Crowninshield, 4 Wheat. Rep. 122.

politic. The question, then, which meets us on the threshold, is this: If the Constitution meant to leave the States the power of establishing systems of bankruptcy to act upon future debts, what great or important object of a political nature is answered by deny-ing the power of making such systems applicable to existing debts?

The argument used in Sturges v. Crowninshield was, at least, a plausible and consistent argument. It maintained that the pro-hibition of the Constitution was levelled only against interferences in individual cases, and did not apply to general laws, whether those laws were retrospective or prospective in their operation. But the court rejected that conclusion. It decided that the Constitution was intended to apply to general laws or systems of bankruptcy; that an act providing that all debtors might be discharged from all creditors, upon certain conditions, was of no more validity than an act providing that a particular debtor, A., should be discharged on the same conditions from his particular creditor, B.

It being thus decided that general laws are within the prohibition of the Constitution, it is for the plaintiff in error now to show on what ground, consistent with the general objects of the Constitution, he can establish a distinction which can give effect to those general laws in their application to future debts, while it denies them effect in their application to subsisting debts. The words are, that "no State shall pass any law impairing the obligation of contracts." The general operation of all such laws is to impair that obligation; that is, to discharge the obligation without fulfilling it. This is ad-mitted; and the only ground taken for the distinction to stand on is, that, when the law was in existence at the time of the making of the contract, the parties must be supposed to have reference to it; or, as it is usually expressed, the law is made a part of the contract. Before considering what foundation there is for this argument, it may be well to inquire what is that obligation of contracts of which the Constitution speaks, and whence it is derived.

2. OBLIGATION OF CONTRACTS CONSIDERED.

The definition given by the court in Sturges v. Crowninshield is sufficient for our present purpose. "A constract," say the court, "is an agreement to do some particular thing; the law binds the party to perform this agreement, and this is the obligation of the contract."

It is, indeed, probable that the Constitution used the words in a somewhat more popular sense. We speak, for example, familiarly of a usurious contract, and yet we say, speaking technically, that a usurious agreement is no contract.

By the obligation of a contract, we should understand the Constitution to mean, the duty of performing a legal agreement. If the contract be lawful, the party is bound to perform it. But bound by what? What is it that binds him? And this leads us to what we regard as a principal fallacy in the argument on the other side. That argument supposes, and insists, that the whole obligation of a contract has its origin in the municipal law. This position we controvert. We do not say that it is that obligation which springs from conscience merely; but we deny that it is only such as springs from the particular law of the place where the contract is made. It must be a lawful contract, doubtless; that is, permitted and allowed; because society has a right to prohibit all such contracts, as well as all such actions, as it deems to be mischievous or injurious. But, if the contract be such as the law of society tolerates—in other words, if it be lawful—then, we say, the duty of performing it springs from universal law. And this is the concurrent sense of all the writers of authority.

3. The duty of performing a contract rests upon universal law.—Illustration of the principle.

The duty of performing promises is thus shown to rest on universal law; and if, departing from this well established principle, we now follow the teachers who instruct us that the obligation of a contract has its origin in the law of a particular State, and is in all cases what that law makes it, and no more, and no less, we shall probably find ourselves involved in inextricable difficulties. A man promises, for a valuable consideration, to pay money in New York. Is the obligation of that contract created by the laws of that State, or does it subsist independent of those laws? We contend that the obligation of a contract, that is, the duty of performing it, is not created by the law of the particular place where it is made, and dependent on that law for its existence; but that it may subsist, and does subsist, without that law, and independent of it. The obligation is in the contract itself, in the assent of the parties, and in the sanction of universal law. This is the doctrine of Grotius, Vattel, Burlamaqui, Pothier, and Rutherforth. The contract, doubtless, is necessarily to be enforced by the municipal law of the place where performance is demanded. The municipal law acts on the contract after it is made, to compel its execution, or give damages for its

violation. But this is a very different thing from the same law
being the origin or fountain of the contract.

Let us illustrate this matter by an example. Two persons contract together in New York for the delivery, by one to the other, of
a domestic animal, a utensil of husbandry, or a weapon of war.
This is a lawful contract, and, while the parties remain in New
York, it is to be enforced by the laws of that State. But, if they
remove with the article to Pennsylvania or Maryland, there a new
law comes to act upon the contract, and to apply other remedies if
it be broken. Thus far the remedies are furnished by the laws of society. But suppose the same parties to go together to a savage wilderness, or a desert island, beyond the reach of the laws of any society.
The obligation of the contract still subsists, and is as perfect as ever,
and is now to be enforced by another law, that is, the law of nature;
and the party to whom the promise was made has a right to take by
force the animal, the utensil, or the weapon that was promised him.
The right is as perfect here as it was in Pennsylvania, or even in New
York; but this could not be so if the obligation were created by the
laws of New York, or were dependent on that law for its existence,
because the laws of that State can have no operation beyond its territory. Let us reverse this example. Suppose a contract to be
made between two persons cast ashore on an uninhabited territory,
or in a place over which no law of society extends. There are such
places, and contracts have been made by individuals casually there,
and these contracts have been enforced in courts of law in civilized
communities. Whence do such contracts derive their obligation, if
not from universal law?

4. A STATUTE WHICH DIMINISHES OR LESSENS AN OBLIGATION IMPAIRS IT.

If these considerations show us that the obligation of a lawful
contract does not derive its force from the particular law of the
place where made, but may exist where that law does not exist, and
be enforced where that law has no validity, then it follows, we contend, that any statute which diminishes or lessens its obligation does
impair it, whether it precedes or succeeds the contract in date.
The contract having an independent origin, whenever the law comes
to exist together with it, and interferes with it, it lessens, we say, and
impairs, its own original and independent obligation. In the case
before the court, the contract did not owe its existence to the particular law of New York; it did not depend on that law, but could

be enforced without the territory of that State, as well as within it. Nevertheless, though legal, though thus independently existing, though thus binding the party everywhere, and capable of being enforced everywhere, yet the statute of New York says that it shall be discharged without payment. This, we say, impairs the obligation of that contract. It is admitted to have been legal in its inception, legal in its full extent, and capable of being enforced by other tribunals according to its terms. An act, then, purporting to discharge it without payment is, as we contend, an act impairing its obligation.

Here, however, we meet the opposite argument, stated on different occasions in different terms, but usually summed up in this, that the law itself is a part of the contract, and, therefore, cannot impair it. What does this mean? Let us seek for clear ideas. It does not mean that the law gives any particular construction to the terms of the contract, or that it makes the promise, or the consideration, or the time of performance, other than is expressed in the instrument itself. It can only mean that it is to be taken as a part of the contract, or understanding of the parties, that the contract itself shall be enforced by such laws and regulations, respecting remedy and for the enforcement of contracts, as are in being in the State where it is made at the time of entering into it. This is meant, or nothing very clearly intelligible is meant, by saying the law is part of the contract.

There is no authority in adjudged cases for the plaintiff in error but the State decisions which have been cited, and, as has already been stated, they all rest on this reason, that the law is part of the contract. Against this, we contend: 1st. That, if the proposition were true, the consequence would not follow. 2d. That the proposition itself cannot be maintained.

5. THE LAW ACTS UPON A CONTRACT ONLY WHEN IT IS BROKEN, BUT FORMS NO PART OF THE CONTRACT ITSELF.

1. If it were true that the law is to be considered as part of the contract, the consequence contended for would not follow; because, if this statute be part of the contract, so is every other legal or constitutional provision existing at the time which affects the contract, or which is capable of affecting it; and especially this very article of the Constitution of the United States is part of the contract. The plaintiff in error argues in a complete circle. He supposes the parties to have had reference to it because it was a binding law, and

yet he proves it to be a binding law only upon the ground that such reference was made to it. We come before the court alleging the law to be void, as unconstitutional; they stop the inquiry by opposing to us the law itself. Is this logical? Is it not precisely *objectio ejus, cujus dissolutio petitur?* If one bring a bill to set aside a judgment, is that judgment itself a good plea in bar to the bill? We propose to inquire if this law is of force to control our contract, or whether, by the Constitution of the United States, such force be not denied to it. The plaintiff in error stops us by saying that it does control the contract, and so arrives shortly at the end of the debate. Is it not obvious, that, supposing the act of New York to be a part of the contract, the question still remains as undecided as ever. What is that act? Is it a law, or is it a nullity? A thing of force, or a thing of no force? Suppose the parties to have contemplated this act, what did they contemplate? Its words only, or its legal effect? Its words, or the force which the Constitution of the United States allows to it? If the parties contemplated any law, they contemplated all the law that bore on their contract, the aggregate of all the statute and constitutional provisions. To suppose that they had in view one statute without regarding others, or that they contemplated a statute without considering that paramount constitutional provisions might control or qualify that statute, or abrogate it altogether, is unreasonable and inadmissible. "This contract," says one of the authorities relied on, "is to be construed as if the law were specially recited in it." Let it be so for the sake of argument. But it is also to be construed as if the prohibitory clause of the Constitution were recited in it, and this brings us back again to the precise point from which we departed.

The Constitution always accompanies the law, and the latter can have no force which the former does not allow to it. If the reasoning were thrown into the form of special pleading, it would stand thus: the plaintiff declares on his debt; the defendant pleads his discharge under the law; the plaintiff alleges the law unconstitutional; but the defendant says, you knew of its existence; to which the answer is obvious and irresistible, I knew its existence on the statute-book of New York, but I knew, at the same time, it was null and void under the Constitution of the United States.

The language of another leading decision is, "A law in force at the time of making the contract does not violate that contract"; but the very question is whether there be any such law "in force"; for, if the States have no authority to pass such laws, then no such law can be in force. The Constitution is a part of the contract as much as the law, and was as much in the contemplation of the parties. So that the proposition, if it be admitted that the law is part of the contract, leaves us just where it found us; that is to say, under the necessity of comparing the law with the Constitution, and of deciding by such comparison whether it be valid or invalid. If the law be unconstitutional, it is void, and no party can be supposed to have had reference to a void law. If it be constitutional, no reference to it need be supposed.

2. But the proposition itself cannot be maintained. The law is no part of the contract. What part is it? the promise? the consideration? the condition? Clearly, it is neither of these. It is no term of the contract. It acts upon the contract only when it is broken, or to discharge the party from its obligation after it is broken. The municipal law is the force of society employed to compel the performance of contracts. In every judgment in a suit on contract, the damages are given, and the imprisonment of the person or sale of goods awarded, not in performance of the contract, or as part of the contract, but as an indemnity for the breach of the contract. Even interest, which is a strong case, where it is not expressed in the contract itself, can only be given as damages. It is all but absurd to say that a man's goods are sold on a *fieri facias*, or that he himself goes to jail, in pursuance of his contract. These are the penalties which the law inflicts for the breach of his contract. Doubtless, parties, when they enter into contracts, may well consider both what their rights and what their liabilities will be by the law, if such contracts be broken; but this contemplation of consequences which can ensue only when the contract is broken, is no part of the contract itself. The law has nothing to do with the contract till it be broken; how, then, can it be said to form a part of the contract itself.

But there are other cogent and more specific reasons against considering the law as part of the contract. (1.) If the law be part of the contract, it cannot be repealed or altered; because, in such case, the repealing or modifying law itself would impair the obligation of the contract. The insolvent law of New York, for example, authorizes the discharge of a debtor on the consent of two-thirds of his creditors. A subsequent act requires the consent of three-fourths; but, if the existing law be part of the contract, this latter law would be void. In short, nothing which is part of the contract can be varied but by consent of the parties; therefore, the argument

runs *in absurdum;* for it proves that no laws for enforcing the contract, or giving remedies upon it, or any way affecting it, can be
changed or modified between its creation and its end. If the law
in question binds one party on the ground of assent to it, it binds
both, and binds them until they agree to terminate its operation.
(2.) If the party be bound by an implied assent to the law, as thereby making the law a part of the contract, how would it be if the
parties had expressly dissented, and agreed that the law should
make no part of the contract? Suppose the promise to have been
that the promisor would pay at all events, and not take advantage
of the statute; still, would not the statute operate on the whole—
on this particular agreement and all? and does not this show that
the law is no part of the contract, but something above it? (3.) If
the law of the place be part of the contract, one of its terms and
conditions, how could it be enforced, as we all know it might be, in
another jurisdiction, which should have no regard to the law of the
place? Suppose the parties, after the contract, to remove to
another State, do they carry the law with them as part of their contract? We all know they do not. Or, take a common case. Some States
have laws abolishing imprisonment for debt; these laws, according
to the argument, are all parts of the contract; how, then, can the
party, when sued in another State, be imprisoned contrary to the
terms of the contract? (4.) The argument proves too much, inasmuch as it applies as strongly to prior as to subsequent contracts.
It is founded on a supposed assent to the exercise of legislative
authority, without considering whether that exercise be legal or
illegal. But it is equally fair to found the argument on an implied
assent to the potential exercise of that authority. The implied
reference to the control of legislative power is as reasonable and as
strong when that power is dormant, as while it is in exercise. In
one case the argument is, "The law existed; you knew it, and
acquiesced." In the other it is, "The power to pass the law existed; you knew it, and took your chance." There is as clear an
assent in one instance as in the other. Indeed, it is more reasonable and more sensible to imply a general assent to all the laws of
society, present and to come, from the fact of living in it, than it is
to imply a particular assent to a particular existing enactment.
The true view of the matter is, that every man is presumed to submit to all power which may be lawfully exercised over him or his
right, and no one should be presumed to submit to illegal acts of
power, whether actual or contingent. (5.) But a main objection to

this argument is, that it would render the whole constitutional provision idle and inoperative; and no explanatory words, if such words had been added in the Constitution, could have prevented this consequence. The law, it is said, is part of the contract; it cannot, therefore, impair the contract, because a contract cannot impair itself. Now, if this argument be sound, the case would have been the same, whatever words the Constitution had used. If, for example, it had declared that no State should pass any law impairing contracts *prospectively* or *retrospectively;* or any law impairing contracts, whether existing or future; or, whatever terms it had used to prohibit precisely such a law as is now before the court,—the prohibition would be totally nugatory if the law is to be taken as part of the contract; and the result would be, that, whatever may be the laws which the States, by this clause of the Constitution, are prohibited from passing, yet, if they in fact do pass such laws, those laws are valid, and bind parties by a supposed assent.

But further, this idea, if well founded, would enable the States to defeat the whole constitutional provision by a general enactment. Suppose a State should declare, by law, that all contracts entered into therein should be subject to such laws as the legislature, at any time, or from time to time, might see fit to pass. This law, according to the argument, would enter into the contract, become a part of it, and authorize the interference of the legislative power with it, for any and all purposes, wholly uncontrolled by the Constitution of the United States.

So much for the argument that the law is a part of the contract. We think it is shown to be not so; and if it were, the expected consequence would not follow.

6. OBJECT AND PURPOSE OF THE CONSTITUTIONAL PROHIBITION.

The inquiry, then, recurs, whether the law in question be such a law as the legislature of New York had authority to pass. The question is general. We differ from our learned adversaries on general principles. We differ as to the main scope and end of this constitutional provision. They think it entirely remedial; we regard it as preventive. They think it adopted to secure redress for violated private rights; to us it seems intended to guard against great public mischiefs. They argue it as if it were designed as an indemnity or protection for injured private rights in individual cases of *meum* and *tuum;* we look upon it as a great political provision, favorable to the commerce and credit of the whole country.   Certainly, we do not deny its application to cases of violated private right.   Such cases are clearly and unquestionably within its operation.   Still, we think its main scope to be general and political.   And this, we think, is proved by reference to the history of the country, and to the great objects which were sought to be attained by the establish-ment of the present government.   Commerce, credit, and confidence were the principal things which did not exist under the old Con-federation, and which it was a main object of the present Constitu-tion to create and establish.   A vicious system of legislation, a sys-tem of paper money and tender laws, had completely paralyzed industry, threatened to beggar every man of property, and, ulti-mately, to ruin the country.   The relation between debtor and creditor, always delicate, and always dangerous whenever it divides society, and draws out the respective parties into different ranks and classes, was in such a condition in the years 1787, 1788, and 1789, as to threaten the overthrow of all government; and a revolution was menaced, much more critical and alarming than that through which the country had recently passed.   The object of the new Constitution was to arrest these evils; to awaken industry by giving security to property; to establish confidence, credit, and commerce, by salutary laws, to be enforced by the power of the whole com-munity.   The Revolutionary War was over; the country had peace, but little domestic tranquillity; it had liberty, but few of its enjoy-ments, and none of its security.   The States had struggled together, but their union was imperfect.   They had freedom, but not an es-tablished course of justice.   The Constitution was, therefore, framed, as it professes, " to form a more perfect union, to establish justice, to secure the blessings of liberty, and to insure domestic tran-quillity."

It is not pertinent to this occasion to advert to all the means by which these desirable ends were to be obtained.   Some of them, closely connected with the subject now under consideration, are obvious and prominent.   The objects were commerce, credit, and mutual confidence in matters of property; and these required, among other things, a uniform standard of value or medium of pay-ments.   One of the first powers given to Congress, therefore, is that of coining money and fixing the value of foreign coins; and one of the first restraints imposed on the States is the total prohibition to coin money.   These two provisions are industriously followed up and completed by denying to the States all power to emit bills of credit, or to make anything but gold and silver a tender in the payment of debts. The whole control, therefore, over the standard of value and medium of payments is vested in the general government. And here the question instantly suggests itself, why should such pains be taken to confide to Congress alone this exclusive power of fixing on a standard of value, and of prescribing the medium in which debts shall be paid, if it is, after all, to be left to every State to declare that debts may be discharged, and to prescribe how they may be discharged, without any payment at all? Why say that no man shall be obliged to take, in discharge of a debt, paper money issued by the authority of a State, and yet say that by the same authority the debt may be discharged without any payment whatever.

We contend that the Constitution has not left its work thus unfinished. We contend that, taking its provisions together, it is apparent it was intended to provide for two things, intimately connected with each other. These are,—1. A medium for the payment of debts; and, 2. A uniform manner of discharging debts, when they are to be discharged without payment.

7. Grants of power to Congress and prohibitions to the States considered.

The arrangement of the grants and prohibitions contained in the Constitution is fit to be regarded on this occasion. The grant to Congress and the prohibition on the States, though they are certainly to be construed together, are not contained in the same clauses. The powers granted to Congress are enumerated one after another in the eighth section; the principal limitations on those powers, in the ninth section; and the prohibitions to the States, in the tenth section. Now, in order to understand whether any particular power be exclusively vested in Congress, it is necessary to read the terms of the grant, together with the terms of the prohibition. Take an example from that power of which we have been speaking, the coinage power. Here the grant to Congress is, "To coin money, regulate the value thereof, and of foreign coins." Now, the correlative prohibition on the States, though found in another section, is undoubtedly to be taken in immediate connection with the foregoing, as much as if it had been found in the same clause. The only just reading of these provisions, therefore, is this : "Congress shall have power to coin money, regulate the value thereof, and of foreign coin; but no State shall coin money, emit bills of credit, or make anything but gold and silver coin a tender in payment of debts."

These provisions respect the medium of payment, or standard of value, and, thus collated, their joint result is clear and decisive. We think the result clear, also, of those provisions which respect the discharge of debts without payment. Collated in like manner, they stand thus: "Congress shall have power to establish uniform laws on the subject of bankruptcies throughout the United States; but no State shall pass any law impairing the obligation of contracts." This collocation cannot be objected to, if they refer to the same subject-matter; and that they do refer to the same subject-matter we have the authority of this court for saying, because this court solemnly determined, in Sturges v. Crowninshield, that this prohibition on the States did apply to systems of bankruptcy. It must be now taken, therefore, that State bankrupt laws were in the mind of the Convention when the prohibition was adopted, and, therefore, the grant to Congress on the subject of bankrupt laws, and the prohibition to the States on the same subject, are, properly, to be taken and read together; and being thus read together, is not the intention clear to take away from the States the power of passing bankrupt laws, since, while enacted by them, such laws would not be uniform, and to confer the power exclusively on Congress, by whom uniform laws could be established?

Suppose the order of arrangement in the Constitution had been otherwise than it is, and that the prohibitions to the States had preceded the grants of power to Congress, the two powers, when collated, would then have read thus: "No State shall pass any law impairing the obligation of contracts; but Congress may establish uniform laws on the subject of bankruptcies." Could any man have doubted, in that case, that the meaning was, that the States should not pass laws discharging debts without payment, but that Congress might establish uniform bankrupt acts? And yet this inversion of the order of the clauses does not alter their sense. We contend that Congress alone possesses the power of establishing bankrupt laws; and, although we are aware of that, in Sturges v. Crowninshield, the court decided that such an exclusive power could not be inferred from the words of the grant in the seventh section, we yet would respectfully request the bench to reconsider this point. We think it could not have been intended that both the States and general government should exercise this power; and, therefore, that a grant to one implies a prohibition on the other. But not to press a topic which the court has already had under its consideration, we contend that, even without reading the clauses of the Constitution in the connection which we have suggested, and which is believed to be the true one, the prohibition in the tenth section, taken by itself, does forbid the enactment of State bankrupt laws, as applied to future as well as present debts. We argue this from the words of the prohibition, from the association they are found in, and from the objects intended.

1. The words are general. The States can pass no law impairing contracts; that is, any contract. In the nature of things a law may impair a future contract, and, therefore, such contract is within the protection of the Constitution. The words being general, it is for the other side to show a limitation; and this, it is submitted, they have wholly failed to do, unless they shall have established the doctrine that the law itself is part of the contract. It may be added that the particular expression of the Constitution is worth regarding. The thing prohibited is called a *law*, not an *act*. A law, in its general acceptation, is a rule prescribed for future conduct, not a legislative interference with existing rights. The framers of the Constitution would hardly have given the appellation of *law* to violent invasions of individual right, or individual property, by acts of legislative power. Although, doubtless, such acts fall within this prohibition, yet they are prohibited also by general principles, and by the constitutions of the States, and, therefore, further provision against such acts was not so necessary as against other mischiefs.

2. The most conclusive argument, perhaps, arises from the connection in which the clause stands. The words of the prohibition, so far as it applies to civil rights, or rights of property, are, that " no State shall coin money, emit bills of credit, make anything but gold and silver coin a tender in the payment of debts, or pass any law impairing the obligation of contracts." The prohibition of attainders, and *ex post facto* laws, refers entirely to criminal proceedings, and, therefore, should be considered as standing by itself; but the other parts of the prohibition are connected by the subject-matter, and ought, therefore, to be construed together. Taking the words thus together, according to their natural connection, how is it possible to give a more limited construction to the term " contracts," in the last branch of the sentence, than to the word " debts," in that immediately preceding? Can a State make anything but gold and silver a tender in payment of future debts? This nobody pretends. But what ground is there for a distinction? No State shall make anything but gold and silver a tender in the payment of debts, nor pass any law impairing the obligation of contracts. Now, by what

6

reasoning is it made out that the debts here spoken of are any debts, either existing or future, but that the contracts spoken of are subsisting contracts only? Such a distinction seems to us wholly arbitrary. We see no ground for it. Suppose the article, where it uses the word *debts*, had used the word *contracts*. The sense would have been the same then that it now is; but the identity of terms would have made the nature of the distinction now contended for somewhat more obvious. Thus altered, the clause would read that no State should make anything but gold and silver a tender in discharge of *contracts*, nor pass any law impairing the obligation of *contracts;* yet the first of these expressions would have been held to apply to all contracts, and the last to subsisting contracts only. This shows the consequence of what is now contended for in a strong light. It is certain that the substitution of the word *contracts* for *debts* would not alter the sense; and an argument that could not be sustained, if such substitution were made, cannot be sustained now. We maintain, therefore, that, if tender laws may not be made for future debts, neither can bankrupt laws be made for future contracts. All the arguments used here may be applied with equal force to tender laws for future debts. It may be said, for instance, that, when it speaks of *debts*, the Constitution means existing debts, and not mere possibilities of future debt; that the object was to preserve vested rights; and that, if a man, after a tender law had passed, had contracted a debt, the manner in which that tender law authorized that debt to be discharged became part of the contract, and that the whole debt, or whole obligation, was thus qualified by the pre-existing law, and was no more than a contract to deliver so much paper money, or whatever other article might be made a tender, as the original bargain expressed. Arguments of this sort will not be found wanting in favor of tender laws, if the court yield to similar arguments in favor of bankrupt laws.

These several prohibitions of the Constitution stand in the same paragraph; they have the same purpose, and were introduced for the same object; they are expressed in words of similar import, in grammar, and in sense; they are subject to the same construction, and, we think, no reason has yet been given for imposing an important restriction on one part of them, which does not equally show that the same restriction might be imposed also on the other part.

We have already endeavored to maintain that one great political object intended by the Constitution would be defeated, if this construction were allowed to prevail. As an object of political regulation, it was not important to prevent the States from passing bankrupt laws applicable to present debts, while the power was left to them in regard to future debts; nor was it at all important, in a political point of view, to prohibit tender laws as to future debts, while it was yet left to the States to pass laws for the discharge of such debts, which, after all, are little different in principle from tender laws. Look at the law before the court in this view. It provides that, if the debtor will surrender, offer, or tender to trustees, for the benefit of his creditors, all his estate and effects, he shall be discharged from all his debts. If it had authorized a tender of anything but money to any one creditor, though it were of a value equal to the debt, and thereupon provided for a discharge, it would have been clearly invalid. Yet it is maintained to be good, merely because it is made for all creditors, and seeks a discharge from all debts; although the thing tendered may not be equivalent to a shilling in the pound of those debts. This shows, again, very clearly, how the Constitution has failed of its purpose, if, having in terms prohibited all tender laws, and taken so much pains to establish a uniform medium of payment, it has yet left the States the power of discharging debts, as they may see fit, without any payment at all.

To recapitulate what has been said, we maintain, first, that the Constitution, by its grants to Congress and its prohibitions on the States, has sought to establish one uniform standard of value, or medium of payment. Second, that, by like means, it has endeavored to provide for one uniform mode of discharging debts, when they are to be discharged without payment. Third, that these objects are connected, and that the first loses much of its importance, if the last, also, be not accomplished. Fourth, that, reading the grant to Congress and the prohibition on the States together, the inference is strong that the Constitution intended to confer an exclusive power to pass bankrupt laws on Congress. Fifth, that the prohibition in the tenth section reaches to all contracts, existing or future, in the same way that the other prohibition, in the same section, extends to all debts, existing or future. Sixthly, that, upon any other construction, one great political object of the Constitution will fail of its accomplishment.

UNCERTAINTY OF LAW.

WILLIAM PALEY.

To a mind revolving the subject of human jurisprudence, there frequently occurs this question : Why, since the maxims of natural justice are few and evident, do there arise so many doubts and controversies in their application ? Or, in other words, how comes it to pass, that although the principles of the law of nature be simple, and for the most part sufficiently obvious, there should exist, nevertheless, in every system of municipal laws, and in the actual administration of relative justice, numerous uncertainties, and acknowledged difficulty ? Whence, it may be asked, so much room for litigation, and so many subsisting disputes, if the rules of human duty be neither obscure nor dubious ? If a system of morality, containing both the precepts of revelation and the deductions of reason, may be comprised within the compass of one moderate volume ; and the moralist be able, as he pretends, to describe the rights and obligations of mankind, in all the different relations they may hold to one another ; what need of those codes of positive and particular institutions, of those tomes of statutes and reports, which require the employment of a long life even to peruse ?

Now, to account for the existence of so many sources of litigation, notwithstanding the clearness and perfection of natural justice, it should be observed, in the first place, that treatises of morality always suppose facts to be ascertained ; and not only so, but the intention likewise of the parties to be known, and laid bare. For example, when we pronounce that promises ought to be fulfilled in that sense in which the promiser apprehended, at the time of making the promise, the other party received and understood it ; the apprehension of one side, and the expectation of the other, must be discovered, before this rule can be reduced to practice, or applied to the determination of any actual dispute. Wherefore, the discussion of facts which the moralist supposes to be settled, the discovery of intentions which he presumes to be known, still remain to exercise the inquiry of courts of justice. And as these facts and intentions are often to be inferred, or rather conjectured, from obscure indications, from suspicious testimony or from a comparison of opposite and contending probabilities, they afford a never failing supply of doubt and litigation. For which reason, the science of morality is to be considered rather as a direction to the parties who are conscious of their own thoughts and motives and designs, to which consciousness the teacher of morality constantly appeals, than as a guide to the judge, or to any third person, whose arbitration must proceed upon rules of evidence, and maxims of credibility, with which the moralist has no concern.—[Moral and Political Philosophy, Book VI, ch. 8.]

[84]

SPEECH OF SEARGENT S. PRENTISS,

In Defense of Hon. Edward C. Wilkinson, of Mississippi, and Others, Indicted for Murder.

At the Mercer County Oyer and Terminer, Held at Harrodsburg, Ky., March Term, 1839.

Analysis of Mr. Prentiss' Speech.

In December, 1838, Hon. Edward C. Wilkinson, his brother Benjamin R. Wilkinson, M.D., and Mr. John Murdaugh, all residents of Mississippi, visited Louisville, Kentucky, for the purpose of making preparations for the marriage of the first-named gentleman, which was about to be celebrated with appropriate ceremonies. The party stopped at the Galt House. In the meantime Doctor Wilkinson ordered a suit of clothes in which to appear at his brother's wedding, from a Mr. Redding, a fashionable Louisville tailor. Two days prior to the time fixed for the nuptials, the three Mississippi gentlemen visited Mr. Redding's establishment for the purpose of obtaining the garments. The coat was a misfit, and not being satisfactory, the tailor promised to alter it. The Doctor was about to pay for the trousers, which had been sent to the hotel, when his brother remarked, that he had better try them on first, as they might be found to fit no better than the coat. Redding remarked that too much had been said about that already. The Judge retorted that he did not come there to be insulted, and seizing a poker struck Redding a violent blow. An altercation ensued. No blood was spilt, however, and the parties separated. Redding, nettled at what had occurred, concluded to take out warrants against the offenders, but was obliged to go to the Galt House to get their names. On his way thither, he related the circumstances to his friends, who became excited over the affair, and that evening armed themselves and proceeded in a body to the Galt House, in company with Redding. Whatever may have been their original intention, the result was a terrible and bloody tragedy. The Mississippians were attacked, knives and pistols were freely used, and two of Redding's companions were killed in the affray. The most intense excitement prevailed, and the Judge and his friends found the jail their only place of safety. Indictments for murder were promptly returned ; but such was the state of public feeling, that an application was made to the Legislature to change the place of trial to Mercer County, and it accordingly took place at Harrodsburg the following March.

The defense was conducted by Seargent S. Prentiss, an old friend of Judge Wilkinson, with whom were associated some of the ablest talent at the Kentucky bar. Mr. Prentiss was at this time but thirty years of age, but his learning and ability had already made for him a national reputation. He had just delivered an argument in Congress, to establish his right to a seat in that body, which Millard Filmore pronounced the most brilliant speech to which he had ever listened. "It elevated him at once," he said, "to the first rank of Congressional orators." Daniel Webster heard it with profound attention during the three days occupied in its delivery, and remarked with characteristic brevity, on leaving the Capitol: "No one can equal it." The peroration of this great speech has become familiar. It was short, but its effect upon the audience was said to have been wonderful. "When you decide," he said, "that she [the State of Mississippi] cannot choose her own representation, at the self-same moment blot from the spangled banner of this Union the bright star that glitters to the name of Mississippi, but leave the *stripe* behind, a fit emblem of her degradation." Judge Bullard remarked of this gifted child of genius, that he could speak the thoughts of poetry with the inspiration of oratory, and in the tones of music. " The fluency of his speech," says Mr. Baldwin, " was unbroken—no syllable unpronounced—not a ripple on the smooth and brilliant tide. Probably he never hesitated for a word in his life. His diction adapted itself without effort to the thought ; now easy and familiar, now stately and dignified, now beautiful and various as the hues of the rainbow, again compact, even rugged in sinewy strength, or lofty and grand in eloquent declamation."[1] In seeking for comparisons and illustrations, to adorn and beautify his rhetoric, Mr. Prentiss did not confine himself to places and incidents made famous by the poets of antiquity. From the jungles of India and the valley of the Nile ; from the plains of Tartary and tropical isles in summer seas, he drew pictures and images which fascinated and delighted his hearers. Yet his speeches are not burdened with a wearisome display of trope and metaphor. He was not, however, content to adopt a style uniformly severe, or to dress his images in solemn black. He arrayed them in gorgeous trappings, in gold and spangles, or in sombre garb, as fitness required, since incongruity was not one of his faults. He never sacrificed an argument for the sake of

---

[1] Baldwin's Flush Times in Alabama and Mississippi.

adornment. His facts were always plainly and tersely stated, and were woven into the text of his address with that consummate skill which indicates powers of analysis of the highest order. Like a meteor blazing across the sky, his genius shone with splendid lustre, dazzling the eyes of men ; and like a meteor he suddenly disappeared forever, the victim of disease and melancholy.

Judge Rowan, who was associated with Mr. Prentiss in the defense of Wilkinson, took occasion in his speech to the jury to pay his colleague the following compliment. In reply to the charge which had been made against Mississippians, that they were " a lordly people, who look down with contempt upon mechanics and the laboring classes of mankind," he remarked : " They looked down upon Mr. Prentiss, who traveled from the far east, and was engaged in teaching school among them—an obscure pedagogue. No; I cannot say he was obscure. He could not be obscure anywhere ; the eruptive flashes of his great mind, like those of Ætna, threw a blaze of light around him, which attracted, or rather exacted, their gaze and admiration. They sent him as their representative to the Congress of the United States. Mr. Prentiss must pardon me for thus going into his private history. I was myself an humble pedagogue. The difference in our condition is, that in my case the people of Kentucky honored me ; in his the people of Mississippi honored themselves."

The trial excited the keenest interest. The Court House was crowded, and it is said that nearly two hundred ladies graced the occasion with their presence, attracted by the name and fame of Mr. Prentiss. The famous Ben. Hardin assisted Mr. Bullock, the prosecuting attorney. The defense was a conspiracy on the part of the tailor and his friends to kill or degrade the Mississippians, and that the latter were justified in defending themselves to the last extremity. Mr. Prentiss spoke as follows :

MAY IT PLEASE YOUR HONOR, AND YOU, GENTLEMEN OF THE JURY :—I rise to address you with mingled feelings of regret and pleasure. I regret the occasion which has caused me thus accidentally and unexpectedly to appear before you, and has compelled you to abandon, for a time, the peaceful and quiet avocations of private life, for the purpose of performing the most important and solemn duty which, in the relations of civilized society, devolves upon the citizen. I regret to behold a valued and cherished friend passing through one of the most terrible ordeals ever invented to try the human feelings, or test the human character ; an ordeal through which, I do not doubt, he will pass triumphantly and honorably, without leaving one blot or stain upon the fair fame that has been so long his rightful portion; but through which he cannot pass unscathed in his sensibilities and feelings. The lightning scar will remain upon his heart; and public justice herself cannot, even though by acclamation through your mouths she proclaims his innocence, ever heal the wounds inflicted by this fierce and unrelenting prosecution, urged on, as it has been, by the demons of revenge and avarice. Most of all do I regret the public excitement which has prevailed in relation to these defendants; the uncharitable pre-judgment which has forestalled the action of law; the inhospitable prejudice aroused against them because they are strangers, and the attempt which has been, and is still making, to mingle with the pure stream of justice the foul, bitter and turbid torrent of private vengeance.

But I am also gratified; gratified that the prosecution under which my friends have labored, is about to cease; that their char-acters, as well as the cause of public justice, will soon be vindi-cated; that the murky cloud which has enveloped them will be dis-sipated, and the voice of slander and prejudice sink into silence before the clear, stern, truthful response of this solemn tribunal. The defendants are particularly fortunate in being tried before such a tribunal. The bearing and character of his Honor who presides with so much dignity, give ample assurance that the law will be correctly and impartially laid down; and I trust I may be permitted to remark, that I have never seen a jury in whose hands I would sooner intrust the cause of my clients, while, at the same time, I am satisfied you will do full justice to the commonwealth.

I came before you an utter stranger, and yet I feel not as a stranger towards you; I have watched during the course of the examination the various emotions which the evidence was so well calculated to arouse in your bosoms, both as men and as Ken-tuckians; and when I beheld the flush of honorable shame upon your cheeks, the sparkle of indignation in your eyes, or the curl of scorn upon your lips, as the foul conspiracy was developed, I felt that years could not make us better acquainted. I saw upon your faces the mystic sign which constitutes the bond of union among honest and honorable men; and I knew that I was about to address those whose feelings would respond to my own. I rejoiced that my clients were, in the fullest sense of the term, to be tried by *a jury of their peers*.

I. REASONS FOR CHANGING THE PLACE OF TRIAL FROM THE COUNTY WHERE THE CRIME WAS COMMITTED.

Gentlemen of the jury, this is a case of no ordinary character, and possesses no ordinary interest. Three of the most respectable citizens of the State of Mississippi stand before you, indicted for the crime of murder, the highest offense known to the laws of the land. The crime is charged to have been committed not in your own county, but in the city of Louisville, and there the indictment was found. The defendants, during the past winter, applied to the Legislature for a change of venue, and elected your county as the place at which they would prefer to have the question of their innocence or guilt investigated.

This course, at first blush, may be calculated to raise in your minds some unfavorable impressions. You may naturally inquire why it was taken; why they did not await their trial in the county in which the offense was charged to have been committed; in fine, why they came here? I feel it my duty, before entering into the merits of this case, to answer these questions, and to obviate such impressions as I have alluded to, which, without explanation, might very naturally exist. In doing so, it will be necessary to advert briefly to the history of the case. My clients have come before you for justice. They have fled to you, even as to the horns of the altar, for protection. It is not unknown to you, that upon the occurrence of the events, the character of which you are about to try, great tumult and excitement prevailed in the city of Louisville. Passion and prejudice poured poison into the public ear. Popular feeling was roused into madness. It was with the utmost difficulty that the strong arm of the constituted authorities wrenched the victims from the hands of an infuriated mob. Even the thick walls of the prison hardly afforded protection to the accused. Crouched and shivering upon the cold floor of their gloomy dungeon, they listened to the footsteps of the gathering crowds; and ever and anon, the winter wind that played melancholy music through the rusty gates, was drowned by the fierce howling of the human wolves, who prowled and bayed around their place of refuge, thirsting for blood.

Every breeze that swept over the city bore away slander and falsehood upon its wings. Even the public press, though I doubt not unwittingly, joined in the work of injustice. The misrepresentations of the prosecutor and his friends became the public history of the transaction; and from one end of the Union to the other, these defendants were held up to public gaze and public execration as foul, unmanly murderers, and that, too, before any judicial investigation whatever had occurred, or any opportunity been afforded them for saying a single word in their own defense.

I recollect well when I received the first information of the affair. It was in some respectable newspaper, which professed to give a full account of the transaction, and set forth with horrible minuteness a column of disgusting particulars.   Instantly, openly, and unhesitatingly, I pronounced the paragraph false, and trampled it under my heels; when rumor seemed to indorse and sustain the assertions of the public prints, I laughed her to scorn.   I had known Judge Wilkinson long and well.   I knew him to be incapable of the acts attributed to him, or of the crime with which he was charged.   Not an instant did I falter or waver in my belief.   I hurled back the charge as readily as if it had been made against myself.   What! a man whom I had known for years as the very soul of honor and integrity, to be guilty, suddenly and without provocation, of a base and cowardly assassination !   One whose whole course of life had been governed and shaped by the highest moral principle; whose feelings were familiar to me; whose breast ever had a window in it for my inspection, and yet had never exhibited a cowardly thought or dishonorable sentiment; that such a one, and at such an era in his life too, should leap at a single bound the wide gulf which separates vice from virtue, and plunge at once into the depths of crime and infamy !   Why it was too monstrous for credence.   It was too gross for credulity itself.   Had I believed it, I should have lost all confidence in my kind.   I would no longer have trusted myself in society where so slender a barrier divided good from evil.   I should have become a man-hater, and, Timon-like, gone forth into the desert, that I might rail with freedom against my race.   You may judge of my gratification in finding the real state of facts in the case so responsive to my own opinion.

I am told, gentlemen, that during this popular excitement, there were some whose standing and character might have authorized the expectation of a different course of conduct, who seemed to think it not amiss to exert their talents and influence in aggravating instead of assuaging the violent passions of the multitude.   I am told that when the examination took place before the magistrates, every bad passion, every ungenerous prejudice was appealed to.   The argument was addressed, not to the court, but to the populace.

It was said that the unfortunate individuals who fell in the affray were *mechanics;* while the defendants were *Mississippians, aristocratic slaveholders,* who looked upon a poor man as no better than a negro.   They were called *gentlemen,* in derision and contempt.   Every instance of violence which has occurred in Mississippi for years past was brought up and arrayed with malignant pleasure, and these defendants made answerable for all the crimes which, however much to be regretted, are so common in a new and rapidly populating country. It was this course of conduct and this state of feeling which induced the change of venue.

2. PRIVATE MEANS EMPLOYED TO PUSH THE PROSECUTION.—MISSISSIPPIANS AND KENTUCKIANS.—DUTY OF THE JURY.

I have made these remarks, because I fear that a similar spirit still actuates that portion of this prosecution, which is conducted, not by the State, but by private individuals.

I am not aware that the commonwealth of Kentucky is incapable of vindicating her violated laws, or unwilling to prosecute and punish the perpetrators of crime. The district attorney has given ample proof that she is provided with officers fully capable for asserting her rights and protecting her citizens; and with the exception of one or two remarks, which fell from him inadvertently, I accord to his observations my most unqualified approbation : he has done equal justice to the State and the defendants; he has acquitted himself ably, honorably, and impartially. But, gentlemen, though the State is satisfied, the prosecutor is not. Your laws have spoken through their constituted agent; now private vengeance and vindictive malice will claim to be heard. One of the ablest lawyers of your country, or of any country, has been employed to conduct the *private part* of this prosecution; employed, not by the commonwealth, but by the real murderer; him whose forehead I intend, before I am done, to brand with the mark of Cain—that in after life all may know and all may shun him. The money of the prosecutor has purchased the talent of the advocate; and the contract is, that *blood* shall be exchanged for *gold*. The learned and distinguished gentleman to whom I allude, and who sits before me, may well excite the apprehension of the most innocent. If rumor speak truth, he has character sufficient, even though without ability, and ability sufficient, even without character, to crush the victims of his purchased wrath.

I said that, with the exception of one or two remarks, I was pleased with the manly and honorable course of the commonwealth's attorney. Those remarks seemed to be more in the spirit of his colleague than in accordance with his own feelings. I was sorry to hear him mention so pointedly, and dwell so long upon the fact that the defendants were *Mississippians*, as if that constituted an ingredient in their crime or furnished a proof of their guilt. If to be a Mississippian is an offense in my clients, I cannot defend them; I am myself *particeps criminis.* We are all guilty; with a malice aforethought, we have left our own beautiful homes, and sought that land, the name of which seems to arouse in the minds of the opposing counsel only images of horror. Truly the learned gentlemen are mistaken in us; we are no cannibals, nor savages. I would that they would visit us, and disabuse their minds of these unkind prejudices. They would find in that far country thousands of their own Kentuckians, who have cast their lot by the monarch stream, in the enjoyment of whose rich gifts, though they forget not, they hardly regret the bright river upon whose banks they strayed in childhood. No State has contributed more of her sons to Mississippi than Kentucky; nor do they suffer by being transplanted to that genial soil. Their native State may well be proud of them, as they ever are of her.

But I do injustice to you and to myself by dwelling upon this matter. Here, in the heart of Kentucky, my clients have sought and obtained an unprejudiced, impartial jury. You hold in your hands the balance of justice; and I ask and expect that you will not permit the prosecution to cast extraneous and improper weights into the scale against the lives of the defendants. You constitute the mirror whose office it is to reflect, in your verdict, the law and the evidence which have been submitted to you. Let no foul breath dim its pure surface, and cause it to render back a broken and distorted image. Through you now flows the stream of public justice; let it not become turbid by the trampling of unholy feet. Let not the learned counsel, who conducts the private part of this prosecution, act the necromancer with you, as he did with the populace in the city of Louisville, when he raised a tempest which even his own wizard hand could not have controlled.

Well may he exclaim, in reference to that act, like the foul spirit in Manfred:

> I am the rider of the wind,
>   The stirrer of the storm;
> The hurricane I left behind
>   Is yet with lightning warm.

Aye, so it is still "with lightning warm." But you, gentlemen, will perform the humane office of a conductor, and convey this electric fluid safely to the earth.

You will excuse these prefatory observations: they are instigated, by no doubt of you, but by a sense of duty to the defendants. I wish to obviate, in advance, the attempts which I know will be made to excite against them improper and ungenerous prejudices. You have seen, in the examination of one of the witnesses, Mr. Graham, this very day, a specimen of the kind of feeling which has existed elsewhere, and which I so earnestly deprecate. So enraged was he, because the defendants had obtained an impartial jury, that he wished the whole Legislature in that place not to be mentioned to ears polite, and that he might be the fireman; and all on account of the passage of the law changing the venue. Now, though I doubt much whether this worthy gentleman will be gratified in his benevolent wishes, in relation to the final destiny of the Senate and House of Representatives of this good commonwealth, yet I cannot but believe that his desires in regard to himself will be accomplished, and his ambitious aspirations fully realized in the ultimate enjoyment of that singular office which he so warmly covets.

3. STATEMENT OF THE DEFENSE, AND THE LAW APPLICABLE TO THE CASE.

Gentlemen of the jury—I ask for these defendants no sympathy, nor do they wish it. I ask for them only justice—such justice alone as you would demand if you occupied their situation and they yours. They scorn to solicit that from your pity which they challenge from your sense of right. I should ill perform towards them the double duty which I have assumed, both of friend and advocate, did I treat their participation in this unfortunate transaction otherwise than candidly and frankly; did I attempt to avoid responsibility by exciting commiseration. I know that sooner than permit deception and concealment in relation to their conduct, they would bare their necks to the loathsome fingers of the hangman; for to them the infamous cord has less of terror than falsehood and self-degradation.

That these defendants took away the lives of the two individuals whose deaths are charged in the indictment, they do not deny. But they assert that they did not so voluntarily or maliciously; that they committed the act from stern and imperative necessity; from the promptings of the common instincts of nature ; by virtue of the broad and universal law of self-defense; and they deny that they have violated thereby the ordinances either of God or man. They admit the act, and justify it.

The ground of their defense is simple, and I will state it, so that it cannot be misapprehended. They assert, and I shall at-

tempt, from the evidence submitted, to convince you that a conspiracy was formed by the prosecutor and various other persons,
among whom were the deceased, to inflict personal violence upon
them; that the conspirators, by preconcerted agreement, assembled
at the Galt House, in the city of Louisville, and attempted to accomplish their object; and that, in the necessary, proper and legal
defense of their lives and persons from such attempt, the defendants caused the deaths of two of the conspirators. After discussing
this proposition, I shall submit another, which is, that even though
a conspiracy on the part of the deceased and their companions, to
inflict personal violence and bodily injury upon the defendants, did
not exist, yet the defendants had *reasonable* ground to suppose the
existence of such a conspiracy, and to apprehend great bodily harm
therefrom; and that upon such reasonable apprehension they were
justified in their action, upon the principle of self-defense, equally
as if such conspiracy had, in point of fact, existed.

The law applicable to these two propositions is simple, being in
fact nothing more than a transcript from the law of nature. The
principles governing and regulating the right of self-defense are
substantially the same in the jurisprudence of all countries—at
least all civilized ones. These principles have been read to you
from the books by my learned and excellent friend, Col. Robertson,
and require no repetition.

That a man has a right to defend himself from great bodily harm,
and to resist a conspiracy to inflict upon him personal violence, if
there is reasonable danger, even to the death of the assailant, will
not, I presume, be disputed. That *reasonable, well-grounded* apprehension, arising from the actions of others, of immediate violence
and injury, is a good and legal excuse for defensive action, proportionate to the apparent impending violence, and sufficient to prevent it, I take to be equally indisputable.

4. THE FACTS SHOWING A MOTIVE FOR A CONSPIRACY TO VISIT VIOLENCE ON THE ACCUSED.

By these plain rules, and upon these simple principles, let us
proceed to test the guilt or innocence of the defendants. First,
then, as to the existence of the conspiracy. Before examining the
direct evidence to this point, you will naturally inquire, was there
any cause for this alleged conspiracy? Motive always precedes
action. Was there any motive for it? If we establish the existence
of the seed, we shall feel less hesitation in being convinced of the

production of the plant. Was there, then, any motive on the part of Mr. Redding and his friends for forming a combination to inflict personal violence upon the defendants? In answering this question, it will be necessary to take notice of the evidence which has been given in relation to events that transpired at the shop of Mr. Redding at a period anterior to the transaction at the Galt House, and which, except for the clue they afford to the motive, and consequently to the subsequent action of the parties, would have no bearing upon the case before you. You will take heed to remember, that whatever of impropriety you may consider as attaching to the conduct of Judge Wilkinson and his friends during this part of the affair, must not be permitted to weigh in your verdict, inasmuch as that conduct is the subject of another indictment which is still pending in this court.

Judge Wilkinson visited Louisville for the purpose of making the preparations necessary for the celebration of his nuptials. The other two defendants had also their preparations to make, inasmuch as they were to act as the friends upon this interesting occasion. Dr. Wilkinson, a brother of the Judge, had ordered a suit of clothes of Mr. Redding, who follows the very respectable occupation of tailor, occasionally relieved and interspersed by the more agreeable pursuits of a coffee-house keeper. On the day but one preceding that fixed for the marriage ceremonies, the Doctor, in company with his brother and friend, Murdaugh, proceeded to the shop of Mr. Redding for the purpose of obtaining the wedding garments. Upon trying on the coat, it was found ill made and of a most ungraceful fit. It hung loosely about his shoulders, and excited by its awkward construction the criticism and animadversion of his friends. Even the artificer did not presume to defend the work of his own hands, but simply contended that he could reorganize the garment, and compel it, by his amending skill, into fair and just proportions. From the evidence, I presume, no one will doubt that it was a shocking bad coat. Now, though under ordinary circumstances the aptitude of a garment is not a matter of very vital importance in the economy of life, and ought not to become the subject of controversy, yet all will admit that there are occasions upon which a gentleman may pardonably indulge a somewhat fastidious taste in relation to this matter. Doctor Wilkinson will certainly be excused, considering the attitude in which he stood, for desiring a well-made and fashionable coat.

I confess I am not a very good judge in concerns of this sort.

I have had no experience on the subject, and my investigations in relation to it have been exceedingly limited. Under favor, however, and with due deference to the better judgment of the learned counsel on the other side, I give it as my decided opinion, that a gentleman who is about to participate in a marriage ceremony is justified in refusing to wear a coat which, by its loose construction and superabundant material, indicates, as in the case before us, a manifest want of good husbandry.

Suffice it to say, Doctor Wilkinson and his friends did object to the garment, and Mr. Redding, after some altercation, consented to retain it. The pantaloons, which constituted a part of the suit, had been sent to the hotel, and the Doctor was in the act of paying for them out of a $100 bill, which he had previously deposited with Mr. Redding, when the Judge remarked that he had better not pay for the pantaloons until he had first tried them on, as they might be found to fit no better than the coat. Mr. Redding, according to his own evidence, responded, that "they had said too much already about the matter;" to which the Judge, he says, replied, that he did not come there to be insulted, and immediately seized the poker and struck him; upon which the Doctor and Mr. Murdaugh also fell on him, with their knives drawn. Redding then seized his shears, but did not succeed in cabbaging therewith any part of his assailants. He was successful, however, in dragging the Judge into the street, where, after a slight scuffle which resulted in no personal injury to any of the parties, they were separated. After the separation, Redding offered, if they would lay down their knives, to fight them all. This kind proposition the defendants declined; but the Doctor returned into the shop, obtained his $100 note, and then the defendants retired from the place.

Such, in substance, is Mr. Redding's own account of the transaction at his shop. The witness Weaver also proves the altercation which occurred in relation to the fit of the coat and the scuffle which ensued in consequence. He, however, avers that Redding, in a very insulting manner, told the Judge that he "was more meddlesome than the other," and that he "was too d—d meddlesome," or words to that effect; which insulting language so excited the Judge that he seized the poker and commenced the assault.

The other witness, Craig, Redding's journeyman, testifies in substance the same as Redding, as to what passed in the shop; corroborates his account of the altercation about the coat; and says that he considered Doctor Wilkinson not as assisting in the affray, but as attempting to separate the parties.   Some of the witnesses think that the Doctor attempted, in the street, to stab Redding, as he was getting the advantage of his brother.   The evidence on this point, as well as in regard to the conduct of Murdaugh, is somewhat contradictory.   In the view, however, which I have taken of the case, the discrepancy is of little importance.

It is clearly proven, take the evidence in any way, that Mr. Redding used insulting language towards Judge Wilkinson, on account of the Judge's expression of an opinion in relation to the fit of his brother's coat.   What was the exact language used it is difficult to ascertain.

There were six persons in the room when the quarrel ensued— on the one side, the prosecutor (Redding), his foreman (Craig), and the boy (Weaver); on the other, the three defendants.

All the evidence on this point has been derived from the first party, and ought, consequently, to be taken with many grains of allowance.   The prosecutor has given you his version of the affair, but his cunning has prevented the defendants from giving you theirs.   Doctor Wilkinson, who was discharged by the examining magistrate, has been included in the indictment, one would judge, for the very purpose of precluding his testimony.   No one can doubt that the conduct of Judge Wilkinson, however reprehensible, resulted from the abusive language and insulting demeanor of Mr. Redding.   The happy facility with which he indulged, on a subsequent occasion, in the use of opprobrious epithets, gives good reason to suppose that his remarks on the present were not very guarded.   The expression deposed to by Weaver is, I presume, but a sample.   " You are too d—d meddlesome," was the observation, accompanied, no doubt, by the overbearing and bullying manner which illustrated his conduct afterwards, and which smacked more of his spiritual pursuit as the Ganymede of a coffee-house, than of his gentle calling as a knight of the shears and thimble.   He certainly did on this occasion " sink the tailor;" for tailors are proverbially polite and gentlemanly in their deportment.

I do not wish to be considered as justifying Judge Wilkinson or his friends, in taking notice of the petulant and insolent conduct of Redding.   I think they would have better consulted their character and feelings by treating him with contempt.   I will go further and candidly admit that I consider their course reprehensible, although it resulted from passion and sudden excitement, and not from deliberate determination.   They were themselves convinced of this in

7

a moment, and left the ground, ashamed, as they still are, of their participation in the matter- Judge Wilkinson rebuking and leading away his young and more ardent friend Murdaugh, who seemed to indicate more disposition to accept the boastful challenge of Mr. Redding, " that he could, if they would lay down their knives, whip them all three." From all the evidence it is perfectly clear that, in the altercation, no personal injury resulted to any of the parties; that the defendants retired voluntarily from the quarrel; while Mr. Redding retained the field, and with boastful taunts and insulting outcries invited a renewal of the fight. The Mississippians were manifestly satisfied. Not so Mr. Redding; he was "full of wrath and cabbage," boiling over with violence, and breathing defiance and vengeance against the retreating foe. He, doubtless, retired to his coffee-house, and attempted to soothe his wounded feelings with some of the delightful beverages which it was occasionally his profitable province to dispense to others. Here his friends gathered around him; he recounted to them his manifold grievances; he grew warm in the recital; the two white-handled pocket-knives, which had been drawn but not used in the affray, danced before his distempered imagination in the shape of trenchant and death-dealing blades. These little instruments of ordinary and general use became at once bowie-knives, " in buckram." He believed, no doubt, and made his friends believe, that he was an injured man, and that some satisfaction was due to his insulted honor. I have presented this part of the case to you simply for the purpose of enabling you to judge of the subsequent action of the parties, and to indicate on which side a desire for vengeance, and a combination to obtain it, were most likely to originate. Upon the conclusion of the first affray, which party would you have suspected of a disposition to renew it ? Where could lie the motive on the part of Judge Wilkinson and his friends for additional violence ? But who that is acquainted with the workings of human nature, or the indications of human feeling, will hesitate a moment in believing that revenge lurked in the bosom of Redding, and sought only a safe opportunity for development? His conduct indicated a state of mind precisely fitted for the formation of a conspiracy.

5. EVIDENCE, DIRECT AND CIRCUMSTANTIAL, DISCLOSING A CON-
    SPIRACY TO DESTROY THE DEFENDANTS.—THE
            DIRECT PROOF.

Having laid the foundation, I will now proceed to the erection of the superstructure. I will show, first by the direct, and then by the circumstantial proofs, the existence of this foul and cowardly conspiracy. I will, however, here remark, that I doubt not the misrepresentations and falsehoods of Mr. Redding, in relation to the transaction, induced several of the persons implicated to join the combination, who, with a correct knowledge of the facts, would never have participated in the affair.

First, then, as to the direct and positive evidence. Mr. Jackson says, that immediately after the first affray he was passing Mr. Redding's, when his attention was attracted by loud talking in the store, which induced him to enter, where he found Redding, Johnson and Meeks. Johnson was expressing his opinion as to the course which should be pursued towards the Mississippians for their conduct, and said they "ought to go to the Galt House and flog them." "Jack," said he to Mr. Redding, "just say the words, and I'll go for Bill Holmes, and we'll give them h—l;" at the same time boasting, in his own peculiar phraseology, "that he was as much manhood as was ever wrapped up in so much hide." Upon some hesitation being evinced at this proposition, Meeks said: "Let's go anyhow, and we'll have a spree."

Mr. Jackson further deposes, that some time after he was stopped by Johnson, on the street, who told him he was going after Holmes; that Jack Redding was a good man, and that he, Jackson, ought to go with them to the Galt House and see him righted. Jackson declined, alleging as an excuse his religious character, and his desire to abstain from fighting; whereupon Johnson exclaimed, in his ardent zeal for enlisting recruits, that "church, hell or heaven ought to be laid aside to right a friend." Jackson says he understood it distinctly, that it was a fight to which he was invited.

Mr. Jackson's testimony is entitled to credit. He did not participate in the affair, and he can have no inducement to speak falsely, for all his prejudices must naturally be enlisted on the side of the prosecution. His character is sustained by unexceptionable testimony, and has been impugned by no one except the salamander gentleman, whose ambition seems to be to pursue in the next world that occupation which in this is principally monopolized by the descendants of Ham.

The next direct evidence of the conspiracy is from Mr. Deering, whose character and testimony are both unimpeachable. He says he was passing down Market street, on the evening of the affray, when he saw, near the Market-house, Johnson in company with

Holmes and others, and that they were discussing the subject of the quarrel between the Mississippians and Redding. This proves that Johnson was carrying into effect his proposition at Redding's store, viz., "to go and get Bill Holmes, and give them h—l." He had already found Bill Holmes, and, we shall presently see, made all his arrangements for "giving them h—l."

Mr. Deering says, that soon after he met Mr. Johnson again, who inquired for Mr. Turner, the City Marshal. Mr. Deering told him he would be too late with his officers, for the Mississippians would be gone; to which Mr. Johnson responded, "*there were enough gone there—that if they came down their hides would not hold shucks.*" What did this mean, if it did not indicate that the conspiracy had already been formed, and a portion of the conspirators assembled at the Galt House for the purpose of preventing the game from escaping, and holding it at bay until the arrival of the rest of the hunters. They had gone, it seems, too, in sufficient numbers to authorize the classical boast of Mr. Johnson, "that if they (meaning the Mississippians) came down their hides wouldn't hold shucks."

There is one more witness whose testimony is positive to the point. It is Mr. Harris. He swears, clearly and unequivocally, that Johnson met him on the evening of the affray, told him that the Mississippians had insulted Mr. Redding, and directly solicited him to go with Redding's friends to the Galt House and see him righted. Mr. Harris says he refused to go, whereupon Johnson exclaimed: "Are you a friend of Redding's?" thereby showing how strong was the feeling where even a mere refusal to participate in the violence was considered as proof that the man refusing was no friend of Redding.

Such, gentlemen, is the positive proof of the conspiracy. It consists of the evidence of three disinterested and honest witnesses, two of whom were directly and strongly solicited to participate in the matter. The testimony of each of these witnesses corroborates that of the other two. The facts sworn to have a natural order and connection. There is verisimilitude about the whole story, which would not belong to either portion by itself. The testimony is entitled to much more weight than if it had been the recital of a single witness; for if you believe one of the witnesses, you must give credit to all. One of them swears that he heard Johnson, in Redding's shop, propose to Redding and his friends that he should get "Bill Holmes" and "give them h—l." The

next witness saw Johnson in the street immediately after, in company with "Bill Holmes," who seems to have been the Achilles of
these Myrmidons, explaining to him his dear Patroclus, Redding,
had been insulted by the hectoring Mississippians, and urging him
to vengeance. Again the same witness met Johnson, and was informed by him that a portion of his banditti had already taken
possession of the passes of the Galt House, and that, if the Mississippians appeared, "their hides wouldn't hold shucks." The third
witness swears to a positive solicitation from Johnson, that he
should join in the affray, and to the expression of strong indignation by this slayer of cattle upon his refusal to do so.

Johnson was the "Malise" of the party, the "messenger of
blood and brand" sent forth to summon the clansmen true. Too
well did he perform his duty. He collected his friends, and conducted them like beasts to the slaughter, while he himself found the
"manhood," which, according to his boast, distended his hide,
rapidly descending to his heels. But enough, for the present, of
this vaporing worthy; I shall pay my respects to him hereafter.

6. The circumstantial evidence showing a conspiracy.

I will now proceed, in pursuance of the plan I had prescribed,
to show the existence of the conspiracy by the circumstantial evidence, which is, if possible, more irrefragable than the direct testimony, but yet most beautifully illustrates and confirms it. I will
exhibit to you a chain of facts, linked together by a natural and
necessary connection, which I defy even the strong arm of the opposing counsel to break. I will weave a cable upon whose unyielding strength the defense may safely rely to ride out the storm of
this furious prosecution.

Mr. Redding went to the Galt House after the affair at his shop,
for the purpose, as he avows, of obtaining the names of the Mississippians, that he might procure process against them from the civil
authorities. On his way, as he confesses, he armed himself with a
deadly weapon, which, however, I am bound in justice to say, he
never had the courage to use. A number of individuals accompanied and followed him, whose manner and strange appearance
excited universal attention, even in the bar-room of the most frequented hotel in the western country. Their strange faces and
strange action excited general apprehension. Nearly every witness
to the unfortunate catastrophe has deposed that he was struck with

the "strange faces" congregated in the bar-room. The learned counsel on the other side has attempted to prove in the examination, and will, no doubt, insist in the argument, that that room is daily crowded with strangers from every part of the country; that the excellence of the fare and the urbanity of its proprietors invite to the Galt House a large portion of the traveling public; and that, consequently, it is nowise remarkable that strange faces should be observed in the bar-room. Though I admit the gentleman's premises, I deny his conclusion. That strangers should frequent the Galt House is not wonderful; they do it every day; and for that very reason strange faces, under ordinary circumstances, arouse neither remark nor attention. That the "strange faces" of Mr. Redding's friends should have excited remark and scrutiny, not only from the inmates of the house, but from strangers themselves, is truly wonderful, and can be accounted for only by admitting that there was something very peculiar in their conduct and appearance.

They went there prepared for preconcerted action. Having a common object, and a well arranged plan, a glance, or a motion, sufficed to convey intelligence from one to the other. Tell-tale consciences spoke from each countenance. Their looks, unlike the mystic sign of the mysterious brotherhood, gave up to the observer the very secret they wished thereby to conceal. There is a strange and subtle influence, a kind of mental sense, by which we acquire intimation of men's intentions, even before they have ripened into word or action. It seems, on such occasions, as if information was conveyed to the mind by a sort of natural animal-magnetism, without the intervention of the senses.

Thus, in this case, all the bystanders were impressed at once with the conviction that violence was intended by the strange men who had attracted their attention. These men, it is proven, were the friends and intimate companions of Redding. Most of them, though living in the city of Louisville, were not in the habit of going to the Galt House, and yet, by singular coincidence, had all assembled there on this occasion.

They were remarkably stout men, constituting the very elite of the thews and muscle of Louisville, and many of them noted for their prowess in the vulgar broils of the city. Why had they thus congregated on this occasion? Why their strange and suspicious demeanor? I will show you why. It will not be necessary to await the actual fight to become fully conversant with their purpose. It found vent in various shapes, but chiefly bubbled out in the unguarded remarks and almost involuntary expressions of the more garrulous of the party.

I shall be compelled, even at the risk of being tedious, to glance at the evidence of a number of the witnesses in showing you the circumstances at the Galt House, which conclusively indicate the existence of the conspiracy.

Mr. Everett, one of the proprietors of the Galt House, says he was admonished by his bar-keeper that a difficulty was about to arise, and he had better persuade Judge Wilkinson out of the bar-room. Accordingly, he went in and took the Judge away, and gives, as a reason, that he was alarmed at the strange faces in the bar-room, and apprehended difficulty; alarmed, not because the faces were those of strangers, but because of something in their appearance which indicated concert and threatened violence.

Mr. Trabue was waiting in the room for supper, and says he heard some one remark, "if the Mississippians had not gone up-stairs, they would have been badly treated;" in connection with which remark Redding was pointed out to him. This, it seems, was after the Judge had retired at the solicitation of Mr. Everett. Now, who were to have treated the Mississippians badly, except Mr. Redding and his friends? Who else had any pretense for so doing? Can you doubt for a moment that the remark had reference to Mr. Redding's party? It was probably made by one of them; but whether by one of them or a stranger, it equally indicated their violent determination. Mr. Trabue also proves, that after Judge Wilkinson retired Mr. Redding also retired; and when the Judge returned into the bar-room Redding presently entered, followed, to use the language of Mr. Trabue, "by a right smart crowd" of his friends. Now, why did Redding thus go out and return with his gang at his heels? Why were his movements thus regulated by the motions of the Judge? Wherefore was it that every one expected a difficulty?

Mr. Redding, according to his own story, went to the Galt House simply for the purpose of obtaining the names of the gentlemen who had insulted him.

He had accomplished his ostensible object. He had obtained the names, and more than that, he had gratified his base appetite by abusing one of the gentlemen in the most indecent and disgusting manner. No rowdy who ever visited his coffee-house could have excelled him in this, to the vulgar mind, sweet mode of vengeance. He had even driven the Judge from the room by the overwhelming torrent of his billingsgate epithets. To use an expression suited to his comprehension and feelings, he remained "cock of the walk." Yet he was not satisfied. He retired and watched the return of the Judge, and then, emboldened by his previous impunity, followed with his cut-throat band to complete the work of vengeance.

But to proceed with the circumstantial evidence. Mr. Montgomery states that he was with Mr. Trabue at the Galt House when Redding came in after the names, and also when he came back just before the conflict; heard him use very rough language, and also heard Halbert remark that there would be "rough work with the Mississippians." Now this fully corroborates the testimony of Mr. Trabue on the same point, who heard the remark, but did not recollect who made it. This Marshall Halbert is the man who boasted, after the affair was over, that he had knocked down one of the Mississippians with a chair, while his back was towards him, and recounted many other feats of daring to the astonishment of the listeners.

I should judge him to be of the blood of honest Jack Falstaff, whose killing, as everybody knows, was always by word of mouth, and whose deeds of desperate valor were so unfortunate as to find neither historian nor believer, except himself. At all events Halbert, according to his own confession, was one of the conspirators, and, I have no doubt, performed his part in the affray as well as he knew how, and with much greater humanity than he pretends. In addition to the above remark of Halbert's, Mr. Montgomery states that he heard several persons say, at a time when the defendants were not in the room, that they would beat the Mississippians well.

General Chambers, who lives opposite the Galt House, and is in the daily habit of visiting it, says he went into the bar-room just before the affray, that he observed persons whom he was not in the habit of seeing there, and that, from their appearance and demeanor, his suspicions were immediately aroused.

I attach great weight to the testimony of General Chambers. His character for intelligence and observation needs no comment from me, and the fact that his suspicions were aroused must convince every one that cause for alarm existed.

The next testimony to which I shall refer, is that of Mr. Oliver. He says that he was acquainted with Mr. Meeks, and was taking a social glass with him on the evening of the affray, when Meeks started off, saying he must go to the Galt House (which was on the opposite side of the street), that he was bound to have a fight that night, and, "by G—d, he would have one." You will recollect that Meeks was one of the persons who collected around Redding immediately after the affair at the shop, and seconded Johnson's proposition to get Bill Holmes and "give them h—l," by saying, "they would go anyhow, and have a spree." Can you doubt, for a moment, that the observation made by this unfortunate man to Mr. Oliver, as just recited, had relation to the previous arrangement with Johnson and others, at Redding's shop? The remark of Meeks, seems to me, taken in connection with his previous and subsequent conduct, is almost conclusive of itself as to the existence of a conspiracy. I had almost forgotten to observe Mr. Oliver's statement that Meeks, before he started, tied a knot in the small end of a cowhide which he carried, manifestly to prevent it from slipping out of his hand in the conflict which he so eagerly courted. His knife, by a sort of pious fraud, had been taken from him by Mr. Oliver, otherwise the result might have been very different. The prudent caution of Mr. Oliver in disarming him of his weapon proves how strong must have been the indications of his violent disposition.

Mr. Reaugh says, he was at the Galt House on the evening of the affray, and saw Redding in conversation with Rothwell and Halbert; he also saw Holmes and Johnson. Something in the demeanor of the party induced him to ask Johnson what was the matter. Johnson replied by relating the affair of the shop. Upon which Reaugh observed, "if the Mississippians fall into the hands of these men, they will fare rather rough." "Yes," replied the worthy butcher, "they would skin them quicker than I could skin a sheep." Mr. Reaugh states that he made the remark to Johnson, because of the remarkable size and strength of the men to whom he alluded, the strange manner in which they had assembled, and the fact that he knew them to be friends of Redding, and that Redding had been in a quarrel with the Mississippians.

Mr. Miller states, that being a member of the grand jury, and having heard of the affray at Redding's, he went into a tin-shop to inquire about the matter, when Mr. Halbert came in and boasted much of what he intended to do. Witness then went to the Galt House for supper, when he heard Redding abusing Judge Wilkinson, and challenging him for a fight. Witness advised Halbert to take Redding away, observing that he, witness, was on the grand jury, had the names, and would have all the matter attended to. Some one, he thinks Johnson, then remarked, that "if he didn't leave the room, he'd see the finest sort of beefsteaks served up." Presently he heard the exclamation, near the counter, "there they are, all three of them!" and the crowd immediately closed in upon the persons so indicated.

Mr. Waggry, also heard the remark about the "steaks," and then heard some one exclaim, "We'll have a h—l of a fight here just now." He also heard Mr. Miller advise Halbert to take Redding away.

Mr. Brown swears that he heard Mr. Miller tell Mr. Redding he was not taking the proper course; he should have the matter before the grand jury; whereupon some one said, "Hush you, Bill Miller, if it comes to handy-cuffs the boys will settle it." The witness then became so apprehensive of a fight that he left the room.

Now, though Miller is not positive as to the person who made use of the expression about "serving up beefsteaks," yet no one, I take it, will hesitate as to his identity. Who but Johnson could speak in such rich and technical language? Who but Johnson could boast of "having as much manhood as was ever wrapped in the same extent of hide?" While, at the same time, he had so arranged it that the "hides" of the Mississippians "would not hold shucks." Who but this unmitigated savage would talk of "skinning" a gentleman "quicker than I could skin a sheep?" Why, he rubs his hands, licks his lips, and talks of serving up Christians in the shape of "steaks," with as little compunction as you or I would exhibit in eating a radish. The cannibal! He should go at once to New Zealand and open his shambles there. His character would suit that country; and I doubt not, he would obtain great custom and find ample demand for his human "steaks." Why, gentlemen, I should be afraid to buy meat out of his stall. He talks as if he supplied it by burking. I should expect some day to swallow an unbaptized infant in the disguise of a reeking pig, or to eat a fellow-citizen, *incog.* in a "steak." Such a fellow should be looked to. But, again, what meant the expression deposed to by Reaugh, "There they are, all three of them, now?" It was the signal for the conspirators to close in. It clearly proves a preconcerted plan; no names were mentioned, and without a previous understanding the expression would have been nonsense. Most of the party did not know the Mississippians; hence it was necessary that some one should give intimation when they entered the room. The expression, "There they are," was the signal for the onset.   What meant the expression sworn to by Waggry, "We'll have a h—l of a fight just now?"

What conclusion do you draw from the response made to Miller, when he advised Redding to bring the matter before the grand jury: "Hush you, Billy Miller, and if it comes to handy-cuffs the boys will settle it?"   If what comes to handy-cuffs?   And who were the boys?   Why, if the quarrel with the Mississippians comes to handy-cuffs, and as for the "boys," there was not a man present who did not know who they were.

Redding was one of the "boys," and a very bad boy, too.   Billy Holmes was another; Marshall Halbert was a "perfect broth of a boy," and, if his own story is entitled to credit, he must have been twins, for he acted the part of at least two in the fight.   Bill John-son was as much of a boy as ever was "wrapped up in the same amount of hide," though his extraordinary modesty has induced him to deny the soft impeachment.   The unfortunate Meeks and Rothwell were two of the "boys;" and last, though not least, comes Harry Oldham, the "Jack Horner" of the party.   He "sat in the corner" till the fight was nearly over, when he "put in his thumb" and "pulled out," not "a plum," but a pistol; and ever since has been exclaiming: "What a brave 'boy' am I."

Yes, gentlemen of the jury, these were the "boys" whose strange appearance aroused the suspicions and excited the apprehensions of all.

Permit me, now, to call your attention to the testimony of Mr. Donahue.   It is clear and conclusive.   He swears, that on the evening of the affray, and just before it occurred, being in the bar-room of the Galt House, he heard Rothwell ask Redding "if they were there?"—upon being answered in the negative, he exclaimed, "Come, let us go up-stairs and bring them down, and give them h—l."   Rothwell was the brother-in-law of Redding, had been in-formed by Redding of his grievances, and had accompanied him to the Galt House.   Whom did he mean when he asked if "they were there?"   The Mississippians, undoubtedly.   Whom did he pro-pose to drag from their rooms, and chastise?   Of course the same persons for whom he had just inquired.   Rothwell asked if "they were there?"   When the defendants came in, some one cried out, "There they are, all three of them!"   These two expressions mani-festly emanated from persons who understood each other, and were engaged in pursuit of a common object.

If these remarks had not relation to some previously concerted plan of action, they would be unmeaning and foolish; but granting the existence of the conspiracy I have supposed, and every word is pregnant with meaning, full of force, weight and effect.

Mr. Raily deposes to the caution given by Miller to Redding; also to the fact that Redding left the room when Judge Wilkinson had retired, and came back again immediately after the Judge had returned. He also saw Oldham after the affair was over, putting a pistol into his pocket, and wiping, with his handkerchief, the blood from a double-edged dirk.

Mr. Pearson says he went to the Galt House just before supper, on the evening of the affray. As he stood behind the bar, one Capt. Rogers observed that there would be a fight. Presently, witness met Marshall Halbert, and told him he ought to stop it, meaning the fight. Halbert said, "no, let it go on." This was before Redding had commenced abusing Judge Wilkinson, and proves that the idea of a fight did not originate from that circumstance. The Judge came, and Redding abused him. He went out, and Redding followed. He returned, and presently so did Redding with a crowd at his heels. Seeing the crowd, and apprehending violence, Mr. Pearson was in the act of leading the Judge out of the room, when the crowd rushed upon Murdaugh; the affray commenced, and the Judge stopped, refusing to leave the room until he saw his friends out of the difficulty. Need I ask you whether he was right in so doing?

Mr. Banks says he saw Redding just after the first affray, and asked him if he was hurt. He says, no, but that "he would have satisfaction," and that "he could whip them, all three."

Dr. Graham says, that after Judge Wilkinson had left the barroom the first time, he heard some one observe, "the d—d coward has run."

Does not Mr. Oldham's testimony prove the conspiracy? I do not mean directly, but circumstantially. He says he was not present at the fight in the bar-room, and knew nothing of the affair, nor of the defendants. He says he was standing in the passage when the door opened, and he received a cut from Dr. Wilkinson, whom he knocked down for his pains.

After fighting in the crowd awhile, he saw Murdaugh retreating up-stairs, and heard him asking for a pistol, whereupon he was reminded of his own pistol, which he immediately drew and discharged at the young gentleman, giving him, not the weapon, but its

contents, to wit, a bullet split in three pieces.   This worthy gentleman, who is certainly

> " as mild a mannered man
> As ever scuttled ship, or cut a throat,"

swears positively that he did not know either of the defendants;
that he belonged to neither party in the affray; and that he fought,
to use his own   descriptive and unrivaled phraseology, entirely
"upon his own hook."

7. Arraignment of Henry Oldham, a witness for the commonwealth.

Surely, Mr. Henry Oldham must be the knight errant of the age;
the Don Quixote of the West; the paragon of modern chivalry.
He fights, not from base desire of vengeance, nor from sordid love
of gold; not even from patriotism or friendship; but from a higher
and a loftier sentiment: from his pure, ardent, disinterested, unsophisticated love of glorious strife.   Like Job's war-horse, he
"smelleth the battle afar off," and to the sound of the trumpet he
saith, ha! ha! To him

> " There is something of pride in the perilous hour,
> Whate'er be the shape in which death may lower,
> For fame is there, to tell who bleeds,
> And honor's eye on daring deeds."

You have heard, gentlemen, of the bright, warm isles which gem
the oriental seas, and are kissed by the fiery sun of the tropics;
where the clove, the cinnamon, and the nutmeg grow; where the
torrid atmosphere is oppressed with a delicious, but fierce and intoxicating influence.   There the spirit of man partakes of the same
spicy qualities which distinguish the productions of the soil.   Even
as the rinds of their fruits split open with nature's rich excess, so
do the human passions burst forth with an overwhelming violence
and prodigality unknown, till now, in our cold, ungentle clime.
There, in the islands of Java, Sumatra, the Malaccas, and others of
the same latitude, cases similar to that of Mr. Henry Oldham are
of frequent occurrence.   In those countries it is called "running a
muck."   An individual becomes so full of fight that he can no
longer contain it; accordingly, he arms himself with a species of
dagger, very similar to that from which Mr. Oldham wiped the
blood with his pocket handkerchief, and rushing into the public

streets, wounds and slays indiscriminately among the crowd. It is true that this gallant exploit always results in the death of the person performing it, the people of the country entertaining a foolish notion that it is too dangerous and expensive a mode of cultivating national bravery. But, in the present instance, I trust this rule will be relaxed. Mr. Oldham is the only specimen we possess of this peculiar habit of the spice islands, and he should be preserved as a curiosity.

But, alas! the age of chivalry has gone by; and, in the performance of my duty, I fear I shall have to exhibit some little defects in the character of Mr. Oldham, calculated in this censorious day to detract from his general merits. It is with great pain, I feel constrained to say (for he is a sort of favorite of mine), that telling the truth is not one of his knightly accomplishments, and that his heroic conduct in the affray at the Galt House was nothing more nor less, according to his own story, than a downright cowardly attempt at assassination.

First, as to his veracity. He says that he was cut in the passage by Doctor Wilkinson, to whose identity he swears positively; yet it is proven, by half a dozen unimpeachable witnesses, that the Doctor was at this time *hors de combat*, beaten to a mummy—almost lifeless, and perfectly limber—while his knife had fallen from his relaxed and nerveless grasp upon the floor of the bar-room, where it was afterwards picked up.

Yet Oldham swears, manfully, that it was the Doctor who cut him; though when asked if his face was not bloody, he replied that the passage was too dark to enable him to distinguish faces. If he could not see whether the face of the person who cut him was bruised or bloody, how dares he swear that it was Doctor Wilkinson, whom he admits he had never seen before?

Yet, though his vision was so dull in regard to this matter, it was almost supernaturally keen upon another. He swears that he was cut by a dirk-knife *with a "white handle."* Now, in this dusky passage, where he could not see the assailant's face, how could he distinguish so accurately the character of the weapon, and, more especially, of the handle? The handle of such a knife as either of those exhibited, would be entirely concealed in the grasp of the holder. But Mr. Oldham could see through the hand, and swear to the color of the handle, even when he could not distinguish the color of the assailant's face.

The prosecution seems to be afflicted with a monomania on the subject of white-handled knives.   The white handles caused them greater terror and excite more of their observation than the blades. One would almost be led to suppose, from the evidence, that the defendants held by the blades and fought with the handles.   These white handles flash before their eyes like the bright inscription upon the dim steel of a Turkish cimeter.   I hope, though with many misgivings, that none of them will ever die of a " white handle."

But, to return to my subject, why, in the name of all that is human or humane, did Oldham shoot at Murdaugh, whom, he acknowledges, he did not know; of whose connection with Doctor Wilkinson he was unacquainted; and who had not attempted to do him the slightest injury ?   According to his own account of the matter, he acted the part of a base and cowardly assassin.   If he tells the truth, he is an assassinating villain; if he does not, he is a perjured villain.   I leave him choice of these two horns of the dilemma, though I doubt not the latter is the one upon which he is destined to hang.   I cannot believe in the existence of such a monster as he would make himself out to be, and have offered his conduct to you as evidence of the existence of a conspiracy, and of his participation in it.   It is better that he should have the excuse of having fought in Redding's quarrel, than no excuse at all.

Gentlemen of the Jury—I have now performed that portion of my task which embraced the circumstantial evidence.   Out of the mouths of fifteen different witnesses, most of them gentlemen of high character and undoubted veracity, I have exhibited to you an almost countless variety of circumstances, the occurrence of which, or of any great portion of them, is absolutely incompatible with any other hypothesis than that of the existence of the conspiracy, which I proposed at the outset to prove.   Upon that hypothesis, all these circumstances are easily explicable, and in perfect accordance with the ordinary principles of human action.

I have combined the scattered strands of evidence; I have finished the cable which I promised; and now challenge the opposing counsel to try their strength upon it.   They may pick it into oakum; but I defy them to break it.

8. The defendants, from their situation, not likely to provoke a quarrel.—Character of the participants compared.

There is one other argument in favor of the view that I have taken of the origin of this unfortunate affray, which may be prop-

erly introduced at this time, and with which I shall close this
branch of the subject.

It arises out of the respective characters and positions in life of
the two parties, and is, in my opinion, entitled to great weight.
Who, in view of his character and situation, was most likely to have
sought and provoked the unfortunate conflict—Judge Wilkinson or
Mr. Redding? The conduct of the Judge, under the opprobrious
epithets heaped upon him by Redding, in the bar-room, sufficiently
indicates that, though he had previously given way to sudden passion, he was now cool, collected and forbearing. His mind had
recovered its balance, and he behaved on this occasion, as well as
subsequently, with philosophical calmness. I doubt, gentlemen,
whether any of you would have permitted Mr. Redding to indulge,
with impunity, in such unmeasured abuse. But the situation of the
Judge was peculiar, and every inducement which could operate
upon a gentleman warned him against participation in broils and
battles. With buoyant feelings and pulse-quickening anticipations,
he had come more than a thousand miles, upon a pilgrimage to the
shrine of beauty, and not of blood; upon an errand of love, and not
of strife. He came to transplant one of Kentucky's fairest flowers
to the warm gardens of the sunny South. The marriage feast was
spread; the bridal wreath was woven; and many bounding hearts
and sparkling eyes chided the lagging hours. The thoughts of the
bridegroom dwelt not upon the ignoble controversy, which, for an
unguarded moment, had occupied his attention, but upon the bright
and glorious future, whose rapturous visions were about to become
enchanting realities.

Under such circumstances Judge Wilkinson could not have desired the conflict. Had the fires of hell blazed in his bosom, they
must have been quenched for a while. The very fiend of discord
would have been ashamed, fresh from a voluntary, vulgar, bloody
quarrel, and reeking with its unsightly memorials, to have sought
the gay wedding banquet.

You cannot believe he coveted or courted the unfortunate affray,
without, at the same time, considering him destitute, not only of all
sentiment of delicacy and refinement, but of every characteristic of
a man. Does his previous character warrant such a conclusion ? He
has, as has been shown to you in evidence, ever maintained the
character of an honorable and upright gentleman. I see, by the
sneer upon the lip of the adverse counsel, that the term grates
harshly upon his sensibilities. But, I repeat it, Judge Wilkinson

has ever maintained the character of a gentleman; a character directly at war with the supposition that his conduct on this occasion resulted otherwise than from necessity. I mean, by a "gentleman," not the broadcloth, but the man; one who is above doing a mean, a cowardly or a dishonest action, whatever may be the temptation; one who forms his own standard of right and will not swerve from it; who regards the opinions of the world much, but his own self-respect more. Such men are confined to no particular class of society, though, I fear, they do not abound in any. I will save the learned counsel the trouble of translating his sneer into language, by admitting that they are to be found as readily among mechanics as elsewhere.

Such a man I believe Judge Wilkinson to be. Such has ever been his character, and he is entitled to the benefit of it on this occasion. It ought to have, and I know will have, very great weight with you. Good character always has been, and ever should be, a wall of strength around its possessor, a sevenfold shield to him who bears it.

This is one of the advantages which virtue has over vice—honorable over dishonorable conduct—an advantage which it is the very highest interest of society to cherish and enforce. In proportion to the excellence of a man's character is, and ever ought to be, the violence of the presumption that he has been guilty of crime. I appeal, then, to Judge Wilkinson's character, to prove that he could not have desired this unfortunate controversy; that it is impossible he should have been guilty, under the circumstances which then surrounded him, of the crime of willful and malicious murder. What, on the other hand, was the condition of the conspirators? Redding had been going about from street to street, like Peter the Hermit, preaching up a crusade against the Mississippians. Johnson, like Tecumseh—but no, I will not assimilate him to that noble warrior—like an Indian runner, was threading each path in the city, inciting his tribe to dig up the tomahawk and drive it, not into the scalps, but the "steaks" of the foe. But I will not pursue this point at greater length.

9. THE DEFENDANTS BELIEVED A CONSPIRACY EXISTED, WHETHER IN FACT IT DID OR DID NOT.

I proposed, after arguing the position, that there actually was a conspiracy to chastise the defendants, and inflict upon them great bodily harm, to show, in the next place, that the defendants had

8

good reason to believe such a conspiracy existed, whether in point
of fact it did or not. Most of the arguments bearing upon this
proposition have been already advanced in support of the other.
These I will not repeat. There are one or two others worthy of notice.
What could Judge Wilkinson have supposed from the conduct of
Redding, but that he sought and provoked a difficulty ? What else
could he conclude from the unmitigated abuse which was heaped
upon him from the opening of the very sluices of vulgarity ? That
the Judge apprehended violence is evident from the warning which
he gave. He told Redding that he might say what he pleased, but
not to lay his hands upon him; if he did, he would kill him. He
could not be supposed to know that Redding came only for the
names. When Meeks stepped up to Murdaugh and struck him
with his clubbed whip, while the crowd closed in around, what
could Murdaugh reasonably expect but violence and bodily harm,
resulting from preconcerted arrangement ? Without going at length
into an argument on this point, I take it for granted, no one will
deny that the defendants had ample grounds for apprehending the
existence, on the part of Mr. Redding and his friends, of a conspiracy to commit upon them personal violence.

Let us now look a moment at the conduct of the defendants, at
the Galt House, and see whether it transcended the bounds of right,
reason or prudence. When Murdaugh and the Doctor entered the
room, the exclamation was made by some one loud enough for all
to hear: "There they are, all three of them, now;" upon which,
according to nearly all the witnesses, Mr. Redding made the remark
to Murdaugh: "You are the man that drew the bowie-knife on me."
You will recollect, Redding had just crossed Judge Wilkinson's
path, and placed himself with his back against the counter, manifestly with the object of bringing on the fight. Murdaugh, indignant at being publicly charged with having drawn a bowie-knife
upon an unarmed man, replied, "that any one who said he had
drawn a bowie-knife told a d—d lie;" whereupon instantly steps up
Meeks, with his knotted cowhide, exclaiming: "You are the d—d
little rascal that did it"—at the same time inflicting upon him a
very severe blow. By-the-by, this assertion of Meeks proves that
he had been at Redding's after the first affray, and heard a full account of it. It is urged against the Judge, that when Mr. Everett
led him to his room, he asked for pistols. I think an argument in
his favor may be drawn from this circumstance. His requisition
for arms proves that he considered himself and his friends in great

personal danger. He manifestly required them not for offense, but for defense. Had he intended an attack, he would not have gone down to the bar-room without first obtaining the weapons he desired. Men do not voluntarily attempt the lives of others without being well prepared. It is evident that Judge Wilkinson and his friends thought only of the protection of their own persons, for they went down-stairs provided only with the ordinary weapons which they were accustomed to bear. Murdaugh and the Doctor had a pocket-knife each; the same they had previously carried. They had added nothing to their armor, either offensive or defensive. The Judge, apprehensive of difficulty, had taken his bowie-knife, which, probably, he had not previously worn. When, at the solicitation of Mr. Everett, he retired, he doubtless informed his friends of what had just transpired in the bar-room, and expressed his fears of violence. This accounts for the readiness with which Murdaugh met the assault of the two powerful men who simultaneously rushed upon him.

10. THE PART TAKEN IN THE AFFRAY BY THE RESPECTIVE DEFENDANTS.

The evidence is conclusive that Meeks commenced the attack upon Murdaugh, by two rapid, violent blows of a cowhide, accompanied by a heavy blow from a stick or cane in the hands of Rothwell. At the same time he seized the hand of Murdaugh, in which, prepared for defense, was an open knife; but Murdaugh, with coolness and celerity, changed the weapon to his left hand, and used it according to the dictates both of law and common sense. The very first blow had driven him to the wall. The crowd closed around him; he could not retreat, and was justified, according to the strictest and most technical principles of even English jurisprudence, to take the life of the assailant. No man but a fool or a coward could have acted otherwise than he did. Was he not, according to the rule read by the District Attorney, in imminent danger of his life or of great bodily harm? Let the unhealed wound upon his head respond. Let his hat, which has been exhibited to you, answer the question. Upon this you may perceive two incisions, which must have been caused by a sharp, cutting instrument. No obtuse weapon was capable of the effect. The blows were manifestly sufficient to have caused death, but for the intervention of the elastic material upon which their principal force was expended. The part, then, taken by Murdaugh in the affray, was clearly defensive and justifiable. It is not pretended that Doctor Wilkinson took any other part in the affray than attempting to escape from its violence, unless you notice the evidence of Oldham, that he cut him as he fled from the room. He was beaten, first by Rothwell, then by Holmes, and if you take their own statements, by those two worthies, Halbert and Oldham. He was crushed almost to atoms. He had not a chance even for self-defense. Rothwell had left Murdaugh, after striking him one blow, in charge of Meeks, and fell upon the Doctor. While beating the Doctor, he was stabbed by the Judge, near the dining-room door. The Doctor fled round the room, still followed by Rothwell, who was again struck by the Judge when upon the opposite side. The two blows paralyzed his powers; when Holmes stepped in and so completely prostrated the Doctor that he was compelled to hold him up with one hand while he beat him with the other.

Neither offensive word nor action, upon this occasion, on the part of Dr. Wilkinson, is proven or pretended. It is perfectly clear that he was beaten by Redding's friends, simply because he was of the Mississippi party. I consider it highly disgraceful to the Grand Jury who found the bill, that he was included in it.

In reference to the part taken by Judge Wilkinson : It is proven beyond contradiction, by Mr. Pearson, a gentleman of undoubted veracity, that the Judge, at his solicitation, was in the act of leaving the room as the affray commenced; when, witnessing the attack upon Murdaugh, he stopped, refusing to leave until he saw the result of the controversy in which his friend was engaged. Standing in the corner of the room, he did not at first take part in the conflict, perceiving, doubtless, that Murdaugh was making good his own defense. Presently, however, he cast his eyes around and saw his brother trodden under foot, entirely powerless, and apparently either dead or in imminent danger from the fierce blows of Rothwell, who, as you have heard, was a man of tremendous physical power, and armed with a bludgeon, some say a sword cane. Then it was he thought it necessary to act; and advancing through the crowd to the spot, he wounded the assailant who was crushing out his brother's life. Gen. Chambers swears positively that Rothwell was beating, with a stick, and with great severity, some one, whom the other witnesses identify as the Doctor, at the time he was stabbed near the dining-room door. This produced a slight diversion in the Doctor's favor, who availed himself of it by retreating, in a stooping posture, towards the passage door. Rothwell, however, pursued and beat him down, but was arrested in his violence by another blow from Judge Wilkinson, which, together with the puncture in his throat, received, in all probability, from a chance thrust of the sword cane in the hands of one of his own party, disabled him and caused his death. About this time Holmes was completing Rothwell's unfinished work, and the Doctor, hunted entirely around the room, fell, utterly exhausted, at the feet of his relentless pursuers. It is wonderful that he had strength enough to escape with Murdaugh and the Judge.

Such, briefly, were the parts enacted by these defendants, respectively, in this unfortunate affray, the result of which none regret more than themselves. Considering the proof of the conspiracy, and the knowledge, or even the reasonable apprehension on the part of the defendants, of its existence, as affording them ample justification for their participation in the matter, I have not thought it necessary to go into a minute analysis of the evidence on this branch of the subject, nor to attempt to reconcile those slight discrepancies which will always occur in the testimony of the most veracious witnesses, in giving an account of the transaction viewed from different positions and at different periods of time.

II. THE LAW OF SELF-DEFENSE.—CIRCUMSTANCES WHICH JUSTIFY THE TAKING OF LIFE.

The law of self-defense has always had and ought to have a more liberal construction in this country than in England. Men claim more of personal independence here ; of course they have more to defend. They claim more freedom and license in their actions towards each other, consequently there is greater reason for apprehending personal attack from an enemy. In this country men retain in their own hands a larger portion of their personal rights than in any other; and one will be authorized to presume an intention to exercise and enforce them, upon grounds that, in other countries, would not excite the slightest suspicion. It is the apprehension of impending harm, and not its actual existence, which constitutes the justification for defensive action. If mine enemy point at me an unloaded pistol or a wooden gun, in a manner calculated to excite in my mind apprehensions of immediate, great bodily harm, I am justifiable in taking his life, though it turn out afterwards that I was in no actual danger.

So, on the other hand, if I take the life of another, without being aware of any intended violence on his part, it will constitute no excuse for me to prove that he intended an attack upon me.

The apprehension must be reasonable, and its reasonableness may depend upon a variety of circumstances—of time, place and manner, as well as of character. The same appearance of danger would authorize greater apprehension, and of course readier defensive action, at night than in the day-time. An attack upon one in his own house would indicate greater violence, and excuse stronger opposing action, than an attack in the street.

Indications of violence from an individual of known desperate and dangerous character will justify defensive and preventive action, which would be inexcusable towards a notorious coward. A stranger may reasonably indulge from the appearance or threats of a mob apprehension that would be unpardonable in a citizen surrounded by his friends and neighbors.

Bearing these observations in mind, let us look at the situation of the defendants. They were attacked at their hotel, which, for the time being, was their house. They were strangers, and a fierce mob had gathered around them, indicating, both by word and deed, the most violent intentions. They were three small, weak men, without friends—for even the proprietor of the house, who should have protected them, had become alarmed, and left them to their fate. Their enemies were, comparatively, giants—dangerous in appearance and desperate in action. Was there not ample ground for the most fearful apprehensions?

12. The propositions advanced by the prosecution, answered.—Illustrations of the law of self-defense.

But the District Attorney says, they are not entitled to the benefit of the law of self-defense, because they came down to supper, and thus placed themselves voluntarily within reach of the danger. According to his view of the case, they should have remained in their chamber, in a state of siege, without the right to sally forth even for provisions; while the enemy, cutting off their supplies, would doubtless soon have starved them into a surrender. But it seems there was a private entrance to the supper table, and they should have skulked in through that. No one but a craven coward, unworthy of the privileges of a man, would have followed such a course. The ordinary entrance to supper was through the bar-room. They had a right to pass this way; no law forbade it.

Every principle of independence and self-respect prompted it. And through that bar-room I would have gone, as they did, though the floor had been fresh sown with the fabled dragon's teeth, and bristling with its crop of armed men.

I care not whether the assailing party had deadly weapons or not; though I will, by-and-by, show they had, and used them, too. But the true question is, whether the defendants had not good reason for believing them armed and every way prepared for a desperate conflict. I have shown already that Dr. Wilkinson and Murdaugh did not transcend the most technical principle laid down by the commonwealth's attorney; not even that which requires a man to run to the wall before he can be permitted to defend himself—a principle which, in practice, is exploded in England, and never did obtain in this country at all. But, says the learned attorney, Judge Wilkinson interfered and took part before he was himself attacked; he had no right to anticipate the attack upon himself; he had no right to defend his friend; he had no right to protect his brother's life. Now I differ from the worthy counsel on all these points: I think he had a right to prevent, by anticipating it, violence upon his person; he had a right to defend his friend, and it was his sacred duty to protect his brother's life.

Judge Wilkinson was the most obnoxious of the party; his friends were already overpowered; he could not expect to escape; and in a moment the whole force of the bandit gang would have turned upon him.

The principles of self-defense, which pervade all animated nature, and act towards life the same part that is performed by the external mechanism of the eye towards the delicate sense of vision —affording it, on the approach of danger, at the same time, warning and protection—do not require that action shall be withheld till it can be of no avail. When the rattlesnake gives warning of his fatal purpose, the wary traveler waits not for the poisonous blow, but plants upon his head his armed heel, and crushes out at once "his venom and his strength." When the hunter hears the rustling in the jungle, and beholds the large green eyes of the spotted tiger glaring upon him, he waits not for the deadly spring, but sends at once through the brain of his crouching enemy the swift and leaden death.

If war was declared against your country by an insulting foe, would you wait till your sleeping cities were wakened by the terrible music of the bursting bomb? till your green fields were trampled by the hoofs of the invader, and made red with the blood of your brethren? No! you would send forth fleets and armies; you would unloose upon the broad ocean your keen falcons; and the thunder of your guns would arouse stern echoes along the hostile coast. Yet this would be but national defense, and authorized by the same great principle of self-protection, which applies no less to individuals than to nations.

13. DEFENDANTS' CONDUCT EULOGIZED.—THEY TOOK LIFE FROM NECESSITY, NOT FROM MALICE.

But Judge Wilkinson had no right to interfere in defense of his brother; so says the commonwealth's attorney. Go, gentlemen, and ask your mothers and sisters whether that be law. I refer you to no musty tomes, but to the living volumes of Nature. What! A man not permitted to defend his brother against conspirators? against assassins, who are crushing out the very life òf their bruised and powerless victim? Why, he who would shape his conduct by such a principle does not deserve to have a brother or a friend. To fight for self is but the result of an honest instinct which we have in common with the brutes. To defend those who are dear to us is the highest exercise of the principle of self-defense. It nourishes all the noblest social qualities, and constitutes the germ of patriotism itself.

Why is the step of the Kentuckian free as that of the bounding deer? firm, manly and confident as that of the McGregor when his foot was on the heather of his native hills and his eye on the peak of Ben Lomond? It is because he feels independent and proud; independent in the knowledge of his rights, and proud in the generous consciousness of ability and courage to defend them, not only in his own person, but in the persons of those who are dear to him.

It was not the blood that would desert a brother or a friend, which swelled the hearts of your fathers in the "olden time," when in defense of those they loved, they sought the red savage through all the fastnesses of his native forest. It was not such blood that was poured out, free as a gushing torrent, upon the dark banks of the melancholy Raisin, when all Kentucky manned her warrior sires. They were as bold and true as ever fought beneath a plume. The Roncesvalles pass, when fell before the opposing lance the harnessed chivalry of Spain, looked not upon a braver or a better band.

Kentucky has no law which precludes a man from defending himself, his brother, or his friend. Better for Judge Wilkinson had he never been born than that he should have failed in his duty on this occasion. Had he acted otherwise than he did, he would have been ruined in his own estimation and blasted in the opinions of the world. And young Murdaugh, too; he has a mother who is looking even now from her window, anxiously watching for her son's return; but better, both for her and him, that he should have been borne a bloody corpse to her arms than that he should have carried to her, unavenged, the degrading marks of the accursed whip.

But there was danger, as well as degradation. Their lives were in imminent hazard. Look at the cuts in Murdaugh's hat and upon his head, the stab received by the Judge, and the wounds inflicted upon the Doctor. Besides the overwhelming superiority in number and strength, the conspirators had very greatly the advantage in weapons. We have proven the exhibition and use by them of knives, dirks, a sword cane, and a pistol, without counting the bludgeons which, in the hands of such men, are weapons little less deadly than the others.

Need I dwell longer upon this point? Need I say that the defendants are no murderers? that they acted in self-defense, and took life from necessity, not from malice?

14. SCATHING REVIEW OF THE CHARACTER AND CONDUCT OF THE
PRINCIPAL WITNESSES FOR THE PROSECUTION.

But there is a murderer; and, strange to say, his name appears upon the indictment, not as a criminal, but as a prosecutor. His garments are wet with the blood of those upon whose deaths you hold this solemn inquest. Yonder he sits, allaying for a moment the hunger of that fierce vulture, conscience, by casting before it the food of pretended regret, and false but apparent eagerness for justice. He hopes to appease the manes of his slaughtered victims —victims to his falsehood and treachery—by sacrificing upon their graves a hecatomb of innocent men. By base misrepresentations of the conduct of the defendants, he induced his imprudent friends to attempt a vindication of his pretended wrongs by violence and bloodshed. His clansmen gathered at his call, and followed him for vengeance; but when the fight began, and the keen weapons clashed in the sharp conflict—where was this wordy warrior? Aye, "Where was Roderick then?" No "blast upon his bugle horn" encouraged his companions as they were laying down their lives in his quarrel; no gleam of his dagger indicated a desire to avenge their fall; with treacherous cowardice he left them to their fate, and all his vaunted courage ended in ignominious flight.

Sad and gloomy is the path that lies before him. You will in a few moments dash, untasted, from his lips the sweet cup of revenge, to quaff whose intoxicating contents he has paid a price that would have purchased the goblet of the Egyptian queen. I behold gathering around him, thick and fast, dark and corroding cares. That face which looks so ruddy, and even now is flushed with shame and conscious guilt, will from this day grow pale, until the craven blood shall refuse to visit his haggard cheek. In his broken and distorted sleep, his dreams will be more fearful than those of the "false, perjured Clarence;" and around his waking pillow, in the deep hour of night, will flit the ghosts of Rothwell and of Meeks, shrieking their curses in his shrinking ear.

Upon his head rests not only all the blood shed in this unfortunate strife, but also the soul-killing crime of perjury; for, surely as he lives, did the words of craft and falsehood fall from his lips, ere they were hardly loosened from the Holy Volume. But I dismiss him, and do consign him to the furies—trusting, in all charity, that the terrible punishment he must suffer from the scorpion-lash of a guilty conscience will be considered in his last account.

Johnson and Oldham, too, are murderers at heart. But I shall make to them no appeal. There is no chord in their bosoms which can render back music to the touch of feeling. They have both perjured themselves. The former cut up the truth as coolly as if he had been carving meat in his own stall. The latter, on the contrary, was no longer the bold and hot-blooded knight, but the shrinking, pale-faced witness. Cowering beneath your stern and indignant gaze, marked you not how "his coward lip did from its color fly;" and how his quailing eye sought from floor to rafter protection from each honest glance.

It seems to me that the finger of Providence is visible in the protection of the defendants. Had this affair occurred at Mr. Redding's Coffee House, instead of the Galt House, nothing could have saved them. Their lives would have been sworn away, without remorse, by Redding and his gang. All that saved them from sacrifice was the accidental presence of gentlemen whose testimony cannot be doubted, and who have given an honest and true account of the transaction.

Gentlemen of the Jury:—I shall detain you no longer. It was, in fact, a matter of supererogation for me to address you at all, after the lucid and powerful exposition of the case which has been given by my respected friend, Col. Robertson. It was doubly so when it is considered that I am to be succeeded by a gentleman (Judge Rowan), who, better perhaps than any other man living, can give you, from his profound learning and experience, a just interpretation of the laws of your State; and in his own person a noble illustration of that proud and generous character which is a part of the birthright of a Kentuckian.

It is true I had hoped, when the evidence was closed, that the commonwealth's attorney might have found it in accordance with his duty and his feelings to have entered at once a *nolle prosequi*. Could the genius of "Old Kentucky" have spoken, such would have been her mandate. Blushing with shame at the inhospitable conduct of a portion of her sons, she would have hastened to make reparation.

Gentlemen:—Let her sentiments be spoken by you. Let your verdict take character from the noble State which you in part represent. Without leaving your box, announce to the world that here the defense of one's own person is no crime, and that the protection of a brother's life is the subject of approbation rather than of punishment.

Gentlemen of the Jury:—I return you my most profound and sincere thanks for the kindness with which you have listened to me, a stranger, pleading the cause of strangers. Your generous and indulgent treatment I shall ever remember with the most grateful emotions. In full confidence that you, by your sense of humanity and justice, will supply the many defects in my feeble advocacy, I now resign into your hands the fate of my clients. As you shall do unto them, so, under like circumstances, may it be done unto you.

————

The jury returned a verdict of not guilty as to all of the defendants.

IMPORTANCE OF THE DOCTRINE OF STARE DECISIS.

LUTHER BRADISH.

The people, in forming the organic law of the government of this State, very wisely foresaw that, in its action and progress, questions of interpretation of the settlement of legal principles, and of their application, would frequently arise ; and thence the necessity of constituting some tribunal with general appellate and supervisory powers, whose decisions should be final and conclusively settle and declare the law. This was supposed to have been accomplished in the organization of this court. Heretofore this court, under the Constitution, has been looked to by the people as the tribunal of the last resort in the State ; and it has hitherto been supposed, that when this court had decided a case upon its merits, such decision not only determined the rights of the parties litigant in that particular case, but that it also settled the principles involved in it, as permanent rules of law, universally applicable in all future cases embracing similar facts, and involving the same or analogous principles. These decisions thus became at once public law, measures of private right, and landmarks of property. They determined the rights of persons and of things. Parties entered into contracts with each other with reference to them, as to the declared and established law ; law equally binding upon the courts and the people. But the doctrine recently put forth would at once overturn this whole body of law founded upon the adjudications of this court, built up as it has been by the long continued and arduous labors, grown venerable with years, and interwoven as it has become with the interests, the habits, and the opinions of the people. Under this new doctrine all would again be unsettled— nothing established. Like the ever returning but never ending labors of the fabled Sisyphus, this court, in disregard to the maxim of " *stare decisis*," would, in each recurring case, have to enter upon its examination and decision as if all were new, without any aid from the experience of the past, or the benefit of any established principle or settled law. Each case with its decision being thus limited as law to itself alone, would in turn pass away and be forgotten, leaving behind it no record of principle established, or light to guide, or rule to govern the future.—[Hanford v. Archer, 4 Hill, 321.]

[124]

SPEECH OF DAVID PAUL BROWN,

In Defense of Alexander William Holmes, Indicted for Manslaughter on the High Seas.

[1 Wallace, Jr., 1.]

AT A CIRCUIT COURT OF THE UNITED STATES, HELD AT THE CITY OF PHILADELPHIA, APRIL TERM, 1842.

LAW OF THE OCEAN.—It is a sailor's duty to protect persons intrusted to his care, not to sacrifice them; and this obligation rests upon him at all times, in every emergency of his calling. He must expose himself to every danger, and protect the life of the passenger to the last extremity.

Where two persons who owe no mutual duty to each other, are by accident placed in a situation where both cannot survive, neither is bound to save the other's life by sacrificing his own; nor would either commit a crime in saving his own life, in a struggle for the only means of safety. In applying this principle, therefore, not only the jeopardy, but the relations in which the parties stand, should be considered, because the slayer must be under no obligation to make his own safety secondary to the safety of others. [United States v. Holmes, 1 Wall. Jr.]

ANALYSIS OF MR. BROWN'S SPEECH.

1. Heroic conduct of the defendant.
2. Rejected indictments.—No quarter to be given or received.
3. Circumstances under which alone a true verdict could be reached.
4. Realistic description of the scenes surrounding the alleged crime.
5. Legal character of the charge.—The authorities discussed.
6. Propositions advanced by the prosecution answered.
7. The prisoner bound to obey the mate's order; otherwise all were in a state of nature when artificial distinction cease to prevail.
8. The defendant acted under the apprehension of immediate peril and pressing necessity.
9. Vindication of the captain of the lost vessel.
10. Narration of the facts, and evidence in the case.
11. The impulses which led to the catastrophe considered.
12. Self-preservation the first law of nature.
13. The survivors saved, solely through the instrumentality of the defendant.

The circumstances surrounding the remarkable case of the United States v. Holmes, present the melancholy romance and painful details which invariably attach to stories of marine disaster. It is, we believe, the only case on record in which the rights of sailor and passenger, and their relative duties and obligations in the hour of peril and shipwreck, have come directly under judicial consideration. It would seem at first blush as if the old maxim, that self-preservation is the first law of nature, a principle enunciated by Lord Bacon and

[125]

approved by elementary and speculative writers for nearly three centuries, had been disregarded here. The familiar illustration given by the high authority referred to, is that of two persons being shipwrecked and getting on the same plank, one of whom, finding it not able to save both, thrusts the other from it, whereby he is drowned. And this is declared to be excusable homicide. A careful examination of the case, however, shows that Mr. Justice Baldwin has adopted this rule, so far as it applies to those who are under no legal obligations to each other. But where such obligations exist, as between sailor and passenger, they remain in force at all times and under all circumstances. The facts of the case are as follows :

On the 13th day of March, 1841, the good ship "William Brown" left Liverpool, bound for Philadelphia. She had on board sixty-five passengers, mostly Irish and Scotch emigrants, and a crew of seventeen, including officers and seamen, making a total of eighty-two souls. On Monday night, the 19th of April, while about two hundred and fifty miles southeast of Cape Race, off the coast of Newfoundland, the vessel struck an iceberg and began to sink. The life-boats were launched. The first mate, eight seamen and thirty-two passengers were crowded into the long boat; the captain, second mate, six of the crew and one passenger got into the jolly boat. The ship went down an hour and a half after she struck, carrying with her thirty-one passengers, who, being unable to get into the boats, perished. At the last moment, just before the wreck disappeared, the frail shells, burdened to the water's edge with human freight, were cut loose and set adrift upon the trackless waste of waters. The boats remained together during the night, and parted company Tuesday morning. Before separating, the mate in the long boat, realizing the extreme peril in which he was placed, tried to prevail on the captain to take some of the passengers from the long boat into the jolly boat, as the former was unmanageable, and said that, unless he did so, it would be necessary to cast lots and throw some overboard. "I know what you'll have to do," said the captain ; "don't speak of that now. Let it be the last resort." As a parting injunction he directed the seamen in the long boat to obey the orders of the mate as they would his own.

The long boat was 22 feet long, 6 feet in the beam, and from 2½ to 3 feet deep. She had provisions for six or seven days, close allowance, consisting of 75 pounds of bread, 6 gallons of water, 8 or 10 pounds of meat, and a small bag of oat meal. The boat, however, was leaky; the plug in the bottom was insufficient for the purpose, and it became necessary to commence bailing the moment she touched the water.

During the forenoon of Tuesday it began to rain, and the rain continued during the remainder of the day and night. The sea was quite calm, however, until towards evening, when the wind freshened and it became rough, and at times washed over the sides of the boat. Great masses of ice were floating about, and during the day icebergs had been seen. As the shades of night began to thicken, the ocean became more and more tempestuous, and the peril of destruction became imminent. The gunwale was within from five to twelve inches of the water. The crew rowed turn-about, and the passengers bailed. About ten o'clock Tuesday night, as the sea grew heavier and the chances of keeping afloat began to diminish, the mate, who had been bailing steadily, cried out : "This work won't do. Help me, God ! Men, go to work." No attention was paid to this order. Some of the passengers then exclaimed: "The boat is sinking. The plug's out. God have mercy on our poor souls!" In a few minutes after, the mate again said : "Men, you *must* go to work, or we shall all perish."

ALEXANDER WILLIAM HOLMES, one of the crew to whom these orders were addressed, was a Finn by birth, and had followed the sea from his youth. He was the last man of the crew to leave the sinking ship, and had become conspicuous for courage and daring in his endeavors to rescue the passengers from the wreck. The following incident will illustrate : A widowed mother and three daughters got into the long boat, but just as it was about being cut loose from the sinking hulk, to escape going down in the vortex, it was discovered that one of the daughters, who was sick and helpless, had been left behind. The mother, half distracted, called the child's name. "Isabel! Isabel! Come! Come!" she cried, but the poor creature was too feeble to stir. William Holmes heard the mother's grief, and climbing up the ship's side, at the peril of his life, he rescued the sick girl, and placing her on his shoulder, swung himself with one arm by the tackle into the boat. This scene is vividly portrayed by his counsel in his address to the jury. He had also parted with nearly all his clothing to protect the shivering women in the boat. Nevertheless, Holmes, the hardy and courageous sailor, in response to the command of the mate to "go to work," assisted in throwing the passengers into the sea. No lots were cast. The passengers were not consulted, the only orders were not to throw over any women, and not to separate man and wife. Holmes and his associates threw overboard fourteen males and two women.

After three persons had been thrown out, Holmes came to FRANCIS ASKIN, who offered him five sovereigns to spare his life till morning, saying : "If God don't send us help by morning, we'll draw lots, and if the lot falls on me, I'll go over like a man." Holmes answered, "I don't want your money, Frank," and cast him into the sea. There was a violent struggle, but the boat did not sink. The two women above referred to as having been thrown over, were the sisters of Askin, and there was some doubt as to whether they were thrown out or voluntarily sprang into the water, choosing to share their brother's fate.

The murder of Askin constituted the offense for which Holmes was indicted and brought to trial in the Circuit Court of the United States, on the 13th day of April, 1842.

The sequel of the catastrophe is soon told. Holmes was the ablest and most experienced seaman on board, and the mate concluded to take his judgment entirely as to what course to pursue. He advised not to make for Newfoundland, that it would never be reached, but to steer south where it was warmer, and take the chances of being picked up. He encouraged everybody, and bade them not despair. He tried to make a sail with a quilt, but the wind was too strong. On Wednesday morning the weather cleared. Holmes kept a sharp lookout, and long before any one else saw it, his trained and experienced eye descried a sail. He at once raised a sign of distress. The approaching vessel proved to be the ship Crescent, which, seeing the signal, put about and picked up the survivors. The captain and second mate with the persons in the jolly boat, after beating about for six days, were rescued by a French fishing lugger.

Holmes was indicted under the act of April 30th, 1790, entitled "An Act for the punishment of certain crimes against the United States (1 Story's Laws U. S.

p. 83), the 12th section of which provides, that if any seaman shall commit *manslaughter* upon the high seas, he shall be imprisoned not exceeding three years, and fined not exceeding one thousand dollars.

The trial created great excitement and attracted universal attention. The prosecution was conducted by William M. Meredith (U. S. District Attorney), Oliver Hopkinson, and George M. Dallas. For the prisoner appeared David Paul Brown, Edward Armstrong, and Isaac Hazlehurst.

For forty years, David Paul Brown was one of the brightest ornaments of his profession, and his attainments and abilities have acquired for the Quaker lawyer enduring fame. He was a scholarly and accomplished advocate, and invariably brought to his task the wealth of his classical learning to adorn and beautify his work. His success at the bar was instantaneous, and it is said that, during the first fifteen years of his professional life, his fees aggregated the handsome sum of $100,000. In his defense of Holmes he urged with great power, that when the vessel went down, the voyage, with all its contemplated conditions and possibilities, was at an end, and whatever duties or obligations might ordinarily attach to the mariner, were absolved under circumstances of extreme peril, when all men were reduced to a state of nature. The Court, however, ruled against him on these points, and afterwards denied a motion for a new trial, involving the correctness of the position taken in his charge. Mr. Brown addressed the jury as follows :[1]

WITH DEFERENCE TO THE COURT :—How wonderful and mysterious, gentlemen of the jury, are the vicissitudes of human life. How frail and precarious are our best holds upon human happiness. Man, the boasted lord of creation, is the sport of every wind that blows, of every wave that flows. He appears like the grass of the field, flourishes and is cut down, and withers ere the setting sun ; like the dews of the morning he sparkles for a brief moment and is exhaled. There is nothing earthly *certain* but *uncertainty ;* there is nothing *true* but HEAVEN.

What a salutary practical commentary is supplied by the present intensely interesting occasion upon the truth of this melancholy doctrine. On the thirteenth day of March, in the last year, a staunch and gallant ship, with a competent commander and a noble crew, with sixty-five passengers on board, sailed from the port of Liverpool, destined for that of Philadelphia ; a destination, alas ! which was never accomplished.

For more than a month, notwithstanding she encountered storms and tempests, she outrode them all ; and like a thing of life held on her way rejoicing. On the 19th of the succeeding month, she arrived in fairer climes and enjoyed more propitious gales ; but even

---

[1] For this full report of Mr. Brown's speech, we are indebted to Mr. Robert Eden Brown, who has collected and edited a volume of his father's speeches. King & Baird, Philadelphia, 1873.

then, when every heart throbbed with the anticipated joy of a speedy arrival, the angel of destruction spread his broad black wings above her, and while traversing the ocean with all sails set, at the rate of ten knots an hour, she came into collision with an island of ice, and in a moment her pride was prostrate, and the doomed ship was reduced to an actually sinking condition, affording scarcely time for the unhappy inmates, in the moment of their extremest need, to cry GOD BLESS US. The ocean, her favored element, of which for years she had been the pride, became her sepulchre ; and the winds that had borne her upon many a prosperous voyage, sung her last sad, only requiem. Here is a scene strikingly presented, in which the theories of philosophy are reduced at once to a frightful reality.

1. HEROIC CONDUCT OF THE DEFENDANT.

But there is still another picture to which I would invite, and upon which I would fasten your attention. On that dreadful night, the crew and half the passengers having taken to the boats, the agonizing voice of a mother is heard even beyond the tumult and the clamor, calling for the preservation of her daughter, who in the consternation of the moment had been forgotten, and remained on board the fated ship. In an instant, you may see a gallant, athletic and powerful sailor, passing hand over hand, by dint of a slender rope, until he regains the vessel. And you may further behold him upon the quarter deck, in the depth of the night, surrounded by the wild and wasteful ocean, with one arm entwined around a sickly and half naked girl, while, with the other, he bravely swings himself and his almost lifeless burden, by means of the "boat tackle falls," from the stern of the sinking ship into the boat below, and at once restores the child to the open arms and yearning heart of the mother. Yet to-day, I say it to the disgrace of the law, after months of solitary imprisonment, you here see that self-same heroic sailor arraigned upon the odious charge of having voluntarily and wantonly deprived a fellow-creature of his life ; and THAT, gentlemen of the jury, is the charge that I am to argue and you are to determine. I say this is what you are to determine.

2. REJECTED INDICTMENTS.—NO QUARTER TO BE GIVEN OR RECEIVED.

It may not be inappropriate, however, though certainly not vital to this cause, that I should ask your attention, in passing to the real

9

subject in controversy, to two other indictments which stain the records of this court, referring to portions of the same transaction: the first charging the defendant with murder, which the grand jury promptly ignoramused ; and the second, in the impotency of disappointed revenge, accusing him of larceny in having stolen *a quilt* of the alleged value of three dollars, which charge shared the same fate. You can form some idea of the dignity of the United States and its value, while observing how it has been cheapened by itself. This very quilt, permit me to remind you, is that which was converted by Holmes into a sail for the boat, in a moment of the extremest peril, in order that he might save the lives of those very beings who gratefully appeared before the grand jury upon the first opportunity, in order to convict their benefactor of these imputed crimes. I shall speak of this hereafter ; for the present I merely advert to it, and pass at once to more important matters.

In approaching the consideration of this case, which I do with pride and pleasure and confidence, I cannot but express my regret, to adopt a military phrase, that I am called into conflict not only with the regular troops of the United States, but with her recently enlisted *volunteers*. I am sorry that my gallant friend[1] who led on the attack so boldly yesterday, and who is a legitimate leader everywhere, should so far have returned to his first love as to desert the white banner of innocence (under which he has lately so successfully fought) to engage once more beneath the bloody flag of such a prosecution as this. Since it is so, however, let him nail that flag to the mast. We should be happy to abide by every principle of civilized warfare ; but in a mortal controversy, in a death struggle like this, we shall neither ask nor will we receive any *quarter*.

3. CIRCUMSTANCES UNDER WHICH ALONE A TRUE VERDICT COULD BE REACHED.

This case, in order to embrace all its horrible relations, ought to be decided in a long boat, hundreds of leagues from the shore, loaded to the very gunwale with forty-two half naked victims; with provisions only sufficient to prolong the agonies of famine and of thirst ; with all the elements combined against her ; leaking from below, filling also from above ; surrounded by ice, unmanageable from her condition, and subject to destruction from the least change of the wind and the waves—the most variable and most terrible of all the elements. Decided at such a tribunal, nature—

[1] Mr. Dallas.

intuition—would at once pronounce a verdict, not only of acquittal, but of commendation.   The prisoner might, it is true, obtain no outward atonement for nine months of suffering and of obloquy; but he would at least enjoy the satisfaction always to be derived from a consciousness of rectitude, in which the better part of the world sympathize, and in which it confides.

Are the United States to come here now, a year after the events, when it is impossible to estimate the elements which combined to make the risk, or to say to what extent the jeopardy was imminent; are they, with square, rule and compass, deliberately to measure this boat, in this room ; to weigh these passengers ; call in philosophers ; discuss specific gravities ; calculate by the tables of a life insurance company the chances of life ; and because they, the judges, find that, by their calculation, this unfortunate boat's crew might have had the thousandth part of one poor chance to escape, to condemn this prisoner to chains and a dungeon for what he did in the terror and darkness of that dark and terrible night ?   Such a mode of testing men's acts and motives is monstrous !

Alas ! how different is the scene now exhibited ?   You sit here, the sworn twelve, the center of that society which you represent, surrounded by the sanctions of those laws which for a time you administer ; reposing amidst the comforts and delights of sacred homes ; directed and instructed by a judge who, being full of light himself, freely imparts it to all he approaches ; to decide upon the impulses and motives of the prisoner at the bar, launched upon the bosom of the perilous ocean ; surrounded by a thousand deaths in their most hideous forms, with but one plank between him and destruction.   What sympathies can be inspired by relative positions so remote, so opposite as these.

4. Realistic description of the scenes surrounding the alleged crime.

Translate yourselves if you can, by the power of imagination, to those scenes, those awful scenes to which this proceeding refers. Fancy yourselves in a frail barque, encompassed by towers of ice Olympus high, and still magnified by the fear natural to man ; exposed to bleak and pitiless winds, surrounded by forty wretches as miserable as yourself, deepening your own afflictions by the contagion of grief ; removed a hundred leagues from land, and still further removed by a destitution of those means by which alone it could possibly be reached.

Nay, further, superadd to these horrors the apprehension of famine, of storm, bearing assured destruction on its wing; and connect all these with the scenes and terrors of the night just past, enough to appal the stoutest heart and overthrow the firmest brain, and then tell me, not what the defendant should have done, but what the most severe and rigid would have done, in trials and perils and calamities like these. It is easy to scorn the tempest while sporting with the zephyr; to laugh at the ocean while secure from its ravages and horrors; to expatiate upon the harmlessness of ice while indulging in it, perhaps as a luxury; or to underrate famine in the abundance of your supplies; but may that Power that " rides on the whirlwind and directs the storm," protect you against the sad reality of those afflictions which in their mere theory are often so readily overcome by your self-secure, cold-blooded and reckless philosophy. Philosophy readily triumphs over past and future and remote ills; but present and immediate ills grapple closely with the heart, and triumph over philosophy.

5. Legal character of the charge.—The authorities discussed.

Let us now come to those facts which distance and defy all the powers of fancy. Before doing this, however, you will pardon me in examining the legal character of his charge : First, as relates to the act of Congress; secondly, as regards the inherent defects of the indictment; thirdly, as respects its inconsistency with the evidence in the cause. I have for the present but a word to say upon each of these subjects, rather to show that they have not been overlooked, than with any intention elaborately to discuss them.

The act of Congress leaves manslaughter where it was at common law, so far as regards its definition; it only modifies its punishment. The punishment is not more than three years, with a penalty not exceeding one thousand dollars. You have been truly told by the opposite counsel that the court may reduce their sentence to a merely nominal punishment. That is the business of the court, however, and after your verdict is found, your influence is extinct. Whether the punishment is to be an hour or a year, it is an infamous punishment; and you should be equally cautious in resting your verdict upon unquestionable and unsatisfactory proof. I marvel, indeed, that my learned friend, while haranguing you upon the enormity of this offense, should attempt soothing you into a verdict by the suggestion that it would probably be attended with no evil to the defendant. Allow me to deprecate this questionable mercy. It is calculated, if not designed, to seduce you from allegiance to your duties. If the defendant be guilty, he should meet the rigor of the law ; if innocent, his rights should not be compromised by the imaginary insignificance of his anticipated punishment. I make no claims upon your charity ; my appeals are to your justice.

Now, as to the internal defects of the indictment. The indictment contains four counts for manslaughter. That is, for unlawfully, but without malice, depriving a fellow-creature of his life. Malice would elevate what would otherwise be manslaughter, into murder.

The first count charges the homicide on board of the ship William Brown, belonging to Stephen Baldwin. The second—on board of a vessel, name unknown, belonging to Stephen Baldwin. The third and fourth are the same, with the exception of Thomas Vogel's name being substituted for that of Stephen Baldwin's.

Now, these charges are incompatible with each other, and are calculated to bewilder the prisoner in his defense. They cannot all be true, and as there has been no election on the part of the prosecution, a verdict upon all will involve an inconsistency obviously illegal, if not utterly fatal. The doctrine of Milton, as applied to angelic existences, that, vital in every part, they cannot, but " by annihilation, die," is not true in its application to indictments. They are mortal in every part, and the destruction of one part of a count is the destruction of all parts of the same count. One count, it is true, does not destroy another when they are at all compatible with each other, and when an election has been made ; but when the charges contained in an indictment are, as in this case, totally inconsistent, if the jury should find a verdict of guilty upon the indictment generally, it will be subject to a motion in arrest of judgment, and it can never stand.

Lastly, I say, if the indictment were unquestionable in itself, it is not supported by the proof. I say nothing in regard to the error in the time stated, which, in *some* cases, might be fatal, but probably not in *this*. The ship, as appears by the evidence, neither belonged to Baldwin nor Vogel, but to McCrea, who is not even referred to. Baldwin, however, it is said, held a claim to her, a mortgage upon her as collateral security. That does not improve the case of the prosecution. Special property may be sufficient, but it must be special property accompanied by possession, or at all events possession itself, actual or constructive. Suppose a person were indicted for committing a burglary upon the house of A. B., and upon the trial it appeared that the house was the dwelling of E. F., and that the person whose name was introduced into the indictment was merely the mortgagee, certainly the charge could not be sustained for a moment. I merely, for the present, hint at rather than press these objections. I shall, if necessary—which it probably will not be—have the benefit of them hereafter.

We pass now to the law more immediately connected with the facts of this case. Russell, Paley, Rutherford, Blackstone, and, above all, Lord Bacon, are the authorities upon which the entire law of the case rests.

As to Puffendorf, Grotius, Heineccius, and others who have been quoted, with all their lofty pretensions, they do not contain as much wisdom or light as may be found upon each and every page of "the wisest and brightest of mankind." So far as regards the present subject, they exhibit more pedantry and casuistry than either learning or common sense.

We contend, that what is honestly and reasonably believed to be certain death, will justify self-defense in the degree requisite for excuse. According to Dr. Rutherford,[1] "this law"—*i. e.*, the law of nature—"cannot be supposed to oblige a man to expose his life to such dangers as may be guarded against, and to wait till the danger is just coming upon him, before it allows him to secure himself." In other words, he need not wait till the certainty of the danger has been proved, past doubt, by its result. Yet this is the doctrine of the prosecution. They ask us to wait till the boat has sunk; we may then make an effort to prevent her from sinking. They tell us to wait till all are drowned; we may then make endeavors to save a part. They command us to stand still till we all are lost, past possibility of redemption, and then we may rescue as many as can be saved! "Where the danger is instantaneous, the mind is too much disturbed," says Rutherford, in a passage heretofore cited, "to deliberate upon the method of providing for one's own safety, with the least hurt to an aggressor." The same author then proceeds: "I see not, therefore, any want of benevolence which can be reasonably charged upon a man in these circumstances, if he takes the most obvious way of preserving himself, though, perhaps, some other method might have been found, which would have preserved him as effectually, and have produced less hurt to the aggressor, if he had been calm enough, and had been

[1] Inst. of Nat. Law, book I, chap. 16.

allowed time enough to deliberate about it."[1] Nor is this the language of approved text-writers alone. The doctrine has the solemnity of judicial establishment. In Grainger *v.* The State,[2] the Supreme Court of Tennessee deliberately adjudge, that "if a man, though in no great danger of serious bodily harm, through fear, alarm, or cowardice, kill another, under the impression that great bodily injury is about to be inflicted on him, it is neither manslaughter nor murder, but self-defense." "It is a different thing," say the Supreme Court of the United States, in the Mariana Flora, "to sit in judgment upon the case, after full legal investigations, aided by the regular evidence of all parties, and to draw conclusions at sea, with very imperfect means of ascertaining facts and principles, which ought to direct the judgment."[3] The decision in the case just cited carried out this principle into practice, as the case of Le Louis, decided by Sir William Scott, had done before.[4]

The counsel cited Lord Bacon, likewise.[5] But the prospect of sinking was not imaginary ; it was well founded. It is not to be supposed that Holmes, who, from infancy, had been a child of the ocean, was causelessly alarmed ; and there being no pretense of animosity, but the contrary, we must infer that the peril was extreme.

I have thus given you the law. There is but little difficulty between us in regard to it. The labor is in the application of the law.

6. PROPOSITIONS ADVANCED BY THE PROSECUTION ANSWERED.

I maintain that a well-founded apprehension of peril to life justifies self-defense, to the extent of destroying the adversary. The opposite counsel maintain that the peril must be actually inevitable. This I deny, and say that it is enough if it be *honestly* and reasonably *supposed* to be so. An *inevitable* danger I don't understand.

They maintain that the peril must be not only inevitable, but immediate. I answer, it need be neither ; but it must reasonably be supposed to be both.

Suppose, upon an indictment for manslaughter, a plank be

[1] Rutherford, Inst. of Nat. Law, book I, chap. 16, § 5.
[2] 5th Yerger's Rep. p. 459.
[3] 11th Wheaton's Rep. p. 51.
[4] 2d Dodson's Admiralty Rep. p. 264.
[5] Works by Montague, vol. 13th, p. 160; London, 1831 ; and 4th Blackstone's Com. p. 160.

measured in court, with square, rule and compass, and it be found that it would have sustained two persons ; still, is he, who in his terror supposes it would not, to be liable for conviction ? Certainly not.

The prosecution contends that if there be a doubt as to the inevitable peril, the defendant is to be convicted. I say it is presumed to have been considered inevitable, from the fact itself ; there being no pretense of animosity, but clear evidence of the greatest kindness and sympathy.

They say, that if the danger were inevitable, still the defendant had no right to make selection. To this I reply, that this argument involves the necessity of throwing *all* overboard. The selection would have been just the same if they had destroyed those who are living now, and permitted the others to remain.

But, say they, lots might have been cast. If the peril were inevitable and immediate, that could not have been done. We hear for the first time of casting lots in a sinking boat, where the question is whether any can be saved, rather than who shall be lost. Lots in cases of famine, where means of subsistence are wanting for the number of the crew, are matters which, horrible as they are, are comparatively familiar to us. But to cast lots to see who shall go first, when all are going, is reserved for the ingenuity of the counsel, who constructs a raft on board of ship, in the depth of the night, with the prospect of her going down before he drives the first nail, or plies the first rope.

The danger was instantaneous ; "a case," says Rutherford,[1] "where the mind is too much disturbed to deliberate ;" and where, if it were "more calm," there is no time for deliberation. The sailors adopted the only principle of selection which was possible in an emergency like theirs ; a principle more humane than lots. Man and wife were not torn asunder ; and the women were all preserved. Lots would have rendered impossible this clear dictate of humanity.

7. THE PRISONER BOUND TO OBEY THE MATE'S ORDER ; OTHERWISE ALL WERE IN A STATE OF NATURE WHEN ARTIFICIAL DISTINCTIONS CEASE TO PREVAIL.

But, again, the crew either were in their ordinary and original state of subordination to their officers, or they were in a state of

---

[1] Inst. of Nat. Law, book I, chap. 16, § 5.

nature.   If in the former state, they were excusable in law for having obeyed the order of the mate ; an order twice imperatively
given.   Independent of the mate's general authority in the captain's
absence, the captain had pointedly directed the crew to obey all
the mate's orders as they would his (the captain's), and the crew
had promised to do so.

It imports not to declare that the crew is not bound to obey an
unlawful order ; for to say that this order was unlawful, is to postulate what remains to be proved.   Who is to judge of the unlaw-
fulness ?   The circumstances were peculiar.   The occasion was
emergent, without precedent or parallel.   The lawfulness of the
order is the very question we are disputing, a question about which
the whole community has been agitated, and is still divided ; the
discussion of which crowds this room with auditors past former
example ; a question which this court, with all its resources, is now
engaged in considering, as such a question demands to be considered, most deliberately, most anxiously, most cautiously.   It is no
part of a sailor's duty to moralize and to speculate, in such a
moment as this was, upon the orders of his superior officers.   The
commander of a ship, like the commander of an army, "gives
desperate commands."   He requires instantaneous obedience.   The
sailor, like the soldier, obeys by instinct.   In the memorable, immortal words of Carnot, when he surrendered Antwerp, in obedience to a command which his pride, his patriotism, and his views
of policy all combined to oppose : " The armed force is essentially
obedient ; it acts, but never deliberates."   The greatest man of
the French Revolution did here but define, with the precision of
the algebraist, what he conceived with the comprehension of a
statesman ; and his answer was justification with every soldier in
Europe !   How far the principle was felt by this crew, let us witness the case of this very mate, and of some of these very sailors,
who, by the captain's order, left the jolly boat, which had ten persons, for the long boat, with more than four times that number.
They all regarded this as going into the jaws of death ; yet, not a
murmur !   It is a well-known fact, that in no marine on the ocean
is obedience to orders so habitual and so implicit as in our own.
The prisoner had been always distinguished by obedience.   Whether
the mate, if on trial here, would be found innocent, is a question
which we need not decide.   That question is a different one from
the guilt or innocence of the prisoner, and one more difficult.

But if the whole company were reduced to a state of nature,

then the sailors were bound to no duty not mutual to the passengers. The contract of the shipping articles had become dissolved by an unforeseen and overwhelming necessity. The sailor
was no longer a sailor, but a drowning man. Having fairly done
his duty to the last extremity, he was not to lose the rights of a
human being, because he wore a roundabout instead of a frock-
coat. We do not seek authorities for such doctrine. The instinct
of these men's hearts is our authority ; the best authority. Whoever opposes it must be wrong, for he opposes human nature. All
the contemplated conditions, all the contemplated possibilities of
the voyage were ended. The parties—sailors and passengers—were
in a new state. All persons on board the vessel became equal ; all
became their own law-givers ; for artificial distinctions cease to
prevail when we are reduced to the equality of nature. The law
which did prevail on that awful night, having been the law of necessity and the law of nature, too, it is the law which will be upheld by
this court to the liberation of this prisoner.

Now I have shown, if these views be sound, that apart from the
preservation of the rest of the passengers, and themselves, these
men could have had no inducement to take life. That the
magnanimity, gallantry and tenderness of Holmes utterly forbid
the idea. That, therefore, it is honestly and fairly to be inferred,
that they apprehended immediate peril, and were sustained by the
laws of nature in acting accordingly.

8. The defendant acted under the apprehension of immediate peril and pressing necessity.

As to the circumstance of Frank Askins offering five guineas to
preserve his life till morning, and its being refused ; that so far
from making against us, makes for us. If they had complied with
that request, they must either have sold the lives of all on board for
five sovereigns, or have offered conclusive evidence that they did
not conceive the peril to be immediate. If they had even received
the money, and afterwards deprived him of life, the money itself
would have been an indication, either of a corrupt motive, or a reliance on their own security, incompatible with the doctrine for
which I contend. It was a terrific deed, to be sure, consider it
which way you will ; and the very horror of the deed constitutes
part of its defense : as it is fairly to be presumed it would not have
been resorted to, except in a case of a *horrible* necessity.

The fate of the two sisters is spoken of with peculiar pathos.

I maintain their lives were never sacrificed by the crew. (1st.) Because there is no positive proof to that effect—mere loose suggestions or inferences. (2d.) Because there was not a hand laid upon any other woman in the boat. (3d.) Because never mentioned by witnesses upon previous examinations. (4th.) Because the conduct of the sisters shows that it was an act of self-devotion, which is almost admitted, indeed ; and which adds another bright page to the records of time, exhibiting the fidelity, affection and devotion of a woman's heart.

Considering it in this point of view, its glory is almost equal to its horrors, neither of which is attributable to the defendant. But it is said, that if the passengers had been allowed to live until the next morning, a ship was at hand.

First, I answer, that the probability was that they could not have survived the night ; and, secondly, that, without prescience they could not know of the ship being at hand.

Now let us look to the next morning. The boat is still filled with water, the peril is not abated, and two more half frozen wretches are removed ; some few hours after this, the vessel is discerned, and Holmes, and the passengers, through the instrumentality of Holmes, are saved.

As to the notion that there is any distinction between sailors and other men, in their natural rights of self-defense, it is not to be tolerated. If the peril were not imminent, no man has a right to destroy the life of another for the preservation of his own. If it were imminent and apparently inevitable, any man, without regard to condition, vocation or degree, had that right. A state of nature implies the absence of all but natural law ; and natural law is not to be affected by artificial distinctions. A sailor is upon equality with passengers ; nay, he is upon an equality with his captain in emergencies like this. With these views of the law let us turn to the facts.

9. VINDICATION OF THE CAPTAIN OF THE LOST VESSEL.

On the 13th of March, 1841, as has been said, the ship sailed from Liverpool to Philadelphia ; she came in contact with the ice on the 19th of April, and in one hour and less was reduced to a sinking condition.

The captain having unavailingly attempted the pumps, ordered the boats to be launched from the ship. Thirty-three passengers and nine sailors entered the long boat, and the captain, seven sailors and one passenger entered the jolly boat. The boats were moored at the stern of the ship, by dint of a ten fathom rope, attached to the vessel. And in a few minutes the ship sunk forever ; the rope being severed at that very moment by Holmes, who was posted for that purpose.

The counsel, at this point of the case, indulged in a severe and unmeasured attack upon Captain Harris, for having deserted the vessel ; maintaining that he was bound to have sunk with her, that he has disgraced the American name by not having done so, and that he presents by his conduct a shameful contrast to Grace Darling, who placed her life in peril to redeem the passengers and crew from a wreck, in the neighborhood of a light-house of which her father was the keeper.

Now this is all very poetical, very beautiful, and what embraces more, very gallant on the part of my learned friend. Rather than take the *laurel* from the brow of Grace Darling or any other darling, I would wear the *cypress* round my own ; but you will still allow me to say, there is a vast difference between an experiment in a life-boat and almost within hail of the shore, and the scene to which our attention is here called—one hundred leagues from land —in the darkness of night and surrounded by icebergs. The captain was not bound to do more than he did ; he was bound to do all that he did. His calmness and composure in the midst of these horrible scenes contributed to save the lives of upwards of fifty human beings ; although it is true that he was not enabled to rescue those who remained on board of the ship. Their temporary rescue would have resulted finally in the loss of *all*.

As to his sacrificing his own life, sympathy for others forbade it. If he and all of the sailors had perished, so far from its operating to the benefit of the passengers, it would have proved their inevitable and total destruction.

But, says the gentleman, why didn't he construct a raft ? he had an hour to do it in. He had no assurance of a moment ; the ship was laden with iron ; two columns of water of the thickness of a man's body were pouring through the stem of the ship into her very vitals. And although nearly an hour elapsed after leaving her, and before she sunk, how was he to determine upon the probability of her surviving the shock ? The learned counsel's argument is quite consistent throughout the case. He says a raft should have been constructed, because it turned out that the vessel did not sink for an hour ; as he says that the men should not have perished, because a ship afterwards hove in sight.

But it is further said by the learned gentleman, that the captain might have taken off more of the passengers. That suggestion is in direct opposition to the evidence. The gunwales of the boat were within six or eight inches of the water ; a single additional person would have swamped them ; and thus *all* must have perish, perhaps, from an ill-judged effort to save *one*. The conduct of the captain was not only judicious, but humane. If he had returned alongside of the ship, he would have been ingulfed by the vortex produced by her sinking, or subjected to a calamity scarcely less terrible, by some of the inmates of the ship jumping into the boats. As to the suggestion that he might have at least rescued the children in the ship, that attempt would have resulted in the same consequence, even supposing that the perishing parents would have been willing to sever themselves, in this moment of direst emergency, from offspring more precious than even life itself.

I have deemed it my duty to say this much in behalf of an absent man, and a most meritorious and exemplary officer ; not that it was by any means essential to the defense, but simply because it was an act of justice. If the captain is so disgracious now in the eyes of the prosecution, so culpable in the eye of the law, why have not our learned adversaries instituted legal proceedings against him, instead of attempting to transfer the burden of his imputed guilt to the shoulders of the prisoner. The captain's deposition was taken ; he was examined in the office of the attorney for the United States ; he was within the very jaws of the *Royal Tiger*, yet those jaws did not close upon him, with all their thirst for blood. Now, however, that his march is o'er the mountain wave, the counsel speak of his escape from justice, and the horrible retribution that awaits his return. This is the thunder without the bolt, or the power of Jove to wield it.

10. NARRATION OF THE FACTS, AND EVIDENCE IN THE CASE.

We pass now to other scenes. In the morning of the 20th of April, which was ushered in in darkness and in gloom, the two boats separated from each other ; the captain and eight others directing their course, in the jolly boat, for Newfoundland, and the mate and thirty-three passengers and crew remaining in the long boat. At the time of separation, which was on Tuesday morning, the captain directed his first officer, who had left the jolly boat for the long boat, to endeavor to steer for the nearest point of land, which was two hundred and fifty miles off ; and then having taken a list of

those on board of the long boat, he bade them a melancholy adieu.
In parting, the mate begged him to take some of the passengers into the jolly boat; the captain refused it as a matter of impossibility ; the mate declared that his boat would sink, or they should
have to cast lots ; and the captain, clearly acquiescing in that probable necessity, begged that it might be the last resort.

Shortly after the departure of the jolly boat, the sad series of
disasters commenced, which terminates in the lamentable catastrophe in which this trial originated. Nothing before this point of
time bears directly upon this question, although there is much in
the scenes referred to, calculated to touch the most callous heart.

At the time the boats parted company, or shortly after, it was
raining heavily ; the air was very cold, from the proximity of the
ice ; and the miserable, half naked passengers were benumbed by
exposure and hardships to which they had been subjected the preceding night. The long boat had leaked from the time she left the
ship ; the plug had, in some way, been removed, and another was
substituted. The second plug was lost, and a variety of expedients
were from time to time resorted to to supply its place, as well as to
stop the other leaks. Added to this, the long boat was, in her situation, entirely unmanageable. The testimony of the mate and captain, which is not contradicted by any of the witnesses, places this
beyond the reach of doubt. Parker, the mate, says : " I have followed the sea for twenty-one years. I think the long boat was too
unmanageable to be saved, from the experience I have had. If
there had been no leak, I do not think they would have been able
to save themselves." Again, upon the cross-examination : " The
long boat being unmanageable, I thought she would have sunk the
first night. By unmanageable I mean they could not put her head
from one point to another—she was going round like a tub ; she
was like her own mistress—they could not keep her head any one
way, not even for a minute."

And Captain Harris is equally clear and explicit upon the subject, when he informs us : " That the long boat leaked, that they
attempted to bail, but could not make out anything; they were so
thronged in the boat. She would not have supported one-half she
had in her, had there been a moderate blow, even without a leak.
The gunwale was about twelve inches above the surface of the sea."

Again, speaking on the same subject, the captain says : "I
found she was unmanageable, and that it was useless for me to
waste further time with them ; they could not use the oars ; they

could not steer the boat," &c.   And, further: "A very little irregularity in stowage would have capsized the long boat; a moderate flaw would have swamped her very quickly."

On Tuesday it rained heavily all day; the sailors were employed in rowing at times; the passengers took their turns in bailing, and it is perfectly apparent from the proof, that this course continued, with but little intermission or relaxation, until the dreary night closed in.   At this time the wind increased, the waves ran high, at times dashing into the boat, depositing ice upon the already half frozen passengers and crew; and at the same time calling for renewed exertion, while impairing the ability to make it.   At length, abandoned to despair, the water increasing in the boat, and the peril of death being imminent and apparently inevitable, a cry of horror is heard from various quarters, exclaiming: "We are sinking!   We are sinking!"   Then it was that the mate, who, unmurmuringly had taken his post in the very throat of death, at the command of the captain, perceiving that everything was reduced to a state of utter hopelessness, and unable longer to repress his emotions, cried out: "Help me, God! this will not do; men, go to work."   The witnesses all agree in regard to these expressions of the mate; some, however, say they were thrice repeated before they were obeyed, and finally the obedience of the crew was the death of sixteen of the passengers, by which, alone, in all human probability, the remaining seventeen passengers and nine seamen were saved.

II. The Impulses Which Led to the Catastrophe Considered.

Here let us pause, to ascertain, if we can, what were the impulses, the secret impulses, the direct impulses that led to this deplorable catastrophe.   I deny, emphatically, the correctness of the doctrine of the prosecution, that if there be any doubts of the sufficiency of the cause which led to the death, the defendant should be convicted.   This inverts the whole current of the philosophy of criminal jurisprudence.   Doubts of motive, doubts of acts, are always doubts of guilt; and reasonable doubts of guilt must result in acquittal.   I am strengthened in this position by the indisputable fact that Holmes, the prisoner, during the whole voyage, was upon the kindest and most harmonious terms with all the passengers; that he preserved the same friendly relation to them after the loss of the ship; that he had periled his life more than once to preserve them ; that he had literally stripped himself of his apparel for their comfort : in short, his desire to save them seemed to absorb all consideration of mere personal or individual safety. In these circumstances, to suppose anything cruel or wanton upon his part, is to run counter to everything that is possible or natural. I infer, therefore, that he supposed the peril to be imminent and instantaneous, or he never would have complied with the orders of the mate; and that the mate who gave the order, did it under the impression of direct necessity, is too obvious to require or admit of argument.

On Tuesday night, I say, about 10 o'clock, the boat filled with water from above and below ; the wind having risen ; the waves having increased ; the ice accumulating, and the passengers shrieking with horror at the prospect of drowning ; the final, fatal order was given. It is not to be supposed that these hardy sons of the sea were unnecessarily alarmed. That Holmes, particularly, was a brave, resolute, and determined seaman, as well as a most humane man, no one will venture to deny ; that he had but one supposable object, which was to save such as might be saved, is equally clear. I maintain, therefore, that the most favorable construction is to be placed upon his motives ; and it is justly to be inferred that he acted upon the impression that the danger was imminent, and that death was inevitable to all, except by resorting to those means which he actually adopted.

We are told, however, that he is not the judge. I ask, who is the judge ? There is a vast deal of difference between judging in a storm and judging of a representation of a storm ; and, therefore, it was that I said, that, in order to a righteous determination of this case, your verdict should be rendered in the midst of perils such as have been described, instead of being pronounced while surrounded by all the securities and sanctions of the law. I agree that if you can conceive of any other inducement than the desire of self-preservation, and that of the majority of the passengers, inducing this act, which I defy you to do, you may then imagine that that inducement led to the act, and thereby divest the prisoner of his present defense ; but even taking all the statements of the witnesses for the prosecution, highly colored—I will not say discolored—as they are, and torture them as you may, it is impossible for you to arrive at any other conclusion than that Holmes was actuated by the kindest and most generous influences ; and certainly I need not say that kindness and generosity are opposed to wantonness and barbarity.

I repeat, then, that in these circumstances of terror men are left to their honest determinations.   They are not to resort to mere imaginary evils as a pretext, nor are they to be *supposed* to resort to them as a pretext.   If they err in their determination, according to the rules adopted by a cold system of reasoning, their error, as thus detected, is not to be visited upon them as a crime.

12. SELF-PRESERVATION THE FIRST LAW OF NATURE.

Suppose two men, occupying perfectly friendly relations to each other, should be cast away, and both seize the same plank (to me the favorite illustration), and one should thrust the other off ; would it not be monstrous, upon the trial of the alleged offender, that the plank should be brought into court and submitted to some men of approved skill, and measured and examined by square, rule and compass ; its specific gravity ascertained, and the possibility of its sufficiency to sustain two men discussed and decided ; and, upon the basis of such calculation as that, the prisoner should be deprived of his liberty or his life ; when, if you had placed the witnesses in his precise situation, and they had been called upon to act upon a sudden emergency, they would have done precisely what he did, and what every principle of natural law abundantly warrants.   It is worse than idle to suppose, that in such a critical juncture as this men are to cast lots or toss up for their lives.   In such peril a man makes his own law with his own right arm.

But, say the learned counsel, had the passengers been permitted to remain until the morning, they might have been saved by the Crescent.   I answer, had they remained a single hour, they would have never seen the morning ; every man, woman and child, would have weltered in the coral caves of the ocean.   The approach of the Crescent could not, even in point of fact, have operated to alleviate their fears ; without prescience, they could have anticipated no such relief.   Men are to act upon the past and the present ; the future belongs to God alone.

You are told, however, that the condition of the boat was not hopeless ; that she was on " the great high road of nations," and that there was every prospect of her being picked up.   The gentleman speaks of the great high road of nations over the pathless ocean, as if it were the Chesapeake and Delaware canal, in which two vessels could scarcely pass abreast.   The " President," steamer, sunk probably upon this great high road, leaving no voice to tell her fate.   Surrounded, as the boat was, by mountains of ice, no

10

ship would probably ever have reached her, if steering in that direct course. Fate itself seemed to forbid it ; nay, no vessel, says the captain, would have ventured among the ice, had the position of the boat been known ; as no commander, however philanthropic, would have so far periled his own hopes in order to redeem the lives of others. The chances of rescue were entirely too remote then—ninety-nine chances against one, say the witnesses—to enter into the calculation of the mate and crew, had their circumstances even been such as to allow them dispassionately to reason upon the subject ; but as it was, terror had assumed the throne of reason, passion became judgment, and you know the sequel.

I have now briefly and imperfectly passed over that part of the case upon which your decision must mainly turn ; but before I close, let me direct your attention to another circumstance which casts a reflected light upon the matters already adverted to. I refer to the occurrence of the next day ; and this leads me to present to your view another picture in this nautical gallery.

13. THE SURVIVORS SAVED, SOLELY THROUGH THE INSTRUMEN-
TALITY OF THE DEFENDANT.

On Wednesday, the 21st of April, the morning dawns ; yet the sun still shrouds his face amidst shadowy clouds and darkness, from the traces of horror which the past night had left. You may see, gentlemen of the jury, without any extraordinary stretch of fancy, on that awful morning, a small boat, in the center of the ocean, with a single sailor, apparently engaged in an effort to rig out a sail, baring his brow and his breast to the bleak winds that howl around him, with no one to impart encouragement or aid, deserted by earth and frowned upon by Heaven. That man was Holmes, the prisoner at the bar. His messmates have sunk exhausted into the bottom of the boat ; the mate is lost in dismay ; the passengers are buried in hopelessness and horror :

> Silent they sit,
> All faculties absorbed by black despair ;
> The world is banish'd, and the soul is dead
> To earthly sympathy—to earthly care,
> Brooding alone on its eternal fate,
> And prostrate in the presence of its God.

And there, amidst this solemn and harrowing scene, the defendant stands, toiling and struggling to the last, not for himself, but

for those very persons who, having forgotten their *gratitude* with their *danger*, now appear before you to pay for *their own life* by depriving their preserver of *his*.   Whether this mode of discharging obligations shall meet with your approval, it will remain for your verdict to decide.

I have now done.   I am perfectly sensible of the power of the learned counsel opposed to me ; and if this case is to be determined by the comparative strength or skill of the advocates, I have much cause for alarm.   My gallant friend who opened the conflict, appeared like Apollo, radiant in his glory, balancing his body, adjusting his bow, and directing his shaft—*his golden pointed shaft*—at the very heart of his intended victim.   By and by, his colleague, who may be compared to Hercules, will take the field with his club, and exert all his stupendous powers to demolish this defense.   Still, armed in the panoply of justice, I entertain no fear, for after all, gentlemen of the jury, what is a giant when wrapped up in a QUILT ?   Against all these odds, therefore, I stand firmly by the side of that man, who always stood firmly by others.   The destiny, the worldly destiny, of the prisoner is now confided to your hands. Do with him as you would be done by.

N. B.—The prisoner's counsel requested the Court to charge, that in a state of imminent and deadly peril all men are reduced to a state of nature ; that when the vessel went down the voyage was at an end, and that there was then no longer any distinction between the rights of sailors and passengers. The Court declined so to charge.   His statement of the law was substantially as follows : The passenger stands in a position different from that of officers and seamen.   It is the sailor's duty to encounter the hardships and perils of the voyage.   The passenger owes no duty but submission ; he is under no obligation to protect and keep the conductor in safety; he is not bound to labor, except in cases of emergency, where his services are required by unanticipated and uncommon danger.   This relation is not changed when the ship is lost by tempest or other dangers of the sea, because impending danger cannot absolve from duty.   Should the danger become extreme, so as to require the sacrifice of human life, the rule of law is the same.   Since the passenger is not bound to labor or incur the risk of life, he is not bound to sacrifice his existence to preserve the sailor.   The captain and a sufficient number of seamen to navigate the boat must be preserved, "for except these abide in the ship all shall likewise perish ;" but *supernumerary* sailors have no right to sacrifice the passengers to secure their own safety.   In the eye of the law, the positions of sailor and passenger are not equal ; nor are the relations between them absolved by the law of nature, or the laws of necessity, under any circumstances.   As between sailor and sailor, or passenger and passenger, they may lawfully struggle with each other for the same plank which can save but one ; but if the passenger is on the plank, even the law of necessity justifies not the sailor who takes it from him. As between those in equal relations, they must have an equal chance of life when the destruction is ascertained to be certain, and must arrive in the near future. As, for example, when all sustenance has been exhausted, and a sacrifice of one person is necessary to appease the hunger of the others, the fairest mode of selection is by lot, which all writers have regarded as just, being in one sense an appeal to God for the selection of the victim.

The jury retired, and after sixteen hours deliberation returned a verdict of guilty. The defendant was sentenced to six months imprisonment at hard labor, and to pay a fine of twenty dollars.

SPEECH OF WILLIAM H. SEWARD,

In Defense of the Negro, William Freeman, Indicted for
the Murder of John G. Van Nest.

AT THE CAYUGA OYER AND TERMINER, HELD AT THE VILLAGE OF AUBURN, N. Y., JULY TERM, 1846.

Analysis of Mr. Seward's Speech.

1. The execution of a madman is murder.
2. The defense is interposed in behalf of justice and humanity, for society and mankind.
3. The preliminary verdict as to the prisoner's sanity, imperfect and unjust.
4. The standard of intelligence by which the prisoner must be judged.
5. Insanity, though often counterfeited, is a perfect defense.—How the truth of the plea may be tested.
6. Relations of the law towards the insane. —Review of Kleim's case.
7. Public security does not require the sacrifice of the prisoner.
8. Difficulty of detecting insanity.—The human mind incapable of complete obliteration.
9. Insanity defined.
10. Why the prisoner could not possibly simulate madness.
11. Insanity of the prisoner demonstrated.— The various causes of insanity discussed.
12. Delusion, when shown, incontestable proof of insanity.—Illustrations of the subject.
13. The circumstances of the murder tested by scientific rules.
14. The personal appearance and demeanor of the prisoner the strongest proof of his insanity.

William Freeman was born at Auburn, in the county of Cayuga, in the year 1824. When he arrived at the age of sixteen, he was accused of having stolen a horse belonging to a Mrs. Godfrey. He stoutly protested his innocence, and after an examination before a magistrate, was discharged. The horse was afterwards found. It had been purchased, it was said, from a negro answering the description of one Jack Furman, who was accordingly arrested. The latter, knowing that Freeman had been previously suspected of the offense, now renewed the charge against him, and offered to implicate Freeman, provided he should himself be released. Freeman was convicted on Furman's evidence, and the latter, the real thief, was discharged as a reward for his perjury; for it afterwards became clear that Freeman was at another place the night the horse was stolen. The conviction affected Freeman's mind. He could not comprehend why he should be shut up in prison for no offense. He pleaded his innocence, and begged in vain to be released, but received no sympathy. His patience finally became exhausted; he grew restive and quarrelsome; and met only with ill-treatment and abuse. One day, his keeper, with whom he had a difficulty, struck him a terrible blow on the temple with a heavy basswood board, from the effects of which he never recovered. To use his own words, " It knocked all the hearing off so that it never came back." He became deaf, grew sullen,

[149]

downcast and morose. A post mortem examination revealed the fact that the drum of his left ear had been broken, and his left temporal bone was carious and diseased. He was considered deranged before his release. He brooded over his unjust imprisonment, and talked of nothing but getting his pay for the time he had spent in prison. The mania grew upon him, and when he was finally discharged at the expiration of his term, he applied, on several occasions, for warrants against persons in order, he said, to get " his pay," but his language was incoherent and broken; and he grew weak and foolish.

John G. Van Nest, a wealthy and respectable farmer, lived with his family in the town of Fleming, on the western border of the Owasco Lake, about three and a half miles south of the village of Auburn. At about half past nine o'clock on the evening of the 12th of March, 1846, Mr. Van Nest, who was about to re-tire, heard proceeding from the back yard the shrieks of his wife. He opened the door, and almost instantly received a fatal wound from the hand of an assassin, and died without a struggle. Helen Holmes, a domestic, in another apartment, hearing the noise, opened the door, when Mrs. Van Nest, pale, haggard and covered with blood, staggered into the house, fell upon the floor, and expired. Mrs. Wyckoff, a member of the family, in her attempt to escape,was struck down by the murderer, who had, by this time, entered the dwelling. The wretch, in passing, slew an infant sleeping in the room, but, in attempting to ascend the stairs, was confronted by Mr. Van Arsdale, a farm laborer employed by Mr. Van Nest, who succeeded in driving his assailant from the premises, though he re-ceived a terrible wound in the encounter. The murderer stole a horse close by and made good his escape. Before he had gone far, he stabbed the animal, pro-cured another, and continued his flight into Oswego county, and was captured the next day, a distance of forty miles from the scene of the tragedy. The assassin was William Freeman.

The conduct of Mr. Seward, in undertaking the defense of Freeman, when he was arraigned for the murder, was an exhibition of moral courage almost without a parallel. The crime charged was terrible and appalling, and wrought upon the public mind to such a degree, it was almost a miracle how the pris-oner escaped swift destruction at the hands of the mob. He was without money and without friends. He sprung from a race socially and politically de-based. His father had been a slave, and the son was a person of idle and in-temperate habits, and, though only twenty-three, had spent five years of his life in State prison. Yet Mr. Seward was convinced that the poor wretch was, at the time of the offense, destitute of reason, and suffering from dementia ap-proaching to idiocy. He believed the execution of such a being would be mur-der, and he determined to spare the community the disgrace of hanging a mad-man, even at the cost of his own popularity. The storm of public indignation beat so fiercely about him, that at one time, fears were entertained for his per-sonal safety. In a letter to a friend, he thus referred to the subject: " There is a busy war around me to drive me from securing a fair trial for the negro Free-man. . . . No priest (except one Universalist), no Levite, no lawyer, no man, no woman, has visited him. He is deaf, deserted, ignorant, and his con-duct is unexplainable on any principle of *sanity*. It is natural he should turn to me to defend him. If he does, I shall do so. This will raise a storm of preju-dice and passion which will try the fortitude of my friends. But I shall do my duty. I care not whether I am to be ever forgiven for it or not."

In addressing the jury upon the preliminary trial, to test the question as to the prisoner's sanity, he said: "In due time, gentlemen of the jury, when I shall have paid the debt of nature, my remains will rest here in your midst, with those of my kindred and neighbors. It is very possible they may be un-honored, neglected, spurned ! But perhaps, years hence, when the passion and excitement which now agitate the community shall have passed away, some wandering stranger, some lone exile, some Indian, some negro, may erect over them an humble stone, and thereon this epitaph, HE WAS FAITHFUL."

On the 18th of May, 1846, indictments were found against Freeman, at the General Sessions of Cayuga county, which were, under the statute, sent to the Oyer and Terminer on the 1st of June following. When about to be arraigned, Mr. Seward voluntarily interposed in his behalf a plea of insanity, upon which issue was joined, and on the 24th of June the Court directed the question to be tried by a jury. After quite a lengthy trial, on the 5th of July the following verdict was rendered : "We find the prisoner sufficiently sane in mind and memory to distinguish between right and wrong." Mr. Seward excepted to the verdict, and requested the Court to instruct the jury to find whether the prisoner was sane or insane, which was refused. The next day (Monday), July 6th, the prisoner was brought up for trial. Mr. Seward objected to his being required to plead, because the verdict on the preliminary trial did not determine the question as to the prisoner's sanity. Objection overruled. When asked if he demanded a trial, the prisoner answered "no." The Court, however, directed a plea of "not guilty" to be entered for him, and ordered the trial to proceed. Mr. Sew-ard volunteered to remain counsel for the prisoner until his death. He con-ducted the case with great ability, and called many witnesses to establish his only defense, insanity. The following counsel appeared on the trial. For the people, John Van Buren (Attorney-General) and Luman Sherwood. For the prisoner, William H. Seward, David Wright and Christopher Morgan. Hon. Samuel Blatchford was associated with Mr. Seward in the preliminary trial.

In closing the case, in behalf of the prisoner, Mr. Seward addressed to the jury the following powerful appeal :

MAY IT PLEASE THE COURT,—*Gentlemen of the Jury :*—"Thou shalt not kill," and, "Whoso sheddeth man's blood by man shall his blood be shed," are laws found in the code of that people who, although dispersed and distracted, trace their history to the crea-tion; a history which records that murder was the first of human crimes.

The first of these precepts constitutes a tenth part of the juris-prudence which God saw fit to establish, at an early period, for the government of all mankind throughout all generations. The latter, of less universal obligation, is still retained in our system, although other States as intelligent and refined, as secure and peaceful, have substituted for it the more benign principle that good shall be re-turned for evil. I yield implicit submission to this law, and ac-knowledge the justice of its penalty, and the duty of courts and juries to give it effect.

In this case, if the prisoner *be* guilty of murder, I do not ask remission of punishment. If he be guilty, never was murderer *more* guilty. He has murdered, not only John G. Van Nest, but his hands are reeking with the blood of other, and numerous, and even more pitiable victims. The slaying of Van Nest, if a crime at all, was the cowardly crime of assassination. John G. Van Nest was a just, upright, virtuous man, of middle age, of grave and modest demeanor, distinguished by especial marks of the respect and esteem of his fellow citizens. On his arm leaned a confiding wife, and they supported, on the one side, children to whom they had given being, and, on the other, aged and venerable parents, from whom they had derived existence. The assassination of such a man was an atrocious crime, but the murderer, with more than savage refinement, immolated on the same altar, in the same hour, a venerable and virtuous matron of more than three-score years, and her daughter, wife of Van Nest, mother of an unborn infant. Nor was this all. Providence, which, for its own mysterious purposes, permitted these dreadful crimes, in mercy suffered the same arm to be raised against the sleeping orphan child of the butchered parents, and received it into Heaven. A whole family, just, gentle and pure, were thus, in their own house, in the night time, without any provocation, without one moment's warning, sent by the murderer to join the assembly of the just; and even the laboring man, sojourning within their gates, received the fatal blade into his breast, and survives through the mercy, not of the murderer, but of God.

For William Freeman, as a murderer, I have no commission to speak. If he had silver and gold accumulated with the frugality of Crœsus, and should pour it all at my feet, I would not stand an hour between him and the avenger. But for the innocent, it is my right, my duty to speak. If this sea of blood was *innocently* shed, then it is my duty to stand beside him until his steps lose their hold upon the scaffold.

I. THE EXECUTION OF A MADMAN IS MURDER.

"Thou shalt not kill" is a commandment addressed, not to him alone, but to me, to you, to the Court, and to the whole community. There are no exceptions from that commandment, at least in civil life, save those of self-defense, and capital punishment for crimes in the due and just administration of the law. There is not only a question, then, whether the prisoner has shed the blood of his fellow man, but the question whether we shall unlawfully shed his blood. I should be guilty of murder if, in my present relation, I saw the executioner waiting for an insane man and failed to say, or failed to do in his behalf, all that my ability allowed. I think it has been proved of the prisoner at the bar, that during all this long and tedious trial, he has had no sleepless nights, and that even in the day time, when he retires from these halls to his lonely cell, he sinks to rest, like a wearied child, on the stone floor, and quietly slumbers till aroused by the constable with his staff, to appear again before the jury. His counsel enjoy no such repose. Their thoughts by day and their dreams by night are filled with oppressive apprehensions that, through their inability or neglect, he may be condemned.

I am arraigned before you for undue manifestations of zeal and excitement. My answer to all such charges shall be brief. When this cause shall have been committed to you, I shall be happy indeed, if it shall appear that my only error has been, that I have felt too much, thought too intensely, or acted too faithfully.

If *my* error would thus be criminal, how great would yours be if you should render an unjust verdict? Only four months have elapsed since an outraged people, distrustful of judicial redress, doomed the prisoner to immediate death. Some of you have confessed that you approved that lawless sentence. All men now rejoice that the prisoner was saved for this solemn trial. But this trial would be as criminal as that precipitate sentence if, through any willful fault or prejudice of yours, it should prove but a mockery of justice. If any prejudice of witnesses, or the imagination of counsel, or any ill-timed jest shall at any time have diverted your attention; or if any prejudgment which you may have brought into the jury box, or any cowardly fear of popular opinion shall have operated to cause you to deny to the prisoner that dispassionate consideration of his case which the laws of God and man exact of you, and if, owing to such an error, this wretched man fall from among the living, what will be your crime? You have violated the commandment, "Thou shalt not kill." It is not the form or letter of the trial by jury that authorizes you to send your fellow man to his dread account, but it is the spirit that sanctifies that glorious institution; and if, through pride, passion, timidity, weakness, or any cause, you deny the prisoner one iota of all the defense to which he is entitled by the law of the land, you yourselves, whatever his guilt may be, will have broken the commandment, "Thou shalt do no murder."

There is not a corrupt or prejudiced witness, there is not a thoughtless or heedless witness, who has testified what was not true in spirit, or what was not wholly true, or who has suppressed any truth, who has not offended against the same injunction.

Nor is the Court itself above the commandment. If these judges have been influenced by the excitement which has brought this vast assemblage here, and under such influence, or under any other influence, have committed voluntary error, and have denied to the prisoner, or shall hereafter deny to him, the benefit of any fact or any principle of law, then this Court will have to answer for the deep transgression, at the bar at which we all shall meet again. When we appear there, none of us can plead that we were insane and knew not what we did; and by just so much as our ability and knowledge exceed those of this wretch, whom the world regards as a fiend in human shape, will our guilt exceed his, if we be guilty.

2. THE DEFENSE IS INTERPOSED IN BEHALF OF JUSTICE AND HUMANITY, FOR SOCIETY AND MANKIND.

I plead not for a murderer. I have no inducement, no motive to do so. I have addressed my fellow-citizens in many various relations, when rewards of wealth and fame awaited me. I have been cheered on other occasions by manifestations of popular approbation and sympathy; and where there was no such encouragement, I had at least the gratitude of him whose cause I defended. But I speak now in the hearing of a people who have prejudged the prisoner, and condemned me for pleading in his behalf. He is a convict, a pauper, a negro, without intellect, sense, or emotion. My child, with an affectionate smile, disarms my care-worn face of its frown whenever I cross my threshold. The beggar in the street obliges me to give, because he says "God bless you" as I pass. My dog caresses me with fondness if I will but smile on him. My horse recognizes me when I fill his manger. But what reward, what gratitude, what sympathy and affection can I expect here? There the prisoner sits. Look at him. Look at the assemblage around you. Listen to their ill-suppressed censures and their excited fears, and tell me where, among my neighbors or my fellow men, where, even in his heart, I can expect to find the sentiment, the thought, not to say of reward or of acknowledgment, but even of recognition. I sat here two weeks during the preliminary trial. I stood here, between the prisoner and the jury, nine hours,

and pleaded for the wretch that he was insane and did not even
know he was on trial; and, when all was done, the jury thought, at
least eleven of them thought, that I had been deceiving them, or
was self-deceived. They read signs of intelligence in his idiotic
smile, and of cunning and malice in his stolid insensibility. They
rendered a verdict that he was sane enough to be tried—a con-
temptable compromise verdict in a capital case; and then they
looked on, with what emotions God and they only know, upon his
arraignment. The district attorney, speaking in his adder ear,
bade him rise, and, reading to him one indictment, asked him
whether he wanted a trial, and the poor fool answered no. Have
you counsel ? No. And they went through the same mockery,
the prisoner giving the same answers, until a third indictment was
thundered in his ears, and he stood before the Court silent, motion-
less, and bewildered. Gentlemen, you may think of this evidence
what you please, bring in what verdict you can, but I asseverate,
before Heaven and you, that, to the best of my knowledge and belief, the prisoner at the bar does not, at this moment, know why it
is that my shadow falls on you instead of his own.

I speak with all sincerity and earnestness, not because I expect my opinion to have weight, but I would disarm the injurious
impression that I am speaking merely as a lawyer speaks for his
client. I am not the prisoner's lawyer. I am, indeed, a volunteer
in his behalf, but society and mankind have the deepest interest at
stake. I am the lawyer for society, for mankind, shocked, beyond
the power of expression, at the scene I have witnessed here of trying a maniac as a malefactor. In this, almost the first of such
causes I have ever seen, the last I hope that I shall ever see, I wish
that I could perform my duty with more effect. If I suffered myself to look at the volumes of testimony through which I have to
pass, to remember my entire want of preparation, the pressure of
time, and my wasted strength and energies, I should despair of ac-
quitting myself as you and all good men will hereafter desire that
I should have performed so sacred a duty. But, in the cause of
humanity, we are encouraged to hope for divine assistance where
human powers are weak. As you all know, I provided for my way
through these trials, neither gold nor silver in my purse, nor scrip;
and when I could not think before hand what I would say, I remembered that it was said to those who had a beneficent commission, that they should take no thought what they should say when
brought before the magistrate, for, in that same hour, it should be

given them what they should say, and it should not be they who should speak, but the spirit of their Father speaking in them.

You have promised, gentlemen, to be impartial. You will find it more difficult than you have supposed. Our minds are liable to be swayed by temporary influences, and above all, by the influences of masses around us. At every stage of this trial, your attention has been diverted, as it will be hereafter, from the only question which it involves, by the eloquence of the counsel for the people, reminding you of the slaughter of that helpless and innocent family, and of the danger to which society is exposed by relaxing the rigor of the laws. Indignation against crime, and apprehensions of its recurrence, are elements on which public justice relies for the execution of the law. You must indulge that indignation. You cannot dismiss such apprehensions. You will, in common with your fellow-citizens, deplore the destruction of so many precious lives, and sympathize with mourning relations and friends. Such sentiments cannot be censured when operating upon the community at large, but they are deeply to be deplored when they are manifested in the jury box.

3. THE PRELIMINARY VERDICT AS TO THE PRISONER'S SANITY, IMPERFECT AND UNJUST.

Then, again, a portion of this issue has been tried, imperfectly tried, unjustly tried, already. A jury of twelve men, you are told, have already rendered their verdict that the prisoner is *now* sane. The deference which right-minded men yield to the opinions of others, the timidity which weak men feel in dissenting from others, may tempt you to surrender your own independence. I warn you that that verdict is a reed which will pierce you through and through. That jury was selected without peremptory challenge. Many of the jurors entered the panel with settled opinions that the prisoner was not only guilty of the homicide, but sane, and all might have entertained such opinions for all that the prisoner could do. It was a verdict founded on such evidence as could be hastily collected in a community where it required moral courage to testify for the accused. Testimony was excluded upon frivolous and unjust pretenses. The cause was submitted to the jury on the fourth of July, and under circumstances calculated to convey a malicious and unjust spirit into the jury box. It was a strange celebration. The dawn of the day of independence was not greeted with cannon or bells. No lengthened procession was seen in our streets, nor were the voices of orators heard in our public halls. An intense excitement brought a vast multitude here, complaining of the delay and the expense of what was deemed an unnecessary trial, and demanding the sacrifice of a victim who had been spared too long already. For hours that assemblage was roused and excited by denunciations of the prisoner, and ridicule of his deafness, his ignorance, and his imbecility. Before the jury retired, the Court was informed that they were ready to render the verdict required. One juror, however, hesitated. The next day was the Sabbath. The jury were called, and the Court remonstrated with the dissentient, and pressed the necessity of a verdict. That juror gave way at last, and the bell which summoned our citizens to church for the evening service was the signal for the discharge of the jury, because they had agreed. Even thus a legal verdict could not be extorted. The eleven jurors, doubtless under an intimation from the Court, compromised with the twelfth, and a verdict was rendered, not in the language of the law, that the prisoner was "not insane," but that he was "sufficiently sane, in mind and memory, to distinguish between right and wrong;" a verdict which implied that the prisoner was at least *partially* insane, was diseased in other faculties besides the memory, and partially diseased in that, and that, although he had mind and memory to distinguish between right and wrong in the abstract, he had not reason and understanding and will to regulate his conduct according to that distinction; in short, a verdict by which the jury unworthily evaded the question submitted to them, and cast upon the Court a responsibility which it had no right to assume, but which it did nevertheless assume, in violation of the law. That twelfth juror was afterwards drawn as a juror in this cause, and was challenged by the counsel for the people for partiality to the prisoner, and the challenge was sustained by the Court, because—although he had, as the Court says, pronounced by his verdict that the prisoner was sane—he then declared that he believed the prisoner insane, and would die in the jury box before he would render a verdict that he was sane. Last and chièf of all objections to that verdict now, it has been neither pleaded nor proved here, and therefore, is not in evidence before you. I trust, then, that you will dismiss, to the contempt of mankind that jury and their verdict, thus equivocating upon law and science, health and disease, crime and innocence.

4. The standard of intelligence by which the prisoner
must be judged.

Again. An inferior standard of intelligence has been set up
here as the standard of the negro race, and a false one as to the
standard of the Asiatic race. The prisoner traces a divided lineage. On the paternal side his ancestry is lost among the tiger
hunters on the gold coast of Africa, while his mother constitutes a
portion of the small remnant of the Narragansett tribe. Hence, it
is held, that the prisoner's intellect is to be compared with the
depreciating standard of the African, and his passions with the
violent and ferocious character erroneously imputed to the
aborigines. Indications of manifest derangement, or at least of
imbecility, approaching to idiocy, are therefore set aside, on the
ground that they harmonize with the legitimate but degraded
characteristics of the races from which he is descended. You,
gentlemen, have, or ought to have, lifted up your souls above the
bondage of prejudices so narrow and so mean as these. The color
of the prisoner's skin and the form of his features are not impressed upon the spiritual, immortal mind which works beneath.
In spite of human pride, he is still your brother, and mine, in form
and color accepted and approved by his Father, and yours, and
mine, and bears equally with us the proudest inheritance of our
race—the image of our Maker. Hold him then to be a man.
Exact of him all the responsibilities which should be exacted under
like circumstances if he belonged to the Anglo-Saxon race, and
make for him all the allowances which, under like circumstances,
you would expect for yourselves.

5. Insanity, though often counterfeited, is a perfect
defense.—How the truth of the plea may be tested.

The prisoner was obliged—no, his counsel were obliged, by law,
to accept the plea of *not guilty*, which the Court directed to be entered in his behalf. That plea denies the homicide. If the law
had allowed it, we would gladly have admitted all the murders of
which the prisoner was accused, and have admitted them to be as
unprovoked as they were cruel, and have gone directly before you
on the only defense upon which we have insisted, or shall insist, or
could insist, that he is irresponsible, because he was and is insane.
We labor, not only under these difficulties, but under the further embarrassment that the plea of insanity is universally sus-

pected. It is the last subterfuge of the guilty, and so, is too often abused. But, however obnoxious to suspicion this defense is, there have been cases where it was true; and when true, it is, of all pleas, the most perfect and complete defense that can be offered in any human tribunal. Our Saviour forgave his judges because "they knew not what they did." The insane man who has committed a crime knew not what he did. If this being, dyed with human blood, be *insane*, you and I, and even the children of our affections, are not more guiltless than he.

Is there reason to indulge a suspicion of fraud here? Look at this stupid, senseless fool, almost as inanimate as the clay moulded in the brick-yard, and say, if you dare, that you are afraid of being deceived by him. Look at me. You all know me. Am I a man to engage in a conspiracy to deceive you and defraud justice? Look on us all, for although I began the defense of this cause alone, thanks to the generosity, to the magnanimity of an enlightened profession, I come out strong in the assistance of counsel never before attached to me in any relation, but strongly grappled to me now, by these new and endearing ties. Is any one of us a man to be suspected? The testimony is closed. Look through it all. Can suspicion or malice find in it any ground to accuse us of a plot to set up a false and fabricated defense? I will give you, gentlemen, a key to every case where insanity has been wrongfully and yet successfully maintained. Gold, influence, popular favor, popular sympathy, raise that defense and make it impregnable. But you have never seen a poor, worthless, spiritless, degraded negro like *this* acquitted wrongfully. I wish this trial may prove that such an one can be acquitted rightfully. The danger lies here. There is not a white man or white woman who would not have been dismissed long since from the perils of such a prosecution, if it had only been proved that the offender was so ignorant and so brutalized as not to understand that the defense of insanity had been interposed.

If he feign, who has trained the idiot to perform this highest and most difficult of all intellectual achievements? Is it I? Shakspeare and Cervantes only, of all mankind, have conceived and perfected a counterfeit of insanity. Is it I? Why is not the imposition exposed, to my discomfiture and the prisoner's ruin? Where was it done? Was it in public, here? Was it in secret, in the jail? His deafened ears could not hear me there, unless I were overheard by other prisoners, by jailers, constables, the sheriff, and a cloud of witnesses. Who has the keys of the jail? Have I? You have had sheriff, jailer, and the whole police upon the stand. Could none of these witnesses reveal our plot? Were there none to watch and report the abuse? When they tell you, or insinuate, gentlemen, that this man has been taught to feign insanity, they discredit themselves, as did the Roman sentinels, who, appointed to guard the sepulchre of our Saviour, said, in excuse of the broken seal, that while they slept men came and rolled away the stone.

6. Relations of the law towards the insane.—Review of Kleim's case.

I advance towards the merits of the cause. The law which it involves will be found in the case of Kleim, tried for murder in 1844, before Judge Edmonds, of the first circuit, in the city of New York, reported in the *Journal of Insanity* for January, 1846, at page 261. I read from the report of the judge's charge:

" He told the jury that there was no doubt that Kleim had been guilty of the killing imputed to him, and that under circumstances of atrocity and deliberation which were calculated to excite in their minds strong feelings of indignation against him. But they must beware how they permitted such feelings to influence their judgment. They must bear in mind that the object of punishment was not vengeance, but reformation; not to extort from a man an atonement for the life which he cannot give, but, by the terror of the example, to deter others from the like offenses, and that nothing was so likely to destroy the public confidence in the administration of criminal justice, as the infliction of its pains upon one whom Heaven has already afflicted with the awful malady of insanity."

These words deserve to be written in letters of gold upon tablets of marble. Their reason and philosophy are apparent. If you send the lunatic to the gallows, society will be shocked by your inhumanity, and the advocates for the abolition of capital punishment will find their most effective argument in the fact that a jury of the country, through ignorance, or passion, or prejudice, have mistaken a madman for a criminal.

The report of Judge Edmonds' charge proceeds: " It was true that the plea of insanity was sometimes adopted as a cloak for crime, yet it was unfortunately equally true, that many more persons were unjustly convicted, to whom their unquestioned insanity ought to have been an unfailing protection." This judicial answer to the argument that jurors are too likely to be swayed by the plea of insanity, is perfect and complete. Judge Edmonds further charged the jury, "that it was by no means an easy matter to discover or define the line of demarkation where sanity ended and insanity began," and that it was often "difficult for those most expert in the disease to detect or explain its beginning, extent or duration; that the classifications of the disease were in a great measure arbitrary, and the jury were not obliged to bring the case of the prisoner within any one of the classes, because the symptoms of the different kinds were continually mingling with each other."

The application of this rule will render the present case perfectly clear, because it appears from the evidence that the prisoner is laboring under a combination of *mania* or excited madness, with *dementia* or decay of the mind. Judge Edmonds furnishes you with a balance to weigh the testimony in the case in these words: ' It was important that the jury should understand how much weight was to be given to the opinions of medical witnesses. The opinions of men who had devoted themselves to the study of insanity as a distinct department of medical science, and studied recent improvements and discoveries, especially when to that knowledge they added the experience of personal care of the insane, could never be safely disregarded by courts and juries; and, on the other hand, the opinions of physicians who had devoted their particular attention to disease were not of any more value than the opinions of common persons."

This charge of Judge Edmonds furnishes a lamp to guide your feet, and throws a blazing light on your path. He acknowledges, in the first place, with distinguished independence for a judge and a lawyer, that "the law, in its slow and cautious progress, still lags far behind the advance of true knowledge. An insane person is one who, at the time of committing the act, labored under such a defect of reason as not to know the nature and quality of the act he was doing, or if he did know it, did not know he was doing what was wrong; and the question is not whether the accused knew the difference between right and wrong *generally*, but whether he knew the difference between right and wrong in regard to the very act with which he is charged. If some controlling disease was, in truth, the acting power within him, which he could not resist, or if he had not a sufficient use of his reason to control the passions which prompted him, he is not responsible. But it must

11

be an absolute dispossession of the free and natural agency of the mind. In the glowing but just language of Erskine, it is not necessary that reason should be hurled from her seat; it is enough that distraction sits down beside her, holds her trembling in her place, and frightens her from her propriety."

Judge Edmonds proceeded: "And it must be borne in mind that the *moral* as well as *intellectual* faculties may be so disordered by the disease as to deprive the mind of its controlling and directing power. In order then, to establish a crime, a man must have memory and intelligence to know that the act he is about to commit is wrong; to remember and understand, that if he commit the act he will be subject to punishment; and reason and will to enable him to compare and choose between the supposed advantage or gratification to be obtained by the criminal act, and the immunity from punishment which he will secure by abstaining from it. If, on the other hand, he have not intelligence enough to have a criminal intent and purpose, and if his moral or intellectual powers are either so deficient that he has not sufficient will, conscience or controlling mental power, or if, through the overwhelming violence of mental disease, his intellectual power is for the time obliterated, he is not a responsible moral agent." The learned judge recommended to the jury, "as aids to a just conclusion, to consider the extraordinary and unaccountable alteration in the prisoner's whole mode of life; the inadequacy between the slightness of the cause and the magnitude of the offense; the recluse and ascetic life which he has led; his invincible repugnance to all intercourse with his fellow creatures; his behavior and conduct at the time the act was done, and subsequently during his confinement; and the stolid indifference which he alone had manifested during the whole progress of a trial upon which his life or death depended."

Kleim was acquitted and sent, according to law, to the State Lunatic Asylum at Utica. The superintendent of the asylum, in a note to this report, states that Kleim is uniformly mild and pleasant; has not asked a question, or spoken or learned the name of any one; seems very imperfectly to recollect the murder or the trial; says he was put in prison; does not know what for; and was taken to the court, but had no trial; that his bodily health is good, but that his mind is nearly gone—quite demented.

You cannot fail, gentlemen of the jury, to remark the extraordinary similarity between the case of Kleim, as indicated in the charge of Judge Edmonds, and that of the prisoner at the bar. If I were sure you would receive such a charge, and be guided by it, I might rest here, and defy the eloquence of the attorney-general. The proof of insanity in this case is of the same nature, and the disease in the same form as in the case of Kleim. The only difference is, that the evidence here is a thousand times more conclusive. But Judge Edmonds does not preside here. Kleim was a white man, Freeman is a negro. Kleim set fire to a house, to burn only a poor obscure woman and her child. Here the madman destroyed a whole family, rich, powerful, honored, respected and beloved. Kleim was tried in the city of New York, and the community engaged in their multiplied avocations, and heedless of a crime not infrequent there, and occurring in humble life, did not overawe and intimidate the Court, the jury, or the witnesses. Here a panic has paralyzed humanity. No man or woman feels safe until the maniac shall be extirpated from the face of the earth. Kleim had the sympathies of men and women, willing witnesses, advocates sustained and encouraged by popular favor, and an impartial jury. Freeman is already condemned by the tribunal of public opinion, and has reluctant and timorous witnesses, counsel laboring under embarrassments plainly to be seen, and a jury whose impartiality is yet to be proved.

7. PUBLIC SECURITY DOES NOT REQUIRE THE SACRIFICE OF THE PRISONER.

The might that slumbered in this maniac's arm was exhausted in the paroxysm which impelled him to his dreadful deeds. Yet, an excited community, whose terror has not yet culminated, declare, that whether sane or insane, he must be executed, to give safety to your dwellings and theirs. I must needs then tell you the law, which will disarm such cowardly fear. If you acquit the prisoner, he cannot go at large, but must be committed to jail, to be tried by another jury, for a second murder. Your dwellings, therefore, will be safe. If such a jury find him sane, he will then be sent to his fearful account, and your dwellings will be safe. If acquitted, he will be remanded to jail, to await a third trial, and your dwellings will be safe. If that jury convict, he will then be executed, and your dwellings will be safe. If they acquit, he will still be detained, to answer a fourth murder, and your dwellings will be safe. Whether the fourth jury acquit or convict, your dwellings will still be safe; for, if they convict, he will then be cut off, and if they acquit, he must, according to the law of the land, be sent to the lunatic asylum, there to be confined for life. You may not slay him then for the public security, because the public security does not demand the sacrifice. No security, for home or hearth, can be obtained by judicial murder. God will abandon him, who, through cowardly fear, becomes such a murderer. *I* also stand for the security of the homes and hearths of my fellow citizens, and have as deep an interest, and as deep a stake as any one of them. There are my home and hearth exposed to every danger that can threaten theirs, but I know that security cannot exist for any, if feeble man undertakes to correct the decrees of Providence.

8. DIFFICULTY OF DETECTING INSANITY.—THE HUMAN MIND
INCAPABLE OF COMPLETE OBLITERATION.

The counsel for the people admit, in the abstract, that insanity excuses crime, but they insist on rules for the regulation of insanity, to which that disease can never conform itself. Dr. Fosgate testified that the prisoner was insane. He was asked by the attorney-general, "what if the law, nevertheless, hold to be criminal that same state of mind which you pronounce insanity?" He answered with high intelligence and great moral firmness, "The law cannot alter the constitution of man as it was given him by his Maker." Insanity, such as the counsel for the people would tolerate, never did and never will exist. They bring its definition from Coke, Blackstone and Hale, and it requires that by reason either of natural infirmity or of disease, the wretched subject shall be unable to count twenty, shall not know his father or mother, and shall have no more reason or thought than a brute beast.

According to the testimony of Dr. Spencer, and the claim of the attorney-general, an individual is not insane if you find any traces or glimmerings of the several faculties of the human mind, or of the more important ones. Dr. Spencer has found in the prisoner memory of his wrongs and sufferings, choice between bread and animal food, hunger to be appeased, thirst to be quenched, love of combat, imperfect knowledge of money, anger and malice. All of Dr. Spencer's questions to the accused show, that in looking for insanity, he demands an entire obliteration of all conception, attention, imagination, association, memory, understanding and reason, and everything else. There never was an idiot so low, never a diseased man so demented.

You might as well expect to find a man born without eyes, ears, nose, mouth, hands and feet, or deprived of them all by disease, and yet surviving, as to find such an idiot, or such a lunatic, as the counsel for the people would hold irresponsible. The reason is, that the human mind is not capable, while life remains, of such complete obliteration. What is the human mind? It is immaterial, spiritual, immortal; an emanation of the divine intelligence, and if the frame in which it dwells had preserved its just and natural proportions, and perfect adaptation, it would be a pure and heavenly existence. But that frame is marred and disordered in its best estate. The spirit has communication with the world without, and acquires imperfect knowledge only through the half-opened gates of the senses. If, from original defects, or from accidental causes, the structure be such as to cramp or restrain the mind, it becomes or appears to be weak, diseased, vicious and wicked. I know one who was born without sight, without hearing, and without speech, retaining the faculties of feeling and smell. That child was, and would have continued to be an idiot, incapable of receiving or communicating thoughts, feelings or affections; but tenderness unexampled, and skill and assiduity unparalleled, have opened avenues to the benighted mind of Laura Bridgman, and developed it into a perfect and complete human spirit, consciously allied to all its kindred, and aspiring to Heaven. Such is the mind of every idiot, and of every lunatic, if you can only open the gates and restore the avenues of the senses; and such is the human soul when deranged and disordered by disease, imprisoned, confounded, benighted. That disease is insanity.

Doth not the idiot eat? Doth not the idiot drink? Doth not the idiot know his father and his mother? He does all this because he is a man. Doth he not smile and weep? and think you he smiles and weeps for nothing? He smiles and weeps because he is moved by human joys and sorrows, and exercises his reason, however imperfectly. Hath not the idiot anger, rage, revenge? Take from him his food, and he will stamp his feet and throw his chains in your face. Think you he doth this for nothing? He does it all because he is a man, and because, however imperfectly, he exercises his reason. The lunatic does all this, and if not quite demented, all things else that man, in the highest pride of intellect, does or can do. He only does them in a different way. You may pass laws for his government. Will he conform? Can he conform? What cares he for your laws? He will not even plead; he cannot plead his disease in excuse. You must interpose the plea for him, and if you allow it, he, when redeemed from his mental bondage,

will plead for you, when he returns to your Judge and his. If you
deny his plea, he goes all the sooner, freed from imperfection, and
with energies restored, into the presence of that Judge. You must
meet him there, and then, no longer bewildered, stricken and dumb,
he will have become as perfect, clear and bright as those who reviled him in his degradation, and triumphed in his ruin.

9. INSANITY DEFINED.

And now what is insanity ? Many learned men have defined it
for us, but I prefer to convey my idea of it in the simplest manner.
Insanity is a disease of the body, and I doubt not, of the brain.
The world is astonished to find it so. They thought for almost six
thousand years, that it was an affection of the mind only. Is it
strange that the discovery should have been made so late ? You
know that it is easier to move a burden upon two smooth rails on
a level surface than over the rugged ground. It has taken almost six
thousand years to learn that. But moralists argue that insanity
shall not be admitted as a physical disease, because it would tend
to exempt the sufferer from responsibility, and because it would expose society to danger. But who shall know, better than the
Almighty, the ways of human safety, and the bonds of human
responsibility ?

And is it strange that the brain should be diseased ? What
organ, member, bone, muscle, sinew, vessel or nerve is not subject
to disease ? What is a physical man, but a frail, perishing body,
that begins to decay as soon as it begins to exist ? What is there
of animal existence here on earth exempt from disease and decay ?
Nothing. The world is full of disease, and that is the great agent
of change, renovation and health.

And what wrong or error can there be in supposing that the
mind may be so affected by disease of the body as to relieve man
from responsibility ? You will answer it would not be safe. But
who has assured you of safety ? Is not the way of life through
dangers lurking on every side, and though you escape ten thousand
perils must you not fall at last ? Human life is not safe, or intended to be safe, against the elements. Neither is it safe, or intended to be safe, against the moral elements of man's nature. It
is not safe against pestilence or against war, against the thunder-
bolt of Heaven, or against the blow of the maniac. But comparative safety can be secured, if you will be wise. You can guard
against war, if you will cultivate peace. You can guard against

the lightning, if you will learn the laws of electricity, and raise the protecting rod. You will be safe against the maniac, if you will watch the cause of madness, and remove them. Yet after all, there will be danger enough from all these causes to remind you that on earth you are not immortal.

Although my definition would not perhaps be strictly accurate, I should pronounce insanity to be a derangement of the mind, character and conduct, resulting from bodily disease. I take this word derangement, because it is one in common every day use. We all understand what is meant when it is said that anything is ranged or arranged. The houses on a street are ranged, if built upon a straight line. The fences on your farms are ranged. A tower, if justly built, is ranged; that is, it is ranged by the plummet. It rises in a perpendicular range from the earth. A file of men marching in a straight line are in range. "Range yourselves, men," though not exactly artistical, is not an uncommon word of command. Now what do we mean when we use the word "*de*ranged"? Manifestly that a thing is not ranged, is not arranged, is out of range. If the houses on the street be built irregularly, they are deranged. If the fences be inclined to the right or left, they are deranged. If there be an unequal pressure on either side, the tower will lean, that is, it will be deranged. If the file of men become irregular, the line is deranged. So if a man be insane. There was a regular line which he was pursuing, not the same line which you or I follow, for all men pursue different lines, and every sane man has his own peculiar path. All these paths are straight, and all are ranged, though all divergent. It is easy enough to discover when the street, the fence, the tower, or the martial procession is deranged; but it is quite another thing to determine when the course of an individual life has become deranged. We deal not then with geometrical or material lines, but with an imaginary line. We have no physical objects for land marks. We trace the line backward by the light of imperfect and satisfactory evidence, which leaves it a matter almost of speculation whether there has been a departure or not. In some cases, indeed, the task is easy. If the fond mother becomes the murderer of her offspring, it is easy to see that she is deranged. If the pious man, whose steps were firm and whose pathway led straight to Heaven, sinks without temptation into criminal debasement, it is easy to see that he is deranged. But in cases where no natural instinct or elevated principle throws its light upon our research, it is often the most difficult and delicate of all human investigations to determine when a person is deranged.

We have two tests. *First*, to compare the individual after the supposed derangement with himself as he was before. *Second*, to compare his course with those ordinary lines of human life which we expect sane persons, of equal intelligence and similarly situated, to pursue.

If derangement, which is insanity, means only what we have assumed, how absurd is it to be looking to detect whether memory, hope, joy, fear, hunger, thirst, reason, understanding, wit, and other faculties remain ! So long as life lasts they never cease to abide with man, whether he pursue his straight and natural way, or the crooked and unnatural course of the lunatic. If he be diseased, his faculties will not cease to act. They will only act differently. It is contended here that the prisoner is not deranged, because he performed his daily task in the State prison, and his occasional labor afterwards; because he grinds his knives, fits his weapons, and handles the file, the ax, and the saw, as he was instructed, and as he was wont to do. Now the lunatic asylum at Utica has not an idle person in it, except the victims of absolute and incurable dementia, the last and worst stages of all insanity. Lunatics are almost the busiest people in the world. They have their prototypes only in children. One lunatic will make a garden, another drive the plow, another gather flowers. One writes poetry, another essays, another orations. In short, lunatics eat, drink, sleep, work, fear, love, hate, laugh, weep, mourn, die. They do all things that sane men do, but do them in some peculiar way. It is said, however, that this prisoner has hatred and anger, that he has remembered his wrongs, and nursed and cherished revenge; wherefore, he cannot be insane. Cowper, a moralist who had tasted the bitter cup of insanity, reasoned otherwise:

> " But violence can never longer sleep
> Than human passions please.   In ev'ry heart
> Are sown the sparks that kindle fiery war;
> Occasion needs but fan them and they blaze,
> The seeds of murder in the breast of man."

Melancholy springs oftenest from recalling and brooding over wrong and suffering.   Melancholy is the first stage of madness, and it is only recently that the less accurate name of monomania has been substituted in the place of melancholy.   Melancholy is the foster-mother of anger and revenge.   Until 1830, our statutory definition of lunatics was in the terms "*disorderly persons, who, if left at large, might endanger the lives of others.*" Our laws now regard them as *merely* disorderly and dangerous, and society acquiesces, unless madness rise so high that the madman slay his imaginary enemy, and then he is pronounced sane.

The prisoner lived with Nathaniel Lynch, at the age of eight or nine, and labored occasionally for him during the last winter. Lynch visited him in the jail, and asked him if he remembered him, and remembered living with him. The prisoner answered yes. Lynch asked the prisoner whether he was whipped while there, and by whom, and why. From his answers it appeared that he had been whipped by his mistress for playing truant, and that he climbed a rough board fence in his night clothes and fled to his mother. Upon this evidence, the learned professor from Geneva College, Dr. Spencer, builds an argument that the prisoner has conception, sensation, memory, imagination, and association, and is most competent for the scaffold. Now here are some verses to which I would invite the doctor's attention:

" Shut up in dreary gloom, like convicts are,
   In company of murderers! Oh, wretched fate!
   If pity e'er extended through the frame,
   Or sympathy's sweet cordial touched the heart,
   Pity the wretched maniac who knows no blame,
   Absorbed in sorrow, where darkness, poverty, and every curse impart."

Here is evidence, not merely of memory and other faculties, but of what we call genius. Yet these verses are a sad effusion of Thomas Lloyd, a man-slaying maniac in Bedlam.

10. WHY THE PRISONER COULD NOT POSSIBLY SIMULATE MADNESS.

The first question of fact here, gentlemen, as in every case where insanity is gravely insisted upon, is this: Is the prisoner feigning or counterfeiting insanity? What kind of a man is he? A youth of twenty-three, without learning, education or experience. Dr. Spencer raises him just above the brute; Dr. Bigelow exalts him no higher; and Dr. Dimon thinks that he has intellectual capacity not exceeding that of a child of ten years, with the knowledge of one of two or three. These are the people's witnesses. All the witnesses concur in these estimates of his mind.

Can you conceive of such a creature comprehending such a plot, and standing up in his cell in the jail, hour after hour, day after day, week after week, and month after month, carrying on such a fraud; and all the while pouring freely into the ears of inquisitors curious, inquisitors friendly, and inquisitors hostile, without discrimination or alarm, or apparent hesitation or suspicion, with "child-like simplicity," as our witnesses 'describe it, and with "entire docility," as it is described by the witnesses for the people, confessions of crime which, if they fail to be received as evidences of insanity, must constitute an insurmountable barrier to his acquittal?

I am ashamed for men who, without evidence of the prisoner's dissimulation, and in opposition to the unanimous testimony of all the witnesses, that he is sincere, still think that this poor fool may deceive them. If he could feign, and were feigning, would he not want some counsel, some friend, if not to advise and assist, at least to inform him of the probable success of the fraud? And yet no one of his counsel or witnesses has ever conversed with him, but in a crowd of adverse witnesses; and for myself, I have not spoken with him in almost two months, and during the same period, have never looked upon him elsewhere than here, in the presence of the Court and the multitude. Would a sane man hold nothing back? admit everything? to everybody? affect no ignorance? no forgetfulness? no bewilderment? no confusion? no excitement? no delirium?

Dr. Ray, in his Treatise on the Medical Jurisprudence of Insanity, p. 333, gives us very different ideas from all this, of those who can feign, and of the manner of counterfeiting: "A person who has not made the insane a subject of study, cannot simulate madness, so as to deceive a physician well acquainted with the disease. Mr. Haslam declares, that 'to sustain the character of a paroxysm of active insanity, would require a continuity of exertion beyond the power of a sane person.' Dr. Conolly affirms, that he can hardly imagine a case which would be proof against an efficient system of observation. The grand fault committed by impostors is that they *overdo* the character they assume. The really mad, except in the acute stage of the disease, are, generally speaking, not readily recognized as such by a stranger, and they retain so much of the rational as to require an effort to detect the impairment of their faculties. Generally speaking, after the acute stage has passed off, a maniac has no difficulty in remembering his friends and acquaintances, the places he has been accustomed to frequent, names, dates, and events, and the occurrences of his life. The

ordinary relations of things are, with some exceptions, as easily and
clearly perceived as ever, and his discrimination of character seems
to be marked by his usual shrewdness.   .   .   .   . A person simulating mania will frequently deny all knowledge of men
and things with whom he has always been familiar."

And now, gentlemen, I will give you a proof of the difference
between this real science and the empiricism upon which the counsel for the people rely in this cause.   Jean Pierre was brought before the Court of Assizes in Paris, in 1824, accused of forgery,
swindling, and incendiarism.   He feigned insanity.   A commission
of eminent physicians examined him, and detected his imposture
by his pretended forgetfulness, and confusion in answering interrogatories concerning his life and history.   The most prominent of
these questions are set down in the books.   (Ray, p. 338.)   I submitted these questions and answers, with a statement of Jean
Pierre's case, to Dr. Spencer, and he, governed by the rules which
have controlled him in the present cause, pronounced the impostor's
answers to be evidence of insanity, because they showed a decay
of memory.

Again, gentlemen, look at the various catechisms in which this
prisoner has been exercised for two months, as a test of his sanity.
Would any sane man have propounded a solitary one of all those
questions to any person whom he believed to be of sound mind?
Take an instance.   On one occasion, Dr. Willard, a witness for the
people, having exhausted the idiot's store of knowledge and emotion,
expressed a wish to discover whether the passion of fear had burned
out, and employing Mr. Morgan's voice addressed the prisoner
thus: "Bill, they're going to take you out to kill you.   They're going to take you out to kill you, Bill."   The poor creature answered
nothing.   "What do you think of it, Bill?"   Answer: "I don't
think about it—I don't believe it."   "Bill," continues the inquisitor with louder and more terrific vociferation, "they're going to
kill you, and the doctors want your bones; what do you think of it,
Bill?"   The prisoner answers: "I don't think about it—I don't
believe it."   The doctor's case was almost complete, but he thought
that perhaps the prisoner's stupidity might arise from inability to
understand the question.   Therefore, lifting his voice still higher,
he continues: "Did you ever see the doctors have any bones?
Did you ever see the doctors have any bones, Bill?"   The fool answers, "I have."   "Then, where did you see them, Bill?"   "In
Dr. Pitney's office."   And thus, by this dialogue, the sanity of the

accused is, in the judgment of Dr. Willard, completely established. It is no matter that if the prisoner had believed the threat, his *belief* would have proved him sane; if he had been terrified, his *fears* would have sent him to the gallows; if he had forgotten the fleshless skeleton he had seen, he would have been convicted of *falsehood*, and of course have been sane.   Of such staple as this are all the questions which have been put to the prisoner by all the witnesses.   There is not an interrogatory which any one of you would have put to a child twelve years old.

Does the prisoner feign insanity?   One hundred and eight witnesses have been examined, of whom seventy-two appeared on behalf of the people.   No one of them has expressed a belief that he was simulating.   On the contrary, every witness to whom the inquiry has been addressed, answers that the sincerity of the prisoner is beyond question.

Mr. Seward here reviewed the testimony of the witnesses to establish the proposition that the prisoner could not feign, and never attempted to simulate insanity.   He then continued :

I submit to you, gentlemen of the jury, that by comparing the prisoner with himself, as he was in his earlier, and as he is in his later history, I have proved to you conclusively that he is visibly changed and altered in mind, manner, conversation and action, and that all his faculties have become disturbed, impaired, degraded and debased.   I submit, also, that it is proved: *First*, that this change occurred between the sixteenth and the eighteenth years of his life, in the State prison, and that, therefore, the change thus palpable was not, as the attorney-general contends, effected by mere lapse of time and increase of years, nor by the natural development of latent dispositions; *Secondly*, that inasmuch as the convicts in the State prison are absolutely abstemious from intoxicating drinks, the change was not, as the attorney-general supposes, produced by intemperance.

11. INSANITY OF THE PRISONER DEMONSTRATED.—THE VARIOUS
CAUSES OF INSANITY DISCUSSED.

I have thus arrived at the *third* proposition in this case, which is, that the prisoner at the bar is insane.   This I shall demonstrate: *First*, by the fact already so fully established, that the prisoner is changed; *Secondly*, by referring to the predisposing causes which might be expected to produce insanity; *Thirdly*, by the incoherence and extravagance of the prisoner's conduct and conversation, and the delusions under which he has labored.

And now as to the predisposing causes.   The prisoner was born in this village, twenty-three years ago, of parents recently emerged from slavery.   His mother was a women of violent passions, severe discipline, and addicted to intemperance.   His father died of *delirium tremens*, leaving his children to the neglect of the world, from which he had learned nothing but its vices.   *Hereditary insanity* was added to the prisoner's misfortunes, already sufficiently complicated.   His aunt, Jane Brown, died a lunatic.   His uncle, Sidney Freeman, is an acknowledged lunatic.

All writers agree, what it needs not writers to teach, that *neglect of education* is a fruitful cause of crime.   If neglect of education produces crime, it equally produces insanity.   Here was a bright, cheerful, happy child, destined to become a member of the social state, entitled by the principles of our government to equal advantages for perfecting himself in intelligence, and even in political rights, with each of the three millions of our citizens, and blessed by our religion with equal hopes.   Without his being taught to read, his mother, who lives by menial service, sends him forth at the age of eight or nine years to like employment.   Reproaches are cast on his mother, on Mr. Warden, and on Mr. Lynch, for not sending him to school, but these reproaches are all unjust.   How could she, poor degraded negress and Indian as she was, send her child to school?   And where was the school to which Warden and Lynch should have sent him ?   There was no school for him.   His few and wretched years date back to the beginning of my acquaintance here, and during all that time, with unimportant exceptions, there has been no school here for children of his caste.   A school for colored children was never established here, and all the common schools were closed against them.   Money would always procure instruction for my children, and relieve me from the responsibility.   But the colored children, who have from time to time been confided to my charge, have been cast upon my own care for education.   When I sent them to school with my own children, they were sent back to me with a message that they must be withdrawn, because they were black, or the school would cease.   Here are the fruits of this unmanly and criminal prejudice.   A whole family is cut off in the midst of usefulness and honors by the hand of an assassin.   You may avenge the crime, but whether the prisoner be insane or criminal, there is a tribunal where this neglect will plead powerfully in his excuse, and trumpet-tongued against the " deep damnation " of his " taking off."

Again. The prisoner was subjected, in tender years, to severe and undeserved *oppression*. Whipped at Lynch's; severely and unlawfully beaten by Wellington, for the venial offense of forgetting to return a borrowed umbrella; hunted by the police on charges of petty offenses, of which he was proved innocent; finally convicted, upon constructive and probably perjured evidence, of a crime of which it is now universally admitted he was guiltless, he was plunged into the State prison at the age of sixteen, instead of being committed to a House of Refuge.

Mere *imprisonment* is often a cause of insanity. Four insane persons have, on this trial, been mentioned as residing among us, all of whom became insane in the State prison. Authentic statistics show that there are never less than thirty insane persons in each of our two great penitentiaries. In the State prison the prisoner was subjected to severe corporeal punishment, by keepers who mistook a decay of mind and morbid melancholy for idleness, obstinacy and malice. Beaten, as he was, until the organs of his hearing ceased to perform their functions, who shall say that other and more important organs connected with the action of his mind, did not become diseased through sympathy? Such a life, so filled with neglect, injustice and severity, with anxiety, pain, disappointment, solicitude and grief, would have its fitting conclusion in a mad-house. If it be true, as the wisest of inspired writers hath said, " Verily oppression maketh a wise man mad," what may we not expect it to do with a foolish, ignorant, illiterate man ! Thus it is explained why, when he came out of prison, he was so dull, stupid, morose; excited to anger by petty troubles, small in our view, but mountains in his way; filled in his waking hours with moody recollections, and rising at midnight to sing incoherent songs, dance without music, read unintelligible jargon, and combat with imaginary enemies.

How otherwise than on the score of madness can you explain the stupidity which caused him to be taken for a fool at Applegate's, on his way from the prison to his home? How else, the ignorance which made him incapable of distinguishing the coin which he offered at the hatter's shop? How else, his ludicrous apprehensions of being re-committed to the State prison for five years, for the offense of breaking his dinner knife? How else, his odd and strange manner of accounting for his deafness, by expressions, all absurd and senseless, and varying with each interrogator: as to John De Puy, " that Tyler struck him across the ears with a plank, and knocked his hearing off, and that it never came back; that they put salt in his ear, but it didn't do any good, for his hearing was gone—all knocked off"; to the Rev. John M. Austin, "the stones dropped down my ears, or the stones of my ears dropped down"; to Ethan A. Warden, "got stone in my ear; got it out; thought I heard better when I got it out"; to Dr. Hermance, "that his ears dropped"; and to the same witness on another occasion, "that the hearing of his ears fell down"; to his mother, "that his ear had fell down"; to Deborah De Puy, "that Tyler struck him on the head with a board, and it seemed as if the sound went down his throat"; to Dr. Brigham, "that he was hurt when young, it made him deaf in the right ear"; also, "that in the prison he was struck with a board by a man, which made him deaf"; and also, "that a stone was knocked into, or out of his ear"?

It is now perfectly certain, from the testimony of Mr. Van Arsdale and Helen Holmes, that the prisoner first stabbed Mrs. Van Nest, in the back yard, and then entered the house and stabbed Mr. Van Nest, who fell lifeless at the instant of the blow. And yet, sincerely trying to give an account of the dreadful scenes, exactly as they passed, the prisoner has invariably stated, in his answers to every witness, that he entered the house, stabbed Van Nest, went into the yard, and then, and not before, killed Mrs. Van Nest. It was in this order that he related the transaction to Warren T. Worden, to John M. Austin, to Ira Curtis, to Ethan A. Warden, to William P. Smith, to Dr. Van Epps, to James H. Bostwick, to Dr. Brigham, to Nathaniel Lynch, to Dr. Willard, to Dr. Bigelow, and to Dr. Spencer. How else than on the score of madness can you explain this confusion of memory? and if the prisoner was sane, and telling a falsehood, what was the motive?

How else than on the score of a demented mind will you explain the fact, that he is without human curiosity; that he has never, since he came out of prison, learned a fact, or asked a question? He has been visited by hundreds in his cell, by faces become familiar, and by strangers, by fellow prisoners, by jailers, by sheriff, by counsel, by physician, by friends, by enemies, and by relations, and they unanimously bear witness that he has never asked a question. The oyster, shut up within its limestone walls, is as inquisitive as he.

How else will you explain the mystery that he, who seven years ago had the capacity to relate connectively any narrative, however extended, and however complex in its details, is now unable to continue any relations of the most recent events, without the prompting of perpetual interrogatories, always leading him by known land-marks; and that when under such discipline he answers—he employs generally the easiest forms—"Yes," "No," "Don't know"?

Then mark the confusion of his memory, manifested by contra-dictory replies to the same question. Warren T. Worden asked him: "Did you go in at the front door? Yes. Did you go in at the back door? Yes. Were you in the hall when your hand was cut? Yes. Was your hand cut at the gate? Yes. Did you stab Mrs. Wyckoff in the hall? Yes. Did you stab Mrs. Wyckoff at the gate? Yes. Did you go out at the back door? Yes. Did you go out at the front door? Yes."

Ethan A. Warden asked him: "What made you kill the child?" "Don't know any thing about that." At another time he answered: "I don't think about it; I didn't know it was a child." And again, on another occasion: "Thought—feel it more;" and to Dr. Bigelow, and other witnesses, who put the question, whether he was not sorry he killed the child, he replied: "It did look *hard*—I rather it was bigger." When the ignorance, simplicity and sincerity of the pris-oner are admitted, how otherwise than on the ground of insanity can you explain such inconsistencies as these?

The testimony of Van Arsdale and Helen Holmes, proves that no words could have passed between the prisoner and Van Nest, except these: "What do you want here in the house?" spoken by Van Nest before the fatal blow was struck. Yet, when inquired of by Warren T. Worden what Van Nest said to him when he entered the house, the prisoner said, after being pressed for an answer, that Van Nest said to him: "If you eat my liver, I'll eat yours;" and he at various times repeated to the witness the same absurd ex-pression. To the Rev. John M. Austin he made the same state-ment, that Van Nest said: "If you eat my liver, I'll eat your liver;" to Ira Curtis the same; to Ethan A. Warden the same; to Lans-ingh Briggs the same; and the same to almost every other witness. An expression so absurd under the circumstances, could never have been made by the victim. How otherwise can it be explained than as the vagary of a mind shattered and crazed?

The prosecution, confounded with such evidence, appealed to Dr. Spencer for relief. He, in the plentitude of his learning, says, that he had read of an ancient and barbarous people, who used to feast upon the livers of their enemies; that the prisoner has not imagination enough to have invented such an idea, and that he

must somewhere have heard the tradition. But when did this demented wretch, who reads " woman " for " admirable," and " cook "
for " Thompson," read Livy or Tytler, and in what classical circle
has he learned the customs of the ancients? Or, what perhaps is
more pertinent, who were that ancient and barbarous people, and
who was their historian?

Consider now the prisoner's earnest and well-attested sincerity
in believing that he could read, when either he never had acquired,
or else had lost, the power of reading. The Rev. Mr. Austin visited him in jail, at an early day, asked him whether he could read,
and being answered that he could, gave him a testament. In frequent visits afterwards, when the prisoner was asked whether he
had read his testament, he answered, " Yes," and it was not until
after the lapse of two months that it was discovered that he was
unable to spell a monosyllable.

Mr. Seward here reviewed the testimony to show that the prisoner could not
read, though he pretended to be able to do so, and claimed, that from various
other circumstances respecting his conduct, it had been clearly established that
the prisoner was hopelessly demented. He showed also that he was insensible
to corporal pain or suffering. He then referred with regret to the fact that his
offer to allow the jury, personally, to examine the prisoner had been rejected.
He continued :

I have thus shown you, gentlemen, the difficulties which attended you in this investigation, the law concerning insanity, the nature
and characteristics of that disease, the great change which the prisoner has undergone, and some of those marked extravagances
which denote lunacy. More conclusive evidence yet remains; and
first, the delusion by which the prisoner was overpowered, and
under whose fearful spell his crimes were committed.

12. DELUSION, WHEN SHOWN, INCONTESTABLE PROOF OF INSAN-
ITY.—ILLUSTRATIONS OF THE SUBJECT.

Delusion does not always attend insanity, but when found it is
the most unequivocal of all proofs. I have already observed, that
melancholy is the first stage of madness, and long furnished the
name for insanity. In the case of Hatfield, who fired at the king
in Drury-Lane Theatre, Lord Erskine, his counsel, demonstrated
that insanity did not consist in the absence of any of the intellectual
faculties, but in delusion; and that an offender was irresponsible, if
his criminal acts were the immediate, unqualified offspring of such
delusion. Erskine there defined a *delusion* to consist in deductions
from the *immovable* assumption of the matters *as realities*, either

12

without any foundation whatever, or so distorted and disfigured by fancy as to be nearly the same thing as their creation.

The learned men here have given us many illustrations of such delusions; as that of the man who believes that his legs are of glass, and therefore refuses to move, for fear they will break; of the man who fancies himself the king of the French; or of him who confides to you the precious secret that he is emperor of the world. These are palpable delusions, but there are others equally, or even more fatal in their effects, which have their foundation in some original fact, and are thus described by Dr. Ray, at page 210 of his work: "In another class of cases, the exciting cause of homicidal insanity is of a moral nature, operating upon some peculiar physical predisposition, and sometimes followed by more or less physical disturbance. Instead of being urged by a sudden imperious impulse to kill, the subjects of this form of the affection, after suffering for a certain period much gloom of mind and depression of spirits, feel as if bound by a sense of necessity to destroy life, and proceed to the fulfillment of their destiny with the utmost calmness and deliberation. So reluctant have courts and juries usually been to receive the plea of insanity in defense of crime, deliberately planned and executed by a mind in which no derangement of intellect has ever been perceived, that it is of the greatest importance that the nature of these cases should not be misunderstood."

Our learned witnesses have given us various definitions of a delusion. Dr. Hun's is perhaps as clear and accurate as any: "It is a cherished opinion opposed by the sense and judgment of all mankind." In simple speech, it is what is called the predominance of one idea, by which reason is subverted. I shall now show you such a predominance of one idea, as will elucidate the progress of this maniac from the first disturbance of his mind, to the dreadful catastrophe on the shores of the Owasco Lake. That delusion is a star to guide your judgment to an infallible conclusion, that the prisoner is insane. If you mistake its course and consign him to a scaffold, it will rest over his grave, indicating him as a martyr, and you as erring or unjust judges.

In April, 1840, Mrs. Godfrey, who resides in the town of Sennett, on the middle road, four miles northeast of Auburn, lost a horse. One Jack Furman, a hardened offender, stole the horse. For some purpose not now known, he put him in the care of the prisoner, who was seen with him. Both Furman and Freeman were arrested. The former was the real thief and Freeman constructively guilty. Freeman was arrested by Vanderheyden, taken into an upper chamber, and *there declared his innocence of the crime.* He was nevertheless committed to jail. *All* the police, and the most prejudiced of the witnesses for the people, have testified their entire conviction that the prisoner was innocent. Furman was selected by favor as a witness for the people. Freeman, while in jail, comprehending his danger, and conscious of his innocence, dwelt upon the injustice, until, having no other hope, he broke prison and escaped. Being retaken, he assigned as the reason for his flight, that Jack Furman stole the horse, and was going to swear him into the State prison. The result was as he apprehended. He was convicted by the perjury of Furman, and sentenced to the State prison for five years. This was the *first* act in the awful tragedy of which he is the hero. Let judges and jurors take warning from its fatal consequences. How deeply this injustice sank into his mind, may be seen from the testimony of Aretas A. Sabin, the keeper, who said to him on the day he entered the prison, " I am sorry to see you come here so young." The prisoner wept. Well would it have been if this, the last occasion on which the prisoner yielded to that infirmity, had, ominous as it was of such fatal mischief, been understood and heeded. A year passed away, and he is found in the prison, neglecting his allotted labor, sullen and morose.

Mr. Seward next traced the progress of the mental derangement of the accused while he was in prison. He then reviewed, in elaborate detail, his conduct and actions from the time he left prison down to the night of the murder, and claimed that it had been shown that a sense of his wrongs had taken complete possession of him, and whatever of mind, conscience or reason remained, had been finally overthrown. His conduct after the murder was next taken up, for the purpose of showing that his past misfortunes were the burden of his life, it having appeared that he always confessed the deed, and in answer to questions put to him to ascertain his motive, the answers were broken and incoherent, but invariably referred to his being in prison innocently, and could get no pay for it.

It would be tedious to gather all the evidence of similar import. Let it suffice, that the witnesses who have conversed with the prisoner, as well those for the people as those for him, concur fully in the same statement of facts, as to his reasons and motives for the murders. We have thus not merely established the existence of an insane delusion, but have traced directly to that overpowering delusion, the crimes which the prisoner has committed.

How powerful that delusion must have been, may be inferred from the fact that the prisoner, when disabled, desisted from his work and made his retreat to his friends in Oswego county, not to escape from punishment for the murders, but, as he told Mr. E. A. Warden, to wait till his wounded hand should be restored, that he might resume his dreadful butchery; and, as he told Dr. Bigelow, because he couldn't "handle his hand." The intenseness of this delusion exceeds that under which Hatfield assailed the king; that which compelled Henriette Cornier to dissever the head of the child entrusted to her care; and that of Rabello, the Portuguese, who cut to pieces with his axe, the child who trod upon his feet.

13. THE CIRCUMSTANCES OF THE MURDER TESTED BY SCIENTIFIC RULES.

The next feature in the cause which will claim your attention, gentlemen of the jury, is the MANNER AND CIRCUMSTANCES OF THE ACT ITSELF.

In Ray's Medical Jurisprudence, at page 224, are given several tests by which to distinguish between the homicidal maniac and the murderer. We shall best consider the present case by comparing it with those tests:

I. "There is the *irresistible*, *motiveless* impulse to destroy life." Never was homicide more *motiveless*, or the impulse more completely irresistible, than in the present case, as we have learned from the testimony already cited.

II. "In nearly all cases the criminal act has been preceded, either by some well marked disturbance of the health, or by an irritable, gloomy, dejected, or melancholy state; in short, by many of the symptoms of the incubation of mania." How truly does this language describe the condition of the prisoner during the brief period of his enlargement!

III. "The impulse to destroy is powerfully excited by the sight of murderous weapons—by favorable opportunities of accomplishing the act—by contradiction, disgust, or some other equally trivial and even imaginary circumstance."

While we learn from Hersey's testimony, that the prisoner kept a store of knives fit for such a deed, we find in the denial of his demands for settlement, for pay, and for process, by Mrs. Godfrey and the magistrates, the contradiction and causes of disgust here described.

IV. "The victims of the homicidal monomaniac are either entirely unknown or indifferent to him, or they are amongst his most loved and cherished objects."

Freeman passed by his supposed oppressors and persecutors, and fell upon a family absolutely indifferent, and almost unknown to him, while he reserved the final stroke for his nearest and best friend, and brother-in-law.

V. " The monomaniac sometimes diligently conceals and sometimes avows his purpose, and forms schemes for putting it into execution, testifying no sentiment of grief."

The prisoner concealed his purpose from all but Hersey. He purchased the knife which he used, in open day, at a blacksmith's shop, in the presence of persons to whom he was well known, and ground it to its double edge before unsuspecting witnesses, as coolly and deliberately as if it were to be employed in the shambles. He applied at another blacksmith's shop, where he was equally well known, to have another instrument made. He shaped the pattern in a carpenter's shop, carried it to the smith, disagreed about the price, and left the pattern upon the forge in open sight, never thinking to reclaim it, and it lay there until it was taken by the smith before the coroner's inquest, as an evidence of his design. So strange was his conduct, and so mysterious the form of the knife which he required, that Morris, the smith, suspected him, and told him that he was going to *kill somebody;* to which he answered with the nonchalance of the butcher: "*that's nothing to you if you get your pay for the knife."* On the two days immediately preceding the murder, he is found sharpening and adjusting his knives at a turner's shop, next door to his own dwelling, in the presence of persons to whom he is well known, manifesting no apprehension, and affecting no concealment.

The trivial concerns of his finance and occupation are as carefully attended to, as if the murder he was contemplating had been an ordinary and lawful transaction. Hyatt demands three shillings for the knife. The prisoner cheapens until the price is reduced to eighteen pence, with the further advantage that it should be sharpened and fitted to a handle. Hyatt demands sixpence for putting a rivet into his knife. He compromises, and agrees to divide the labor and pay half the price. He deliberately takes out his wallet and lays down three cents for Simpson, the turner, for the use of the grindstone. On the very day of the murder, he begs some grease at the soap factory to soften his shoes, and tells Aaron Demun that he is going into the country to live in peace. At four o'clock in the afternoon he buys soap at the merchant's for Mary Ann Newark, the poor woman at whose house he lived. He then goes cautiously to his room, takes the knives from the place of their concealment under his bed, throws them out of the window, to avoid exposure to her observation, and when the night has come, and the bells are ringing for church, and all is ready, he stops to ask the woman whether there is any *chore* to be done. She tells him, none, but to fill the tub with snow. He does it as carefully as if there were no commotion in his mind, and then sallies forth, takes up his instruments, and proceeds on his errand of death. He reconnoiters the house on the north of Van Nest's, Van Nest's house, and Brooks' house on the south, and finally decides upon the middle one as the place of assault. It does not affect his purpose that he meets Mr. Cox and Mr. Patten, under a broad, bright moonlight. He waits his opportunity, until Williamson the visitor has departed, and Van Arsdale the laboring man has retired to rest. With an energy and boldness that no sane man with such a purpose could possess, he mortally stabs four persons, and dangerously wounds a fifth, in the incredibly short space of five minutes. Disabled, and therefore desisting from further destruction, he enters the stable, takes the first horse he finds, mounts him without a saddle, and guiding him by a halter, dashes towards the town. He overtakes and passes Williamson the visitor, within the distance of three-fourths of a mile from the house which he had left in supposed security. Pressing on, the jaded beast, worn out with age, stumbles and brings him to the ground. He plunges his knife into the breast of the horse, abandons him, scours forward through the town, across the bridge and on the middle road to Burrington's; there seizes another horse, mounts him, and urges forward until he arrives among his relations, the De Puys, at Schroeppel, thirty miles distant. They, suspecting him to have stolen the horse, refuse to entertain him. He proceeds to the adjoining village, rests from his flight, offers the horse for sale, and when his title to the horse is questioned announces his true name and residence, and refers to the De Puys, who had just cast him off, for proof of his good character and conduct. When arrested and charged with the murder he denies the act.

VI. Now the sixth test given by Dr. Ray is, that "while most maniacs having gratified their propensity to kill, voluntarily confess the act and quietly give themselves up to the proper authorities, a very few only, and those to an intelligent observer show the strongest indications of insanity, fly and persist in denying the act."

VII. " Murder is never criminally committed without some *motive* adequate to the purpose in the mind that is actuated by it,

while the insane man commits the crime without any motive whatever, strictly deserving the name."

VIII. "The *criminal* never sheds more blood than is necessary
for the attainment for his object. The *monomaniac* often sacrifices
all within his reach, to the cravings of his murderous propensity."

IX. "The *criminal* either denies or confesses his guilt; if the
latter, he sues for mercy, or glories in his crimes. On the contrary,
the *maniac*, after gratifying his bloody desires, testifies neither remorse, repentance, nor satisfaction."

X. "The *criminal* has accomplices; the maniac has none."

XI. "The murderer never conceives a design to murder without projecting a plan for concealing his victim, effecting his escape,
and baffling pursuit. The maniac prepares the means of committing the crime, with calmness and deliberation, but never dreams
of the necessity of concealing it when done, or of escape, until his
victim lies at his feet."

Dr. Bigelow and others state, that the prisoner told them, as obviously was the case, that he sought no plunder; that he thought
not of escape or flight, until his *things* were broken, and his hand
was cut, so that he could not continue his WORK. He seized the
nearest and the most worthless horse in the stable, leaving two fleet
animals in their stalls. He thought only of taking Burrington's
horse when the first failed; all he cared for was to get out of the
county, there to rest until his hand was cured, so that he could
come back and do more *work*. He rested from flight within thirty
miles from the seat of his crimes, and, in selling his horse, was depriving himself of the only means of making his escape successful.
When the person of Van Nest was examined, his watch, pocket-
book, money and trinkets were found all undisturbed. Not an
article in the house had been removed; and when the prisoner was
searched upon his arrest, there was found in his pockets nothing
but one copper coin, the hundredth part of a dollar. Without further detail, the parallel between the prisoner and the tests of madness established by medical jurisprudence, is complete.

It remains, gentlemen, to conclude the demonstration of the
prisoner's insanity, by referring to the testimony of the witnesses
who have given their opinion on that question.

Mr. Seward then reviewed the testimony. He claimed, upon this point, that
the evidence of the State was feeble and unsatisfactory, while that adduced by
the defense was conclusive and overwhelming, and established beyond all doubt
the fact that the prisoner was insane. In discussing the statements of Dr. Spen-

cer, the principal expert for the State, he proceeded to demolish the theories advanced by that scientific gentleman after the following fashion :

He heralds himself as accustomed to teach, and informs us that he has visited the principal hospitals for the insane in London, Paris, and other European capitals. How unfortunate it was, that on his cross-examination, he could not give the name or location of any asylum in either of those cities! Even the names and locations of the " Charenton " and " Bicetre " had escaped his memory. But it is no matter. The doctor overwhelms us with learning, universal and incomprehensible. Here is his map [1] of the mental faculties, in which twenty-eight separate powers of mind are described in odd and even numbers.

The arrows show the course of ideas through the mind. They begin with the motives in the region of the highest odd numbers in the southwest corner of the mind, marked A, and go perpendicularly northward, through Thirst and Hunger to Sensation marked B; then turn to the right, and go eastward, through Conception, to Attention, marked C, and then descend southward, through Perception, Memory, Understanding, Comparison, Combination, Reason, Invention and Judgment; wheel to the left under the Will, marked D, and pass through Conscience, and then to V, the unascertained center of Sensation, Volition, and Will. This is the natural turnpike road for the ideas when we are awake and sane. But here is an open shunpike, X, Y, Z, on which Ideas, when we are asleep or insane, start off and pass by Conscience, and so avoid paying toll to that inflexible gatekeeper. Now all this is very well, but I call on the doctor to show how the fugitive Idea reached the Will at D, after going to the end of the shunpike. It appeared there was no other way but to dart back again, over the shunpike, or else go cringing, at last, through the iron gate of Conscience. Then there was another difficulty. The doctor forgot the most important point on his own map, and could not tell, from memory, where he had *located " the unascertained center."*

The doctor pronounces the prisoner sane because he has the chief intellectual faculties, Sensation, Conception, Attention, Imagination, and Association. Now here is a delicate piece of wooden cutlery, fabricated by an inmate of the lunatic asylum at Utica, who was acquitted of murder on the ground of insanity. He who fabricated it evinced in the manufacture, Conception, Perception,

[1] For the Map, see Appendix, p. 717.

Memory, Comparison, Attention, Adaptation, Co-ordination, Kindness, Gratitude, Mechanical Skill, Invention, and Pride. It is well for him that Dr. Spencer did not testify on his trial.

Mr. Seward then referred to the overwhelming preponderance of medical and other testimony for the prisoner, which he proceeded to analyze with great ability, and concluded by directing attention to the personal conduct and demeanor of the accused, which he claimed was the strongest proof of his insanity. This may, perhaps, be considered the most touching and powerful part of his address:

14. THE PERSONAL APPEARANCE AND DEMEANOR OF THE PRISONER THE STRONGEST PROOF OF HIS INSANITY.

There is proof, gentlemen, stronger than all this. It is silent, yet speaking. It is that *idiotic smile* which plays continually on the face of the maniac. It took its seat there while he was in the State prison. In his solitary cell, under the pressure of his severe tasks and trials in the workshop, and during the solemnities of public worship in the chapel, it appealed, although in vain, to his taskmasters and his teachers. It is a smile, never rising into laughter—without motive or cause—the smile of vacuity. His mother saw it when he came out of prison, and it broke her heart. John De Puy saw it and knew his brother was demented. Deborah De Puy observed it and knew him for a fool. David Winner read in it the ruin of his friend Sally's son. It has never forsaken him in his later trials. He laughed in the face of Parker, while on confession at Baldwinsville. He laughed involuntarily in the faces of Warden and Curtis, and Worden and Austin, and Bigelow and Smith, and Brigham and Spencer. He laughs perpetually here. Even when Van Arsdale showed the scarred traces of the assassin's knife, and when Helen Holmes related the dreadful story of the murder of her patrons and friends, he laughed. He laughs while I am pleading his griefs. He laughs when the attorney-general's bolts would seem to rive his heart. He will laugh when you declare him guilty. When the judge shall proceed to the last fatal ceremony, and demand what he has to say why the sentence of the law should not be pronounced upon him, although there should not be an unmoistened eye in this vast assembly, and the stern voice addressing him should tremble with emotion, he will even then look up in the face of the Court and laugh, from the irresistible emotions of a shattered mind, delighted and lost in the confused memory of absurd and ridiculous associations. Follow him to the scaffold. The executioner cannot disturb the calmness of the idiot.

He will laugh in the agony of death. Do you not know the significance of this strange and unnatural risibility? It is a proof that
God does not forsake even the poor wretch whom we pity or despise. There are, in every human memory, a well of joys and a
fountain of sorrows. Disease opens wide the one, and seals up the
other forever.

You have been told, gentlemen, that this smile is hereditary
and accustomed. Do you think that ever an ancestor or parent of
the prisoner, or even the poor idiot himself, was in such straits as
these? How then can you think that this smile was ever before
recognized by these willing witnesses? That chaotic smile is the
external derangement which signifies that the strings of the harp are
disordered and broken, the superficial mark which God has set
upon the tabernacle, to signify that its immortal tenant is disturbed
by a divine and mysterious commandment. If you cannot see it,
take heed that the obstruction of your vision be not produced by
the mote in your own eye, which you are commanded to remove
before you consider the beam in your brother's eye. If you are
bent on rejecting the testimony of those who know, by experience
and by science, the deep afflictions of the prisoner, beware how you
misinterpret the handwriting of the Almighty.

I have waited until now, gentlemen, to notice some of the animadversions of the counsel for the people. They say that drunkenness will explain the conduct of the prisoner. It is true that John
De Puy discovered that those who retailed poisonous liquors were
furnishing the prisoner with this, the worst of food for his madness.
But the most laborious investigation has resulted in showing, by the
testimony of Adam Gray, that he once saw the prisoner intoxicated,
and that he, with some other persons, drank spirits in not immoderate quantity on the day when Van Nest was slain. There is no
other evidence that the prisoner was ever intoxicated. John De
Puy and Adam Gray testify, that, except that one time, he was
always sober. David Winner proves he was sober all the time the
witness lived at Willard's; and Mary Ann Newark says he was entirely sober when he sallied forth on his fatal enterprise. The only
value of the fact of his drunkenness, if it existed, would be to account for his disturbed nights at De Puy's, at Gray's and at Willard's. It is clearly proved that his mind was not beclouded, nor
his frame excited, by any such cause on any of those occasions;
and Doctor Brigham truly tells you, that while the maniac goes
quietly to his bed, and is driven from it by the dreams of a dis-

turbed imagination, the drunkard completes his revels and his orgies before he sinks to rest, and then lies stupid and besotted until nature restores his wasted energies with return of day.

He then spoke of the assaults which had been made upon the credibility of several of the witnesses for the defense, and the attempts to discredit them on acconut of their social position and low standard of intelligence, and continued as follows :

The testimony of Sally Freeman, the mother of the prisoner, is questioned. She utters the voice of NATURE. She is the guardian whom God assigned to study, to watch, to learn, to know what the prisoner was, and is, and to cherish the memory of it forever. She could not forget it if she would. There is not a blemish on the person of any one of us, born with us or coming from disease or accident, nor have we committed a right or wrong action, that has not been treasured up in the memory of a mother. Juror ! roll up the sleeve from your manly arm, and you will find a scar there of which you know nothing. Your mother will give you the detail of every day's progress of the preventive disease. Sally Freeman has the mingled blood of the African and Indian races. She is, nevertheless, a woman and a mother, and nature bears witness in every climate and every country, to the singleness and uniformity of those characters. I have known and proved them in the hovel of the slave, and in the wigwam of the Chippewa. But Sally Freeman has been intemperate. The white man enslaved her ancestors of the one race, exiled and destroyed those of the other, and debased them all by corrupting their natural and healthful appetites. She comes honestly by her only vice. Yet when she comes here to testify for a life that is dearer to her than her own, to say she knows her own son, the white man says she is a drunkard ! May Heaven forgive the white man for adding this last, this cruel injury to the wrongs of such a mother ! Fortunately, gentlemen, her character and conduct are before you. No woman has ever appeared with more decency, modesty and propriety than she has exhibited here. No witness has dared to say or think that Sally Freeman is not a woman of truth. Dr. Clary, a witness for the prosecution, who knows her well, says, that with all her infirmities of temper and of habit, Sally "was always a truthful woman." The Roman Cornelia could not have claimed more. Let then the stricken mother testify for her own son.

> " I ask not, I care not—if guilt's in that heart,
>   I know that I love thee, whatever thou art."

The learned gentlemen who conduct this prosecution have attempted to show that the prisoner attended the trial of Henry Wyatt, whom I defended against an indictment for murder, in this Court, in February last ; that he listened to me on that occasion, in regard to the impunity of crime, and that he went out a ripe and complete scholar. So far as these reflections affect me alone, they are unworthy of an answer. I pleaded for Wyatt then, as it was my right and my duty to do. Let the counsel for the people prove the words I spoke, before they charge me with Freeman's crimes. I am not unwilling those words should be recalled. I am not unwilling that any words I ever spoke in any responsible relation should be remembered. Since they will not recall those words, I will do so for them. They were words like those I speak now, demanding cautious and impartial justice; words appealing to the reason, to the consciences, to the humanity of my fellow men; words calculated to make mankind know and love each other better, and adopt the benign principles of Christianity, instead of the long-cherished maxims of retaliation and revenge. The creed of Mahomet was promulgated at a time when paper was of inestimable value, and the Koran teaches that every scrap of paper which the believer has saved during his life, will gather itself under his feet, to protect them from the burning iron which he must pass over while entering into Paradise. Regardless as I have been of the unkind construction of my words and actions by my cotemporaries, I can say in all humility of spirit, that they are freely left to the ultimate, impartial consideration of mankind. But, gentlemen, how gross is the credulity implied by this charge ! This stupid idiot, who cannot take into his ears—deaf as death—the words which I am speaking to you, though I stand within three feet of him, and who even now is exchanging smiles with his and my accusers, regardless of the deep anxiety depicted in your countenances, was standing at yonder post, sixty feet distant from me, when he was here, if he was here at all, on the trial of Henry Wyatt. The voice of the district attorney reverberates through this dome, while mine is lost almost within the circle of the bar. It does not appear that it was not that voice that beguiled the maniac, instead of mine; and certain it is, that since the prisoner does not comprehend the object of his attendance here now, he could not have understood anything·that occurred on the trial of Wyatt.

Gentlemen, my responsibilities in this cause are discharged. In the earnestness and seriousness with which I have pleaded, you will find the reason for the firmness with which I have resisted the popular passions around me. I am, in some degree, responsible, like every other citizen, for the conduct of the community in which I live. They may not inflict on a maniac the punishment of a male-factor, without involving me in the blame, if I do not remonstrate. I cannot afford to be in error abroad, and in future times. If I were capable of a sentiment so cruel and so base, I ought to hope for the conviction of the accused; for then the vindictive passions, now so highly excited would subside, the consciences of the wise and the humane would be awakened, and in a few months the in-vectives, which have so long pursued me, would be hurled against the jury and the Court.

You have now the fate of this lunatic in your hands. To him as to me, so far as we can judge, it is comparatively indifferent what be the issue. The wisest of modern men has left us a saying, that "the hour of death is more fortunate than the hour of birth," a saying which he signalized by bestowing a gratuity twice as great upon the place where he died as upon the hamlet where he was born. For ought that we can judge, the prisoner is uncon-scious of danger and would be insensible to suffering, let it come when it might. A verdict can only hasten, by a few months or years, the time when his bruised, diseased, wandering and be-nighted spirit shall return to Him who sent it forth on its sad and dreary pilgrimage.

The circumstances under which this trial closes are peculiar. I have seen capital cases where the parents, brothers, sisters, friends of the accused surrounded him, eagerly hanging upon the lips of his advocate, and watching in the countenances of the Court and jury, every smile and frown which might seem to indicate his fate. But there is no such scene here. The prisoner, though in the greenness of youth, is withered, decayed, senseless, almost lifeless. He has no father here. The descendant of slaves, that father died a victim to the vices of a superior race. There is no mother here, for her child is stained and polluted with the blood of mothers and a sleeping infant; and "he looks and laughs so that she cannot bear to look upon him." There is no brother, or sister, or friend here. Popular rage against the accused has driven them hence, and scattered his kindred and people. On the other side I notice the aged and venerable parents of Van Nest, and his surviving children, and all around are mourning and sympathizing friends. I know not at whose instance they have come. I dare not say they ought not to be here. But I must say to you that we live in a Christian and not in a savage State, and that the affliction which has fallen upon these mourners and us, was sent to teach them and us mercy and not retaliation; that although we may send this maniac to the scaffold, it will not recall to life the manly form of Van Nest, nor reanimate the exhausted frame of that aged matron, nor restore to life, and grace, and beauty, the murdered mother, nor call back the infant boy from the arms of his Saviour. Such a verdict can do no good to the living, and carry no joy to the dead. If your judgment shall be swayed at all by sympathies so wrong, although so natural, you will find the saddest hour of your life to be that in which you will look down upon the grave of your victim, and "mourn with compunctious sorrow" that you should have done so great injustice to the "poor handful of earth that will lie mouldering before you."

I have been long and tedious. I remember that it is the harvest moon, and that every hour is precious while you are detained from your yellow fields. But if you shall have bestowed patient attention throughout this deeply interesting investigation, and shall in the end have discharged your duties in the fear of God and in the love of truth justly and independently, you will have laid up a store of blessed recollections for all your future days, imperishable and inexhaustible.

———

John Van Buren, attorney-general, closed the case for the people, and the Hon. Bowen Whiting delivered the charge. The jury, after consultation, on the 23d of July, returned a verdict of guilty, and the prisoner was, at 6:30 o'clock the next morning, sentenced to be hanged on the 18th of September. Mr. Seward obtained a writ of error, and the conviction was afterwards reversed and a new trial ordered. (Freeman v. The People, 4 Denio.) After the reversal by the General Term, the prisoner was visited by the Circuit Judge, with reference to the propriety of having him arraigned, and it is said he declined to try him again. The prisoner died in his cell August 21st, 1847. A post mortem examination was had, which revealed the fact that his brain had been long diseased, and that he must have been insane before the murder.

ARGUMENT OF CHARLES O'CONOR,

For the Claimants, in the Case of the Brig-of-War General Armstrong.

[Armstrong *v.* The United States, Dev. Ct. of Cl. 22]

BEFORE THE UNITED STATES COURT OF CLAIMS, AT WASHINGTON, D. C., NOVEMBER 27th, 1855.

INTERNATIONAL LAW.—Where the claim of a citizen upon a foreign government has been submitted to arbitration, without his consent, or without an opportunity to be heard, and the award is adverse to him, the government must respond to the claimant in damages.

ANALYSIS OF MR. O'CONOR'S ARGUMENT.

1. Unprecedented character of the claim, and the court.
2. Origin and growth of jurisprudence.— Classification of rights and remedies.
3. Object and purposes of legal tribunals.
4. Early struggles of the English chancellors in framing a system of equity.
5. Character and importance of the Court of Claims.
6. Power of the court to create remedies, and grant relief.
7. Condition of the republic in 1812.
8. Story of the destruction of the " American Privateer."
9. Liability of Portugal.
10. The United States could look to Portugal alone for redress.
11. Rights of belligerents in neutral territory.
12. A nation like an individual bound absolutely to discharge its obligations.
13. Portugal bound to prevent hostilities within its jurisdiction.
14. Extent of the liability of a neutral.
15. Such liability absolute.
16. Such liability not affected by the strength of the government.
17. Neither poverty nor weakness a ground of exemption.
18. Government bound to enforce a subject's claim for damages against a foreign power.
19. The government responsible for its failure to enforce such claim.
20. In its prosecution the government is not the agent of the claimant.
21. Submission of the claim to arbitration creates no estoppel.
22. Government failed to present the facts to the arbitrator.
23. Claimant forbidden to argue his cause before Napoleon.
24. The award invalid since it turned upon a question not submitted to the arbitrator.
25. A single question of law all that was intended to be referred.
26. The question as to who was the aggressor a matter of national honor or shame.
27. There was no question of fact before Napoleon.
28. Circumstances under which the Armstrong fired the first gun.
29. Napoleon's award should have been rejected as void for want of jurisdiction.

The battle of Fayal will be remembered as one of the most brilliant naval engagements in the second war between the United States and Great Britain. It was fought on the night of the 26th of September, 1814, in the port of Fayal, one of the Azores islands, in the dominions of Portugal. In this famous action the damages were sustained, which form the subject of the very interesting and able argument of Mr. O'Conor here presented. The legal controversy lasted for more than forty years, having engaged public attention from the time of James Monroe, down to the administration of James Buchanan. Some of the most distinguished men in the United States, Portugal, England, and France conducted the protracted diplomatic correspondence. The claim was pressed with such zeal and ardor, that hostilities seemed at one time inevitable. President Taylor sent a fleet to Portugal, and, had he lived, the hero of Buena Vista would, doubtless, have sustained his country's honor, and enforced payment, even through the intervention of war, if necessary.

During our second memorable struggle with Great Britain, in 1812, the American brig General Armstrong was fitted out as a privateer. She sailed from Sandy Hook, on the evening of the 9th of September, 1814, under command of Captain Sam. C. Reid, of New York, with a crew of ninety men ; and, on the 26th, ran into Fayal roads for a supply of fresh water. Portugal, being a neutral power, the vessel was entitled, under the law of nations, to protection while within neutral territory. It is an elementary principle, that the property of belligerents, while within neutral jurisdiction, is inviolable. It is not lawful to make neutral territory the scene of hostility, or to attack an enemy while within it ; and if the enemy be attacked, or any capture is made under neutral protection, the neutral is bound to redress the injury, and effect restitution.[1]

The American privateer, having learned that none of the enemy's cruisers had been seen in that latitude for several weeks, cast anchor, supposing, of course, in case she was surprised by the arrival of a hostile squadron, or by superior strength and numbers, that the laws of civilized warfare would be observed, and the neutrality of the port respected. About sunset a British brig, the Carnation, hove in sight. Two more of the enemy's vessels, the Rota and Plantagenet, were sighted, and signalled, and appeared suddenly in the roads. The hostile squadron closed in upon Captain Reid's gallant little vessel, and, in utter violation of every principle of good faith and national honor, determined to overpower the Americans and capture their ship. Shortly after dusk, Captain Reid, noticing some suspicious movements, began to haul his vessel close under the guns of the castle. The

---

[1] Kent's Com. vol. 1, p. 117; Vattel, book 3d, ch. 7, § 132.

moon was near its full, riding in the heavens like a ball of silver, and the clear light revealed to the American commander every movement of the enemy. The Carnation, about eight o'clock, lowered all her boats, which were manned with an armed force, and moved rapidly towards the "Armstrong." Seeing this hostile demonstration, Captain Reid, after warning them to keep off, cleared the decks for action. The boats, however, paid no attention to the warning, and, when they got nearly alongside, the Americans opened a murderous fire, which was promptly returned. The enemy cried for quarter, and hauled off, having lost upwards of twenty killed and wounded. Aboard the Armstrong one man was killed, and the first lieutenant wounded. They now prepared for a more formidable attack. The inhabitants of the island crowded to the shore to witness the magnificent and exciting spectacle about to take place. The little vessel floating the stars and stripes carried but seven guns. The Carnation carried 18 guns, the Rota 38, and the Plantagenet 74. About midnight the attack was renewed with twelve boats, and about four hundred men. As this fleet approached the Americans opened a heavy fire, which was promptly returned. This continued until the enemy was alongside, and attempted to board the vessel. They were driven back with great slaughter. The Armstrong's second lieutenant had died of his injuries, and the third lieutenant was badly wounded, consequently the fire was slackened at the forecastle ; but the gallant captain, rallying his entire force, succeeded in beating off the enemy in a hand to hand conflict, in which swords, pikes, pistols and muskets were freely used. The attack was renewed a third time with a wild shout, and, after a decided conflict, the enemy were routed, and many of their boats entirely destroyed. The action lasted about forty minutes. The British lost nearly two hundred men. The American loss was two killed and seven wounded. Captain Lloyd, commanding the British squadron, finding himself unable to capture the privateer, soon after began to cannonade her. The Americans, finding further resistance useless, scuttled and abandoned their vessel, which was soon after set on fire by the British.

The vessel having been destroyed in violation of the neutrality of the port, Portugal became liable for the damages sustained, while England, in turn, became liable to Portugal. Conceding her liability, Portugal at once demanded redress from England, which she failed to obtain. At the request of the owners of the privateer, the United States, in 1835, made a demand on Portugal for the loss. After protracted negotiations, it was finally agreed, by treaty concluded on the 24th of February, and ratified on the 10th of March, 1851, to submit the claim to arbitration, and Napoleon III, then president of France, was chosen as referee. On the 3d of November, 1852, he rendered an award in favor of Portugal, which was accepted and acquiesced in by our government. Captain Reid, in behalf of himself, and the owners, officers and crew of the privateer, then presented a claim against the United States for $131,600. The grounds upon which the liability of the government was based are discussed by Mr. O'Conor with great learning and ability. The case was finally brought on for argument on the 17th of November, 1855, before the United States Court of Claims at Washington, present Hon. John J. Gilchrist, C. J., Hon. Isaac Blackford, and Hon. George P. Scarburgh. Mr. O'Conor was successful. The views advanced by the great advocate were afterwards adopted by the court which rendered judgment in favor of his clients. The claimants were represented by Charles O'Conor and

13

Sam. C. Reid, Jr., of New York; Hon. P. Phillips of Alabama; and Hon. Charles Naylor of Pennsylvania.   Hon. Montgomery Blair, U. S. Solicitor, represented the government.   After all the counsel had spoken, Mr. O'Conor, on the 27th of November, closed the case for the claimants as follows :

MAY IT PLEASE THE COURT:—The claim now presented for adjudication may be placed upon several distinct grounds.   In the first place, we contend that the General Armstrong was employed by her officers and crew in the service of the United States, and against the public enemy, under such circumstances that, on being advised of the facts and of the great benefits which resulted therefrom to the country, it became the government, as a matter of equity, to adopt the act and to indemnify the parties against the expense incurred.

Our second general head embraces the following elements: The General Armstrong, whilst lying in the port of Fayal, was entitled to absolute protection from the Portuguese government.   That protection was not afforded; in violation of the neutrality of that port, she was destroyed by the forces of a British squadron; and for this delinquency on the part of Portugal, her owners had a perfect right, by the law of nations, to be fully indemnified.   The owners had themselves no legal capacity to prosecute this claim directly; but, on establishing its validity, they were entitled to redress through the action of their own government against that of Portugal.   The United States, accordingly, investigated the claim, decided in favor of its justice, assumed the control of it, and entered upon the duty of enforcing it.   Instead, however, of prosecuting it to an issue by legitimate means, the government receded from its duty in that respect, and actually extinguished the claim, whereby a right has accrued to the owners to demand compensation from the public treasury.

Each step in the argument by which these conclusions are arrived at, seems to us quite clear and intelligible; but the learned solicitor for the government has advanced a great variety of objections, and it is principally in answering these that we shall engage the time and attention of your honors.

1. UNPRECEDENTED CHARACTER OF THE CLAIM, AND THE COURT.

The absence of precedents has been urged against us, and we have been called upon to produce from the books of the common law some instance of an action brought, a trial had, and a judgment rendered for the plaintiff upon a claim like the present.   We cannot comply with this unreasonable demand; but neither can we admit that our claim should suffer on that account. The nation itself is here a defendant, responding to the claim of a private suitor for reparation of injuries sustained—a thing unparalleled in jurisprudence. The court itself is the first-born of a new judicial era. Consequently, we cannot hope to find among the narrow rules and practical formulæ which ordinarily govern in determining mere questions of property between citizen and citizen, the lights which are to guide its judgment. As a judicial tribunal, it is not merely new in the instance; it is also new in principle. So far as concerns the power of courts to afford redress, it has heretofore been fundamental that the sovereign can do no wrong. This court was erected as a practical negative upon that vicious maxim. Henceforth our government repudiates the arrogant assumption, and consents to meet at the bar of enlightened justice every rightful claimant, how lowly soever his condition may be.

Whence is such a tribunal to extract the principles by which its action is to be governed—by which it shall test and allow or disallow the claims which may come before it? In ordinary cases of specific rights declared by some particular statute or regulation, its path may be easy. But in those extraordinary cases which are dependent upon principles not hitherto falling within the judicial authority, which has never been enforced against the State, and which, consequently, courts have never declared in their judgments or illustrated in their opinions, difficulties may be encountered at the outset. To meet and surmount these, if they exist, is one of the high and responsible duties devolved upon your honors, as pioneers in this newly opened chapter of juridical science.

Though without exact precedents, you are not wholly without chart or compass. A reference to the origin and growth of jurisprudence, in instance the most analogous, will furnish a sufficient guide.

2. ORIGIN AND GROWTH OF JURISPRUDENCE.—CLASSIFICATION OF RIGHTS AND REMEDIES.

Rights and their correlative duties are divided into two classes, that is to say, the perfect and the imperfect. The only difference between these classes is in external circumstances—intrinsically or morally there is none. Perfect rights are those which may be enforced by established remedies; perfect duties are those the performance of which may be coerced; a right of imperfect obligation

is one for the enforcement of which no remedy is provided. Jurisprudence, as administered by human tribunals, deals only with the
means of enforcing rights which are recognized as perfect; but like
all moral sciences, it is capable of improvement. As the general
mind of a nation advances in that freedom which is the result of
increased knowledge, the legislative authority will constantly enlarge the sphere of action assigned to jurisprudence, and increase
its power of establishing justice. Jurisprudence is only the means,
justice is the end. Jurisprudence is of human origin; justice is an
attribute of divinity, pre-existent of all created things, eternal and
immutable. Its authority is not derived from any human code,
either of positive institution or of customary reception; its decrees
are found in the voice of God speaking to the heart which faith
has purified to receive and reason enlightened with capacity to understand.

When thus aided by the legislature, jurisprudence is enabled to
enlarge the circle of perfect rights, by furnishing, from time to
time, new instrumentalities for enforcing justice. *Est boni judicis
ampliare jurisdictionem*, is a sound and unexceptionable maxim;
for the exercise of jurisdiction is but giving to men in a practical
form the behests of divine justice, and enforcing their observance.
This is well illustrated by the rise and progress of the English law.
In the lofty growth of equity, by the side of its stunted rival, the
common law, we see by what means rights founded in justice and
conscience, but not yet recognized by positive law, may rise in
grade, acquire recognition, and become enforceable by adequate
remedies. In that example this court will find the best lights for
its government. In our early law books we find it urged and admitted, that "every right must have a remedy." But Lord Chief
Justice Vaughan stripped this common place of all its force, by
replying, "where there is no remedy, there can be no right." The
common law judges of England always acted upon the principle
embodied in this remark. From their rigid adherence to it arose
the necessity of a distinct jurisdiction—the power of equity to
compel an observance of those duties which conscience enjoined,
but which positive law had provided no means of enforcing.

3. OBJECT AND PURPOSES OF LEGAL TRIBUNALS.

The ordinary courts of law are not created to declare or enforce
justice in the abstract, or justice in general.[1] Their function is to

[1] See note *a* to De Bode *v.* Regina, 13 Queen's Bench R. p. 387.

effectuate such human rights only as, in the existing stage of its progress, jurisprudence is enabled to bring within the sphere of its remedial forms, leaving all others to be sought by entreaty and yielded by free will.   The judge is obliged to dismiss every claim, however just, for enforcing which he cannot find an appropriate writ in the register; and, consequently, the regret of the bench and a deep censure upon the defendant is often expressed in the same breath with a judgment denying the remedy sought.

This was strikingly exemplified in the case of Jackson *v.* Bartholomew.[1]   An honest farmer seeing his neighbor's wheat-stack on the verge of being consumed by fire in the owner's absence, voluntarily assumed the task of saving it, and did so at a slight cost.   Reimbursement being churlishly refused, he brought an action in a justice's court, and the rustic magistrate, not learned enough to know that legal policy sometimes stifles the voice of conscience, decided in favor of the plaintiff.   The defendant appealed; and when reversing the decision on the ground that for a service, however beneficial, rendered without a previous request, no action lay, the Supreme Court of New York denounced the defendant's conduct as "most unworthy."   In this censure all honest men must concur.   No one could doubt that, had the owner of the wheat been present at the moment of peril, he would have requested aid and promised compensation.   An honest man would have conceded this, ratified his neighbor's kind intervention, and promptly repaid his expenditure; but selfishness saw that this was a duty of imperfect obligation, and a callous conscience dishonorably refused to perform it.

4. Early struggles of the English chancellors in framing a system of equity.

The equity jurisdiction of Great Britain has been considered as an anomaly in legal science.   Continental jurists seem never to have comprehended it; though it could easily be shown that no civil society ever existed in which there were not some remediable forms of injustice which *lex non exacte definit sed arbitrio boni viri permittit.*[2]   Institutions which are novel in form, will always excite criticism and opposition, however harmonious they may be, in principle, with what has gone before.   But the difficulties which may beset the path of this court, at the outset of its high career, can-

[1] 20 Johnson's Reports, p. 28.   [2] Story's Eq. Jur. §§ 8, 9.

not be greater than those which surrounded the early English chancellors in their efforts to mitigate the rigor and supply the imperfections of positive law. They had no judicial precedents to guide them in stilling the waves of contention; the great unwritten law of natural justice alone governed. They claimed to deal with matters binding in conscience only, and the power to enforce its dictates. At every step they had to contend with the argument now urged against us, that there was no legal remedy, and consequently the law left it optional with the defendant how to demean himself in the premises. As in the present case, the law—the law was dinned into the ears of the court, by the advocates of wrong, with loudness and pertinacity; but the clamor was unavailing. Without aid from precedents, but guided by principles, the courts grappled with and mastered the devices of iniquity. Justice! Equity! Conscience! words without definition, and incapable of being defined, alone prescribed their jurisdiction, and neither legal nor political science had any further connection with the new cases arising before them, than to aid in solving the question how far State policy would admit of right being done to the injured suitor.

To the precise extent which a due regard to public policy would admit, the masters of equity encroached upon the territory of imperfect duties, making firm land wheresoever they trod. Thus they gradually redeemed from the outlawry to which ignorance or inexpertness had consigned them, a large class of imperfect rights, and enforced a large class of duties before deemed imperfect—because not enforceable—but which were always obligatory in the eyes of God, and were always voluntarily performed by honest men.

5. Character and importance of the Court of Claims.

Prior to the institution of this court, all rights, as against the nation, were imperfect in the legal sense of the term; every duty of the nation was a duty of imperfect obligation. There was no judicial power capable of declaring either; no private person possessed the means of enforcing the one or coercing the other. These rights may be deemed still to remain, in one sense, imperfect; for the decrees of this court cannot be carried into execution by authority of the court itself. But effectual progress has been made toward giving form and method to the administration of justice between the nation and the individual. This court enables the latter to obtain an authoritative recognition of his right. No more is needed; for in no case can a State, after such a recognition, withhold payment and yet retain its place in the great family of civilized nations. The ordinary jurisdiction of the court bears a strong resemblance to the narrow cognizance at common law; but its extraordinary jurisdiction over " all claims which may be referred to it by either house of Congress," extends its power to the utmost limits attainable by juridical science in its fullest development. In this aspect, its dignity and importance as a governmental institution cannot be too highly appreciated. As a means by which rightful claims against the government may be readily established, and those not founded in justice promptly driven from the portals of Congress, it must exercise a most healthful influence. But we are authorized to look higher than the mere convenience of suitors and the dispatch of public business. Enlightened patriotism will contemplate other and more important consequences. Caprice can no longer control. Here equity, morality, honor and good conscience must be practically applied to the determination of claims, and the actual authority of these principles over governmental action ascertained, declared and illustrated in permanent and abiding forms. As step by step, in successive decisions, you shall have ascertained the duties of government toward the citizen, fixed their precise limits upon sound principles, and armed the claimant with means of securing their enforcement, a code will grow up, giving effect to many rights not heretofore practically acknowledged. In it will be found enshrined for the admiration of succeeding ages an honorable portraiture of our national morality, and a full vindication of the eulogium recently pronounced upon our people by the highest authority in the parent State. " Jurisprudence," says Lord Campbell, in the Queen v. Millis,[1] "is the department of human knowledge to which our brethren in the United States of America have chiefly devoted themselves, and in which they have chiefly excelled."

6. Power of the Court to Create Remedies, and Grant Relief.

Whilst we assert that this court does not stand *super antiquas vias* in anything which concerns mere procedure, and, consequently, that the call for judicial precedents is idle and unreasonable, we admit that cases arising here must be determined in conformity

---

[1] 10 Clarke & Finnelly, p. 777.

with established principles. It has been truly said, that "you have no power to invent rights," but it must be conceded that you have express power to invent remedies. The seventh section of the act creating the court, provides that you shall prepare to be laid before Congress for enactment, the requisite bill or bills in those cases which shall have received your "favorable decision, in such form as, if enacted, will carry such decision into effect." This, according to Mr. Justice Ashhurst, in Pasley v. Freeman,[1] is the precise mode of dealing with cases which are without precedent in the known practice of judicial tribunals.

We agree that you have jurisdiction only over that class of cases which are claims properly so called. The applicant for bounty must go elsewhere. Grace and favor, if it is ever proper to bestow them, must be bestowed as heretofore, by Congress, without your interference. But claims—claims which would be entitled, as between individuals, to recognition and enforcement according to known principles of law, or upon known principles of equity, are to be vindicated and established by this court. We assert no more than this, except so far as the nature of things may warrant a practical distinction between a sovereign State and an individual. In this way the sphere of equity may, as against the government, admit of some expansion. In a case like that of the wheat-stack, cited from Johnson's Reports, a court constituted as this is, could find no difficulty in enforcing the claim against the government. If a large quantity of public property, or any other great public interest, were, at this moment, in danger of being sacrificed, under circumstances rendering it impossible to apply to the executive for instructions or for the means of saving it, we insist that a reference of the voluntary salvor's claim would enable this court, as keeper of the nation's conscience, to award remuneration. We say that government could not, any more than the owner of the wheat-stack, conscientiously withhold compensation in such a case; and that, if the claim should be sent here, this court would be bound to enforce it. State policy may forbid that equity should go so far in a case between individuals as to compel a man to make a request, as it were *nunc pro tunc.* But why may not government ascertain, through a proper judicial investigation, the existing and binding force in equity of a claim upon it, which, in a private case, no honest man would hesitate to acknowledge; which no gentleman could repudiate without dishonor ?

[1] 3 T. R. p. 63.

7. CONDITION OF THE REPUBLIC IN 1812.

When war was declared in 1812, this republic was yet in the infancy of her power. We could scarcely be said to possess either an army or a navy. Though in the achievement of our independence we had won high renown, yet physical strength, the only attribute which can enforce respect for the rights of a nation, was not ours to any great extent, and was not imputed to us by any. Our commercial marine had often been plundered with impunity. Even our ships of war had not been exempt from search and impressment. War with France, our early friend, had failed to protect us from insult, and it was in an absolutely necessary defense of our existence as an independent State, that we were compelled to venture upon hostilities with the greatest power of ancient or modern times. The invasion of our neutral rights in navigating the ocean induced the measure, the vindication of them was its immediate aim and object.[1]

Our naval reputation at that time may be judged by the romantic temerity with which the Alert, a pitiful little English gunboat, in the first month of the war, bore down upon the Essex, a 32-gun frigate.

Perhaps we seized upon an opportune moment, for Britain was engaged in an European war which tasked her utmost energies. Even with this advantage on our side, the contest was very unequal; but when at length the gigantic power of Napoleon was prostrated, what was our condition ? The patroness of France, under her restored dynasty, the foremost of a holy alliance of all monarchical Christendom, with her thousand ships and her victorious legions relieved from every other occupation, Britain stood prepared to "crush us at a blow." Such, all will remember, was the language of the times; and naught seemed to interpose between her resolve and its execution but a brief time, as much as might be needed to conquer intervening space.

Her force was soon felt. The sacred capitol of our Union, the spot consecrated to liberty by the immortal Washington, fell into the hands of her mercenaries. The thunder of her vauntings was heard along our coasts, and at what vital point her apparently resistless force was next to fall upon us, none could tell.

[1] Annals of Thirteenth Congress, pp. 1419–1427, 1431.

8. Story of the destruction of the "American Privateer."

At that critical juncture (September 9th, 1814), the General Armstrong set sail from New York upon a cruise designed to harass our powerful antagonist. On the seventeenth day out she cast anchor in the neutral port of Fayal, for the purpose of taking in a supply of water. Soon after, on the same day, a British squadron, under the command of Captain Lloyd, consisting of a seventy-four-gun ship, a frigate of thirty-eight guns, and a sloop of war carrying eighteen guns, entered that port for the same purpose. Two conflicts took place between the American privateer and a body of armed men sent in boats from the British fleet to assail her, which terminated in the destruction of the privateer.

This violation of neutrality, and the consequent loss of our property, entitled us to demand compensation as claimants upon the justice of Portugal.

Questions of law have been raised as to this asserted liability of Portugal. These we must dispose of in the first place.

9. Liability of Portugal.

It is said that Captain Reid, having himself resorted to violence and struck the first blow, must be deemed the aggressor, however apparent it may have been that such resort was necessary to save his vessel from capture. It is also said, that the obligation of a neutral to make compensation in such cases is not absolute; that if a neutral, at the time and place of the aggression, employs all the means in his power to prevent it, this is all that can be required. Of course, in this connection, it is conceded that if there be negligence in providing, at such time and place, the amount of defensive force which might, under all circumstances, be reasonably required, or if there was a failure in the due and effectual employment of such force, from pusillanimity, gross ignorance, or want of skill on the part of the neutral, responsibility might ensue. What singular questions for discussion between nations would arise in the investigation of these points! In following out its consequences, this idea of limiting national responsibility within the compass of national power, it is said that property unlawfully seized by a third power, within the territory of a neutral, must be restored by the courts of the latter, in case it should come within their reach; but that when the property is destroyed, or for any other reason cannot be thus subjected to legal process, the neutral is only bound to use his best exertions to procure compensation.

To illustrate what is meant by this employment of his best exertions, it is argued that a neutral is not bound to go to war in such a case; that it would be unreasonable and, consequently, unjust to require a feeble State to involve itself in hostilities with a powerful aggressor merely for the sake of obtaining justice for the stranger; that friendly negotiation and urgent entreaty for compensation constitute the whole duty of a weak neutral State, whose territory has been unlawfully converted into a theater of war by a powerful belligerent.

Notwithstanding their palpable absurdity, these doctrines are gravely insisted on. From a perusal of the correspondence between the two governments, it might be thought that some of the able and patriotic negotiators who, from time to time, sought the enforcement of the claim against Portugal, conceded these doctrines; for they condescended, in arguing against them, to discuss the evidence, relying, as they well might, upon its insufficiency to excuse Portugal, even if the rule of law was as contended for. We shall adopt the same line of argument; but we protest, at the outset, against any such inference as against us. We do not acquiesce in any of these doctrines. They are founded in the grossest misconception of public law, and a singular blindness to the plainest dictates of common sense. We proceed to prove this, seeking thereby to establish that, in point of law, our claim was perfectly valid against Portugal, until that government was released by the acquiescence of the United States in Louis Napoleon's award.

10. The United States could look to Portugal alone for redress.

England could in no event be held responsible to the United States or to the aggrieved parties. As between belligerents themselves, it is the right of each to make war upon the other, his subjects and property, wheresoever he can find them. " A capture made within neutral waters is, as between enemies, deemed to all intents and purposes rightful. It is only by the neutral sovereign that its legal validity can be called in question. The enemy has no rights whatever; and if the neutral omits or declines to interpose a claim, the property (so captured) is condemnable, *jure belli*, to the captor." " This," says the Supreme Court in The Ann, 3d Wheaton's R. p. 435, "is a clear result of the authorities, and the doctrine rests on well established principles of public law." True it is, that Great Britain was responsible over to Portugal for any sum which she might be obliged to pay; and hence, no doubt, the British influence in procuring Louis Napoleon's award. But that was a question altogether between Portugal and Great Britain; we had no claim whatever against the latter.

It is affirmed, on all hands, that belligerents are bound to abstain from hostilities within neutral territory, and that any violence, except in self-defense, committed by them within such territory is unlawful. It is unlawful as between the neutral and each of the belligerents. The injured belligerent may claim indemnity from the neutral, the neutral may demand reimbursement from the aggressor. We refer to the case last cited, and also to 1 Wheaton, p. 405; 4 Wheaton, p. 52; Ibid. p. 298.

II. RIGHTS OF BELLIGERENTS IN NEUTRAL TERRITORY.

The rule requiring a total abstinence from hostilities within neutral territory has, of course, the same limitation which is imposed by reason and necessity in every other case where violence is prohibited. The right of self-defense is rightly called the first law of nature. The arm of the civil magistrate cannot always be extended to prevent injury to the citizen, and when it is not present for his defense, he is not bound to submit unresistingly to death or wounds. When the danger is imminent, and safety cannot otherwise be purchased, the assailed party may always defend himself, repelling force by force. The same authorities which assert that a belligerent forfeits all claim to protection from a neutral sovereign by commencing hostilities within his territory, admit this right of self-defense. And this, let it be noted, is not the privilege of returning a blow; that, indeed, is revenge or retribution, not self-defense. Self-defense must foresee, anticipate, and defeat the unlawful design whilst only threatened or mediated. Nothing else is defense. Chief Justice Marshall says, in The Ann,[1] that "whilst lying in neutral waters," a ship is "bound to abstain from all hostilities, except in self-defense." Again he says, that no vessel in such waters "is bound to submit to search, or to account (to the belligerent) for her conduct or character." In a case somewhat analogous to the present, The Marianne Flora,[2] Mr. Justice Story says, in reference to defensive force used by the commander of a ship

---

[1] 3 Wheaton, p. 435.   [2] 11 Wheaton, p. 1.

menaced by another: " He acted, in our opinion, with entire legal propriety. He was not bound to fly or to wait until he was crippled. His was not a case of mere remote danger, but of imminent, pressing, and present danger. He had the flag of his country to maintain and the rights of his cruiser to vindicate." It will be seen, therefore, that Captain Reid's acts in defense of his vessel were lawful; that they involved no breach of duty on his part towards Portugal, and that they in no degree lessened the duty of Portugal to protect him.

12. A NATION LIKE AN INDIVIDUAL BOUND ABSOLUTELY TO DISCHARGE ITS OBLIGATIONS.

What is sometimes called local and temporary allegiance, but is more properly termed obedience, is due to every government from aliens and strangers sojourning within its jurisdiction. The neutral State forbids hostilities within its territories between the armies or navies of belligerents, precisely as the civil magistrate forbids violence between individual enemies. By his laws and regulations, he absolutely supersedes the law of nature, and promises absolute protection in return for obedience. We may admit the truism that neither men nor nations can go further in the performance of their obligations than the employment of their utmost ability. But an obligation like that under consideration is never, in itself, theoretically, nor for any practical purpose, subject to any such limitation. A private man's obligations are no longer enforceable in fact, when his whole means of payment are exhausted; but after that event he remains charged with the residue of his indebtedness precisely in the same degree as before. Until relieved by death, or released by bankruptcy, he is still bound to his creditor. Poverty and weakness may plead for indulgence, but neither can rightfully demand a release. The obligation remains. So it is with nations; they must perform their duties or cease to exist. There is no bankrupt act for them; political extinction is their only refuge from the penalties of unredeemed responsibility.

Although some crude remarks of publicists may be found affording a slight pretext for the argument, it cannot be maintained, that the duty of a sovereign to afford full protection to the stranger within his gates, whose presence he permits, is anything less than absolute, or that the duty in this respect of a weak nation is any less than that of a strong and powerful one.

When a private individual breaks the peace and does an injury to another, the sovereign power subjects him, by due process of law, to mulcts and penalties. His whole estate, if necessary, is sequestered for the remuneration of the injured party. Precisely the same measure of retribution is to be meted out for the like offense when committed against persons or property by a foreign nation.

13. PORTUGAL BOUND TO PREVENT HOSTILITIES WITHIN ITS JURISDICTION.

Belligerents are not permitted to fit out ships of war or augment their force in the ports of a neutral; but all nations allow their ports to be visited by the vessels of those with whom they are in amity, for the purpose of obtaining those necessaries of life which are equally useful in peace or war. Therefore, it was entirely proper for the American privateer and the British squadron to enter the friendly port of Fayal, as they did, to supply themselves with water. But it was the duty of both to preserve the peace while there, and that duty was enforced to the utmost against the privateer by the Portuguese authorities. After the first attack upon the General Armstrong, and in anticipation of the second, Captain Reid sought the governor's permission for thirty of his countrymen, then on shore at Fayal, to come on board and assist in the defense of his vessel. The application was peremptorily refused; and Louis Napoleon, in his award, commends as worthy of all praise the act of the governor, in thus effectually preventing an augmentation of the American force. We agree that this was performing precisely, and to the letter, the duty of Portugal towards England. But we insist, however excusable the governor may have been from want of power, that the supreme government of Portugal was bound effectively to have prevented hostilities against those who were restrained by its laws from employing their own means of self-defense.

The learned solicitor asserted, that the Portuguese government was not bound to protect strangers, any more than it was bound to protect its own people. Perhaps it was not. It is the duty of every government to protect its own people, and when violence has been committed upon them, to enforce redress from the wrong-doer to the whole extent of such wrong-doer's ability. The same duty exists to preserve the peace within neutral territory between belligerent nations. The reason is obvious; the local authority compels the belligerent parties to keep the peace, and it is therefore bound to protect them. This seems to us so plain, so obvious, that no argument is necessary to enforce it.   Indeed, the general proposition is not denied; we have only to combat an attempt to fritter it away in practice by subtle distinctions.

14. Extent of the liability of a neutral.

The extent of the liability upon the part of the neutral power, to furnish compensation from its own treasury for the losses incurred in consequence of its failure to keep the peace within its territories, is alone disputed.   If full reparation is not due to the stranger, what is he entitled to?   The attempts to answer this question are ludicrous!   It is said, that if a vessel is captured in neutral territory, and afterwards comes within the same territory, it should be restored to the original owner; but if it is carried off and does not return within the neutral territory, then the neutral is not liable.   If this is true, then the total destruction of property involves no liability at all, for the neutral cannot deliver up that which has ceased to exist.   As violence cannot always be prevented, what is the duty of the neutral in those cases where destruction ensues?   The learned solicitor says, the nation whose territory has been invaded is to remonstrate with the aggressor; it is to appeal to him in the name of justice, reason and friendship, to make amends to the injured party.   And it is said, if these means fail, the injured party can claim no further redress.   Can this be law?   The sovereign to whom the application is made, is the unrighteous transgressor; he knows that the reparation sought is for his enemy.   He knows also that he has only to refuse, and the obligation of his neutral friend will be satisfied.   By a simple refusal he can close the transaction and settle the account forever.   If this were really the extent of the neutral liability, the whole notion of a right to indemnity would be the merest farce.

We insist that the obligation of the neutral power is to prevent hostilities, if practicable; and, if that be impracticable, then to make compensation for the injury sustained.

15. Such liability absolute.

The notion of limiting the duty to prevention or to the employment of such force as may happen to be at the spot for that purpose, is extremely absurd.   It can rarely be in the power even of the greatest States to maintain at every point of their territories a force adequate to prevent violations of their neutrality.   Indeed, when the force exists, the local officer is not always justifiable in employing it. If the commander of a dozen British seventy-four-gun ships, lying in one of our ports, where they had touched for provisions, should seize a Russian ship, refuse to surrender her to the marshal, and, as Lloyd did at Fayal, threaten, in case of interference with his capture, to bombard the town and slaughter its inhabitants, would the local authorities be bound to plunge at once into the horrors of irregular war? In most cases the force on the spot would be wholly inadequate to effective resistance. But when it happens otherwise, we doubt the expediency of such a resort. Vastly less mischief would result, in ordinary cases, from leaving the wrong to be redressed by the supreme power. Then, if war should come, it would be met with fitting preparation. The armed warrior, not the women and children of a peaceful town, would encounter its brunt. We deny that the governor of the Azores could properly have employed his military force in open war upon the fleet of a powerful nation, which was not only the friend and ally, but, it may be said, the protector of his sovereign. Even if his force had been adequate, the act would have been rash and injudicious. It is quite clear that in such cases the local authorities should most generally submit to the violence, leaving it to the supreme government to apply the proper remedy. And it is equally clear that indemnity is the only remedial justice which can ordinarily be had. If the neutral State has any duty to perform, it is the procurement of such indemnity.

16. SUCH LIABILITY NOT AFFECTED BY THE STRENGTH OF THE GOVERNMENT.

In the obligations which thus rest upon neutrals, there is no difference between strong and weak nations. We commonly say, that in the eye of the law all men are equal. So, in international law, all sovereigns are on a perfect equality. Consequently a State, however feeble, cannot maintain its rank and position in the family of nations without performing its public duties When it fails in this respect, it must necessarily fall exactly into the same condition as an individual engaged in trade, who, failing to pay his debts and to perform the duties of his station, loses all credit and position among his fellow-men. This doctrine is reasonable; no other would be tolerable. A feeble State has at its command a suitable remedy for every such case. When wronged by a powerful nation, it may invoke the reprobation of mankind by a proper exposition of the act. The force of opinion is great, and nations have been constrained to respect it in the worst of times. If this resort should fail, it may form an equal alliance with other States of its own class, or it may seek the protection of one more powerful. If it can be supposed that none of those means would enable it to redeem its obligations, nothing can be clearer than that it should declare itself bankrupt and relinquish its pretensions to sovereignty.

To prove that for injuries to property sustained by a belligerent, within the territory of a neutral, from hostilities there unlawfully prosecuted against him by his enemy, the neutral sovereign is only bound to afford the measure of redress which may be within his ability, your honors are referred to the text of certain treaties between the United States, England, France, Russia, and Holland. We there find stipulations to the effect that each nation engages to "use its utmost endeavors to obtain from the offending party full and ample satisfaction for the vessel or vessels so taken," or to "protect and defend by all means in its power the vessels, &c., and restore the same to the right owner." These treaties are relied upon as full evidence of the sense entertained by the great maritime States, as to the extent of the obligations of neutrals in the particular now under consideration. It is claimed that they are not merely strong, but decisive evidence of the *jus gentium.* We admit the proposition in its broadest extent. It only remains, then, to inquire what is meant by the "utmost endeavors" of a nation, or by the employment of "all means in its power." Our government is one party to these treaties. Do we, when promising to use our utmost endeavors and all means in our power, intend to say that we will humbly pray for justice and earnestly expostulate against injustice? Does this involve a complete exhaustion of all the means in our power? And if, indeed, we are so weak and so degraded as this, is Great Britain, is powerful and martial France, with more than forty millions of warlike subjects, equally so? The small kingdom of Holland is also a party to these treaties. Surely these same words, in the same treaty, do not mean one thing as applied to one party, and a different thing as applied to the other party. We respectfully insist that the rule, as expressed in the text of our writers on international law, and in these treaties, means nothing less than that the neutral State is bound to obtain or to make restitution for every outrage committed upon friendly nations within its limits, peacefully if it can, forcibly if it must.

14

17. NEITHER POVERTY NOR WEAKNESS A GROUND OF EXEMPTION.

A few words in Mr. Wheaton's comment upon these treaties are thought to favor the doctrine of limited liability now contended for. In Mr. Lawrence's edition of the Elements of International Law, p. 497, the author says: "They were not bound to make compensation, if all the means in their power were used and failed in their effect." But he does not, by example or otherwise, give the least clue to his notions concerning the means which must be used by the "high contracting parties" in order to fulfill the obligation created by these words. Observing upon the jurisdiction over captures in neutral territory exercised by the admiralty courts of the neutral, he says, it is "exercised only for the purpose of restoring the specific property, and does not extend to the infliction of vindictive damages, as in ordinary cases of maritime injuries." This sentence is the learned solicitor's leading authority for the position, that when the specific property is destroyed the neutral has no duty to perform. An important distinction, however, exists between the obligations of a sovereign power, which are to be recognized and performed through its executive, and the much more limited field of admiralty jurisdiction. Of course, a court of admiralty could neither draw upon the public treasury, nor levy war upon a foreign power. But we can find in Mr. Wheaton's work no evidence that he ever intended to sanction the doctrine that sovereign power can excuse itself from performing the duties of sovereignty on the plea of weakness.

We have been asked, whether we mean to insist that Portugal was bound to go to war? We answer, certainly not. Portugal owed us no such obligation. The question, so far as war is concerned, was, whether she owed that measure to herself? Her obligation was to yield us protection, and having failed in that, to indemnify us. Whether she would prosecute a claim against Great Britain by the sword or otherwise, for reimbursement, was altogether her own affair. If she was so weak or so pusillanimous as to waive her rights in this respect, we certainly could not complain. We only say that her high state amongst the powers of earth required her to protect or indemnify us, and forbid her to plead weakness or poverty as a ground of exemption.

The unlimited liability of the neutral in such cases is asserted by the highest authorities on international law. It is asserted in the published speeches of nearly every legislator who has spoken

upon this claim.   All our administrations, without exception, have
maintained it.   Portugal herself conceded it in 1814, and even
Louis Napoleon admits it.   He says, in his award, that, if Captain
Reid had not released her by his own conduct, Portugal was under
an obligation "to afford him protection by other means than peaceful intervention." The original liability of Portugal is therefore
manifest, unless Captain Reid, by some misconduct on his own
part, forfeited the protection which she owed him.   Whether he so
misbehaved, is a question of fact which we will discuss hereafter.

18. Government bound to enforce a subject's claim for damages against a foreign power.

The next question of law is, whether the enforcement of this
claim against Portugal devolved upon the United States as a public duty.

In return for the allegiance claimed by the sovereign, says Mr.
Justice Blackstone, the sovereign "is always under an obligation to
protect his subjects at all times and in all countries." And that
this right of the subject "can never be forfeited by any distance of
place or time, but only by misconduct." [1]

The Lord Chancellor of England, on the argument of Baron de
Bode's case,[2] says: "It is admitted law that, if the subject of a
country is spoliated by a foreign government, he is entitled to obtain redress through the means of his own government.   But if,
from weakness, timidity, or other cause on the part of his own government, no redress is obtained from the foreigner, then he has a
claim against his own country."

These are the maxims of monarchy at his day.   It was the pride
of her who, in ancient times, gave law to men and nations, that, in
the most distant climes and among the most barbarous people, " I
am a Roman citizen " was a certain passport to safety.   Shall it be
said that our republic yields a less perfect protection to her citizens?   We trust not.   Mr. Justice Parker, one of the most eminent
of American jurists, recognizes the rule that in such cases there
rests an "obligation on the government of the United States to
procure redress for its citizens, or itself to reimburse them." [3]   On

---

[1] Wendell's Blackstone, pp. 370, 371, and notes.
[2] 16 Eng. L. & Eq. Reports, p. 23.
[3] Farnam v. Brooks, 9 Pickering's Reports, p. 239.

this head, there is no lack of precedents. Half the diplomacy of nations has been devoted to obtaining securities for their merchants when subjected in person or property to the jurisdiction of other States; half the treaties on record contain provisions for ascertaining dues and making compensation on account of past failures in this respect, and all of them abound with mutual pledges of protection for the future. From the father of his country to our present chief magistrate, no executive has sent to Congress an annual message unmarked with recognitions of this duty. We defy reference to a single instance in which the President has failed annually to apprise Congress of his progress in pending efforts to obtain for our citizens redress of grievances suffered by the acts or omissions of other nations.

The duty of our government in this respect cannot be denied. It is not denied. The questions are, how far did that duty extend ? was there any failure in performing it ? and, if so, is the government responsible for the consequences ?

19. THE GOVERNMENT RESPONSIBLE FOR ITS FAILURE TO ENFORCE SUCH CLAIM.

Responsibility is denied on many grounds. In the first place, we are told, the government of the United States, in prosecuting claims against foreign powers for redress of grievances suffered by our citizens, is merely the agent of the injured individual; and, assuming as applicable the same rules which obtain in the common law, concerning the private relation of principal and agent, or, more exactly speaking, master and servant, it is said that the claimants did not object to the treaty with Portugal before it was made, or afterwards so protest against it, or against the action had under it, as to screen themselves from the imputation of having ratified the act of their servant by implied consent or acquiescence. It is said the subsequent action of the claimant amounts to acquiescence; acquiescence is assent; assent is ratification, and then comes, in this common maxim of servile law, " a subsequent assent is equivalent to an original command."

On the other hand, and with equal confidence, it is asserted, that the government is the sole judge what claim of the citizen it will enforce ; in what manner, at what time, by what means, and to what extent, it will enforce them. It may, says our learned opponent, relinquish them, submit them to arbitration, and to any kind of arbitrament it judges to be expedient in reference to the general interests of the republic; it may accept a compromise, or it may release them without compensation, or for a consideration of benefit or convenience to the public.   In fine, its power over the whole subject is claimed to be absolute in the most comprehensive sense of the word, no responsibility attaching to its action, whatever that action may be.

It is true, that when laying down this latter proposition, the government solicitor became appalled by the enormity of his own doctrine.   First, relieving his conscience by an empty admission that it would be wrong, nay, iniquitous, to sacrifice a private right to the public convenience, he endeavored to close this part of the discussion by asserting that nothing of the kind had ever been done in the whole practice of the government.   But feeling, as he reached it, that this assertion begged the very question before the court, he returned like a stout-hearted champion to his starting point, and insisted that the power was vested in our government thus to deal with, traffic in, and for its own benefit dispose of the private right of the citizen, without any responsibility whatever.

The two heads of exemption from liability thus advanced for the government, are manifestly inconsistent.   It must be admitted that they cannot stand together; we hope to show that neither of them is well founded.

20. In its prosecution, the government is not the agent of the claimant.

How can the government be an agent or mere servant, liable to be restrained by the master's prohibition, or affected by his subsequent censure, and, at the same time, possess absolute discretionary power over the whole subject, free from control, restraint or responsibility?   The inconsistency is too glaring.

An individual despoiled by the rapacity, or aggrieved by the negligence of a foreign power, cannot lawfully wage war, or in any other form prosecute directly a claim for indemnity.   His only remedy is to invoke the aid of his own government.   By a fundamental rule of the social compact, sanctioned by immemorial practice, every community is bound to afford this kind of protection to its members.   And when a sovereign State, in the performance of this duty, appears as a prosecutor for redress of injuries, the claimant and respondent are equal in power and dignity.   The individual wrong-doer, and the individual sufferer, are alike lost sight of.   The responding State cannot avoid liability by delivering up for sacrifice its agent or subject; neither is the claiming State to be deemed a mere agent of the aggrieved person. It does not act in the name or by the authority of the injured individual, but in its own name and right, as ultimate and paramount lord proprietor of all things, and sovereign of all persons, within its jurisdiction. Between these "high contracting" or high contending parties is the suit and the trial; between them must be the judgment, whether obtained by negotiation, awarded by arbitrament, or won by the sword.[1]

As the respective nations are the parties, and the only known or recognized parties to the controversy, it necessarily follows that any act of the claiming power, which bars its right of farther prosecuting the claim, works an extinguishment of the claim itself; is, in substance and effect, a release to the respondent.

The methods of pursuing such a claim are negotiation, and failing that, war, or, if the respondent will consent, arbitration. In all cases which admit of its application, the latter is a resort favored by wisdom and humanity. When a claim is mutually submitted to arbitrament and determined by the arbiter, that law of honor and good faith which nations must obey,[2] declares the award to be final, unless a just and defensible cause can be assigned for disregarding it. If, upon its publication, neither party protest against it, the award becomes conclusive, whatever may be its moral or legal vices.

21. SUBMISSION OF THE CLAIM TO ARBITRATION CREATES NO ESTOPPEL.

In the present case, a perfectly valid claim against Portugal has been destroyed by the action of the government. We will prove this by the evidence before your honors. The award of Louis Napoleon stands in our way, and is relied upon as an estoppel. In connection with our review of the merits, we hope to show that the award is void as against us: first, for want of jurisdiction; secondly, because the government did not place before the arbiter, but expressly withheld from his view, important evidence, which afforded him an opportunity to decide upon facts from his own notions or *ex parte* stories, and sanctioned his availing himself thereof; thirdly, because it refused us permission to be heard before the arbiter, or to present an argument to him; and lastly, because even upon the

---

[1] 5 Howard's U. S. R. p. 397.   [2] 8 Paige, p. 534.

imperfect proofs presented to him, the award is manifestly partial and unjust.

Pursuant to the treaty with Portugal, by which this claim was to be submitted to the arbitrament of a third power, the Secretary of State, on the 20th of March, 1851, "in accordance," as he states, "with suggestions made by M. de Figaniere" (the minister of Portugal) instructed Mr. Hadduck, our representative at Lisbon, to prepare a protocol, with certain documents annexed, to be authenticated by the respective governments, and laid before the arbiter. The President of the French Republic was first named; and in case he should decline the office, King Oscar, of Sweden, was to be chosen in his place.

This letter of instructions contains a very singular passage; it is in these words: "You will understand, of course, that these copies (*i. e.*, the papers to be annexed to the protocol) are limited to such communications as have passed between the American legation and the Portuguese government at Lisbon, and between this department and the Portuguese legation in Washington." The historical fact, that at the time of the occurrence, and when the proofs in support of the claim were first made up and presented, the Portuguese government was seated not at Lisbon, but at Rio Janeiro, renders it easy to perceive why the Portuguese minister suggested this singular limitation of the proofs to be laid before the arbiter. His suggestion was craftily made and unwarily adopted. Its effect was to carry into the record to be submitted to the arbiter only so much and such parts of the evidence as happened to be incorporated with a renewed correspondence on the subject, which was commenced in 1834, about twenty years subsequently to the occurrence of the outrage for which redress was sought. We will presently show that this instruction caused to be suppressed at least one piece of evidence which was of great force, and, as we conceive, perfectly conclusive upon the very point of Louis Napoleon's judgment. By the 12th July, 1851, the Department of State was apprised of its mistake, and, in a dispatch of that date to Mr. Hadduck, after calling his attention to the restrictive phraseology used in his previous instructions, Mr. Webster says: "To provide, however, against the omission of any important part of the earlier portion of the correspondence, I mean that which passed in 1814 and 1815 in Rio Janeiro, where the court of Portugal at that time resided, and which it could not have been intended to exclude, I transmit you herewith " copies, &c.

The latter instructions were issued from the Department of State, at Washington, on the 12th July, 1851; but on the 9th day of the same month, three days previously, the protocol had been completed at Lisbon, signed and sealed by the respective agents of Portugal and of the United States, and forwarded to the arbiter. This is expressly stated in Mr. Hadduck's letter to the State Department, dated 17th July, 1851.

If any important part of the evidence was left out by this misadventure in preparing the documents, it must be confessed that the case was not properly prepared. The solicitor has felt the pressure of this circumstance. He could not help feeling it; for we have read from the dispatch of July 12th, 1851, an express admission by the Department of its own error. The answer now given to this objection is, that everything material in the prior correspondence was, in some form, repeated in that which was annexed to the protocol. But the fact is otherwise.

22. Government failed to present the facts to the arbitrator.

Louis Napoleon's award admits expressly, or impliedly, every proposition of law for which we contend. So far as the law is concerned, it asserts but a single position against us, to wit: that a belligerent who commences hostilities within the territory of a neutral, thereby forfeits all claim to protection; and this we have never denied. The Supreme Court of the United States has often so decided, and we have never set up any pretense to the contrary.[1] The point of the award is, that Captain Reid and his gallant companions were the first aggressors. It goes upon a mere naked question of fact. How manifestly important, then, was it that the contemporaneous correspondence, and all the testimony taken at the time and bearing on this point, should have been laid before the arbiter.

It seems that Commodore Lloyd, the commander of the British squadron, soon after the transaction, caused to be prepared and verified by Lieutenant Fausset, an affidavit giving the British view of the facts. No full copy of this affidavit was furnished to the arbiter. A portion of it is found in the letter of Mr. James B. Clay, our minister at Lisbon, to Count Tojal, Portuguese Minister of Foreign Affairs, dated November 2d, 1849. That part is mani-

---

[1] The Ann, 3 Wheaton's R. p. 435.

festly false; but great aid in developing its falsehood would almost necessarily have resulted from a review of its whole contents. Here was a serious failure on the part of our government in its obligation to properly collect and present the proofs.

Immediately after the occurrence at Fayal, the Marquis D'Aguiar, the Portuguese minister of foreign affairs, addressed a letter to Lord Strangford, the minister plenipotentiary of Great Britain, resident at the court of Rio Janeiro, in which he denounced the outrage upon the General Armstrong as an "audacious" and an "unprovoked attack." He also called upon the British government to make "satisfaction and indemnity, not only to the subjects of Portugal, but for the American privateer, whose security was guaranteed by the safeguard of a neutral port." In the same letter, the Portuguese minister "nails to the counter," as a base falsehood, the pretense of Captain Lloyd, embodied in Lieutenant Fausset's affidavit, and which Louis Napoleon has sought to consecrate as truth, thereby, as far as in him lay, falsifying American history and dishonoring the American name.

Thus speaks the Marquis D'Aguiar: "His Excellency (Lord Strangford) will likewise observe the base attempt of the British commander, at the time he commenced the unprovoked attack on the American privateer, to attribute those violent measures to the breaking of the neutrality on the part of the American in the first instance, by repelling the armed barges that were sent for the purpose of reconnoitering that vessel, advocating, with the most manifest duplicity, that they (the Americans) were consequently the aggressors; but what appears still more surprising, is the arrogance with which the British commander threatened to consider the territory of his royal highness (the prince-regent of Portugal) as enemies, should the governor adopt any measures to prevent them from taking possession of the American privateer, which they subsequently plundered and set on fire."

Some allusions to this letter were, indeed, contained in the correspondence submitted to the arbiter; but no copy of it, or of these important parts of it, was laid before him. This, the learned solicitor tells us, was an unimportant omission, because the Portuguese minister of State could only judge from the evidence; that his view of it, if erroneous, was not conclusive upon his government, and that Louis Napoleon was bound to exercise an independent judgment on the evidence itself. Admitting, for the sake of the argument, that all the facts were laid before Louis Napoleon (which was not the case), it cannot be maintained that this letter did not contain important matter for his consideration. He had assumed to decide a contested fact of considerable antiquity. The witnesses were not personally produced before him; no truth-eliciting cross-examination could be had, no oral dissection or discussion of the proofs was allowed. Was it an unimportant fact that the defendant in the cause—Portugal herself—had, through her highest authorities, solemnly, and at the very moment of the transaction, acknowledged the truth of Captain Reid's statement, and stamped as base duplicity and falsehood the story of Captain Lloyd and his lieutenant? Contemporaneous opinion is strong evidence as to ancient facts. When it is considered that this opinion came from our opponent in the cause under arbitrament, and that, at the time of pronouncing it, Portugal was not only the friend and the ally, but, it may be said, a dependent of Great Britain, its force as evidence cannot be too highly appreciated. If not technically conclusive, who will say that it was not very persuasive?

Here was another grievous failure in the duty of duly presenting the proofs in support of the claim on Portugal.

There was another, and, as we regard it, still a greater failure. It is a very fair presumption that Captain Lloyd conceived the design of seizing the Armstrong for a special purpose. To facilitate aggressions upon our coast and in our rivers, small vessels were greatly needed. The desire to supply this need has always seemed the most probable solution of Lloyd's flagitiously illegal conduct. It so happens that one document included in the Rio Janeiro correspondence, and wholly omitted in the protocol, distinctly proves this motive. Immediately after the principal or midnight combat, William Greaves, the British consul at Fayal, addressed to the Portuguese governor of the Azores a letter in which is found this statement: "The (British) commander will send a brig from his squadron to fire on the American schooner; and if the said brig should encounter any hostilities from the castle, or your Excellency should allow the masts to be taken from that schooner (the General Armstrong), he will regard this island as an enemy of his Britannic majesty, and will treat the town and castle accordingly."

Lloyd threatened to bombard the town and castle of a friend and ally of his sovereign, in case the authorities should permit the Americans to dismantle or destroy their own vessel so as to unfit her for service. Anxiety to save an enemy from suicide proves some other motive than revenge. The desire to reduce him to captivity and servitude can alone account for it.

All these important proofs having been suppressed, it cannot be said that the claimant's case was fairly tried before Louis Napoleon. According to the recorded admission of that great jurist and statesman, Daniel Webster, contained in his official letter of July 12th, 1851, it was submitted in an imperfect and improper manner.

The failure to arrange the proofs properly so called, separately from the mere arguments contained in the correspondence, seems to have misled Louis Napoleon as to the nature of the submission, or to have furnished him with a pretense for assuming a power which our government could not have intended to confer.

The whole frame of his award implies that, in respect to the facts, he did not consider himself bound by the documentary proofs annexed to the protocol, and that he assumed the power of ascertaining them *aliunde*.

For this purpose, we may fairly presume that he rambled whithersoever he pleased—into British history or into British table-talk. He recites that he proceeded to judgment "after having caused himself to be correctly and circumstantially informed in regard to the facts which have been the cause of the difference, and after having minutely examined the documents, duly signed in the names of the two parties, which have been submitted to our inspection by the representatives of both powers."

These words certainly imply that he sought proof of the facts elsewhere, and afterwards examined the protocol with its attached documents, as an additional or supplemental act. He did not obtain what he calls his correct and circumstantial information solely and exclusively by a perusal of these papers.

Thus it appears that, after having submitted the claim to an arbiter, the government failed in its first duty as *promovent*. It not only omitted to produce the evidence in its power, but expressly withheld it at the instigation of the adverse party. It also furnished the partial umpire with an excuse for assuming powers not granted to him, and not intended to be conferred upon him.

23. Claimant forbidden to argue his cause before Napoleon.

To cap the climax of injustice in the measures by which this claim was sacrificed, the claimants were refused a hearing before the arbiter, or even the liberty of presenting to him a written argument in support of their claim. This was one of those flagitious violations of justice against which every honest mind must revolt.

To reject without a hearing may be well enough, as between a despot and his bond-slave; it is not within the capacity of a judge. Precedent, authority, reason and sentiment unite in condemning it.

The Supreme Court of Pennsylvania, in Falconer & Montgomery,[1] says: "The plainest dictates of natural justice must prescribe to every tribunal the law that 'no man shall be condemned unheard.' It is not merely an abstract rule or positive right, but it is the result of wise experience, and of a wise attention to the feelings and dispositions of human nature. An artless narrative of facts, a natural and ardent course of reasoning will sometimes have a wonderful effect upon a sound and generous mind; an effect which the cold and minute details of a reporter can neither produce nor supplant. Besides, there is scarcely a piece of written evidence, or a sentence of oral testimony, that is not susceptible of some explanation or exposed to some contradiction. To exclude the party, therefore, from the opportunity of interposing in any of these modes (which the most candid and the most intelligent of disinterested persons may easily overlook), is not only a privation of his right, but an act of injustice to the umpire, whose mind might be materially influenced by such interposition."

The case of Sharp v. Bickerdike[2] arose upon an award made in Scotland. The award was not impeached for any other fault than the neglect of the arbitrator to hear the party, under a mistaken belief that he had consented to waive that right. The positive law of Scotland was, that no award should be set aside, at the instance of either party, for any cause or reason whatever, unless it was for bribery, falsehood or corruption in the arbitrator. Lord Eldon, delivering the judgment of the House of Lords, said, that by the great principle of eternal justice, which was prior to all these acts, &c., it was impossible that the award could stand. He added: "Even if he had decidedly *rightly*, he had not decidedly *justly*." In these cases, and in Elmendorf v. Harris, decided by the court of *dernier* resort, in New York,[3] the awards in question were unanimously set aside upon this principle. Following this line of precedent, the Court of Queen's Bench, in the very recent case of Oswald v. Grey,[4] annulled an award for this cause, saying: "A more glaring departure from the rules that ought to regulate the

---

[1] 4 Dallas' Reports, p. 233.
[2] 3 Dow's Parliamentary Reports, p. 102.
[3] 23 Wendell, p. 633.
[4] 23 Eng. Law & Eq. R. p. 88.

proceedings of persons sitting in the character of judges, it is impossible to conceive."

24. THE AWARD INVALID SINCE IT TURNED UPON A QUESTION NOT SUBMITTED TO THE ARBITRATOR.

Another and conclusive objection to this award appears.

As has been before observed, it goes upon a mere question of fact; that is to say, the question whether the Americans, on the occasion in question, resorted to force before they were assailed, or subjected to any indignity or peril?

It never could have been the intent of the executive or the Senate in framing the treaty with Portugal, to submit that question to arbitrament. A total insensibility to national honor would have been manifested in adopting such a course.

The correspondence between Portugal and the United States shows that the former denied its liability on legal grounds. It was affirmed, on the part of Portugal, that the duty of a State to afford protection to foreigners within its territory was not absolute; that, if such State employed the means of protection in its power, it was not responsible for the inefficacy of such means. The absurdity of this position, as applicable to the case in hand, has been already shown; but suffice it to say, in this connection, that Portugal gravely insisted on it. The treaty (Art. 2) recites, as the cause of the arbitrament, that "the high contracting parties had not been able to come to an agreement upon the question of public law involved in the case of the American privateer, General Armstrong, destroyed by British vessels in the waters of the island of Fayal, in September, 1814."

25. A SINGLE QUESTION OF LAW ALL THAT WAS INTENDED TO BE REFERRED.

This recital proves that the intent was to refer a question of law only, not to refer a question of fact. Only two questions of law can be imagined as arising in the case: first, the silly pretense of immunity from the duties of sovereignty, on the ground of weakness, set up by Portugal; and, secondly, whether, if the General Armstrong was the first assailant, she had thereby forfeited her claim to protection. The latter point, as we have shown, was well settled in the affirmative by our own courts, and was never disputed by us; consequently it is plain that but one question of law was in dispute. This question it might have been the part of wisdom to refer, for no third power could ever have decided it against us. Louis Napoleon himself was obliged to determine it in our favor.

Did the Department of State, when preparing the protocol, intend to submit the question of fact to Louis Napoleon? We have shown that the treaty gave it no authority so to do; but we ask whether, through misapprehension of his powers, temporary inadvertence, or from any other cause, Daniel Webster, in the exercise of his high functions as representative of the honor and interests of his country, did really intend to submit to the arbitrament of a third power the question of fact, whether the British or the Americans were the aggressors in the memorable combat of September, 1814, at Fayal? We cannot believe that such an intention existed. We could not admit it without abandoning forever our deep and unfeigned admiration of that illustrious jurist and statesman. Such an act would have been the extreme of folly. It involved, by an inevitable necessity, the loss of the claim and, what was far worse, a lasting reproach upon our country.

26. THE QUESTION AS TO WHO WAS THE AGGRESSOR A MATTER OF NATIONAL HONOR OR SHAME.

In that midnight conflict, a little American privateer of two hundred and forty tons burthen, carrying seven guns and ninety men, defeated the force of a whole British fleet, killing of her assailants, according to the English historians themselves, within one-sixth as many men as Britain lost in the great naval victory off Cape St. Vincent.

The strength of this comparison will be best exhibited by the facts. In that action, there were fifty ships of war engaged, and Britain's immortal Nelson captured the Santissima Trinidada of 136 guns, and three other three-deckers.

Making due allowance for the disparity of the forces engaged, looking with severely exact justice to precise facts, and judging by results, there is not a transaction in the whole history of naval warfare which reflects such signal lustre upon the gallantry of the actors as the defense of the General Armstrong. True, the heroes who perished in the fight had moldered into dust, and no monument honored their resting places. Those who survived it had nearly all passed from earth, and the very few yet alive were near the close of their earthly pilgrimage, and were pining in want and penury—were memorials of that neglect which is proverbially the recompense of public benefactors.   But the glory of their achievements was not forgotten.   It belonged to the American name; it had irradiated our naval diadem for forty years, and had become a matter of history.   Was an American Senate likely to forget its duty towards these recollections?   Was Daniel Webster the man to deliver over this bright page in our annals, to be obliterated by the dictum of an European prince?

Honor cannot attend or result from unlawful violence.   Unable to deny the physical results, Britain had sought to stigmatize the conduct of Captain Reid as an unprovoked aggression in breach of Portuguese neutrality, contrary to the law of nations, and deserving only the contempt and abhorrence of mankind.   Desperate as may seem the folly of imputing to this little cock-boat aggressiveness against a whole fleet, any resort was preferable to a confession of the facts.   Accordingly this pitifully absurd tale was placed upon the records of the British Admiralty, and thence transferred to the annals of the royal navy.   Britain had sat in judgment on the fact, in her national capacity, and sanctioned this story with her high approval.   On the other hand, the government of the United States, in all its departments, and under several successive administrations, had testified its full belief in the statement of Captain Reid.   From these sources, the literature of the respective nations had taken opposing opinions.   The respective historians of Britain and of the United States stood before the world in direct conflict as to the fact, and were, of course, to descend to future times as rival claimants of credibility on this question.   Its solution involved no matter of mere pecuniary interest, territorial aggrandizement or other worldly profit of any kind; it was a question of national honor or shame.

Did any nation ever submit such a question to the arbitrament of an umpire?   To admit it to be a question for trial was to embrace infamy?   As well might a high-toned gentleman charged with some scandalous act by a known and avowed enemy, refer the slander to a mutual friend, with authority to decide, upon proofs, whether or not he was a scoundrel.   Honor decides such questions for itself, reposes on its own known rectitude for a protection, or vindicates itself by more active means.   It never reposes in a trustee, an agent, or an umpire, the power of consigning it to infamy.

27. THERE WAS NO QUESTION OF FACT BEFORE NAPOLEON.

One of our reasons for denying that Mr. Webster could ever have intended to refer to Louis Napoleon the question of fact whether the Armstrong was the aggressor, is that the result must necessarily have been against his country and his fellow-citizens.

It is a principle of universal law, that the affirmative must be proven by a preponderance of evidence. Equal colliding forces produce a state of rest, as equal weights in the scales produce an equipoise. It follows that whenever the opposing proofs as to a disputed fact are equal, the party who asserts the fact must fail. This, however true in theory, is rarely, if ever, applied in practice. Some circumstance affecting the credit of a witness or of a document produced on the one side or the other, almost always turns the scale; and the verdict or decision goes, accordingly, upon the theory of full credence being given to one side and denied to the other. Thus a judicial forum decides between parties, and resolves the doubtful point upon a nice scrutiny of the proofs, responding according to its view of the right, notwithstanding that its decree may possibly wound the honor of one party and his witnesses, by impliedly imputing to them intentional misrepresentation.

Now it so happens, as any one can in a moment see, that if the question of fact as to who was the first aggressor was to be submitted in this case, the United States would hold the affirmative, and the witnesses would be in direct conflict. Consequently a judgment could not be formed in our favor without thus implicating the witnesses of our adversary; whilst, on the other hand, the arbiter could decide against us upon the mere philosophical principle that, a perfect balance being produced, it did not become him, as a friend and ally of each, to disbelieve either.

The treaty provided that the submission should be made " to a sovereign potentate or chief of some nation in amity with both the high contracting parties." It was well known that the true party for whom Portugal appeared in the case was Great Britain. Whatever Portugal might be compelled to pay to us, Great Britain would, of course, be held to reimburse. But, besides all this—and hence this bitter, long-continued, unyielding opposition to this claim by Portugal, her ally—the honor of Great Britain was deeply involved in the issue. Great Britain, for a wonder, was then " in amity " with the whole civilized world. She was on terms of the closest amity with both the chrysalis royalty of France and with Oscar of

Sweden, the only potentates contemplated by the protocol of submission.   The witnesses on our side were private citizens.   They
had not even an official recognition to connect them with our government, in the technical consideration of an European sovereign,
so that discrediting them might be deemed a direct offense to the
nation.   On the other hand, the opposing witnesses were public
officers, servants and agents of Great Britain.   Without taking into
view, as additional reasons, or make-weights, toward the same conclusion, the intimate relations for mutual support and protection
which exist between the sovereigns of Europe, is it not manifest to
the most simple-minded observer, that no one of them, consistently
with a prudent regard for his own high interests, could ever assume the office of arbiter upon a matter of fact between two independent sovereign powers, and pronounce a decree stigmatizing the
public agents of either as perjured?

28. Circumstances under which the Armstrong fired the first gun.

It was never denied that Captain Reid fired the first gun.
Prima facie, then, he was the aggressor.   To justify this and fix
upon the British forces the inception of hostilities, it was necessary
to prove affirmatively the menacing approach of an armed enemy.
This was an affirmative of the class which it is most difficult to
establish by proof.   Captain Reid and his men could do no more
than swear to it, as they did, and by way of confirmation affirm
the distinct fact that the fire was returned from the British boats.
But the defeated commandant of the assailing force could easily
deny this, and he had denied it.   Nor was this a case in which,
from the nature of the thing, affirmative testimony has a superiority
over negative.   There was no room for mistake or oversight on the
British side.   Lieutenant Fausset knew whether his men were
armed or not; and he swore they had no arms.   Of course, if they
had no arms, they could not have returned the American fire.   In
addition to the rule that the affirmative must be proved by a preponderance of testimony, there was a principle in close affinity to
it, which any one could see led inevitably to our defeat in the
umpirage.   As to the hostile intent of the approaching British
flotilla, Captain Reid could only act upon circumstances affording
a presumption of such intent.

Had he abstained from firing any longer than he did, it is probable that his deck would have been covered with an overwhelming

15

armed force before a blow was struck. Perhaps no wound would ever have been given on either side. Perhaps every privateersman would have been suddenly seized and pinioned by superior numbers, and the gallant little Armstrong, instead of perishing gloriously amid her vanquished enemies, might have been employed to carry rapine and desolation to our defenseless homes and firesides. As it was always admitted that in the first combat Captain Reid repelled the assailing force whilst it yet held no more commanding position than that of a menace, proof of an aggressive intent by those in the British boats was indispensable to our success; and the proof on that head could only be circumstantial. On the other hand, Lieutenant Fausset could swear positively that no such intention existed. He could say Captain Reid was mistaken, and thus, in the most polite style imaginable, entitle his side to the imperial award.

How hopelessly desperate, then, was the case—treated as a question of fact—considering who was the arbiter and the consequences to result from the decision.

In this connection, we do not question the equal fitness of Louis Napoleon as an arbiter with any other European potentate. It was not to be expected that any sovereign of Europe would convict the British officers of perjury. He could not otherwise conform to the known policy of his class than by finding, as he did, that the fact was not proved. Consequently it would have been a gross error to submit a fact of this kind to the determination of such an arbiter. He could not afford to act judicially, to scrutinize the evidence fairly, or to determine the fact justly. It would have been not only a grievous error in national policy, but a palpable failure in duty to the country, and to the claimants. No American who regards the honor of his country will ever admit that the Senate of the United States intended to submit to any earthly arbitrament the question of national honor which Louis Napoleon has assumed to decide. No friend or honest admirer of Daniel Webster will ever admit that he could have so far mistaken the import of the treaty as to suppose that he had power to submit it, or that he could have been so blind to the dictates of reason and common sense, or so ignorant of the motives of State policy which govern European potentates, as not to have seen that such submission was equivalent to what lawyers call a *retraxit*. He never could have intended thus to sacrifice at a blow the private interests committed to his charge, and the national honor he so deeply cherished.

29. NAPOLEON'S AWARD SHOULD HAVE BEEN REJECTED AS VOID
FOR WANT OF JURISDICTION.

If we are right in this, it will be seen that Louis Napoleon's assumed jurisdiction over the facts was an usurpation of power not granted. Upon this ground alone his award was wholly void in every legal and moral sense, and should have been rejected by our government immediately after its publication.

The tendency to usurpation was pretty strong in the mind of the arbiter at the time, as may be perceived by reference to contemporaneous events. But in reference to this case, he not only assumed powers not granted, but undertook to overrule and negative the very facts agreed upon by the high contracting parties, and which, of course, he was expressly forbidden to adjudge.

In the second article of the treaty, it is stated in so many words, that the General Armstrong was "destroyed by British vessels in the waters of the island of Fayal." (Article 2.) Yet, the award, in reciting this part of the submission, studiously omits the words "by British vessels," and, in its finding upon the facts, it states that the act of destruction was by Captain Reid in consequence of the hostile demonstration made. Even if it was within his judicial province to set aside a fact agreed by the parties, he could not justify this finding. The proofs are clear that Captain Reid merely fired a shot through the vessel's bottom, in order to sink her in the harbor, thus placing her for the time beyond the enemy's reach, and reserving the chance of raising her at a future period. But the British, being thus baulked in their original design, set fire to her, and thereby effected her complete destruction.

30. WHEN THE AWARD WAS ACCEPTED, THE LIABILITY OF POR-
TUGAL WAS EXTINGUISHED, AND THE LIABILITY
OF OUR GOVERNMENT AROSE.

Thus it will be seen that, independently of the deeper moral objection to it, Louis Napoleon's award was not entitled to any respect whatever, and was wholly void, because he based it upon a question of fact not submitted to him. It may be well, therefore, to state here the legal grounds on which we insist that its acceptance wrought an extinguishment of our claim against Portugal, and gave rise to a claim in its place against the treasury of the United States. We had, originally, a just claim for indemnity upon Portugal, which, under the circumstances, it was the imperative duty of our government to enforce, and which, as against us, the government had no right to surrender or annul.　The power of prosecuting that claim was vested in the government alone, and consequently the award of Louis Napoleon thereon—whether just and lawful or not—on being accepted by the department to which is intrusted our foreign affairs, worked a complete extinguishment of the claim as against Portugal.[1]　That acceptance deprived us of all recourse except upon the public treasury.　We claim that the award of Louis Napoleon was partial and unjust; we have shown that it was void for want of jurisdiction, because not warranted by the submission, and that it was void as against us, because important evidence was withheld from him, and because the right to be heard in support of our claim before himself or his council was denied to us.

31. Ground of the liability of the government.

The withholding of evidence, the denial of a hearing, and the unwarrantable acceptance of the award, are relied upon as involving a liability of the government, because they are not acts of a subordinate official who might be personally responsible at law to the citizen for the injury produced by his malversation, but are acts of State, performed by the supreme executive in the exercise of a high discretionary authority which no court could control or correct, at the suit of an individual.　Hence the liability of the nation.

An opinion of Mr. Attorney-General Cushing has been cited, showing that the government is not responsible for the acts of marshals, collectors, pilots, and other subordinate officers who are appointed to facilitate the business operations of the citizens.　We acquiesce unhesitatingly in this opinion.　But it has no application to the President, the heads of departments, or other high public functionaries who are themselves the government.　These officers are intrusted with the power of representing the nation and acting for it.　They cannot be arraigned in a court of law, or elsewhere made responsible to the private citizen who may be injured by acts of State, performed through their agency.　For these the nation itself must answer, in its collective and sovereign capacity.　Indeed, the departments constantly recognize this rule.　Collectors of the customs are in the daily habit of seizing goods and performing

[1] See Secretary Marcy's Letter, dated Dec. 10th, 1854.

other acts of direct interference with the property of individuals, in conformity with instructions from the treasury founded upon a construction of the law which is subsequently condemned by the courts as erroneous; and, as a necessary result, they are frequently made liable for damages and expenses.   On all such occasions, it is the established practice to indemnify the subordinate out of the public treasury.   Though selected with especial reference to their fitness for high station, the heads of departments are mortal, and must sometimes err through haste, inadvertence or misconception. When such errors occur, there being no other remedy, it is altogether just that the government should make the reparation. Though the act directed to be done is unlawful, though the direction itself is, of course, a violation of law, still it is impossible to conduct public affairs, at all times, with absolute accuracy, and there must be somewhere a discretionary power to act for the public upon emergencies and in doubtful cases.   When that discretion is rightly exercised, the nation takes the benefit; when erroneously exercised, it should sustain the resulting loss.

These same principles apply here.   Our claim is against the public treasury, because the injury complained of resulted from acts of the government itself, performed through its highest functionaries, in the exercise of an irresponsible discretion.   The maxim *respondeat superior*, is eminently applicable to such cases.   For acts of State, the State itself must answer.   The government of the United States did not protest against the award of Louis Napoleon, but, on the contrary, expressly declared its acquiescence through the department of State, and thus released Portugal from all further responsibility.   Had the award been rejected, we should now stand in the same attitude which we had occupied for forty years.   We would still hold a valid and subsisting claim against Portugal, neither abandoned nor released by our government, and still in due course of prosecution by the proper authority.   Although, in such a condition of things, we might well murmur at the delay, perhaps mere delay, even amounting to neglect, would not entitle us to maintain here or elsewhere a pecuniary demand against the United States.

The right to reject the award of a mutual friend has been exercised by our government, and is fully recognized in the law of nations.   Vattel says, that where there is flagrant partiality, or where the arbitrator exceeds his power by determining a matter not submitted to him, it will not bind.   "If, by a sentence manifestly unjust, and contrary to reason, the arbitrator has stripped himself of his quality, his judgment deserves no attention."—Book 11, ch. 18, § 239.—In the same section, that writer illustrates his views by very apposite instances. He says: "In case of a vague and unlimited submission, in which the parties have neither precisely determined what constitutes the subject of the quarrel, nor marked out the limits of their opposite pretensions, it may often happen that the arbitrator may exceed his power and pass judgment on what has not really been submitted for his decision." In this case the submission was framed without the requisite precision as to the point submitted, or Louis Napoleon, without that apology, transcended the authority granted. In either case, the award should have been rejected.

32. Review of the evidence as to who was the aggressor.

We will now consider the evidence with a view to the question whether Captain Reid was the aggressor.

Here Mr. O'Conor read from James' Naval History of Great Britain, vol. 6, p. 349, which may be regarded as the British version, and the conflicting authority from Ingersoll's History of the Second War, vol. 1, pp. 44, 45. He referred to the affidavits of Lieut. Faussett and Captain Reid, which were also conflicting, the former averring that the men in the boat first fired upon by the privateer had no arms, the latter alleging that they were armed, and when warned refused to keep off. He then showed that Reid's statements were correct, and were corroborated by the facts and circumstances, and that the English version was inconsistent throughout. He then continued:

The primary fact in dispute was this: Did Faussett approach the Armstrong peacefully and unarmed, in a single small boat, to ask a question, or did he approach, with several large boats, thereby displaying and employing such a force as to justify apprehensions of a hostile attack? Louis Napoleon concedes it to be "clear," that this first approach to the General Armstrong was by "some English long-boats, commanded by Lieutenant Robert Faussett of the British navy." Disbelieving him as to the main and primary fact, what honest court, sitting to determine this case between man and man, could have found, upon his evidence, that his crews were not armed, in opposition to the unimpeached oath of Captain Reid and his officers, confirmed by the voice of all indifferent spectators? The whole story is a palpable falsehood. The case is eminently one for the application of the rule *falsus in uno falsus in omnibus.* Any impartial and competent arbitrator would have applied it.

Nothing but Louis Napoleon's total incapacity to sit in judgment on the case, in consequence of his political relations with Great Britain—the party most deeply implicated in the transaction—can account for the award.

Upon reason and authority, the claim against Portugal appears to have been well founded in fact and valid in law. We had, by the law of nations and the principles of justice, an absolute right to full indemnity from that country. That right has been sacrificed, and the remaining question is this: Are we remediless?

33. THE ARBITRATION NEVER RATIFIED BY THE CLAIMANTS.

Whilst we deny the authority or force of this award, and question the whole course of the government in respect to the reference, we wish to be understood as standing not in the least behind the learned solicitor in our admiration for the character of Daniel Webster. That great man had been just called into the State department, upon the sudden and wholly unexpected advent of a new administration. General Taylor's warlike spirit, as it was supposed, had brought the country to the verge of a war with Portugal. The civilian who succeeded him preferred peace, and, of course, his judgment controlled. Acting in harmony with the policy of the new executive, and perhaps without having given to the subject that careful examination which it required, Mr. Webster assented to the reference for the sake of peace. In this way, the rights of the claimants were sacrificed for what was deemed the public weal.

But it is contended that the United States, in prosecuting these claims against foreign powers, acts only as agent for the individuals aggrieved, and that, as principals, we have ratified the act of submission to Louis Napoleon.

We have already denied, *in toto*, the applicability of this doctrine. There can be no implied ratification, because the case is not one of principal and agent. The nation has the whole power; it is the principal, not the agent. In defending the rights of the citizen, it is no more an agent than a father is in avenging an insult offered to his child. It acts in vindication of its own honor and sovereignty. But we need not have denied the doctrine, for there is no evidence of ratification.

On the first rumor that an arbitrament was in contemplation,

Mr. Sam. C. Reid, Junior, the counsel for the claimants, addressed to the Secretary of State a letter inquiring of its truth, and praying to be heard on the subject before any such action should be had. The gallant old sailor himself, who had never known fear of personal danger, shrank with a wisely instinctive horror from the bare thought of submitting his own and his country's honor to the arbitrament of an European despot. The keenness with which he felt upon this subject is but thinly veiled by the modest courtesy of his respectful remonstrance. Let it be read; it deserves a place in the annals of his country. Let the personal characteristics of the hero, as exhibited in peaceful action, adorn the same page which bears to future times his illustrious deeds. They will alike challenge admiration and reflect honor upon all who may be so happy as to imitate.

"New York, August 26, 1850.
"Hon. Daniel Webster:

"*Sir*,—By the recent daily journals, rumors are rife that the claims of the General Armstrong are about to be referred to some power for arbitration. This mode at best being considered somewhat problematical, we, the claimants, would respectfully suggest, whether or not a settlement by treaty or convention may not in your opinion be preferable, as being most likely to enable us to obtain our demands without the risk of a failure?

" Feeling, as we do, that we are in very safe and very able hands, we have no great fears for the future, if we be allowed to compare what you have already done for us with what is to be expected on future occasions.

"After so much negotiation, controversy, and anxiety, for a long series of years, we now look to you, sir, with every confidence for a final and favorable termination of this affair. And should you be pleased to honor us with your views, we shall esteem ourselves under additional obligations.

"With great respect, &c.,
"S. C. Reid,
"Late Commander of the G. A.,
"In behalf of the claimants."

Before either of these letters reached the department of State, the negotiations had been brought to a close, and consequently our government could not recede. This had been done without notice to the claimants, without either knowledge or assent on their part, and it was contrary to their wishes.

As it was too late to prevent the arbitrament, the claimants did all that remained in their power. They solicited permission, first, that young Mr. Reid, their counsel, might proceed to France with competent authority to obtain a due advocacy of the case. This was not granted. They next had prepared a written argument, and prayed that it might be laid before the arbiter. This request was also denied. It seems to have been understood that it was beneath the dignity of a monarch to hear the party. As an act of State, this refusal may have been according to established forms, but, if it was, how manifest becomes our position that the case never should have been referred. Royal grants usually run *ex certa scientia et mero motu.* This royal arbitrament seems to have been in like manner understood by all parties, except the unsubmitting claimants, as an appeal to absolute, irresponsible monarchical volition!

These rejected solicitations for common justice, and these disregarded remonstrances constitute the whole evidence relied upon to prove a ratification. If they have that effect, we ask, in the name of conscience and reason, what could the claimants have done in the premises which would not have been a ratification? Was it necessary to levy war against the government? Was it necessary to appear at the State department and rail at the secretary like a common scold? Ought we to have hired penny-a-liners and filled the journals of the day with invective? Surely none of these things will be pretended. We objected to the policy pursued. When overruled, and no other resource was left to us, we resolved, in humble submission to the omnipotence of the State department, to make the most of a bad position and to devote every means in our power to the attainment of success.

It may be presumed that our objections to the submission are not relied upon as acts of ratification. Perhaps that point is mainly founded on our prayer to be heard before Louis Napoleon. What else could we have done at that stage of the affair? Silence would have been deemed assent. Any omission on our part to do and suggest whatever was in our power and which could possibly conduce to success, would have been disrespectful toward our government, and might justly have been condemned. Desperate as the case may have seemed to us, it did not appear so to the government, and surely we were right in straining every nerve to secure success. The spirit which animated our gallant tars in the midnight combat at Fayal secured neither safety nor entire success; but it inflicted upon the enemy an irreparable wound. It reflected lustre upon our country. The same wise, gallant, persevering and indomitable spirit presided over this last effort to sustain a righteous cause sinking under the combined influence of artifice in the enemy, partiality in the judge and oversight in the prosecutors. It did not succeed; but this court will not permit it to prejudice the man who made it. On the contrary, it was on his part a performance of duty. Instead of justifying his condemnation to perpetual silence as a willing participator in this unwise submission, it is precisely the act which secures him still a standing in court as a claimant, and entitles him this day to ask a judicial sentence against the unjust arbiter. *Judex damnatur cum nocens absolvitur.*

There is something most irrational in the pretense that this prayer for leave to be heard, although rejected, was a ratification by us of all that had been done. A gladiator cast naked and weaponless into the arena, would instinctively call for a sword as the lion approached him. According to our learned adversary's notions of justice, this last prayer of the predestined victim, although cruelly denied, would be an approval of his sentence to the unequal conflict. We dismiss, without further comment, this idlest of all idle pretenses.

34. CAPTAIN REID BOUND IN LAW AND HONOR TO PURSUE THE COURSE HE DID.

It has been urged that Captain Reid ought to have surrendered; that he would have suffered no dishonor in yielding without a blow. Suppose it to be so, was there neither merit nor honor in the opposite course? But we cannot agree with the learned solicitor in this. An act of Congress passed at the commencement of the war, directed the President to prepare instructions and to cause a copy to be delivered to the captain of every private armed cruiser.[1] Our copy was lost in the Armstrong. Knowing that a line of conduct very different from tame and unresisting submission was commanded, we have sought for the original among the archives of the department, but without success. The same remorseless enemy who destroyed the copy at Fayal, at about the same moment destroyed the original record at this capitol. We cannot, therefore, produce it, but we submit that this court should infer the fact. The instructions undoubtedly were to use the utmost exertions to defeat the military and naval forces of the enemy, whenever and wherever encountered. The ninth section of the same act gave

---

[1] 2 Statutes at Large, p. 761, § 8.

a bounty to each person on board when any privateer burned, sunk or destroyed an armed vessel of the enemy of equal force.

Pensions are also allowed by the acts of Congress to every officer, seaman and marine belonging to a privateer, disabled in any engagement with the armed vessels of the enemy.[1]

This point ought not to have been urged by the counsel for the government.   Indeed the fact that it is here urged with a hope of success, considering the ground of the arbiter's decision against us, gives great and, we conceive, conclusive force to a distinct equity entitling us to compensation from the public treasury.

The facts and circumstances in proof show clearly that Captain Lloyd's object was to possess himself of the General Armstrong, for the purpose of employing her against the unprotected villages and hamlets upon our sea-board.

We have shown that the first approach was by many boats, and that the men in them must have been armed.   Louis Napoleon admits the former fact; indubitable results make manifest the latter. The letter of Consul Graves proves Lloyd's desire to capture the vessel in an uninjured state, and the first approach, as proved by Faussett himself, shows a design to carry her by surprise.   His pinnace, as he calls it, when fired into, was immediately alongside of the Armstrong, so near that he employed a boat-hook to direct her motions.

These circumstances are, we say, entirely satisfactory proof of the design imputed.

How great, then, was the merit of Captain Reid; how deep were our obligations to him and his gallant companions for having defeated it.

35. THE CLAIM FOUNDED ON PRINCIPLES OF JUSTICE AND EQUITY.

Independently of the right to reimbursement from Portugal, they have a direct claim upon the equity and justice of their country.

When the boats first approached, symptoms of this design, in the judgment of Captain Reid, were manifest.   If Captain Reid had preserved a pusillanimous or selfishly pacific demeanor, submitted to capture and allowed his vessel to become a weapon of offense

[1] 2 Statutes at Large, p. 799, § 2.

against his country, the validity of his claim against Portugal never could have been effectually questioned. But he acted on appearances, defeated the design, crippled a whole British fleet, and conducted his operations in a manner at once so judicious and so gallant that, whilst considering the forces employed, they excel in martial glory and fearful consequences to the enemy, any event of the whole war; every spectator, including even the Portuguese allies of our enemy—many of whom were injured in person and property during the conflict—justified them as acts of imperiously necessary self-defense, warranted by the great principles of natural and international law, notwithstanding that they were conducted within a neutral territory. His motive could only have been to defeat this pernicious design, his acts could not have been dictated by rashness and temerity, or by any selfish purpose. All the circumstances repel the imputation of rashness; selfishness would have counselled submission to the enemy. He acted on a belief which we can now see was amply justified; he defeated the hostile intent: no mortal can set limits to the benefits which may probably have resulted to these United States from that defeat.

Yet the very nature of the case rendered proof that that intent actually existed extremely difficult. Counter-evidence must of course be very accessible to the unprincipled assailant. The intent itself was fraudulent and dishonorable. Those engaged in it could not be very conscientious. Falsehood, deception and prevarication are the invariable allies of fraud. In submitting himself to the government of his well-founded opinion on this point, Captain Reid performed an act of disinterested devotion to the defense of his country. It was a departure from what the solicitor now calls "the private business speculation in which he was engaged." It was a voluntary act of national defense. By entering upon it, he threw away his certain claim of reimbursement from the Portuguese government, for it exposed him to that very judicial condemnation by which the claim has been sacrificed. Upon any proofs which could ever be produced it might be to a partial arbitrator, nay, to any tribunal, quite "uncertain" that the hostile and aggressive intent which he anticipated and repelled, had any existence except in his own imagination.

In thus judging and acting, Captain Reid performed a great public benefit. He carried on war against the enemy at his own expense; and it was only necessary to satisfy the constituted authorities of his country that the act was a proper one to be ratified and adopted, in order to give him a perfect claim in equity for reimbursement of the cost from the public treasury.

A government at war always contemplates carrying on hostilities at the public cost by the employment of force against the enemy at such points as may seem most likely to prove effectual. And, although it is true that no citizen is authorized to assume the direction of war measures, yet whenever a private individual, with no motive but the public good, voluntarily avails himself of a favorable opportunity, and bears the brunt of a contest which government would gladly have assumed, could it have foreseen the occasion, we conceive that there arises in his favor an equitable claim to reimbursement.

The principles of enlarged equity and good conscience illustrated by the voluntary service in rescuing the stack of wheat from impending peril mentioned in 20th Johnson's Reports, apply to such cases, and require the government to indemnify the patriotic actors.[1]

36. PRIVATE PROPERTY CANNOT BE TAKEN FOR PUBLIC USE WITHOUT JUST COMPENSATION.

There is still another distinct head under which our claim should be allowed.

It is asserted by the learned solicitor, and cannot be denied, that the government has entire and absolute control over such claims as that which existed in this case against Portugal, and is alone competent to prosecute them. Of course, we admit this proposition. But whilst we concede the power, we deny that the government has the right deliberately and intentionally to work an inevitable shipwreck, or an express extinction of the private citizens' claim, for its own ease in the administration of public affairs, to secure the favor or appease the resentment of a foreign power, or to attain any object or purpose beneficial only to the public at large, except upon full compensation to the person whose right is thus devoted to the use of the nation. This denial is sustained by the eternal principles of justice. And these principles, so far as they touch this question, do not rest merely upon the authority of reason or even of precedent. They are consecrated as

---

[1] The point of law here contended for was affirmed by the Commissioners of Claims under the late convention with Great Britain, *in re* The Hudson's Bay Company; President's Message of Aug. 11, 1856, p. 165. See also opinion of Denio, Ch. J., 3 Kernan's N. Y. Reports, p. 149.

law by the fifth amendment to the Constitution. It provides that "private property shall not be taken for public use without just compensation." No one will pretend that a right to reimbursement for an injury is not property, or that the extinguishment of all remedy for the enforcement of such a right, is not taking away the right from him who possessed it.

This fundamental rule has been violated by the government of the United States, in respect to the claim now before your honors; and we insist that, whenever the heel of power tramples in this way upon the interests of a private citizen, a reference of his claim to this court vests it with the means, and charges upon it the duty of vindicating the right and exacting justice from the conscience of the republic.

37. GENERAL OBSERVATIONS AS TO THE DUTY OF THE GOVERNMENT.

Some further general observations relative to the powers and duty of government in prosecuting against foreign powers claims for redress of grievances suffered by its citizens may here be proper.

Though its action is representative, and bears a certain analogy to that of an agent, yet, unlike any other agency, its power over the subject is supreme. Whatever the government could do in its legislative capacity, it could properly have done in reference to this claim. Undoubtedly, in pursuing demands against foreign States, the government must be the sole judge of the measures to be adopted. It is the judge whether war shall be made, and how long the negotiations shall be permitted to progress before resort shall be had to extreme measures. The interests of particular individuals are not to be preferred to the interests of the whole; nor are the horrors of war to be rashly invoked. It is also the sole and the competent judge whether the claim actually exists. It has the right to take adequate measures for investigating the facts, and ascertaining not only the existence of the claim, but whether it is of such a nature as to be properly enforceable by governmental agency. This may be done in any tribunal, or by any officer or instrumentality the government may think fit to select. This is manifestly so, because in the nature of things the government cannot otherwise act intelligently. As a consequence, we must concede that when the official inquiry thus instituted results adversely to the claim, the suitor is obliged to submit. Even though his claim be just, he must relinquish its prosecution. In such a case he is in no worse plight than the owner of any other righteous demand, who, from want of evidence or other accident, has failed to persuade a court and jury of its justice or legality.

Even when a claim has been found upon due examination to be just, we concede that the suitor must submit to such delay in the prosecution of it as the exigencies of public affairs may occasion; nor is there any greater right to complain of delays than belong to suitors in our ordinary courts of justice. Much time is often required to carry their cases through, and consequently mere delay cannot be considered a neglect of duty.

Questions of more difficulty may arise in respect to the powers of government to compromise a claim which it has pronounced to be just. For instance, whether in consideration of some special circumstances government would be authorized, in a class of cases, to accept as in full a portion of the sum due? Perhaps there are grounds which might justify the exercise of such a discretion. We do not mean to deny or dispute it, because the inquiry is altogether irrelevant to this case.

It has been contended that, when prosecuting claims against a foreign State, government has a right to discriminate between those equally meritorious, to prosecute some and abandon others. Perhaps this may be so. But there is an universally received notion of justice which forbids such a course. The learned solicitor may, if he pleases, pronounce it a vulgar prejudice; certainly its condemnation is usually expressed in a somewhat vulgar form of speech. It is called "making fish of one, and flesh of another." Even in matters of gift or courtesy it is disapproved. Equality is approved by the universal sense of mankind—in the distribution of alms, the bestowal of complimentary gifts, and the tender of courtesy, as well as in the administration of justice. When a parent's testament discriminates between his children, it often leaves a "plague-spot" upon the testator's memory, and lights the baleful fires of hatred amongst his posterity. How far a simple discrimination between claims of precisely equal merit might be competent, need not be determined. No such case is before the court. This claim was never thus simply discriminated against and abandoned. We will consider hereafter what may be the just result of that which did take place, that is to say, an abandonment of it by the government for a valuable consideration received by the public.

The right of the government as prosecutor of claims for the

spoliation of its citizens, to discriminate, to a certain extent, between classes of claims, might safely be conceded, and perhaps
could not be denied. For instance, in negotiating with a foreign
State, all claims existing prior to a certain date, or to some public
event, might perhaps be deferred; all claims constituting a class,
and, as such, falling within certain principles apparently detracting
from their merit, might perhaps be relinquished. This line of
action would not always involve a manifest violation of the rule
that government should afford equal protection, and extend equal
benefits to all beneath its sway. In imposing taxes and other
burdens, the legislative power often selects certain classes. Particular trades or occupations hitherto lawful may, by an exercise of
legislative discretion, be adjudged to be prejudicial to the public
interest, and henceforth prohibited or restrained within new and
more confined limits. The legislative power decrees that only
males between certain ages shall be sent to bare their bosoms to the
enemy and ward off his assaults, thus exempting all others from
military duty. Inequalities in administration like these which go
upon some reason, wisely or not, assumed to be just, have not the
impress of unfairness and favoritism. We need not in this case
deny their lawfulness. But whilst we concede to the government,
in its legislative action and in its executive administration, this
right of discriminating between large classes of cases or persons,
in the imposition of burdens and the granting or withholding of
privileges, we deny its right to single out for sacrifice a single individual or one particular claim. Such an act is repugnant to the
general sense of mankind; and, if it be designed for the public interest, is forbidden by the Constitution, unless upon full compensation made from the public treasury.

38. The claim against Portugal sacrificed for public ends.

In the first place, the government investigated the merits of this
claim, and determined that it was valid. It was in the power of the
government, on obtaining new lights, to have revoked this decision;
but it never has done so. It never can do so ; the facts forbid.
As *parens patriæ*, it assumed the duty of enforcing against Portugal
this claim, together with several others of equal, but not of greater
validity. Negotiations were commenced accordingly, and after
many years they reached a conclusion. The ultimatum of Portugal
was, that, although she denied the justice of all the claims, yet,

for the sake of peace, she would recede from her opposition to all the others, and would pay them in full, provided our government would refer this one to arbitration. Whether she could be driven from this position by anything less than actual compulsion, was to some extent tested by General Taylor's administration. The United States could not separate the several parts of the offer; they were obliged to accept it or reject it *in toto*.[1] Mr. Clay, our minister, by authority of his government, rejected it, demanded his passports, and sailed from the Tagus.

At this critical moment in the history of our claim, the heroic head of our government was summoned from mortal to immortal life. His more cool successor, armed with a higher degree of prudence, shrunk from the responsibilities of a war with that nation which had been pleading her own weakness and incapacity for half a century. He at once relinquished the high ground taken by his predecessor, and accepted the offer of Portugal.

The treaty thereupon made, singled out the case of the General Armstrong for umpirage, and the other claims were paid accordingly.

We do not deny that our government might fairly have submitted any mere question of law involved in the case even to a third power, since, on that part of the case, error seems to have been impossible. Perhaps we could not complain of an investigation of the facts by a jury or by any responsible and impartial individual. But inasmuch as, from the outset, it was plainly manifest to the commonest understanding, that a reference of the claim, as a question of fact, or as a mixed question of law and fact, to any potentate of Europe, necessarily involved its rejection, we insist that this treaty, taken in connection with the subsequent unwarrantable acquiescence of our government in Louis Napoleon's award, was a sacrifice of the claim for the sake of accomplishing ends deemed to be important to the public, that is to say, the recovery of other claims and the restoration of amity with Portugal. If we are mistaken in the views which have been expressed to the contrary, and the treaty did, indeed, contemplate a submission of the facts, our point is only made the more brief and direct. Then the treaty itself was a substantial surrender of our claim. All that followed was "leather or prunella," the mere ceremonial of the release. Louis Napoleon was the scrivener, chosen by the high

[1] 2 Sandford's Chancery Reports, p. 244.

16

contracting parties, to select the phrase and apply the forms required for a solemn authentication of their preconceived design.
We do not mean that, in a common and vulgar sense, our government designed this relinquishment; but it is sound law and conformable to reason, that parties are always held to intend the necessary result of their acts. Portugal saw that arbitration and
release were practical synonyms; the claimants saw it and remonstrated against the measure; our government ought to have seen it,
was bound to have seen it, and must, therefore, be adjudged to
have seen it.

Thus we establish our point that this claim being private property, was devoted to destruction for purposes of State, which fact,
by the Constitution and by the elementary principles of general
justice, entitles the owners to compensation from the public
treasury.

39. OBSERVATIONS AS TO THE ANTIQUITY OF THE CLAIM AND ITS ALLEGED REJECTION.

The great antiquity of this claim has been urged against it.
That is certainly not the fault of the claimants. They presented
it in their protest on the very day the General Armstrong was destroyed; they have patiently but respectfully pressed it by every
means in their power from that day to the present. If it has been
neglected by the government, which alone had the means of enforcing it, that fact, so far from being an objection to the claim as
now presented to this court, is the very basis on which it rests.

Here Mr. O'Conor showed that the claim never had been rejected, as was
claimed by the government. He referred to the report of the Senate Committee
in 1817, when it was declared " that indemnity from Portugal ought to be insisted on as an affair of State." Next he showed that it was again referred to
the State Department in 1846. He then referred to the action of Congress after
the decision of Louis Napoleon, when a bill providing that the matter be referred to the court, having passed the house, was tabled in the Senate by one
vote. He then continued :

The claim was once allowed by a strong vote, and the utmost
that can be alleged against it is, that it was once indefinitely postponed by a majority consisting of one single vote. It is true, the
claimants have been delayed and postponed; they have been turned
over to Portugal for redress, and sent muzzled and fettered to the
footstool of Louis Napoleon for justice; but their merit has never
been denied. Every congressional report upon the subject, and

they amount to four in number, covering a period of nearly forty years, is in their favor.

40. PERSONAL MOTIVES OF CAPTAIN REID.—A COMPARISON WITH WASHINGTON.

Captain Reid has been reproached with sordid motives in mingling with the glorious history of his achievement the acceptance of a pecuniary recompense. Is it dishonorable in the war-worn veteran to accept from the overflowing treasury of his happy and prosperous country the means of subsistence in his old age, and of decent sepulture when his hour of parting shall arrive? Surely not. The learned solicitor accompanied his lecture on this head with a reference to the example of him whose deeds and memory are deemed the best illustrations of all that is heroic in patriotism, and exalted in honor and moral rectitude. Though Captain Reid presumes not to challenge a comparison, we must say that this allusion of the learned solicitor was most unfortunate. Though there be no comparison, neither is there in this particular any contrast. Though Washington never descended to the grade of a hireling, and persisted to the last in refusing compensation, though he did not even accept reimbursement of his personal expenses from our impoverished treasury during the conflict; yet it is one of the recorded proofs of his practical wisdom, of his freedom from mere sentimentality, and of his precision and exactitude in the details of duty, that, when his country had achieved her independence and was able and willing to do justice, he rendered, in his own handwriting, a minute statement of his expenses in the public service, and received from Congress a full pecuniary indemnity. This parallel, which, but for the learned solicitor's introduction of it, we would not have ventured to exhibit, refutes another of his arguments. He says that all claims allowed by government ought to be founded in some prescribed rule of law. Washington declined that very payment for his time and services which the law allowed, and accepted the indemnity which no known law directly sanctioned, but which, being due on principles of natural justice, was conceded by the enlightened equity of Congress and the gratitude of his country.

Captain Reid asks no gratuity; he asks neither pay nor reward for his personal toil, sufferings or achievements. Simple indemnity for the actual pecuniary losses of himself and his brave companions is all that he seeks for himself or them.

Here and elsewhere, it has been again and again urged that the allowance of this claim would be bad policy and "a dangerous precedent."

Paying a just indemnity for such losses, it is said, would lead to numerous claims of the kind. When claims are not founded on meritorious services, they can be rejected. But we cannot see that any mischief will result to our country or its interests from allowing indemnity for the cost of achievements in war, so signal in themselves and so beneficial in their consequences as that now under review. May such "precedents" never be wanting. They must ever redound to the profit and honor of our country, and can never prove dangerous, except to our enemies.

It is said, if we repudiate the award of Louis Napoleon, it will disturb our amicable relations with France and prevent European potentates from ever acting as umpires for us. France cannot easily make a national quarrel out of our awarding compensation to our gallant tars for doing their duty. And if the effect of your decision should be to deter, for all future time, American statesmen from submitting to the arbitrary determination of an European potentate, without evidence and without argument, questions of fact involving our national honor, so much the better. If it shall also deter European rulers from ever again assuming the decision of such questions, it will render them an important service. He who by position and circumstances is disqualified from exercising an impartial judgment, sins against his best interests and his own honor in assuming the office of judge.

The award is founded in error. It seeks to falsify American history, to fix a stigma upon our national character, and, at our expense, to rescue our enemy from merited opprobrium. Unless by some competent authority repudiated upon our part, we must be deemed, through all future time, as having subscribed to its truth and our own dishonor. Instead of allowing it to seem thus acquiesced in, this court, as it may do consistently with truth and justice, ought to stamp upon the page of history its indignant reprobation of both the reference and the award.

Let it not be said that posterity will prefer to the judgment of this court the award of the impartial referee. In what degree he was impartial may be gathered from the facts. He assumed powers not granted. He gave credit to the denial of a witness whose positive assertion he discredited and solemnly found to be untrue. At the very time of forming his award he was secretly progressing in negotiations for an alliance with Great Britain, the nation chiefly interested against us in the controversy.   The importance of that alliance, and the necessity of securing it, may be judged by the stupendous objects it had in view, and is now struggling to accomplish.[1]   Neither will it be overlooked that he was chosen to arbitrate as president of the republic of France, and that, when preparing the award, he was actively engaged in undermining the foundations of that government, which, as chief magistrate, he was pledged to maintain.   Though the reference was to a president, the award came from a king.   With the hand which signed it, he had just stricken down the liberties of his country; that hand was yet reeking with the life-blood of a republican constitution.

It may not seem strange if to gratify a monarchical ally, he sacrificed the rights of a republic.

You have been asked to avoid scrutinizing too nicely the justice of this award, from considerations of deference to the chief of a sovereign State now in amity with us.   We ask you to scrutinize it closely, to judge it fearlessly, and, as becomes an American tribunal, to discard considerations of policy when justice and national renown are involved.   If the arbiter were all that his most obsequious admirers would venture to assert, his merits have been sufficiently acknowledged and amply rewarded.   The liberties of one republic have been sacrificed to his ambition, let us not immolate the fame of another upon the same unholy altar.

[1] At the time when this speech was delivered, the seige of Sebastopol, by the combined forces of France and Great Britain, was in active progress.—EDITOR.

THE GROWTH OF PRINCIPLES.

HON. JOSEPH NEILSON.

Chief Justice of the City Court of Brooklyn.

At the sea shore you pick up a pebble, fashioned after a law of nature, in the exact form that best resists pressure, and worn as smooth as glass. It is so perfect that you take it as a keepsake. But could you know its history from the time when a rough fragment of rock fell from the over-hanging cliff into the sea, to be taken possession of by the under currents, and dragged from one ocean to another, perhaps around the world, for a hundred years, until in reduced and perfect form it was cast upon the beach as you find it, you would have a fit illustration of what many principles, now in familiar use, have endured, thus tried, tortured and fashioned dur-ing the ages. We stand by the river and admire the great body of water flowing so sweetly on; could you trace it back to its source, you might find a mere rivulet, but meandering on, joined by other streams and by secret springs, and fed by the rains and dews of heaven, it gathers volume and force, makes its way through the gorges of the mountains, plows, widens and deepens its channel through the provinces, and attains its present majesty. Thus it is that our truest systems of science had small begin-nings, gradual and countless contributions, and finally took their place in use, as each of you, from helpless childhood and feeble boyhood, have grown to your present strength and maturity. No such system could be born in a day. It was not as when nature in fitful pulsations of her strength suddenly lifted the land into mountain ranges, but rather, as with small accretions, gathered in during countless years, she builds her islands in the seas.

It took a long time to learn the true nature and office of governments; to discover and secure the principles commonly indicated by such terms as "Magna Charta," the "Bill of Rights," "Habeas Corpus," and the "Right of trial by jury;" to found the family home, with its laws of social order, regulating the rights and duties of each member of it, so that the music at the domestic hearth might flow on without discord; the household gods so securely planted that "Though the wind and the rain might enter, the king could not"; to educate noise into music, and music into melody; to infuse into the social code and into the law a spirit of Christian charity, something of the benign temper of the New Testament, so that no man could be persecuted for conscience sake, so that there should be an end of human sacrifice for mere faith or opinion; the smouldering fires at the foot of the stake put out, now, thank God, as effectually as if all the waters that this night flood the rivers had been poured in upon them. It took a long time to learn that war was a foolish and cruel method of settling international differences as compared with arbitration; to learn that piracy was less profitable than a liberal commerce; that un-paid labor was not as good as well-requited toil; that a splenetic old woman, falling into trances and shrieking prophecies, was a fit subject for the asylum rather than to be burned as a witch.

It took a long, long time after the art of printing had been perfected before we learned the priceless value, the sovereign dignity and usefulness of a free press.

But these lessons have been taught and learned; taught for the most part by the prophets of our race, men living in advance of their age, and understood only by the succeeding generations. But you have the in-heritance.—[From an address delivered at Saratoga, August 1, 1875.]

SPEECH OF RUFUS CHOATE,

On behalf of Helen Maria Dalton, in the Dalton Divorce Case.

BEFORE Mr. JUSTICE MERRICK, AND A JURY, IN THE SUPREME JUDICIAL COURT, HELD IN THE CITY OF BOSTON, MAY, 1856.

Analysis of Mr. Choate's Speech.

[247]

Near the close of his life, and in the fullness of his fame, Rufus Choate made his great argument in defense of Helen Maria Dalton, in an action brought by her husband for a divorce. He was, at the time, regarded as the head of the American bar, and one of the most eloquent men living. The cause furnished materials upon which to display his power as a lawyer and an advocate.

On the 11th of June, 1855, in the city of Boston, Frank Dalton married Helen Maria Gove, a pretty, blushing school-girl of seventeen summers. Dalton was then a young man of twenty-two, of good family and excellent prospects. He stood high in the estimation of the mercantile firm with whom he was associated, and earned a handsome yearly income, the reward of his talents and industry. He lived with his young wife at a stylish boarding-house in a fashionable part of the city, and for about five months was one of the happiest men in the world; a kind and affectionate husband, and loved and esteemed by all within the circle of his acquaintance. The period of the honeymoon, however, had scarcely passed when the clouds began to lower, his domestic happiness was broken and destroyed, and proceedings for divorce was the result. It appears that his wife, who was quite handsome, became familiar with a young man named William Sumner, who succeeded in stealing her affections to such an extent that she finally accepted presents and corresponded with him, and on several occasions went out driving in his company. When the husband made the discovery, he brought his wife and Sumner face to face, at the house of his brother-in-law, Mr. Coburn, in Shawmut avenue, to ascertain the exact truth, for he hoped and trusted that his wife, though foolishly indiscreet, was guilty of no crime. He heard their story, and, though in deep distress and agony of spirit, he believed his wife, until Sumner, for some reason becoming alarmed, threw himself at her feet for protection. This so exasperated the husband that he thrashed Sumner severely, and would perhaps have seriously injured him had he not succeeded in making his escape. Sumner left Boston and went to his home in Milton, where shortly afterwards he sickened and died. The newspapers got hold of the story, the affair was greatly exaggerated, created a sensation, and the result was that Dalton and Coburn, for the latter was present at the beating, were arrested on the charge of having caused his death, were indicted and lodged in jail. It is a remarkable coincidence that the unfortunate young husband was put in the same cell previously occupied by Albert J. Tirrell, whose life was saved by Mr. Choate in a defense supposed to have been the most skillful and remarkable in the history of the American bar. The grand jury refused to find a bill against the prisoners for murder, but they were indicted for manslaughter, tried, and acquitted. Upon the charge of assault, however, Dalton was convicted and sentenced to five months' imprisonment. During his confinement he still believed his wife innocent of actual criminality with Sumner. Then there came a confession by the wife; whether a confession of her folly or something more, is not exactly clear. Counsel for the defense argued, that from his conduct the husband did not consider that it embraced his wife's guilt. Then a sad circumstance occurred. Mrs. Dalton became very ill. The theory of the plaintiff was that she attempted to prematurely destroy her offspring to hide the evidence of her guilt. Counsel for the defense insisted that she had suffered a miscarriage, and seem to have established this fact upon the trial. They claimed that the husband believed his wife innocent, and would have lived with her, but his friends, in order to poison his mind against her forever, circulated the story which it was endeavored to establish at the trial. Whether the last great charge was true or false, certain it is that Frank Dalton came to believe his wife guilty. He was, however, a man with a kind heart and generous impulses, and it was thought by his father-in-law, that if proper influences could be brought to bear, a reconciliation might be effected. In response, however, to the overtures of Mr. Gove, the offer of money and the proposition to go to California, Mr. Dalton wrote: "Were she innocent, if heaven had made me such another world of one entire and perfect chrysolite, I would not have sold her for it; but as I know her to be what she has been obliged to confess to me she is, the world is not rich enough to buy me! I have loved her, but no more can she be wife of mine. I cannot any longer confide to her the guardianship of my honor; she has unfitted herself to be any longer the keeper of any man's honor and his peace of mind. I cannot take her to be the mother of my children; if the law does not compel me to do it, I cannot do it." It was then that Dalton showed his splendid manhood, for he paid back to Mr. Gove the $3,000 which he had advanced as a marriage portion, and having thus swept away every seeming incumbrance, he came into court and asked that the marriage contract he had made might be dissolved, because his wife had failed faithfully to keep and perform it.

Notwithstanding the strong circumstances pointing to the defendant's criminality, Mr. Choate unquestionably showed that, putting plaintiff's proof in the strongest possible light, the entire evidence was at least consistent with a theory of defendant's innocence, even if also consistent with a theory of guilt, and he claimed that, under the circumstances as matter of law, the plaintiff was not entitled to a verdict. (Bishop on Mar. & Div. § 423; Ferguson v. Ferguson, 3 Sandford, 307.) Despite the good name and character of the plaintiff, and the exceedingly able and brilliant argument of Richard H. Dana, Jr., in his behalf, Mr. Choate split the jury and won the case.

The crowning point of this wonderful effort was the manner in which he disposed of the story that the defendant had destroyed her offspring. On that portion of the evidence—after he had finished his searching analysis of the testimony, pronounced his terrible and scathing arraignment of the witnesses relied upon to establish it, and made his conclusive argument to show that there was not the shadow of a foundation for a motive for the crime—he had demolished the strong part of the plaintiff's case, and made an impression upon a portion of the jury that could not be effaced. All the resources of his well-stored mind and fervid imagination were brought to bear and made to contribute to his advantage and success. He knew how to touch the springs of knowledge at the right time and in the right way, without straining, without effort, without vain display, without show of pedantry. His work was the work of a master. The strong parts of plaintiff's evidence crumbled away beneath his searching investigation. His power to persuade and convince was irresistible.

It will be noticed with what tenderness and regard he treated not only his adversary, for whom he entertained high esteem, but the plaintiff also. He never stooped to employ invective; but his arraignment of an untruthful witness, when opportunity offered, was fearful and terrific. Mr. H. F. Durant was associated with Mr. Choate, and opened for the defendant. Richard H. Dana, Jr., conducted the cause for the plaintiff with very great ability. When the evidence on both sides was all in, Mr. Choate arose and addressed the jury as follows:

Mr. Foreman and Gentlemen:—I congratulate you, on approaching, at least, the close of this case, so severe and painful to all of us. One effort more of your indulgence I have to ask, and then we shall retire from your presence, satisfied and grateful that everything which candor and patience and intelligence can do for these afflicted suitors has been done. It very rarely, indeed, happens, gentlemen, in the trial of a civil controversy, that both parties have an equal, or rather a vast interest that one of them—in this case the defendant—should be clearly proved to be entitled to your verdict. Unusual as it is, in the view I take of this case, such an one is now on trial.

I. A verdict for defendant equally desirable by both parties.

To both of these parties, it is of supreme importance, in the view I take of it, that you should find this young wife, erring, indiscreet, imprudent, forgetful of herself, if it be so, but innocent of the last and greatest crime of a married woman. I say, to both parties it is important. I cannot deny, of course, gentlemen, that her interest in such a result is perhaps the greater of the two. For her, indeed, it is not at all too much to say, that everything is staked upon the result. I cannot, of course, hope, I cannot say, that any verdict which you can render in this case, can give her back again the happy and sunny life which seemed opening upon her two years ago; I cannot say it, because I do not think that any verdict you can render will ever enable her to recall those weeks of folly, and frivolity, and vanity, without a blush, without a tear; I cannot desire that it should be so. But, gentlemen, whether these grave and impressive proceedings shall terminate by sending this young wife from your presence with the scarlet letter upon her brow; whether in this, her morning of life, her name shall be thus publicly stricken from the roll of virtuous women—her whole future darkened by dishonor and waylaid by temptation; her companions driven from her side; herself cast out, it may be, upon common society, the sport of libertines, unassisted by public opinion or sympathy or self-respect—this certainly rests with you. For her, therefore, I am surely warranted in saying, that more than her life is here at stake. "Whatsoever things are honest, whatsoever things are lovely, whatsoever things are pure, whatsoever things are of good report, if there be any virtue, if there be any praise," all the chances that are to be left her in life, for winning and holding these holy, beautiful and needful things, rest with you.

I cannot, therefore, with my impression of the importance of this inquiry, turn away from her, even to these parents whose hearts are bleeding also. But is there not another person, gentlemen, interested in these proceedings, with an equal, or at least a supreme interest with the respondent, that you shall be able by your verdict to say that Helen Dalton is not guilty of the crime of adultery, and is not that person her husband? I do not say, gentlemen, that he ought to feel or would feel grateful for a verdict that should acquit her on any ground of doubt or technicality, leaving everybody to suspect her guilty; I do not say that he would feel contented with such a verdict as that, though I say it would be her sacred right that such a verdict should be rendered, if your minds were left in that state. He must acquiesce, whether the verdict is satisfactory to him in that particular or not. But, gentlemen, if you can here and now, on this evidence, acquit your consciences and render a verdict that shall assure this husband that a jury of Suffolk, men of honor and spirit, some of them his personal friends, believe that he has been the victim of a cruel and groundless jealousy; that they believe that he has been led by that scandal that circulates about him, and has influenced him everywhere; that he has been made to misconceive the nature and over-estimate the extent of the injury his wife has done him; if he could be made to believe and see, as I believe you see and believe, and every other human being sees and believes, that this story of abortion, by which he has been induced to institute these proceedings, is falser than the coignage of hell; if you can thus enable him to see that, without dishonor, he may again take her to his bosom, let me ask you if any other human being can do another so great a kindness as this? If by your verdict you can assure him that his first thoughts on this subject were right; that the steadiness and constancy with which he held her to his heart, from the 17th of November down to the morning of the 26th of February; the steadiness and constancy with which he held her to his affections, after he became aware of every credible fact and circumstance that has been put in evidence in this case; if you can teach him that this steadiness and constancy were just and honorable and true; if you thus restore him to his former and better self, before he was maddened by these falsehoods and this malignant conspiracy by which he has been surrounded: will it not be he, rather than she, that will have occasion to bless you for your judgment?

Sensitiveness to public opinion, if I understand the character of

Dalton at all, is what has misled him; it is other men's judgments, not his own, which have led him to this proceeding; it is through others' eyes, not his own, that he has looked; and now I submit that, if you can only assist him to follow in the impulses of his own heart without dishonor, permit me to say, you may live long and do much, but to no human being can you do such a kindness as this.

> " Not poppy, nor mandragora,
> Nor all the drowsy syrups of this world,
> Can ever med'cine thee to that sweet sleep
> That thou ow'd'st yesterday."

It seems to me, therefore, gentlemen, if my learned friend on the other side will not deem it arrogance in me to say so, that I am here to maintain the cause, not of the wife against the husband, but of both of them. I am here to say, that the husband has a right to his wife, and the wife has a right to her husband. What is their case, gentlemen, as it now rests, in my own mind at least, and I trust in yours, as far as the result is affected by the whole evidence now before us ? Permit me to state that case exactly as I apprehend it; and when I have done, that I shall be obliged to turn a little more particularly and more methodically to what the libellant has to prove, and by what evidence he has attempted to establish it; but first let me give you the position of the case as at last it rests, I hope, upon your minds, certainly rests upon my own.

2. THE NARRATION.

These parties were married in June, 1855; he was very young, I believe not more than 22 or 23 at the time, and she was only a child, not yet eighteen, at school as late as the January previous, which she left in consequence of her engagement, and to make preparations for her marriage. She was comely, of remarkable modesty—on the testimony of Dalton himself and of Mr. Richard-son—affectionate and fond in her nature and disposition, a little quick sometimes, as has been testified to, but instantly herself again, and instantly hastening, whenever a momentary difference had occurred between herself and her husband, to make all up by throwing her arms around his neck—herself making the approach to a reconciliation. She was the child, I hope I may be allowed to say, notwithstanding the testimony of Mrs. Joseph Coburn given here yesterday, of respectable, Christian parents, somewhat beyond the middle of life, their youngest and not their least beloved, and they had been diligent to afford her all those opportunities of education, moral and mental, which our commonwealth offers to all its daughters, and they had afforded her, what perhaps is of more importance to remember here, the still more inestimable privileges and blessings of the family altar and worship, and a Christian, constant parental example. This was Helen Dalton that day—pure as the falling flake of snow, pure as any child, as any bride that was ever given in marriage at any altar. They began their married life by living at a grave and decorous boarding-house of the first class—Mrs. Le Cain's, in Summer street—full of servants, full of boarders, and of the highest respectability in all particulars. They were affectionately fond of each other, and there was never, in the history of married, bridal life, a happier beginning. Such is the universal testimony in this case.

About the 20th or 25th of September she became, or knew herself to be, pregnant; the father of that child, beyond a particle of controversy, was her lawful husband. This was the last of September, a month before she ever saw young Sumner, two months before that ride to Brighton or Watertown, previous to the outrage on Shawmut avenue, where, if at all, they are to locate the crime.

3. Helen Dalton's acquaintance with Sumner.

It happened, as has been stated by counsel on both sides, in the opening, that not being at housekeeping, and her husband necessarily and without the least fault on his part—creditable rather to him—detained from home about his business, she was very much alone and had very little to do, and having a sister very nearly her own age, and a very respectable friend, Miss Snow—to whose deposition, given so long ago you may have forgotten it, I shall have occasion to revert—having friends as pure as she was then, she was, in that pleasant waning summer and beginning of autumn, very much abroad. I hope I shall be excused for saying to the married men upon the jury, that the very restlessness of incipient pregnancy may have induced a desire to be abroad. It was during this time that she made the acquaintance of young Sumner, whose name, from his connection with this case, recalls many sad thoughts and memories of the disappointed hopes that cluster about him and rest upon his grave. He also was nothing more than a boy, with some capacity, I may say, for refinement of sentiment, a certain pleasing address and manner, with some susceptibility of disposition—not that he was debauched or dissolute—for his friends' sake

I thank God there is not a particle of evidence that he was a seducer by profession or design, only that once or perhaps twice he was hurried away by impulse into the offer of a familiarity, revealing a warmer and more ungovernable sentiment, which was instantly repelled and instantly and forever abandoned. If evil into that immature nature came and went, as evil will, it perished in the blossom and bore no fruit.

4. Insincerity of counsel as to offering Sumner's dying declarations.

Gentlemen, my learned brother, in opening his case, was pleased to say that he was not at liberty, by the rules of law, to give in evidence certain imaginary confessions made by young Sumner on his death-bed. My learned brother will excuse me for saying that he has not been quite so scrupulous in the offer of incompetent and inadmissible testimony, as to warrant a belief in it here. But lest there should be any, you will remember that my associate, after consultation with myself, in his opening argument, challenged the learned counsel—pledging us to waive every objection on the ground of incompetency or the order of trial—challenged him to produce the brother of Mr. Sumner, who hung over his dying bed and received his last words. The witness was before you, gentlemen, called on two or three comparatively unimportant points in this case, and constantly under the eye of the counsel on the other side. We challenged him to produce him, to say whether or not, in that last hour, in that moment of unutterable solemnity, just when he was passing into the presence of the All-seeing One, he went out of the world confessing or denying that he had committed this act. Gentlemen, let the fact that my learned brother has not ventured to meet this challenge, go for the proof. Men may live fools, but fools they cannot die.

5. No evidence of improper intimacy.

Well, gentlemen, this acquaintance began the middle of October; I pray you, as I may not think it worth while to spend time to recur to it again—I pray you take it here that there is not a scintilla of evidence that she ever saw him in her life until the middle of October. She was then pregnant by her husband six weeks. What the nature of their acquaintance was, so far as it consisted in outside, visible evidence, I think we have been able to lay before you exactly. They met occasionally in the streets;

sometimes at Fera's and Vinton's saloons. I think we hear of two rides in omnibuses, in which were all four (Mr. Sumner and Mr. Porter, Mrs. Coburn and Mrs. Dalton), the omnibuses full of passengers; they drove once to Cambridge in a carriage, according to the testimony of the driver Burns, four together, the windows all open; and once only rode out alone. That she was ever out walking with him after the sun went down, that they ever met but in the broadest daylight, that he ever insulted or astonished her by an invitation to a house of assignation, that they ever met anywhere but in the broad light of day, but in the presence of everybody, except on the single occasion of the ride to Brighton, there is not a particle of proof. I advert now to the deposition of Miss Snow. Perhaps you have forgotten that they asked that respectable witness, called by themselves, whether she ever knew or heard of Helen Dalton's going with Sumner to a house of assignation or a house of pleasure, and she denied that she had ever heard or known such a thing in her life. Therefore I have the honor to repeat, in order that we may not exaggerate the matter, and may have the whole of this part of the cause before us—I say I have the honor to repeat that these interviews, Mr. Foreman, were no walks by dusk or moonlight, no meetings by the insidious and seductive light and music of the house of pleasure, no walk, no meeting, anywhere, on any occasion, alone, but a single ride on the 15th or 16th of November.

6. Mrs. Dalton's love for her husband.

Gentlemen, of this intimacy between Helen Dalton and Mr. Sumner, I hold the same opinion with regard to it that the father expressed through his tears upon the stand. I look upon it with abhorrence. I regard it exactly as Helen Dalton everywhere, in every word she uttered, in every line she wrote, whenever her bursting tears enabled her to speak her thoughts, shows that she regarded it. But we are here on a charge of adultery, and I have the honor to submit to you, gentlemen, after the most careful and thoughtful consideration and weighing of evidence in this case, under responsibilities professionally as severe and as oppressive as those under which I ever assisted to try a case in my life; I respectfully submit, on a review of that evidence, these two views will have the approbation of every candid mind. I submit that she never came to love young Sumner with that impulsive, absorbing, engrossing love that endangers virtue and conquers shame. I submit also, gentlemen, that there was never a moment, during their whole intercourse, when the thought of criminal connection was entertained by her for a moment—never one. Young, comely, vain, as may be with her sex and in her condition, in her father's family, trained to but little intercourse with the world, the society and pleasing manners of this young man tickled her, afforded her pleasure, playing round the head, but going not near the heart. But I mean to maintain, and I shall base the defense—a triumphant defense in this case, unless I deceive myself upon it—that her husband had her heart at first, and has it to-day; that this attachment (if you please to call it so) was merely a transient and superficial feeling, a false, fickle light on the surface of the stream, whose depths were unchanged, untroubled, undisturbed. How well she loved him we shall see, if you will permit me to go a little into the argument of the cause. The whole case is full of evidence to show the affection of the earlier period of their married life. There are the three weeks after the Shawmut avenue tragedy; those two days when, during those three weeks, her husband having absented himself, she knew not why, she went for him, half distracted, everywhere, going at a late hour in the evening to his mother's house; her following him to jail, hovering about that cell, a beam of light, a dove of constant presence; those letters—in the whole history of the human heart there is nothing to equal the depth of feeling, the beautiful, inexpressible, undimmed affection they exhibit, down even to the very last, in which she breathes out the thoughts of a breaking heart; how well she loved him from the first, how constantly she loved him through the whole, and how light and transient and superficial was this intimacy with Mr. Sumner, I shall have the pleasure, by and by, of stating my opinion.

7. Sumner's desires indignantly repelled.

I say, also, for the second view of this intercourse between her and Sumner, that it is beyond all reasonable controversy, that the very first time that Sumner suffered himself to be hurried away by a momentary impulse into expressions that revealed the existence of warmer desires, she instantly met and instantly repelled them. Will you ever forget, gentlemen, that only a day or two before the Shawmut avenue tragedy, having discovered by, it may be, a touch of the foot or of the hand, the existence of these warm emotions, she thereupon repelled him, snatched her letters from his hands, tore them up, and threw them out the window?

Have you forgotten that one of the letters of Sumner to her was never opened by her, but found unopened? Well did Dalton comment upon that fact when he said to Mr. Richardson, she could not much have loved him to have left his letter unopened. And I submit to you further, gentlemen,—the evidence will show you whether I am warranted in these strong introductory statements—that when at Brighton or at Watertown, he, probably for the first time in his life, distinctly conveyed an intimation of his wishes, how she started back from him, burst out crying—on the testimony of Mrs. E. O. Coburn, their witness, and to be believed by them—and commanded that he should instantly drive her home again to Boston.

8. DEFENDANT'S FULL AND COMPLETE REVELATIONS.

The letters were found; the Shawmut avenue tragedy was enacted; Sumner was brought into her presence and made certain statements. The next Sunday night, in the presence of the Daltons, of whom I am bound to say, although they have, perhaps with the best motives towards their kinsman, perhaps intentionally and perhaps unintentionally, urged him to this proceeding; notwithstanding this, I have the greatest pleasure in saying that they stand out in extraordinary comparison, as a family of witnesses and of blood, with that other family which figures so largely and, as I shall show you by and by, so disgracefully in the case. In their presence, on the Sunday night after the tragedy, she made a full and complete revelation of her way of life with Sumner, in the presence of her husband and of his family; admitted there, as everywhere, her own grief, shame and compunction for what had taken place, but protested her absolute innocence of the last and greatest crime, just as she had once before, when Dalton proposed that test, sunk down on her knees, with her hand on her father's gift, the Bible, and solemnly swore her innocence of that charge; just as she had, in that even more solemn moment when the pains of premature birth were upon her, in the presence of Mr. Richardson, adjured her Maker that she was innocent.

9. DALTON, WITH KNOWLEDGE OF ALL THE FACTS, BELIEVED HIS WIFE INNOCENT.

This brings me to that great fact which I apprehend you will believe to be decisive in the case, that the libellant—with the knowledge of every single credible fact and circumstance which is laid before you in this cause, and with the full and perfect knowledge

17

of everything but this enormous and outrageous and barbarous falsehood of abortion, which was an after-thought; with a full and perfect knowledge of her intimacy with Sumner, her rides with him, her going to saloons, her exchange of rings and letters, the gift of a book, and the knowledge of the still further fact that on one occasion Sumner, in a moment of passion, had reached his hand into her bosom; with the knowledge of every fact and declaration on which this jury will place a particle of reliance—declared, not merely by his language, but by acts and conduct the most unequivocal, that he believed her innocent of that crime, and loved and trusted her still. And so I have to repeat, for it seems to me that in this view the argument will appear to be conclusive; I repeat that down to that time, through all that interval, from the 17th of November down to the 14th of January, with the knowledge of every credible fact and circumstance, Dalton, who knew his wife so much better than we can know her, who knew how pure as an angel she came to his bed, who knew when she spoke the truth, who knew how tenderly she had loved him, who knew so much better than we can know how to probe her, how to practice upon her, how to surprise her into confession; he who had even a chance to watch over her sleep and hear the revelations of her dreams, he loved her and believed her innocent of this charge down to the 14th of January— down to that date, I respectfully submit, the fact will not admit of controversy. Once for all, gentlemen, remember that series of letters from the jail, so honorable to his first thoughts, showing him still so well worthy to be the husband of this wife; those letters from the jail, so beautiful, so manly—unless he was deceiving her, which, of course, he was not—one long, unbroken strain of music, the burden of which is "home, sweet home, and you, my loved one, my fond one, dearer and better for what has happened, you again to fill and illumine and bless it." So it stood down to the 14th of January, which brings us to a great epoch in the history of this case.

10. WHY PLAINTIFF DID NOT MEET HIS WIFE PENDING HIS TRIAL FOR HOMICIDE.

We come now, Mr. Foreman and gentlemen, to this law suit. The grand jury found no bill against Mr. Dalton and Mr. Coburn for murder, but indicted them for manslaughter. On the charge of murder they were to be released, and were released. They came abroad on the 14th of January, and then at once they were to pre-

pare for their trial, which promised, at that time, to be a very severe
one. The punishment for manslaughter may be twenty years in
the State prison, and of manslaughter both these parties were at
that time believed by the public to be guilty; they were believed to
have aided in sending that boy to his dishonored and untimely
grave. Public opinion, whatever that is worth, was undoubtedly
against them both, especially against E. O. Coburn, as the oldest
and probably the leader in that tragedy; and he having taken it
into his head to console his domestic grief by stealing $1,700 from
his father-in-law's safe, by keys false, or otherwise, was somewhat
distrusted and as likely to undergo a pretty severe trial at the bar
of public opinion. To change that public opinion, and in order
to a defense against the charge of manslaughter, it became necessity that there should be a belief, or at least an appearance of belief, in the guilt of Sumner. And therefore, gentlemen, at some
time, the precise time is not practicable nor is it necessary to fix,
but at some time, and at some short time, too, before leaving the
jail, it was arranged, unquestionably through the influence of counsel (not of my brother Dana, who, I believe, was not engaged in
this early stage of the case), that when Dalton and Coburn should
go abroad, they should not publicly meet their wives. To go into
court and maintain that Sumner had attempted or committed adultery, and to maintain that in the sincere belief of his guilt they had
killed him, and at the same time publicly consort with their wives,
would seem inconsistent and impolitic; and so it was arranged—
I do not know as I have to complain of it as an impolitic or inex-
pedient arrangement—that they should not meet their wives at all.
Therefore it is that you hear from Mr. Richardson, that Mr. Dalton wrote to him that, although he had arranged to meet his wife
at once, it would not be expedient for him to meet her until after
the trial; otherwise he should be very glad to see her. They came
abroad, and although in almost the very last letter which he wrote
to his wife from the jail, he expressed a desire to fly to her arms, he
refused to see her, and did not see her at all.

II. Influences which prejudiced the husband.

So it remained down to the 25th of February. I said, and I
repeat, that I do not know that this was very impolitic or inexpe-
dient, or that it is to be complained of at all; but I pray you now
to see the history of the libel. The very moment he places himself in this position, he comes to be in an antagonistic and false

position towards her from the nature of the case; the habit of dwelling on the offenses or supposed offenses of Sumner very naturally brought his mind into something like suspicion or belief that Sumner was guilty, and that brought him to a willingness or necessity to believe that his wife was guilty too. At all events, it brought him into a condition of complete perplexity of mind, and surrounded him with ten thousand influences which poured into his abused ears and loaded his bosom with jealous doubts. His family and friends, insidious enemies pretending to be friends, gossipers and scandal-mongers right and left, the whisper of public opinion to which Dalton is emphatically sensitive, the laugh of by-standers, all came around him as an atmosphere, and brought him to that condition so strikingly represented by the greatest master of the heart—"Perplexed in the extreme"—"*Perplexed in the extreme.*" He came to know what I trust few hearts know—

> " What damned minutes tells he o'er,
> Who dotes yet doubts, suspects, yet strongly loves."

Gentlemen, there is not in the whole history of human nature, in fact or fiction, a more remarkable and affecting illustration of the degree of perplexity to which the human mind can be brought, than this of the condition of Mr. Dalton's mind at that time.

12. Defendant's alleged confession explained.

Then we have another important fact in this case. You remember how he wrote along all the way down to the 12th of January, how fondly he loved and trusted her, and how happy he hoped they would yet be. As early as the 5th of February, before he heard one solitary fact or circumstance of which we have a particle of credible evidence, so far as we can discern, before the story of the abortion was concocted to poison his mind, my brother Dana was called upon to give us notice of the libel. And then, more strongly to bring to mind another illustration of the perplexed condition of his mind at that time, do you remember that Mr. Richardson testified that Mr. Dalton told him, with all the sincerity in the world, that his wife had actually confessed to him that she had committed adultery with Sumner in Fera's saloon ? " I believe her innocent," he says, and then comes on the revulsion which is the natural result of the perplexed condition of his mind, and he says, "she confessed to me that she committed adultery in Fera's saloon." Did she ever confess to adultery in Fera's saloon ? You know perfectly well she never did. "When did she confess it?" "At the time of the flogging affair." And yet, after the flogging affair, he holds her to his heart and his bed for three weeks, and writes her these tender and manly letters from jail. He understood exactly what she confessed then. She confessed then what she has everywhere confessed, by her words and letters, temptation, wrong, sin, but no adultery—*no adultery !* Accordingly, gentlemen, he lived with her and wrote to her, and she was his wedded and trusted wife for a month afterward. But now, in this perplexed and false position in which he stood towards her, preparing for his trial, with ten thousand whisperers at his elbow, he actually brought himself to the belief that she had confessed it! How striking an illustration that is, by the way, of the danger of these confessions! What a lesson of candor and caution and good sense it teaches a jury, as to weighing alleged confessions put in evidence.

However, there he was, from the 14th of January down to the 25th of February, away from her, among her enemies, his heart encrusted over, though, as we shall see in a moment, a deep fountain of love and trust was there even yet.

13. MEETING OF THE HUSBAND AND WIFE, AFTER THEIR SEPARATION.

We come now to the 25th of February. What happened then, gentlemen? This wife had been kept from his sight from the time he left jail, on the 14th of January down to the 25th of February; more than a month she had never seen him. On that night, winged by that love which was stronger than the malignity of the Coburns, that love which is said (if I may be excused the expression in a cause so grave as this) to "laugh at locksmiths," she forced her way to his presence in the very house of her enemies, his enemies, and the enemies of truth. Gentlemen, what took place there on that evening of the 25th of February can never, of course, be perfectly known until all secrets, large and small, shall be revealed; but I have no fear but that the intelligence of this jury will penetrate that interview, and I have no fear but that, turning with disgust from the perjury of John H. Coburn, you will see that these were the transactions of this evening: They met there after a long separation. The meeting, at the commencement was most painful, beginning in a review of the past, interrupted, of course, by sobs and tears, in which she again reviewed and reiterated, and prayed him to forgive her for what she had done, the very same story she had told at the house of his mother the Sunday after the tragedy;

and then and there, I respectfully submit, you will find on the proof that the husband trusted her again completely, as he had done from the beginning, and surrendered his heart and person to her; that they then locked that door, and there remained alone until some one, rapping upon the outside, reminded them of what they seemed to have forgotten, so fast had the hours flown by that it was past nine o'clock. Instead of meeting there to make arrangements for a separation of husband and wife, which is the theory of the other side—instead of that it was a still more sad and self-reproachful confession of all that she had ever done, asseverating and constantly avowing her innocence of guilt; and he, then and there, finding he had no criminal guilt to pardon, pardoned and forgave the rest, and they locked their door and sat down to sketch out the plan of their future troubled life. It was not expedient or practicable that they should meet publicly, for his sentence was still hanging over his head; but they sat down then and there to arrange their future life, as he in terms told her father. They parted with the understanding that the first meeting, somewhat privately from the Daltons and Coburns, was to take place at the house of Mrs. Richardson, her sister, on the night following.

I cannot possibly abstain, as I see it lying under my eye, from recurring to that mutilated letter which, because it had been mutilated, his honor declared inadmissible, but which came in by our consent last night. I ask you to turn to that, and see if it does not reveal that this "poor creature" (as even Mary Hunter was constrained to call her) went away from that interview, walking in the air, in the clouds; a new world, a recovered husband, a happy future opening before her. Hear her, and not my colder language:

"My much loved husband: In our meeting yesterday, I see a bright hope and prospects of a happy future before me. Oh! dear Frank, I hope that the day will come when we shall be happy soon. I feel much happier than I did yesterday. [Why "much happier?" Because she has told everything? Because she has a great load off her conscience? No, gentlemen!] I feel now as if I had a dear husband to live for; before I felt as if I did not care to live; I had nothing to live for. But oh! what a beautiful thought now fills my heart—that I have him, dear Frank, to live for; him to build all my future hopes on; his strong arm to lean on; his dear words and sweet smiles to encourage me; and if I should ever falter, I have Frank to say, cheer up, Nellie, we shall soon be happy. It seems as if I could not express on paper my thoughts; but I long to fly to his arms, and lay my face close to his, and then tell him all my heart."

Judge you, gentlemen, judge you, whether or not that letter was written the morning after a confession that must have wrung tears from the eyes, and drops of ruddy blood from the heart of the husband who parted them forever! No, gentlemen! I repeat, they met; the meeting was sorrowful at first; at first it was a review of the melancholy past; it was repentant of that past; it was the assertion of innocence; it was the delicious belief of innocence; it was the arrangement of a future life, based upon that belief; and therefore it is that when she awakes the next morning a new sun is shining, there is a new heaven and a new earth.

14. OBJECT AND PURPOSE OF THE STORY OF THE WIFE'S CRIME EXPOSED.

But what followed? He could not be publicly seen with her, and Edward O. Coburn went home with her that night, and Edward O. Coburn had discernment enough to find out how it was with them—that she had won her husband back again; and even he, although he is a man who will mutilate her letters and turn them by forgery as far as he can into a lie, even he was obliged to admit upon the stand that she told him that she felt better that night, for she was going to see her husband again the next night. Then it was that these parties, the Coburns, finding that the husband and wife were going to come together again at last, and that all was likely to be over, then and there it was, I respectfully submit to you, that they fabricated and reported to Dalton this hideous and unutterable falsehood of the abortion by the instrument of Dr. Calkins. I submit to you, gentlemen, that then and there it was that they approached his abused and ready ear with that infamous story of abortion. There was exactly enough of truth for falsehood and malignity to work upon. The truth had been exactly this: Mrs. Dalton had suffered a premature birth. Grief and care which were entirely adequate to produce the effect, according to the testimony of the medical witnesses who have been upon the stand, had prematurely nipped in its bud of life her progeny. Three times, including the last one, she had been attacked by the pains of miscarriage, and three times that Christian matron, mother, of whose credibility I shall by and by have the honor to say something, but on whose credibility I with undoubting confidence rely—this Christian mother, when these attacks came on, herself familiar with that agony and pain, applied to her a mother's care and a mother's love, and along with these, those old mother remedies, warm water for the feet and composition powders; not to produce miscarriage, because that event was believed to be inevitable, but in the vain idea—for Dr. Clark has told you that they were worthless for this purpose—that they might a little relax the system and diminish the agony, and if miscarriage must happen, a little relieve the sufferings of her child. If for that this Christian mother is to stand condemned and judged as a party to the murder of that young life, God have mercy upon us! I hope there is no one on that jury who is a victim, as I am, periodically, to sick headache, as I should just as soon expect to have my wife accused of murder, because when that torture is upon me, she is in the habit of coming to me with a little warm water and bathing my head, in the hope that possibly it may relieve in some degree the agonizing throbs. Is it administered to cause sick headache—judge you as you would be judged— or in the hope that the pain would be assuaged, the system relaxed, the time of suffering shortened? This is what they have done. The two first cases of this difficulty passed off. While she was suffering from the third attack, her brother-in-law broke in upon her and told her that her husband had refused to see her and to live with her, and then, after an agony of tears and another appeal to her Maker that she was innocent, the miscarriage took place.

On that foundation I say, gentlemen, I submit it is perfectly true that these men then and there fabricated, out of whole cloth, the story of an intentional abortion by the agency of Dr. Calkins. I shall by and by have occasion to show you how unutterably false is that story; false everywhere, disproved by the weight of irresistible evidence in this case. But I advert to it here and now only for the purpose of showing you how it was that the last blow was struck, and Mr. Dalton was, for the present at least, if not forever, separated from his wife. And that fiction did the business, and he thenceforward surrenders himself to his friends, as they called themselves—his enemies, as I think—and here he is, upon such testimony as they enable him to lay before you.

Here Mr. Choate spoke of the painful duties of counsel and the jury. He then referred to the subject of public trials, as follows :

15. NECESSITY AND PROPRIETY OF PUBLIC TRIALS.

Our habits are for public trial and investigation, and our liberties will last just as long as our trials are public, and not a moment more. We agree in that; we have this love of a public trial from our ancestors. Who does not remember a remarkable case a few years ago, when her majesty the queen of England was arraigned before the House of Lords on a charge, and assailed by a body of trash, compared with which the evidence of Mrs. Coburn is as innocent as one of Dr. Watts' psalms or hymns. And here I would like to ask your honor and this public, whether or not, if it had been proposed to try that cause under lock and key at a long table covered with baize and by lamp light, the people of England would have borne it? They would have thrown every lord and bishop into the river, and piled the stones of the parliament house on their heads; but they would have seen that trial and heard that trial. Do you think that was for the love of offensive exhibitions, gentlemen? I have the honor to believe, for the country of my descent and yours, that was the old English love of fair play. They wanted to see how this was to be done, and how it was that a set of Italian rascals and villains that ought to have been hanged forty years before they came over to England to testify, were going to prove that the greatest of queens could become the wickedest of women. It was an inclination to see that done; and if John H. Coburn must separate this man and wife, people want to know how it is brought about, and surround the jury to see with their eyes and take something of the benefit of their judgment. Shame to him who evil thinks. I said, and say again, no man is hurt by this trial who was worth saving when he came into court. Shame to him who evil thinks! The man, the mind, the heart that could go through such cases as this, listen to this sad, melancholy story of bridal love, of jealousy, of misery, of sorrow, of broken hearts, of willful perjury, and carry away no impression but of its obscenity, reminds one of an expression used by the pastor of your Brattle street church, who said he could go through a gallery of art, containing the pictures of heroes and demi-gods, with no impression but that they were all stark naked. Shame to him who evil thinks. Let us, gentlemen, not suffer our delicacy to prevent our doing our duty; the result is to be one which may interest the heart and affections and improve the life.

16. The presumption of innocence.

We begin this trial, Mr. Foreman and gentlemen, by taking with us a familiar principle of the law—by the presumption that everybody, and especially the defendant, is innocent until clearly proved guilty. We begin with the presumption that it is in the last degree

improbable that a young bride, in the fifth month of her marriage
and the second month of her pregnancy, affectionate, modest, of
Christian training, has committed the greatest crime of woman.
We take with us, gentlemen, merely that the circumstance that she
has been engaged in what Edward O. Coburn said he thought was
a flirtation, and nothing more, with young Sumner, does not prove
that the last great step is taken. We believe this, and take this
with us, because we know it to be so, perfectly well. We ourselves
and those we love best, rejoice to know that it does not follow because one step has been taken, all have been. We take with us the
ordinary principle, too, by which circumstantial and other evidence
of adultery is to be weighed. I had the honor to call the attention
of the court just now to an authority upon this subject. It is not
worth while to trouble you with it, but I pray his honor to take
notice, that throughout, the burden is upon the libellant to prove his
case clearly and undoubtedly; that every invisible fact and circumstance goes for nothing at all; and that throughout, if everything
that has been established by credible evidence is fairly reconcilable
with the innocence of the party, in reference to the great ultimate
charge, there is not a tittle of proof in the case.

17. No proof of defendant's guilt.

With this we start. It is the crime of adultery, Mr. Foreman.
It is an intentional and deliberate surrender of the person unlawfully to another. No surprise at the window, no sudden placing
of the hand within the bosom, instantly and by a flood of tears repelled, is adultery. There must be some intentional, intelligent,
voluntary and consummated surrender of the body; and this established by evidence clear and undoubted, or there is no case. No
such case is established or begun to be established before you. It
would express my opinion, gentlemen—and if I should allow myself, what I would prefer to do, to make a very short address upon
this evidence, I should leave it upon that—it would express my
opinion exactly of the state of the proof, if I should say that, until you come down to the alleged confession of John H. Coburn,
there is not a particle of proof, not one fact, not one declaration,
that tends in the least degree to prove the guilt of the defendant;
and of John H. Coburn's testimony I should say, it was the most
barbarous, beastly, incredible, impossible perjury that was ever attempted to be passed upon a jury. And if my object, as I said before, were merely a verdict of acquittal upon this charge, I would

leave it there, or rather I would proceed at once to the discussion of the testimony upon that fact. But the importance of the cause and the novelty of the trial make it necessary to go a little further; and therefore I beg leave to submit my commentary upon the whole proof under this arraignment, and I commend it to your attention, as it will enable you to see where I am in the progress of the discussion; and I will enable you to give me credit for believing that if I do not at once place, or in one moment, reply to a piece of evidence that lies in your own mind, according to the arrangement I have proposed, I shall do it in another.

I have, therefore, to submit to you that every particle of credible evidence in this case, until you come down to the testimony of John H. Coburn and the alleged confession of the 25th of February, is perfectly consistent with the innocence of Helen Dalton; and I shall respectfully submit that if it rested there, on the whole case as it existed down to that evening, you would not leave your seats to find a verdict for the defendant. I shall then have the honor to submit to you that Mr. Coburn's evidence is not entitled to a moment's belief. I want you, gentlemen, first to try all that evidence yourself, and after you and I have conferred a little upon it, I shall respectfully once more ask you to appreciate the great fact, that upon every single word of it, every fact and circumstance, Mr. Dalton himself pronounced his own judgment, and declared that it did not convict her of guilt.

18. No proof of proximate acts of adultery.

In the first place, let us look at it for ourselves. It is usual in cases of alleged adultery for the libellant or the commonwealth, or whoever has the burden of proof, to begin by what is called positive proof of what are called proximate acts; that is to say, direct positive evidence of certain acts committed by which a party approximates to a surrender, evidencing an immediate commission of the crime. Direct evidence of the commission of adultery is of course very rare, and is never demanded. Positive evidence of these proximate acts, such I mean, of course, as the parties being found very near each other and apparently surprised, rising hastily, dress discomposed, one running one way and another another, confusion, hesitancy, embarrassment—positive evidence of that kind of proximate acts is ordinarily the evidence by which adultery is established in a court of law. Accordingly, on a late occasion, in the immediate neighborhood, of which everybody, except perhaps

my brother Dana, may have heard something, that was the admitted
line of proof—positive proof of alleged proximate acts.

The first remark that I have to make here is, that there is not
the first particle of evidence of any proximate act.

Here Mr. Choate carefully analyzed the testimony to show that no proximate acts of adultery had been shown. He then continued:

19. RULES AS TO WEIGHING CIRCUMSTANTIAL EVIDENCE.

The burden being then upon the libellant to establish beyond a
reasonable doubt the fact of the adultery, and the libellant failing
altogether to produce the ordinary evidence of a positive character
of proximate acts, we pass on—still, as you understand, gentlemen,
confining ourselves entirely to the state of the proof, before we arrive at the alleged confessions—we pass on to see what is the nature
of the proof relied upon by the libellant. And you see that it is
circumstantial evidence only of adultery. They rely wholly upon
circumstantial evidence to prove the alleged fact of adultery. I
speak of this intermediate and earlier period, let me say, in order
that I may be perfectly appreciated by the jury, before and independent of the alleged offense sworn to by the Coburns, and I remind you that it is no more, at the best, than circumstantial evidence of adultery. I need not pause to remind you how much
caution, how much candor, and how much intelligence are requisite in appreciating circumstantial evidence in any case. That
kind of evidence may clearly prove guilt. That many times, however, it has also shed innocent blood, and many times it has stained
a fair name, I need not pause for a moment to illustrate or remind
you. Instead of doing that, I think I shall be better occupied,
under the direction of his honor, in reminding you of the two
great rules by which circumstantial evidence is to be weighed, appreciated and applied by the jury. Those rules, gentlemen, are
these :

In the first place, that the jury shall be satisfied, beyond a
reasonable doubt, that the circumstances relied upon to prove the
fact really existed; and then, when these circumstances are clearly
and certainly established.

In the second place, it is a rule of equal, or even more importance in this case, that the jury shall be satisfied that they conduct,
as a necessary result and conclusion, to the inference of guilt. It
is a rule that may be called a golden rule in the examination and
application of this kind of evidence which we call circumstantial,

that should it so turn out that every fact and circumstance alleged and proved to exist is consistent on the one hand with the hypothesis of guilt, and on the other hand consistent, reasonably and fairly, with the hypothesis of innocence, then those circumstances prove nothing at all. Unless they go so far as to establish as a necessary conclusion this guilt which they are offered with a view to establish, they are utterly worthless and ineffectual for the investigation of truth. I had the honor to read to the court this morning, and possibly in your hearing, an authority in which that familiar and elementary doctrine was laid down, a doctrine every day applied, everywhere recognized as primary in the appreciation of this kind of evidence. It is not enough that the circumstances relied upon are plainly and certainly proved. It is not enough to show that they are consistent with the hypothesis of guilt. They must also render the hypothesis of innocence inadmissible and impossible, unreasonable and absurd, or they have proved nothing at all.

20. THE CIRCUMSTANCE RELIED ON BY PLAINTIFF.

I might illustrate this by reference to cases, and by reference to the practice and experience of courts of law. But there is no need at this moment to detain you upon this subject, and I pass at once to the examination of the circumstances relied upon by the counsel for the libellant to prove the charge of adultery. I think I may very well put first, as the foremost upon which they here insist, as the capital fact and circumstance upon which they mean to rely, that Helen Dalton, having been conscious of the guilt of adultery, practiced, by the aid, assistance and advice of her mother, the crime of intentional abortion by the agency of Calkins' instrument, to conceal that guilt. That, I respectfully submit, is the fact, and the great fact that the libellant insists upon in this case. That is the circumstance I have had the honor already to submit to you, by which they at last determined the yet undoubting mind and heart of Dalton. That was the capital suggestion by which they at last approached him, and persuaded him to abandon his wife and institute this libel. That circumstance is also the first and main one through which, from the first three days of this trial, they appeared to gain the ear of the public and the press, and by which they made an impression upon you.

I have the honor to insist upon the evidence, by leave of the court, that a more enormous and manifest falsehood, in the color of circumstantial proof, was never laid before a jury. What is this circumstance, exactly as the libellant, by his testimony, brings it before you? We learn from the testimony that Helen Dalton, having been threatened with a natural miscarriage in the manner indicated in the evidence upon the stand by her mother, and corroborated more particularly by other testimony; having been threatened with a natural miscarriage once, twice, and a third time, was assisted by her mother by some of those feeble and accustomed old woman's remedies, warm water applied to the feet—composition powder to be taken. It is not the charge, and I understand that the learned counsel will not venture to take the ground, if it be true in point of fact, as upon the evidence has been shown to you, that she was merely threatened with a natural miscarriage, and in order to break its force, alleviate its pangs, and, if it was inevitable, abridge its duration, her mother applied the remedies; but the charge is this exactly: that, being perfectly well, liable to bear a child, whose countenance might tell the story of guilt, fearing the revelation of a natural birth, under the advice of her mother, attended by her mother and counselled by her father, she was conducted at first to an irregular operator who performed an artificial operation for abortion. That is the ground taken by the other side; and it is between these two theories, upon this part of the case, that I have the honor of comparing the weight of the evidence and invoking the intelligence of the jury. I ask, gentlemen, which theory it is that commends itself to you? Is it the one propounded by the respondent, proved by her mother, father, Mrs. Richardson, Margaret Ware, Mrs. Emerson, Dr. Calkins, and by everybody, that it was a natural miscarriage, three times developing the threat of its approach, three times vainly sought to be alleviated by those trivial remedies of the mother, three times feared, three times provided against, and at last, happening under the anguish of the communication made to her by Dalton through Mrs. Richardson? Is it this, or is it, as they put forward; that being perfectly well, pregnant, and about to be naturally delivered, but not knowing who was the father of the child, and fearing that its birth might reveal her guilt, for the purpose of concealment she resorted to this abortion? If it is the explanation which we lay before you, of course this is all perfectly worthless as circumstantial evidence in the case. But if, on the other hand, they have established their theory, these are circumstances, I admit, of great strength; and I have, therefore, the honor to repeat that this is the capital fact or circumstance offered by the learned counsel, and attempted to be proved by his witnesses, and by which they persuaded Dalton to resort to this libel, by which they stand or fall, upon the judgment of this jury, in their whole case.

21. No motive to induce defendant to destroy her offspring.

I pray your attention, therefore, for a moment somewhat more carefully, particularly to the weight of the evidence upon this point. And the very first thing to which your attention is likely to be called, is the question: Where was the motive which induced Helen Dalton, or the mother of Helen Dalton, to commit this crime of abortion ? Where was the motive to stifle the birth of life of her unborn babe in the circumstances imputed in the libel ? Where was the motive ? My learned friend is very well aware of the importance of that part of the case, and therefore he made it substantially the groundwork of the case, saying that he should prove, by certain evidence more clearly to be brought before you, that Helen Dalton stated that she could not tell who was the father of her child, and to secure herself from that shame, abortion was practiced upon her by the knowledge of some of her family and through the instrumentality of a low physician. My learned brother put forward the motive and took the issue; but having gone through with the evidence in this part of the case, I ask you where is the particle of evidence, credible or incredible, that Helen Dalton ever stated to any human being that she did not know who was the father of her child ? Where is the witness, Edward Coburn, John Coburn, Mary Hunter, or anybody, who comes forward here to give the least color to a charge so cruel and yet so decisive as this ? If they told my learned friend so, upon consultation with him, before they appeared upon the stand, I can only say that when they came before this court, and into the light of this room, they did not dare to repeat it. I can only say, that if anybody told him so anywhere, when they came here, that which was a mere fiction in the beginning, their memory refused to enable them to repeat in your presence; for I have the honor again to submit to you that, from the first to the last, there is not a scintilla of evidence from any witness, even from the most disreputable and untrustworthy of them all, that Helen Dalton ever breathed a doubt to mortal man or woman of the paternity of her yet unborn babe. On the contrary, if it were necessary to consume your time upon this point, I

might show you by Miss Dalton and other witnesses, that it was
known to everybody, or assumed by everybody, that Dalton was
the father of the child. Mary Hunter tells you that this savin,
about which she gives you so much information, the leaves of
which may be as large as your thumb-nail, or as large as the New
York *Courier & Enquirer*, she don't know which, was given to
bring along Dalton's child. It was Dalton's child, by the testimony of all, that was to be made to be born before its time; and
from the testimony of no one, in view of the evidence, light or
dark, is there a suggestion that she ever feared in her life that it
should prove otherwise. Where then, I ask you, does my learned
brother find a warrant for that opening which made such a lodg-
ment in your minds and in the minds of the community a fortnight ago, when this case commenced, the assertion that she said
she did not know who was the father, and not knowing what father's
face might be painted upon its infancy, she decided to destroy it?
I respectfully submit, upon the other hand, that it is demonstrated
in the course of the evidence, so as to leave no doubt upon the
mind of a human being, that whatever else there may be in this
case to regret, and whatever else there may be to investigate, Dalton was the father of that child; that it was known to him, that it
was known to her, that it was known or believed to be so by everybody. And therefore the foundation of this most cruel and yet in-
fluential pretense is struck from under their feet.

Here Mr Choate reviewed the evidence to support his statement, and to
show that this testimony was not contradicted. He then continued:

Can it be that rights like these, that affections like these, are to
be determined by the jury against proof or without proof, and in
the face of a body of such proof as that with which we confront
it? On the other hand, we have the honor to lay before you, first,
the testimony of three witnesses swearing to the matter, directly
and distinctly as within their own knowledge; and, secondly, that
of two experts, who apply their knowledge of science to this subject, and who declare that the knowledge of conception must have
dated back as far as the last of September or the first of October.

Starting from that, the next inquiry in this case is, when and
where did Helen Dalton first become acquainted with Sumner?
That at that time she had ever known such a man as Sumner, not
a human being contends. And yet the time of that acquaintance
has a very material bearing upon the alleged statement that she

said she did not know who was the child's father; and in order to show you the utter groundlessness of that charge, I have only to remind you that they have not produced one scrap of evidence that she ever saw the person of Sumner in her life before the middle of October. And she bore in her bosom a pregnancy of a month, or at least of two or three weeks, before she ever saw him in her life. I contend that nobody's suspicions have ever dreamed that there was any colorable pretense for the charge of an unlawful connection with Sumner until the 16th of October, when certainly she was one or two months advanced in this pregnancy. There is no proof which they have been able to bring upon that point.

But I do not rest it upon the absence of evidence. How stands the matter, so far as regards the direct testimony? They have introduced two direct witnesses who certainly are entitled to credit; Miss Snow, a respectable young lady, and friend of Helen Dalton, and willing to be her friend and to avow herself to be her friend; and Mrs. Coburn, her sister, who would know, if any human being would know, the fact; and both declare that, to their best knowledge and belief, Helen Dalton never saw Sumner in her life up to the middle of October. Miss Snow declares that all the knowledge she has of their acquaintance begins about the middle of October, when she was introduced to him; and Mrs. Coburn, in her deposition read to you last night, makes the declaration that it was the middle of October before she ever saw him. Are not the facts undoubted that she was pregnant, that it was known to her husband, known to her mother and her sisters?

22. TESTIMONY REVIEWED TO SHOW ABSENCE OF MOTIVE.

And now, turning again to my learned friend, who says that she declared she did not know who was the father of her child, I ask him, as I asked before, where was the motive to stifle his unborn babe in the birth of life, and to add this crime of murder to all the other incidents with which this case is connected? Where was the motive? Do you think it probable, Mr. Foreman—I pray your attention to the evidence—do you think it probable that this young wife, suspected by her husband and stricken to her heart because her husband suspected; who knew perfectly well that she was innocent; who hoped that it might live to be a tie and pledge to them in the days of their reunion; who knew perfectly well that she carried in her bosom, upon her infant's eloquent features, what might one day testify to the legitimacy of the child, the honor of the hus-

18

band, and the virtue of the wife—do you believe that then and there she would surrender her body to this operation, to this peril, to stifle and destroy her means of proof; her most eloquent of advocates, the most powerful means by which a mother expecting and hoping for progeny could look forward to restore the alienated heart of a once loving husband, with whom she must either live or bear no life? I turn upon him, in total absence of proof of these alleged facts, and I ask what motive could she have had? I appeal, to borrow the language of the Queen of France, when, in that great trial which terminated with the sacrifice of her life, being accused of everything else, she was accused of pandering the vices of her son, she exclaimed, and that shriek went through France and through Europe: " I appeal to mothers, if it be possible ! " I appeal to you if it be possible that this daughter should be led out by her mother, and trotted across the street like an unclean beast, for an operation which was to destroy the hopes of both. I appeal to you if it be possible that that mother and grandmother can be believed to have cared so little about the operation for intentional abortion, as was testified by one witness, that she had performed it herself half a dozen times upon the person of Mrs. Emerson, so that she would do it as lightly and unfeelingly as a boy would shake green apples from a tree. I appeal to you, gentlemen, if our hearts and our reasons do not pronounce and denounce the whole story as a fabrication, an ingenious falsehood, without a single element of grave truth?

Here Mr. Choate showed that the only proof to the contrary was that of John H. Coburn, Edward O. Coburn, and Mary Hunter, whose testimony he showed was conflicting and unworthy of belief. He then continued :

Now, what have we upon the other side? I do not know but the trial will end in the severance of this tie; and in a general conviction of a body of perjury committed in the court-house under your eye, most hideous, most enormous, most unparalleled in the administration of criminal justice. But if it is not to come to that, then I put upon one side of this case of the charge of abortion this great fact: that we produce the positive and direct testimony of five witnesses—for I include Mr. and Mrs. Emerson, inasmuch as it is just as fully proved that the operation for abortion has been practiced upon Mrs. Emerson for six times as upon Helen Dalton once—five witnesses, hitherto respectable in the eyes of the community, who have come before you with every apparent title to your confidence, and who have opposed the declarations which the other side have brought forward, by declarations of matters of fact strictly within their personal knowledge. Three of them say that no abortion was practiced upon Helen, and two of them testified that no abortion was practiced upon Mrs. Emerson. Five witnesses swear directly as to a matter of fact, most striking and painful if it ever happened within their recent experience, which they will remember as long as their moral nature exists, if it occurred at all; and these five tell you that the story is false and scandalous and groundless from beginning to end.

23. DEFENDANT'S PROOF SHOWING FALSITY OF THE CHARGE NARRATED.

I think I should hardly be warranted in an ordinary case in detaining you another moment, if it were not very material, if it were probable, if it were not attended with consequences which I think will settle this controversy. If it were a mere naked question whether abortion was procured or not, I should leave it here; but inasmuch as, if it were not done, if that story is as false, every part of it, as any fabrication from the infernal world, this whole case goes down with it, I ask you to pause a moment longer. If there was no abortion, permit me to say, better were it for John H. Coburn, Edward O. Coburn, and Mary Hunter, if they from an untimely birth had never seen the light, than that they should come here and commit this great sin, if they die without repentance and without forgiveness. I submit that it will follow inevitably, in every aspect of this case, that if that story is untrue, there is not a particle of foundation to rest their case upon from the beginning.

I am not blaming Dalton. Do not understand me as blaming Dalton because he brings forward their charge of abortion. They vanquished him by it. They made a child of him by it. They made him believe that story. He took it as it was told to him, and it was no folly for him to lay it before you. It is they who fabricated it, and who by means of it have won him to this pursuit, who are deserving of our censure. Upon that I have something further to say by and by.

Now I ask you, first and foremost, whether you believe our five positive witnesses. I would not in any ordinary case consume time upon it; but if you will bear with me, I think there is a capital distinction between the testimony of the other side and that of these five witnesses, who swear to matters of fact within their own positive knowledge. If that matron mother led that blooming and

innocent child across the street for the performance of this operation, she knows it.   If Mr. Gove was consulted about it, or counselled it either before he went West or after his return, he knows it
perfectly.   If this happened at all, I submit to you that Dr. Calkins
knows it perfectly.   And if it was ever practiced upon the pure,
youthful, matron form of Mrs. Emerson, does not she and does not
her husband know it ?   And yet they all declare it to be an absolute
falsehood upon the stand.   Can there possibly be any escape for
them if they are wrong ?   Is not here an absolute certainty that, if
they are honest and state what they believe to be true, they cannot
be mistaken ?   Allow me for a moment to run over this part of the
evidence, that you may perceive its entire strength; for I want this
matter put completely at rest, to put at rest your judgment; and I
want your verdict to express your opinion upon this point.   Let me
then go over this evidence a little more in detail.

24. Mrs. Gove—her character and testimony.

We call Mrs. Gove, who declares upon her solemn oath in your
presence, that she never advised an operation, that she never accompanied her daughter for that purpose, and that she never
suspected or dreamed that it was ever charged until a late period
in the history of this case.   You remember her testimony upon the
stand, and I ask you whether you believe her a willful perjurer.   I
know the deep feeling with which she testifies in the case.   I know
that she has arrived at a time of life when the future is abridged as
well as uncertain and doubtful, and I believe that at any time of
life she would give her own for her child; and I submit to you, if
there is any ground to say or any ground to suspect that she comes
here willing to peril her soul—and she sustains, I believe, a Christian character—in swearing to a falsehood.   Do you believe that
story to be true ?   Grief may have impaired her faculties to some
extent.   Her memory may be occasionally somewhat defective.
Some exceptions may have been taken as to her manner upon the
stand.   But the solemnity and dignity of that Christian matron as
a witness here must, I think, have given to you all the assurance
you could desire that she meant to tell the truth.   Is there any
escape for her upon the ground of forgetfulness ?   Can it be that
she could take part in such a transaction, and not be able to remember it ? or that she does so much of it in her own house that a
particular case of that kind makes no impression upon her memory?
Could she be mixed up with a domestic agony so sharp as this—

could she possibly have taken part in it, led her child to the knife, and carried her back to a premature delivery—and have forgotten it? Gentlemen, there is no such escape for my learned friend as this. There is the most dreadful perjury, or she has told the truth.

But you observe, still further, that there is no excuse left upon the score of forgetfulness, for another reason. You cannot have forgotten with how much minuteness of detail she traced the history of this case. She fixed the period of the pregnancy, announced the fact that she was three times threatened with miscarriage, fixed the number of weeks as nearly as the time may be fixed, a time corroborated by the testimony in the case of the final miscarriage. You will remember that she stated with the utmost precision the kind of remedies which she applied, the periods she applied them, the effects that followed; that one attack passed away, and then, after a considerable interval, another came on; that these attacks were subdued under the influence of some applications made by her maternal care; and at last the third and decisive attack followed, hurried to its inevitable consummation by that sharpest of afflictions, announced by Mr. Richardson, that her husband refused to meet her again. I respectfully submit, therefore, that there is no room—none in the world—for escape, upon the score of forgetfulness, from the charge of perjury, if she has not told you the truth.

25. MR. GOVE,—HIS CHARACTER AND TESTIMONY.

Permit me now to say something of Mr. Gove. He stands before you convicted of a violation of truth and a most deliberate perjury, if he had any agency, direct or indirect, or if he ever suspected in his life that the crime of abortion was committed, until he heard it in the anonymous communication of which he has spoken. I know very well that Mr. Gove's testimony is liable to criticism. With this burden upon his mind, and this long agony, threatened as he is with the lopping off the lowest and fairest branch of the family tree, I know how full his heart is, and I respect him the more for it. I know, gentlemen, that he does not dismiss it from his thoughts an hour; that it is in his prayers; that it goes with him to his bed; that it attends him in the streets; that it lies heavy upon his heart everywhere; that it makes him forget the proprieties of his general character, in the presence of one of the jury. I know that it haunts his dreams—dreams, gentlemen; he has no sleep but the sleep which anodynes supply him;

and I know very well, therefore, that in regard to the trifling matters of detail, or concerning proprieties of conduct, Mr. Gove has not appeared advantageously. The father has been too strong for the citizen, in certain respects and to a certain extent; and I need not appeal to you, gentlemen, who may expect or fear also yourselves to be judged, to say whether or not he would commit a willful perjury upon a matter of fact like this. Is not that a wholly delusive theory, in everybody's judgment? May he not be imprudent and talkative, wish to hear whether one man or another man is to pass upon this trial which affects more than his life, because it affects what is treasured in his heart? May he not want to know about what this witness says, or what that witness says? May he not talk imprudently or even foolishly, but yet, past the middle of life, a man whose gray hairs and bald head give evidence of an approach to that time when we should be walking, thoughtful and silent, upon the solemn shore of that vast ocean upon whose waves we are to sail so soon, would he not put truth and good words on board? Is that the correct inference that a man like Mr. Gove—grown up before you, a boy from the country, of respectable and pious parentage, one of the disciples and children of John and Charles Wesley, who sings their hymns, utters their prayers daily and nightly—comes to swear deliberately and willfully to a falsehood? God forbid, gentlemen, that we should thus judge one another in judgment! I do not appeal to your charity, to your hearts, but I put it to your knowledge of life—and you may be parents—whether you cannot appreciate perfectly how the father should be talkative, and forward, and imprudent; willing to forget, or at any rate forgetful of smaller and minute details, and yet shrink back as if hell opened under his feet from the utterance of a lie?

Here Mr. Choate reviewed the evidence to show the falsity of the crime charged against the defendant and against her father, and continued:

26. Dr. Calkins.—Inference from his refusals to answer.

There is another single witness who, if anybody upon the face of the earth, must have known whether this charge was true or false, and that is Dr. Calkins. We who did not know who he was, or care what he was, produced him here; because we knew that whatever he was, he would not dare to stand before the face of that mother and child, and tell you that that mother ever practiced abortion or assisted in it. We called him and placed him before

you, and you know that, unless he adds to the other black list the
guilt of perjury, the charge is groundless. As Dr. Calkins is a
stranger, he was entitled to be heard before you, and I submit to
you that he is entitled to be believed upon his oath, upon every
principle of law and common sense, until it is shown why he should
not be believed.   Every witness is entitled to be believed upon his
oath with regard to a matter within his knowledge, unless we have
some certain ground upon which to discredit him.   I ask you, if
there is one scintilla of evidence that should warrant you upon
your oaths in saying that Dr. Calkins has sworn to a word of un-
truth ? What is there against Dr. Calkins ? This only. My learned
brother addressed certain inquiries to ascertain whether he had not
at some other period procured an irregular abortion.   Dr. Calkins
took his constitutional privilege and declined to answer.   What is
the inference ? It is that he so respects his oath, that he dares
not answer untruly; and that he could not answer untruly, without
criminating himself, he took his constitutional privilege and declined to answer.   What was to hinder him from giving my brother
information about that bamboo-bottomed chair ? What was to
hinder him from denying everything, but the fear of Almighty
God on the oath he had taken ?   And why does he stand here and
swear that he did not practice an abortion upon Helen, but because
he can truly do it ? I submit to you, that the very fact that he
made this distinction, that he claimed this constitutional privilege
in the one instance, upon which his honor instantly extended to
him its protection, and answered freely in the other instance,
showed that he could negative one inquiry as a man of conscience
under oath, and respected his oath too much to negative the other.
Although I disapprove of what we may conjecture his practice to
have been, I thank God that herein we may see another illustration
that a man may do one wrong and commit one irregular act, or one
breach of the law, and yet that he is not necessarily a devil incar-
nate, a perjurer, or an adulterer.

     I go further for Dr. Calkins and say this: Disapproving alto-
gether of his bamboo-bottomed chair, unless it is an easier one than
I have been accustomed to, I have this to say for him, that there is
not a scrap of evidence in here that he has taken an infant's life,
or endangered a human mother—not one.   In coming before you,
I know nothing of reputation, and you know nothing of reputation;
we know nothing but the evidence of the facts, as they have been
by law laid regularly before you.

27. DEFENDANT'S EVIDENCE STRONGLY CORROBORATED.

Three witnesses, then, the only ones who have spoken upon the subject, declare this charge of abortion against Helen Dalton to be false. Are they not corroborated?

Here Mr. Choate stated the corroborating testimony, and continued :

I should be glad to know, also, if there is any corroboration of the assertion that here was an intentional abortion, and not the natural progression of a miscarriage. I should like to know why we have not further evidence about it from this family. How comes it to pass that this young woman, passing to Pleasant street and going to Dr. Calkins, no human being in or about the house ever heard or dreamed of it? Mrs. Richardson did not know it; and how comes it to pass that Mrs. Emerson, who spent that very Friday there, upon the evidence of the mother and daughter, who heard her mother say that she feared a miscarriage—how comes it to pass that she knows nothing at all about it? It negatives it. If Mrs. Coburn is not willfully perjured, and that will hardly be contended here, you have this striking fact. The testimony of all these parties refers to the successive attacks, and to the fact that the mother feared a miscarriage; it shows that she called upon Helen to lie down and keep still in order to prevent it; she kept her still and recumbent, and in two cases it all passed away; she administered the harmless foot-bath and composition powder, to diminish its pangs if it should not pass away. I think, too, there is corroboration in the testimony of Dr. Clark; and in this whole case, if her story is corroborated anywhere, I think you will find that corroboration here, that it is an ordinary case of natural miscarriage, the result, it may be, of grief or care. Dr. Storer and Dr. Jackson have testified that it belongs to this great trial of woman, extraordinary and mysterious, this bearing of children in pain; it is a part of the law that not only physical disease, accident, physical calamity, but the labor of the heart, sorrow and anguish, fear and doubt, and mental pain, may produce this effect—it is the ordinary history. These remedies rather mark the purpose of the mother to soothe her nerves for the purpose either of securing her from miscarriage, or conducing to her comfort in that untoward event.

Here Mr. Choate reviewed more corroborative testimony. He then continued :

I intend, if my feelings will allow me, to bring this whole series of correspondence, by and by, in its order before the jury, in demonstration of the merits in this case. It will be useless to turn to that correspondence now. Suffice it for the present to say this: What becomes of this theory of abortion upon the other side? The story is that, being well enough, feeling herself pregnant, and not knowing who was the father of the child, she decided to submit to this operation, and put it to death. And upon this view of the case, this whole operation should be conducted secretly and without the knowledge of her husband; whereas we see by his letters, as I will show you more completely and regularly by and by, she apprised him from attack to attack, exactly or substantially what was the matter, exactly or substantially what they all feared, exactly or substantially what her mother was giving in order to alleviate her pains if the miscarriage was to happen, and after all, she congratulates herself, congratulates Dalton, that she will give him a child at last, and moots the little playful conjugal question, " Shall it be a boy or a girl?" I will not trust myself now to read from her letter, but the result is an ample demonstration that her father, mother, sisters, all knew of it.

Here Mr. Choate stated other corroborating testimony, and continued :

28. THE TESTIMONY OF THE PARTIES CONTRASTED.

I now put it to you, as I said before, that if our confidence in human testimony is not to be abandoned, that apparently just, pure, comely, intelligent and still young wife, swore to the truth when she said that she never had abortion practiced upon her by instruments, or by purpose, in her lifetime; that she had suffered one certainly natural miscarriage, and possibly another, may be true; but the whole story as it was told here, in every part and parcel, in substance and in color, was wholly false. We must believe that somebody tells the truth, and we must believe that one or another swears falsely. I do not think it a very wise position to maintain that a witness upon one side swears intentionally to a falsehood. It is a hard charge to bring—a dreadful crime to impute. Better is it to adopt almost any supposition, to solve the case, than that supposition. But we are here in this painful and remarkable position—somebody has perjured himself or herself before God Almighty. That we know. We have only by our best lights to say who, the one or the other, has done it. You are not, therefore, brought at all to the painful dilemma of being obliged to take a certain theory of a case, or to say that an individual has sworn untruly.   Edward O. Coburn and John H. Coburn have perjured themselves, or five respectable witnesses have perjured themselves; and I put it to you, upon this solemn responsibility of your oaths, to declare whether you do not believe Mrs. Emerson and her husband, and these other witnesses.

Here Mr. Choate referred to the vindictive cross-examination of Mr. Emerson, showing that it was unwarranted, and that the witness had no other motive than to tell the truth.

29. Evidence of flirtation no proof of crime.

What do they go to next?   It is said—and this brings me to an interesting and very important part of the case—that there was an intimacy between Helen and Sumner : walks, drives, rings exchanged, a book given, an intimacy of some weeks, a light, frivolous, objectionable intimacy, one which, as long as she is a living woman, is to be the sorrow and repentance of her life; and so there was.   They will say, as Edward O. Coburn expresses it to Mr. Matthews (that was the witness, I think), that there was a " flirtation " between Mr. Sumner and Mrs. Dalton.   I answer, gentlemen, yes, there was; and I answer also, exactly in the words of Edward O. Coburn and Mr. Matthews, in the same conversation, that it was only a flirtation—that it went no farther than a flirtation—that it might have gone farther, but was stopped.   I answer thus this great piece of circumstantial evidence on which they rely, therefore, in the words of their witness, that it was a flirtation only, and there it stops.

I answer in my own language also, in the next place, gentlemen, which I greatly prefer, that this intimacy, which since the days of Joseph Addison, has been called a flirtation—a vulgar, coarse word, but one that best expresses the idea—this series of conduct, however, which we call flirtation, as circumstantial evidence to prove the fact of adultery, is wholly worthless.   And this is a point on which I hope, gentlemen, at some little length, with some care—not unmindful of my duties as a parent, a citizen—to lay before you my views also as a lawyer, and in a court.   I repeat, and I submit to your honor's direction, and upon the authorities, that this kind of intimacy that is characterized, as Mr. Coburn characterizes it also between the parties, as circumstantial evidence of the crime of adultery, is wholly worthless; and for this decisive reason—founded upon the nature of circumstantial evidence—that it may perfectly well consist with innocence of that great crime. With propriety, with decorum, with a proper respect and regard to reputation, I agree it cannot consist, and does not consist; but with innocence of the least degree of the crime of adultery, I submit that, as circumstantial evidence, it is absolutely worthless, and upon the broad ground that it may perfectly well exist and be committed, and yet no crime of adultery shall have been committed.

I have to ask your attention, gentlemen, a little more particularly to the exhibition of this proposition of evidence under the rules of law, and then to a brief examination of this case; and I submit what I have to say here under three views. But, notwithstanding my entire concurrence with the counsel on the other side, and with the father and with the child in regard to the indecorous, the light, the frivolous character of this kind of conduct, or anything characterized as flirtation, I submit to you, on the whole course of this evidence, it is perfectly clear that Helen Dalton never came to love Sumner with that engrossing, impulsive and absorbing love that endangers virtue and conquers the instincts of shame. I shall submit it to you on the consideration of the evidence applicable to the case. I shall submit to you, further, that it is perfectly clear, that the very moment she discovered that in his case his warmer feelings were carrying him beyond the line of propriety, and threatening a solicitation of personal guilt, she started in a moment from his advances. And I shall submit, thirdly and lastly, that this Mr. Dalton himself, with that knowledge of every single fact and circumstance that made up that entire series of intimacies between Sumner and his wife, came deliberately and intelligently to the judgment that she was wholly innocent of the crime for which she is arraigned here to-day.

30. OBSERVATIONS ON EVILS OF FLIRTATION.

Under these three views I beg leave to submit to you some thoughts on this part of the case. Now I had the honor to say— and I shall in a moment refer to the authority that warrants what I insist upon in that behalf—that this matter of intimacy which is characterized by this name, as a circumstantial evidence of the crime of adultery, is not entitled to the least consideration. I have the honor to submit to you that there is no fact in all our social life better established than this: that a young married woman may admit that kind of intimacy and accept a certain degree of pleasure from it, and yet at heart shall never be touched for an instant by the sentiment of a dangerous love, and start back when the proposition of crime is intelligibly made to her, as if hell was opening under her feet. I submit as the result of all our observation of life and of books—our Edgeworths, our Walter Scotts—all that we have observed everywhere, proceeds upon this distinction and reasons upon it—every observer puts the flirt in one class and the adulterer in another, and everybody understands that they belong to a totally distinct species of characters, that a totally distinct moral and censorial treatment of them applies to them everywhere. We ridicule and satirize her whom we call vain, light, coquettish; from the adultress we turn away with aversion and tears. We satirize one as foolish, and turn from the other as wicked. We hold up one as a warning to herself for her own correction; of the other we say: "O no, we never mention her." One is weak, the other is wicked; one has a right, I submit to you, gentlemen, to the benefit of the exhortation of parents, the protection of law, the protection of public opinion, the care of a husband; from the other, duty, public opinion, religion itself commands us to turn away and to tear her from the heart, although its fibres part and its blood follows in the effort. Is it not a fact, gentlemen, not very pleasant, not very creditable, but perfectly well known to us all through our observation of life, that many a woman, married woman, may hover and flutter for half a lifetime in this region of vanity, flattery and coquetry, and yet never dream of taking the dark descent below? Is it not a fact as well established as any other, that falls within our observation? How many of them will flutter their plumage and incline their ear to the music of flattery, and even allow it to be polluted by the whisper of a half suppressed warmer passion, and yet, when the romance is broken by the solicitation of chastity, will start and put their hands upon their ears, and fly as if a goblin damned was revealed before them! I submit to you, gentlemen, that it is a fact perfectly established by all our observation of life, that many a woman may indulge in this sentiment, and accept this treatment and feel this pleasure, whose heart is never touched by an illicit love, and I need not, I think, submit to you—your knowledge of life is enough for it, gentlemen—that, unless the heart is conquered, adultery is utterly impossible.

I return, gentlemen, to maintain my proposition. On the law, I respectfully submit that this conduct on which my brother is by and by to insist as evidence circumstantially proving the commission of the last crime, is worthless as circumstantial evidence to establish it. And while I place myself on that ground, I know, gentlemen, that you cannot by possibility misunderstand me so much as to suppose I am defending this kind of conduct. I believe I go as far as any one of you in my judgment of it; I believe I know I ought at least to go as far as you in my moral condemnation of it. I believe to adopt in advance every word of the polished and expressive exhortation of my friend who will address you on this subject. I agree with him in every word he says of its indecorum and its levity, its frivolity and its danger. But I meet him as a lawyer and on the judgment of this jury, on the knowledge of life, on the language of every observer of life and all we know of it, we know that many women have gone so far and yet could never be suspected of having taken that last final step.

31. APPLICATION OF THE LAW TO THE CASE AT BAR.

In that immediate connection, permit me to remind you of his honor's direction of the course of law which should govern this case. The learned judge, in the case I had the honor to refer to this morning, had occasion to comment upon certain letters that go beyond any letters to be relied upon in this case—to comment upon them and the conduct on the part of the wife. I am permitted by the court to read the passage to you; it is from one of my learned brother's ecclesiastical judges, and I think he at least will approve of their judgment. He was a man, a good man, who knew life too well to make an illogical, a barbarous, a beastly inference from conduct that he disapproved; we knew that ten thousand fashionable women came home at midnight, one o'clock, two o'clock, from a party at which they supposed themselves to be honored, to find their husbands asleep, aye, and to be conscious of a truer pleasure and deeper love when they lay down by his side, than they received from the admirers of an evening. It is a pleasure only too agreeable to a light, susceptible and easily flattered nature, playing around the head, but coming not near the heart; and, therefore, gentlemen, I feel no doubt or difficulty that we should be able to agree in our judgment of the act on its true quality as a ground of inference in relation to the grave charge they have brought here. But let me read the charge of the learned judge:

"The letters have been much examined and commented upon. I have read them over and over again; but I do not intend to follow the counsel in their comments. They are written in an ardent and romantic strain; Bushe soliciting interviews for criminal pur-

poses, for it is impossible his object, in thus addressing a married
woman, could have been other than criminal, or that when a married woman receives such letters from a married man, but that she
must know they were for licentious purposes.   Still, however some
women will go a great way without proceeding to the last extremity
of guilt; and the court must be satisfied, not only that there has
been a surrender of the mind, but of the person."

"Women will go a great way without proceeding to the last extremity of guilt;" therefore, that she has gone a little way or a
great way is not proof of guilt by the oaths of this jury in point of
law.   It is not proof of guilt, it will not warrant an inference, and
it is beyond all manner of controversy, therefore, that here and
now, unless they can go further, much further than to those moral
and ordinary platitudes in which my brother will by and by indulge, about the impropriety of such conduct as this—which he
cannot by possibility paint in anything like the strength of condemnation in which it shows its effects here to-day—an answer to
all that is, that we agree with him perfectly, but that is worthless
for his argument.   Unless, therefore, he can go further than that,
and show you beyond the fact of intimacy and beyond the fact of
flirtation, that there was this consummated act of guilt established
by other collateral and stronger proof, then I respectfully submit
that he totally fails on this part of the case, on the doctrine of circumstantial evidence.

32. The evidence of flirtation entirely worthless.

Now, gentlemen, I have been laying down the law, so to speak,
under the direction of the court, in regard to this kind of evidence, and I have only now to say, leaving the point and proceeding to the proof, that if there ever was a case in the world where a
young married woman might feel a certain degree of pleasure in
this description of intercourse, and yet not commit a great crime,
I think it would be this.   I ask you if you believe it probable that
a young wife, eighteen years of age, in the fifth month of her marriage and the second month of her pregnancy, modest to an extraordinary degree, as her husband attests, a child of schools, a child
of religion, has all at once committed this great crime?   If a writer
of romance should put forward such a case, would you not say he
did not understand his own foolish business, and that his case was
extraordinary and unnatural?   Do you believe it probable, do you
believe it credible, that those instincts of shame, those lessons of

virtue, those lessons of childhood, those words of the holy man by
whom they had just been united in marriage, those prayers, those
hymns, those hopes, were all lost in a moment? I admit, gentlemen, not very much accustomed to this kind of society, probably
never in her life having received the attention and address of a
young man like this, she very naturally felt a certain degree of
pleasure in it—that kind of pleasure that applies to the head, but
does not come near the heart, to which the heart which is wise replies: Can this be joy? But the instant the mask was attempted
to be or was thrown off, that instant she saw it was not her beauty,
or her conversation, or her manners that made the attraction, but
that the aims were lust, she resisted and fled. If then, gentlemen,
I am warranted in my position—as I think you will agree with me ;
as I know I am upon the law—that this series of conduct which we
call a flirtation is not circumstantial evidence of guilt at all, this
case presents the strongest possible illustration of that fact.

33. Evidence of flirtation consistent with a theory of innocence.

There is a cardinal rule for the interpretation of circumstantial
evidence which I referred to yesterday, and which I deem of such
vital importance in the case that I will read it to you again:

"When the facts relied upon are equally capable of two interpretations, one of which is consistent with the defendant's innocence, they will not be sufficient to establish guilt."

That they are irreconcilable with positiveness of guilt, as well
as of innocence, gives them no value as proof of the fact. It will
not, therefore, be enough for my learned brother, when he comes
to comment upon the circumstantial evidence in this case, that the
facts are always and throughout consistent with the supposition of
the crime of adultery. Unless he can go further and show that they
necessarily lead to that conclusion, and that they are utterly irreconcilable with the hypothesis of innocence, they are worth nothing
for any purpose. We take with us also, gentlemen, in this investigation, what I had the honor to lay before you yesterday as a universal maxim of life and society, that that kind of intercourse between a married woman and another not her husband, without his
knowledge, which we generally denominate as a flirtation, is utterly
unavailing to prove the crime of adultery, for the reason that it has
been universally observed, that it may be entirely consistent with

the innocence of the accused. I had the honor in bringing that
maxim to your recollection yesterday, to advert to Addison, Edge-
worth and Scott. It has been recorded and proved, and, by
the kindness of my learned friend, I am enabled to bring to your
recollection another recognition of that fact, in one of those
pregnant and solid judgments of that great and stern moralist,
Dr. Johnson: "Depend on it, sir," said he, "there is a vast
distance from familiarity to that great and last crime—a vast
distance." It is quite apparent, therefore, that in order to make
anything of this series of conduct on the part of Mrs. Dalton, the
libellant is called on to go a great deal further. And I submit it is
perfectly clear that he is to go so far and take this step; that taking
her entire little life as before us, from January, 1855, down to the
last letters which she wrote to her husband in answer to the cruelty
of this libel, he must show you that she had conceived a passion of
illicit love, so vehement and so absorbing towards Sumner as necessarily, when opportunity was afforded, would lead to the commission of the offense with which she is charged. They must take
that step, or they do not advance in the least degree the inference
of guilt from the circumstantial evidence of this trial.

Now, I am about to have the pleasure to lay before you conclusive proofs, that if you take that life from January down to the
last period to which the evidence in the case has traced it, it is perfectly manifest that the general and habitual tone of her sentiment,
of her affection, was steadfastly for her husband; that she loved
him affectionately, deeply, constantly, and always, and although she
might have been a little influenced, her love a little suspended, by
this intimacy, which she and all of us so greatly regret, that it revived again, in all its original strength, the moment the sharp realities of life brought her back again completely to herself. And I
shall respectfully submit, in the next place, that whatever your
opinion may be as to the extent to which this intimacy with Sumner
had proceeded, and how far her interest in him had been carried,
it is perfectly plain, on the evidence introduced by the libellant
himself, that it stopped short, wholly short, of the commission of
the last great offense.

Here Mr. Choate referred to two letters put in evidence by plaintiff, written
by Sumner to defendant, one of which was never opened by her, and both found
in an exposed place. From these facts, he claimed that the letters could not be
relied upon as proof that the defendant loved Sumner, but implied a contrary inference. He explained why the evidence of defendant's letters to Sumner

had been ruled out.   He then reminded the jury that their oaths forbade them to consider testimony which the court had excluded, in arriving at a verdict.   He contended at great length that none of the letters contained evidence of defendant's love for Sumner, nor of guilt between them, and that this theory had not been sustained.   He then commented on the circumstances of the defendant's last ride with Sumner, to Brighton and Watertown, and claimed that this testimony revealed nothing criminal or unnatural.   He then continued:

34. Crime cannot be inferred from proof of unlawful love and opportunity.

I suppose my learned friend's argument will be upon this point, to bring in his ecclesiastical law books to prove that they have somewhere broached the doctrine, that if there is proved to have been unlawful love and opportunity, the jury may infer the crime. I ask your honor to instruct the jury that whatever such authority may be quoted, we have no such law as that in this commonwealth; and upon this point I pray your honor's attention to the case of Dunham v. Dunham.   I claim that we are not bound by it, whatever those works may declare.   They seem to be of the opinion that where there is unlawful love and an opportunity, adultery is necessary as a sort of chemical result.   Do they forget that there is such a thing as free will, such a thing as conscience, such a thing as recollection of the teachings of religion, such a thing as shame, such a thing as a point at which to stop and a point from which to go back ?   They forget the inherent virtue that pervades the nature of woman.   They forget such a word as that.   And therefore I say that the doctrine is old, poor, monkish, artificial, and has never been adopted in this State, and never, as my learned brother will present it to you, in any country; for I believe the work holds that if it turns out that the opportunity did not as a matter of fact carry the parties to the guilt, there is an end of it.   I contend that there is no divorce to be granted for loving or for having an opportunity, if the parties do not indulge.   There is no proof of such indulgence; and therefore every word of the evidence that I have brought before you this morning, is proof to the contrary.   Upon this case it stands demonstrated, and I entreat your judgments upon your oaths to say, that whatever fancy or vanity there may have been, her heart was not affected, at all events she did not yield so far as to carry her beyond the line of perfect personal innocence.   I imagine, gentlemen, that this is pretty nearly the end of the case, and I might here invoke your judgment and leave it.

19

Here Mr. Choate referred to the exchange of rings and presents to show that those acts were open and unconcealed, and were not evidence against defendant. He continued:

35. CIRCUMSTANCES SHOWING THAT DEFENDANT NEVER DECLARED SHE LOVED SUMNER.

I do not know whether my learned brother will think it worth his while to comment upon a little evidence, which, however, they introduced, and I cannot therefore pass entirely unnoticed. Some of it, particularly that of Miss Coburn, may be deserving of our attention; while that of Mary Hunter I maintain to be unworthy of it in the least degree. Upon that they may argue some interest in Sumner. You will scarcely have forgotten that Mary Hunter told you that on the day of the flogging affair, between the time when Porter was beaten and the time when Sumner was brought in to be beaten also, she heard the respondent tell her husband that he was no husband of hers; that he should not be or would not be her husband; that she hoped a dagger or two would be stuck in his heart; and all the rest of that testimony. They gravely produce such trash as that, to show you that she shamelessly avowed to his face that she preferred Sumner to him. I do not believe that if I had passed this over, my learned friend would have said anything about it; but it was introduced, and I suppose was intended to make an impression. To be sure, Mary Hunter is compelled to admit that, on that very night, Dalton, who had heard it all, slept with his wife; and that from that time forward for three weeks he held her upon his own pillow to his heart, which had not yet con- demned. You are glad, I apprehend, to remember, gentlemen, that it is established by the series of letters we have laid before you, that he continued to declare his love for her, and his full belief that she reciprocated that love. And yet this woman is brought here to make you believe that under the circumstances that took place that night, she turns round and tells him to his head : You are no husband to me, and Sumner is the man I love.

Mr. Choate then referred to the testimony of Adelaide Coburn on this point, and claimed that the wife's language on that occasion, when she entreated her husband to remain with her, and added "you are no husband of mine if you leave me now," was not inconsistent with a warm affection on her part toward him. With great ingenuity he sought to turn the evidence to his advantage, and pointed his argument by an illustration from Virgil's famous epic. He said:

36. Dido's entreaty with Æneas.

My friend is welcome to the evidence, if he will only make the proper use of it. Have we not seen ten thousand parallel cases, and is not that exactly what we should expect to find; her praying him not to go, presenting to him every inducement not to go, and even adding, in the language of frantic and imprudent impreca- tion upon him: I hope you will get killed if you go; for God's sake stay with me; stay with me or you are no husband; I hope you will get killed if you go. Is it not a fine touch of human nature in the heart? I submit it to my learned friend, and pray his commentary upon it. And inasmuch as he meets my explana- tion with a smile, may I be permitted to ask him if it has not been regarded a fine touch and true to nature, in the Roman poet when he drew the Carthagenian queen; when she had been driven even to unsex herself in entreating Æneas to remain, and appealed to the memory of that secret meeting in the cave during the storm, when she entreated him by his offspring unborn and by the future of Carthage to stay; and then, when she found him still fixed and determined upon his departure, breaking out before the tempest of her passion and praying that he might perish by the storm and the whirlwind and the flood, without the care of friends or gods, upon the angry sea; and again, when another reaction came, falling back fainting, and carried by her servants to her couch! And do we not find that same fine touch of nature in the mother or the affectionate sister, every day of our lives, when she says to the froward boy, "Stay at home, or I hope you will have your head broke for going out at such a time as this?" That is all there is of it. It is ex- actly that outbreak of human nature which we constantly witness; and I ask you if this is not ten thousand times more probable than the enormous, foolish and barbarous explanation which Mary Hun- ter affords of it.

37. Defendant's love for her husband.

I believe I have now gone over all the evidence upon which the learned counsel have relied here to show how far, to what extent this affection of Mrs. Dalton for Sumner proceeded. I have re- spectfully submitted to you that it was a light, transient, superficial fancy, and no more; for the very instant she discovered that his designs went further than her virtue and her instincts approved, they were met and repelled. If that be the result of the evidence, of course all this part of the case is at an end. But I am only too happy to call to your remembrance, that in regard to the whole body of evidence which is laid before you, if you take her entire life as it is brought before you from January, 1855, when their courtship began, until her very last letter in answer to his libel, which terminates the series, you will find it marked by a sweet, passionate and beautiful love for her husband, as an entire little life, one long, true, constant love, never interrupted, never displaced. Once and for a few weeks losing somewhat of its entire control, but recovering it again in a moment and flowing strongly and beautifully as ever. Let me remind you how the evidence stands in relation to that fact, which is of a good deal of importance and authority, in appreciating all parts of this case, and may do very much towards determining whether she is yet a wife fit for the arms of Dalton and deserving your favorable verdict. Weighing all the circumstances, what do they show us?

She was a child at school when Dalton sought her honorably in marriage. There is no doubt, for Dalton feelingly and strongly so declared, and I think we had other testimony to the same effect, that she was modest, uncommonly so, and to such an extent that, although he met her often, he sought in vain to catch her eye in the street as she walked to and from school. It was only when addressed honorably and openly for marriage, that she yielded him her heart. I submit that it is perfectly clear that Dalton had secured that great thing, a pure and modest young woman's first love. Look at her after life, trace it from the hour of marriage, and you find a uniform concurrence of the evidence in every quarter that she was ever affectionate and fond; that she made his house and his home like another garden of Eden. We have the universal testimony uncontradicted, of everybody everywhere, that she was ever affectionate, ever fond, never away for a moment when she might hope to have the pleasure of his society there, never absent from a meal, never away at the hour of supper, never neglecting a solitary duty of the wife, even to the stitching of a button upon his shirt-collar, but always faithful, always affectionate, always tender. It will add much to a correct understanding of this part of the case to read Dalton's letters to her from the jail, to see whether he then had anywhere any reason to remind her that she was during those few weeks becoming absent-minded, engrossed, or irritable, or that she was at all changed. Not a word of it. There is not a little of evidence to show it, but everything on the contrary demonstrates

that at every moment of time which she could find she devoted to
her husband, that all that time she appeared the same, and manifested that unchanged and affectionate tenderness and care; that
she was never moody, never gloomy, never apparently thinking of
somebody, never apparently sorry to see him; never neglectful of
the ten thousand little cares through which the demonstration of
love exercises and enjoys itself; never absenting herself, but always
there, always there through it all.   I confess that I attach an importance to all this beyond my own power of language to tell or
convey to you, because I put it to your own hearts and your
own knowledge of life, if her heart had not been his, could she not
have changed during those five or six weeks in her husband's eye.
Could she love God and Mammon?   Could her heart own two
loves at once?   No, gentlemen; she would have been changed, she
would have been away at his meals, inattentive to his wants, un-
moved and unregardful of his care—a changed wife in all.   But
what is the fact?   I submit that it stands entirely demonstrated
here, through that whole critical period, upon the testimony of her
husband himself, again and again, most fully and unequivocally
delivered in his letters from the jail, that she was not changed to
him for one hour.   This all follows close upon the affair of the
Shawmut avenue tragedy; and I entreat your attention that there
was no mourning, no tears over Sumner's untimely grave.   Was
there anything in the three weeks following to show that she did
not through all this cling to her old love exactly as before?   Did
not her husband leave her every morning with a kiss, take her
upon his knee, find her there every evening when he came home?
A striking evidence how affectionate was their intercourse is found
in the fact that when Mr. Gove, hearing the rumor of this scandal
and this misery while in the West, coming home distracted and
anxious to see what it was that was threatened, is greeted on his
return by that first sight which he sees—the wife sitting still upon
her husband's knee.   And thus those three weeks passed away.
One or two little irritations arose, it is true, because she thought he
was a little hasty in requiring her to disown her own beloved sister,
but yielding in a moment she throws her arms about him and says:
"I yield it all; I will do it if you say so; I don't see the reason of
it, but I will do it if you say so."   And when once he left her upon
a certain Friday, we have the testimony of Mrs. Richardson how
distracted she was during that absence, how she wandered almost
at midnight to her mother's house to seek an explanation, and to

complain and cry out that the Daltons were getting away her husband from her. And then, when she goes to the jail, she is like a
light in the jail, that every day when she can drag one foot after
the other, in order to give him every possible provision which she
could afford, asking him to have his clothes returned, bringing him
bouquets to give him pleasure in his cell—pansies "for remembrance," as poor Ophelia says—every hour, every moment, down to
the very last, when he goes from the jail and declines to meet her.
I take that whole life together, that little rounded life from January, 1855, to January, 1856, and I say that there is not in the history of womanhood, a history of married life, a year more beautiful, true, constant. I ask you, is not a love like this worth having?
Is it not the evidence of a good heart, a rich heart, a wealth for
him who knows how to cultivate it?

Taking this body of evidence, we find on the other hand as
miserable a piece of folly and nonsense as could well happen, weeks
of shame afterwards looked upon with abhorrence, weeks of sin as
she calls it herself a thousand times over, explaining and asseverating every moment that she was innocent of the great crime; weeks
of sin, but no week, hour or moment of illicit love; even if there
could have been an illicit love, one which stopped short, far short,
of its final consummation of guilt.

Here Mr. Choate read the first letter written by defendant to her husband
in jail, indicating her affection for him. He then showed that, with a knowledge of all the facts in the case, except the charge of abortion, which he claimed
to be a conspiracy against her, Dalton believed his wife, and continued to love
her. He continued:

38. A CONVICTION ASKED ON THE EVIDENCE ON WHICH PLAINTIFF REGARDED HER INNOCENT.

I call your attention particularly to one or two of these last
letters of Dalton from the jail, because they, in my judgment, put
an end to this case. If he, upon all this evidence, believes her to
be innocent of adultery, can he stand before the jury to-day and ask
you upon the very same evidence to believe her guilty of adultery?
Is not he of all human beings the best qualified to judge of the evidence and to judge of its effect? When, therefore, you look upon
his letters, and compare them with the evidence in this case, all of
it known to him when these letters were written, I shall expect you
to use it in his way. In the first place you will say, Dalton had
heard every word of this evidence, and if it really and necessarily

conducts us to an inference of guilt, it must come to us exaggerated. Was not the husband's ear quick to hear, and the husband's
eye quick to see? Would he not know if she had said that which
was to strike a dagger into his heart? Did not he hear it, if she
ever exclaimed, I love Sumner? Certainly he must have heard it,
if it had been said. You will say, then, that there is exaggeration
in the testimony as reported to you, if it conducts you to a more
severe judgment than the husband himself, who, if anybody, could
hear and interpret it aright. But there is another view of this evidence of Dalton's, the just and full import of which I pray you to
weigh. I have touched upon it again and again, but I cannot tear
myself from it. I cannot divest myself of the impression that it
disposes of the controversy. It is the circumstance that Dalton of
all human beings had the best means of judging of the guilt or innocence of his wife, and that his judgment is conclusive upon ours.
Not that you may not find him a poor, silly, trifling and fond fool,
overcome by her blandishments; not but you may be driven to it,
in coming to the conclusion that he could not judge whether she
was guilty or innocent. But there is not a little of evidence to
show that he has not the average and ordinary share of intelligence,
or that he is not altogether qualified to judge for himself. Was not
the husband, under the nature of the circumstances, the best and
the severest of judges? Had not jealousy quickened his apprehension, and even colored his eye against her? Had he not beaten
Sumner almost to death for improper familiarities tendered by him
and not sufficiently promptly repelled by her? Was he not jealous
and suspicious, and therefore exactly in the mood to look upon her
with more distrust than your hearts would allow to entertain? And
when he came to probe the whole matter to the bottom, what
human being so well as Dalton is entitled to belief? When he
looks back and sees that modest eye, averted in the street, that coy
reluctance to yield her virgin heart, that sweet chastity of her original virgin person, who could know as well as he could know how
truly she had loved him always? Who could know as he must
have known how to catch her in a lie, how to probe her for the
truth, how to come suddenly upon her, how to practice a little deception and take her unawares, how to hang upon her sleep and
see what she said when conversing only with her heart and her
spirit, without the assistance of her reason and her judgment?
Who could tell so well as he how sincere was her repentance, and
how that repentance was confined to a mere acknowledgment of

imprudence, joined with a protestation of innocence or guilt? Who could read that heart, who try that case, like Dalton? I hope I do not underrate the intelligence of the jury, upon whose intelligence so much is depending; I do not fear the action of the tribunal which for her I have invoked; but, with the profoundest respect for you, gentlemen of the jury, and for the court, I ask what one human being could best investigate the facts and most surely know how to interpret them, could most certainly draw the right deductions from this whole body of circumstances, if it were not he whom jealousy had exasperated and aroused. He has judged, and he has found her not guilty, upon every particle of evidence in this case but this hideous, incredible, barbarous allegation to which I am coming in a moment.

39. The influences which changed the husband's demeanor.

What changed Dalton when he came out of the jail? I briefly adverted to it yesterday, and may remind you of it again to-day. It was the necessity of his unhappy position. He was on trial for manslaughter, and the penalty threatened to be a severe one. It was necessary that they should be separated; and when they were separated, he fell a victim to the influences which were brought inevitably to bear upon him. You remember the passage in one of his letters, date of December 19th, in which he says:

"My dear wife, if the world could understand your case as I do, I should feel happy; but as they do not, we must make the best of it."

There it is; there is his judgment. For myself I have tried you; for myself I approve you; you gave me your virgin heart and person; you should make me the father of my first child; I have appreciated your error; I have investigated its origin, the extent to which it was carried, and I find you the same dear Nellie that won my heart, and would to God that the judgment of the world was as my judgment, would to God that the opinions of the world would enable me to stand before them and avow thus publicly what I assure you is the settled conviction of my heart and judgment. To show you how long this continued, how long and how steadily he held these opinions, I have to call your attention to letters which he wrote towards the close of the time when he was in jail. We heard something about forged letters. It is to be stated for the thorough understanding of these last letters of his, that he had heard of those forged letters, that he had heard from Nellie that they were forgeries, as by law you are bound to take them to have been. You will see that they never altered his sentiment in the slightest degree, nor colored in the least degree the expression of his affection for her. I shall ask you to take those last letters which he wrote her from the jail; and I entreat you to remember that there is not a line in those letters from beginning to end, there is no intimation that some dark speech had reached his ear and changed his mind. There is an intimation that necessities control him and make it proper for them not to meet quite so openly or immediately as he had anticipated; but there is not a suggestion, from first to last, that down to that hour he had heard a single thing to change his mind—not one. I submit, therefore, that the explanation is entirely in accordance with what I assumed yesterday, that having been compelled by the necessities of his position, as he believes, to live away from her, his mind was perplexed and distracted by the scandal which abused his ear and at last reached and changed his feelings towards her. Now let us see that in these last letters written from the jail, he still loved her, and still promised to meet her, when they could arrange their plans for their future life. The first is dated January 8th.

Here Mr. Choate read passages from several letters written by Dalton to his wife, dated in the early part of January, 1856. Court then took a recess, after which he resumed his argument as follows :

40. EVIDENCE OF THE ALLEGED CONFESSIONS.—A CONFESSION OF GUILT IMPOSSIBLE UNDER THE CIRCUMSTANCES.

We have arrived, in the course of the argument, gentlemen, to the evening of the 25th of February. The case of the libellant, if it can be maintained at all, is to be maintained on this, that although down to that night the respondent had continued constant in her asseveration of innocence of the great crime, and her husband has implicitly believed it, on that night, not having succeeded in forcing an interview with him at the house of Coburn, she confesses to him that she had been guilty of adultery. Unless this part of the case is established by credible and undoubted testimony to your reasonable conviction, it is certain that there is no case for the libellant. We are brought at once, then, to the examination of that important part of the case. And perhaps I cannot better begin what I have to say in relation to it, than by asking you whether

it is at all conceivable, as a matter of probability, that this respondent on that night all at once falls into a confession of guilt.   Down
to that hour, remember, her story had been uniform, and repeated,
and constant; down to that hour, on her oath, in the pangs of premature childbirth, with tears and attestations to God Almighty, she
had declared herself innocent; down to that time her husband had
a hundred times said he had believed her to be so.   And the allegation on the part of the libellant is, that then and there, under the
influence of some incomprehensible motive or another, she suddenly and instantly changes her tone and admits her guilt.   I think,
gentlemen, that the first thought which would present itself to your
mind, with which you should most naturally begin this inquiry, is,
whether or not it is at all conceivable, as a matter of probability, on
any view of the case, that she could then and there go and confess
it.   Those of you who believe with me on this survey of the evidence, and on the judgment of the libellant himself, that she was
wholly innocent of guilt, will of course reject it as entirely incredible and impossible.   But I respectfully submit to those of you who
may feel any degree of doubt in regard to the matter, who might
still think it in any degree an open question whether she was or
was not possibly guilty, although there is no proof of it—I ask
you whether you believe it to be possible that then and there she
makes the confession?   May I ask you, gentlemen, with very great
earnestness and confidence, if you can discover a conceivable motive for it?   I can very well understand, assuming for a moment
the hypothesis of guilt, that although she had down to that hour
continued steady and constant in her asseveration of innocence,
upon a death-bed, in a moment of anticipated final separation from
her husband, wishing to make a clean and clear breast and reveal
everything—if she had down to that time kept so perilous a secret
as this in her bosom, that she would have declared it.

But how stands the admitted fact; for what purpose is it on the
confession of everybody in this case, that she seeks this interview
with her husband?   Everybody tells you—John H. Coburn tells you,
that in that interview she proposes to fly with him to California,
where they can live away and alone.   Every particle of evidence in
this case, entitled or not entitled to confidence, makes it perfectly
clear to a demonstration, that she solicited that interview because,
tortured by his extraordinary absenting himself from her since he
left jail, she was anxious to make one more effort to win him back.
From the hour he left the prison, down to the night of the 25th of

February, she had expected to see him; down to that time she had
been kept from him by influences incomprehensible to herself;
down to that time she felt scandal and slander were keeping them
apart; that his ear had been abused, and that he only wanted one
more assurance from her lips that she had told all the truth, and
he would come back to her. For that purpose, the result of all
the evidence in this case proves, she seeks him, and then and
there—I respectively submit to you in advance—that it is a stupendous moral improbability, which nothing can sustain, that on
any possible theory of this case, she should meet him and fall into
a confession of adultery. For what conceivable purpose, I ask
you again, on any theory of the case, should she do it? She was
dying to live with him; her heart craved him; she must live there
or bear no life, and the whole object of the interview, obtained partially, they say, by stratagem—and I dare say it is so, for they did
not intend to meet—was to remove any lingering doubt or uncertainty on his mind in regard to her supposed guilt. The very object of it was to overcome any obstacle that scandal and slander
had placed between their reunion, and therefore I submit it is prov-
able by no amount of evidence, that meeting him for that purpose,
she falls instantly into a confession of guilt. Whether she was
guilty or innocent, I submit to you; we know, as men of common
intelligence, that she would have continued, then and there, steadfast in her assertion of innocence; was she so great a fool as to
think for a moment, that if after so many and such solemn assevera-
tions of her innocence she could not win her husband back, a little
confession of adultery would do it? If he would not live with her
an innocent woman, would he live with her a guilty woman? If he
would not live with her believing her heart to be his and her body
to be his, would he live with her after he learned that she had surrendered both to his pollution? I put it to you, in advance, gentlemen, that if an angel from heaven, a being assuming to come in
the guise of an angel, should appear before you with such a story
as this, it would bring his origin, mission and character into great
question with you. Was she afraid at that time of any new revelation? Certainly none at all. The forged letters, if she had heard
of them, she declared to be forgeries, and her husband believed it.
Sumner was in his grave; the last voice that accused her was
hushed in death; and therefore, if down to that hour, fearless of
exposure, fearless of detection anywhere, or from any quarter, she
had continued steadfast in this assertion of innocence, I submit

that every motive that could weigh with the human mind, would have kept her constant in it to the end; and if down to that time, while Sumner was still living, and these letters, if they were not forged, might have been invoked against her and proved to be genuine, she had never faltered in that assertion, and if every motive of fear had gone, and every motive for persistence in her original statement had remained in all its force, I repeat, even upon the testimony of John H. Coburn and Edward O. Coburn, and from all the facts and circumstances in this case, she seeks that interview for the single purpose of disabusing the ear of her husband of this scandal and slander, by which he was kept so mysteriously away from her, and therefore it is not possible, under the ordinary and known laws of human nature, that she should not have persisted in her innocence still. Those of you who believe with me all the evidence in this case as judged by Dalton himself, will declare her innocent; those of you who are in any degree of doubt upon that subject, will also say she is innocent. I have therefore to call your attention directly to the nature of the evidence by which they attempt to overcome our claim of the improbability of this confession.

41. Nature and character of confessions as evidence.

And this makes it necessary and proper that I should say a word in advance in regard to the nature and danger of this kind of evidence on which they are now relying. It is the evidence of confession, and confessions on the reported words of the speaker. It is very common to say, and it has passed into a maxim of the law, and it is one, I dare say, upon which his honor will give you the results of his own experience in his instructions to the jury, that it is a kind of evidence in all circumstances extremely dangerous, and to be most critically and carefully considered by the jury. The evidence of confession may sometimes be the highest and most satisfactory in a judicial investigation; and, on the other hand, it may be, according to the circumstances of the case, the most worthless by which human rights are ever brought in peril in a court of law.

Gentlemen, if we can feel undoubted confidence that the exact words of the speaker are brought before us as they were uttered; if we can feel undoubted confidence that we have them all in their proper order and according to their sense and meaning as they were spoken; if we can feel undoubted confidence that nothing has been omitted, nothing has been colored, the right collocation has been pursued from first to last, and that the true substantial sense and effect, as it was intended when they were uttered, has been given, we may then, with great confidence and certainty, proceed to the most solemn of adjudications. But if, on the other hand, there is reason to fear that the words themselves may have been imperfectly heard; if they come reported to us by untrustworthy and unreliable witnesses; if they are testified to by persons under strong temptation to color, to exaggerate, to forget, to drop the appropriate qualifications, to change the order of them as they are spoken; if they come before us under such circumstances as these, gentlemen, there is no weaker or more worthless or more pernicious description of proof on which an intelligent jury are called upon to investigate a case.

I think we need not go further than such a case as this to indicate the danger of such a species of evidence. Had you not had it proved, by the most undoubted testimony in the case, that Mr. Dalton, with apparent sincerity, declared in the country, that Mrs· Dalton had confessed to him that she committed the crime of adultery in Fera's saloon. You remember the testimony of William Richardson to this point; and to those of you who know him and his character, and to all of you who have seen and heard him on the stand, I am sure there cannot be a particle of doubt that Dalton made the declaration with apparent sincerity. That he did so, is the evidence of Mr. Richardson, under circumstances that give it entire credit in the minds of the jury; that he did so submit, made it perfectly clear by the fact that the allegation in the libel charges in terms adultery in Fera's saloon. Dalton then made that declaration—and as I believe that Dalton, with all his faults, all his mistakes (and as much as I pity him, I have to the same extent to censure him), is still an honest, intelligent man—you have it before you that he himself, an honester man than either of these Coburns, a thousand times told, verily believed, and seriously declared that his wife had confessed to his face adultery in Fera's saloon. That you have heard from him. Did she ever make such a confession as this to Dalton? Did she ever say a word to him which, as he understood it, at a time when his mind was fairly and freely under the influence of no sinister motive or biases or cause of disturbance—did she ever make such a declaration as this to him in her life? Gentlemen, let his own conduct answer that question. I had occasion to advert to it yesterday, but it is necessary again to call your attention to it. Dalton himself declared that the confession was

made to him about the time of the flogging affair of the 17th of
November. That it was made then, if it was ever made, there is
no matter of controversy or doubt in this case. If any fact is
established, it is this one: that from the 14th of January until the
evening of the 25th of February, he never met her at all. This
confession of his wife, therefore, thus distinctly and deliberately
affirmed by him to have been made to him, was made on or before
or about the 17th of November, and within three or four days following that tragedy. Did Dalton at that time understand that to
be a confession of guilt in Fera's saloon? Didn't he live with her
for the three weeks following as a loving and trusting husband?
Didn't he write her letters which have been so much the subject of
commentary before you? Is it not, therefore, perfectly clear, as he
heard them first when his ear was unabused, and his mind capable
of judging, and his memory capable of accurately reporting, that
he understood her perfectly? What did he understand her to say
then? Just what she has said everywhere, just what she has said
a hundred times over in her letters, more forcibly and more strongly
everywhere against herself than there—that she had sinned with
Sumner; that she had had improper intercourse and intimacy with
him, and that she had met in the course of that intimacy at Fera's
saloon. That was exactly the confession as she made it; that was
exactly the manner in which he understood it then, proved by his
subsequent, unequivocal acts; and yet afterwards, when he came
abroad and began to look back upon it from some time subsequent,
when he began to conjecture that public opinion began to proscribe this and proscribe that, when his real or false friends had
come to whisper another story in his ear; even then it was, for the
first time, that, attempting to recall the conversation and to find in
it somewhat to justify him for the course public opinion, not his
own convictions, was compelling him to adopt, exceedingly doubtful, perplexed in the extreme, and endeavoring to recall those words,
he recalls them as a confession of actual guilt.

I submit that you have there an illustration and a warning that
should put you upon your guard from first to last, and if you find
such a mind as Dalton's incapable of recalling a confession made
to him deliberately and distinctly, and on which he acted for two
months, incapable to remember, incapable to repeat—judge you
whether or not great caution is not needed in weighing this kind of
evidence, when you appreciate the source from which it comes before us. Always, therefore, gentlemen—and I pray his honor's at-

tention and approbation to the remark—this species of evidence is to be weighed with the utmost degree of care and caution; and I suppose, sir, that I speak the universal language of the books and the universal experience of every lawyer, when I say to you that in the nature of the case no well founded reason to apprehend that the words spoken were equivocal in their nature, that they were meant by the person speaking them in one sense, and yet so uttered that there is danger that they should be taken in another, and when they come before you on the report of witnesses untrustworthy, testifying under strong apparent bias and motive to color and exaggerate, and omit and put them out of their order, it is the weakest and least reliable testimony ever given in a court.

That is true, gentlemen, of this kind of evidence, under all circumstances; but may I not now remind you a little more formally and earnestly, how these confessions all come in.

42. APPLICATION OF THE RULES OF EVIDENCE TO THE FACTS.

May I not remind you that every one of them is made by a party believing and admitting herself to be guilty of something; by a party who, under that consciousness of having been guilty to some extent, through sighs and bursting tears, makes confession of that guilt, intending to make no confession of guilt beyond that. Is there not extreme danger that the extent and nature of the confession, which is insisted upon, will be exaggerated and colored when it comes to be reported to you by parties with a disposition and temper to report unfavorably. Helen Dalton did not stand in a position in which she could deny all impropriety and all guilt; on the contrary, her case is—and it has this affecting and this important peculiarity—that she had much wrong to confess, that she had much guilt to own, that she had many temptations to acknowledge, that she had much sin to pray God and her husband to forgive; therefore, when she is making confessions to this extent, is there not danger the most extreme, unless we can place the most undoubted reliance on the kind of testimony and the character of witnesses by whom it comes to be reported to us, that it will come exaggerated, and misconceived and overrated, perilously and fatally, at the cost of truth.

Here Mr. Choate argued that the letters of defendant in evidence contained confession of impropriety and wrong, but not of the great crime charged. He then continued :

Therefore, you see, even in the interpretation of writing, where the party is making a confession to some extent, there is great danger that we shall interpret those confessions beyond the meaning. And therefore I have to call your attention to that great rule by which not all circumstantial evidence, but in a very extraordinary degree any evidence of confession, is to be judged—that great rule which applies and governs this part of the case, which is that, if the language employed, whether spoken or written, is fairly and reasonably susceptible of a twofold construction, it is the duty of the jury to take it in the milder. It is not at all a matter of feeling, it is not a matter of the heart, it is not a matter of charity, it is not a matter of inclination, but it is a clear rule of the law, that where the language is equivocal, and where circumstances (and her own folly among the rest) have placed the party in a condition in which she must speak in equivocal expression, you are bound everywhere to adopt the milder interpretation; and yet you see that when testimony like that, not resting upon letters, comes to be reported to you by witnesses under strong bias and feeling, to color, exaggerate and overstate, it is all but impossible that it should come before you in form false and distorted.

43. ARRAIGNMENT OF THE WITNESSES TO THE CONFESSION.

The first general remark, then, which I have to make to you on this evidence is, that before the law advises a jury to pay the slightest regard to reported verbal confessions, they ought to have the clearest conviction that the witnesses who come here to report it are perfectly cool, unbiased, impartial, fair, just, and under the influence of no motive and no temptation which should induce them to color, exaggerate or distort it. The law makes it, I submit, and I pray the observation of the court upon this, almost an indispensable prerequisite that they should come before you through a source perfectly trustworthy; through witnesses whose character is undoubted and justly unsuspected by the jury, so that they should feel satisfied that they cannot by any possibility have lost or gained by their representation before you. And I submit that we come to the evidence of confessions in this case, evidence of a fact so improbable in itself, by this great uncertainty standing out on the face of it, that there is not a scintilla of testimony of confession against Helen Dalton, but of the confession of that indiscretion and loss of self-respect about which there is no controversy in the case, except from witnesses who are not apparently entitled to the least degree of regard from the jury.

John H. Coburn, who admits here in this case that he attempted to obtain money by written false pretenses of Mr. Gove, a State's prison offense that ought to destroy his testimony in a moment; Edward O. Coburn, who has to admit in the outset of the cause that he is a robber to the amount of seventeen hundred dollars of his father's money, and Mary Hunter, that brawny stranger of whom we know that she is a wet nurse and a mother without a husband—these are the witnesses who come before you. I say nothing of conspiracies or of families, but I do have the honor to say to you for the rights of my client, in regard to evidence so delicate, requiring to be weighed and handled with such accuracy and care, that it is a body of proof which should put it out of the consideration of the jury in a moment. These witnesses to confession cannot so much as bring a written letter of my client to this case without mutilating it as a forger; they cannot carry a letter to her husband without taking a pen and striking out eleven lines of it, and thus change the whole statement into a lie which she has never uttered. Does not that fact stand outside of this case? Was not his honor, a week or a fortnight ago, obliged by the undoubted rules of law to reject a letter offered in evidence by the counsel on the other side, because it appeared on the evidence addressed to the court, that one of the leading witnesses had by mutilation turned the whole letter into a falsehood, and poisoned her own proofs at the very source. Are they witnesses to be trusted with the report of evidence by words? Are they witnesses to remember words where everything may depend upon the exact expression, upon the order of the language, upon dropping an epithet here and inserting an epithet there, by which the guilt of adultery is confessed? Is this a body of witnesses that are to be trusted to report words, that are the issues of life, with certainty and accuracy? I submit that, on the outside of it, the whole case of confession to be listened to by this jury, is a conclusive and rational distrust which would leave my client in no fear at all of the result. Here is a man that cannot be trusted to carry ten bushels of yellow flat cord across the city for fear that he would steal half of it; who cannot be trusted to take a hat full of uncounted bills to New York. A man who has not honesty enough, or fairness enough, to weigh the hind quarter of an ox—shall he be trusted to weigh out gold dust and dimes, and count the pulses of life? A man not honest

20

enough, a combination not honest enough, to carry a letter without mutilating it into a falsehood, to prove words in which honesty, intelligence and fairness may be entirely omitted!

We come, then, to this examination of confession exactly in this state of the case: It is a probability, amounting almost to a miracle, that a confession should be made under any circumstances at all. Confessions themselves are never to be acted upon by the jury, unless they know, upon their oaths, that they have the very words spoken in the sense in which they came. They never can have that assurance if they have not a clear and undoubting confidence in the speaker that reports them. And their case opens, I say, with this: that a moral miracle is to be established on the testimony of confessions, by the evidence of witnesses, as a body, manifestly and apparently, undeserving a moment's confidence.

44. CREDIBILITY OF WITNESSES.—ARRAIGNMENT OF JOHN H. COBURN.

But, gentlemen, we must go now into this miserable detail a little more fully. My client has been in great danger of being ruined by the evidence of witnesses, every one of whom I submit is worse than the other, and every one of whom is less trustworthy than the other. And it becomes, therefore, my painful duty to ask your attention for a few moments on the evidence to some of these grounds on which the law declares it to be your duty to lay the evidence aside. I hope you know me too well, by this time, gentlemen, at any rate, if not it is too late to make professions about it, to think that I have any pleasure in railing against witnesses; that I expect to gain anything in the least degree by mere sarcasm against witnesses; that I do not recognize in the fullest manner the general presumption of the law that a witness means to speak the truth; that I am not, therefore, bound to show you on this proof that, according to the established and recognized tests by which the credibility of evidence is to be weighed and appreciated, these witnesses are not entitled to confidence.

If I don't go to that extent, do not hear me; if I do not go to that extent, I give my eloquent friend leave to reply that I have brought a mere railing accusation. If I shall show you, according to those standards which the law has provided to discriminate between truth and falsehood, between trustworthiness and untrustworthiness, that these witnesses are not entitled to the full and undoubting confidence of the jury, I then demand of you, on your oaths, gentlemen, that you disbelieve every one of them.

I may be permitted, in this same connection, to repeat a remark I made yesterday, which is, that somebody or another in this case has perjured himself. It is not a vague, a general charge of perjury, to be made out by me against the other side; it is a call on the jury to choose and say, according to recognized tests of credibility by which the credit of witnesses is to be weighed in a court of law, which of the witnesses they will believe and which they will not believe.

I begin, therefore, with the foundation witness in this case, John H. Coburn, and I respectfully submit to you, that, tried by every test of credibility which the law recognizes, on your oaths you are bound to disbelieve him. It is not that a laugh can be raised against Coburn or his testimony—that is nothing; it is that, according to those tests which are founded on the longest and widest experience the law deems satisfactory, to show whether a jury can safely believe or not, he is not to be believed. I submit, then, that John H. Coburn is not an honest man, and is not, therefore, entitled to be heard in so delicate a work as bringing every word my client spoke on that evening to her husband; he is not an honest man, and I put it on your solemn oath to you, that there is not a man on that jury who, on the exhibition of John H. Coburn, would entrust him to carry a bundle worth five dollars from this court-house to the depot. There is not a man of you who would take him into your service for any wages or for no wages; there is not a man of you who would have his own life, his own character, his own good name, still less the life of his child or the good name of his child, to rest on the tongue of that witness for a moment. How does he come into this transaction at all? I will tell you exactly. He found out very well that Mr. Gove was extremely exercised on the subject of this attack upon his daughter; he found that this father, alarmed and apprehensive, receiving anonymous letters, his nights made sleepless, his fears becoming his master, was looking for and fearing evidence in every direction; and says Coburn to himself: "I will have something of this; I will make something out of that, or my name's not John H. Coburn, nor John S. Perkins, nor John S. 'Serkins.'" Here he found the tenderest sensibilities of the human heart tortured. I will not call, as my learned friend did the other day, Mr. Gove an "old fool," but he was an old parent tormented by his heart's love, ready in a moment to believe everything, ready to run to the fortune teller, ready to take counsel with dreams when his anodyne would give him a dream to consult. And says he: "I will have a jacket and trowsers out of this business; I see pantaloons there; I will have a game of billiards and a suit of clothes, or I am nobody." That is the way he comes into the case. He comes and tells Mr. Gove the most treacherous, beastly falsehood by which an exercised, and tender, and apprehensive heart and imagination can be solicited and imposed upon. Says he: "I was in the court-house the other day, very much absorbed in the trial of the cause, and somebody whispered in my ear that one John Simpson saw these people commit adultery out in Brighton." "Now," says he, "I don't think John Simpson will stick to that; I don't know that it is true, but if you will furnish me money enough I will go and find John Simpson, and he can be brought to see whether it is true or not." Every word of that was as black a lie as if it had been uttered by four pirates. He never had heard a word in the court-house about John Simpson; there was no such man as John Simpson; the whole is a pure and sheer coinage of his own bad heart to practice upon this father and furnish himself with the miserable means of a night or two's dissipation in Providence, and a suit of clothes that he had not credit for at a second-hand shop. It is a sheer fabrication—there is no such man as John Simpson on the face of the earth; if there is, now is his time, now is his last time; I call for John Simpson, out of this court or out of this community, to show his head; aye, or any human being that ever heard of him in his life. It would not be extraordinary if, looking over the directories of ten thousand cities, States and kingdoms, you might find such a man; but that John Coburn ever heard of such a name, that the name of such a man was ever reported to him in his life, that he believed for an instant he had any such testimony to give, that it was anything but downright scandal and falsehood—for which, if I was not in a court-house and was not responsible to the law, I should say a horsewhip was the remedy and not the State prison—is preposterous. No such man ever existed. Why do I say this? Does not Coburn come here and say somebody told him about Simpson? Yes; but who told him? Do we rely on what Coburn heard? Here he is: a little money, and he who agreed to go down and make that report through the telegraph will swear to it just as solemnly as he has done it on the stand? Do you believe him on the stand on his oath, or because you believe the principle of veracity is there? I hope the solemnity of an oath will never be dispensed with. I believe it is not likely to be; but I am bound to regard it as a foolish and idle ceremony if it is taken by a heart and head that does not recognize out of doors the principle of truth. I say once more, that you have no more evidence of the existence of John Simpson than you have that Coburn met him at Providence and was about putting him over the wires when he wanted him for evidence. He lied then for money; he may now lie for malignity and consistency. There is not, therefore, a title of evidence, and I call on you who are charged with the administration of justice in this case, who should know by this time that our rights are only as our proofs—and that you don't own your house any more than I own it but upon evidence—that you have no right to your life or good name, no right to entertain a belief in the good name of your wife or child in law, but according to the proofs by which the law is administered—I call upon you here and now to say, this man is a rogue, a liar, a forger of false telegraphic communications. A party comes into this case for the purpose of making money by falsehood; therefore he is to be laid entirely out of the consideration of the jury. Do you suppose that anybody whispered to him in the court-house about John Simpson? Next to John Simpson, I should like to see the man who made the whispered communication in the court-house. He hadn't the curiosity to look over his shoulder, so absorbed was he in the proceedings; somebody whispered in his ear, "Simpson saw all this at Brighton," and he never looked over his shoulder to see who it was. I would like to know if he thought he was a man with a "venerable gray beard," whether he was all right about the feet. He should be suspicious of that, I should think—whether there was nothing cloven anywhere—and to be quite sure whether it was not the suggestion of the devil himself or his own bad heart. Never looked over his shoulder to see the man! If the person who gave that information is within the sound of my voice to-day, let me tell him now is his time, and that he would bring a hundred times more than he was probably ever worth in his life if he would show his head. There never was such a communication; the whole was simply false, and you have no doubt of it as it stands before you.

Gentlemen, you have as little pleasure as I have—and I have little pleasure in remarking upon any human being, who, upon the responsibility of his oath, has given his testimony. But we are here to defend a great right in a court of law, and upon the proofs it would be a mistake of duty if we did not follow this matter up, and hunt up to the whole extent the character of this witness. I say you do not know whether he tells the truth, because he lied down there; and didn't he lie here, and didn't he come up to the Tremont and the Parker House and book himself with a false name —for a charge which remained unliquidated, for all he knows— and then send down a communication in the name of John Simpson, to bring this poor, credulous, terrified heart to a hotel to be cheated? Is there a man who doubts that he had some scoundrel whom it was intended to pass off to Mr. Gove as this Simpson, who was willing to declare to the falsity of the charge? Didn't he twice by writing declare that Simpson was there, and wasn't it a palpable and repeated lie? And this man to save his head and conscience and sacrifice his heart. He is so malignant a creature that if the mere joke of this exquisite falsehood should bring this father up there, merely to give him the trouble of walking to the hotel and an additional walk upstairs—no, I give John H. Coburn credit for not quite so much malignity as this; and I have reason to suppose that if it was not for a little money to play billiards with and a suit of new clothes, he would hardly go so far as that. Practice a joke under those circumstances! Is this the character of Coburn? Why, he admitted all this falsehood on the stand in such a winning, ingenious and loving way—that he was a great rogue and liar, and had been everywhere, that we were almost attracted to him. It is, therefore, fit and proper we should know that this winning confession of Coburn on the stand was not quite so voluntary after all, but if it becomes necessary to bring another incident into the trial, he is ready to furnish it.

This Coburn, about six days ago, was attacked by a very bad erysipelas in his ankle. I do not wonder at that; after his five hours' examination on that stand I think he might get it. But he was attacked with a very bad erysipelas in his foot or ankle. In my humble judgment, it was an erysipelas of apprehension about coming into the court-house to testify under the eye of the court and jury. But he was attacked, and accordingly we sent a couple of eminent physicians, Drs. Dana and Durant, up to see what they could do for him, and they put him through a course of warm water or composition powder, or one thing or another, until they cured the erysipelas beyond all doubt, gentlemen. They killed the witness and they cured the patient. So the man came upon the stand, and admitted he sent this communication by telegraph, and the message from the Parker and Tremont. He swore forty times very deliberately that he never wrote one of them—deliberately and repeatedly over and over again, and it was not till my friend, the Doctor here, had turned that screw about a hundred times, with from forty to fifty interrogations, that he was beaten out of one covert into another, from another into another, until at last he was obliged to confess, although he began with most peremptorily denying it altogether, that he sent the telegraph and wrote the forged communication from the Tremont and Parker House.

That deposition has been read to you, gentlemen, and perhaps it may be within your recollection, and I will not take a great deal of time to verify what I have said. I do maintain—and I call upon my brother who was present and who can tell whether what I say is exactly true or not—I call your attention to the fact, that instead of then and there admitting he recollected it in the prompt manner he did on the stand, he meant to lie it through and deny it, and he did deny again and again in the most deliberate, positive and peremptory terms that he sent the telegraph or sent the message. And his honor will instruct you—and I ask the court for that instruction—that if you found him then and there intentionally uttering a willful and deliberate falsehood, you will not look at his testimony, you will not weigh it, you will not remember that he has testified in the case. You will throw him out of view and put the merits of the case upon testimony that is credible.

Here Mr. Choate analyzed Coburn's testimony in detail to show that he was unworthy of belief. He then continued :

Can I, gentlemen of the jury, possibly pursue the detail of such an examination as that ? I ask you, as you value your rights, that you instantly, if you take the rule which the court will unquestionably prescribe to you, if the witness has intentionally falsified in any one thing, he is to be taken to be false in all things. He may be innocently mistaken in one case, and yet you may give him credit in another part of the case, but the moment that you find him deliberately falsifying, his opinion is of no consequence, it has no meaning, and he is regularly laid out, and there is an end of him, and the case is thenceforward to go on without him. The only escape for this man is for him to say, that he goes to Providence and telegraphs these falsehoods; comes back to Boston and hires two rooms at different hotels, under false names; causes false letters to be sent under false names, enters his own name falsely—

and that transaction had entirely faded from his memory—and therefore he could not recollect it. I say it would be to trifle with the oaths of the jurors, with the administration of the law, the rights of the parties, to give the least degree of credit to such an explanation as that. I submit to you, therefore, there is an end to the witness John H. Coburn, and there is no testimony to that hideous confession which he comes here to report—none whatever. It is not sworn to, there was no confession to the judgment of the jury under the subtle rules of law. Do you not all see that in the course of this argument I have carefully avoided all mere professional raillery at the witness? I am bringing him up to the golden tests and standards by which the law weighs proof, or the assayer weighs gold. I am helping you to see him by the light of the rule of law, and I cannot allow you for a moment to suppose that I am indulging in a professional habit of abusing witnesses when I am simply declaring to you—with all truth and soberness, under my responsibility to my profession and my oath of office, and with the sanction of this bench—the great rule of law by which the credibility of evidence is to be passed on; and I declare the law to be, if you find a witness to have sworn deliberately to a falsehood, knowing and believing it to be a falsehood, that he is no longer a witness, and on this ground I submit that the testimony of John H. Coburn is not to engage your attention for a moment. There is a great deal of commentary that might be made on this, a great deal tending to show the utter incredibility of the witness to the jury, with which I will not detain you. He is laid out, and is to be viewed as a discarded, false and perjured witness.

Here Mr. Choate went on to point out particular instances and portions of the testimony which he argued were absolutely false. He continued:

45. THE HUSBAND'S CONDUCT A REFUTATION OF COBURN'S EVIDENCE.

There is one answer to this man's testimony, which puts an end to him on this case, and I submit that we gain on the merits of our own case by this commenting on the worthlessness of the evidence offered by the libellant, and I answer this story that the conduct of Dalton that night, as we have it revealed to us by credible testimony in this case, gives this story to the hissing and contempt which it deserves from every intelligent man.

I ask you to look at the conduct of Dalton; take the unquestionable circumstances, then all the positive testimony; take the beautiful letter in which the next morning she breathed out her expectation of that new life of promise resulting from the interview, and I ask if you believe for one single moment that such a hideous communication was made.   Remember that down to that time, even after Dalton left the jail, he declared that he believed she was innocent, that he loved and trusted her, and wished to God that he could trust her completely.   Remember that down to that night, on her oath, with her hand on the Bible, and in the pains of the threatened miscarriage, she had declared herself to be innocent; and remember, that she then comes into his presence to play her last card for his heart, and then, according to this man's testimony, makes such a confession.   I put it to you that, exasperated as Dalton was, hoping, yet fearing, manifestly determined to fly at once, if the evidence of her guilt should come from her lips, would he not have started from his feet at such a declaration, and cried, "Oh! ruin! ruin!" and fled from the door?

You are soon to be appealed to to give a divorce, because those sensibilities which are respected and which are to be religiously cared for, these susceptibilities of the husband have been outraged.

Try him, then, as a husband; try him on the supposition that he has those sensibilities and feels them keenly, and then give him credit for this character.   I have to ask you, if one man of you doubts, on hearing such a communication from his wife, he would have exclaimed: "May God forgive you, I cannot!   All is over now!" and have left her forever.   There is not a husband on the panel that would not have done it; nor a husband who recognizes the marriage tie on the face of the earth who would not have done it.   Yet does John H. Coburn hear him utter one word?   Not one. He seems very desirous of knowing what Fanny has been doing. But is that all?   No, gentlemen.   By all the admitted testimony of this case coming to us by the witnesses for the libellant, and therefore open to no criticism from them, the doors are softly drawn to and locked, and there they are for two hours and a half—there they would have been till daylight if this same John H. Coburn had not knocked at the door and said it was nine o'clock, and asked them if they were aware of the lateness of the hour.   What was he doing there?   How is the confession just then made for the first time? What has become of that?   I submit that it is too clear for a moment's controversy, that the conversation began with the door open, and was the free, full, heart-breaking revelation of actual wrong, and an asseveration of actual innocence; that it was full of sorrow, grief and earnest pathos on her part; that she at last caused him to believe the truth, and then the door was closed, and then and there she gave her love to her husband. I have adverted to this more than once. You may take it as coming from my client, or on my suggestion, as you please. In that sweet recognition they spent two hours, two hours and a half. He was satisfied that there had been nothing but imprudence, and no guilt; and in that sweet moment of reconciliation, after an absence of two months—do not be quite sure that he did not then and there give her all that a husband can; whether he did so or not, it is entirely immaterial to my argument, which is, that his conduct was utterly and instantly a decisive refutation of Coburn's story about the confession. I go further, and show you, by a body of positive and circumstantial evidence, that they there made a provisional arrangement for their troubled and yet possible future. They fell into an arrangement, and although he could not live with her openly until the sentence was imposed, yet he was entirely ready to do everything for his wife, and then and there commenced arrangements for their troubled future; and I submit it to you, it was agreed that they should meet the next Thursday night to mature their arrangements, when they should lay out a scheme of life for the future.

Remember, in the next place, that Edward O. Coburn admitted, that when they were going home, that she said she felt better now —not because she had made a clean breast of guilt, but because she expected to meet him the next Thursday night.

46. The mutilated letter.

The next piece of evidence is that mutilated letter; that eloquent orator, that truthful and decisive witness—the mutilated letter. They bring it and offer it as a letter written by her the next morning after the transaction, and they do not dare lay it before you without first erasing eleven lines, which, though incapable of being fully read, clearly show that this poor thing was then and there making provision for every contingency of this meeting on the next Thursday night. They found that she was making too strong a point of it, in taking too much pains that nothing should prevent the meeting, and so they struck out a portion of it. I submit that you take a microscope of a hundred horse power, and you will find a meaning in the erasure, and will see that it is a clear recognition of the arrangement for the proposed meeting; and if you cannot find it in this way, I think you will do so by your reason.

Here Mr. Choate showed from the evidence and Mrs. Dalton's letters to her husband, that at their meeting, after she had told him everything, he promised to live with her, and was prevented by his family from doing so. That the alleged confessions, even if true, revealed no crime, but the evidence, on the contrary, disclosed that plaintiff after all believed his wife innocent. Mr. Choate next reviewed the testimony of Edward O. Coburn and Mary Hunter at great length, to show, first, that it was false, and, second, that, even if any part of it were true, it failed to establish the confession of adultery sought to be proved by plaintiff. He then continued:

47. EDWARD O. COBURN'S STORY OF THE CAKE AND WINE AN INVENTION.

This Mr. Coburn began to find after a time that his excuse of standing at a window would not quite answer the purpose, and he began to think, under my brother Durant's cross-examination, that, as the excuse of standing at the window might perhaps be sufficiently explained and deemed to be adequate, it would be well for him to volunteer to add to that excuse that she had been taking a little cake and wine, and probably that was the reason. Mark the hypocritical malignity of that testimony. He had stated before that she had been surprised in an unexpected position, and that she resisted the moment she found she was surprised. He perceived that that was a perfect defense everywhere; he therefore thought he would give her a treat of a little cake and wine of his own. It was the cake, the wine, the champagne, which was to account for it; he had not said a word about taking cake, or wine, or champagne—not a word; the whole of it was a sudden, extemporaneous, hypocritical, malignant invention of the witness to color, change, qualify and turn to falsehood his whole story upon the stand, which had attributed to her the excuse of being surprised at the looking out of a window, resisting in a moment, her virtue never yielding. He says to himself: " That is a complete and perfect defense, but if she were to be brought under the influence of a stimulant, wine or champagne, she might have yielded to that surprise;" and so he finds his occasion, and treats her at his own expense, as it costs him nothing—to cake and wine and champagne upon the stand. I submit to you, gentlemen, whether it was not as sheer, as malignant, as hypocritical a falsehood as has occurred in the testi-mony of any witness in this whole case. I am inclined to think that Mary Hunter's story came rather suddenly across his memory, and so he volunteered it, although he was compelled to admit that she had herself said not a single syllable about it.

I put it to you again, gentlemen, with great earnestness, that if the testimony of this witness was entirely trustworthy, making rea-sonable allowance for the difficulty of reporting language, the state of the case which he makes out against her is no more than can be made out against any young daughter of Boston, pure as the flakes of snow when it falls, standing at the Athenæum and looking out upon a graveyard, upon whom an intoxicated rowdy should sud-denly break in and allow his hand to stray lasciviously upon her bosom, from whom instantly she turns, shrieks, bursts into tears and falls hysterically—not a particle, and that is the state of testi-mony before you. Is there anything in the evidence of John H. Coburn which in the least degree resembles it? He places it at a time when she is conducting an earnest expostulation to a com-plaint of her husband—at a time when she is making an argument to show that she is entitled to have him back again; and I there-fore put it to you as beyond a particle of doubt, that she means so to conduct that argument as to make out a case. Of the two Co-burns at confession give me John H. Coburn, for he gets up some-thing which nobody believes. The principles of the two Coburns remind me of Pope's classification:

> " John struts, a perjurer, open, bold and brave,
> Ned sneaks, a liar, an exceeding knave."

That is the difference between them exactly. Is Edward O. Coburn entitled in the least degree to the credit of the jury? Need I say anything more than to ask you whether Edward O. Coburn is an honest man and fit to be trusted upon a question of this im-portance—affecting life, or character, or good fame?

Here Mr. Choate referred to the fact that credit was claimed for Edward O. Coburn, because he wanted to run away and not testify. He branded him as a hypocrit, and showed that he did not wish to be questioned about robbing his father-in-law's safe as the reason why he desired to absent himself. He con-tinued:

48. ARRAIGNMENT OF EDWARD O. COBURN.

There is a general public rumor current in this community that a thief is not an honest man, and Edward O. Coburn is a thief.

He was obliged to admit under your eye, that he took false or true keys, broke into his father's safe, and took all there was. Of the amount he was not certain, but it was about $1,700. He went away and denied it—that is to be a thief, and to be a thief is not to be an honest man. He who would steal his father-in-law's money is not to be believed when he gives testimony against his sister-in-law, the child of the father-in-law. He is not an honest man. You heard the explanation that he attempted to give here, and the malignity and intellectual hypocrisy by which that explanation was marked. He was called upon to admit the fact, and he did so. He was called upon for his reasons, and he said that in consequence of his irregularities he had contracted debts, which he wanted to pay. He wanted a little money, and as some defense of himself against this charge he said it was under the influences of certain wild ideas; that the memory of this affair had done him great injury. When he was asked how much money he wanted to pay his debts, he said he did not know, but he took all there was; and then he went away and denied that he had taken a dollar. And yet to put himself upon this jury—I care nothing about his defense—as entitled to some confidence from the jury, he undertakes to account for taking this money by certain wild ideas. How contemptible a hypocrisy is this! I can very well understand, from what I have read and what I have discovered, that a husband suddenly made aware or made to believe in his wife's guilt, and made jealous by it, might be urged in the tempest to the murder of the adulterer, or to the murder of the adulteress, and the digging of his own grave. That I can understand, for it is altogether a new mode which he seems to have taken of solacing his grief—that of stealing by means of false keys. It has generally been considered a great stroke of nature in the poet, where he represents Othello—when those billows were raging and those storms blowing in that great bosom—as going to the bed, kissing his wife, and then stifling her to death; and after that comes the superb speech beginning,

Soft now, a word or two before we part,

and he kills himself. But what should we think of Shakespeare, to adopt Mary Hunter's expression, if he had represented Othello as "blowing off a little," in the first place, by stealing seventeen or eighteen hundred dollars of his father's money? It is hypocrisy, gentlemen, and no truth, no manhood. I submit that the witness is not entitled to the confidence and credit of this jury.

Here Mr. Choate went on at great length to show that the witness testified falsely from malignant motives. He continued:

This man comes here to report words and confession when he cannot carry a letter from one house to another without sitting down and forging it into a falsehood. He stands here, let me say, in the judgment of this court on the evidence in this position. He receives a letter from the respondent which he agrees to carry to her husband, that letter which was filled up with new life and new hopes—a new and a dear husband to live for, a future opening before her, a happy meeting next Thursday which she is anxious by all possible attentions to secure to herself—and he cannot bring it before the court without having first elaborately erased from it every word which goes to show an arrangement for such a meeting as that. I repeat that such a man who has not honesty and fairness enough to keep his hands from forgery, is not entitled to bring in words.

There is that beautiful letter, not a word of confession in it; there it is with a key at the end, opening all its sense, and he broke in and stole the key—*stole the key;* not this time a key for the robbery of his father's store, but for the destruction of the daughter's proofs. I pray your judgment, gentlemen, that this is the end of Edward O. Coburn.

49. Arraignment of Mary Hunter.

From John H. Coburn and Edward O. Coburn to Mary Hunter, whether ascending or descending, is easy—with or without the Latin maxim on that subject. I believe if you leave the two Coburns out of the case, you will not be troubled by Mary Hunter. I submit that her testimony was mixed for her exactly as a man mixes rum and water to drink, and she drank it. In that bronze, strange woman, what do we behold? From her appearance and her account of herself upon the stand, what do we know that would warrant us to give credit to what she swears to for a moment? Where she came from, with whom she has lived, what has been her way of life, who is the father of her child, to every question which my brother Durant puts under the settled practice of the court, the only means by which perjury of an unknown stranger can be detected—to all these she answers, with her arms akimbo, " It is none of your business." I submit to you, gentlemen, that the inference is inevitable, if she could truly and properly answer those questions on her oath, a chaste, well ordered life and conversation, she would have leaped to do it. She would have rejoiced at the opportunity; my learned brother would have instructed her, it would have been his duty to so instruct her to take her earliest opportunity to tell her history, perhaps a humble one; and I submit to you that no other inference can be made from her reiterated refusal to tell us anything about herself, than that she knows perfectly well that it is one of those rare cases, but which sometimes happen, where "the least said is soonest mended;" and therefore she tells us, "it is none of your business," and that is the end. Is that a ground for railing at the witness? No; but it is a ground for saying that we do not know whether that woman knows anything, or respects in the least degree the sanctity of an oath. We have not a particle of evidence that that foreigner and stranger ever had a lesson from the Bible in her life, that she ever heard a word of counsel from priest or minister, that she ever heard a mass "by bell, book or candle," that she ever saw a domestic example of purity, that she remembers a father or mother, that she had ever received one single lesson or one single influence which enables us to believe that she, here and now, feels the obligation of an oath. That she is a foreigner is nothing against her; that, being a foreigner, we should naturally inquire something about her antecedents, was not strange, but it was nothing against her; and if then and there she had frankly disclosed them to us, we might have found her entitled to belief. But she buries herself up, she refuses to tell you anything; and I repeat that you do not know whether from her childhood to this hour she ever had a lesson of virtue from anybody, ever came to understand the importance of truthfulness, the virtue of chastity and the value of character and reputation.

She stands before you here and now, gentlemen, only as a wet nurse and mother, without a husband, whom she will not confess, and it is for you to say, if standing on her alone, if the cause rests on her alone, whether or not she is entitled in the least degree to credit by this jury. The matter and manner of her testimony may be briefly adverted to, and with that I complete all I have to say with regard to her.

Here Mr. Choate showed that her evidence about purchasing savin, &c., was unworthy of belief, and wholly uncorroborated. He then continued:

50. ALL THE LETTERS TAKEN TOGETHER SHOW DEFENDANT INNOCENT.

I need not, in the view I have been taking of this case, call your attention to one fact. I apprehend it has already been anticipated and long since disposed of. That on reading this entire series of letters, you will find, everywhere, from first to last, perhaps strongest in the first, certainly no stronger in the last, continual and reiterated expressions of remorse, and regret, and grief by Helen Dalton for what she had done. I do not believe my learned brother, upon a collation of that series of letters, will stand up here and contend for a moment, and say, that she ever dreamed of supposing for a moment, she meant to confess by any strong expression, that she had committed the crime of adultery; but, on the contrary, I hold it to be one of the best points in this case for that young wife, I hold it to be a satisfactory evidence, that there is yet a heart and character worth cultivating and saving, that there is yet a wife whom Dalton might be proud and happy to take again to his bed, that no strength of language seems to herself sufficient to express her own remorse and shame for what she has done. She knew when she penned every one of those letters, she knew perfectly well, from her conversation with her husband and the Daltons on the Sunday evening after the Shawmut avenue tragedy, that he understood perfectly well that all her strong expressions, all her tears, all her prayers to Almighty God to forgive her for her sin, all her regret that she had failed to make him happy, and failed to be worthy of him, were only the confessions of a pure and a chaste heart, that judged itself more harshly than God in his infinite mercy will surely judge it, more harshly than the generous and manly heart could judge it. As she looked back to that time, no language seemed too strong, no compunction seemed too severe, no prayer to God seemed too profound, no promise of a better life too warm, too strong, too heartfelt, to express it all. And now I say, for my learned brother to cull out a single one of that series, and put it forward without its context, by itself, and call on you to interpret it as no letter ought to be interpreted, out of its connection, without the *usus loquendi* of the parties themselves, who perfectly understood it, and without which it could not be appreciated— to do that would be a cruelty tremendous, an injustice from which I think he would shrink back. No, gentlemen, you will take this series from first to last, and I will take my chance of a verdict, or disagreement, as you shall find, that the strongest and clearest expressions of compunction, grief, guilt, and sin, shall be found at the beginning of the series. After he had seen them, and studied them, and understood them perfectly well, he writes her again and again that he truly loves her, looks to a happier life yet with the loved one, the trusted one. I might read a sentence or two, but one is enough, for she had clearly and distinctly put him in possession of her mind on this point. I submit that the purer she was, the more confident she felt that her body had been preserved as a vessel of honor for her husband, at the same time, the more distinctly and clearly she appreciated the deep wrong she had actually done. I submit that it is according to the nature of love that she shall even overstate, she shall exaggerate, shall make more of it than it deserves, even of that miserable flirtation which did not end in adultery. It is to lay herself at his feet; it is to show how wholly she feels with him; it is to assure him of her whole heart laid bare, her whole soul probed to the bottom; and, therefore, it is that you shall find here exaggerated expressions, which, unless you know perfectly well, as the correspondents themselves must have known, their true signification. I apprehend under the rule of law they must be subject to the mildest interpretation which can be put upon them. Here you have the key to the whole, and thank God, they have not stolen this bar if they have stolen the others. "God knows I love you, darling, forgive that vein of folly, although I have sinned—yet not criminal;" that is the key; that is the interpretation of the language. And thenceforward it is perfectly understood between the parties that when she says she has sinned, that she has been wicked, that she has been tempted, that the tempter is in his grave, and she is sorry he had not been there before he presented the temptation; it is all perfectly understood between them from beginning to end. It is the most dreadful cruelty and injustice here and now to desert that perfect understanding; that what she meant was: "I have been sinful by my vanity; I have been secretly tempted by the influence of this young man now in his grave, and I have so far done you a wrong which I shall acknowledge for sin, and pray God while life lasts to forgive me for, but not crime, dear Frank, not crime "—the whole course of the correspondence perfectly understood by them—and to read half-a-dozen extracts from those letters, to show much more strength of affection and a sin which he can never forgive. It is hardly necessary to illustrate my proposition with regard to the meaning of language, the *usus lo-*

21

quendi of the parties in the interpretation of a writing. "Frank, you know and God knows that when I married you I was as pure as a child could be, and I am now. If you do not know it, your folks know it. Father will not allow his daughter, if she has committed a wrong thing, which no one upholds her in, to be treated thus. Darling Frank, pray our heavenly Father to forgive me my sins, and let us also feel that in a great degree he has. Frank, when you pray, pray that God will forgive your erring wife. I never expect to have any one love me, I have been so naughty; but then I know Frank will love me, if no one else, won't you, darling?" After that he writes to her again and again and again: "My own sweet Nelly, my darling, I fly to your arms; we shall be happy yet. Courage; trust your own affectionate husband." Then, gentlemen, I submit that the selection of a single paragraph from such a letter as the last, written manifestly under the impression of the great joy the communication of the day before in its results had given her, will not be pursued, or if pursued, will be ineffectual with a candid jury.

I therefore, gentlemen, bring this argument to a close. Positive evidence on behalf of the respondent from the nature of the case we cannot bring. Sumner is in his grave; we cannot bring him. We could not bring in evidence of his declarations, but in that silence we have these two persuasive tests: the testimony of a dying man to his innocence—testimony on that solemn occasion when men and women speak the truth if they ever speak it; and the testimony of Helen Dalton, who declared herself innocent of this crime; once when her husband, who knew that she was to be trusted, who knew that he could entitle himself to have the joy of belief in her, proposed to her to sink down upon her knees upon the family Bible, and call upon her heavenly Father to witness whether she spoke the truth, upon which oath propounded by her she declared herself to be innocent; and over again, when the pains of premature delivery came upon her, when, therefore, she was in the very danger and peril of death, in that state where, according to a statute of law in this commonwealth, a certain artificial credit is always to be given to the oath of a witness declaring her innocence then. We submit the proof that from the testimony in this case, she has been uniformly and steadily constant in that declaration.

The charge of abortion by which they poisoned your own minds for a time, and the public mind for a time, is wholly false and

wholly disproved. There is no question whatever about this. The
testimony of these Coburns and Mary Hunter, all three, will not
weigh a feather for a moment in your minds. And then upon
every thing else, from one end of the case to the other, every particle of credible testimony, you have the deliberate judgment of the
best witnesses on our side.

I leave her case, therefore, upon this statement, and respectfully submit that for both their sakes you will render a verdict
promptly and joyfully in favor of Helen Dalton—for both their
sakes. There is a future for them both together, gentlemen, I
think; but if that be not so—if it be that this matter has proceeded
so far that her husband's affections have been alienated, and that a
happy life in her case has become impracticable, yet for all that,
let there be no divorce. For no levity, no vanity, no indiscretion,
let there be a divorce. I bring to your minds the words of Him
who spake as never man spake: "Whosoever putteth away his
wife"—for vanity, for coquetry, for levity, for flirtation?—"whosoever putteth away his wife for anything short of adultery, intentionally, willingly indulged, and that established by clear, undoubted
and credible proof—whosoever does it, 'causeth her to commit
adultery.'" If they may not be dismissed then, gentlemen, to live
again together, for her sake and her parents' sustain her; give her
back to self-respect and the assistance of that public opinion which
all of us require.

There was a time in the progress of this cause when that father,
unaware of what might be produced against her, or by what instruments of defense it would be necessary here to protect his daughter's
honor, set on foot an inquiry of recrimination to be instituted
against the libellant. Information was brought to his ears on which
he directed a certain inquiry; the result was communicated to
counsel, and that result has been stated on the files of the court.
On that allegation of recrimination we have had occasion to produce no evidence; it was contrary, as Mr. Gove has sworn, to the
wishes of his daughter from first to last, that the attempt should
be made at all. There is, therefore, by her request—and it is
gratifying to the counsel in that respect to be able to indulge that
request—not a tittle of evidence upon which it can ever be predi-
cated that he was guilty; as to that he must be found to be innocent. Permit me to say that she would have thought it the last
drop in this bitterest cup if her own frivolities and vanities had
done anything to tempt or even to bring into suspicion the chastity

of her husband. It would have been the bitterest drop in her cup. She would say by me, as she said to him in her last letter to Frank: "You have done all you can to disgrace me, but no matter now— I will not blame you. You are my husband for the present; I will not talk against you nor say aught that can make you unhappy. Wishing you much happiness and peace with much love, if you will accept it, I remain, your wife." So may she remain until that one of them to whom it is appointed first to die, shall find the peace of the grave.

I thank you for your kind indulgence and leave the case in your hands.

It is perhaps proper here to state, that when this speech was delivered, re-porters did not always possess the skill they now have. Mr. Choate, when ex-cited and in the full tide of his argument, spoke with great rapidity—a vehement and onward rush of thoughts. It was, therefore, difficult, often impossible, to take down fully and accurately all he said; and Professor Brown, in speaking of this argument, remarks, that the mere reading of it can give but a feeble idea of its beauty and cogency. A reporter once remarked, he would as soon undertake to report "chain-lightning." It is related of Mr. Choate, that after reading one of his addresses, a friend asked him whether it had been correctly given. The reply was, "not verbally, not verbally, but the general nonsense of the thing they have got."

The effect of the powerful appeal in the Dalton Case went farther than the jury box. It brought conviction in a strange direction. Mr. Choate, we have reason to believe, convinced the plaintiff. It is certain, at all events, that soon after the trial Dalton began paying attentions to his wife, sending her bouquets, and exhibiting other tokens of his affection. Both shortly left Boston, were re-united, and lived together in harmony.

ARGUMENT OF EDWIN M. STANTON,

In Defense of Hon. Daniel E. Sickles, Indicted for the Murder of Philip Barton Key.

IN THE CRIMINAL COURT FOR THE DISTRICT OF COLUMBIA, WASHINGTON, D. C., APRIL 23d, 1859.

Analysis of Mr. Stanton's Argument.

1. Homicide defined.
2. Theory of the defense.
3. Effects of the crime of adultery upon the home circle.—Sanctity of the nuptial bond.
4. The hallowed relation as between parent and child.
5. The tie between brother and sister.
6. The punishment of adultery under the Levitical law.
7. Conduct embraced within the act of adultery.

8. The husband legally justified in slaying the adulterer.
9. Review of Manning's case.
10. Slaying the adulterer no crime under the law.
11. The wife's consent no qualification of the adulterer's guilt.
12. The English and American authorities discussed.
13. The wife's consent cannot be invoked to shield the adulterer.
14. The prisoner's right to slay further based on the law of self-defense.

" Whether a homicide committed by a man smarting under a sense of dishonor is murder or manslaughter," says Mr. Wharton in his work on homicide, " depends upon the question whether the killing was in the first transport of passion or not. In the latter case the offense is murder ; in the former manslaughter." Those not familiar with legal principles may regard this as an extremely harsh rule. Many will, no doubt, consider that a man is not only blameless, but justified in taking the life of the adulterer, and that, in doing so, he discharges a duty which he owes to the community. The rule, however, is a wise one, and salutary in its operation. Chief Justice Ruffin, of North Carolina, in a very able opinion, illustrates the wisdom of the law on this subject. He says: " Where a husband only hears of the adultery of his wife, no matter how well authenticated the information may be, or how much credence he may give the infórmer, and kills either the wife or her paramour, he does it not upon present provocation, but for a past wrong—a grievous one, indeed; but it is evident he kills for revenge. Let it be considered how it would be if the law were otherwise. How remote or recent must the offense be ? How long or how far may the husband pursue the offender ? If it happen that he be the deluded victim of an Iago, and, after all, that he has a chaste wife, how is it to be then ? These inquiries suggest the impossibility of acting on any rule but that of the common law, without danger of imbruing men's hands in innocent blood, and certainly of encouraging proud, headstrong men to slay others for vengeance, instead of bringing them to trial and punishment by law." [1]　The act of adultery, therefore, furnishes no excuse for the homicide. Its effect, at most, is to reduce the grade of killing from murder to manslaughter.

It is only under the common law of England, however, that the slaying of the adulterer caught in the act, is regarded as manslaughter. Such killing was justified by the laws of the Greeks, the Romans, the ancient Goths, and other nations of antiquity. If a burglar enters my dwelling to spoil my goods, and I kill him, the authorities all agree that I am justified. I am not guilty of any offense, because the circumstances will excuse the homicide. Applying this principle, it was urged in the Sickles case, that if a libertine destroys his friend's home, if he spoils his domestic happiness, ruins the wife's chastity and the mother's virtue, the husband would be justified in taking his life. The burglar seeks that which is material and perishable. What the adulterer destroys is more precious than gold or rubies, and cannot be restored. Hon. Edwin M. Stanton discussed the law upon this subject in a masterly manner, and made perhaps the most powerful argument that has ever been attempted upon the subject. On behalf of his client he claimed, that if such killing was manslaughter under the common law as it existed in England, it should not be followed here, nor declared as part of our American jurisprudence. He urged that both in law and in morals Mr. Sickles was justified in taking the life of the adulterer, for he insisted that, in the eye of the law, he slew him in the act. The facts of the case are briefly told.

On Sunday afternoon, on the 27th of February, 1859, Sickles shot and killed Key in a public thoroughfare, in the city of Washington. The night before the homicide, he learned that Key, who had been his friend and companion, had violated the sanctity of his friendship and betrayed his hospitality, and had been for a long time criminally intimate with Mrs. Sickles. The truth of this terrible revelation was confirmed the next morning. While Mr. Sickles was seated near his front window, he saw Key drive past and wave his handkerchief, the signal that he desired to meet Mrs. Sickles away from the roof of her husband. Within a very few hours the opportunity presented itself, and the husband, enraged and mortified beyond endurance, shot and killed the seducer upon the public street. "Key, you scoundrel," he exclaimed, "you have dishonored my house; you must die," whereupon he fired three shots, all of which took effect in the body of the victim.

The inquiry before the court was not as to how far the accused was blameless in the eye of his maker for inflicting vengeance upon the destroyer of his domestic happiness. However interesting such a discussion might be to the mind of the casuist, it did not necessarily arise before a human tribunal. Could the slayer be convicted under the law? Was the fact that he took the life of an adulterer, because he had committed adultery, a legal excuse for the homicide? Mr. Stanton undertook to show, as matter of law, that the prisoner was justified; that those decisions which sustained a contrary doctrine had their origin in an age which for vice and profligacy has no parallel in the history of the Anglo-Saxon race, and that the law declared during that period had no precedent in the past, and had not been followed since. He argued the question in all its bearings, not only as affected by the common law of

[1] State v. Neville, 6 Jones (N. C.) Law, 433.

England, but the aspect in which the prisoner's acts would have been regarded under other systems of jurisprudence which have prevailed among men since the morning of time.   He cites the law of Moses for the government of the Jews, a people whose statutes were ordained not by any human legislature, but by divine authority.   And so under the law of all civilized countries of which we have any account in ancient history, either sacred or profane, there is but one answer to the question as to the punishment of the adulterer.   When, however, Mr. Stanton justifies his client's conduct upon the broad principles of self-protection, which he asserts as a natural right, his argument is great.   His eloquent description of the sanctity, the beauty and purity of the family relation, and the importance of family influence as the great factor in social life, upon which alone the existence of civil society depends, commands admiration and is rendered powerful and effective; while the conclusion is irresistible, that the crime of adultery brings destruction not only upon the individual, but upon society itself.   The argument was not upon the facts to the jury, but upon the law to the court, in order to sustain the position taken by the prisoner's counsel upon the requests to charge the jury.   In order that the argument may be thoroughly understood, the reader will find the requests submitted by the prosecution and the defense, and the rulings of the court, at page 718 of the Appendix.

Before Mr. Stanton filled the office of attorney-general of the United States, his reputation as a lawyer was established in connection with the Wheeling Bridge Case, and the Pennsylvania Railroad *v.* The Canal Commissioners, reported in 9th of Harris.   A brilliant advocate and profound lawyer, he possessed also the qualities of a great judge.   By his early demise, shortly after his appointment to the bench of the Supreme Court of the United States, the world has lost the benefit of his ripe learning, wide research and experience.

The trial of Mr. Sickles was commenced on Monday, April 4th, 1859, in the Criminal Court for the District of Columbia, at the city of Washington, before Hon. T. H. Crawford and a jury.   Robert Ould, U. S. District-Attorney, was assisted on behalf of the prosecution by Mr. J. M. Carlisle, of Washington.   The following gentlemen appeared for the prisoner: James T. Brady and John Graham, of New York, Edwin M. Stanton, Mr. Radcliff, Mr. Clinton, Mr. Magruder, and Mr. Phillips, of Washington.   The trial lasted twenty days, and resulted in verdict of acquittal.   Mr. Stanton addressed the court as follows:

MAY IT PLEASE YOUR HONOR:—It becomes my duty to present some considerations in support of the points of law which have been submitted by the defense, and which points are in conformity with those which may be given to a jury.[1]   The event which has brought the jury and the prisoner at the bar into solemn relations, and made the court and counsel participators in this momentous trial, is the death of Mr. Key at the hand of Mr. Sickles, which took place on Sunday, the 27th of February.   The occasion of this event was an adulterous intrigue between Mr. Key and the wife of Mr. Sickles.   The law rising on the case must depend on

[1] For the points submitted, see Appendix, p. 718.

the relations each held to the other at the time the occurrence took place. Two theories have been presented—one by the prosecution, the other by the defense. Those theories, as in all such cases, are opposite; and it will be for the court, by a comparison of those theories with the known principles of law, to give to the jury the instruction.

1. Homicide defined.

The act of taking human life is designated in law by the general term of homicide, which may be either with malice or without malice. The act of Congress which governs in this district, designates two grades of unlawful homicide, namely, murder and manslaughter. "Murder," says Blackstone, "is now thus defined, or rather described, by Sir Edward Coke: 'When a person of sound memory and discretion unlawfully killeth any reasonable creature in being, and under the king's peace, with malice aforethought, either express or implied.'" The same author defines manslaughter to be "the unlawful killing of another without malice, either express or implied; which may be either voluntary, upon a sudden heat, or involuntary, but in the commission of some unlawful act." In some States the law designates other grades of unlawful homicide, but only two are designated by the act of Congress before referred to; but life may be taken under circumstances which the law will excuse or justify. This must depend on a variety of circumstances, neither foreseen nor enumerated, and must be judged by wise tribunals and by maxims which form the common law of the land, and are essential to peace and security. They are illustrated by examples and cases, whence the reason of the law can be derived, and by these the true rule of judgment is ascertained.

There are two classes of cases in which a man may be exempted from judicial punishment for killing, namely, self-protection, which is a natural right, and, secondly, the defense of one's household from the thief or robber. But there is a third class, arising from the social relation, for the law holds family chastity and the sanctity of the marriage bed, the matron's honor and the virgin's purity, to be more valuable and estimable in law than the property or life of any man. The present case belongs to that class. On it rests the foundation of the social system. As it involves the life of the prisoner, it cannot be too carefully considered. Indeed this principle has never come before a judicial tribunal in a form more im-

pressive than now.   Here, in the capital of the nation, the social
and political metropolis of thirty millions of people, a man of
mature age, the head of a family, a member of the learned profession, a high officer of the government, intrusted with the administration of the law, and who for years at this bar has demanded
judgment of fine, imprisonment and death against other men for
offenses against law, has himself been slain in open day in a public
place, because he took advantage of the hospitality of a sojourner
in this city.   Received into his family, he debauched his house,
violated the bed of his host, and dishonored his family.   On this
ground, alone, the deed of killing was committed.

2. Theory of the defense.

The instructions presented by defendant bring to the view of
the court two consistent lines of defense—one, that the act of the
prisoner at the bar is justified by the law of the land, under the circumstances of its commission; the other, that, whether justified or
not, it is free from legal responsibility by reason of the state of the
prisoner's mind.   When the crime was committed against him by
the deceased, in both points of view, the relations which the deceased and the prisoner at the bar bore to each other at the moment
of the fatal act are to be observed—one, as a husband outraged in
his house, his family, and his marital rights; the other, an adulterer
in *flagrante delicto*.   While counsel for the prisoner insist that the
act is justified by the law, the counsel for the prosecution assert
that the act is destructive of the existence of society, and demand
judgment of death against him as a fitting penalty.

3. Effects of the crime of adultery upon the home circle.—Sanctity of the nuptial bond.

The very existence of civil society depends not on human life,
but on the family relations.   "Who knows not," says John Milton,
"that chastity and purity of living cannot be established or continued, except it be first established in private families, from
whence the whole breed of men come forth?"   "The family," says
another distinguished moralist, "is the cradle of sensibility, where
the first lessons are taught of that tenderness and humanity which
cement mankind together; and were they extinguished, the whole
fabric of society would be dissolved."   In a general sense, the

family may embrace various degrees of affinity, more or less near; but in a strictly legal sense it embraces the relations of husband and wife, parent and child, brother and sister. The first and most sacred tie, however, is the nuptial bond. "Eternal discord and violence," says a great moralist, "would ensue if man's chief object of affection were secured to him by no legal tie." No man could enjoy any happiness or pursue any vocation if he could not enjoy his wife free from the assaults of the adulterer. The dignity and permanence of the marriage are destroyed by adultery. When the wife becomes the adulterer's prey, the family is destroyed, and all family relations are involved in the ruin of the wife. When a man accepts a woman's hand in wedlock, he receives it with a vow that she will love, honor, serve and obey him in sickness or in health, and will cleave only to him. This bond is sanctified by the law of God. "What God hath joined together let no man put asunder." By a marriage, the woman is sanctified to the husband, and this bond must be preserved for the evil as well as for the good. It is the blessing of the marital institution that it weans men from their sins and draws them to the performance of their duties. This seal of the nuptial vow is no idle ceremony. Thenceforth the law commands the adulterer to beware of disturbing their peace. It commands that no man shall look on woman to lust after her.

The penalty for disobedience to that injunction did not originate in human statutes; it was written in the heart of man in the Garden of Eden, where the first family was planted, and where the woman was made bone of man's bone, flesh of man's flesh. No wife yields herself to the adulterer's embrace till he has weaned her love from her husband; she revolts from her obedience, and serves the husband no longer. When her body has been once surrendered to the adulterer, she longs for the death of her husband, whose life is often sacrificed by the cup of the poisoner, or the dagger or pistol of the assassin.

4. THE HALLOWED RELATION AS BETWEEN PARENT AND CHILD.

The next greatest tie is that of parent and child. If in God's providence a man has not only watched over the cradle of his child, but over the grave of his offspring, and has witnessed earth committed to earth, ashes to ashes, and dust to dust, he knows that the love of a parent for his child is stronger than death. The bitter lamentation—"Would to God I had died for thee"—has been wrung from many a parent's heart. But when the adulterer's shadow comes between the parent and child, it casts over both a gloom darker than the grave. What agony is equal to his who knows not whether the children gathered around his board are his own offspring or an adulterous brood, hatched in his bed. To the child it is still more disastrous. Nature designs that children shall have the care of both parents; the mother's care is the chief blessing to her child—a mother's honor its priceless inheritance. But when the adulterer enters a family, the child is deprived of the care of one parent, perhaps of both. When death, in God's providence, strikes a mother from the family, the deepest grief that preys upon a husband's heart is the loss of her nurture and example to his orphan child; and the sweetest conversation between parent and child is when they talk of the beloved mother who is gone. But how can a father name a lost mother to his child, and how can a daughter hear that mother's name without a blush? Death is merciful to the pitiless cruelty of him whose lust has stained the fair brow of innocent childhood by corrupting the heart of the mother, whose example must stain the daughter's life.

5. The tie between brother and sister.

The pride and glory of the family is its band of brothers and sisters. Sprung from the same love, with the same blood coursing in their veins, their hearts are bound together by a cord which death cannot sever; for, wide asunder as may be the graves of a household, varied as may be their life here on earth, when life's rough ocean is passed, sooner or later they will rejoice on the heavenly coast—a family in heaven. But when the adulterer puts a young wife asunder from her husband, her child is cut off from all kindred fellowship. The companionship and protection of a brother of the same blood can never be hers. No sister of the same blood can ever share her sorrow or her joy. Alone, thenceforth, she must journey through life, bowed down with a mother's shame. Nor does the evil stop here. It reaches up to the aged and venerable parents of the wretched husband and of the ruined wife, and stretches around to the circle of relatives and friends that cluster around every hearth. Such are the results of the adulterer's crime on the home—on the home, not as it is painted by the poet's fancy, but home as it is known and recognized by the law—as it exists in the household, and as it belongs to the family of every

man. They show that the adulterer is the foe of every social relation, the destroyer of every domestic affection, the fatal enemy of
the family, and the desolator of the home. The crime belongs to
the class known in law as *mala in se*—evil in itself—fraught with
ruin to individuals and destruction to society.

6. THE PUNISHMENT OF ADULTERY UNDER THE LEVITICAL LAW.

Such being its nature, we can easily perceive why it is that in
Holy Writ the crime of the adulterer is pronounced to be one
which admits of no ransom and no recompense. We can perceive
why it is that in every book of the Old and New Testament it is
denounced; why it is that by every holy lawgiver, prophet and
saint, it is condemned. We can understand why it is that twice it
is forbidden in the Ten Commandments, and why it is that Jehovah
himself, from the tabernacle in the midst of the congregation, declared that "the man who committeth adultery with another
man's wife, even he who committeth adultery with his neighbor's
wife, shall surely be put to death." By God's own ordinance he
was to be stoned to death, so that every family in Israel, every man,
woman and child might have a hand in the punishment of the
common enemy of the family. By the Levitical law, the adulteress
was subject to the same punishment. But the Redeemer of mankind, when on earth, is supposed to have mitigated the punishment
of the adulteress by requiring him who was without sin to cast at
her the first stone. No such condition, however, was imposed in
favor of the adulterer. There was no mitigation of his crime, and
we know the Saviour's judgment of the sin when he declared that
"he who looketh at a woman to lust after her committeth adultery
in his heart." From the silence of Scripture on the occasion recorded in the Gospel of John, it is to be inferred that, as the adulterer and adulteress had been taken in the act, the adulterer on
that day in Jerusalem had been put to death by the husband, as he
might be by the Roman law, before the adulteress had been brought
to the Saviour's feet. This case has been cited here, as it often is
in favor of the adulterer and against the husband. But the argument of Dr. Paley, alluded to by counsel on the other side, conclusively shows that that case cannot be cited in favor of the adulterer. On that day, in Jerusalem, the laws of Moses, as a civil
and political institution, had passed away and the Roman law had
taken its place.

Why was it that the men of Jerusalem brought not to the Saviour the adulterer who had been taken at the same time, if they wanted to know the Saviour's judgment of the sin of adultery. By the Roman law, while the adulterer suffered death, that punishment does not seem to have been inflicted on the adulteress. This woman, therefore, was brought to the Saviour's feet to hear what would be his judgment. If he had undertaken to say that the laws of Moses ought not to prevail then, an accusation might be brought against him in the synagogue; and if, on the other hand, he had said that the laws of Moses should be enforced, then ready accusation would have leaped to their lips that he was usurping judicial functions, and he would have been brought before the judgment seat of the Roman authorities. As Dr. Paley observes, the case only serves to show that the Saviour meant to rebuke those who tempted him, but that he never designed to shield the adulterer from the just doom of the law.

7. Conduct embraced within the act of adultery.

What, then, is the act of adultery? It cannot be limited to the fleeting moment of sexual contact; that would be a mockery; for then the adulterer would ever escape. But law and reason mock not human nature with any such vain absurdity. The act of adultery, like the act of murder, is supposed to include every proximate act in furtherance of, and as a means to, the consummation of the wife's pollution. This is an established principle in American and English law, established from the time of Lord Stowell, as will be hereafter shown. If the adulterer be found in the husband's bed, he is taken in the act, within the meaning of the law, as if he was found in the wife's arms. If he provide a place for the express purpose of committing adultery with another man's wife, and be found leading her, accompanying her, or following her to that place for that purpose, he is taken in the act. If he not only provides, but habitually keeps such a place, and is accustomed by precon-certed signals to entice the wife from the husband's house, to be-siege her in the streets, to accompany him to that vile den; and if, after giving such preconcerted signal, he be found watching her, spy-glass in hand, and lying in wait around a husband's house, that the wife may join him for that guilty purpose, he is taken in the act.

If a man hire a house, furnish it, provide a bed in it for such a purpose, and if he be accustomed, day by day, week by week, and month by month, to entice her from her husband's house, to tramp with her through the streets to that den of shame, it is an act of adultery, and is the most appalling one that is recorded in the annals of shame; if, moreover, he has grown so bold as to take the child of the injured husband, his little daughter, by the hand, to separate her from her mother, to take the child to the house of a mutual friend while he leads the mother to the guilty den, in order there to enjoy her, it presents a case surpassing all that has ever been written of cold, villainous, remorseless lust.

8. The husband legally justified in slaying the adulterer.

If this be not the culminating point of adulterous depravity, how much farther could it go? There is no one point beyond. The wretched mother, the ruined wife, has not yet plunged into the horrible filth of common prostitution, to which she is rapidly hurrying, and which is already yawning before her. Shall not that mother be saved from that, and how shall it be done? When a man has obtained such a power over another man's wife that he can not only entice her from her husband's house, but separate her from her child for the purpose of guilt, it shows that by some means he has acquired such an unholy mastery over that woman's body and soul that there is no chance of saving her while he lives, and the only hope of her salvation is that God's swift vengeance shall overtake him. The sacred glow of well-placed domestic affection, no man knows better than your Honor, grows brighter and brighter as years advance, and the faithful couple whose hands were joined in holy wedlock in the morning of youth find their hearts drawn closer to each other as they descend the hill of life to sleep together at its foot; but lawless love is short-lived as it is criminal, and the neighbor's wife so hotly pursued, by trampling down every human feeling and divine law, is speedily supplanted by the object of some fresher lust, and then the wretched victim is sure to be soon cast off into common prostitution, and swept through a miserable life and a horrible death to the gates of hell, unless a husband's arm shall save her.

Who, seeing this thing, would not exclaim to the unhappy husband: Hasten, hasten, hasten to save the mother of your child. Although she be lost as a wife, rescue her from the horrid adulterer; and may the Lord, who watches over the home and the family, guide the bullet and direct the stroke.[1]   And when she is delivered, who would not reckon the salvation of that young mother cheaply purchased by the adulterer's blood ?   Aye, by the blood of a score of adulterers ?   The death of Key was a cheap sacrifice to save one mother from the horrible fate which, on that Sabbath day, hung over this prisoner's wife and the mother of his child.

Mr. Stanton here reviewed the authorities, both English and American, bearing upon the question of adultery as a justification for homicide.   He then proceeded:

Under the laws of Maryland, as they descended to the District of Columbia, at the time of the cession in 1801, it has never been adjudged by this or any other court, that the man who destroyed the violator of his family chastity was guilty of a crime.

9. REVIEW OF MANNING'S CASE.[2]

Manning was a married man, who, entering his house one day, found his wife in the arms of a neighbor who was committing adultery with her.   The husband snatched up a stool and struck a blow over the adulterer's head, and killed him on the spot; and for this was arraigned as a prisoner for murder.   As an Englishman it was his birthright to have the act passed upon by a jury of his country, and his innocence or guilt determined by them in accordance with the common law.   But this was in the dark day of judicial tyranny and corruption; the day when jurors were fined and sent to jail, as the authorities show, for refusing to find verdicts against their consciences, in accordance with the charge of the court; in a day when, from the King's Bench, from Westminster Hall, it was declared that the judge was intrusted with the liberties of the people, and that his saying was the law.   That was the day when it was adjudged that the husband was a felon for killing a man caught in adultery with his wife.   In Manning's case, Judge Twisden directed a special verdict, and determined the degree of guilt himself; and Manning was punished by being branded on the hand as a felon.

10. SLAYING THE ADULTERER NO CRIME UNDER THE LAW.

There were four epochs in which killing in such cases went unpunished: it was justified under the Jewish dispensation, by the

[1] Here the audience broke into an unrestrainable burst of applause, which the officers of the court vainly endeavored to check.

[2] Sometimes cited Maddy's Case, Ventris's R. p. 158; Sir T. Raymond's R. p. 212; 2 Keble's R. p. 829.

laws of Solon, by those of the Roman empire, and by the Gothic institutions which have given shape to our own. By the mere force of frequent repetition in the books, of Manning's case, it has come to be believed that a man must stand by the bed of his wife and behold the adulterer polluting his bed, and not raise his hand against him. From the time of Edward II to King Charles—three hundred and sixty odd years—no word is to be found in the common law, no word imputing guilt to the slayer of the violator of the chastity of his wife. This right to kill was never denied till now. There is one fact I have never before seen related, except by Paley, that by the laws of the commonwealth, immediately preceding the time of Charles, adultery was punished by death.

MR. CARLISLE.—Blackstone mentioned it. In 1650, at a period before the judgment in Manning's case, it was punishable by death.

MR. STANTON.—The age of Charles was an age of adultery and gross corruption; the palace was filled with harlots and thronged with adulterers and adulteresses; the judges were the panderers, partakers and protectors of the corruptions of the age, and the same court which adjudged the husband to be a felon for slaying the adulterer on his bed, fined and sent jurors to prison for refusing to find verdicts in accordance with its instructions. It was the same court which hunted Quakers, Catholics and Nonconformists to death; the same court which persecuted John Howe and Richard Baxter, and which sent to the pillory and prison John Bunyan for preaching the gospel to the poor.[1]

This was the state of the laws and social life at the time the principle was introduced into the common law of England, that to kill an adulterer in the act is a crime. And when society in this district is reduced to the same condition, and when the government offices are filled by open and avowed adulterers, when the professions of law and medicine shall be thronged with libertines, when the wife's purity and family chastity shall become a jest, then it will be time to introduce here a principle of common law never before heard from the judgment-seat; then it will be necessary for the court to extend the shield of law over its attorneys to save their lives from the hands of the husbands whose wives they have violated, whose homes they have destroyed, and whose families they have made desolate.

[1] For a history of those times, Mr. Stanton referred to Macaulay, vol. I, p. 140.

11. THE WIFE'S CONSENT NO QUALIFICATION OF THE ADULTER-
ER'S GUILT.

I claim, then, on this proposition, that the expression or rule of
the common law in regard to the consent of the wife had its origin
in a state of manners and of social life that do not exist in this
country, and that that rule is not applicable here. It is founded
on the principle that the wife's consent can qualify the degree of
the adulterer's guilt, and determines the husband to be a criminal.
In American society, there is a freedom from restraint and super-
vision that exists nowhere else, and this results from various causes:
husbands, fathers and brothers devote a large share of time to the
cares of life and to the duties of providing for the family, during
which time the female portion of the family are left to themselves
without protection. The frequent changes of habitation and the
equality of our social condition lead to a frankness of intercourse
which requires, for the sanctity of the home and the security of the
marriage bed, a rigorous personal responsibility to the death. The
peculiar conditions of society in this District are also to be noted
before any principle like that of social law can be introduced.

Families come hither from all parts of the Union to remain for
a shorter or a longer period of time. To enjoy any social life here,
the intercourse must be frank, without suspicion. The time which,
in long established communities, may enable individuals to choose
and pick out those with whom they may associate, is not had here.
Besides, it has been the custom here for officers of the government,
and those in the public employment, to throw open their doors with
a wide hospitality that exists nowhere else. This forms a peculiar
feature and attraction in Washington society, and by the population
that it attracts here and the stimulus thus given to business, the
wealth and prosperity of the city and District are promoted. But
if these social occasions are to be made the means of guilty as-
signations; if they are to become the means by which the adulterer
pursues his lust, then the doors of families must be swiftly closed.
No man would be willing to have his hospitality made the means of
an assignation, or the social occasions, when he desires to give his
friends and neighbors pleasure, converted into opportunities for
corrupting the innocent wife of his friend.

I repeat, then, that the doctrine on which this prosecution rests,
is founded on the Manning case, copied by Hale and Foster and
Blackstone. But it is lso to be observed that, from the day in which
22

Manning's case was decided to the present hour, it has not been followed by the conviction of a husband in England. No husband since then has been punished as a felon for taking the life of an adulterer. In three cases the doctrine of that case has been declared from the bench, but only by two judges: the case of the Queen against Fisher, the case of the Queen against Kelly, and another case. Two of these were tried by Justice Pare, and the other by Baron Rolfe. In the one, there was no adultery of the wife; in the other, no marriage, and in the third, the crime was of a totally different nature.

12. THE ENGLISH AND AMERICAN AUTHORITIES DISCUSSED.

As, from the time of Alfred to the time of Charles the Second, there is no evidence that a husband was regarded as a felon in common law for slaying an adulterer, so from the time of Charles the Second to the present hour that principle has never been enforced by the punishment of any man in England.

Counsel then proceeded to argue that in the three cases cited by the prosecution from the North Carolina and South Carolina reports, there were entirely distinct questions at issue; that, so far as the marital relations of slaves were concerned, they were not recognized by the laws of those States, and that, therefore, the adjudications or rulings in the case of slaves did not govern or apply to this case.

There is another case cited in Jones—the case of a white man; but there was sufficient evidence to show that the killing proceeded from preceding malice. The case, however, which was cited from Hill's Reports, has some analogy to this case. There the adulterer slew a husband who was endeavoring to rescue his wife, and it was held that the murderer could not set up the plea of self-defense. The American common law on this subject is shown in the cases of Singleton Mercer, of Myers, of Jacob Green, the case of John Stump, and the case of Jarboe, where, in each instance, the slayer of the seducer was acquitted. I also refer your Honor to Smith's case and Sherman's case in Philadelphia, Boyer's case in Virginia, and Ryan's case reported in vol. 2 Wheeler's Criminal Cases, p. 47. Where, then, I ask, does the adulterous doctrine of Charles the Second prevail in America? Not where the stars and stripes wave; not even where the royal banner of England floats; for it was not long since, in Canada, a husband had followed his wife's seducer from city to city till he found and slew him; and there the doctrine of Charles the Second was repelled and the man instantly acquitted.

By the American law the husband is always present by his wife; his arm is always by her side; his wing is ever over her. The consent of the wife cannot in any degree affect the question of the adulterer's guilt; and if he be slain in the act by the husband, then it is justifiable homicide. I will pass, then, to the question of what constitutes the act. I understood one of the learned counsel for the prosecution to claim, in accordance with the very loose language of Baron Parke, that it is necessary for the husband to have ocular demonstration.

MR. CARLISLE.—" Finding " is the word.

MR. STANTON.—It does credit to the frankness as well as to the good sense of the counsel not to claim that doctrine, but that is the doctrine of Manning's case. The wife could not only consent to the act, but the husband, if he came in in the dark, could not lay his hand on the adulterer until he lit the candle and saw his shame; and then if he slew the adulterer he must have the felon's branding on his hand. The object was to erect before the husband the gallows and branding iron, so that the courtiers and corrupt men of that age might pursue with impunity the wives and daughters of the people; hence they demanded not only that the wives should not consent, but that the husband should see his shame. As late as within the last few years, Baron Parke, sitting in the judgment-seat of England, said that the husband must have ocular inspection of the act. What is the act, and what is necessary? It is the fact of adultery that constitutes the guilt of the individual and the justification of the husband. The fact is to be manifested according to the rules of evidence that apply in regard to other facts. It is claimed by the defense that the evidence was brought directly to the visual senses of the prisoner at the bar; but whether it was so or not, the fact is only to be determined by the ordinary rules of evidence.

Counsel here referred to the rules of evidence in regard to adultery, as laid down in Poynter on Marriages, p. 187; Collins *v*. The State, vol. 14 Alabama Reports, p. 608; The State *v*. Jolly, vol. 3 Devereux and Battle (N. C.) Law, p. 110.

13. THE WIFE'S CONSENT CANNOT BE INVOKED TO SHIELD THE ADULTERER.

My last proposition is, that the wife's consent cannot shield the adulterer, she being incapable by law of consenting to any infraction of her husband's marital rights, and that, in the absence of consent and connivance on his part, every violation of the wife's chastity is, in the contemplation of law, forcible and against his will, and may be treated by him as an act of violence and force on his wife's person. It follows, as a logical consequence, from the relation of husband and wife, as stated in the first proposition, because her very being and existence is suspended, that is to say, "incorporated and consolidated," says Blackstone, into that of the husband during marriage, that any invasion of the husband's right or chastity of the wife is a forcible act.

The law does not look to the degree of force; it looks to the forcible movement; and being an act of force, it follows that the right of the husband to resist that force is clear and undoubted on the highest principles of law. My friend here,[1] says, he condemns the adulterer as much as any one, but that he abhors lawless violence. So do I; but the question is here whether the violence be lawless? In undertaking to designate the act of the prisoner here as an act of violence, as an act of personal justice, he assumes the very question that is involved, because on no theory of law, on no system of jurisprudence recognized among men, has the defense of a right, the maintenance of possession in a right, the protection of a right, been recognized either as a revengeful act or an act of lawless violence. By the contemplation of law, the wife is always in the husband's presence, always under his wing; and any movement against her person is a movement against his right, and may be resisted as such.

14. THE PRISONER'S RIGHT TO SLAY FURTHER BASED ON THE LAW OF SELF-DEFENSE.

We place the ground of defense here on the same ground and limited by the same means as the right of personal defense. If a man be assailed, his power to slay the assailant is not limited to the moment when the mortal blow is about to be given; he is not bound to wait till his life is on the very point of being taken; but any movement towards the foul purpose plainly indicated justifies him in the right of self-defense, and in slaying the assailant on the spot. The theory of our case is, that there was a man living in a constant state of adultery with the prisoner's wife, a man who was daily, by

---

[1] Mr. Carlisle.

a moral—no, by an immoral power—enormous, monstrous, and al-together unparalleled in the history of American society, or in the history of the family of man, a power over the being of this woman —calling her from her husband's house, drawing her from the side of her child, and dragging her, day by day, through the streets in order that he might gratify his lust. The husband beholds him in the very act of withdrawing his wife from his roof, from his pres-ence, from his arm, from his wing, from his nest; meets him in that act and slays him, and we say that the right to slay him stands on the firmest principles of self-defense.

I have endeavored, as briefly as I could, to explain the prin-ciples of social law and jurisprudence on which the defense is planted, and I trust that, on examination, it will not be found to be any visionary ground of defense, or any such mere theory as was apprehended by my learned friend[1] who opened the argument. He says that society could not exist on such principles, because this was the exercise of the right of private judgment; and if it was to be established as a principle, the land would be a scene of blood, as the punishment of adultery would be followed by the punish-ment of other crimes. Now, if it were so, if this land were to be a scene of blood, and if it were necessary to make it so, I ask whether blood had not better run in torrents through our streets than that the homes of men should be destroyed by the adulterer at will? But it is not so. Neither your Honor nor I will be frightened by any such appaling picture. Thank God, adultery is a crime that is usually a stranger to American society. It is but rarely in our history that some great event like this occurs to startle society and lead it to the examination of the principles on which it is founded. That has been the case, and should it lead to the examination of the principles of law on which home and family rest, should it result in planting around that home and family the safeguards of the law, in breaking through the bonds by which the adulterous court of Charles the Second undertook to bind the arm of the husband; then some good will grow out of that great evil that has been produced by this event.

It is not my purpose to pursue this discussion in reference to the other points. I shall leave them to my colleague.[2] I thank your Honor for the patience with which you have heard me in the discussion of this question. I have endeavored to discuss it on

---

[1] Mr. Carlisle.   [2] Mr. James T. Brady.

principles which I believe, as a man, as a father, and as a husband, to be essential to the peace and security of your home and mine. I have endeavored to discuss it on principles which are essential to the peace and prosperity of the society in which my home is planted as well as yours; and I hope that, by the blessing of God, as it has been your Honor's good fortune to lay down the law which secures the family, in one aspect, from the seducer of the sister, you may also plant on the best and surest foundations the principles of law which secure the peace of the home, the security of the family, and the relations of husband and wife, which have been in the most horrid manner violated in this case.

SPEECH OF JAMES T. BRADY,

In Defense of the "Savannah Privateers," Indicted for Piracy.

AT A CIRCUIT COURT OF THE UNITED STATES, HELD AT THE CITY OF NEW YORK, OCTOBER TERM, 1861.

Analysis of Mr. Brady's Speech.

1. Piracy. — Nature and character of the crime.
2. Piracy under the law of nations, and under the acts of Congress.—The "Enchantress" case.
3. The question of intent one of fact for the jury.
4. Intent can not be inferred, but must be proved.
5. Consequences of defendants' acts not necessarily criminal.
6. Legal presumption of intent may be overcome. --Narration of facts.
7. Larceny and trespass distinguished.—Illustrations.

8. The letter of marque a valid defense.
9. The "Liberty Boys" of New York before the revolution.
10. Rebellion as distinguished from revolution.
11. The right of revolution a legal right.
12. Secession synonymous with revolution; right synonymous with power.
13. Evidences of the existence of civil war.
14. During civil war, the combatants are entitled to all the rights of war.—Blockade defined.
15. The duties of an advocate require the highest moral courage.

The trial of the officers and crew of the Confederate privateer Savannah forms an interesting episode in the history of the late war of the rebellion, involving, as it did, a discussion of the legal aspects of that memorable conflict; the right of revolution within the law of nations, and the rights of revolutionists under the laws of war. The Savannah, a schooner of about fifty-three tons burden, armed with cannon and small arms, and manned by a crew of twenty persons, including her officers, sailed from under the shadows of Fort Sumter, on the morning of Sunday, the 2d day of June, 1861, and pushed out into the Atlantic, bound for no port, and without any particular point of destination in view. Her commander, Thomas Harrison Baker, carried a letter of marque bearing date the 18th of May, 1861, issued by Jefferson Davis, signing himself "President of the Confederate States of America," whereby the Savannah was commissioned and authorized "to act as a private armed vessel of the Confederate States, on the high seas, against the United States of America, their ships, vessels, goods and effects, and those of her citizens, during the pendency of the war now existing between the said Confederate States and the said United States."

On Monday, the 3d of June, the Savannah descried a sail and gave chase, flying the American colors. The vessel proved to be the American brig Joseph,

laden with sugar, from Cardenas, in Cuba, bound for Philadelphia. When within hailing distance, Captain Baker ran up the confederate flag, and ordered the
master of the Joseph on board his vessel, with his papers, by authority of the
Confederate States, saying, in response to an inquiry from the Joseph, " I am
sorry for it, but you make war upon us, and we have, in retaliation, to make war
upon you." A prize crew was put on board the Joseph, and she was run into a
confederate port and sold as a prize. Upon the same day, however, the Savannah
was captured by the United States brig-of-war Perry. The prisoners were afterwards transferred to the Minnesota, which ran into Hampton Roads, and were
there placed on board the Harriet Lane, which carried them to New York, where
they were indicted by the United States grand jury, and tried upon a charge of
piracy.

Twelve prisoners were arraigned : Thomas Harrison Baker, Charles Sydney
Passalaigue, John Harleston, Henry Cashman Howard, Joseph Cruse del Carno,
Patrick Daly, John Murphy, Martin Galvin, Henry Oman, William Charles
Clarke, Richard Palmer, Alexander Carter Coid, and Albert G. Ferris. The first
four named were citizens of the United States; the others were foreigners, and
had never been naturalized.

Piracy is of two kinds : national and municipal. The former is a crime under the common law of nations; the latter is an offense under the statutes of a
particular State or nation. Under the former, the element of intent must be
broad enough to cover property of every nation ; under the latter, the offense is
made out by showing an intent to depredate upon the property of the particular
State, to the exclusion of all others. A pirate, according to the general definition, offends against the universal laws of society; he is deemed an enemy of the
human race, making war indiscriminately upon all mankind, and the vessels of
every nation have a right to seize and punish him. National piracy is defined to
be "the offense of depredating on the seas, without being authorized by any
sovereign State, or with commissions from different sovereigns at war with each
other." [1] It is a rule of international law, that in a state of war existing between
two nations, either may commission "privateers," or private armed vessels to
carry on war against the enemy on the high seas; and such commission will afford
protection, even in the courts of the enemy's country, against a charge of robbery
or piracy.

Congress, under the power given by the Constitution,[2] to define and punish
piracies and felonies committed on the high seas, and offenses against the law of
nations, passed an act, on the 30th of April, 1790, entitled "An Act for the punishment of certain crimes against the United States," commonly known as " The
Crimes Act." On the 15th of May, 1820, an additional law was passed making
further provision for punishing the crime of piracy. The third section of the act
of 1820 declares, " that, if any person shall, upon the high seas, commit the
crime of robbery, in or upon any ship or vessel, or upon any ship's company of
any ship or vessel, or the lading thereof, such person shall be adjudged to be a
pirate." Under this statute, a commission from a State or nation at war with another, would, according to the law of nations, constitute a defense.

The ninth section of the act of 1790 declares, " that if any *citizen* shall com-

---

[1] Wheaton's Int. Law, p. 184.   [2] Article 1, sec. 8.

mit any piracy or robbery aforesaid, or any act of hostility against the United States, or any citizen thereof, upon the high seas, under color of any commission from any *foreign* prince or State, or on pretense of authority from any person, such offender shall, notwithstanding the pretense of any such authority, be deemed, adjudged, and taken to be a pirate, felon and robber." It was claimed by the prisoners, that this statute could only apply to acts done under authority of a foreign power or person; that, if Jefferson Davis represented that power or person, then the defendants were subjects of that power, not citizens of the United States, and not within the act; if he did not represent a foreign power, the act had no application.

The indictment charged the prisoners with the robbery of an American vessel upon the high seas, and contained ten counts : the first five were framed under the act of 1820; the other five under the ninth section of the act of 1790, charging all the prisoners with being citizens, and with having committed the acts set forth on pretense of authority from one Jefferson Davis. On behalf of the foreign defendants, it was claimed, that it was a settled principle of international law that one nation could not make that piracy which was not piracy under the law of nations, except so far as their own subjects were concerned,[1] and hence there could be no conviction under the act of 1820, since there was no intent to seize any but American vessels. It was further claimed, in behalf of all the defendants, that the commission from Jefferson Davis was a defense, because the right of revolution for cause was a legal right, and the position occupied by the Confederacy towards the United States was such that they were justified in adopting the means of retaliation or aggression recognized in a state of war, and entitled to all the privileges and immunities existing under the laws of war.

The questions presented upon this trial, it will be seen, were of the first magnitude and importance, and required for their solution a familiarity with the most profound legal principles and the highest professional knowledge. The case was conducted by distinguished counsel, among whom were some of the ablest lawyers in the land. E. Delafield Smith, United States District Attorney, was assisted by William M. Evarts, Samuel Blatchford (now U. S. Circuit Judge), and Ethan Allen; for the defense appeared Jeremiah Larocque, Daniel Lord, James T. Brady, Algernon S. Sullivan, Joseph H. Dukes, Isaac Davega, and Maurice Mayer. Hon. Judges Nelson and Shipman presided.

The character and genius of James T. Brady made him the most popular advocate of his time, for in him were combined the most superb qualities of the head and heart. The following remark illustrates his genuine manhood : " I honor greatness, genius and achievements," he said, " but I honor more those qualities in a man's nature which show that, while he holds a proper relation to the Deity, he has also a just estimate of his fellow-men, and a kindly feeling towards them. I would rather have it said of me, after death, by my brethren of the bar, that they were sorry I had left their companionship, than to be spoken of in the highest strains of gifted panegyric." He was esteemed by all, but to those who were so fortunate as to share his acquaintance, he was endeared by the warmest ties of friendship and affection. That man will always be loved

---

[1] Wheaton's Int. Law, vol. 6, p. 85; 1 Kent's Com. p. 195; 1 Phillemore, 381; Hefter on Modern Int. Law (4th ed.), p. 191.

who believed, as did Mr. Brady, that the highest, purest, and most unselfish of all earthly affections is man's love for man. He was a successful and accomplished lawyer. His intellectual power will appear upon a perusal of his very able and interesting address for the defense of this case. After all the other counsel for the prisoners had spoken, Mr. Brady summed up as follows :

MAY IT PLEASE THE COURT,—*Gentlemen of the Jury:*—I feel quite certain that all of you are much satisfied to find that this important trial is rapidly drawing to a close; and I think it would be unbecoming in me, as one of the counsel for the accused, to proceed a step farther in my address to you without acknowledging to the court the gratitude which we feel for their kindness in hearing so largely discussed the grave legal questions involved in this controversy; to the jury, for their unvarying patience throughout the investigation; and to our learned opponents, for the frank and open manner in which the prosecution has been conducted. Our fellow-citizens at the South—certainly that portion of them who cherish affection for this part of the Union—will find in the course of this trial most satisfactory evidence that respect for law, freedom of speech, freedom of discussion, liberty of opinion, and the rights of all our countrymen, here exist to the fullest extent. All of us have heretofore been connected with interesting and exciting trials. I am warranted in saying that, considering the period at which this trial has occurred, and all the facts and circumstances attending it, the citizens of New York have reason to be proud that such a trial could proceed without one word of acerbity, without one expression of angry feeling, or one improper exhibition of popular sentiments.

1. PIRACY.—NATURE AND CHARACTER OF THE CRIME.

The great question for this jury, absorbing all others, is: Have the twelve men named in the indictment, or has either of them, committed piracy, and thus incurred the penalty of death? It is a very interesting inquiry, gentlemen—interesting in its historical, national, judicial and political aspects; interesting, too, because of the character and description of the accused. We discover that eight of them are foreigners, who have never been naturalized, and do not judicially come under the designation of citizens of the United States. Four of them are what we call natural-born citizens: two from the State of South Carolina, one from North Carolina, and one from Philadelphia. Two of them are in very feeble health; and I am sorry to say, some are not yet of middle age, some quite young, including Passalaigue, who has not yet attained his eighteenth year. I know my fellow-citizens of New York quite well enough to be quite sure that, even if there had been any exhibition of popular prejudice, or feeling, or fury, with a view to disturb their judgments in the jury-box, the sympathy that arises properly in every well-constituted heart and mind, in favor of the accused, their relatives and friends, would overcome any such wrong impulse as might be directed to deprive them of that fair trial which, up to this point, they have had, and which, to the end, I know they will have.

Are they pirates and robbers? Have they incurred the penalty of death? Gentlemen, it is a little curious that, during the present reign of Victoria, a statute has been passed in England softening the rigor of the punishment for piracy, and subjecting the person found guilty to transportation, instead of execution, unless arms have been used in the spoliation, or some act done aggravating the offense. I have used the term "pirate," and the term "robber." There is another which, strangely enough, was employed by a judge of the Vice-Admiralty Court in South Carolina, in 1718, who calls these pirates and robbers, as we designate them, "sea thieves;" and I am very glad to find that phrase, because the words robber and pirate have fallen into mere terms of opprobrium; while the word "thief" has a significance and force understood by every man. You know what you thought a "thief" to be when a boy, and how you despised him; and you are to look at each prisoner mentioned in this indictment, and say, on your consciences as men, in view of the facts and of the law, as expounded by the learned court, do you consider that the word "thief" can be applied to any one of the men whom I have to assist in defending? That is the great practical question which you are to decide.

Here Mr. Brady briefly adverted to the question of jurisdiction, as having been already very fully discussed. After some observations on the case of Hicks, the pirate, he continued :

2. PIRACY UNDER THE LAW OF NATIONS, AND UNDER THE ACTS
OF CONGRESS.—THE "ENCHANTRESS" CASE.

This indictment charges two kinds of offense: Piracy, as that crime existed by the law of nations, which law may be said to have been incorporated into the jurisprudence of the United States; and piracy under the ninth section of the act of 1790. Piracy by the law of nations is defined by Wheaton, the great American commentator on international law, on page 184 of his treatise on that subject. "Piracy," says that eminent gentleman, who was an ornament to the country which gave him birth, and an honor to my profession, "piracy is defined by the text-writers to be the offense of depredating on the seas, without being authorized by any sovereign State, or with commissions from different sovereigns at war with each other." The last part of the definition you need not trouble yourselves about, as I only read it so as not to quibble the text. I will read the passage without the latter part. "Piracy is defined to be the offense of depredating on the seas, without being authorized by any sovereign State." Other definitions will hereafter be suggested.

This leads me to remark upon certain judicial proceedings in Philadelphia against men found on board the Southern privateer "Jefferson Davis," and who were convicted of piracy for having seized and sent away as a prize the "Enchantress." Now, my way of dealing with juries is to act with them while in the jury-box as if they were out of it. I never imitate that bird referred to by the gentleman who preceded me—the ostrich which supposes that when he conceals his head, his whole person is hidden from view. I know, and every gentleman present knows, that a jury in the city of Philadelphia has convicted the men arrested on the "Jefferson Davis" of piracy. We are a nation certainly distinguished for three things: for newspapers, politics, and tobacco. I do not know that the Americans could present their social individualities by any better signs. Everybody reads the papers, and everybody has a paper given him to read. The hackman waiting for his fare consumes his leisure time perusing the paper. The apple-woman at her stall reads the paper. At the breakfast table, the dinner table, and the supper table, the paper is daily read. I sometimes take my meals at Delmonico's, and have there observed a gentleman who, while refreshing himself with a hasty meal, takes up the newspaper, places it against the castor, and eats, drinks and reads all at the same time. Gentlemen, I say that a people so addicted to newspapers must have ascertained that the men in Philadelphia were convicted; and how the jury could have done otherwise upon the charge of Justices Grier and Cadwalader, I am incapable of perceiving. I have the pleasure of knowing both those eminent judges. My acquaintance with Judge Cadwalader is slight, it is true, but of sufficient standing to insure him the greatest respect for his learning and character. With Judge Grier the acquaintance is of longer duration; and as he has always extended to me in professional occupations before him courtesies which men never forget, I cannot but speak of him with affection. I have nevertheless something to say about the law laid down by those judges on that case. No question on the merits was left to the jury, as I understand the instructions. The jurymen were told that if they believed the testimony, then the defendants were guilty of piracy.

3. THE QUESTION OF INTENT ONE OF FACT FOR THE JURY.

Now, as to the aspect of this case in view of piracy by the law of nations, the question for the jury is, in the first place: Did these defendants, in the act of capturing the Joseph, take her by force, or by putting the captain of her in fear, with the intent to steal her? That is the question as presented by the indictment, and in order to convict under either of the first five counts, the jury must be satisfied, beyond all reasonable doubt, that, in attacking the Joseph, the defendants were actuated as described in the indictment, from which I read the allegation that they, "with force and arms, piratically, feloniously, and violently, put the persons on board in personal fear and danger of their lives, and in seizing the vessel did, as aforesaid, seize, rob, steal and carry her away." In this the indictment follows the law. Another question of fact, in the other aspect of the case, under the ninth section of the act of 1790, will be, substantially, whether the existence of a civil war is shown. That involves inquiry into the existence of the Confederate States as a *de facto* government or as a *de jure* government.

The *animus furandi*, so often mentioned in this case, means nothing but the intent to steal. The existence of that intent must be found in the evidence, before these men can be called pirates, robbers, or thieves; and whether such intent did or did not exist, is a question entirely for you.

To convict under the ninth section of the act of 1790, the prosecution must prove that the defendants, being at the time of such offense citizens of the United States of America, did something which by that act is prohibited. You will bear in mind that the act of 1790, in its ninth section, has no relation except to American-born citizens, and as to that part of the indictment the eight foreigners charged are entirely relieved from responsibility.

Mr. Brady here read the special verdict in the case of U. S. *v.* Smith (5 Wheat. 104), as illustrating what piracy is, and continued:

According to the evidence in the case of Smith, the defendants were clearly pirates. They had no commission from any government or governor, and were mere mutineers, who had seized a vessel illegally, and then proceeded to seize others without any pretense or show of authority, but with felonious intent. For these acts they were justly convicted.

4. INTENT CAN NOT BE INFERRED, BUT MUST BE PROVED.

Now, we say, that this felonious intent as charged against these defendants, must be proved. But what say my learned friends opposed? Why (in effect), that it need not be proved to a jury by any evidence, but must be inferred, as a matter of law, or by the jury first, from the presumption that every man knows the law; and these men, in this view, are pirates—though they honestly believed that there was a valid government called the Confederate States, and that they had a right to act under it—because they ought to have known the law; ought to have known that, although the Confederate States had associated for the purpose of forming, yet they had not completed a government; ought to have known that, though Baker had a commission signed by Jefferson Davis, the so-called President of the Confederate States, under which he was authorized to act as a privateer, yet the law did not recognize the commission.

There is, indeed, a rule of law, said to be essential to the existence of society, that all men must be taken to know the law, except, I might add, lawyers and judges, who seldom agree upon any proposition until they must.

The whole judicial system is founded upon the theory that judges will err about the law, and thus we have the courts of review to correct judicial mistakes and to establish permanent principles. Yet it is true that every man is presumed to know the law; and the native of Manilla (one of the parties here charged), *Loo Foo*, or whatever his name may be, who does not, probably, understand what he is here for, is presumed to know the law as well as one of us. If he did not know it better, considering the differences between us, he might not be entitled to rate high as a jurist. One of my brethren read to you an extract from a recent German work,[1] which presents a different view of this subject as relates to foreign subjects in particular cases. I was happy to hear Mr. Mayer on the law of this case, more particularly as he declared himself to be

[1] Hefter on Modern Int. Law.

a foreign-born citizen; for it is one of the characteristics of this government—a characteristic of our free institutions—that no distinction of birth or creed is permitted to stand in the way of merit, come from what clime it may.

5. Consequences of defendants' acts not necessarily criminal.

There is another presumption. Every man is presumed to intend the natural consequences of his own acts. Now, what are the natural consequences of the acts done by these defendants? The law on this point is illustrated and applied with much effect in homicide cases. Suppose a man has a slight contention with another, and one of the combatants, drawing a dagger, aims to inflict a slight wound, say upon the hand of the other; but, in the struggle, the weapon enters the heart, and the injured party dies. The man is arrested with the bloody dagger in his hand, the weapon by which death was unquestionably occasioned; and the fact being established that he killed the deceased, the law will presume the act to be murder, and cast upon the accused the burden of showing that it was something other than murder.[1] I hope, gentlemen, to see the day when this doctrine of law will no longer exist. I never could understand how the presumption of murder could be drawn from an act equally consistent with murder, manslaughter, justifiable or excusable homicide, or accident, but such is the law, and it must be respected.

I say, that neither of the defendants intended, as the ordinary and natural consequence of his act, to commit piracy or robbery, though what he did might, in law, amount to such an offense. He intended to take legal prizes, and no more to rob than the man in the case I supposed designed to kill. The natural consequences of his acts were, to take the vessel and send her to a port to be adjudicated upon as a prize.

6. Legal presumption of intent may be overcome.— Narration of facts.

Now, I state to my learned friends and the court this proposition: that, though a legal presumption as to intent might have ex-

---

[1] Now, under the New York statutes, the rule is changed. The law no longer presumes malice from proof of killing merely. The jury must determine the grade of the offense from all the evidence of the case. Stokes *v.* The People, 53 N. Y. 164.

isted in this case, if the prosecution had proved merely the forcible
taking, yet if, in making out a câse for the government, any fact be
elicited which shows that the actual intent was different from what
the law, in the absence of such fact, would imply, the presumption
is gone. And when the prosecution made their witness detail a
conversation which took place between Captain Baker and the captain of the Joseph, with reference to the authority of the former to
seize the vessel, and when you find that Captain Baker asserted a
claim of right, that overcomes the presumption that he despoiled
the captain of the Joseph with an intent to steal. The *animus
furandi* must, in this case, depend on something else than presumption. I will refer you for more particulars of the law on this
point to 1 Greenleaf on Evidence, sections 13 and 14, and I make
this citation for another purpose. When an act is in itself illegal,
sometimes, if not in the majority of cases, the law affixes to the
party the intent to perpetrate a legal offense. But this is not the
universal rule. In cases of procuring money or goods under false
pretenses, where the intent is the essence of the crime, the prosecution must establish the offense, not by proving alone the act of receiving, but by showing the act and intent; so both must be proved
here.

Now, I ask, has the prosecution entitled itself to the benefit of
any presumption as to intent? What are the facts—the conceded
facts? Baker, and a number of persons in Charleston, did openly
and notoriously select a vessel called the "Savannah," then lying
in the stream, and fitted her out as a privateer. Baker, in all of
these proceedings, acted under the authority of a commission signed
by Jefferson Davis, styling and signing himself President of the
Confederate States of America. Baker and his companions then
went forth as privateersmen, and in no other capacity, for the purpose of despoiling the commerce of the United States, and with
the strictest injunction not to meddle with the property of any other
country. The instructions were clear and distinct on this head, as
you know from having heard them read. They went to sea and
overhauled the Joseph, gave chase with the American flag flying—
one of the ordinary devices or cheats practiced in naval warfare;
a device frequently adopted by American naval commanders to
whose fame no American dare affix the slightest stigma. On near-
ing the Joseph, the Savannah showed the secession flag, and Baker
requested Captain Meyer to come on board with his papers. The
captain asked by what authority, and received for answer: "The

authority of the Confederate States." The captain then went on board with his papers, when Baker, helping him over the side, said: "I am very sorry to take your vessel, but I do so in retaliation against the United States, with whom we are at war." Baker put a prize crew on board the Joseph, and sent her to Georgetown; the captain he detained there as a prisoner. She was then duly submitted for judgment as a prize. These are the facts upon which they claim that piracy at common law is established.

7. LARCENY AND TRESPASS DISTINGUISHED.—ILLUSTRATIONS.

My learned associate, Mr. Larocque, cited a number of cases to show that, though a man might take property of another, and appropriate it to his own use, yet if he did so under color of right, under a *bona fide* impression that he had authority to take the property, he would only be a trespasser; he would have to restore it or pay the value of it, but he could not be convicted of a crime for its conversion.

Let me state a case. You own a number of bees. They leave your land, where they hived, and come upon mine, and take refuge in the hollow of a tree, where they deposit their honey. They are your bees, but you cannot come upon my land to take them away; and though they are in my tree, I cannot take the honey. Such a case is reported in our State adjudications.[1] But, suppose that I did take the bees and appropriate the honey to my own use: I might be unjustly indicted for larceny, because I took the property of another, but I am not, consequently, a thief in the eye of the law; the absence of intent to steal would insure my acquittal.

That is one illustration. I will mention one other, decided in the South, relating to a subject on which the South is very strict and very jealous. A slave announced to a man his intention to escape. The man secreted the slave for the purpose of aiding his escape and effecting his freedom. He was indicted for larceny, on the ground that he exercised a control over the property of the owner against his will. The court held that the object was not to steal, and he could not be convicted. In Wheaton's Criminal Proceedings, page 397, this language will be found, and it is satisfactory on the point under discussion: "There are cases where taking is no more than a trespass. Where a man takes another's goods

---

[1] Goff *v.* Kilts, 15 Wend. 550; and see Gillet *v.* Mason, 7 Johns. 161; Ferguson *v.* Miller, 1 Cow. 243.

openly before him, or where, having otherwise than by apparent robbery, possessed himself of them, he avows the fact before he is questioned. This is only a trespass."

Now all these principles are familiar and simple, and do not require lawyers to expound them, for they appeal to the practical sense of mankind. It is certainly a most lamentable result of the wisdom of centuries, to place twelve men together and ask them, from fictions or theories, to say, on oath, that a man is a thief when every one of them knows that he is not. If any man on this jury thinks the word pirate, robber or thief can be truly applied to either of these defendants, I am very sorry, for I think neither of them at all liable to any such epithet.

8. The letter of marque[1] a valid defense.

But, suppose that the intent is to be inferred from the act of seizing the Joseph, and the defendants must be convicted, unless justified by the commission issued for Captain Baker, let us then inquire as to the effect of that commission. We say that it protects the defendants against being treated as pirates. Whether it does or not depends upon the question whether the Confederate States have occupied such a relation to the United States of America that they might adopt the means of retaliation or aggression recognized in a state of war.

It is our right and duty, as advocates, to maintain that the confederate government was so situated, and to support the proposition by reference to the political and judicial history and precedents of the past, stating for these men the principles and views which they and their neighbors of the revolting States insist upon; our personal opinions being in no wise called for, nor important, nor even proper, to be stated at this time and in this place.

If it can be shown that the Confederate States occupy the same position towards the government of the United States that the thirteen revolted colonies did to Great Britain in the war of the revolution, then these men cannot be convicted of piracy.

I do not ask you to decide that the Southern States had the right to leave the Union, or secede, or to revolt—to set on foot an insurrection, or to perfect a rebellion. That is not the question here. I will place before the jury such views of law and of history as bear upon the case, endeavoring not to go over the ground

---

[1] For a copy of the letter, see Appendix, p. 722.

occupied by my associates. I will refer you to a small book published here in 1859, entitled "The History of New York from the
Earliest Time," a very reliable and authentic work. In this book
I find a few facts to which I will call your attention, one of which
may be unpleasant to some of our friends from the New England
States, for we find that New York, so far as her people were concerned—exclusive of the authorities—was in physical revolt against
the parent government long before our friends in New England,
some of whom often feel disposed to do just what they please, but
are not quite willing to allow others the same privilege.

9. The "liberty boys" of New York before the revolution.

I will refer to it to show you what was the condition of things long
before the 4th of July, 1776, and to show that, though we now hurl
our charges against these men as pirates—who never killed anybody, never tried to kill anybody; who never stole and never tried
to steal—yet the men of New York city who committed, under the
name of "Liberty Boys,"what England thought terrible atrocities, in
New York, were never touched by justice, not even so heavily as if
a feather from the pinion of the humming bird had fallen upon
their heads. I find that, about the year 1765, our people here began to grumble about the taxes and imposts which Great Britain
levied upon us. And you know, though the causes of the revolutionary war are set forth with much dignity in the Declaration of
Independence, the contest originated about taxes. That was the
great source of disaffection, directing itself more particularly to
the matter of tea, and which led to the miscellaneous party in Boston, at which there were no women present, however, and where
salt water was used in the decoction. I find that the governor of
the city had fists, arms, and all the means of aggression at his command; but at length, happily for us, the government sent over a
young gentleman to rule us (Lord Monckford), who, when he did
come, appears to have been similar in habits to one of the accused,
who is described as being always idle. The witness for the prosecution explained that separate posts and duties were assigned to
each of the crew of the Savannah; one fellow, he said, would do
nothing. But he will be convicted of having done a good deal, if
the prosecution prevail. A state of rebellion all this time and
afterwards existed in this particular part of the world, until the
British came and made themselves masters of the city. In the

course of the acts then committed by the citizens, and which the British government called an insurrection, a tumultuous rebellion and revolution, they offered, or it was said they offered, an indignity to an equestrian statue of George III. The British troops, in retaliation, and being grossly offended at the conduct of Pitt, who had been a devoted friend of the colonists, mutilated the statue of him which stood on Wall street. The remains of the statue are still with us, and can be seen at the corner of West Broadway and Franklin street, where it is preserved as a relic of the past—a grim memento of the perfect absurdity of charging millions of people with being all pirates, robbers, thieves, and marauders.

When the British took possession of this city, they had at one time in custody five thousand persons. That was before any formal declaration of independence; before the formation of a government *de jure* or *de facto;* and yet did they ever charge any of the prisoners with being robbers? Not at all. Was this from any kindness or humane spirit? Not at all: for they adopted all means in their power to overcome our ancestors. The eldest son of the Earl of Chatham resigned his commission, because he would not consent to fight against the colonies. The government did not hesitate to send to Germany for troops. They could not get sufficient at home. The Irish would not aid them in the fight. The British did not even hesitate to employ Indians; and when, in Parliament, the Secretary of State justified himself, saying that they had a perfect right to employ " all the means God and nature " gave them, he was eloquently rebuked. Even, with all this hostility, such a thing was never thought of as to condemn men, when taken prisoners, and hold them outside that protection which, according to the law of nations, should be extended to men under such circumstances, even though in revolt against the government.

10. Rebellion as distinguished from revolution.

In October, 1774, the king, in his message to Parliament, said that a most daring spirit of resistance and disobedience to the laws existed in Massachusetts, and was countenanced and encouraged in others of his colonies.

Now, I want you to keep your minds fairly applied to the point, on which the court will declare itself, as to whether I am right in saying, that the day when the message was sent to Parliament, the colonies occupied towards the old government a position similar to that of the Confederate States in the hour of revolt to the United

States.   But we will possibly see that the Confederate States occupy a stronger position.

In the course of the discussion which ensued upon the message, the famous Wilkes remarked: "Rebellion, indeed, appears on the back of a flying enemy; but revolution flames on the breastplate of a victorious warrior."

If an illegal assemblage sets itself up in opposition to the municipal government, it is a mere insurrection, though ordinary officers of the law be incapable of quelling it, and the military power has to be called out.   That is one thing.   But when a whole State places itself in an attitude of hostility to the other States of a confederacy, assumes a distinct existence, and has the power to maintain independence, though only for a time, that is quite a different affair.

We remember how beautifully expressed is that passage of the Irish poet, so familiar to all of us, and especially to those who, like myself, coming from Irish ancestry, know so well what is the name and history of rebellion:

> " Rebellion—foul, dishonoring word,
>   Whose wrongful blight so oft hath stained
>   The holiest cause that tongue or sword
>   Of mortal ever lost or gained !
>   How many a spirit born to bless
>   Has sunk beneath thy withering bane,
>   Whom but a day's—an hour's success,
>   Had wafted to eternal fame ! "

A remarkable instance, illustrating the sentiment of this passage, is found in the history of that brave man, emerging from obscurity, stepping suddenly forth from the common ranks of men, whose name is so generally mentioned with reverence and love, and who so lately freed Naples from the rule of a tyrant.   This brave patriot was driven from his native land, after a heroic struggle in Rome.   History has recorded how he was followed in this exile by a devoted wife, who perished because she would not desert her husband; and how he came to this country, where he established himself in business until such time as he saw a speck of hope glimmer on the horizon over his lovely and beloved native land.   Then he went back almost alone.   Red-shirted, like a common toiling man, he gathered round him a few trusty followers who had unlimited confidence in him as a leader, and accomplished the revolution which dethroned the son of Bomba, and placed Victor Emanuel in his stead. You already know that I speak of Garibaldi.[1] And yet, Garibaldi, it seems, should have been denounced as a pirate, had the sea been the theater of his failure; and a robber, had he been unsuccessful upon land.

What do you think an eminent man said, in the British Parliament, about the outbreak of our revolution, and the condition of things then existing in America? "Whenever oppression begins, resistance becomes lawful and right." Who said that? The great associate of Chatham and Burke, Lord Camden. At that time Franklin was in Europe, seeking to obtain a hearing before a committee of parliament in respect to the grievances of the American people. It was refused.

The Lords and Commons, in an address to the king, declared in express terms, that a "rebellion actually existed in Massachusetts;" and yet, in view of all that, no legal prosecution of any rebel ever followed. So matters continued till the war effectively began, Washington having been appointed commander-in-chief. Then some Americans were taken by the British and detained as prisoners. Of this Washington complained to General Gage, then in command of the British army. Gage returned answer that he had treated the prisoners only too kindly, seeing that they were rebels, and that "their lives, by the law of the land, were destined for the cord." Yet not one of them so perished.

11. THE RIGHT OF REVOLUTION A LEGAL RIGHT.

In view of these things, even so far as I have now advanced; in view of the sacrifices of the southern colonies in the revolution; in view of the great struggle for independence, and the great doctrine laid down, that, whenever oppression begins, resistance becomes lawful and right—is it possible to forget the history of the past, and the great principles which gleamed through the darkness and the perils of our early history? Are we to assert that the Constitution establishing our government is perfect in all its parts, and stands upon a corner-stone equivalent to what the globe itself might be supposed to rest on, if we did not know it was ever wheeling through space? Is all the history of our past, its triumphs and reverses, and the glorious consummation which crowned the efforts

[1] Garibaldi's sympathies were not with the Confederacy, as appears by his letter, read by Mr. Evarts, in his reply. See *post*, p. 419, and Appendix, p. 723.

of the people, all alike to be thrown aside now, upon the belief that we have established a government so perfect, and a Union so complete, that no portion of the States can ever, under any circumstances, secede, or revolt, or dispute the authority of the others, without danger of being treated as pirates and robbers? The Declaration of Independence has never been repudiated, I believe, and I suppose I have a right to refer to it as containing the political creed of the American people. I do not know how many people of the old world agree with it, and a most eminent lawyer of our own country characterized the maxims stated at its commencement as "glittering generalities." But I believe the American people have never withdrawn their approbation from the principles and doctrines it declares. Among those we find the self-evident truth, that man has an inalienable right to life, liberty, and the pursuit of happiness; that it is to secure these rights that governments are instituted among men, deriving their just powers from the consent of the governed; and that whenever any form of government becomes destructive of those ends, it is right and patriotic to alter and abolish it, and to institute a new government, laying its foundations on such principles, and conferring power in such a form, as to them may seem most likely to secure their safety and happiness. Is this a mockery? Is this a falsehood? Have these ideas been just put forward for the first time? There has been a dispute among men as to who should be justly denominated the author of this document. The debate may be interesting to the historian; but these principles, though they are embodied in the Constitution, were not created by it. They have lived in the hearts of man since man first trod the earth. I can imagine the time, too, when Egypt was in her early glory, and in fancy see one of the poor, miserable wretches, deprived of any right of humanity, harnessed, like a brute beast, to the immense stone about being erected in honor of some monarch, whose very name was destined to perish. I can imagine the degraded slave pausing in his loathsome toil to delight over the idea that there might come a time when the meanest of men would enjoy natural rights, under a government of the multitude formed to secure them.

Now, what says Mr. Blackstone, the great commentator on the law of England, when speaking of the revolution which dethroned James II: "Whenever a question arises between the society at large and any magistrate originally vested with powers originally delegated by that society, it must be decided by the voice of the

society itself. There is not upon earth any other tribunal to resort to." [1]

Prior to the 23d of March, 1776, the Legislature of Massachusetts authorized the issuing of letters of marque to privateers upon
the ocean, and when my learned friend, Mr. Lord, in his remarks
so clear and convincing, called attention to the lawfulness of privateering, my brother Evarts attempted to qualify it by designating
the granting of letters of marque as reluctantly tolerated, and as
if no such practice as despoiling commerce should be permitted,
even in a state of war.

I will not again read from Mr. Marcy's letter, but I will
say here that the position he took gratified the heart of the
whole American people. He said, in substance: If you, England and France, have the right to despoil commerce with
armed national vessels, we have a right to adopt such means of
protection and retaliation as we possess. We do not propose, if
you make war upon us, or we find it necessary to make war upon
you, that we, with a poor, miserable fleet, shall not be at liberty to
send out privateers, but yield to you, who may come with your
steel-clad vessels and powerful armament to practice upon us any
amount of devastation. No. We never had a navy strong enough
to place us in such a position as that with regard to foreign powers.
Look at it. Do you think that France or England has any feeling
of friendship towards this country as a nation? I do not speak of
the people of these countries, but of the cabinets and governments.
No. Nations are selfish. Nearly all the laws of nations are founded
on interest. Nations conduct their political affairs on that basis.
They never receive laws from one another, not even against crime.
And when you want to obtain back from another country a man
who has committed depredations against society, you do it only by
virtue of a treaty, and from no love or affection to the country demanding it. And if this war continues much longer, I, for one,
entertain the most profound apprehension that both these powers,
France and England, will combine to break the blockade, if they
do not enter upon more aggressive measures. If they for a moment
find it their interest to do so, they will, and no power, moral or
physical, can prevent them.

I say, then, the right of revolution is a right to be exercised,
not according to what the government revolted against may think,
but according to the necessities or the belief of the people revolting.

[1] Black. Com. vol. I, p. 211.

If you belonged to a State which was in any way deprived of its rights, the moment that oppression began resistance became a duty. A slave does not ask his master when he is to have his freedom, but he strikes for it at the proper opportunity. A man threatened with death at the hands of another, does not stop to ask whether he has a right to slay his assailant in self-defense. If self-preservation is the first law of individuals, so also is it of masses and of nations. Therefore, when the American Colonies made up their minds to achieve independence, whether their reasons were sufficient or not, they did not consent to have the question decided by Great Britain, but at once decided it for themselves. Very early in our history, in 1778, France recognized the American government. England, as you know, complained, and the French government sent back an answer, saying: Yes, we have formed a treaty with this new government; we have recognized it, and you have no right to complain; for you remember, England, said France, that during the reign of Elizabeth, when the Netherlands revolted against Spain, you, in the first place, negotiated secret treaties with the revolutionists, and then recognized them; but, when Spain complained of this, you said to Spain: The reasons which justify the Netherlands in their revolt entitle them to our support. Was success necessary? Was the doctrine of our opponents correct, that, though people may be in absolute revolt against the parent government, with an army in the field, and in exclusive possession of the territories they occupy, yet they have no right to be recognized by the law of nations, and are not entitled to the humanities that accompany the conditions of a war between foreign powers? Is success necessary? Why was it not necessary in the case of the colonies when recognized by France? Why not necessary in the case of the Netherlands when recognized by England? Never has been put forward such a doctrine for adjudication since the days of Ogden and Smith, tried in this city in 1806.

Here Mr. Brady referred to the argument of Thomas Addis Emmett, in defense of Smith and Ogden, charged with aiding General Miranda and the people of Caraccas in a revolt against Spain, as showing that the right of revolution rested upon sound legal principles. He then cited extracts from a work of James D. Torrey on "The Southern Rebellion, and the War for the Union," showing that the view taken by the South was analogous to the notions entertained by New England in the war of 1812, and could not be considered as novel or wicked. He then proceeded:

12. Secession Synonymous with Revolution; Right Synonymous with Power.

Now, this enables me to repeat, with a clearer view derived from history, the proposition that the Confederate States are—under the law of nations, and the principles embodied in the Declaration of Independence, sustained in the revolution, and recognized by our people—in a condition not distinguishable from that of the colonies in 1776, except that, if there be a difference, the position of the confederates, in reference to legality, as a judicial question, is more justifiable, as it is certainly more formidable. This word "secession" is, after all, only a word; a word, as Mr. Webster said in one of his great speeches, answering Mr. Calhoun, of fearful import; a word for which he could not, according to his views, too strongly express condemnation. But whether you use the word "secession," or the familiar expression, "going out of the Union," or, "not consenting to remain in the Union," the idea is one and the same. Much acumen and ingenuity have been displayed, even by a mind profound as that of Mr. Calhoun, a most acute man and a pure man, as Mr. Webster eloquently attested in the Senate chamber, after the decease of that South Carolina statesman. I say a good deal of acumen had been spent on the question whether a State, or any number of States, have a right under the Constitution to secede from the Union. It is a quarrel about phrases. It is not necessary in any point of view, political, philological or moral, to use the word "secession" as either excusing or justifying the act of the Confederate States. Suppose I grant, as a distinct proposition, in accordance with what I admit to be the opinion of the great majority of jurists, and orators, and statesmen at the North, that there is no right in a State, under the Constitution, to secede from the Union—what then? I shall not stop to give you the argument with which the South presents a view of the question entirely different from that of the North. Of what consequence is it, practically, whether the right of the State to go out be found in any part of the compact called the Constitution, or be derived from a source extrinsic of it? You (let me suppose) are twelve States, and I am the thirteenth. There is the original confederacy of States, pure and simple, under the agreement with each other; and there, according to the views of Mr. Webster and the prosecution here, we became constituted in a general government, or, as Wheaton says, in a "composite government," giving great power to the general center. Now, what difference does it make, if you twelve States conclude to leave me, whether you do it by virtue of anything contained in the Constitution, or inferable from the Constitution, or in virtue of some right or claim of right that resides out of the Constitution? It is not of the least consequence. I do not care for the word "secession." It would be, at the worst, revolution. In that same great speech of Mr. Webster's against Calhoun, in which I think I am justified in saying he exhausts the subject and makes the most formidable argument against the theory of secession that was ever uttered in the United States, all the conclusion he comes to is this: "'Peaceable secession!' I cannot agree to such a name. I cannot think it possible. It would be revolution." Very well. Of what consequence is the designation? Who cares for the baptism or the sponsors? It is the thing you look to. And if they have either the right or the power to secede or revolutionize, they may do it, and there is no tribunal on earth to sit in judgment upon them; though we have the right and the power, on the other hand, to battle for the maintenance of the whole Union.

Our friend, Mr. Justice Grier, says: "No band of conspirators can overcome the government merely because they are dissatisfied with the result of an election." Now, gentlemen, with the deference he deserves, I would ask the learned Justice Grier, or any other justice, or my learned friend, Mr. Evarts, how he will proceed to dispose of the case which I am about to put? Suppose that all but one of our States meet in their legislatures, and, by the universal acclaim, and with the entire approval of all the people, resolve that they will remain no longer in association with the others—what will you do with them? That solitary State, which may be Rhode Island, says: "I have in me the sovereignty; I have in me all the attributes that belong to empire or national existence; but I think I will have to let you go. Whether you call it secession, or rebellion, or revolution, you may go, because you have the power to go, if there be no better reason." And power and right become, in reference to this subject, the same thing in the end. Do they not? Is there any relation on earth that has a higher sanction than marriage? So long as two parties, who have contracted that holy obligation, have, in truth, no fault to find with each other, is there any right in either to go away from the other? There is no such right, either by the law of God or of man. But there is a power to do it; is there not? And if the wife flee from her husband, instead of towards him, or if a husband go from his wife, is there any law of society that can compel them to unite? And why not? Because mankind, though they have perpetrated many follies, have, at least, recognized that this was a remedy utterly impossible. In the relation of partnership between two individuals, does not the same state of things exist? and do not the same arguments suggest themselves? I ask my learned brother what he can do in reference to the ten States that have claimed to secede from the Union, and have organized themselves into a government? I will give him all the army he demands, and will let him retain in the chair of State this honest, pleasant Mr. Lincoln, who is not the greatest man in the world—nobody will pretend that—but is as good and honest a person as there is in the world. There is not the slightest question but that, in all his movements, he only proposes what he deems consistent with the welfare and honor of the country. I will give my learned brother the army now on the banks of the Potomac, doing nothing, and millions of money, and then I desire him to tell us how, with all these aids, he can coerce those ten States to remain in the confederacy. What was said by Mr. Buchanan on the subject, in his message of December last? "I do not propose," said he, "to attempt any coercion of the States. I believe that it would be utterly impossible. You cannot compel a State to remain in the Union. They may refuse to send Senators to the Senate of the United States. They may refuse to choose electors, and the government stops." Well, I grant you that this is not the view of other men quite as eminent as Mr. Buchanan. I grant you that the great Chief Justice Marshall—a man to whom it would be bad taste to apply any other word than great, because that includes everything which characterized him—I grant you that brilliant son of Virginia met an argument like this with the great power that distinguished all his judgments, when a question arose in the Supreme Court of the United States, affecting the State of Virginia and a citizen. But of what importance it is what any man thinks about it? What is your theory as compared with your practice? Now, I will give my friend all the power he wants, and ask him to deal with these ten States. Do you believe it to be within the compass of a possibility to compel them to remain in the Union, as States, if they do not wish it?

Thus I reach the conclusion, on even the weakest view of the case for us, that the power to secede, and the power to organize a government existing, there is no power on earth which, on any rule of law, can interfere with it, except that of war, conducted on the principles of civilized war.

Now, then, let us look at those Confederate States a little more closely. What says Vattel, in the passage referred to by my learned friend, Mr. Larocque, and which it is of the utmost importance, in this connection, to keep in mind.

Here Mr. Brady cited Vattel (Book 3, chap. 18, §§ 287, 292, 293), to show the distinction between rebellion and civil war,[1] and claimed that the Confederate States were clearly within the rule, and entitled to the benefits of the established laws of war. He continued:

Is not that clearly expressed and easy to understand? All of us comprehend and can readily apply it in this case. That resolves the question, if indeed this be the law of the land, into this: Have the Confederate States, on any show of reason, or without it—for that does not affect the inquiry—attained sufficient strength, and become sufficiently formidable, to entitle them to be treated, under that law of nations, as in a condition of civil war, even if they have not constituted a separate, sovereign and independent nation? Really, it seems to me, too clear for doubt, that they have. We had, in the revolution, thirteen colonies, with a limited treasury, almost destitute of means, and with some of our soldiers so behaving themselves, in the early part of the struggle, that General Washington, on one memorable occasion, threw down his hat on the ground and asked: "Are these the men with whom I am to defend the liberties of America?" And those of you, gentlemen, who have read this correspondence, know how constantly he was complaining to Congress about the inefficiency of the troops and their liability to desertion. I remember that he says something like this: "There is no doubt that patriotism may accomplish much. It has already effected a good deal. But he who relies on it as the means of carrying him through a long war will find himself, in the end, grievously mistaken. It is not to be disguised that the great majority of those who enter the service do so with a view to the pay which they are to receive; and, unless they are satisfied, desertions may be expected." He also remarked, at another period, in regard to the troops of a certain portion of our country, which I will not name, that they would have their own way; that, when their term of enlistment expired, they would go home; and that they would

---

[1] For the sections cited see Appendix, p. 723.

sometimes go before that period arrived. That, I am mortified to say, has been imitated in the present struggle.

Such was the early condition of the colonies.

Now, the Southern Confederacy have ten States; they had seven when this commission was issued, with about eight millions of people. They have separate State governments, which have existed ever since the Union was formed, and which would exist if this revolution were entirely put down. They have excluded us from every part of their territory, except a little foothold in the eastern part of Virginia, and "debatable ground" in western Virginia. We have not yet been able to penetrate farther into the Confederate States. We cannot send even food to the hungry or medicine to the afflicted there. We cannot interchange the commonest acts of humanity with those of our friends who are shut up in the South. I do think, with the conceded fact looking directly into the face of the American people that, with all the millions at the command of the administration, there is yet found sufficient force and power in the Confederate States to maintain their territory, their government, their legislature, their judiciary, their executive, and their army and navy, it is vain and idle to say that they are not now in a state of civil war, and that they ought to be excluded from the humanities incident to that condition. Such an idea should not, I think, find sanction in either the heart, the conscience or intelligence of any right-minded man.

13. Evidences of the existence of civil war.

Not only are the facts already stated true, but the Confederate States have been recognized as a belligerent power by France and England, as we have proved by the proclamations placed before you; and they have been recognized by our government as belligerents, at least. That I submit, as a distinct question of fact, to the jury, unless the court conceive that it is a pure question of law, in which case I am perfectly content that the court shall dispose of it.

And where do I find this? I find it in the admission of Mr. Lincoln, in his inaugural address, that there is to be no attempt at any physical coercion of these States; a concession that it is a thing not called for, not consistent with the views of the administration, or with the general course of policy of the American people. According to his view, there was to be no war. I find it in the correspondence of General Anderson with Governor Pickens, which has been read in the course of the trial[1]—which, of course, has been communicated to the government, will be found among its archives, and of which no disapprobation has been expressed. And here I borrow a doctrine from the district attorney, who said, when I declared that the legislative branch of the government had not given their declaration as to what was the true condition of the South, that their silence indicated what it was; and so, the silence of the government, in not protesting against this correspondence, is good enough for my purpose.

The proclamation of the President, calling for 75,000 troops, and then calling for a greater number, would, in any court in Christendom, outside of the United States, be regarded, under international law, as conclusive evidence that those troops were to be used against a belligerent power. Who ever heard of eight millions of people, or of one million of people, being all traitors, and being all liable to prosecution for treason at once. I find this recognition in the exchange of prisoners, which we know, as a matter of history, has occurred. I find it in the capitulation of Hatteras, at which, and by which, General Butler, of his own accord, when he refused the terms of surrender proposed by Commodore Barron, declared that the garrison should be taken as prisoners of war; and that has been communicated to the government, and no dissatisfaction expressed about it.

And, gentlemen, I rest it, also, as to the recognition by our government, on the fact to which Mr. Sullivan so appropriately alluded: the exchange of flags of truce between the two contending forces, as proved by one of the officers of the navy. A flag of truce sent to rebels—to men engaged in lawless insurrection, in treasonable hostility to the government, with a view to its overthrow! Why, gentlemen, it is the grandest, as it is the most characteristic, device by which humanity protects men against atrocities which they might otherwise perpetrate upon each other: that little white flag, showing itself like a speck of divine snow on the red and bloody field of battle; coming covered all over with divinity; coming in the hand of peace, who rejoices to see another place where her foot may rest; welcome as the dove which returned to the ark; coming, I say, in the hand of peace, who is the great conqueror, and before whom the power of armies and the bad ambitions and great struggles of men must ultimately be extinguished,

---

[1] For an abstract of the documentary evidence, see Appendix, p. 725.

This, of itself, will be regarded by mankind, when they reflect wisely, as sufficient to show that our government must not be brutal; and we seek to rescue the administration from any imputation that it wants to deny to the South the common humanities which belong to warfare, by your refusing to let men be executed as pirates, or to make a distinction between him who wars on the deep and him who wars upon the land.

It is very strange if the poor fellows who had no means of earning a meal of victuals in the city of Charleston, like some of those who composed the crew of this vessel, shut up as if in a trap, should be hanged as pirates for being on board a privateer, under a commission from the Confederate States, and that those who have slain your brothers in battle should be taken as prisoners of war, carefully provided for, and treated with the benevolence which we extend to all prisoners who fall into our hands ; the same humanities that, as you perceive, are provided for in the instructions from Jefferson Davis, found on board the privateer, directing that the prisoners taken should be dealt with gently and leniently, and to give them the same rations as were supplied to persons in the confederate service.

Mr. Brady here referred to the proposition advanced by Vattel, that some reason must exist for a revolt or a civil war, in order to distinguish it from an insurrection merely.   He claimed that if any reason existed, there was no common superior to judge who was right or wrong.   He then stated the reasons assigned by the South in justification of its course.   They claimed, he said, that the government had no right to interfere with slavery, or limit its extension, or to nullify the fugitive slave laws in New England.   He referred to Mr. Webster's speech of the 7th of March, 1850, to show that no section of the country had a right to refuse obedience to the fugitive slave law, and that such refusal was a wrong towards the South.   He referred to the "Creole Case," to show that the courts did not afford them ample remedy, and that, therefore, their only course was revolution.   He then continued :

14. DURING CIVIL WAR, THE COMBATANTS ARE ENTITLED TO ALL
     THE RIGHTS OF WAR.—BLOCKADE DEFINED.

Let me now cite to you Wheaton's International law, page 30, in which he says, that "sovereignty is acquired by a State, either at the origin of the civil society of which it is composed, or when it separates itself from the community of which it previously formed a part, and on which it was dependent." Then he says, that "civil war between the members of the same society is, by the general usages of nations, such a war as entitles both the contending parties to all the rights of war as against each other, and as against neutral nations."

This, if your Honors please, seems to me an answer to the doctrine put forward in this case, that the judges are to treat this question in reference to the seceding States as it has been viewed by the executive and legislative branches of the government. If it be true that when a state of civil war exists, as stated by Wheaton, both the contending parties have all the rights of war as against each other, as well as against neutral nations, then it follows very clearly that the seceding States, as well as our own, have all the rights of war; and there is no such rule as that they must have those rights determined only by the executive or legislative branches of the government, or by both.

And here, gentlemen, let us refer to the matter of blockade, which I take to be the highest evidence of a distinct recognition, by the general government, of a state of war as between the United and the Confederate States. I see no escape from that conclusion. It is true that a learned judge in New England, an eminent and pure man, has determined, as we see from the newspapers, that, in his judgment it is not a blockade which exists, but merely the exercise by the general government of its authority over commerce and territory in a state of insurrection ; that it is a mere police or municipal regulation. Well, gentlemen, that is not the view taken by the judges elsewhere. Certainly it is not adopted in this district, where prize cases have arisen, instituted by the government, which calls this a blockade; and I undertake to say that, in the history of the human race, that word, blockade, never was applied except in a state of war; and the exercise of that power never can occur except in a state of war, because, as the writers inform us, blockade is the right of a belligerent affecting a neutral, and only allowable in a state of war. Why is it that France and England, and all the other countries of the world, do not attempt to send their vessels to any of the ports in guard of which we place armed vessels ?

A word more about piracy: A pirate is an offender against the law of nations. He is called in the Latin, and by the jurists, the enemy of the human race. Any nation can lay hold of him on the high seas, take him to its country, and punish him. Now, if a ship of war—British, French, Russian, or of any other nation— should meet with a piratical craft, she would capture and condemn it in the courts of her country, and the crew would suffer the pun-

24

ishment of pirates. No one will dispute that proposition. But if such a ship of war had met with the privateer Savannah, even in the very act of capturing the Joseph, would she have captured the Savannah or attempted to arrest her crew as pirates? If not, does it not follow, as a necessary consequence, that the Savannah was not engaged in piratical business? and does it not involve a palpable absurdity to say, that a vessel on the high seas, cruising under a privateer's commission, can be treated as a pirate by the power with which it is at war, and yet be declared not a pirate by all the other powers of the earth? This must be so, if there is anything in the idea that piracy is an offense against the law of nations.

There is not a case in our books where any man, under a commission emanating from any authority or person, was ever treated as a pirate, and so condemned, unless the actual intent to steal was proved. In the case of Aurey such was the fact, as in many other cases which have been cited. And so it seems, that, if the Confederate States were either an actual government, established in virtue of the principles of right to which I have referred; or if a government *de facto*, as distinguished from one having that right; or if these men believed that the commission emanated from either kind of government—was lawfully issued—we claim that it is impossible in law, and would be wrong in morals, and unjust in all its consequences, to hold them as pirates, or to treat them otherwise than as prisoners of war. And, gentlemen, I am sorry to say, or rather I am glad to say, that if they should be acquitted of the crime of piracy, they would yet remain as prisoners of war. The worst thing to do with them is to hang them. By preserving their lives we have just their number to exchange for prisoners taken by the enemy.

You, gentlemen, will do your duty under the law, whatever be the consequences. If you have no doubt that these men have committed piracy, they should be convicted of piracy. No threat of retaliation from any quarter should or will influence right-minded men in the disposition to be made of cases where they have to give a verdict according to their conscience, the evidence, and the law of the land.

But the fact of retaliation, as a danger that may ensue from treating as pirates men engaged in war, is referred to by Vattel in his treatise on the laws of nations. It is one of the considerations which enjoin on courts and governments the duty of seeing that,

when people are prosecuting civil war, they shall enjoy the humanities of war.

Mr. Brady here discussed the case under the ninth section of the act of 1790.
He claimed it had no application to the four Americans, since they owed allegiance to another government. That, as construed by the prosecution, the act was
unconstitutional, because it could only apply to acts done under authority of a
foreign power or person, and if Jefferson Davis was or represented that power, the
defendants were his subjects, and not citizens; if he did not represent a foreign
power, the act did not apply at all. He then referred to the subject of variance
between the proof and the indictment, and cited Wharton's Crim. Law, pp. 78,
91, 93, 94 and 96, and U. S. v. Hardiman, 13 Peters, 176. He claimed also that
the status of the Confederacy was a judicial question, and must be considered by
the court and jury. After referring to the trial of McLeod, he concluded as
follows:

Gentlemen, I will detain you but a few moments longer. I have
endeavored to show, in the first place, that these men cannot be
convicted of piracy, because they had not the intent to steal, essential to the commission of that offense, and that you are the judges
whether that intent did or did not exist. If it did not, then the
accused men are entitled to acquittal on that ground. If the act
of 1790 be constitutional, and if it can be construed to extend to
a case like this, then eight of the prisoners are to be discharged,
being foreigners, not naturalized; and the other four also, having
acted under a commission issued in good faith by a government
which claimed to have existence, acted upon in good faith by themselves, and with the belief that they were not committing any lawless act of aggression. In this connection I hold it to be immaterial whether the confederate government was one of right, established on sufficient authority according to the law of nations, and
to be recognized as such, or whether it was merely a government in
fact. We claim, beyond all that, and apart from the question of
government in law or government in fact, that there exists a state
of civil war, which entitles these defendants to be treated in every
other manner than as pirates; which may have rendered them
amenable to the danger of being regarded as prisoners of war, but
which has made it impossible for them to be ever dealt with as
felons.

15. The duties of an advocate require the highest
moral courage.

I am sorry that it has become necessary in this discussion to
open subjects for debate, any inquiry about which, at this partic-

ular juncture in our history, is not likely to be attended with any great advantage. But, like my brethren for the defense, I have endeavored to state freely, fearlessly, frankly and correctly, the positions on which the defendants have a right to rely before the court and before you. It would have been much more acceptable to my feelings, as a citizen, if we had been spared the performance of any such duty. But, gentlemen, it is not our fault. The advocate is of very little use in the days of prosperity and peace, in the periods of repose, in protecting your property, or aiding you to recover your rights of a civil nature. It is only when public opinion, or the strong power of government, the formidable array of influence, the force of a nation, or the fury of a multitude, is directed against you, that the advocate is of any use.

Many years ago, while we were yet colonies of Great Britain, there occurred on this island what is known as the famous negro insurrection—the result of an idle story told by a worthless person, and yet leading to such an inflammation of the public mind that all the lawyers who then practiced at the bar of New York (and it is the greatest stigma on our profession of which the world can furnish an example) refused to defend the accused parties. One of them was a poor priest, of, I believe, foreign origin. The consequence was, that numerous convictions took place, and a great many executions. And yet all mankind is perfectly satisfied that there never was a more unfounded rumor, never a more idle tale, and that judicial murders were never perpetrated on the face of the earth more intolerable, more inexcusable, more without palliation. How different was it in Boston, at the time of what was called the massacre of Massachusetts subjects by British forces! The soldiers on being indicted, sought for counsel, and they found two men of great eminence in the profession to act for them. One of them was Mr. Adams, and the other Mr. Quincy. The father of Mr. Quincy addressed a letter, imploring him, on his allegiance as a son, and from affection and duty toward him, not to undertake the defense of these men. The son wrote back a response, recognizing, as he truly felt, all the filial affection which he owed to that honored parent, but, at the same time, taking the high and appropriate ground that he must discharge his duty as an advocate, according to the rules of his profession and the obligation of his official oath, whatever might be the result of his course.

The struggles, in the history of the world, to have in criminal trials an honest judiciary, a fearless jury, and a faithful advocate, disclose a great deal of wrong and suffering inflicted on advocates silenced by force, trembling at the bar where they ought to be utterly immovable in the discharge of their duty—on juries fined and imprisoned, and kept lying in dungeons for years, because they dared, in State prosecutions, to find verdicts against the direction of the court. The provisions of our own Constitution, which secure to men trial by jury and all the rights incident to that sacred and invaluable privilege, are the history of wrong against which those provisions are intended to guard in the future. This trial, gentlemen, furnishes a brilliant illustration of the beneficial results of all this care. Nothing could be fairer than the trial which these prisoners have had; nothing more admirable than the attention which you have given to every proceeding in this case. I know all the gentlemen on that jury well enough to be perfectly certain that whatever verdict they render will be given without fear or favor, on the law of the land, as they shall be informed it does exist, on a calm and patient review of the testimony, with a due sympathy for the accused, and yet with a proper respect for the government, so that the law shall be satisfied and individual right protected.

But, gentlemen, I do believe most sincerely that, unless we have deceived ourselves in regard to the law of the land, I have a right to invoke your protection for these men. The bodily presence, if it could be secured, of those who have been here in spirit by their language, attending on this debate and hovering about these men to furnish them protection—Lee, and Hamilton, and Adams, and Washington, and Jefferson, all whose spirits enter into the principles for which we contend—would plead in their behalf. I do wish that it was within the power of men, invoking the great Ruler of the Universe, to bid these doors open and to let the revolutionary sages to whom I have referred, and a Sumter, a Moultrie, a Marion, a Greene, a Putnam, and the other distinguished men who fought for our privileges and rights in the days of old, march in here and look at this trial. There is not a man of them who would not say to you that you should remember, in regard to each of these prisoners, as if you were his father, the history of Abraham when he went to sacrifice his son Isaac on the mount—the spirit of American liberty, the principles of American jurisprudence, and the dictates of humanity, constituting themselves another Angel of the Lord, and saying to you, when the immolation was threatened, "Lay not your hand upon him."

SPEECH OF WILLIAM M. EVARTS,

For the Prosecution in the Case of the "Savannah Privateers," Indicted for Piracy.

At a Circuit Court of the United States, Held at the City of New York, October Term, 1861.

Analysis of Mr. Evarts' Speech.

Mr. Evarts closed the case for the prosecution. He discussed the various questions raised by the prisoners in an able and masterly manner, weaving an instructive and interesting address, full of information in the departments of legal learning, which pertain to the law of nature and nations, and embracing a consideration of the immunities and privileges recognized by the rules of civilized warfare. When, and under what circumstances, in law and in morals, are a people justified in invoking the scourge of war; and for what causes have they a right to shatter the foundations of government and society? The prisoners claimed, that if cause had been shown, the court must recognize the existence of a state of civil war, and could not treat the belligerents as insurrectionists merely, but as entitled to all the rights of war. That, in a state of civil war, the right to commission privateers was a legal right, and the letter of marque offered in evidence was, therefore, a legal defense. They claimed that the federal government had accorded these rights to the soldiers in the field, and that, therefore, the court should do likewise with regard to those who carried on warfare on the ocean; and, by way of justification, it was sought to establish a parallel between the war of the revolution and the war of the rebellion.

In answer to these arguments Mr. Evarts claimed, that the wrongs complained of by the South, as constituting just cause for rebellion against the government, did not proceed from the government. That there was no parallel between the present controversy and the war with Great Britain in 1776; because the causes for that revolution embraced an exercise of tyranny towards the colonies by the mother country, and an absolute denial of representation in the government. Here there was no pretense either of oppression by the general government, or of any limitation of the right of representation. This branch of the defense was discussed under two heads, the right of secession, and the right of revolution. Under the first, Mr. Evarts gave a historical sketch of the causes and results of the revolution, to show that the war was carried to a successful termination by the people, as one people, and not as independent sovereignties. That although the diplomatic history of the country showed that in some of the early treaties each State was separately named, yet they were invariably grouped as one nation, and the treaties always referred to the commerce of the two countries. Under the second head, he argued, that where a government was defective or vicious in its operations, there an inherent right existed to alter or abolish it. But where a government was universally regarded as the most perfect of all human governments, it was unjust and wicked to rebel against it. As proof of the perfection of our system he quoted the encomiums that had been passed upon it by some of the wisest statesmen at the South, at the hour of its birth, and at the hour of its attempted dissolution. Owing to the great length of this speech, it became necessary to give that portion of it relating to right of revolution only. The technical portions relative to the bearing of the act of 1790, and some minor topics, have been necessarily omitted, from both the arguments of Mr. Brady and Mr. Evarts, though referred to in the notes, together with the authorities cited.

The question of jurisdiction was argued at various stages of the case. It arose from the following language of the statute: "The trial of all offenses which shall be committed upon the high seas, or elsewhere, out of the limits of any State or district, shall be in the district where the offender is apprehended, or into which he may be first brought." It was claimed that the prisoners were first brought into Hampton Roads, in the eastern district of Virginia, and that this court had no jurisdiction. The court held that the clause was in the alternative, and jurisdiction might be exercised either in the district where the prisoners were first brought, or in the district where they were apprehended under lawful authority for trial. Mr. Evarts spoke as follows:

MAY IT PLEASE YOUR HONORS, AND GENTLEMEN OF THE JURY:—A trial in a court of justice is a trial of many things be-

sides the prisoners at the bar. It is a trial of the strength of the
laws, of the power of the government, of the duty of the citizen,
of the fidelity to conscience and the intelligence of the jury. It is
a trial of those great principles of faith, of duty, of law, of civil
society, that distinguish the condition of civilization from that of
barbarism. I know no better instance of the distinction between
a civilized, instructed, Christian people, and a rude and barbarous
nation, than that which is shown in the assertions of right where
might and violence and the rage of passion in physical contest
determine everything, and this last sober, discreet, patient, intelligent, authorized, faithful, scrupulous, conscientious investigation,
under the lights of all that intelligence with which God has favored
any of us; under that instruction which belongs to the learned and
accredited expounders of the law of an established free government; under the aid of, and yet not misled by, the genius or eloquence of advocates on either side.

But, after all, the controlling dominion of duty to the men before you in the persons of the prisoners, to the whole community
around you, and to the great nation for which you now discharge
here a vital function for its permanence and its safety; your duty
to the laws and the government of your country (which, giving its
protection, requires your allegiance, and finds its last and final
resting-place, both here and in England, in the verdicts of juries);
your duty to yourselves requires you to recognize yourselves not
only as members of civil society, but as children of the " Father of
an Infinite Majesty," and amenable to His last judgment for your
acts. Can any of us, then, fail to feel, even more fully than
we can express, that sympathies, affections, passions, sentiments,
prejudices, hopes, fears, feelings and responsibilities of others than
ourselves are banished at once and forever, as we enter the threshold
of such an inquiry as this, and never return to us until we have
passed from this sacred precinct, and, with our hands on our
breasts and our eyes on the ground, can humbly hope that we have
done our duty, and our whole duty.

Something was said to you, gentlemen of the jury, of the un-
wonted circumstances of the prosecution, by the learned counsel
who, many days ago, and with an impressiveness that has not yet
passed away from your memory, opened on behalf of the prisoners
the course of this defense.

I. LIMITATION OF THE RESPONSIBILITY OF THE JURY.

He has said to you, that the number of those whose fate, for life or for death, hangs on your verdict, is equal to your own; hinting a ready suggestion that that divided responsibility by which twelve men may sometimes shelter themselves, in weighing in the balance the life of a single man, is not yours. Gentlemen, let us understand how much of force and effect there is in the suggestion, and how truly and to what extent the responsibility of a jury may be said to include this issue of life and death. In the first place, as jurymen, you have no share or responsibility in the wisdom or the justice of those laws which you are called upon to administer. If there be defects in them; if they have something of that force and severity which is necessary for the maintenance of government and the protection of peace and property, and of life on the high seas: you have had no share in their enactment, and have no charge at your hands of their enforcement. In the next place, you have no responsibility of any kind in regard to the discretion of the representatives of this government in the course which they choose to take, as to whether they will prosecute or leave unprosecuted. You do not, within the limits of the inquiry presented to you, dispose of the question, why others have not been presented to you; nor may that which has been done in a case not before you, serve as a guide for the subject submitted to your consideration. So, too, you have no responsibility of any kind concerning the course or views of the law which this tribunal may give for your guidance. The court does not make the law, but Congress does. The court declares the law as enacted by the government, and the jury find the facts, giving every scrutiny, every patient investigation, every favor for life, and every reasonable doubt as to the facts, to the prisoners. Having disposed of that duty, as sober, intelligent and faithful men, graduating your attention only by the gravity of the inquiry, you have no further responsibility. But I need not say to you, gentlemen, that if any civilized government is to have control of the subject of piracy, if pirates are to be brought within the jurisdiction of the criminal law, the very nature of the crime involves the fact that its successful prosecution necessarily requires that considerable numbers shall be engaged in it. I am quite certain that, if my learned friends had found in the circumstances of this case nothing which removed it out of the category of the heinous crime of private plunder at sea, exposing property and life, and breaking up commerce, they would have found nothing in the fact that a ship's crew was brought in for trial, and that the number of that crew amounted to twelve men, that should be pressed to the disturbance of your serene judgment, in any disposition of the case. Now, gentlemen, let us look a little into the nature of the crime, and into the condition of the law.

2. PRINCIPLES GOVERNING THE PUNISHMENT OF CRIME.

The penalty of the crime of piracy or robbery at sea stands on our statute books heavier than the penalty assigned for a similar crime committed on land; which is, in fact, similar, so far as concerns its being an act of depredation. It may be said, and it is often argued, that, when the guilt of two offenses is equal, society transcends its right and duty when it draws a distinction in its punishments; and it may be said, as has been fully argued to you, at least, by implication, in the course of this case, that the whole duty and the whole responsibility of civil governments, in the administration of criminal law and the punishment of crime, has to do with retributive vengeance, as it were, on the moral guilt of the prisoner. Now, gentlemen, I need not say to you, who are experienced at least in the common inquiries concerning governments and their duties, that, as a mere naked and separate consideration for punishing moral guilt, government leaves, or should leave, vengeance where it belongs—to Him who searches the heart and punishes according to its secret intents—drawing no distinction between the wicked purpose which fully plans, and the final act which executes that purpose. The great, the main duty; the great, the main right of civil society, in the exercise of its dominion over the liberties, lives, and property of its subjects, is the good of the public, in the prevention, the check, the discouragement, the suppression of crime. And I am sure that there is scarcely one of us who, if guilt, if fault, if vice could be left to the punishment of conscience and the responsibility of the last and great assize, without prejudice to society, without injury to the good of others, without, indeed, being a danger and a destruction to all the peace, the happiness, and the safety of communities, would not readily lay aside all his share in the vindictive punishments of guilty men. But society, framed in the form and for the purposes of government, finds, alas! that this tribunal of conscience, and this last and future accountability of another world, is inadequate to its protection against wickedness and crime in this.

You will find, therefore, in all, even the most enlightened and most humane codes of laws, that some necessary attention is paid to the predominant interest which society has in preventing crime. The very great difficulty of detecting it, the circumstances of secrecy, and the chances of escape on the part of the criminal, are considerations which enter into the distribution of its penalties. You will find, in a highly commercial community, like that of England, and to some extent—although, I am glad to say, with much less severity—in our own, which is also a highly commercial community, that frauds against property, frauds against trade, frauds in the nature of counterfeiting and forgery, and all those peaceful and not violent, but yet pernicious interferences with the health and necessary activity of our every-day life, require the infliction of severe penalties for what, when you take up the particular elements of the crime, seems to have but little of the force, and but little of the depth of a serious moral delinquency.

3. Wisdom and justice of the pardoning power.

The severity of the penalties for passing counterfeit money are inflicted upon the poor and ignorant who, in so small a matter as a coin of slight value, knowingly and intelligently, under even the strongest impulses of poverty, are engaged in the offense. Now, therefore, when commercial nations have been brought to the consideration of what their enactments on the subject of piracy shall be, they have taken into account that the very offense itself requires that its commission should be outside of the active and efficient protection of civil society; that the commission of the crime involves, on the part of the criminals, a fixed, deliberate determination and preparation; and that the circumstances under which the victims, either in respect of their property or of their lives, are exposed to these aggressions, are such as to make it a part of the probable course of the crime, that the most serious evils and the deepest wounds may be inflicted. When a crime, not condemned in ethics or humanity, and which the positive enactments of the law have made highly penal, yet contains within itself circumstances that appeal very strongly to whatever authority or magistrate has rightful control of the subject for a special exemption, and special remission, and special concession from the penalty of the law, where and upon what principle does a wise and just, a humane and benignant government, dispose of that question? I agree that, if crimes which the good of society requires to be subjected to harsh penalties, must stand, always and irrevocably, upon the mere behest of judicial sentence, there would be found an oppression and a cruelty in some respects, that a community having a conscientious adherence to right and humanity would scarcely tolerate. Where, then, does it wisely bestow all the responsibility, and give all the power that belongs to this adjustment, according to the particular circumstances of the moral and personal guilt, which must be necessary, and is always conceded? Why, confessedly, to the pardoning power alluded to on one side or the other—though chiefly on the part of the prisoners' counsel—in the course of this trial. You will perceive at once what the difference is between a court or a jury, or a public prosecuting officer, yielding to particular circumstances of actual or of general qualification of a crime charged, so that the law shall be thwarted, and the certainty and directness of judicial trial and sentence be made the sport of sympathy, or of casual or personal influences, and placing the pardoning power where it shall be governed by the particular circumstances of each case, so that its exercise shall have no influence in breaking down the authority of law, or in disturbing the certainty, directness and completeness of judicial rules. For, it is the very nature of a pardon, committed to the chief magistrate of the federal Union in cases of which this court has jurisdiction, and to the chief magistrate of every State in the Union in cases of which the State tribunals take cognizance, that it is a recognition of the law, and of the sentence of the law, and leaves the laws undisturbed, the rules for the guidance of men unaffected, the power and strength of the government unweakened, the force of the judiciary unparalyzed, and yet disposes of each case in a way that is just, or, if not just, is humane and clement, where the pardon is exercised.

Now, gentlemen, I shall say nothing more on the subject of pardon. It is a thing with which I have nothing to do; with which this learned court has nothing to do; with which you, as jurymen, have nothing to do, beyond the fact that this beneficent government of ours has not omitted from its arrangement, in the administration of its penal laws, this divine attribute of mercy.

4. ELEMENTS OF THE CRIME OF PIRACY.

Now, there being the crime of piracy or robbery on the high seas, which the interests of society, the protection of property and of life, the maintenance of commerce, oblige every State and every nation, like ours, to condemn—what are the circumstances, what are the acts, that, in view of the law, amount to piracy? You will understand me that, for the present, I entirely exclude from your consideration any of the particular circumstances which are supposed to give to the actual crime perpetrated a public character, lifting it out of the penal law that you administer, and out of the region of private crime, into a field of quite different considerations. They are, undoubtedly, that the act done shall be with intent of depriving the person who is in possession of property, as its owner, or as the representative of that owner, of that property. That is what is meant by the Latin phrase, with which you are quite as familiar now, at least, as I, *animo furandi*—with the intention of despoiling the owner of that which belongs to him. And, to make up the crime of robbery on land, in distinction from larceny or theft, as we generally call it (though theft, perhaps, includes all the varieties of crime by which the property of another is taken against his will), robbery includes, and piracy, being robbery at sea, includes the idea that it is done with the application, or the threat, or the presence of force. There must be actual violence, or the presence and exhibition of power and intent to use violence, which produces the surrender and delivery of the property. Such are the ingredients of robbery and piracy. And, gentlemen, these two ingredients are all; and you must rob one or the other of them of this, their poison, or the crime is completely proved, when the fact of the spoliation, with these ingredients, shall have been proved. The use that the robber or the pirate intends to make of the property, or the justification which he thinks he has by way of retaliation, by way of injury, by way of provocation, by way of any other occasion or motive that seems justifiable to his own conscience and his own obedience to any form whatever of the higher law, has nothing to do with the completeness of the crime, unless it come to what has been adverted to by the learned counsel, and displayed before you in citations from the law-books—to an honest, however much it may be mistaken and baseless, idea that the property is really the property of the accused robber, of which he is repossessing himself from the party against whom he makes the aggression.

5. OPINIONS OR VIEWS AS TO PROPERTY RIGHTS IN GENERAL, NO DEFENSE.

Now, unless, in the case proved of piracy, or robbery on land, there be some foundation for the suggestion that the willful and intentional act of depriving a party of his property rests upon a claim of the robber, or the pirate, that it is his own property (however baseless may be the claim), you cannot avoid, you cannot defeat, the criminality of the act of robbery, within the intention of the law, by showing that the robber or the pirate had, in the protection of his own conscience, and in the government of his own conduct, certain opinions or views that made it right for him to execute that purpose.   Thus, for instance, take a case of morals: A certain sect of political philosophers have this proposition as a basis of all their reasoning on the subject of property, that is, that property, the notion of separate property in anything, as belonging to anybody, is theft; that the very notion that I can own anything, whatever it may be, and exclude other people from the enjoyment of it, is a theft made by me, a wrongful appropriation, when all the good things in this world, in the intention of Providence, were designed for the equal enjoyment of all the human race.   Well, now, a person possessed of that notion of political economy and of the moral rights and duties of men, might seek to avail himself of property owned and enjoyed by another, on the theory that the person in possession of it was the original thief, and that he was entitled to share it.   I need not say to you, that all these ideas and considerations have nothing whatever to do with the consideration of the moral intent with which a person is despoiled of his property.

Now, with regard to force, I do not understand that my learned friends really make any question, seriously, upon the general principles of what force is, or upon the facts of this case, that this seizure of the Joseph by the Savannah had enough of force—the threat, the presence and exhibition of power—and of the intent to use it, to make the capture one of force, if the other considerations which are relied upon do not lift it out of that catalogue of crime.

6. An exhibition of force sufficient evidence.

It is true that the learned counsel who last addressed you, seemed to intimate in some of his remarks, near the close of his very able and eloquent and interesting address, that there was not any force about it, that the master of the Joseph was not threatened, that there was no evidence that the cannon was even loaded, and that it never had been fired off.   Well, gentlemen, the very illustration which he used of what would be a complete robbery on land—the aggressor possessing a pistol and asking, in the politest manner, for your money—relieves me from arguing that you must fire either a cannon or a pistol before you have evidence of force. If our rights stand on that proposition, that when a pistol is presented at our breast, and we surrender our money, we must wait for the pistol to be fired before the crime is completed, you will see that the terrors of the crime of robbery do not go very far towards protecting property or person, which is the object of it.

7. NATURE OF THE DEFENSE AND PROVINCE OF THE JURY.

When, gentlemen, the government, within a statute which, in the judgment of the court, shall be pronounced as being lawfully enacted under the Constitution of the United States, has completed the proof of the circumstances of the crime charged, it is entitled at your hands to a conviction of the accused, unless, by proof adduced on his part, he shall so shake the consistency and completeness of the proof on the part of the government, or shall introduce such questions of uncertainty and doubt, that the facts shall be disturbed in your mind, or unless he shall show himself in some predicament of protection or right under the law (and by "under the law" I mean, under the law of the land where the crime is punishable, and where the trial and the sentence are lawfully attributed to be), or unless he shall introduce some new facts which, conceding the truthfulness and the sufficiency of the case made by the government, shall still interpose a protection, in some form, against the application of the penalty of the law. I take it that I need not say to you that this protection or qualification of the character of the crime must be by the law of the land; and whether it comes to be the law of the land by its enactment in the statutes of the United States, or by the adoption and incorporation into the law of the land of the principles of the law of nations, is a point quite immaterial to you. You are not judges of what the statutes of the United States are, except so far as their interpretation may rightfully become a subject of inquiry by the jury, in the sense of whether the crime is within the intent of the act, in the circumstances proved. You are not judges of what the law of nations is, in the first place; nor are you judges of how much of the law of nations has been adopted or incorporated into the system of our government and our laws, by the authority of its Congress or of its courts.

Whether, as I say to you, there is a defense, or protection, or qualification of the acts and transactions which, in their naked nature and in their natural construction, are violent interferences with the rights of property, against the statute, and the protection of property intended by the statute; whether the circumstances do change the liability or responsibility of the criminal, by the introduction of a legal defense under the law of nations, or under the law of the land in any other form, is a question undoubtedly for the court, leaving to you always complete control over the questions of fact that enter into the subject. So that the suggestion also dropped by my learned friend, at the close of his remarks, that any such arrangement would make the jury mere puppets and give them nothing to do, finds no place. It would not exclude from your consideration any matters of fact which go to make up the particular condition of public affairs, or of the public relations of the community towards each other, in these conditions which disturb the land, provided the court shall hold and say that, on such a state of facts existing, or being believed by you, there is introduced a legal qualification or protection against the crime charged. But if it should be held that all these facts and circumstances, to the extent and with the effect that is claimed for them by the learned counsel as matter of fact, yet as matter of law leave the crime where it originally stood, being of their own nature such as the principles of law do not permit to be interposed as a protection and a shield, why, then you take your law on the subject in the same way as you do on every other subject, from the instructions of the learned and responsible bench, whose errors, if committed, can be corrected; while your confusion between your province and the province of the court would, both in this case and in other cases, and sometimes to prejudice of the prisoner, and against his life and safety when prejudices ran that way, confound all distinctions; and, in deserting your duty to usurp that of another portion of the court, you would have done what you could, not to uphold, but to overthrow the laws of your country and the administration of justice according to law, upon which the safety of all of us, at all times, in all circumstances, depends.

Mr. Evarts here reviewed the evidence showing the facts, substantially as stated at page 343. He then spoke of the imperative duty which devolved upon government to protect its citizens and their property. He claimed upon the evidence that the acts of the prisoners were entirely voluntary, that their motives were selfish, and proceeded from a desire for private gain and not patriotic devotion ; and argued that there was nothing in the acts of Congress relating to piracy contrary to humanity or common sense. That the United States, by treaty with France and the Netherlands, agreed that any person of either nations taking letters of marque or commissions from any country with which either might be at war, should be punished as pirates. (Citing Treaty of Commerce with France, Feb. 6th, 1778, art. 21, Stat. at L. vol. 8, p. 24 ; Treaty between Netherlands and U. S., 1872, art. 19, Stat. at L. vol. 8, p. 44.) That it was the uniform policy of our government to extirpate private war from the ocean. After referring to the evidence to show that there has been sufficient exhibition of force on the part of the defendants, he continued :

8. PRIVATEERING UNDER THE LAW OF NATIONS, AND LAWS OF WAR.

I do not know that I need say anything to you about privateering, further than to present somewhat distinctly what the qualifications, what the conditions, and what the purposes of privateering are. In the first place, privateering is a part of war, or is a part of the preliminary hostile aggressions which are in the nature of a forcible collision between sovereign powers. Now, what is the law of nations on this subject, and how does there come to be a law of nations; and what is its character, what are its sanctions, and who are parties to it? We all know what laws are when they proceed from a government and operate upon its citizens and its subjects. Law, then, comes with authority, by right, and so as to compel obedience; and laws are always framed with the intent that there shall be no opportunity of violent or forcible resistance to them, or of violent or forcible settlement of controversies under them, but that the power shall be submitted to, and the inquiry as to right proceed regularly and soberly under the civil and criminal tribunals. But when we come to nations, although they have relations towards each other, although they have duties towards each other, although they have rights towards each other, and although, in becoming nations, they nevertheless are all made up of human beings, under the general laws of human duty, as given by the common lawgiver, God, yet there is no real superior that can impose law over them or enforce it against them. And it is only because of that, that war, the scourge of the human race—and it is the great vice and defect of our social condition that it cannot be avoided—comes in as the only arbiter between powers that have no common superior. I am sure that the little time I shall spend upon this topic will be serviceable; as, also, in some more particular considerations as to what is called a state of war, and as to the conditions which give and create a war between the different portions of our unhappy country and its divided population.

So, then, nations have no common superior whom they recognize under this law, which they have made for themselves in the interest of civilization and humanity, and which is a law of natural right and natural duty, so far as it can be applied to the relations which nations hold to one another. They recognize the fact that one nation is just as good, as matter of right, as another; that whether it be the great powers of Russia, of England, of France, of the United States of America, or of Brazil, or whether it be one of the feeble and inferior powers, in the lowest grade, as one of the separate Italian kingdoms, or the little republic of San Marino, whose territories are embraced within the circuit of a few leagues, or one of the South American States, scarcely known as a power in the affairs of men; yet, under the proposition that the States are equal in the family of nations, they have a right to judge of their quarrels, and, finding occasions for quarrel, have a right to assert them, as matter of force, in the form of war. And all the other nations, however much their commerce may be disturbed and injured, are obliged to concede certain rights that are called the rights of war. We all understand what the rights of war are on the part of two people fighting against each other. A general right is to do each other as much injury as they can; and they are very apt to avail themselves of that right. There are certain meliorations against cruelty, which, if a nation should transgress, probably other nations might feel called upon to suppress the extravagance. But, as a general thing, while two nations are fighting, other nations stand by and do not intervene. But the way other nations come to have any interest, and to have anything to say whether there is war between sovereign powers, grows out of certain rights of war which the law of nations gives to the contending parties against neutrals. For instance : Suppose Spain and Mexico were at war. Well, you would say, what is that to us? It is this to us. On the high seas, a naval vessel of either power has a right, in pursuit of its designs against the enemy, to interrupt the commerce of other nations to a certain extent. It has a right of visitation and of search of vessels that apparently carry our flag. Why ? In order to see whether the vessel be really our vessel, or whether our flag covers the vessel of its enemy, or the property of its enemy. It has also a right to push its inquiries farther, and if it finds it to be a vessel of the United States of America, to see whether we are carrying what are called contraband of war into the ports of its enemy; and if so, to confiscate it and her. Each of the powers has a right to blockade the ports of the other, and thus to break up the trade and pursuits of the people of other nations; and that without any quarrel with the other people. And so you see, by the law of nations, this state of war which might at first seem to be only a quarrel between the two contending parties, really becomes, collaterally, and in some cases to a most important extent, a matter of interest to other nations of the globe. But however much we suffer, however much we are embarrassed (as, for example, in the extreme injury to British commerce and British interests now inflicted in this country — the blockade keeping out their shipping and preventing shipments of cotton to carry on their industry), we must submit, as the English people submit, in the view their government has chosen to take of these transactions.

Now, gentlemen, this being the law of nations, you will perceive that, as there is no human earthly superior, so there are no courts that can lay down the law, as our courts do for our people, or as the courts of England do for their people. There are no courts that can lay down the law of nations, so as to bind the people of another country, except so far as the courts of that country, recognizing the sound principles of morality, humanity and justice obtaining in the government and conduct of nations towards each other, adopt them in their own courts. So, when my learned friends speak of the law of nations as being the law that is in force here, and that may protect these prisoners in this case against the laws of the United States of America, why, they speak in the sense of lawyers, or else in a sense that will confuse your minds, that is to say, that the law of nations, as the court will expound and explain it, has or has not a certain effect upon what would be otherwise the plain behests of the statute law.

9. RIGHTS OF NEUTRAL POWERS, WITH RESPECT TO PRIVATEERS, IN A STATE OF CIVIL WAR.

Now, it is a part of the law of nations, except so far as between themselves they shall modify it by treaty (two instances of which I have read in the diplomacy of our own country, and a most extensive instance of which is to be found in the recent treaty of Paris, whereby the law of nations, in respect to privateering, has been so far modified as to exclude privateering as one of the means of war), outside of particular arrangements made by civilized nations, it was a part of the original law of war prevailing among nations, that any nation engaged in war might fit out privateers in aid of its belligerent or warlike purposes or movements. No difficulty arose about this when war sprang up between two nations that stood before the world in their accredited and acknowledged independence. If England and France went to war, or if England and the United States, as in 1812, went to war, this right of fitting out privateers would obtain and be recognized. But there arises, in the affairs of nations, a condition much more obscure and un-certain than this open war between established powers, and that is, when dissension arises in the same original nation; when it pro-ceeds from discontent, sedition, private or local rebellion, into the inflammation of great military aggression; and when the parties assume, at least (assume, I say), to be rightfully entitled to the po-sition of powers, under the law of nations, warring against one another. The South American States, in their controversy which separated them from the parent country, and these States when they were colonies of Great Britain, presented instances of these domestic dissensions between the different parts of the same gov-ernment, and the rights of war were claimed. Now, what is the duty of other nations in respect to that? Why, their duty and right is this, that they may either accord to these struggling, rebellious, revolted populations the rights of war, so far as to recognize them as belligerents, or not; but whether they will do so or not, is a question for their governments, and not for their courts sitting un-der and by authority of their governments. For instance, you can readily see that the great nations of the earth, under the influences upon their commerce and their peace which I have mentioned, may very well refuse to tolerate the quarrel as being entitled to the dignity of war. They may say: No, no; we do not see any occa-sion for this war, or any justice or benefit that is to be promoted by it; we do not see the strength or power that is likely to make it successful; and we will not allow a mere attempt or effort to throw us into the condition of submitting to the disturbance of the peace, or the disturbance of the commerce of the world. Or, they may say: We recognize this right of incipient war to raise itself and fairly contend against its previous sovereign—not necessarily from any sympathy, or taking sides in it, but it is none of our affair; and the principles of the controversy do not prevent us from giving to them this recognition of their supposed rights. Now, when they have done that, they may carry their recognition of right and power as far as they please, and stop where they please. They may say: We will tolerate the aggression by public armed vessels on the seas, and our vessels shall yield the right of visitation and search to them. They may say: We will extend it so far as to include the right of private armed vessels, and the rights of war may attend them; or they may refuse to take this last step, and say: We will not tolerate the business of privateering in this quarrel. And, whatever they do or say on that subject, their courts of all kinds will follow.

10. THE FACT THAT THE SOUTH HAD BEEN RECOGNIZED AS BELLIGERENTS, IMMATERIAL.

Apply this to the particular trouble in our national affairs that is now progressing to settle the fate of this country. France and England have taken a certain position on this subject. I do not know whether I accurately state it (and I state it only for the purpose of illustration, and it is not material), but, as I understand it, they give a certain degree of belligerent right, so that they would not regard the privateers on the part of the Southern rebellion as being pirates, but they do not accord succor or hospitality in their ports to such privateers. Well, now, suppose that one of these privateers intrudes into their ports and their hospitalities, and claims certain rights. Why, the question, if it comes up before a court in Liverpool or London, will be: Is the right within the credit and recognition which their government has given? And only that. So, too, our government took the position in regard to the revolting States of South America, that it would recognize them as belligerents, and that it would not hang, as pirates, privateers holding commissions from their authority. But when other questions came up, as to whether a particular authority from this or that self-styled power should be recognized, our government frowned upon it, and would not recognize it. With regard to Captain Aury, who styled himself Generalissimo of the Floridas, or something of that kind, when Florida was a Spanish province, our courts said: We do not know anything about this; his commissions are good for nothing here; our government has not recognized any such contest or incipient nationality as this. So, too, in another case, where there was an apparent commission from one struggling power, the court say: Our government does not recognize that power, and we do not, in giving any rights of war to it; but the court say, it appears in the proof that this vessel claims to have had a commission from Buenos Ayres, another contending power; if so, that is a power which our government recognizes; and the case must go down for further proof on that point.

I confess that, if the views of my learned friends are to prevail in determining questions of crime and responsibility under the laws and before the court, and are to be accepted and administered, I do not see that there is any government at all. For you have every stage of government: first, government of right; next, a government in fact; next, a government trying to make itself a fact; and, next, a government which the culprit thinks ought to be a fact. Well, if there are all these stages of government, and all these authorities and protections, which may attend the acts of people all over the world, I do not see but every court and every jury must, finally, resolve itself into the great duty of searching the hearts of men and putting its sanctions upon pure or guilty secret motives, or notions, or interpretations of right and wrong—a task to which you, gentlemen of the jury, I take it, feel scarcely adequate.

II. THE CONDITION OF BELLIGERENTS NO PROTECTION TO CITIZENS.

Now, gentlemen, I have perhaps wearied you a little upon this subject; because it is from some confusion in these ideas: first, of what the law of nations permits a government to do, and how it intrudes upon and qualifies the laws of that government; and, second, upon what the rights are that grow out of civil dissensions, as towards neutral powers, that some difficulty and obscurity are introduced into this case.

If the court please, I maintain these propositions in conformity with the views I have heretofore presented: first, that the law of the land is to determine whether this crime of piracy has been committed, subject only to the province of the jury in passing upon the facts attending the actual perpetration of the offense; and, second, upon all the questions invoked to qualify, from the public relations of the hostile or contending parties in this controversy, the attitude that this government holds towards these contending parties is the attitude that this court, deriving its authority from this government, must necessarily hold towards them.

I have argued this matter of the choice and freedom of a government to say how it will regard these civil dissensions going on in a foreign nation, as if it had some application to this controversy, in which we are the nation, and this court is the court of this nation.

But, gentlemen, the moment I have stated that, you will see that there is not the least pretense that there is any dispensing power in the court, or that there has been any dispensing power exercised by our government, or that there has been any pardon, or any amnesty, or any proclamation, saving from the results of crime against our laws any person engaged in these hostilities, who at any time has owed allegiance and obedience to the government of the United States. Therefore here we stand, really extricated from all the confusion, and from all the wideness of controversy and of comment that attends these remote considerations of this case, that have been pressed upon your attention, as if they were the case itself, on the part of our learned friend.

Mr. Evarts here discussed the constitutionality of the act of 1790, and claimed that a citizen who accepted a commission, even from a foreign power, nevertheless continued to be a citizen within the meaning of the act. (Citing U. S. *v.* Pirates, 5 Wheat. 202 ; " The Invincible," Opinions Atty.-Gen. vol. 3, p. 120.) He argued that Congress had power to govern its citizens on the high seas, notwithstanding it had no common-law jurisdiction on the subject of crimes. He then continued :

12. Statement of the views advanced by the defense.

Now, gentlemen, if the court please, I come to a consideration of the political theories or views on which these prisoners are sought to be protected against the penalties of this law. In that argument, as in my argument, it must be assumed that these penalties, but for those protections, would be visited upon them; for we are not to be drawn hither and thither by this inquiry, and to have it said, at one time, that the crime itself, in its own nature, is not proved, and, at another time, that, if it be proved, these are defenses. I have said all I need to say, and all I should say, about the crime itself. The law of the case on that point will be given to you by the court, and if it should be, as I suppose it must, in accordance with that laid down by the court in the circuit of Pennsylvania, then, as my learned friend Mr. Brady has said of that, that he could not see how the jury could find any verdict but guilty, it necessarily follows, if that is a sound view of the law, that you cannot find any other verdict but guilty. I proceed, therefore, to consider these other defenses which grow out of the particular circumstances of the piracy.

Now, there are, as I suggested, three views in which this subject of the license, or authority, or protection against our criminal laws in favor of these prisoners is urged, from their connection with particular occurrences disclosed in the evidence. One is, that they are privateers; but I have shown you that, to be privateers, their commission must come from an independent nation, or from an incipient nation which our government recognizes as such. Therefore, they fail entirely to occupy that explicit and clear position under the law of the land and the law of nations. But, they say, they are privateers either of a nation or a power that exists, as the phrase is, *de jure*, that has a right the same as we, or England, or France; or of a power that has had sufficient force and strength to establish itself, as matter of fact. Without considering the question of right, as recognized under the system of nations, they contend, and with a great deal of force and earnestness in the impression of their views upon the jury, and great skill and discretion in handling the matter; they contend that there is a state of civil war in this country, and that a state of civil war gives to all nations engaged in it, against the government with which they are warring, rights of impunity, of protection, of respect, of regard, of courtesy, which belong to the laws of war; and that, without caring to say whether they are a government or ever will be a government, so long as they fight they cannot be punished.

That is the proposition; there is nothing else to it. They come down from the region of *de jure* government and *de facto* government, and have nothing to prove but the rage of war on the part of rebels, in force enough to be called war. Then they say that, by their own act, they are liberated from the laws, and from their duty to the laws, which would otherwise, they admit, have sway over them, and against which they have not as yet prevailed. That is the proposition.

Another proposition on which they put themselves is, that whatever may be the law, and whatever the extent of the facts, if any of these persons believed that there was a state of war, rightful to be recognized and believed, in good faith, that they were fighting against the United States government, they had a right to seize the property of United States citizens; and that, if they believed that they constituted part of a force co-operating, in any form or effect, with the military power which has risen up against the United States of America, then, so long as they had that opinion, they, by their own act, and their own construction of their own act, impose the law upon this government, and upon this bench, and upon this jury, and compel you to say to them that if, in taking, in a manner which would have been robbery, this vessel, the Joseph, they were also fighting against the United States of America, they have not committed the crime of piracy.

13. THE EVIDENCE, AS TO CIVIL WAR, AND THE RIGHT OF REVOLUTION.

Now, if the court please, and gentlemen of the jury, let us, before we explore and dissect these propositions; before we discover how utterly subversive they are of any notions of government, of fixity in the interpretation of the law, or certainty in the enforcement of it; let us see what you will fairly consider as being proved, as matter of fact, concerning the condition of affairs in this country. Let us see what legal discrimination or description of this state of things is likely to be significant and instructive, in determining the power and authority of the government, and the responsibility of these defendants. They began with an ordinance of South Carolina, passed on the 20th of December of last year, which in form and substance simply annulled the ordinance of that State with which, as they say, they ratified or accepted the Constitution of the United States. They then went on with similar proceedings on the part of the States of Georgia, Alabama, Mississippi, and Florida, showing the establishment and adoption of a provisional Constitution, by which they constituted and called themselves the Confederate States of America. They proved, then, the organization of the government, the election of Mr. Davis and Mr. Stephens as President and Vice-President, and the appointment of secretaries of war and of the navy, and other portions of the civil establishment. They proved, then, the occurrences at Fort Sumter, and gave particular evidence of the original acts at Charleston—the firing on the Star of the West, and the correspondence which then took place between Major Anderson and the governor of South Carolina. They then went on to prove the evacuation of Fort Moultrie; the storming of Fort Sumter; the proclamation of the President of the United States, of the 15th of April, calling for 75,000 troops; Mr. Davis' proclamation, of the 17th of April, inviting privateers; and then the President's proclamation, of the 19th of April, denouncing the punishment of piracy against privateers, and putting under blockade the coasts of the revolted States. The laws about privateering passed by what is called the Confederate government, have also been read to you; and this seems to complete the documentary, and constitutional, and statutory proceedings in that disaffected portion of the country. But what do the prisoners prove further? That an actual military conflict and collision commenced, has proceeded, and is now raging in this country, wherein we find not one section of the country engaged in a military con-

test with another section of the country; not two contending factions, in the phrase of Vattel, dividing the nation for the sake of
national power; but the government of the United States, still
standing, without the diminution of one tittle of its power and dignity; without the displacement or disturbance of a single function
of its executive, of its legislative, of its judicial establishments;
without the disturbance or the defection of its army or its navy;
without any displacement in or among the nations of the world;
without any retreat, on its part, or any repulsion, on the part of
any force whatever, from its general control over the affairs of the
nation, over all its relations to foreign States, over the high seas,
and over every part of the United States themselves, in their whole
length and breadth, except just so far as military occupation and
military contest have controlled the peaceful maintenance of the
authority and laws of the government.

Now, this may be conceded for all sides of the controversy. I
do not claim any more than these proofs show, and what we all
know to be true; and I am but fair in conceding that they do show
all the proportions and extent which make up a contest by the
forces of the nation, as a nation, against an armed array, with all
the form and circumstances, and with a number and strength,
which make up military aggression and military attack on the part
of these revolting or disaffected communities or people.

14. THE FACT OF ACTUAL EXISTENCE OF WAR IMMATERIAL.

Now, some observations have been made, at various stages of
this argument, of the course the government has taken in its declaration of a blockade, and in its seizure of prizes by its armed
vessels, and its bringing them before the prize courts; and my
learned friend, Mr. Brady, has done me the favor to allude to some
particular occasion on which I, on behalf of the goverment, in the
admiralty court, have contended for certain principles which would
lead to the judicial confiscation of prizes under the law of the land,
or under the law of nations adopted and enforced as part of the
law of the land. Well, gentlemen, I understand and agree that,
for certain purposes, there is a condition of war which forces
itself on the attention and the duty of governments, and calls on
them to exert the power and force of war for their protection and
maintenance. And I have had occasion to contend—and the
learned courts have decided—that this nation, undertaking to suppress an armed military rebellion which arrays itself, by land and

by sea, in the forms of naval and military attack, has a right to exert—under the necessary principles which control and require the action of a nation for its own preservation, in these circumstances of danger and of peril—not only the usual magisterial force of the country; not only the usual criminal laws; not only such civil posses or aids to the officers of the law as may be obtained for their assistance; but to take the army and the navy, the strength and the manhood of the nation, which it can rally around it, and in every form, and by every authority, human and divine, suppress and reduce a revolt, a rebellion, a treason, that seeks to overthrow this government in, at least, a large portion of its territory, and among a large portion of its people. In doing so, it may resort, as it has resorted, to the method of a warlike blockade, which, by mere force of naval obstruction, closes the harbors of the disaffected portion of the country against all commerce. Having done that, it has a right, in its admiralty courts, to adjudicate upon and condemn as prizes, under the laws of blockade, all vessels that shall seek to violate the blockade. Nor, gentlemen, have I ever denied, nor shall I here deny, that, when the proportions of a civil dissension or controversy come to the port and dignity of war, good sense and common intelligence require the government to recognize it as a question of fact, according to the actual circumstances of the case, and to act accordingly. I, therefore, have no difficulty in conceding that, outside of any question of law and right; outside of any question as to whether there is a government down there, whether nominal or real, or that can be described as having any consistency of any kind, under our law and our government, there is prevailing in this country a controversy, which is carried on by the methods, and which has the proportions and extent, of what we call war.

15. WAR DEFINED.—THE PLEA OF WAR A CONFESSION OF TREASON.

War, gentlemen, as distinguished from peace, is so distinguished by this proposition: that it is a condition in which force on one side and force on the other are the means used in the actual prosecution of the controversy. Now, gentlemen, if the court please, I believe that that is all that can be claimed, and all that has been claimed, on behalf of these prisoners, in regard to the actual facts and the condition of things in this country. And I admit that, if this government of ours were not a party to this controversy; if it looked on it from the outside, as England and France have done, our government would have had the full right to treat these contending parties, in its courts and before its laws, as belligerents, engaged in hostilities, as it would have had an equal right to take the opposite course. Which course it would have taken, I neither know, nor should you require to know.

But I answer to the whole of this, if the court please, that it is a war in which the government recognizes no right whatever on the part of the persons with whom it is contending; and that, in the eye of the law as well as in the eye of reason and sound political morality, every person who has, from the beginning of the first act of levying war against the United States until now, taken part in this war, actively and effectively, in any form; who has adhered to the rebels; who has given aid, information, or help of any kind, wherever he lives, whether he sends it from New Hampshire or New York, from Wisconsin or from Baltimore, whether he be found within or without the armed lines, is, in his own overt actions or open espousal of the side of this warring power against the government of the United States, a traitor and a rebel. I do not know that there is any proposition whatever, of law, or any authority whatever, that has been adduced by my learned friends, in which they will claim, as matter of law, that they are not rebels. I invited the attention of my learned friends, as I purposed to call that of the court, to the fact that the difficulty about all this business was, that the plea of authority or of war, which these prisoners interposed against the crime of piracy, was nothing but a plea of their implication in treason. I would like to hear a sober and solemn proposition from any lawyer, that a government, as matter of law, and a court, as matter of law, cannot proceed on an infraction of a law against violence either to person or property, instead of proceeding on an indictment for treason. The facts proved must, of course, maintain the personal crime; and there are many degrees of treason, or facts of treason, which do not include violent crime. But to say that a person who has acted as a rebel cannot be indicted as an assassin, or that a man who has acted on the high seas as a pirate, if our statutes so pronounce him, cannot be indicted, tried and convicted as a pirate, because he could plead, as the shield of his piracy, that he committed it as part of his treason, is, to my apprehension, entirely new, and inconsistent with the first principles of justice.

This very statute of piracy is found in a general crimes act.

The first section is: "If any person or persons owing allegiance to the United States of America shall levy war against them, or shall adhere to their enemies, giving them aid and comfort within the United States, or elsewhere, and shall be thereof convicted," "such person or persons shall be adjudged guilty of treason against the United States, and shall suffer death."

16. TREASON NO DEFENSE AGAINST PIRACY.

Now, you will observe that treason is not a defense against piracy; nor is good faith in treason a defense against treason, or a defense against piracy. What would be the posture of these prisoners, if, instead of being indicted for piracy, they were indicted for treason? Should we then hear anything about this notion that there was a war raging, and that they were a party engaged in the war? Why, that is the very definition of treason. Against whom is the war? Against the United States of America. Did you owe allegiance to the United States of America? Yes, the citizens did; and I need not say to you, gentlemen, that those residents who are not citizens owe allegiance. There is no dispute about that. Those foreigners who are living here unnaturalized are just as much guilty of treason, if they act treasonably against the government, as any of our own citizens can be. That is the law of England, the law of treason, the necessary law of civilized communities. If we are hospitable, if we make no distinction, as we do not, in this country between citizens and foreigners resident here and protected by our laws, it is very clear we cannot make any distinction when we come to the question of who are faithful to the laws. So, therefore, if they were indicted for treason, what would become of all this defense? It would be simply a confession in open court that they were guilty of treason. Well, then, if they fell back on the proposition: "We thought, in our consciences and judgments, that either these States had a right to secede, or that they had a right to carry on a revolution; that they were oppressed, and were entitled to assert themselves against an oppressive government, and we, in good faith, and with a fair expectation of success, entered into it;" what would become of them? The answer would be: "Good faith in your attempt to overthrow the government does not excuse you from responsibility for the crime of attempting it." Our statute is made for the purpose of protecting our government against efforts made, in good faith or in bad faith, for its overthrow.

17. The authority of Vattel in harmony with the prosecution.

And now, in this connection, gentlemen, as your attention, as well as that of the court, has been repeatedly called to it, let me advert again to the citation from that enlightened public writer, Vattel, who has done as much, perhaps, as our learned friends have suggested, to place on a sure foundation the ameliorations of the law of nations in time of war, and of their intercourse in time of peace, as any writer and thinker whom our race has produced. You remember that he asks: How shall it be when two contending factions divide a State in all the forms and extent of civil war; what shall be the right and what the duty of a sovereign in this regard? Shall he put himself on the pride of a king, or on the flattery of a courtier, and say, I am still monarch, and will enforce against every one of this multitude engaged in this rebellion the strict penalties of my laws? Vattel reasons, and reasons very properly: You must submit to the principles of humanity and of justice; you must govern your conduct by them, and not proceed to an extermination of your subjects because they have revolted, whether with or without cause. You must not enforce the sanctions of your government, or maintain its authority, on methods which would produce a destruction of your people. And you must not further, by insisting, under the enforced circumstances which surround you, on the extreme and logical right of a king, furnish occasion for the contending rebels, who have their moments of success and power as well as you, to retaliate on your loyal people, victims of their struggle on your behalf, and thrown into the power of your rebellious subjects; to retaliate, I say, on them the same extreme penalties, without right, without law, but by mere power, which you have exerted under your claim of right.

And now, gentlemen of the jury, as the court very well understands, this general reasoning, which should govern the conduct of a sovereign, or of a government, against a mere local insurrection, does not touch the question as to whether the law of the nation in which the sovereign presides, and in violation of which the crime of the rebels has been perpetrated, shall be enforced. There has been, certainly, in modern times, no occasion when a sovereign has not drawn, in his discretion and under the influence of these principles of humanity and justice, this distinction, and has not interposed the shield of his own mercy between the offenses of misled and misguided masses of his people and the offended laws. We know the difference between law and its condemnation, and mercy and its saving grace; and we know that every government exercises its discretion.   And I should like to know why these learned counsel, who are seeking to interpose, as a legal defense on the part of a criminal, the principles of policy and mercy which should guide the government, are disposed to insist that this government, in its prosecutions and its trials, has shown a disposition to absolve great masses of criminals from the penalties of its laws?   I should like to know, when my learned friend Mr. Brady, near the close of his remarks, suggested that there had been no trial for treason, whether this government, from the first steps in the outbreak down to the final and extensive rage of the war, has not foreborne to take satisfaction for the wrongs committed against it, and has not been disposed to carry on and sustain the strength of the government without bloody sacrifices for its maintenance and for the offended justice of the land?   But it is certainly very strange if, when a government influenced by those principles of humanity of which Vattel speaks, and which my learned friends so much insist upon, has foreborne, except in signal instances, or, if you please, in single instances that are not signal, to assert the standard of the law's authority and of the government's right, that it may be seen that the sword of justice, although kept sheathed for the most part, has yet not rusted in its scabbard, and that the government is not faithless to itself, or to its laws, its powers or its duties, in these particular prosecutions that have been carried, one to its conclusion, in Philadelphia, and the other to this stage of its progress, here; it is strange, indeed, that the appeal is to be thrust upon it: "Do not include the masses of the misguided men!" and when it yields so mercifully to that appeal and says, "I will limit myself to the least maintenance and assertion of a right," that the answer is to come back: "Why, how execrable, how abominable, to make distinctions of that kind!"

But, gentlemen, the mercy of the government, as I have said to you, remains after conviction, as well as in its determination not to press numerous trials for treason; but it is an attribute, both in forbearing to try and in forbearing to execute, which is safely left where the precedents that are to shape the authority of law cannot be urged against its exercise.   Now, I look upon the conduct and duty of the government on somewhat larger considerations than have been pressed before you here.   The government, it is said, does not desire the conviction of these men, or, at least, should not desire it. The government does not desire the blood of any of its misguided people. The government—the prosecution—should have no passion, no animosities, in this or in any other case; and our learned friends have done us the favor to say that the case is presented to you as the law should require it to be; that you, and all, are unaffected and unimpeded in your judgment; and that, with a full hearing of what could be said on the part of these criminals, you have the case candidly and openly before you.

18. DUTY OF GOVERNMENT TO PROTECT ITS COMMERCE AND ITS CITIZENS.

Now, gentlemen, the government, although having a large measure of discretion, has no right, in a country where the government is one wholly of law, to repeal the criminal law, and no right to leave it without presenting it to the observation, the understanding, and the recognition of all its citizens, whether in rebellion or not, in its majesty, in its might, and in its impartiality. The government has behind it the people, and it has behind it all the great forces which are breathing on our agitated society, all the strong passions, all the deep emotions, all the powerful convictions, which impress the loyal people of this country as to the outrage, as to the wickedness, as to the perils of this great rebellion. Do you not recollect how, when the proclamation of Mr. Davis invited marauders to prey upon our commerce, from whatever quarter and from whatever motives (patriotism and duty not being requisite before they would be received), the cry of the wounded sensibilities of a great commercial people burst upon this whole scene of conflict? What was there that as a nation we had more to be proud of, more to be glad for in our history, than our flag? To think that in an early stage of what was claimed to be first a constitutional, and then a peaceful, and then a deliberate political agitation and maintenance of right, this last extreme act, the arming of private persons against private property on the sea, was appealed to before even a force was drawn on the field on behalf of the United States of America! The proclamation of the President was but two days old when privateers were invited to rush to the standard. The indignation of the community, the sense of outrage and hatred was so severe and so strong, that at that time, if the sentiment of the people had been consulted, it would have found a true expression in what was asserted in the newspapers, in public speeches, in private conversations: that the duty of every merchantman and of every armed vessel of the country, which arrested any of these so-called privateers, under this new commission, without a nation and without authority, was to treat them as pirates caught in the act, and execute them at the yard-arm by a summary justice.

Well, I need not say to you, gentlemen, that I am sure you and I and all of us would have had occasion to regret, in every sense, as wrong, as violent, as unnecessary, and, therefore, as wholly un-justifiable, on the part of a powerful nation like ourselves, any such rash execution of the penalties of the law of nations, and of the law of the land, while our government had power on the sea, had authority on the land, had courts and laws and juries under its au-thority, to inquire and look into the transaction.

The public passions on this subject being all cool at this time, after an interval of four months or more from the arrest, we are here trying this case. Yet my learned friends can find complaint against the mercy of the government and its justice, that it brings any prosecution; and great complaint is made before you, without the least ground or cause as it seems to me, that the prosecution is pressed in a time of war, when the sentiments of the community are supposed to be inflamed.

Well, gentlemen, what is the duty of government, when it has brought in prisoners arrested on the high seas, but to deliver them promptly to the civil authorities, as was done in this case; and then, in the language of the Constitution, which secures the right to them, to give them a speedy and impartial trial? That it is impartial they all confess. How speedy is it? They say they regret that it proceeds in time of war. Surely, our learned friends do not wish to be understood as having had denied to them in this court any application which they have made for postponement. The promptness of the judicial and prosecuting authorities here had produced this indictment in the month of June, I believe the very month in which the prisoners were arrested, or certainly early in July; and then the government was ready to proceed with the trial, so far as I am advised. But, at any rate, an application—a very proper and necessary application—was made by our learned friends, that the trial should be postponed till, I believe, the very day on which it was brought on. That application was not ob-jected to, was acquiesced in, and the time was fixed, and no further suggestion was made that the prisoners desired further delay; and if the government had undertaken to ask for further delay, on the ground of being unprepared, there was no fact to sustain any such

26

application. If it was the wish of the prisoners, or for their convenience, that there should be further delay, it was for them to
suggest it. But, being entitled by the Constitution to a speedy as
well as an impartial trial, and the day being fixed by themselves on
which they would be ready, and they being considered ready, and
no difficulty or embarrassment in the way of proof having been
suggested on the part of the government, it seems to me very
strange that this regret should be expressed, unless it should take
that form of regret which all of us participate in, that the war is
not over. That, I agree, is a subject of regret. But how there
has ever been any pressure, or any—the least—exercise of authority adverse to their wishes in this matter, it is very difficult for me
to understand.

19. THE NOVEL POLITICAL QUESTIONS PRESENTED BY THE DEFENSE.

Now, gentlemen, I approach a part of this discussion which I
confess I would gladly decline. I have not the least objection—no
one, I am sure, can feel the least objection—to the privilege or
supposed duty of counsel who are defending prisoners on a grave
charge—certainly not in a case which includes, as a possible result,
the penalty of their clients' lives, to go into all the inquiries, discussions and arguments, however extensive, varied, or remote, that
can affect the judgment of the jury, properly or fairly, or that can
rightly be invoked. But I confess that, looking at the very interesting, able, extensive and numerous arguments, theories and illustrations that have been presented in succession by, I think, in one
form or another, seven counsel for these prisoners, as the introduction into a judicial forum, and before a jury, of inquiries concerning the theories of government, the course of politics, the occasion
of strife on one side or the other, within the region of politics and
the region of peace, in any portion of the great communities that
composed this powerful nation; in that point of view, I aver, they
seem to me very little inviting and instructive, as they certainly are
extremely unusual in forensic discussions. Certainly, gentlemen of
the jury, we must conceive some starting point somewhere in the
stability of human affairs, as they are intrusted to the control and
defense of human governments. But in the very persistent and
resolute views of the learned counsel upon this point: first, on the
right of secession as constitutional; second, if not constitutional,
as being supposed by somebody to be constitutional; third, on the

right of revolution as existing on the part of a people oppressed, or deeming themselves oppressed, to try their strength in the overthrow of the subsisting government; fourth, on the right to press the discontents inside of civil war; and then finally and at last, that whoever thinks the government oppresses him, or thinks that a better government would suit his case, has not only the right to try the venture, but that, unsuccessful, or at any stage of the effort, his right becomes so complete that the government must and should surrender at once and to every attempt: I see only what is equivalent to subversion of government, and to saying that the right of revolution, in substance and in fact, involves the right of government in the first place, and its duty in the second place, to surrender to the revolutionist, and to treat him as having overthrown it in point of law and in contemplation of its duty. That is a proposition which I cannot understand.

Nevertheless, gentlemen, these subjects have been so extensively opened, and in so many points attacks have been made upon what seems to me not only the very vital structure and necessary support of this, our government, but the very necessary and indispensable support of any government whatever, and we have been so distinctly challenged, both on the ground of an absolute right to overthrow this government whenever any State thinks fit; and, next, upon the clear right, on general principles of human equity, of each State to raise itself against any government with which it is dissatisfied; and upon the general right of conscience, as well as on the complete support by what has been assumed to have been the parallel case, on all those principles, of the conduct of the colonies which became the United States of America and established our government—that I shall find it necessary, in the discharge of my duty, to say something, however briefly, on that subject.

Now, gentlemen, these are novel discussions in a court of justice within the United States of America. We have talked about the oppressions of other nations, and rejoiced in our exemption from all of them, under the free and benignant and powerful government which was, by the favor of Providence, established by the wisdom and courage and virtue of our ancestors. We had, for more than two generations, reposed under the shadow of our all-protecting government with the same conscious security as under the firmament of the heavens. We knew, to be sure, that for all that made life hopeful and valuable, for all that made life possible, we depended upon the all-protecting power and the continued favor of Divine Providence. We knew just as well, that without civil society, without equal and benignant laws, without the administration of justice, without the maintenance of commerce, without a suitable government, without a powerful nationality, all the motives and springs of human exertion and labor would be dried up at their source. But we felt no more secure in the Divine promise that "summer and winter, seed-time and harvest," should not cease, than we did in the permanent endurance of that great fabric established by the wisdom and the courage of a renowned ancestry, to be the habitation of liberty and justice for us and our children to every generation. We felt no solicitude whatever that this great structure of our constituted liberties should pass away as a scroll, or its firm power crumble in the dust. But, by the actual circumstances of our situation, and, if not by them, certainly by the destructive theories which are presented for your consideration, it becomes necessary for us as citizens, and, in the judgment at least of the learned counsel for these prisoners, for you, and for this learned court, in the conduct of this trial and in the disposition of the issue of "guilty" or "not guilty" as to these prisoners, to pay some attention to these considerations. If, in the order of this discussion, gentlemen, I should not seem to follow in any degree, or even to include by name, many of the propositions, of the distinctions, and of the arguments which our learned friends have pressed against the whole solidity, the whole character, the whole permanence, the whole strength of our government, I yet think you will find that I have included the principal ideas they have advanced, and have commented upon the views that seem to us, at least so far as we think them to be at all connected with this case, suitable to be considered.

Here Mr. Evarts discussed the right of secession, showing that such a doctrine as contended for by the defense was utterly antagonistic with the theory of the American revolution out of which the nation was born, and that it was only upon the idea of unity that *the people* of the colonies succeeded. He then proceeded to discuss the right of revolution as follows:

20. THE RIGHT OF REVOLUTION.

And now, gentlemen, having done with this doctrine of secession, as utterly inconsistent with the theory of our government, and utterly unimportant as a practical right for any supposable or even imaginable case that may be suggested, I come to consider the question of the right of revolution. I have shown to you upon what principles and upon what substantial question, between being subjects as slaves or being participants in the British government, our colonies attempted and achieved their independence. As I have said to you, a very brief experience showed that they needed, to meet the exigencies of their situation, the establishment of a government that should be in accordance with the wishes and spirit of the people in regard of freedom, and yet should be of such strength and such unity as would admit of prosperity being enjoyed under it, and of its name and power being established among the nations of the earth.

Without going into the theories of government and of the rights of the people, and of the rights of the rulers, to any great extent, we all know that there has been every variety of experiment tried, in the course of human affairs, between the great extreme alluded to by my learned friend (Mr. Brady), of the slavery of Egyptians to their king—the extreme instance of an entire population scarcely lifted above the brutes in their absolute subjection to the tyranny of a ruler, so that the life and the soul, and the sweat and the blood of a whole generation of men are consumed in the task of building a mausoleum as the grave of a king—and the later efforts of our race, culminating in the happy success of our own form of government, to establish, on foundations where liberty and law find equal support, the principle of government, that government is by, and for, and from all the people; that the rulers, instead of being their masters and their owners, are their agents and their servants; and that the greatest good of the greatest number is the plain, practical and equal rule which, by gift from our Creator, we enjoy.

21. The problem of self-government.

Now this, you will observe, is a question which readily receives our acceptance. But the great problem in reference to the freedom of a people, in the establishment of their government, presents itself in this wise: The people, in order to maintain their freedom, must be masters of their government, so that the government may not be too strong, in its arrangement of power, to overmaster the people; but yet the government must be strong enough to maintain and protect the independence of the nation against the aggressions, the usurpations and the oppressions of foreign nations. Here you have a difficulty raised at once. You expose either the freedom of the nation by making the government too strong for the preservation of individual independence, or you expose its existence by making it too weak to maintain itself against the passions, interests and power of neighboring nations. If you have a large nation, counting its population by many millions and the circumference of its territory by thousands of miles, how can you arrange the strength of government, so that it shall not, in the interests of human passions, grow too strong for the liberties of the people? And if, abandoning in despair that effort and that hope, you circumscribe the limits of your territory and reduce your population within a narrow range, how can you have a government and a nation strong enough to maintain itself in the contests of the great family of nations, impelled and urged by interests and passions?

22. Practical object and spirit of government.

Here is the first peril which has never been successfully met and disposed of in any of the forms of government that have been known in the history of mankind, until, at least, our solution of it was attempted, and unless it has succeeded and can maintain itself. But, again, this business of self-government by a people has but one practical and sensible spirit and object. The object of free government is, that the people, as individuals, may with security pursue their own happiness. We do not tolerate the theory that all the people constituting the nation are absorbed into the national growth and life. The reason why we want a free government is, that we may be happy under it, and pursue our own activities according to our nature and our faculties. But you will see at once that it is of the essence of being able to pursue our own interests under the government under which we live, that we can do so according to our own notions of what they are, or the notions of those who are intelligently informed of, participate in, and sympathize with those interests. Therefore it seems necessary that all of the every-day rights of property, of social arrangements, of marriage, of contracts—everything that makes up the life of a social community —shall be under the control, not of a remote or distant authority, but of one that is limited to and derives its ideas and principles from a local community.

Now, how can this be in a large nation, in a nation of thirty millions, distributed over a zone of the earth? How are we to get along in New York, and how are others to get along in South Carolina, and others in New England, in the every-day arrangements that proceed from government and affect the prosperity, the freedom, the independence, the satisfaction of the community with the condition in which it lives ?   How can we get along if all these minute and every-day arrangements are to proceed from a government which has to deal with the diverse opinions, the diverse sentiments, the diverse interests of so extensive a nation ?   But if, fleeing from this peril, you say that you may reduce your nation, you fall into another difficulty.   The advanced civilization of the present day requires for our commercial activity, for our enjoyment of the comforts and luxuries of life, that the whole globe shall be ransacked, and that the power of the nation which we recognize as our superior shall be able to protect our citizens in their enterprises, in their activities, in their objects all over the world.   How can a little nation, made up of Massachusetts, or made up of South Carolina, have a flag and a power which can protect its commerce in the East Indies and in the southern ocean ?   Again, we find that nations, unless they are separated by wide barriers, necessarily, in the course of human affairs, come into collision; and, as I have shown to you, the only arbitrament for their settlement is war. But war is a scourge, an unmitigated scourge, so long as it lasts, and in itself considered.   But for objects which make it meritorious and useful, it is a scourge never to be tolerated.   It puts in abeyance all individual rights, interests and schemes, until the great controversy is settled.

23. Political results of war.

If, then, we are a small nation, surrounded on all sides by other nations, with no natural barriers, with competing interests, with occasions of strife and collision on all sides, how can we escape war, as a necessary result of that miserable situation ?   But war strengthens the power of government, weakens the power of the individual, and establishes maxims and creates forces that go to increase the weight and the power of government, and to weaken the rights of the people.   Then we see that, to escape war, we must either establish a great nation which occupies an extent of territory and has a fund of power sufficient to protect itself against border strifes and against the ambition, the envy, the hatred of neighbors; or else one which, being small, is exposed to war from abroad to subjugate it, or to the greater peril to its own liberties, of war made by its own government, thus establishing principles and introducing interests which are inconsistent with liberty.

I have thus ventured, gentlemen, to lay before you some of these general principles, because, in the course of the arguments of my learned friends as well as in many of the discussions before the public mind, it seems to be considered that the ties, the affections and the interests which oblige us to the maintenance of this government of ours, find their support and proper strength and nourishment only in the sentiments of patriotism and duty, because it happens to be our own government; and that, when the considerations of force or of feeling which bring a people to submit to a surrender of their government, or to a successful conquest of a part of their territory, or to a wresting of a part of their people from the control of the government, shall be brought to bear upon us, we shall be, in our loss and our surrender, only suffering what other nations have been called upon to lose and to surrender, and that it will be but a change in the actual condition of the country and its territory.

24. WISDOM AND ADVANTAGES OF OUR POLITICAL SYSTEM.

But you will perceive that, by the superior fortune which attended our introduction into the family of nations, and by the great wisdom, forecast and courage of our ancestors, we avoided, at the outset, all the difficulties between a large territory and a numerous population on the one hand, and a small territory and a reduced population on the other hand, and all those opposing dangers of the government being either too weak to protect the nation, or too strong and thus oppressive of the people, by a distribution of powers and authorities, novel in the affairs of men, dependent on experiment, and to receive its final fate as the result of that experiment. We went on this view, that these feeble colonies had not, each in itself, the life and strength of a nation; and yet these feeble colonies and their poor and sparse population were nourished on a love of liberty and self-government. These sentiments had carried them through a successful war against one of the great powers of the earth. They were not to surrender that for which they had been fighting to any scheme, to any theory of a great, consolidated nation, the government of which should subdue the people and re-introduce the old fashion in human affairs: that the people were made for the rulers, and not the rulers by and for the people. They undertook to meet, they did meet, this difficult dilemma in the constitution of government, by separating the great fund of power and reposing it in two distinct organizations. They reserved to the local communities the control of their domestic affairs, and attributed the maintenance and preservation of them to the State governments. They undertook to collect and deposit, under the form of a written Constitution, with the general government all those larger and common interests which enter into the conception and practical establishment of a distinct nation among the nations of the earth, and determined that they would have a central power which should be adequate, by drawing its resources from the patriotism, from the duty, from the wealth, from the numbers of a great nation, to represent them in peace and in war; a nation that could protect the interests, encourage the activities and maintain the development of its people, in spite of the opposing interests or the envious or hostile attacks of any nation. They determined that this great government, thus furnished with this range of authority and this extent of power, should not have anything to do with the every-day institutions, operations and social arrangements of the community into which the vast population and territory of the nation were distributed. They determined that the people of Massachusetts, the people of New York, and the people of South Carolina, each of them, should have their own laws about agriculture, about internal trade, about marriage, about apprenticeship, about slavery, about religion, about schools, about all the every-day pulsations of individual life and happiness, controlled by communities that moved with the same pulsations, obeyed the same instincts, and were animated by the same purposes. And, as this latter class of authority contains in itself the principal means of oppression by a government, and is the principal point where oppression is to be feared by a people, they had thus robbed the new system of all the dangers which attend the too extensive powers of a government. They divided the fund of power to prevent a great concentration and a great consolidation of the army of magistrates and officers of the law and of the government, which would have been combined by an united and consolidated authority, having jurisdiction of all the purposes of government, of all the interests of citizens, and of the entire population and entire territory in these respects. They thus made a government, complex in its arrangements, which met those opposing difficulties, inherent in human affairs, that make the distinction between free governments and oppressive governments. They preserved the people in their enjoyment and control of all the local matters entering into their every-day life, and yet gave them an establishment, springing from the same interests and controlled by the same people, which has

sustained and protected us in our relations to the family of nations
on the high seas and in the remote corners of the world.

Now, this is the scheme and this is the purpose with which this
government was formed; and you will observe that there is contained in it this separation and this distribution. And our learned
friends, who have argued before you respecting this theory and
this arrangement and practice of the power of a government as inconsistent with the interests and the freedom of the people, have
substantially said to you that it was a whimsical contrivance, that
it was an impossible arrangement of inconsistent principles, and
that we must go back to a simple government composed of one of
the States, or of a similar arrangement of territory and people,
which would make each of us a weak and contemptible power in
the family of nations; or we must go back to the old consolidation
of power, such as is represented by the frame of France or England
in its government, or, more distinctly, more absolutely, and more
likely to be the case, for so vast a territory and so extensive a population as ours, to the simple notion of Russian autocracy.

That, then, being the object, and that the character of our institutions, and this right of secession not being provided for, or
imagined, or tolerated in the scheme, let us look at the right of
revolution as justifying an attempt to overthrow the government;
and let us look at the occasions of revolution which are pretended here as giving a support before the world, in the forum of
conscience, and in the judgment of mankind, for the exercise of
that right.

And first let me ask you whether, in all the citations from the
great men of the revolution, and in the later stages of our history,
any opinion has been cited which has condemned this scheme as
unsuitable and insufficient for the freedom and happiness of the
people, if it can be successful? I think not. The whole history
of the country is full of records of the approval, of the support,
of the admiration, of the reverent language which our people at
large and the great leaders of public opinion, the great statesmen
of the country, have spoken of this system of government. Let
me ask your attention to but two encomiums upon it, as represented by that central idea of a great nation, and yet a divided
and local administration of popular interests, to wit, one in the first

stage of its adoption, before its ratification by the people was complete; and the other, a speech made at the very eve of, if not in the very smoke of, this hostile dissolution of it.

26. Views of William Pinkney on the perfection of our government.

Mr. Pinkney, of South Carolina, who had been one of the delegates from the State in the national convention, and had co-operated with the northern statesmen, and with the great men of Virginia, in forming the government as it was, in urging on the convention of South Carolina the adoption of the Constitution and its ratification, said:

"To the Union we will look up as the temple of our freedom—a temple founded in the affections and supported by the virtue of the people. Here we will pour out our gratitude to the Author of all good, for suffering us to participate in the rights of a people who govern themselves. Is there, at this moment, a nation on the earth which enjoys this right, where the true principles of representation are understood and practiced, and where all authority flows from and returns, at stated periods, to the people? I answer, there is not. Can a government be said to be free where those do not exist? It cannot. On what depends the enjoyment of those rare, inestimable rights? On the firmness and on the power of the Union to protect and defend them."

Had we anything from that great patriot and statesman of this right of secession, or independence of a State, as an important or a useful element in securing these rare, these unheard of, these inestimable privileges of government, which the author of all good had suffered the people of South Carolina to participate in? No; they depended "on the firmness and the power of the Union to protect and defend them." Mr. Pinkney goes on to say:

"To the philosophic mind, how new and awful an instance do the United States at present exhibit to the people of the world? They exhibit, sir, the first instance of a people who, being thus dissatisfied with their government, unattacked by a foreign force and undisturbed by domestic uneasiness, coolly and deliberately resort to the virtue and good sense of the country for a correction of their public errors."

That is, for the abandonment of the weakness and the danger of the imperfect confederation, and the adoption of the constitutional and formal establishment of federal power. Mr. Pinkney goes on to say:

"It must be obvious that, without a superintending government, it is impossible the liberties of this country can long be secure. Single and unconnected, how weak and contemptible are the largest of our States! how unable to protect themselves from external or domestic insult! how incompetent, to national purposes, would even the present Union be! how liable to intestine war and confusion! how little able to secure the blessings of peace! Let us, therefore, be careful in strengthening the Union. Let us remember we are bounded by vigilant and attentive neighbors"—(and now Europe is within ten days, and they are near neighbors)—"who view with a jealous eye our rights to empire."

27. VIEWS OF ALEXANDER H. STEPHENS ON THE SANCTITY OF THE UNION.

Pursuing my design of limiting my citations of the opinions of public men to those who have received honor from, and conferred honor on, that portion of our country and those of our countrymen now engaged in this strife with the general government, let me ask your attention to a speech delivered by Mr. Stephens, now the Vice-President of the so-called Confederate States, on the very eve of, and protesting against, this effort to dissolve the Union. I read from page 220 and subsequent pages of the documents that have been the subject of reference heretofore:

"The first question that presents itself," says Mr. Stephens to the assembled legislature of Georgia, of which he was not a member, but which, as an eminent and leading public man, he had been invited to address, "is, shall the people of the South secede from the Union in consequence of the election of Mr. Lincoln to the Presidency of the United States? My countrymen, I tell you frankly, candidly and earnestly, that I do not think that they ought. In my judgment, the election of no man, constitutionally elected to that high office, is sufficient cause for any State to separate from the Union. It ought to stand by and aid still in maintaining the Constitution of the country. To make a point of resistance to the government, to withdraw from it because a man has been constitutionally elected, puts us in the wrong. We are pledged to maintain the Constitution. Many of us have sworn to support it.

*   *   *   *   *   *   *

"But it is said Mr. Lincoln's policy and principles are against the Constitution, and that, if he carries them out, it will be destructive of our rights. Let us not anticipate a threatened evil. If he violates the Constitution, then will come our time to act. Do not let us break it because, forsooth, he may. If he does, that is the time for us to strike. * * * My countrymen, I am not of those who believe this Union has been a curse up to this time.

True men, men of integrity, entertain different views from me on this subject. I do not question their right to do so; I would not impugn their motives in so doing. Nor will I undertake to say that this government of our fathers is perfect. There is nothing perfect in this world, of a human origin. Nothing connected with human nature, from man himself to any of his works. You may select the wisest and best men for your judges, and yet how many defects are there in the administration of justice? You may select the wisest and best men for your legislators, and yet how many defects are apparent in your laws? And it is so in our government.

"But that this government of our fathers, with all its defects, comes nearer the objects of all good governments than any on the face of the earth, is my settled conviction. Contrast it now with any on the face of the earth." ["England," said Mr. Toombs.] "England, my friend says. Well, that is the next best, I grant; but I think we have improved upon England. Statesmen tried their apprentice hand on the government of England, and then ours was made. Ours sprung from that, avoiding many of its defects, taking most of the good and leaving out many of its errors, and, from the whole, constructing and building up this model republic, the best which the history of the world gives any account of.

"Compare, my friends, this government with that of Spain, Mexico, the South American Republics, Germany, Ireland—are there any sons of that down-trodden nation here to-night?—Prussia, or, if you travel further east, to Turkey or China. Where will you go, following the sun in his circuit round our globe, to find a government that better protects the liberties of its people, and secures to them the blessings we enjoy? I think that one of the evils that beset us is a surfeit of liberty, an exuberance of the price-less blessings for which we are ungrateful.   *   *   *   *

"When I look around and see our prosperity in everything—agriculture, commerce, art, science, and every department of education, physical and mental, as well as moral advancement, and our colleges—I think, in the face of such an exhibition, if we can, without the loss of power, or any essential right or interest, remain in the Union, it is our duty to ourselves and to posterity to—let us not too readily yield to this temptation—do so. Our first parents, the great progenitors of the human race, were not without a like temptation when in the garden of Eden. They were led to believe that their condition would be bettered, that their eyes would be opened, and that they would become as gods. They in an evil hour yielded. Instead of becoming gods, they only saw their own nakedness.

"I look upon this country, with our institutions, as the Eden of the world, the paradise of the Universe. It may be that out of it we may become greater and more prosperous, but I am candid and sincere in telling you that I fear if we rashly evince passion, and, without sufficient cause, shall take that step, that, instead of becoming greater and more peaceful, prosperous and happy—instead of becoming gods—we will become demons, and, at no distant day, commence cutting one another's throats."

Still speaking of our government, he says:

" Thus far it is a noble example, worthy of imitation. The gentleman (Mr. Cobb) the other night said it had proven a failure. A failure in what? In growth? Look at our expanse in national power. Look at our population and increase in all that makes a people great. A failure? Why, we are the admiration of the civilized world, and present the brightest hopes of mankind.

" Some of our public men have failed in their aspirations; that is true, and from that comes a great part of our troubles.

" No, there is no failure of this government yet. We have made great advancement under the Constitution, and I cannot but hope· that we shall advance higher still. Let us be true to our cause."

Now, wherein is it that this government deserves these encomiums which come from the intelligent and profound wisdom of statesmen, and gush spontaneously from the unlearned hearts of the masses of the people? Why, it is precisely in this point, of its not being a consolidated government, and of its not being a narrow and feeble and weak community and government. Indeed, I may be permitted to say that I once heard, from the lips of Mr. Calhoun himself, this recognition, botl of the good fortune of this country in possessing such a government, and of the principal sources to which the gratitude of a nation should attribute that good fortune. I heard him once say, that it was to the wisdom, in the great convention, of the delegates from the State of Connecticut, and of Judge Patterson, a delegate from the State of New Jersey, that we owed the fact that this government was what it was, the best government in the world, a confederated government, and not what it would have been—and, apparently, would have been but for those statesmen—the worst government in the world, a consolidated government. These statesmen, he said, were wiser for the South than the South was for herself.

I need not say to you, gentlemen, that if all this encomium on the great fabric of our government is brought to naught, and is made nonsense by the proposition that, although thus praised and thus admired, it contains within itself the principle, the right, the duty of being torn to pieces whenever a fragment of its people shall be discontented and desire its destruction, then all this encomium comes but as sounding brass and a tinkling cymbal; and the glory of our ancestors, Washington, and Madison, and Jefferson, and Adams; the glory of their successors, Webster, and Clay, and Wright, and even Calhoun, for he was no votary of this nonsense of secession, passes away, and their fame grows visibly paler, and the watchful eye of the English monarchy looks on for the bitter fruits to be reaped by us for our own destruction, and as an example to the world, the bitter fruits of the principle of revolution and of the right of self-government which we dared to assert against her perfect control. Pointing to our exhibition of an actual concourse of armies, she will say: "It is in the dragon's teeth, in the right of rebellion against the monarchy of England, that these armed hosts have found their seed and sprung up on your soil."

28. Marvelous success of our government.

Now, gentlemen, such is our government, such is its beneficence, such is its adaptation, and such are its successes. Look at its successes. Not three-quarters of a century have passed away since the adoption of its Constitution, and now it rules over a territory that extends from the Atlantic to the Pacific. It fills the wide belt of the earth's surface that is bounded by the provinces of England on the north, and by the crumbling and weak and contemptible governments, or no governments, that shake the frame of Mexico on the South. Have nature and providence left us without resources to hold together social unity, notwithstanding the vast expanse of the earth's surface which our population has traversed and possessed? No. Keeping pace with our wants in that regard, the rapid locomotion of steam on the ocean, and on our rivers and lakes, and on the iron roads that bind the country together, and the instantaneous electric communication of thought, which fills with the same facts, and with the same news, and with the same sentiments, at the same moment, a great, enlightened and intelligent people, have overcome all the resistance and all the dangers which might be attributed to natural obstructions. Even now, while this trial proceeds, San Francisco and New York, Boston and Portland, and the still farther east, communicate together as by a flash of lightning; indeed, it may be said, making an electric flash farther across the earth's surface—and intelligible, too, to man—than ever, in the natural phenomena of the heavens, the lightning displayed itself. No; the same author of all good, to whom Pinkney avowed his gratitude, has been our friend and our protector, and has removed, step by step, every impediment to our expansion which the

laws of nature and of space had been supposed to interpose. No,
no ; neither in the patriotism nor in the wisdom of our fathers was
there any defect; nor shall we find, in the disposition and purposes
of divine providence, as we can see them, any excuse or any aid
for the destruction of this magnificent system of empire. No; it is
in ourselves, in our own time and in our own generation, in our
own failing powers and failing duties, that the crash and ruin of
this magnificent fabric, and the blasting of the future hopes of mankind, is to find its cause and its execution.

Here Mr. Evarts showed that there was nothing in the declaration of independence to justify the right of revolution, except for some cause proceeding
from the general government amounting to absolute despotism or a denial of the
right of representation. He then reviewed all the alleged grievances of which
the South complained, to show that none of them proceeded from the federal
government, and that they were without any real foundation, because the South
was fully represented, and slavery was protected by the federal statutes, which
were enforced by the United States courts.

29. DISTINCTION BETWEEN POWER AND RIGHT.

Now, my learned friends, pressed by this difficulty as to the
sufficiency of the causes, are driven finally to this: that there is a
right of revolution when anybody thinks there is a right of revolution, and that that is the doctrine upon which our government rests,
and upon which the grave, serious action of our forefathers proceeded. And it comes down to the proposition of my learned
friend, Mr. Brady, that it all comes to the same thing, the power
and the right. All the argument, most unquestionably, comes to
that. But do morals, does reason, does common sense recognize
that, because power and right may result in the same consequences,
therefore there is no difference in their quality, or in their support,
or in their theory ? If I am slain by the sword of justice for my
crime, or by the dagger of an assassin for my virtue, I am dead,
under the stroke of either. But is one as right as the other ? An
oppressive government may be overthrown by the uprising of the
oppressed, and Lord Camden's maxim may be adhered to, that
"when oppression begins, resistance becomes a right;" but a government, beneficent and free, may be attacked, may be overthrown
by tyranny, by enemies, by mere power. The colonies may be
severed from Great Britain, on the principle of the right of the
people asserting itself against the tyranny of the parent government; and Poland may be dismembered by the interested tyranny

of Russia and Austria; and each is a revolution and destruction of the government, and its displacement by another—a dismemberment of the community, and the establishment of a new one under another government. But do my learned friends say that they equally come to the test of power as establishing the right? Will my learned friend plant himself, in justification of this dismemberment of a great, free and prosperous people, upon the example of the dismemberment of Poland, by the introduction of such influences within, and by the co-operation of such influences without, as secured that result? Certainly not. And yet if he puts it upon the right and the power, as coming to the same thing, it certainly cannot make any difference whether the power proceeds from within or from without. There is no such right. Both the public action of communities and the private action of individuals must be tried, if there is any trial, any scrutiny, any judgment, any determination, upon some principles that are deeper than the question of counting bayonets. When we are referred to the case of Victor Emanuel overthrowing the throne of the king of Naples, and thus securing the unity of the Italian people under a benign government, are we to be told that the same principle and the same proposition would have secured acceptance before the forum of civilization, and in the eye of morality, to a successful effort of the tyrant of Naples to overthrow the throne of Victor Emanuel, and include the whole of Italy under his, King Bomba's, tyranny? No one. The quality of the act, the reason, the support, and the method of it, are traits that impress their character on those great public and national transactions as well as upon any other.

30. GOOD FAITH NO DEFENSE.—CASE OF JOHN BROWN.

There is but one proposition, in reason and morality, beyond those I have stated, which is pressed for the extrication and absolution of these prisoners from the guilt that the law, as we say, impresses upon their action and visits with its punishment. It is said that, however little, as matter of law, these various rights and protections may come to, good faith, or sincere, conscientious conviction on the part of these men as to what they have done, should protect them against the public justice.

Now, we have heard a great deal of the assertion and of the execration of the doctrine of the "higher law," in the discussions of legislation and in the discussions before the popular mind; but I never yet have heard good faith or sincere opinion pressed, in a

27

court of justice, as a bar to the penalty which the law has soberly affixed, in the discreet and deliberate action of the legislature. And here my learned friend furnishes me, by his reference to the grave instance of injury to the property, and the security, and the authority of the State of Virginia, which he has spoken of as "John Brown's raid," with a ready instance in which these great principles of public justice, the authority of government, and the sanction of human law were met, in the circumstances of the trans-action, by a complete, and thorough, and remarkable reliance, for the motive, the support, the stimulus, the solace, against all the penalties which the law had decreed for such a crime, on this in-terior authority of conscience, and this supremacy of personal duty, according to the convictions of him who acts. The great State of Virginia administered its justice, and it found, as its prin-cipal victim, this most remarkable man, in regard to whom it was utterly impossible to impute anything like present or future, near or remote, personal interest or object of any kind: a man in regard to whom Governor Wise, of Virginia, said, in the very presence of the transaction of his trial, that he was the bravest, the sincerest, the truthfulest man that he ever knew. And now let us look at the question in the light in which our learned friend presents it: that John Brown, as matter of theoretical opinion of what he had a right to do under the Constitution and laws of his country, was justified upon the pure basis of conscientious duty to God; and let us see whether, before the tribunals of Virginia, as matter of fact or matter of law, or right or duty, any recognition was given to it. No. John Brown was not hung for his theoretical heresies, nor was he hung for his hallucinations of his judgment and the aberra-tion of his wrong moral sense, if you so call it, instead of the in-terior light of conscience, as he regarded it. He was hung for attacking the sovereignty, the safety, the citizens, the property, and the people of Virginia. And when my learned friend talks about this question of hanging for political, moral or social heresy, and that you cannot thus coerce the moral power of the mind, he vainly seeks to beguile your judgment. When Ravaillac takes the life of good King Henry, of France, is it a justification that, in the inter-ests of his faith, holy to him—of the religion he professed—he felt impelled thus to take the life of the monarch? When the assassin takes, at the door of the House of Commons, the life of the prime minister, Mr. Percival, because he thinks that the course of meas-ures his administration proposes to carry out is dangerous to the country, and falls a victim to violated laws, I ask, in the name of common sense and common fairness, are these executions to be called hanging for political or religious heresies? No. And shall it ever be said that sincere convictions on these theories of secession and of revolution are entitled to more respect than sincere convictions and opinions on the subject of human rights? Shall it be said that faith in Jefferson Davis is a greater protection from the penalty of the law than faith in God was to John Brown or Francis Ravaillac?

Here Mr. Evarts showed that the exchange of flags of truce and capitulations did not constitute such a recognition of the enemy as justified rebellion or a violation of law. That what the government had done in this respect in the past, was no bar to future action. That it was the duty of the government to show that resort to war, as a means of redress, was error; that the remedy for all grievances, real or imaginary, is in the region of debate and opinion and equal representation. He then read a letter from Garibaldi, showing that the Italian patriot did not share the views of the defense in regard to the war, his sympathies being with the federal government.[1] After quoting from Mr. Webster's speech, delivered on the centennial anniversary of the birthday of Washington, in 1832, in which he eulogized the establishment of our government as the greatest achievement in human affairs, he concluded as follows:

If, gentlemen, the eloquence of Mr. Webster, which thus enshrines the memory and the great life of Washington, calls us back to the glorious recollections of the revolution and the establishment of our government, does it not urge every man everywhere that his share in this great trust is to be performed now or never, and wherever his fidelity and his devotion to his country, its government and its spirit, shall place the responsibility upon him? It is not the fault of the government, of the learned district attorney, or of me, his humble associate, that this, your verdict, has been removed, by the course of this argument and by the course of this eloquence on the part of the prisoners, from the simple issue of the guilt or innocence of these men under the statute. It is not the action or the choice of the government, or of its counsel, that you have been drawn into higher considerations. It is not our fault that you have been invoked to give, on the undisputed facts of the case, a verdict which shall be a recognition of the power, the authority, and the right of the rebel government to infringe our laws, or partake in the infringement of them, to some form and extent. And now, here is your duty, here your post of fidelity, not

[1] For the reference to Garibaldi, see *ante*, p. 357; for the letter, see Appendix, p. 723.

against law, not against the least right under the law, but to sustain, by whatever sacrifice there may be of sentiment or of feeling,
the law and the Constitution. I need not say to you, gentlemen,
that if, on a state of facts which admits no diversity of opinion,
with these opposite forces arrayed, as they now are, before you—
the Constitution of the United States, the laws of the United
States, the commission of this learned court, derived from the government of the United States, the venire and the impaneling of
this jury, made under the laws and by the authority of the United
States, on our side; met, on their side, by nothing, on behalf of
the prisoners, but the commission, the power, the right, the authority of the rebel government, proceeding from Jefferson Davis—you
are asked, by the law, or under the law, or against the law, in some
form, to recognize this power, and thus to say that the folly and
the weakness of a free government find here their last extravagant
demonstration, then you are asked to say that the vigor, the judgment, the sense, and the duty of a jury, to confine themselves to
their responsibility on the facts of the case, are worthless and yielding before impressions of a discursive and loose and general nature.
Be sure of it, gentlemen, that, on what I suppose to be the facts
concerning this particular transaction, a verdict of acquittal is
nothing but a determination that our government and its authority,
in the premises of this trial, for the purposes of your verdict, are
met and overthrown by the protection thrown around the prisoners
by the government of the Confederate States of America, actual or
incipient. Let us hope that you will do what falls to your share in
the post of protection in which you are placed, for the liberties of
this nation and the hopes of mankind; for, in surrendering them,
you will be forming a part of the record on the common grave of
the fabric of this government, and of the hopes of the human race,
where our flag shall droop, with every stripe polluted and every
star erased, and the glorious legend of "liberty and Union, now
and forever, one and inseparable," replaced by this mournful confession, "unworthy of freedom, our baseness has surrendered the
liberties which we have neither the courage nor the virtue to love or
defend."

Judge Nelson delivered the charge to the jury, on Wednesday afternoon,
October 30, at the close of Mr. Evarts' address. They remained out all night,
and, being unable to agree, were discharged by the court on the following day.

ARGUMENT OF JOHN K. PORTER,

On the Constitutionality of Legal Tender Acts.—
Metropolitan Bank v. Van Dyck.

[27 N. Y. 400.]

BEFORE THE COURT OF APPEALS OF THE STATE OF NEW YORK, AT ALBANY, JUNE 27th, 1863.

Analysis of Mr. Porter's Argument.

1. Object and purpose of the Constitution, and the powers delegated to give it effect.
2. The exigencies which made it necessary to pledge the public credit for the public defense.
3. Results of the measures adopted by Congress.
4. The power of Congress to declare what shall be a legal tender, not prohibited by the Constitution.
5. Why this power was not conferred in specific terms.
6. How the power to create a legal tender was exercised in Colonial times.
7. Congress, by creating a "uniform" currency, fulfilled a constitutional trust.
8. Enumeration of the incidents of the war power vested in Congress.
9. Review of the events of the war.—An historical retrospect.
10. Nature of the crisis which demanded the passage of the legal-tender acts.
11. The desperate alternative forced upon Congress.
12. The power to pass the legal-tender acts exists by express grant, and by necessary implications.
13. Postulates which those who seek to nullify the legal-tender acts must establish.
14. The power to create a legal tender existed prior to the adoption of the Constitution, and was either vested in Congress or extinguished.
15. The inquiry whether self-preservation is an inherent right rising above constitutional limitations, does not arise.
16. Meaning of the terms "legal tender" and "money" considered and distinguished. — The subject of legal tender.
17. All the attributes of sovereignty presumed to exist, till those who deny it establish the contrary.

The Metropolitan Bank, the party plaintiff in this action, was a banking corporation, located and doing business in the city of New York, and organized under and by virtue of the laws of that State. By its charter, it was authorized to issue circulating notes to a fixed and limited amount, upon depositing with the bank department proper securities for the redemption and payment of its currency so issued. The statute further provided, in case, after lawful demand, default should be made in the payment of any of its notes in "lawful money of the United States," that the holder of such notes should cause the same to be protested; and the bank department was authorized, upon receiving notice of such protest, to institute proceedings as prescribed by the statute to enforce payment out of the securities deposited with him for that purpose, and, if need be,

[421]

to sell the same. On the 26th of March, 1863, one D. Valentine, being the owner and holder of a bill or note of the denomination of ten dollars, issued by the Metropolitan Bank, presented the same to the proper officer and demanded payment thereof in gold or silver coin of the United States, which was refused. The bank, however, tendered to Valentine, and offered to pay the note presented by him for redemption, with a note of the denomination of ten dollars, issued by the Secretary of the Treasury upon the credit of the United States, under and by virtue of an act of Congress, entitled "An act to authorize the issue of United States notes, and for the redemption or funding thereof, and for funding the floating debt of the United States," approved February 25th, 1862. The tender was refused. The note was duly protested, and notice of protest filed with the defendant, Henry H. Van Dyck, Superintendent of the Bank Department, as required by law. The defendant then notified the plaintiff, that the note which Valentine had presented for redemption must be paid within fifteen days in gold or silver coin, or, in default thereof, he would proceed to sell the securities deposited with him, and redeem said note according to the requirements of the statute.

The plaintiff accordingly brought this action to restrain the defendant from taking any steps towards the sale of the stock or trust funds in his hands belonging to plaintiff, on the ground that the money tendered by it to Valentine, by way of redemption, was "lawful money of the United States," and that said tender was a valid and legal tender. The issue involved, therefore, was the validity of the act of February 25th, 1862. If Congress had no power to provide for the payment of the national debt, and to create a currency for that purpose upon the credit of the government, and to make such currency a legal tender in payment of all debts public and private, then the money tendered by the plaintiff in payment of its note was not "lawful money of the United States," and no legal tender had been made. The court below held, that Congress had power to pass the law creating a national currency, and giving it the quality of a legal tender in payment of all debts, and enjoined the defendant from instituting proceedings to sell plaintiff's securities. From that decision this appeal was taken.

The importance of the question presented was, at the critical period when it arose, beyond all calculation, and the result of the decision will be of vital consequence as long as the republic shall endure. The government was engaged in suppressing the most formidable rebellion known to history; a struggle which has been justly regarded as the greatest of modern wars. Congress was consequently obliged to create a currency, and issue its bonds to provide means to maintain and support the fleets and armies enlisted to preserve its existence. If the courts should declare that Congress had no constitutional power to do this, or to make its notes a legal tender for private as well as public debts, the effect of the decision would render its currency and bonds valueless, and thus deprive the government of the only means for protecting itself from utter dissolution. It was an issue, therefore, which concerned the very existence of the nation—whether it could exercise the right of self-preservation under the Constitution. It has been frequently claimed that, independent of express statutory authority, the right of existence is inherent in every sovereignty, outweighing all considerations, and rising above all constitutional limitations. Philosophical and historical writers in different ages, and at different periods, have agreed that self-preservation is the supreme law, the application of which is universal, embracing within its scope communities as well as individuals, nations as well as men. History records instances in which this doctrine has been invoked, and constitutes the only authority upon which the measures of the government could be sustained. But history also teaches, that such a course, however justifiable for the moment, has always been productive of the greatest evils, because men who have exercised power without constitutional authority, even to save a nation's life, have never failed afterwards to make such actions a pretext for the exercise of unlawful authority to further schemes of personal ambition. Judge Porter, however, contended for no such doctrine. He recognized in it principles which were dangerous in the extreme. With marked ingenuity and great power of reasoning, he showed that the framers of our Constitution, in their consummate political wisdom, had provided for the exercise of such a power within that instrument by an express grant to Congress, so that, in the exercise of this most important attribute of sovereignty, it was not necessary to go beyond the organic law. The decision of the lower court was affirmed. Judges Selden and Denio dissented from the opinion of the court, upon the ground that, while Congress had power to issue money, it had no power to make its currency a legal tender in payment of private debts, or to compel an individual to accept it in payment therefor. Mr. J. V. W. Doty and George Ticknor Curtis appeared for the appellant; and William Curtis Noyes and John K. Porter for the respondents. Mr. Porter said:

MAY IT PLEASE THE COURT:—The able and exhaustive argument of my learned associate has left nothing with which I can occupy profitably the portion of time allotted for my part in the discussion, unless it be to submit some general suggestions as to the powers of Congress under the Constitution, in the varying exigencies of peace and of civil and foreign war.

Precisely here is the point from which, in our reasonings, we begin to diverge from my learned friend, Mr. Curtis, who, in his opening argument, has presented with so much perspicuity and learning all that can be urged against the power of the government to uphold itself against treason, and to defend against the violence of rebellion the people by whose authority the Union was ordained.

We submit that there is and can be no bolder constitutional heresy than the proposition which, though not advanced in terms, pervades the entire argument of our adversaries, that the Constitution is a mere compact between the States, or, at most, a mere power of attorney from the people to the federal government.

It is an *ordinance of sovereignty*, framed by the American people through their representatives in national convention, and subsequently ratified in separate conventions by the people of each of the original thirteen States. It has been ratified by the people of each of the younger States which have since presented themselves, from time to time, at the capitol for enrollment as members of the federal Union, and to seek protection and strength beneath the ægis of the Constitution.

In construing this ordinance, it is to be read in view of the unlimited power of those who framed it, and the magnitude of the objects which they proclaimed as intended and secured by its adoption.

The preamble of the Constitution is the *first utterance* of the nation as an organized government. It is the proclamation of their will, their purpose and their act, by the whole American people. In every exigency of national existence, it continues to announce to the government and to the world the sovereign objects the people sought to attain, and the sovereign powers they assumed in the Constitution to confer.

1. Object and purpose of the Constitution, and the powers delegated to give it effect.

In the light thus reflected upon it, by this unanimous and authentic utterance of the popular will, every clause of the ordinance is to be read. Each grant of power is to be expounded with a view to the great ends proclaimed in the preamble. The Constitution furnishes in its first words its own irrevocable rule of judgment.

"We, the People of the United States, in order to form a more perfect Union, establish justice, insure domestic tranquillity, provide for the common defense, promote the general welfare, and secure the blessings of liberty to ourselves and our posterity, do *ordain and establish* this Constitution for the United States of America."

Six objects are proclaimed:

(1.) Cementing the Union; (2.) Establishing justice; (3.) Insuring domestic tranquillity; (4.) Providing for the common defense; (5.) Promoting the general welfare; (6.) Securing to ourselves and our posterity the blessings of liberty.

To secure each of these great ends, in times of peace, of war, of insurrection, of invasion, of public repose, of public danger, the Constitution commits to Congress, as the representative of the popular will, the powers under consideration in this discussion, to be so exercised as to fulfill each and all of these high trusts.

It empowers the representatives of the people, by the enactment of laws, subject to the check of the Presidential veto:

(1.) To lay and collect taxes; (2.) To pay the public debts; (3.) To provide for the common defense; (4.) To regulate commerce; (5.) To coin money; (6.) To borrow money; (7.) To regulate the value of money; (8.) To punish counterfeiters of public securities and current coin; (9.) To declare war; (10.) To support armies; (11.) To maintain navies; (12.) To suppress insurrections; (13.) To repel invasions; (14.) To enact all laws *needful to the execution of these* powers, and of all *other* powers vested in the government, or any of its officers or departments under this Constitution.

Your Honors will observe, that in my abstract I have marshaled these powers, not in the order of their enumeration in the Constitution, but in the order appropriate to the discussion of the questions now submitted for judgment.

2. THE EXIGENCIES WHICH MADE IT NECESSARY TO PLEDGE THE PUBLIC CREDIT FOR THE PUBLIC DEFENSE.

Exigencies have arisen during the present war, which have made it necessary, in order to enable the government to execute these powers and to preserve its own existence, to employ more money than exists in gold and silver coin in the Western Hemisphere, and more than probably exists to-day on the face of the whole earth.

Ours is the wealthiest government in Christendom. Its resources are boundless, but they are not in coin. The people it is charged with the duty of defending, is rich, but not in coin. The country is at war with rebellious States in which *paper money* is the legal currency.

We have debts to pay; armies and navies to support; insurrection to suppress; invasion to repel; a country to defend.

Congress has adjudged, with the concurrence of the President, that an exigency has arisen in which it is "necessary and proper" for the protection of the people and their government, to make the public credit available for the public defense, and to make the notes of the United States, with a pledge of the public faith, a legal tender in payment of public and private debts; and laws have accordingly been enacted with that view, from time to time, as the necessities of the nation have demanded.

The enemies of the government, at home and abroad, denounced these acts, as they have denounced every measure of the war. The people, of course, acquiesced. They appreciated the public necessity. If Congress had *failed* to fulfill its trust, it would have pre-cipitated us into universal bankruptcy; and this, by an almost in-evitable necessity, would have involved the speedy dissolution of the government.

3. RESULTS OF THE MEASURES ADOPTED BY CONGRESS.

The policy adopted by Congress, with the concurrence of the Secretary of the Treasury, has vindicated itself by its works. The public credit has been maintained. We have upheld the army and the navy, while they in turn have upheld the government. We have narrowed the lines of rebellion and compressed the throat of treason. Under the measures adopted by Congress, and to-day arraigned before the judiciary which owes its being to the Consti-tution, the people of the loyal States, in their mere material inter-ests, are more prosperous now, in a time of public war, than any other people on earth in periods of profound peace.

But this acquiescence is not universal. The defendant in this particular case occupies a mere fiduciary relation, and has a record of loyalty which will honorably connect his name with the history of New York during this memorable war. But some half dozen gentlemen of a population of twenty millions, who seem to have personal and private interests which do not harmonize with "the general welfare " of the country, which it is the constitutional duty of Congress to promote; and who would prefer their payments in gold, at the premium it bears in times of civil commotion, have al-most simultaneously invoked the courts, in this and in other States, to nullify these acts of Congress, and to fulfill their oaths of fidelity to the Constitution, to which my learned adversary so impressively referred, by adjudging it to be utterly impotent even for its own salvation.

4. THE POWER OF CONGRESS TO DECLARE WHAT SHALL BE A LEGAL TENDER, NOT PROHIBITED BY THE CONSTITUTION.

There is no allegation, either by these non-contents or their counsel, that Congress is *prohibited* from declaring by law what shall be a legal tender in payment of private or of public debts.

They concede that the *omission* of such prohibition was not in-advertent; for the subject was present in the minds of the framers of the Constitution, and the tenth section of the same article which clothes Congress with the broad powers to which I have referred, expressly prohibits the *States* from making "anything but gold and silver coin a tender in payment of debts."[1]

The omission was confessedly due to no hesitation, either as to the propriety or necessity, of limiting the broad powers conferred on Congress by the eighth section; for the ninth section of the same article contains a series of emphatic and express prohibitions.

Neither can it be claimed that the omission was due to inadvertence on the part of the *people;* for after full discussion of every clause of the Constitution in the conventions of the several States, amendatory articles were proposed, consisting mainly of limitations of the powers of Congress; but no State could be found even to *propose* a prohibition of the exercise of the power, inherent in all sovereignties, of determining by law what should be a tender in payment of private and public debts.

Nor was the omission due to the people's being *unmindful* that this was an inherent right of the law-making power in every government claiming to be supreme. They recognized the *existence* of the power, by prohibiting its exercise by the States—which were not intended to be supreme in matters of national concern. They recognized its *necessity*, by not extending the prohibition to the general government, which, for national purposes, they invested with the high attributes of sovereignty.

5. WHY THIS POWER WAS NOT CONFERRED IN SPECIFIC TERMS.

They did not, indeed, commend and invite its exercise by conferring it in terms, as a separate and specific power; for they regarded a departure from the standard of gold and silver as an evil to be deprecated, unless public exigencies should make it a necessity to avert still greater evils.

To have disarmed the government of a power, which the experience of every civilized nation had shown to be at times a condition of national existence, would have been to deliver it over in bonds to the mercy of its enemies, in periods of civil convulsion or foreign war.

The Constitution was adopted by a people who, before they were organized into a nation, had known the grip of the strong vice of war. They had felt to the quick the mischiefs of a government currency, issued in deference to inexorable necessity, and to an amount far exceeding the means which could be pledged by the

---

[1] Constitution, art. 1, sec. 10.

States for its redemption; and they hoped that no future contingency would impose a like necessity, even on a responsible government. But they also knew that the exercise of the power of making the notes of the Colonies a legal tender in payment of the debts of their citizens, had alone enabled them, even with the aid of the British crown, to struggle through the French and Indian wars, and the hardships and vicissitudes of frontier growth.

6. How the power to create a legal tender was exercised in colonial times.

South Carolina led the van in 1703. New York and Connecticut followed, and made their notes a legal tender in 1709. Rhode Island fell into their wake in 1720; Pennsylvania in 1722; Maryland in 1733; Delaware in 1739; North Carolina in 1748; Virginia in 1755; Georgia in 1760.[1] In two of the States, tobacco and beaver skins were made a legal tender, and your Honors doubtless still retain your schoolboy memories of the celebrated Parson's Case, in which Wirt so charmingly interwove the story of the wrongs of the clergy, with the eloquence of Patrick Henry, in support of the act of the House of Burgesses of Virginia, authorizing the payment in gold and silver of the stipend which, in right of the church, they claimed to be payable only in the narcotic commended by Sir Walter Raleigh even on his way to the scaffold.[2]

In 1751, the imperial parliament, by the act of 24 George II, ch. 53, sec. 2, in the exercise of its unlimited and undoubted power, interdicted the further emission by the Colonies of bills of credit as a legal tender. That country was less benign to our fathers than to its later Colonies; for from 1833 to the present hour, the notes of the Bank of England have been, by act of parliament, a legal tender for private debts in every part of the British empire.[3]

The Colonies were at length relieved from this parliamentary restriction by the Declaration of Independence—a declaration which they found themselves unable to maintain, except by resuming the exercise of the governmental power of making their notes a legal tender for public and private debts.

The continental money has been much maligned; for its issues

---

[1] 11 Peters, 333–7, Briscoe v. Bank of Kentucky; Cong. Globe of 1862, p. 797.

[2] Wirt's Life of Henry, 38, Philadelphia ed. 1836.

[3] 3 & 4 William IV, ch. 98, sec. 6.

were controlled by no central government, and were too inordinate in amount to be redeemed by States reduced to bankruptcy by war.

Yet the continental money, such as it was, was the price paid for our existence as a government; and those only who do not deem liberty worth what it cost denounce the purchase, because it was not cheap enough for the money-changers, some of whom I fear would sell it now for half its cost, and take their pay in confederate scrip.

7. CONGRESS, BY CREATING A "UNIFORM" CURRENCY, FULFILLED A CONSTITUTIONAL TRUST.

Governments cannot *wage* war without the *means* of war. The Colonies were poor. We are rich. We know—the world knows—and our adversaries concede, that every dollar of our debt will be paid. Few men in the loyal States have ventured publicly to intimate a doubt on this subject, and as to-morrow looms higher than yesterday, it would be more grateful even to them, that the intimation should be forgotten, than that it should be remembered.

No man believes that the debt of England will ever be paid, unless on the condition of the downfall of the British monarchy. That debt is the security of the throne. No such security is needed by a free government. Ours is a debt due *to* the people, and *from* the people. It is contracted by the popular will, for the public defense.

Congress, in providing for the issue of treasury notes, was not insensible of the evils that followed in the train of the continental currency which paid the price of American independence. The chief of these was, that, the States having small resources, it became matter of interest to speculators in the misfortunes of their country to depreciate the public credit. Congress resolved, that in this war for *maintaining* our independence, the credit of the government should be upheld by the army, the navy, the people and *the law;* and that the debt we are compelled to incur should neither be multiplied *now* by exactions, nor repudiated *hereafter* on the pretext of such exactions.

A popular government has no interest of its own, apart from the interests of the whole body of the people. Congress imposed on itself, and on every officer of the government, the same burden it imposed on the citizens at large. It held its powers in trust for the nation, which could act through Congress, and through Congress *alone*.

When the government was suddenly summoned in the exigencies of a civil war, to which no parallel is furnished in the history of man, to an expenditure of two millions a day, it would have been a breach of trust to put its bonds *carte blanche* in the hands of speculators and bind the people to pay six millions for each two millions expended.

It would have been faithless if it had not used all its powers to protect them from exactions destructive of every interest.

The constitutional trust was fulfilled. The complaint of our adversaries is that it was not betrayed.

The people, through the House of Representatives and the President—the States, through their Senators in Congress—*adjudged* the existence of a necessity for means for the public defense, unparalleled in the history of nations; and in such an exigency *ordained*, in view of the impending struggle for the salvation of the Constitution and the republic, that there should be a single and uniform currency, alike for the people and the government, resting on the firm foundation of the public faith; and that in this crisis of war and civil convulsion the private creditor should exact no other or better pay than we bestow on the armies whom we charge by law with the duty of defending us, at the peril of mutilation and death, and at the easy rate of thirteen dollars a month payable in treasury notes.

The government held—as I trust this court will hold—that the creditor who remains at home has no higher rights in a period of public war than those whom the law summons to the deck or the camp.

8. Enumeration of the incidents of the war power vested in Congress.

It is conceded that the government can constitutionally compel every citizen to serve in the field; to serve, *with* treasury notes or *without* them; to serve on the public credit; and that it can shoot him, if he refuse, as a deserter.

It can appropriate the property of every citizen, if needful for the purposes of war, and with no security but the credit of the government.

It can levy taxes, not subject to restitution—poll taxes, income taxes, land taxes, partial or general, equal or unequal, measured only by the necessities of war—and this, though debtor and creditor be involved by it in common ruin and bankruptcy.

The government may, if essential to the preservation of its existence and to the public defense, substitute itself for the creditor, and appropriate every debt, pledging the faith of the nation for its payment.

These are propositions too familiar to the court to require argument or authority in their support. They have not been denied. They will not be controverted hereafter, either here or elsewhere, in the progress of a discussion, on the ultimate issue of which is poised the fate of the republic.

I have thus marshaled for the purposes of the present argument, a few of the stern and recognized incidents of the war power which the Constitution has confided, with limitations immaterial to the present issue, to the absolute discretion of Congress, except so far as even that discretion is controlled by the unlimited powers invested in the commander-in-chief for the purposes of public defense, in periods of civil convulsion and foreign war.

And yet, when the American Congress exercises *the first right of war*, by availing itself of the public credit for the public defense, we are told that it is bound by some constitutional implication, to provide a better currency for the defended than for their defenders; that, though the soldier and the sailor must be content with treasury notes, they shall not in the hands of their wives and children be a tender to the landlord for his rent or the baker for his bread; that the rights of more than half a million of citizens in arms are overrode by the more sacred rights of disaffected grocers and mortgagees at home, guaranteed to them, as they claim, by some unwritten clause of the Constitution.

9. REVIEW OF THE EVENTS OF THE WAR.—AN HISTORICAL RETROSPECT.

It becomes material, in one aspect of the discussion, to recur to the circumstances under which the notes of the United States were made a lawful tender by act of Congress.

In November, 1860, Mr. Lincoln was elected to the presidency by the votes of nearly two millions of our citizens. More than a million of votes were cast for Judge Douglas, who was equally true and loyal to the Constitution. One-third of the popular vote was divided between the two remaining candidates, who, after being defeated at the polls, illustrated the honor and good faith of themselves and their adherents, by uniting in a treasonable attempt to subvert the government which the people would not permit them to administer.

On the 10th of December, 1860, Mr. Cobb retired from the treasury department, and the frauds perpetrated with his connivance, in the interest of the conspirators, proved even more serious than had been foreshadowed by his apology six days before, in his report to Congress, for the depletion of an already rifled treasury.

Four days later, General Cass resigned the portfolio of the state department, on account of the refusal of President Buchanan to reinforce Fort Moultrie, which was then menaced by the rebels with guns stolen with the connivance of the Secretary of War. That functionary, though higher on the list of promotion, could not be spared from his present position; and accordingly General Cass was succeeded by Attorney-General Black, who, on the 20th of the preceding month, had favored Mr. Buchanan with an official opinion, announcing in effect, but with much decorous circumlocution, that the government was constitutionally impotent for its own defense, and existed only by the toleration of the South.

On the 24th of December, a convention of South Carolina adopted an ordinance of secession, by which it assumed to dissolve the American Union.

Two days later, Major Anderson, the Kentuckian in command, spiked the guns of Fort Moultrie, and transferred the little band—which represented there the force of the nation—to the narrower and more defensible limits of Fort Sumter.

On the 29th of December, Floyd, having purloined and transferred to the confederates all the national arms and munitions of war which they thought worth their acceptance, and having divided and dispersed the American forces to suit the purposes of his accomplices, resigned his position in the Cabinet to take a commission in the confederate army, alleging as his reason that the President had broken faith with the rebels by not ordering Major Anderson back to Fort Moultrie, where they could have seized him more conveniently.

On the 8th of January, 1861, President Buchanan sent a message to Congress, communicating so much as he thought proper of his personal correspondence with the South Carolina conspirators; announced that "we are in the midst of a great revolution," and gravely recommended to the people of the loyal States to yield to the rebels, and conciliate them by a new appeal "to the ballot box."

The other Cotton States, having in the meantime perfected their conspiracy—having possessed themselves by treachery, by surprise, by theft and by violence of the treasure, the arms and the strong-holds of the nation—followed at the heels of South Carolina, and adopted ordinances of secession.

The rebel flag was raised by Mississippi on the 9th of January, 1861; by Alabama and Florida on the 11th; by Georgia on the 19th, and by Louisiana on the 25th of January.

Six days afterwards, at a convention held at our own State capitol, the memorable announcement went forth from high author-ity, as a response from the North: "Already six States have with-drawn from this confederacy.   Revolution has actually begun."

On the 23d of February, 1861, the President-elect made his way to the capitol; and the enemies of the country continue to this day to reproach him for wearing the Scotch cap and cloak recom-mended by Gen. Scott, which saved him from recognition by the assassins who were awaiting his arrival at Baltimore.

President Buchanan was unfortunately under the influence, and persistently blind to the purposes of those who were in league to remove his successor and to subvert by violence the government each had been chosen by the people to administer.

On the 4th of March, President Lincoln was inaugurated, and was saved again from assassination by the forecast of Gen. Scott, who insisted that his predecessor should accompany him on his way to the capitol, and that the avenue should be guarded by an armed soldiery.

Three days afterwards, Beauregard, a former protégé of the government, was put in command of the army of rebels who had been assembled to seize Fort Sumter.

On the 14th of April, that fortress fell; and if the constitutional theory of our adversaries could be maintained, on that day this government fell.

On the 15th of April, President Lincoln issued his proclamation, summoning 75,000 men to arms, to maintain and defend the Union and the Constitution.

On the 21st of July, the national army was defeated at Bull Run.   On the 20th of August, Gen. McClellan assumed command of the army of the Potomac.   From that time, until long after the enactment of this law, the guns of the rebel army were trained on the capitol, and its tents and watch-fires within view from its cupola.

At the commencement of the then fiscal year, the entire aggre-
28

gate amount of gold and silver coin in the country, north and south, so far as it could be deduced from reliable statistics, was $243,010,103. If your Honors should have occasion to verify this fact, you will find a statement on the subject in detail in the 48th volume of Hunt's Merchants' Magazine, 215, in the number of that work issued in March, 1863.

This was much less than the country needed to borrow for immediate use. Accordingly, on the 25th of February, 1862, an act of Congress was passed to provide means for the immediate payment of the arrears due to the army and navy, by issuing $150,000,000 in United States notes, in addition to the public loans previously made or authorized, making these notes a tender in payment of debts due to and from the people and the government, and providing for the funding of the public debt and payment of the interest in coin.

The particular provisions of that act have been brought to your Honors' notice by my learned associate. I need only make a passing allusion to the circumstances under which it was enacted.

It was voted for within reach of a night assault by 100,000 rebels in arms. The war had been begun against the pillaged nation, under the leadership of those who had rifled its treasury. It had been begun against an unarmed nation, by those who had been trained to the science of war at its expense, and who, after being laden with its honors and enriched by its bounty, banded together as conspirators against its life.

The conspiracy had been well matured. At home and abroad the work was prepared. The courts of Europe had been preoccupied by the able, adroit and busy emissaries of the South. Every purchasable government press had been suborned to the use and interests of the rebels. The North had but one friend among the nations of the earth—that friend the Russian Czar, exercising dominion over portions of three continents, Europe, Asia and America; in sympathy with us, because we had common enemies; but passive, because our controversy had no relation to the interests of his dynasty.

Our credit was undoubted throughout christendom; but no nation on earth had a motive to aid us either with money, with men or with arms. Under these circumstances we had only to rely, as among monarchies every republic must rely, on the patriotism, the fidelity and the resources of our own people. That reliance was not in vain. Three-quarters of a million of men, untrained to arms, interposed their breasts and their bayonets between the government and the public enemy.

The President, unused to the responsibilities of command, was nevertheless faithful and loyal to his trust. He needed, as the head of the nation—what he has hitherto received, and what he will receive to the end—the earnest, constant, enduring support of every cordial friend of the government. Congress coming fresh from the people, was also true and faithful to its trust. It needs no other vindication of its patriotism, its wisdom and its forecast in regard to the enactment now in question, than has been furnished by subsequent events.

I pass over intermediate matters familiar to your Honors, and which have already gone to history, where your judgment is soon to follow them.

10. NATURE OF THE CRISIS WHICH DEMANDED THE PASSAGE OF THE LEGAL-TENDER ACTS.

Congress assembled on the 1st of December, 1862. The President, in his message, communicated the fact that in the fiscal year ending on the 30th of June, 1862, the year in which the law in question was enacted, the disbursements of the government had been $570,841,700 25, of which $529,692,460 50 had been borrowed on the credit of the government. The payment of specie had been suspended, not only by the banks, but by the people. It was a necessity of war, acquiesced in by the common consent of the nation. The President directed the attention of Congress to intervening events, which had demonstrated the wisdom and necessity of the law adopted at the previous session, and submitted for their consideration the claims of the people and the government in the existing exigencies of the nation.

After full deliberation and discussion in Congress, a similar act was passed, which will be found in the Statutes at Large for 1863, page 709, chapter 73. The act was approved by the President, and became a law on the 3d of March, the last day of the third session of the 37th Congress. It was entitled "An act to provide ways and means for the support of the government," an ordinary title, to which events had given an extraordinary significance.

The first section authorized the Secretary of the Treasury to borrow $900,000,000 on bonds of the government, payable in coin, at periods ranging from ten to forty years, with interest semi-annually, payable also in coin. The second section authorized him to issue, on the credit of the United States, $400,000,000 of treasury notes, and $150,000,000 of United States notes, exchangeable for prior issues of a like character, and to be made a legal tender to a similar extent with previous issues. The third section authorized him, if required by the exigencies of the public service for the payment of the army and navy, and other creditors of the government, to issue on the credit of the United States $150,000,000 of United States notes, not bearing interest, which notes so issued should be lawful money, and a legal tender in payment of all debts, public and private, within the United States, except for duties on imports and interest on the public debt.

Thus, on the 3d of March, 1863, by the concurrent and recorded judgment of the popular and the executive departments of the government, $1,600,000,000 were required to meet the current obligations of the nation, beyond the resources it anticipated from the revenues on imports, the sales of the public lands, the proceeds of the stamp acts, and the direct taxes imposed on the incomes and industry of the country. One-third of those bound to contribute to the expenses of the government, had already been reduced by their own rebellion to destitution and bankruptcy; and the property remaining in their possession was protected against federal demands by military ramparts and bayonets. Three-quarters of a million of loyal men were in arms on the land, and a proportionate number on the sea, to maintain the government by force. All must be fed, clothed, and supplied with the munitions of war.

Sixteen hundred millions were to be drawn for the exigencies of the ensuing year alone—and on the theory of our adversaries, this amount was to be drawn in coin, and not from our entire population of 31,000,000, but from 20,000,000 of loyal citizens. On their theory, each soldier, sailor, man, woman, child, must contribute $80 in gold and silver, besides all other State and national burdens, and this to maintain the government to the 1st of January, 1864.

This was the nature of the public crisis, which in the judgment of Congress demanded the enactment of these laws. They are *pari materia*, and stand or fall together. The Supreme Court of the United States has already announced its judgment of the perils which overhung the people and the government, by declaring on our judicial records, simultaneously with the passage of one of these acts, that we were in the crisis of " the greatest civil war known in the history of the human race."[1]

---

[1] The Prize Cases, 2 American Law Register, N. S. 339.

11. The desperate alternative forced upon Congress.

The question presented to Congress for decision was : Shall the government be dissolved ?   The alternative was, the exercise, in a period of public war, of an inherent sovereign power, not prohibited by the Constitution, or a bankrupt treasury, a bankrupt people, and a government overthrown.

Two millions of dollars a day must be paid out by the government for the ordinary disbursements of war.   Its efficient arms had been stolen, and it must replace them from the markets of Europe. It could not borrow abroad, from enemies who looked and longed for its destruction.   It could not borrow at home in gold and silver, without draining the life-blood of commerce, and this by forced loans involving universal bankruptcy.   It could not meet present demands by taxation, for it needed the money to sustain the machinery of taxation, and one-third of those subject to assessment were making war upon the taxing power.   It could not wait, and it could not want.   It might tax, but the people could not pay.   It could sacrifice private property by seizure and forced sales, but there was not enough gold and silver coin on the continent to buy what the government would be compelled to sell.

All powers necessary to the execution of its governmental trusts were expressly granted to Congress by the Constitution.   If the power to enact these laws be incident to the necessity, it existed ; for the necessity was undeniable.   One-third of the nation was using against the other two-thirds the very power, the existence of which for the destruction of the government was recognized and defended by those who denied its existence for the purpose of government protection.

The alternative was plain.   The government, to which alone the creditor could look for protection, must be upheld ; must uphold the Constitution and the laws ; must sustain the people, the debtor, the creditor, the common rights and common existence, by substituting the public credit and the plighted faith of the nation, for the gold and silver coinage, which had formed the theoretical, but at no portion of our history the practical currency of the country.

All individual rights of life, liberty and property, are subordinate to the right of national existence.   Rights of *property* exist only through and under government.   When the government itself is in peril of subversion by war, the Constitution has wisely left its arm of protecting power bare and free. When all rights are endangered, it is better that some be suspended, than that all should perish. The right of the government in the maintenance of its sovereignty, not only to kill its enemies but to compel its citizens to die in its defense, is conceded by those who deny it the power to maintain navies, support armies, suppress insurrections, provide for the common defense, and wage war for the maintenance of its own existence.

The right of Congress to make United States notes a legal tender, in the exercise of the *specific* powers to levy taxes, and to borrow, to coin and to regulate the value of money, has been so fully considered in the numerous briefs and arguments of my learned associates, and so ably discussed in the opinions delivered by the Judges in the Seventh Judicial District, that I shall feel at liberty to confine myself to the single question of the validity of the law, under the *general authority* vested in Congress by the last clause in the eighth section of the first article of the Constitution.

12. THE POWER TO PASS THE LEGAL-TENDER ACTS EXISTS BY EXPRESS GRANT, AND BY NECESSARY IMPLICATION.

The people, after declaring that Congress shall have certain specific powers, conclude the enumeration by an express grant of the broad and plenary power : " To make all laws which shall be necessary and proper for carrying into execution the foregoing powers and all other powers vested by this Constitution in the government of the United States, or in any department or officer thereof."

So clearly does the very idea of government presuppose the existence of power in some of its departments, to do such acts as may be needful to fulfill its trusts and maintain its authority, that some of our earlier statesmen were of opinion that Congress would have possessed it, even without the specific grant, as a necessary and inherent right of sovereignty—and that it, therefore, added nothing more than would have been plainly implied, even in the absence of such a provision. Those who would use the Constitution as a weapon with which to cleave down the government, are fond of quoting these opinions, as authority for expunging this clause from the instrument—while they sturdily reject the postulate that the power would have existed by necessary implication, even without the grant. They are not at liberty to ignore at once the clause and the implication. It is a very easy, but a very illogical process, to strike out the express grant, on the ground that the power was inherent in Congress, and then to deny the power on the ground of the absence of an express grant.

The provision stands. It can neither be expunged nor ignored. *Primus inter pares*, it is second in authority to no other provision of the Constitution. Events have demonstrated the wisdom of those who framed it. Ordinary powers were enumerated, because they were capable of enumeration. Other powers were granted, to be exercised only in case of necessity. As the varying necessities of national existence could not be foreseen, these did not admit of enumeration. As some department of the government must judge of the existence of the necessity, which was the sole condition of the power, it was committed to the concurrent judgment of the representatives of the people, and the representatives of the States, subject to the check of the presidential veto.

The law in question is upheld by this provision of the Constitution, if, in the existing exigencies of the nation, its enactment was "*necessary and proper for carrying into execution*" the powers vested in Congress, "to lay and collect taxes"—"to borrow money on the credit of the United States"—"to regulate the value" of money—"to provide and maintain a navy"—"to raise and support armies"—"to suppress insurrection"—"to pay the debts and provide for the common defense and general welfare of the United States."

If this legislation was necessary and proper to enable Congress to fulfill these high trusts, the law must stand or the Constitution must fall.

13. POSTULATES WHICH THOSE WHO SEEK TO NULLIFY THE LEGAL·
TENDER ACTS MUST ESTABLISH.

When our adversaries invoke the subversion of these acts of Congress by the judiciary, they are charged with the burden of maintaining one of two propositions.

The first is, that there *is* no such necessity as these laws presuppose and recognize : that there is gold and silver coin enough in the loyal States to fulfill all private obligations, and with the surplus to conquer ten millions of men who can command gold in the markets of Europe, closed to us ; who can issue hundreds of millions of confederate scrip for every million of Northern coin, and who recognize and pay no debts among themselves, except by pledging the faith of a league of rebellious States.

As to this, I need only say it is a purely political question, committed to the judgment of another department of the government, whose decision on this state of facts is not subject here to review. The Constitution having intrusted Congress with the duty of determining what may be needful, in the varying exigencies of public necessity, to carry into effect the powers with which it is vested— its judgment, in good faith, and in its own sphere of action, is absolute and subject to no review. This proposition is too clearly settled by authority to require elucidation by argument. I will ask the court to note a reference to a few additional cases not cited in the printed points.[1]

Failing in this, our adversaries must maintain the proposition, that, conceding these laws, by which the notes of the United States are declared a legal tender, to be "necessary and proper for carrying into execution" the specific powers vested in Congress— conceding them to be within the very terms of the general grant of power at the close of the eighth section—they are still in conflict with the Constitution, because they are not specially authorized *elsewhere* in the same instrument, within the ordinary and enumerated powers of Congress, to be exercised irrespective of any public necessity.

They do not advance this proposition in terms; and yet, unless they can establish that we are powerless to pass these laws—though they are demanded for the common defense, as an iron necessity of war, to avert the downfall of the government; though this necessity is adjudged by Congress, with the concurrence of the President; though the fact exists, and is known of all men ; though without the exercise of this power the Constitution itself is paralyzed—we submit that our opponents have not gained a stand-point, from which they can call on the courts to fulfill their trust by scuttling the national ship and going down with the wreck.

As the means adopted by Congress were appropriate to the required ends, and as subsequent events have demonstrated that they precisely met the public necessity to which all other remedies were inadequate, the *onus* is upon those who seek to nullify these laws to establish that the means resorted to were plainly excluded by the Constitution. In the language of Chief Justice Marshall, those who contend that the government " may not select any appropriate

---

[1] The Prize Cases, 2 Am. Law Register, N. S. 335; United States *v.* Probasco, Ib. 419, 430 ; McCulloch *v.* State of Maryland, 4 Wheat. 316, 422 ; Wheaton's Life of Pinkney, 561 ; Martin *v.* Mott, 12 Wheat. 31.

means—that one particular mode of effecting the object is excluded—must take upon themselves the burden of establishing the
exception." [1]

14. THE POWER TO CREATE A LEGAL TENDER EXISTED PRIOR TO
THE ADOPTION OF THE CONSTITUTION, AND WAS EITHER
VESTED IN CONGRESS OR EXTINGUISHED.

The conceded absence of any *express prohibition* on this subject, has peculiar force and significance. The power of making
the paper of the government a legal tender, existed and was exercised in every State, from the Declaration of Independence to the
adoption of the federal Constitution. In the *partition* then made
of governmental powers, this, being one essential for national purposes, would appropriately be conferred upon the national Congress. It was vested in the Congress of the United States, or it
was vested nowhere. It was not one of the powers "reserved to
the States respectively, or to the people" by tenth article of the
amendments to the Constitution. It was not reserved to the States,
for they were expressly prohibited from its exercise. It was not reserved to the people, for it was not personal and popular in its nature. It was a high governmental power—a known and recognized
attribute of national sovereignty. It was either committed to Congress, or annihilated. There is no presumption in favor of the voluntary and deliberate extinguishment of a sovereign power, essential to the authority and existence of every nation, which would
compete on equal terms with the other nations of the earth.

15. THE INQUIRY WHETHER SELF-PRESERVATION IS AN INHER-
ENT RIGHT RISING ABOVE CONSTITUTIONAL LIM-
ITATIONS, DOES NOT ARISE.

The federal government, in its national relations, is invested
with the powers of sovereignty. If the Constitution had failed to
invest it with these, it would, in the language of Chief Justice
Marshall, have been only "a splendid bauble." Mere forms are
nothing. Substance is everything. It was said by Napoleon, that
"a throne is a mere block of wood, covered with velvet." A national Constitution, which failed to organize a nation, would be
even more unmeaning than the throne stripped of its covering.

In the special message of President Monroe, communicated to

[1] 4 Wheaton, 410.

Congress on the 4th of May, 1822, after giving the history of the Constitution, he proceeds to say : "Thus were two separate and independent governments established over our Union—one for *local* purposes, over each State, by the people of the State ; the other for *national* purposes, by the people of the United States. The whole power of the people on the representative principle is divided between them. The State governments are independent of each other, and to the extent of their powers are complete sovereignties. The national government begins where the State governments terminate, except in some instances where there is a concurrent jurisdiction between them. This government is also, to the extent of its powers, a complete sovereignty."[1] On the question of the supremacy and sovereignty of the federal government, within the scope of its powers in all matters of national concern, I beg leave to refer the Court to the opinions of Chief Justice Marshall, in the United States Bank case, and of Mr. Justice Nelson, in the Tax case.[2]

We do not claim that the courts should, in an iota, transcend the limits of the Constitution ; but simply that they should deal with it fairly, with a view to its avowed objects and ends.

The case has not yet arisen—I trust it may never arise—when the judiciary may be compelled to pass on the question of the ultimate power of all governments in maintaining their own existence.

It was in reference to such a question, that Cromwell, in 1656, speaking in behalf of England, addressed language to the British Parliament, which has been deemed worthy of a place in history :

"If nothing should ever be done, but what is *'according to law,'* the throat of the nation may be cut while we send for some one to make a law. Therefore, certainly it is a pitiful beastly notion to think, though it *be* for *ordinary* government to live by law and rule, yet if a government in *extraordinary* circumstances go beyond the law, even for self-preservation, it is to be clamored at, and blattered at. When matters of necessity come, then, without guilt, extraordinary remedies may be applied.   *   *   And I must say I do not know one action of this government—no, not one—but it hath been in order to the peace and safety of this nation."

If, in the progress of events in revolutionary times, that question should ever arise, the courts will have occasion to weigh the

---

[1] 2 Statesman's Manual, 497.
[2] 4 Wheat. 405 ; 25 Howard's Pr. R. 14, 16.

views of an eminent southern civilian, submitted as the result of calm study and a mature reflection, in a posthumous publication on the principles of government. Mr. Calhoun says : " Exigencies will occur, in which the entire powers and resources of the community will be needed to defend its existence. When this is at stake, every other consideration must yield to it. Self-preservation is the supreme law, as well with communities as individuals." [1] If this principle of ultimate governmental power has indeed a foothold in the polity of nations, it could find no exigency in which it would apply with greater force, than immediate peril of national dissolution in the throes of intestine war. The declaration of Vattel, that "a civil war breaks the bands of society and government, or at least suspends their force and effect," is with approval cited in the same opinion of the Supreme Court of the United States, which, in March last, characterized this as " the greatest civil war known in the history of the human race." [2]

I have referred to this mooted question of the inherent governmental right of self-defense, rising in great exigencies above all constitutional limitations, not with a view of discussing it, or expressing any opinion as to its soundness, but for the sole purpose of distinguishing it from the position we maintain, and with which our opponents seem to confound it.

We claim that Congress was authorized by express constitutional grant, to exercise the powers in question, when demanded by governmental necessity, and that the means it employed, having been not only *appropriate* but *efficacious* to meet the necessity, its decision on these questions, purely political in their nature, is not subject to review and reversal in any judicial tribunal, but binds the whole American people, by whose authority and in whose name it was pronounced.

16. MEANING OF THE TERMS "LEGAL TENDER" AND "MONEY" CONSIDERED AND DISTINGUISHED.—THE SUBJECT OF LEGAL TENDER.

The substantial issue is on the right to make the notes of the United States a legal tender. A minor issue is raised as to the power of Congress to declare them to be *money*. That is a question of very trivial moment, as without such a declaration they *are*

[1] 1 Calhoun's Works, p. 10.
[2] The Prize Cases, 2 Am. Law Reg. N. S. 337, 339.

money by the common recognition of all civilized communities.[1] If Congress had failed to make the declaration, the omission would be quite immaterial, as the Supreme Court of the United States had held treasury notes to be money, even before they were made a legal tender.[2]

But on the great question in the case, whether the government can make this money a legal tender, your Honors will not fail to observe that the very term *"legal* tender " imports, that the subject is one by the common understanding of mankind, belonging in every sovereignty to the law-making power. It has been recognized as such in every civilized nation. Gold and silver have been a legal tender with us. Not so in Great Britain. There, except for small sums, it is *gold* coin or notes of the Bank of England. Not so in France. There it is *silver* coin—and government paper in periods of public exigency.

Our first government coinage was copper; of which 300 tons were converted into money, at the mint, during the secretaryship of General Hamilton.

Doubtless, gold and silver, and government paper, have been generally preferred by the law-making powers of the various modern nations. That this was not always so, even with them, is illustrated by the fact that we have the record in British history, of the time when a white woman was money, and when a fair-haired Saxon slave boy was a medium of commercial exchange, and the subject of tender in payment of civil debts; and it is a curious feature of English History, alluded to by Macaulay, that there is no record to be found in the Statutes at Large, to this day, of the abolition in that country of the institution of human slavery.

Whatever, in any country, may happen to be for the time the recognized medium of commercial exchange, whether gold, silver, or government paper, it derives its character as legal tender, not from the material of which it is composed, but from the imprint of the law-making or sovereign power. I may have a chest full of gold bars, but, without the stamp of government authority, it is not a legal tender in payment of a debt for a loaf of bread.

When a penny of Cæsar was brought by a disciple to one wiser

---

[1] Wharton's Law Lexicon; Burrill's Law Dictionary; Webster's and Worcester's Dictionaries; McCulloch's Commercial Dictionary, title Money; Rees' Cyclopedia, title Coin; 4 Webster's Works, 339; Miller *v.* Race, 1 Borrow's R. 452.

[1] United States *v.* Morgan, 11 Howard, 160: WOODBURY, J.

than man, the inquiry he deemed appropriate was, not what metal
is this, but, "whose image and superscription is this?" It was the
recognition by the king of kings, of the authority of human laws,
and the stamp of national sovereignty.

17. ALL THE ATTRIBUTES OF SOVEREIGNTY PRESUMED TO EXIST,
     TILL THOSE WHO DENY IT ESTABLISH THE CONTRARY.

Dealing then, as we are, with a recognized attribute in every
nation of the law-making power, we are entitled to presume its existence, until those who deny it can establish, with irresistible
clearness, its annihilation. It must be shown to be affirmatively
excluded, under all circumstances, in all exigencies, or it will be
deemed to be embraced in a Constitution designed to *distribute* and
not to *destroy* the attributes of representative sovereignty.

In every nation, all the legitimate powers of government are
lodged in some of its various departments, by the necessity of
social and national existence. By the law of human imperfection,
no Constitution ever devised by man, contained a full bill of particulars of all governmental powers. But this proves, not the absence
of the powers, but the imperfection of constitutional enumeration
and forecast.

As this power to make laws for upholding the nation is neither
in the States nor the executive, it is in the people, or the Congress
to which they have deputed authority, to make laws for carrying
into execution all powers belonging to or inherent in the whole
body of the government.

It is to be remembered that the Constitution was framed with
reference to perpetuity; to all the exigencies of human affairs in
the future vicissitudes of the race. Its *general* powers were
granted in terms sufficiently broad and comprehensive to cover
those cases, certain to arise, but which no human foresight could
anticipate and provide for in detail. The establishment of a government with power to perpetuate and maintain itself, was the
primary purpose of the Constitution; as the want of such power
was the primary mischief which led to its adoption.

In the case of McCulloch *v.* The State of Maryland, Chief
Justice Marshall, in the most memorable judicial opinion which il-
lumines the annals of American jurisprudence, established immu-
tably the principles of construction which control the judicial
department of the government in expounding the Constitution. It

was of that unanimous decision of the ultimate tribunal of the nation that William Pinkney said, he saw in it "a pledge of the immortality of the Union." Your Honors will have occasion to recur
to the opinion anew, and without pausing to follow the train of
that luminous argument, I desire only to call the attention of the
court to one or two brief passages which relate to the particular
clause of the Constitution empowering Congress to make all laws
which shall be necessary and proper to carry into execution the
powers of the government. "The subject is, the execution of
those great powers on which the welfare of a nation essentially depends. It must have been the intention of those who gave these
powers to insure, as far as human prudence could insure, their
beneficial execution. This could not be done by confining the
choice of means to such narrow limits as not to leave it in the
power of Congress to adopt any which might be appropriate, and
which were conducive to the end. This provision is made in a
Constitution intended to indure for ages to come, and, consequently, to be adapted to the various *crises* of human affairs. To have
prescribed the means by which government should, in all future
time, execute its powers, would have been to change, entirely, the
character of the instrument, and give it the properties of a legal
code. It would have been an unwise attempt to provide, by immutable rules, for exigencies which, if foreseen at all, must have
been seen dimly, and which can be best provided for as they occur.
To have declared that the best means shall not be used, but those
alone without which the power given would be nugatory, would
have been to deprive the legislature of the capacity to avail itself
of experience, to exercise its reason, and to accommodate its legislation to circumstances. If we apply this principle of construction
to any of the powers of the government, we shall find it so pernicious in its operation that we shall be compelled to discard it.

"We admit, as all must admit, that the powers of the government are limited, and that its limits are not to be transcended. But
we think the sound construction of the Constitution must allow to
the national legislature that discretion, with respect to the means
by which the powers it confers are to be carried into execution,
which will enable that body to perform the high duties assigned to
it, in the manner most beneficial to the people. Let the end be
legitimate, let it be within the scope of the Constitution, and all
means which are appropriate, which are plainly adapted to that

end, which are not prohibited, but consist with the letter and spirit of the Constitution, are constitutional." [1]

We submit, that upon the principles settled by this decision, the laws in question are plainly within the powers expressly vested in Congress by the Constitution. If the question were even one of doubt—one on which, in the language of Chief Justice Marshall, "human reason might pause, and the human judgment be suspended"—you would not on such an issue, bring the judiciary in collision with the other two departments of the government, but would solve the question, by giving your country the benefit of the doubt. Even in such a case, the court would peremptorily refuse, in the language of Justice Grier, "to cripple the arm of the government, and paralyze its powers by subtle definitions and ingenious sophisms." [2]

The question is, not how three members of the convention which framed the Constitution were induced to propose it to the people—but what was the intent evinced by the people in its adoption? The inquiry is, how would it have been read by Washington, Hamilton, and Madison, in the light of the events now transpiring—which have developed the necessity and wisdom of these general grants of power. As George Mason said to John C. Calhoun, "the Constitution has proved to be wiser than the men who made it."

President Madison, in his annual message of December 5, 1815, after the close of the war with Great Britain, introduced a passage, which leaves no doubt how he would have solved the question, in a national exigency like that in which these laws were passed.

"The absence of the precious metals will, it is believed, be a temporary evil ; but until they can again be rendered the general medium of exchange, it devolves on the wisdom of Congress to provide a *substitute* which shall equally engage the confidence and accommodate the wants of the citizens throughout the Union. If the operation of the State banks cannot produce this result, the probable operation of a national bank will merit consideration ; and, if neither of these expedients be deemed effectual, it may be necessary to ascertain the terms upon which the notes of the government, no longer required as an instrument of credit, shall be

[1] 4 Wheaton, 415, 421.
[2] 2 American Law Register, N. S. 339.

issued upon motives of general policy as a common medium of circulation.[1]

It is to be remembered, too, that this is not an issue between the States and the nation—between two clashing sovereignties—but simply a question whether the power we contend for has been annihilated, or whether it exists in the federal government for the common protection of the people and the States. We submit that, in determining this issue, the Constitution is to be read as an ordinance of sovereignty, by the people of a continent, for the maintenance of public law and liberty, and the defense of themselves and their posterity. It is also to be remembered that the paramount duty of every citizen, every officer, every judge, State and federal, is to uphold the government and defend the Constitution. Especially is this our duty when the issue presented is, whether the Constitution, adopted by the people for their protection, shall be so wrested from its objects as to inure only to the benefit of the public enemy. It happens, by a singular coincidence, that the appeal to your Honors, to declare the government impotent for its own defense, is made at a time when the heels of the rebel soldiery are polluting the soil of a free State, between the capitol of New York, in which we hold our deliberations, and the capitol of the nation, where final judgment is to be pronounced.

On the theory we maintain, the Constitution was designed as a citadel to secure public liberty and repose. On the theory of our adversaries, it was to serve as a grave, in which sovereignty should be buried alive, to linger only until life should be extinguished by suffocation.

"*E pluribus unum*" is not a mere rhetorical phrase, but the terse record of the philosophy of our system of government—a stumbling-block only to those who reject even the mathematical postulate that the whole is greater than either of its parts. The effect of yielding to the views of these tenacious friends of the Constitution, would be to relieve them and us from its burdens and its protection. It would be to deliver over the government to its enemies, "*monstrum ingens—cui lumen ademptum*"—nay, more, with its inherent force and its constitutional power of self-defense, bound to helplessness with cords spun from its own fibre.

[1] 1 Statesman's Manual, 330.

ARGUMENT OF WILLIAM A. BEACH,

In Defense of Samuel North and Others, Charged with
Tampering with Soldiers' Votes.

BEFORE A MILITARY COMMISSION AT WASHINGTON, D. C., FEBRUARY, 1865.

Analysis of Mr. Beach's Argument.

Samuel North, Levi Cohn, Marvin M. Jones, and two others, were tried before a military commission, convened at the city of Washington in February, 1865, charged with having falsely and fraudulently signed and issued election blanks, purporting to have been sent by soldiers in the field, to their homes in the State of New York; and for attempting to cast the votes of absent soldiers, in fraud of the rights of the true elector. The accusation was rendered doubly criminal and detestable, in view of the events transpiring at the time, and ex-

29   [449]

cited popular wrath and indignation everywhere. It was during the war of the rebellion, at the critical period, when it became necessary to choose a President of the United States. In the dark and perilous hours of that great conflict, which was to decide the existence of our institutions, any attempt to interfere with the political rights of our country's defenders could not be tolerated or excused upon any pretext.

The circumstances surrounding the case were as follows: The legislature of the State of New York, on the 21st of April, 1864, passed an act to enable qualified electors of the State, absent therefrom, and in the military service of the United States and navy thereof, to vote (Laws 1864, ch. 253). The soldier was required, by the provisions of the act, to authorize any elector of the town or city where he resided to cast his vote for him, such authority to be in writing properly executed and acknowledged. The ballot and the written authority were to be sealed in an envelope, which was to be placed inside of another envelope marked " soldier's vote," and forwarded to the elector authorized to cast it, by mail or otherwise. The delivery or presentation of any forged, altered or changed ballot was declared to be a misdemeanor, subjecting the offender upon conviction to fine and imprisonment.

It was alleged that the defendants had prepared and forwarded spurious votes, and also that they had abstracted genuine votes and inclosed others instead. The charge was, therefore, of the most heinous character, being a political crime and an offense against society, meriting the severest punishment. Public opinion and public prejudice were strongly against the prisoners, and their condemnation was demanded by the press of the country. The accused were arraigned before a military court, sitting at the national capitol, a tribunal which, as the sequel shows, had no power or authority to detain the prisoners, and was without jurisdiction of the offense charged.

Under such circumstances Mr. Beach made his masterly argument in behalf of the defendants. But it was at a juncture when the advocate appears to the best advantage and is of the greatest service. As was truly remarked by Mr. James T. Brady, in his address in defense of the " Savannah Privateers," " the advocate is of very little use in the days of prosperity and peace, in the periods of repose. It is only when public opinion, the strong power of government, the formidable array of influence, the force of a nation, or the fury of a multitude is directed against you, that the advocate is of any use."

The defense presented by Mr. Beach was twofold in its character: first, he contended that the court had no power or authority to detain, try or sentence the prisoners, and, secondly, that from the evidence in the case it appeared that the defendants were innocent of the charges preferred. The result was complimentary, not only to the intellectual powers of the advocate, but to the sterling integrity of the members of the tribunal whom he addressed, who despite the pressure of public opinion and the clamor of an injured community, refused to usurp powers which they did not possess, and discharged the prisoners.

For the prosecution appeared General John A. Foster, the judge advocate. The prisoners were represented by William A. Beach, of New York, and John D. McPherson and Mr. Gillet, of Washington. After the evidence was all in, Mr. Beach addressed the court as follows :

MAY IT PLEASE THE COMMISSION:—I may assume, with propriety, that Your Honors and myself have a common purpose in our present labor. It is, to accomplish essential justice. Of course this is the sole object of this honorable Court. I know the partisanship of counsel, the partial prepossessions of professional effort. But there are occasions of exalted interest, which inspire the spirit of advocacy with something of their own elevation. I deem this one of them. It reaches the domain of executive power. It associates with the cardinal principles of government. It concerns the sacred rights of personal liberty and of trial by jury. It is magnified by the demands of exigent war. We cannot but feel that it is invested with unusual and elevating consequence. While I acknowledge the enlarged sentiments it excites, I greatly regret that it does not confer a corresponding ability for their expression.

I. POWERS ASSUMED BY MILITARY COURTS.

I design no disrespect by the remark, that I speak rather for my cause than for the Court. As an organized tribunal of the country I render to it, personally and collectively, the respect due to its dignified position. Still, I cannot resist the conviction, that this is not the safest judgment seat for civil right and individual liberty. Your Honors are a military tribunal, instructed soldiers, imbued, it is true, with the chivalric characteristics of your profession, but inclined, nevertheless, to the severe and summary conclusions taught by the necessities of the camp and the field. I miss the forms and the principles of civil judicature, the atmosphere of legal experience and thought pervading the courts of common law. I cannot forget, that I stand in the presence of military power, associated with all the terror it brings to the sensitive apprehension of organized and regulated justice. Nor can I forget, that in the progress of this case, this Court has already demonstrated its natural tendencies, manifested the influences which inhere in and surround it. By an excusable association of ideas, one would connect with a military court like this, the trial of military crimes. Propriety would seem to require that its jurisdiction should be limited to the soldier, and the necessities of armies; that, untaught in the profound wisdom of municipal law, unfamiliar with the vast system of rules within which civil right is enshrined, this Court would be content so to administer its office, as to protect military organization and secure military efficiency.

It has adjudged otherwise. It asserts the power to punish a

civilian for an offense against the domestic law of a State. It claims jurisdiction over the citizen of New York, to punish an alleged crime against her dignity and peace. It arrogates the power to supersede her authority not only, but here, in the midst of regular courts, active and efficient in the exercise of all their functions, to assume the trial and punishment, by military law, of private citizens charged only with civil malefaction.

Surely the incongruity of this proceeding cannot fail to excite astonishment and dread. It invests this cause with a new dignity, elevating it far above personal consequences. It will be engrafted upon the history of these deplorable times, not the least among the many indications marking the decay of American liberty.

It is for this cause I speak, with the hope of demonstrating its true character, and exposing dangerous violations of public law and private right.

Your Honors, I am sure, have no desire to usurp authority. You cherish the rights of a common citizenship. You recognize the ancient principles which constitute this government a government of law, and upon which, alone, American freedom can securely rely.

In the great emergency oppressing our country, the fear is, that an ardent patriotism will forget its reverence for the law; that, in eager pursuit of desirable ends, it will be less scrupulous of the means employed. Such is the necessary tendency of war. It is hostile to regulated peace. It is the element of force acting destructively upon civil institutions. Unless restrained within the limits of actual necessity, it grows into turbulent despotism.

2. THE ACTION OF THE COURT CANNOT BE JUSTIFIED ON THE PLEA OF MILITARY NECESSITY.

I do not overlook or deny the prerogatives of military necessity. I acknowledge the presence and rights of war, and would not, if I could, abridge the power which shall arm this government with the amplest ability to maintain its integrity. Purest patriots may differ in the details by which this result may be attained, but to that result every loyal heart is irrevocably pledged. Quite possibly Your Honors and myself might differ as to the circumstances creating the extreme necessity, before which the ordinary functions of government, and the securities of society, are at once prostrated. I raise no abstract issue of principle. Conceding the doctrine in its most liberal sense, I yet insist that it has no principle, either of right or policy, applying to a case like the present.

3. A MILITARY COMMISSION HAS AUTHORITY TO PUNISH ONLY MILITARY OFFENSES.

It is upon the rights of war, either express or customary, that this prosecution proceeds. It is founded upon military jurisdiction alone, and must be upheld by military law. It can gain no support from municipal enactment. Your Honors are not exerting a concurrent jurisdiction. You claim exclusive, absolute power, deriving and seeking no aid from associated authority.

It is desirable, therefore, to ascertain, primarily, the character of the offense charged against the accused, and how far, if at all, it is recognized as a military crime.

4. GENERAL OBSERVATION AS TO THE NATURE OF CRIME, AND THE PHILOSOPHY OF PUNISHMENT.

It will be conceded, that all crime, punishable by human authority, consists in the violation of some rule of conduct declared and published by some competent source. The principle is fundamental. It underlies the administration of criminal justice by all tribunals, whether military or civil. To constitute offense there must be law existing and law violated; and the law which declares it, must be proclaimed and public. If it exist in the form of positive enactment, it must be published. If it be customary law, it must be general, uniform, acknowledged. The citizen cannot be entrapped into crime. He must be notified of the demands of society in all the departments of its action, whether of peace or war, before obedience can be exacted, and disobedience punished. In a government of laws those acts only are criminal which the law condemns; and publicity is one of its material requisites. The idea of secret statutes, withheld from the subject whose conduct they are to regulate, is hostile to every principle of just government, and excites the sternest indignation. Hence the ponderous statutes of our national and State legislatures, declaring and defining crime, publicly enacted and widely promulgated. Hence the principle of antiquity involving immemorial recognition, upon which the common law rests. Hence, also, it is, that all are chargeable with knowledge of the law. Ignorance of its mandate will not excuse the offender. It is the duty of the subject to know it, and knowing, to obey it. The existence of the implication and duty, demands

the correlative obligation of government, to publish its requirements.   Men cannot be required to know that which is unrevealed,
or to obey that which is unannounced.   They cannot be punished
but for sinning with knowledge, or with the means of knowledge.
History has immortalized the shame of the ancient lawgiver, whose
edicts were only published upon the city walls, high above the observation of the people.   And if ever an American citizen shall be
condemned under an unknown law, history will be true to her trust,
and perpetuate the memory and condemnation of the prodigious
wrong.

5. The authority of the court extends only to viola-
tions of military law.

This inquiry into the nature of the offense charged, of necessity involves the jurisdiction of this Court.   If military law has not
been invaded, Your Honors have no power to punish.   It is an inquiry always pertinent and proper.   It may be raised by preliminary plea to the charge and specifications, or upon final submission; and whenever and however presented, imperatively demands
the consideration of the Court.   To this proposition I cite from
O'Brien, p. 248, and De Hart, p. 111.

" The prisoner may make a plea of demurrer by pleading that
even if the facts alleged be true, they do not amount, as stated, to
the offense charged.   When the facts do not amount to any offense
cognizable by a military court, the prisoner may take advantage of
it by a plea of demurrer, by a plea of jurisdiction, or under the
general plea of not guilty." [1]
" For although the prisoner might subsequently plead the want
of relevancy, or perspicuity in the charge, still, as the court is the
judge of its own competency, at any stage of its proceedings, and is
bound to notice questions of jurisdiction whenever raised, the
mode of procedure now suggested, could never, in any instance,
militate against the interests of the accused, and might, in some,
save much useless trouble and individual responsibility." [2]

My position, therefore, is, that to give this Court jurisdiction, the
charge and specifications must impute military crime; and that, to
be so, the acts specified must be declared unlawful by the articles
of war, or be such as are " repugnant to military discipline, and are
pointed out by law; by the general regulations of the army, and by
the customs of war."

[1] O'Brien's Am. Mil. Law, p. 248.
De Hart on Courts-martial, p. 111.

"The charge must enunciate some one general crime provided against by the articles of war.   It must enunciate it clearly and distinctly, so that the prisoner may know precisely the offense of which he is accused." [1]

Here Mr. Beach cited De Hart on Courts-martial, p. 299, to establish the proposition that where the charge itself does not name any crime provided for generally or specifically by any of the articles of war, the court was bound to discharge the prisoner. (For the extract cited, see Appendix, p. 726.) He then continued:

The Court will observe how admirably these citations maintain the idea of published or known law.   They recognize the indispensable ingredient of publicity.   Acts designated as such, by positive law, by general army regulations and the custom of war, are alone crimes.   The adoption of articles of war by Congressional enactment, the promulgation of regulations, the growth of customs, all assume the necessity of established and notified obligation. Their object is to form a military code, prescribing rules of action promotive of the efficiency of the service, and defining the powers of military tribunals.   If there be an undefined jurisdiction, springing from a pretended necessity, roaming unrestrained and unregulated, without law to limit or judge its action, adjudging crime at pleasure and punishing at discretion, what need of articles of war or army regulations?   And how long would the rights of citizenship stand before the bold usurpation?

Your Honors must, therefore, find in these nominated sources of your authority, some provision constituting the acts charged against the defendants' military crimes.   What then is the charge?

6. THE CHARGES AGAINST DEFENDANTS DO NOT EMBRACE A MILITARY CRIME.

It alleges "conduct prejudicial to the military service of the United States, and in fraud of the electoral rights and duties of the soldiers and officers in said service."

It will be perceived that the charge is of conduct having two characteristics or consequences; not of two distinct species of acts. It affirms that the defendants have been guilty of deeds, which are both prejudicial to the service and in fraud of electoral right.   It is not necessary, here, to contend that the proven offense must combine the two alleged results.   The position may be assumed with

[1] O'Brien's Am. Mil. Law, p. 235.

great propriety. The charge and specifications are analogous to an indictment, averments in which, descriptive of the offense, must be proven as laid. The point, however, now is, not the sufficiency of the proof, but the law declaring the things charged to be criminal. If it be conceded that the testimony sustains the charge, it is denied that either affirm a military crime. Grant that the proven acts prejudiced the service, where is the article, or regulation, or custom, declaring them criminal in the civilian? What law prohibits them as to him? Are they forbidden by the provisions devised by the wisdom of Congress, or established by the experience of the past? This is the first essential inquiry.

It is by the specifications that these defendants must be judged. They must sustain the charge not only, but must, in themselves, constitute the crime, or some degree of it, embodied in the charge.

Here Mr. Beach cited O'Brien's American Military Law, pp. 234 and 235, to show that the specifications must not only sustain the charge, but must themselves embody the offense charged. (For the extract cited, see Appendix, p. 728.) He then continued:

7. THE CHARGES NOT SUSTAINED BY THE SPECIFICATIONS.

It is manifest that these specifications do not uphold that branch of the charge which imputes conduct prejudicial to the military service of the United States. The most perverse ingenuity will fail to connect with that service, in the remotest association, the forgery of soldiers' votes, or frauds upon their elective suffrage. They are utterly disconnected with the military character and duty of the soldier. They deprive him of no martial right. They, in no degree, diminish his soldierly ability, or disqualify him for service. They affect him only in his civil relations, impairing none of his obligations to the government, neither seducing him from his duty nor impairing his fitness to perform it. How, then, do these alleged frauds prejudice the military service of the United States? It is for the learned judge advocate to maintain it, and for this Court, intelligently and conscientiously, to adjudge it. No vague and indefinite accusation will answer the demands of justice. No general assertion of injury to the service will satisfy the responsibility of the Court. It must be able to perceive clearly the injurious effect, and to trace it to the alleged cause. If there be any substantial imperfection in the relation, this prosecution falls. The charge and the specifications must harmoniously co-exist, each founded upon and mutually sustaining the other. This is the plain teaching of military law, followed by the uniform practice of its courts.

I respectfully but emphatically ask, then, if these specifications disclose any acts inimical to military service? Can it be that a reputable Court will adjudge a proposition so revoltingly preposterous and false?

8. CIVIL OFFENSES NOT WITHIN THE JURISDICTION OF THE COURT.

The remnant of the charge requires Your Honors to adjudicate that frauds upon the elective rights and duties of soldiers, in no degree affecting the military service of the United States, are crimes punishable by courts-martial. To this complexion this argument must come, at last. It is upon this theory that the defendants must be condemned, if at all. No sophistry can evade the position. You must find in the specifications the elements of the crime you adjudge, and you find in them no other accusation. It is a direct, bold issue, which must be frankly met and responsibly determined. I press it vigorously, in all its bald and repulsive absurdity, upon the consideration of the Court. You are expected to record, by solemn judicial decree, that the forgery of a soldier's vote, or fraud upon his elective franchise, is a military crime, subjecting the offenders to an undefined penalty under military law. The proposition needs but its statement for its refutation. Nay, may it please Your Honors, the statement awakens something more than a mental dissent. It shocks the commonest intelligence, and arouses a bitter resentment. The free sentiment of this country is not so far subdued that it can feel nothing but fear under the threatening pretension. We venerate the institutions of our fathers; we cling to the Union, hallowed by their wisdom and sacrifice; we yield and suffer much for its preservation: but if it is to be saved only by the surrender of the dearest privileges it confers to the dominion of military power; if the purest civil rights are to be grasped by a military jurisdiction, it may be well worth consideration whether the boon deserves the price.

9. NO AUTHORITY CONFERRED UPON THE COURT TO TRY CIVIL OFFENSES.

I pray Your Honors to inquire for the source of your authority, to entertain this indictment. What article of war, what army regulation, what custom of warfare confers it? I search for it in vain.

Your Honors are a Court of special and limited powers. You have no original or general jurisdiction. You are created by the national executive, by virtue of an act of Congress. I look to the act, to the order under which you convene, and I find no special delegation of this authority. I look to the general law, to military usage, and I find there no countenance for your claim. Upon what, then, is it founded? If it exist at all, it must be traceable in some enactment, or regulation, or custom. These all are silent. And the strange anomaly is presented of a special Court, exercising important criminal functions, derived neither from the legislature, the executive, or the customs of mankind. Such a spectacle may well excite profound astonishment and dismay. The assumption is accompanied with a tremendous responsibility. It cannot pass unnoticed in an intelligent community, educated in the midst of authorized courts and mindful of their constitutional rights.

10. MILITARY LAW DEFINED.

In this connection I invite Your Honors' attention to an admirable definition of military law, and the powers of its courts, from O'Brien. He says:

"Military law may be defined to be a body of rules and ordinances prescribed by competent authority for the government of the military state considered as a distinct community. It is an accumulation law. The citizen, on becoming a soldier, does not merge his former character in the latter. He relieves himself from none of his former duties and obligations. Instead of this, he engages to perform other duties in addition to those with which he was formerly charged. He submits himself to a special code of laws which does not supersede or abrogate that to which he was formerly subject, but which, on the contrary, binds him by a new tie to the very same authority which, as a citizen, he previously obeyed. With regard to civil powers and authorities he stands in the precise position he formerly occupied. They lose none of their rights and prerogatives. He still remains subject to them, and is bound to assist and aid them even in the apprehension of his military comrades. There is no principle more thoroughly incorporated, in our military as well as in our civil code, than that the soldier does not cease to be a citizen, and cannot throw off his obligations and responsibilities as such. The general law claims supreme and undisputed jurisdiction over all. The military law puts forth no such pretensions. It aims solely to enforce on the soldier the additional duties he has assumed. It constitutes tribunals for the trial of breaches of military duty only. It attempts not to regulate or adjust the civil rights of those who fall under its cognizance, nor does it affect to redress civil injuries or private wrongs, unless they be, in some degree, connected with the safety and good order of the military state, as having a tendency to disturb its peace and quiet. Civil injuries or private wrongs, not immediately related to the rights of a soldier, as such, are left, like his civil rights, to the redress of the general or common law.

"These two systems of law can, in no case, come in collision. Their spheres of action are different.   The military code commences where the other ends.   It finds a body of men who, besides being citizens, are also soldiers.   Their rights and duties in the former capacity it finds already well established; but, in their latter capacity, their duties are undefined, their rights are unascertained, until it steps in to fill this vacuum, to place the soldier as completely under the cover of law, and to guard him as securely against tyrannical and arbitrary power in his military as in his civil character.   The one code embraces all citizens, whether soldiers or not; the other has no jurisdiction over any citizen as such." [1]

Your Honors perceive how completely the extract justifies my reasoning.   It will impress Your Honors with its obvious propriety. It assigns to Courts like yourselves, their true position.   It enables them to accomplish their full office, without interference, with the ordinary tribunals of the country.   It disturbs none of the relations of civil life.   It assigns to you exclusively the field of military discipline and efficiency.   It maintains a wise harmony between the necessity which called you into existence and the functions you should exercise.

11. RUINOUS CONSEQUENCES WHICH MUST FOLLOW AN ASSUMPTION OF UNLAWFUL AUTHORITY.

Why, then, assume ungranted and dangerous power?   You are created for the good of the army, and for that alone.   Why enlarge the circle of your duty, and that upon a principle which stretches it over every civil right of the soldier?   It is not only unjustifiable; it is profitless.   You accomplish thereby no beneficial result.   The consequences are all evil.   You inaugurate a baleful conflict between civil and military power.   You spread wider the terrors of insurrectionary war, devastate more broadly the institutions of peace, and alienate the confidence of the people.   The bold spirit of the trained commander may mock these unprosperous issues, but Your Honors are upon the judicial bench, not in the field.   You are called to exert the prudence of the judge, not the fearlessness of the veteran.   Wisdom, not courage, is the quality of your posi-

[1] O'Brien's Am. Mil. Law, pp. 26, 27.

tion. We live in perilous times, when it becomes us to act wisely. The foundations of government are fiercely shaken. Recent events seem to assure us that they are rapidly settling to their former solidity; but there is a mighty work of reconstruction before this people. With peace will come the onerous duty of reorganization, and a more sensible appreciation of the accumulated burdens of war. It is well to limit, as far as may be, its devastations upon civil right, and to cultivate amity between the government and the people. This will not be done by needless encroachment upon their privileges, and a reckless and ruthless exertion of military power.

If Your Honors assume this jurisdiction, you are forced, more-over, to devise a punishment for the crime you invent. You en-counter a fresh novelty in this necessity. You have, then, not only a roving commission to try all charges, but plenary discretion to punish. Your Honors are, without guide or limit, the most uni-versal and arbitrary Court on the face of the earth. You may re-vive the barbarity of the ancient law of Britain, or practice the most indulgent lenity. You may discriminate between culprits, and protect friends while you crush enemies. It is a most convenient license. You may choose your subjects at pleasure, and dispose of your selected victims as caprice or interest may dictate; or you may execute submissively the will of the power which made you.

I am not exaggerating the statement. I have proven that there is no law empowering this Court to try the accused upon the mat-ters alleged; and I affirm that there is no law specifying their pun-ishment. With the exception of spies, suttlers, commissaries, camp retainers, and the like, no non-military offender is triable or punish-able under the articles of war, or any other law or custom, except martial law regularly declared. There is no provision for a case like the present. Hitherto it has been uncontemplated by delib-erative or executive wisdom, unrequired by the emergencies of war. If it be true, that Your Honors may try and punish under these specifications, it is the only example under heaven, outside of absolutism, where a citizen may be condemned without law limiting the punishment, either by specified penalty or by a conferred dis-cretion. This fearful prerogative to punish, exposed to all the temptations which beset it—now urging it to vindictive cruelty, and now seducing it to weakness—changing and vacillating and ter-rible, cannot exist where justice is respected. It prostrates per-sonal security at the foot of judicial power. It would multiply in this land the infamous scenes enacted in England by a Scroggs and a Jeffries. Courts like this would be fearful as the inquisition— tremendous and destructive engines, wielded by unsparing hands, against the franchises of liberty.

12. DEFENDANTS ENTITLED TO AN ACQUITTAL.

I know Your Honors are bold and brave men, sinewed and strong "on the perilous ridges of battle," but it requires another hardihood to strike at the integrity of the law—full against the buckler of the Constitution. My clients stand securely under these safeguards. They invoke you, by your respect for these, by your instinctive sense of right, by your veneration for the past and your trust for the future, to stay this ill-judged prosecution. They demand an acquittal, for want of jurisdiction in this Court. Innocent or guilty, it is their lawful due. If they have broken the law, it is not your law. If they deserve punishment, yours are not the hands to inflict it. Meet this issue in the enlarged spirit of the upright judge, enlightened by patriotic forecast. The plaudits and blessings of the country will attend your judgment. It will stand an enduring landmark, illustrative of judicial integrity and independence, amidst the disquieting and disintegrating influences of the present hour.

13. DISTINCTION BETWEEN MARTIAL LAW AND MILITARY LAW.— MARTIAL LAW NOT APPLICABLE.

The position I have argued is not overcome by the prevailing presence of martial law. I raise no question as to the power to declare it in certain emergencies. I concede, that, wherever lawfully existing, it supplants civil authority and consolidates in a single will all the powers of the State. Mr. De Hart thus writes:

"It must be understood, however, that the term martial law has a different interpretation from that of military law. Military law, as has been stated above, is a rule for the government of military persons only, but martial law is understood to be that state of things when, from the force of circumstances, the military law is indiscriminately applied to all persons whatsoever. The distinction is thus expressed by a writer on military law: 'Martial law extends to all persons; military law to all military persons, but not to those in a civil capacity.'" [1]

But, if Your Honors please, this tyrannical and abyssmal law is

[1] De Hart on Courts-martial, p. 17.

only invoked in seasons of the extremest anarchy and peril. It is an act of the last necessity; and it must be proclaimed before the ordinary avenues of justice are closed and the vitality of civil right is strangled in the mailed grasp of military rule. It will not, I think, be pretended that martial law exists here. No proclamation has established it. It does not practically exist. Your streets abound with an armed soldiery, and the commandant issues necessary orders for their government and discipline; but the civil magistracy continue to discharge their appropriate duties, while the higher courts dispense the weightier matters of the law.

I understand the learned judge advocate to maintain that the city of Washington is "in the field," in a sense which introduces martial law. I am not familiar with the technical signification of the term. Unskilled judgment will apply it only to the scene of active operations in presence of an enemy. Such an exigency alone demands the suppression of the usual agencies of social order. Non-combatants would not consider an unbeleaguered garrison "in the field," nor a recruiting station, nor depots for troops. If Washington is "in the field," so is Baltimore and New York, and the large cities of the West, and martial law impends over their peaceable and loyal populations. I submit to Your Honors, this would be an unnecessary and mischievous application of the term, vastly overreaching the necessity from which it originates. It is a palpable misapplication if it implies the consequences claimed by the learned judge advocate.

14. Rule as to the existence of martial law.

I deny, however, that martial law accompanies armies in the field, except in the control of the excrescences which attend them. Mr. De Hart thus states the doctrine:

"Armies, when engaged in active operations, are at all seasons accompanied by a large train of followers who minister to their convenience and comfort. The various descriptions of persons included under that appellation have granted to them certain privileges, such as living within the boundaries of the camp, and protection to their persons and property, dependent necessarily upon the essential conditions of good order, quiet, subordination and fidelity to the State. The great important interest to the nation involved in the movements of an army, which, for certainty of action, uniformity of conduct and ultimate success, must rely mainly upon a system of rigid discipline, has caused the rule which applies everywhere else for the protection of the civilian, to be somewhat modified, or even for the time to be entirely set aside; hence the custom which provides in the field, of trying persons not connected with the army by courts-martial, must have arisen from, as it depends on, necessity. Were any other principle for the regulation of such persons admissible, it is certain that an army might suffer the greatest detriment, and a way might thereby be opened for the easy communication of the enemy, and the acquisition and transmission of intelligence. Disorder, riot and confusion would necessarily also prevail; for it would be quite impossible to exact the observance of different police laws by the enlisted soldier and the follower of the camps, when both parties are confined to the same limits.

"But it must be remembered, that the opposition of such laws to such persons would not be warranted in time of peace, under the ordinary conditions of camps and garrisons; and wherever civil jurisdicture is in force, the followers of the camp who are accused of crimes punishable by the known laws of the land, must be given up to the civil magistrate." [1]

In this form the rule is quite admissible. It secures all the benefit sought, without injury to the general interests of society. It subjects those who voluntarily attach themselves to the army to the imperious necessity which surrounds it with prompt and vigorous subjection. There is justice in it, as well as need of it. But this seems not to appease the rapacious spirit of military consolidation. It is not content with the "field," but aspires to the city. It annexes to an army, quartered in the quiet and luxurious metropolis of the Union, the incidents and necessities which pertain only to the "tented field" and the sulphurous din of war. The ambition is not likely to be gratified. It may encroach somewhat upon the steady movements of our civil organizations, but their majestic revolution will, full soon, repel the aggression.

15. CONSEQUENCES OF THE DOCTRINE ADVANCED BY THE JUDGE ADVOCATE.

If the position be sound, the municipal and judicial institutions of this district exist only by military sufferance. The action of its courts depends entirely upon the indulgence of military grace. It needs but the order of a military governor, and your august national temple will be polluted by the tread of an armed soldiery, and its halls of justice and of legislation be closed. An improvised military commission will occupy the places of the reverend justices who dignify our national tribunal, and military edicts will supplant the deliberations of Congress. This is the legitimate and close

[1] De Hart on Courts-martial, pp. 22, 23.

conclusion of the argument. If Your Honors adjudge the doctrine, you must accept these consequences; and they may follow more speedily than Your Honors would desire. Events quite as wonderful have happened in history.

16. Constitutional rights cannot be suspended.

The learned judge advocate affirms your jurisdiction upon another and still more alarming theory. He invokes your action, because, as he declares, in time of war "the great mass of the provisions of the Constitution are suspended."

It is a startling announcement, coming from the public prosecutor, on behalf of the United States, uttered within sound of Capitol Hill, under the very droppings of the sanctuary. If it were not for its savor of authority, it would be execrated as an appalling sacrilege. I denounce the sentiment as at once unsound in law and atrocious in principle. In a free government, regularly operating in its legitimate sphere, no imaginable condition of things suspends for an instant the constitutional privileges of the citizen. War largely subverts individual right, but war co-exists with the Constitution. It is by the efficient exercise of powers granted by it, not by its subversion, that the calamities of war are to be overcome. Broad and ample provisions anticipate the exigency. It did not escape the prophetic intuition of the fathers of the republic. Just emerged from the strife of the revolution, they were unlikely to forget, in the formation of a government, the necessities of war. It is the wonder of their marvelous work that it grasped and provided for all the possibilities of the future. It was formed for perpetuity; it left nothing to the hazard of a contingency; it confided to the general government the power of making treaties, of declaring war, of suppressing insurrection.

Under and by virtue of the Constitution, Congress and the executive wield the vast resources of the nation. By it our navy is founded and our armies marshaled. Its energies have gathered the triumphant hosts who proudly bear to-day its banner over the ruins of a gigantic rebellion. Obedient to it, a loyal people have lavished upon this government their richest treasures. What more does the rapacity of war demand? And what will be the end of an impaired Constitution? The nature of this government will be essentially changed, and all its invigorating principles necessarily paralyzed. If this be done by military power, and in so far as done, it is military despotism; however done, it is revolutionary.

The Constitution ordains this government, organizes its form and confers and limits its authority. The principle is elemental in the law and statesmanship of the country. The maxim, that government is derived from the consent of the governed, is old but not forgotten. It is graven deep upon our historic record. It is the living principle of our national life. This consent is expressed in the Constitution; through it alone are our rulers empowered. There is no other fountain of power; there cannot be, in a constitutional system. All exercised authority not conferred by its grants, express and implied, is but audacious usurpation, tending in the degree of its departure to the overthrow of free institutions.

In the memorable contests of the past over governmental power, how constantly have our great jurists and statesmen appealed to the Constitution, bowing in reverent submission to its supremacy, recognizing and honoring the obligation and wisdom of its limitations and restraints! The idea of the learned judge advocate is a wild paradox, born of these inauspicious days. Not until now has it been taught that the great charter of American liberty has lost its virtue; that the exigencies of war suspend the fundamental law by which alone government exists. If so, it must then survive by its own inherent strength, and that is a military dictatorship. It is claimed thus to override the Constitution under the pretense of an inexorable necessity. It is the old plea of tyrants, and thus always have encroachments upon waning liberty begun, and the end, unresisted, has ever been sure and fatal.

Half a century ago, the gorgeous genius of Erskine denounced this dogma of Kingcraft. I appropriate his language. On Hardy's trial for treason he thus spoke:

"What is it that distinguishes the government of England from the most despotic monarch? What but the security which the subject enjoys in a trial and judgment by his equals ; rendered doubly secure as being part of a system of law which no expediency can warp, and which no power can abuse with impunity! To the attorney-general's second preliminary observation I equally agree; I anxiously wish with him that you shall bear in memory the anarchy which is desolating France. Before I sit down, I may, perhaps, in my turn, have occasion to reflect a little upon its probable causes; but, waiting a season for such reflection, let us first consider what the evil is which has been so feelingly lamented as having fallen on that unhappy country. It is, that in the dominion of a barbarous State necessity, every protection of law is abrogated and destroyed; it is, that no man can say, amid such a system of alarm and terror, that his life, his liberty, his reputation, or any one

30

human blessing is secured to him for a moment; it is, that, if accused of federalism, or moderatism, or incivism, or whatever else the changing fashions and factions of the day shall have lifted up into high treason against the State, he must see his friends, his family, and the light of heaven no more—the accusation and the sentence being the same, following one another as the thunder pursues the flash." [1]

I deny the necessity. I maintain the ability of the Constitution to support itself. Upon it this government can stand, defiant of all adversity. It is the fertile source of prosperity in war as well as peace. In all emergencies it reconciles the high prerogatives of government with the personal privileges of citizenship. It makes these to harmonize and co-operate in all the diversities of its experience. It is only when the constitutional relation between the government and the citizen is disturbed, that disorder ensues. Maintain that inviolate, restrict power to its prescribed sphere, attaching to it thus the hopes and interests of the people, and you give to this nation immortal life.

17. The doctrine of suspending the Constitution novel and startling.

I appeal from the present to the past, from the learned judge advocate to the venerated sages of America, from the war of to-day to those of history. If I remember aright, this government encountered some stringent necessities in the war of 1812. Patriotism, in a certain quarter, now intensely loyal, was not as fervid then. The heresy of secession was more than dreamed of in those early days, north of Mason and Dixon's line. We were in our youth, struggling with the giant of nations; but the grand specific of the learned judge advocate, through a suspension of the Constitution, was not then administered. The necessity was dire enough. The embargo sat heavily upon New England, and she did more than mutter; but the Constitution was unshaken, and the war was glorious. The modern invention of abrogating and reinstating the organic law, the idea that the Constitution could exist in suspended animation, dandled in the arms of military terrorism, had not then been discovered; it was too near the cradle of the republic.

18. Provisions of the Constitution sufficient for every political possibility.

It will be difficult to mention any necessary operation of war

---

[1] Howell's State Trials, vol. 24, p. 878.

upon civil rights not embraced by the qualifications of the Constitution. The learned judge advocate referred to the deprivation of trial by jury, forgetting that by the Constitution the right is withheld from the military and naval forces when in actual service. I do not stop to urge the implication springing from this express provision. The power to raise armies and wage war carries all authority necessary to do so effectually. The unavoidable incidents of war accompany its existence. By the declaration of the Constitution, government possesses all powers necessary to render effective those specifically granted. What need, then, to assail the Constitution? Whenever actual necessity requires the sacrifice of private property, or individual right, the Constitution authorizes it. Why, then, inculcate the pernicious notion that it is unequal to its great office; that the vigor which has borne it gallantly through two foreign conflicts, is unable to subdue the rebellious outbreaks of its own subjects? It has become fashionable to decry its merits. We have lost our veneration for the political parent which has nursed and protected our infancy and glorified our manhood. We have grown too large and strong for constitutional restraint. It needs but the doctrine of the learned judge advocate to disencumber our maddened passions and ambitions of all embarrassment, and leave us to that career of political profligacy which prophesied and accomplished the fate of the old republics.

19. ALL CONSTITUTIONAL AUTHORITY CLEARLY DEFINED.

I have claimed for government the broadest incidental powers. I believe the Constitution expansive enough for all the possibilities it may meet. This, by no means, concedes that these powers, when their exertion is demanded, are to remain inexplicit and indefinite, dependent upon the caprice of military captains or the arbitrary will of the executive. They mainly appertain to Congress. So far as concerns the necessities of war, they have been expressed and methodized by legislative act and the law of nations. The articles of war define their quality and regulate their exercise; the modes by which they operate, the agencies through which they act, are all nominated, and, beyond these, they remain unexerted in the hands of Congress. The most superficial student knows, that in a representative, constitutional government, its officers have no undefined, discretionary authority, undelegated by the Constitution or the legislature. All official power must originate from these; and this

is the radical distinction between our own system and the simple
monarchies of Europe. When it shall become the expressed will
of the people to eradicate this difference, and not till then, will the
theory of the learned judge advocate be accepted by American
law or by popular favor.

20. CASE OF VALLANDIGHAM DISTINGUISHED.

It has been said that the opinion of Judge Leavitt, in the case
of Vallandigham, intimates it. On the contrary, its reasoning and
avowals are in direct opposition to it. The judge says (p. 263):

" In my judgment, when the life of the republic is threatened, he
mistakes his duty and obligation as a patriot, who is not willing to
concede to the Constitution such a capacity of adaptation to circumstances as may be necessary to meet a great emergency and
save the nation from hopeless ruin."

It is the flexible quality of the Constitution, adapting itself to
the emergencies of war, or rather, it is its sagacious foresight,
anticipating and providing for them, to which the judge appeals.
He concedes both its obligation and its efficiency. He countenances no such abomination as a suspension of " the great mass " of
its powers. Again he says (p. 266) :

" In time of war the President is not above the Constitution,
but derives his power expressly from the provision of that instrument, declaring that he shall be commander-in-chief of the army
and navy.   *   *   *   The occasion which justifies the exercise of this power, exists only from the necessity of the case; and
when the necessity exists, there is a clear justification of the act.
If this view of the power of the President is correct, it undoubtedly implies the right to arrest persons who, by their mischievous
acts of disloyalty, impede or endanger the military operations of
the government."

These sentiments cannot be misunderstood or misapplied.
They recognize the supreme obligations of the Constitution, and
fortify, with singular exactness, the considerations I have submitted to Your Honors. They locate the war power of the government in the Constitution. They do more. They justify its exercise against civil right only " from the necessity of the case." They
confine military arrests to those persons " who, by their mischievous acts of disloyalty, impede or endanger the military operations
of the government."

21. THE OFFENSES CHARGED NOT HOSTILE TO THE MILITARY OPERATIONS OF THE GOVERNMENT.

When Your Honors shall find an imperative necessity requiring the arrest and punishment of these defendants; when any act shall have been proven against them, impeding or endangering the military operations of the government, your jurisdiction may be acknowledged. But where is the necessity? and how have my clients interfered with military action? The great and manifest distinction between the case of Vallandigham and this is, that he was charged with conduct pernicious to the discipline of the army. General Burnside, in his statement to the court, vindicated his order precisely upon this ground. The charge upon the military commission, was "declaring disloyal sentiments and opinions, with the object and purpose of weakening the power of the government in its efforts to suppress an unlawful rebellion."

What analogy is there in the two examples? Have these defendants propagated disloyalty, fomented dissension, alienated the patriotism of the army, or disturbed its harmony? Not at all, Your Honors. They were the commissioned agents of New York in ministering to the wants of her soldiery. Their efforts were auxiliary to the government and in aid of the effectiveness of the army. They are charged with no design or act hostile to military operations. No treasonable sentiment is imputed to them. If they did all of which they are accused, they have violated no military order, endangered no military enterprise, tampered with no military obligation. Be he a traitor or a patriot, they are not fit associates for Vallandigham; his fate furnishes no precedent for their condemnation. This prosecution remains unprecedented and unparalleled. It stands upon no sure foundation of principle or example. It appeals to no impulse of patriotism. You seek, in necessity, some apology for its merciless cruelty, and find none. These defendants have tasted the bitterness of a felon's captivity, felt the dishonoring and savage rigor of military infliction, isolated from the amenities and sympathies of social life. Justice demands a reason for this barbarous invasion of constitutional right. What imminent danger impended? What interest of State was imperiled? What clamoring exigency exacted the sacrifice? None, Your Honors, none. They are the powerless victims of authority mischievously perverted, hopeless, save in the dignified independence and impartial justice of this honorable Court.

22. Whether defendants can be punished under the State law immaterial.

It has been further argued that New York cannot punish these defendants for offenses against her laws, committed beyond her territorial jurisdiction. I differ with the learned prosecutor upon the abstract proposition, although it is not involved in this case. The prisoners are citizens of New York, owing obedience to her authority. They were acting under her laws and in reference to her interests, and it may well be insisted that the obligation of her statutes followed them everywhere. It is not, however, needful to discuss the question. New York, at least, can punish crimes originated abroad, but consummated within her limits. If the offense be set on foot here, but effected or continued there, she has ample power to deal with the offender. Nor is it requisite that the criminal act should have been personally performed by the accused, within her boundaries. It is sufficient that he instigated or assisted its performance. If he planned outside, and another executed within her borders, he is accessary and liable. The injury is inflicted there, and he aided in its infliction. Nothing more is necessary than that he be brought within her actual control.

The argument, at least, is but a lame apology for the intermeddling of military courts with civil obligations. Your Honors cannot derive jurisdiction from the mere absence of authority elsewhere to punish. This Court is not charged with the duty of supplying the imperfections of the law. It is more important to determine how much power Your Honors possess, than how little belongs to New York. The weakness of her jurisdiction does not strengthen yours; and if Your Honors shall undertake to pursue all offenses which would otherwise escape "unwhipped of justice," your judicial functions have a remarkable origin and will have abundant exercise.

23. Duty of government to protect its soldiers considered.

The learned judge advocate justifies the proceedings before this Court upon still another ground. He affirms it to be the "duty" of government to protect the rights of its soldiers, and from this he deduces the power to punish by court-martial frauds upon his electoral privilege. I am at a loss to perceive how this "duty" is imposed. Government cannot gratuitously assume it, and thus gain jurisdiction over civilians and their rights. The duty must be compulsory or undertaken in obedience to law; otherwise, by voluntary and officious assumption of "duty," government might invest itself with the most arbitrary powers, and absorb in one department the functions of all. This is vitally opposed to the protective principle of our institutions. They rest upon a division of authority, upon multiplied responsibilities, upon a watchful system of checks and balances hostile to centralization.

The idea of the learned judge advocate is not altogether visionary. Undoubtedly government owes a duty to its soldiers, but it relates exclusively to their rights in that special character, and which grow immediately out of their military relations. It originates from military character, and must be confined to military subjects. If not, the superintending care of government must necessarily overspread all the business and social interests of each officer and private in the army. If it extends at all beyond strict military associations, it must be comprehensive and complete. It cannot be restricted to New York soldiers and frauds upon her election laws. If the discharge of this universal duty has fallen upon Your Honors, you must be endowed with general jurisdiction, both civil and criminal. If you protect the soldier in the enjoyment of his electoral right simply because he is a soldier, you must, for the same reason, protect all others. If you punish wrongs to one, you must as to all. You must defend his rights of property and pursue the thief who filches his purse, the gambler who robs, and the confidence man who defrauds him. Your Honors must not forget his matrimonial privileges. You must frown upon seduction and adultery, and amuse yourselves with actions for criminal conversation.

24. JURISDICTION OF THE COURT MUST ARISE FROM POSITIVE LAW.

Surely, the authority of this Court cannot depend upon such reasoning. It is held by no such absurd tenure. You are a court of law, like as any other court known to the country. You must find your jurisdiction in the Constitution, and in acts of Congress passed in accordance with it. You can gain it rightfully from no other source. It would be lamentable, indeed, if Your Honors were driven to follow the learned judge advocate, in his devious search, after authority for this proceeding. Powers, such as you wield, should have no dubious origin. They lay strong hold upon the liberty and life of the citizen. They fall with sudden, resistless, merciless energy. The doom is arbitrary, the execution summary. They should be exerted upon no doubtful occasion. They should trace their descent lineally and legitimately from legal parentage. Before Your Honors shall judge these accused, claiming the rights of private citizenship, appealing, as they do, to the sacred guardian-ship of the civil law, to the constitutional privilege of trial by jury, in due course of law, you will examine your judicial lineage, and see to it that you exercise no spurious authority. The occasion has become too marked and conspicuous for inconsiderate action. It looks toward consequences too serious for indifferent unconcern.

I submit to Your Honors this jurisdictional question with an assured confidence, although I feel how unequal to the great theme my argument has been. I have not specifically spoken of the con-stitutional provisions regulating the forms of proceeding in criminal prosecutions, nor of the clear intendments springing from the act of 1863. I have preferred to meet this issue in the limited mode I have pursued. I have sought to impress upon Your Honors the ardent convictions of my own mind, and lead your judgments to a wise conclusion. Notwithstanding your adverse prepossessions, I have faith in the sober reflections of the righteous judge; I have faith in the educated intelligence, the constitutional instincts of this honorable Court, and look to them hopefully to acknowledge the rights of American citizenship.

25. QUESTIONS OF FACT INVOLVED.

My duty, nevertheless, requires a discussion of the issues of facts arising from the evidence. I might well have rested this de-fense upon the poverty of the accusing proof. My clients need no shelter, other than their innocence, against the asserted jurisdiction of this Court. Upon this they have rested with quiet assurance, while the unlimited power of this government has exhausted itself in spasmodic efforts to discover proof of guilt. Always ready, they have endured the ignominy and distress of a loathsome imprison-ment, while this trial has been prolonged by a frantic and fruitless pursuit of criminating testimony. The public prosecutor has thrown his official dragnet over the State of New York, subsidized private malice and partisan hate, agitated every cess-pool of polit-ical garbage in his implacable purpose to convict. The judgment of every thoughtful observer, the public sense of the community, disapproved this prosecution. Indignant, as all true citizens were, at the suspicion of attempted fraud upon the elective franchise, popular conviction, long ago, exonerated these defendants. Magnanimous justice would have accepted the general verdict; but the overheated zeal of the prosecutor, the peril of at once admitting the falsehood and folly of this accusation, inspired anew the flagging zeal which, for its own safety, sought a victim. These defendants have been tortured with the severest prison regimen, in the merciless hope that desperate means would supply a justification. This trial has been delayed, not to procure known evidence, but to hunt it down. Suspicion alone dictated the charge; industry was to obtain the needful testimony, and, in the meantime, a gentleman of cultivated associations, distinguished for probity and position, must await in prison the tardy advance of his accuser. True, the spontaneous sympathy of the just and good has cheered him. From political friend and political foe, his unmerited suffering has drawn prompt and hearty testimonials to his integrity. It is none the less lamentable that such a scene should have been enacted at the center of national authority, at the culminating point of highest law and loftiest power. Speedy trial is due to innocence, speedy judgment to guilt. Government owes to its subjects protection against inquisitorial prosecutions. If the benign provisions of the Constitution to this end are to be "suspended," if the established tribunals of the country are to be superseded, humanity cries aloud against the iniquity which executes before it condemns. Probable cause alone justifies the humiliating incarceration of a citizen. When it shall be tolerated, that military officials may arrest upon suspicion and imprison at will, the worst of tyranny will be felt, because it is the tyranny of abused law.

What, after all, has been accomplished by these unparalleled efforts of the government? It is the power of the United States, with its host of satellites and its prodigal treasures, directed by this rancorous purpose, arrayed against the simple citizen powerless in his cell. What wonder if this mighty influence should prevail over individual weakness! We are not ignorant of the insidious resources of towering dominion. It finds zealous sycophants. Ready instrumentalities are tendered to its service. Obsequious parasites divine its wishes and pander to their gratification. This is a government prosecution. The majesty of the accuser intensifies the charge. The destined victim is a prominent citizen of his native State, more deeply obnoxious from his distinction. The crime alleged is an atrocious attempt to deprave the vital principle of our free institutions. Who will deny that the gravest deliberation, the most cautious investigation, should precede the spectacle this proceeding exhibits? Who could anticipate from it "a most lame and impotent conclusion" which provokes the ridicule and scorn of the world?

I cannot anticipate the judgment of this Court; but in the instincts of a common manhood, I may believe that Your Honors cannot but feel how pitiful is the *denouement* of this miserable tragedy.

If all be conceded that the most embittered malice can claim from the proof, what is the magnitude of the crime which has so aroused the vindictive energies of the government? Frightful developments of gigantic frauds were promised. The press and the rostrum, with glaring italics and vehement denunciation, paraded the coming revelation. The frenzy of political zeal was maddened with spectral visions of ponderous "boxes" and flitting shapes, ominous of political ruin. The State agency of New York, marshalled by Col. North, with huge and stealthy fraud, were corrupting the whole franchise of the Union, and the startled country seemed to see the fabric of government tottering to its fall. Truly, the mountain heaved in painful labor. Your Honors are witnesses to the royal delivery, and are to christen the contemptible progeny.

This State prosecution claims to have revealed the astounding fact, that a dozen preparatory forms for soldiers' votes were signed and certified in blank, by a competent officer, to be executed by the voter at need. With ostentatious fraud they were spread upon a public table, in the absence of the official who alone could properly employ them; and the evidence fails to show a single instance of their effectual use. There is not the slightest proof of a single false ballot deposited. It is pretended that these forms were preserved for an emergency. It is a false pretense; but, if true, they were not used. The diligence of the learned judge advocate has succeeded in raising a suspicion that, during the entire canvass, three attempts were made by somebody to change soldiers' votes. How and by whom made is at the best problematical, but they all signally failed.

In its utmost latitude, this is the "head and front of the offending—no more." That it was not even this, I hope to demonstrate. But grant it this, how far short it is of criminality, how infinitely disproportioned to the direful prelude and the wearisome performance! What stately dignity invests the government of the United States, presiding at this momentous accouchement.

Here Mr. Beach reviewed in detail the testimony to show that the defendants were entitled to an acquittal on the evidence. In discussing the alleged
confession of guilt by Jones, one of the defendants, made in the absence of the
others, he contended that it was not evidence against them, on the ground that
the declarations of a conspirator are not competent against his fellow-conspira-
tors, unless made in pursuit of a common design, which must be first clearly
established, citing from the opinion of Chief Justice Marshall on the trial of
Aaron Burr (Burr's Trials, pp. 93–96). He contended, further, that it did not
implicate Col. North, and that to convict, all the circumstances must be inconsistent with the theory of innocence, citing from the opinion of Chief Justice
Shaw in the case of Prof. Webster (5 Cush. p. 317). After reviewing the evidence
of all the witnesses, he continued :

If Your Honors please, this comprises, in detail, all the evidence,
direct and remote, against Col. North. It is, with no sentiment of
disrespect to this Court, that I express my amazement that he
should be still held as a criminal. However just his original arrest
may have seemed; whatever colorable suspicions or fears may have
instigated it; surely, after the developments of this trial, the instructed justice of this government should have given him an
honorable discharge. I do not reflect upon its exertion by the
statement that he has been pursued by the keenest vigilance.
Grant that it was due to the nature of the accusation. He has
suffered, in advance, the doom of the convicted malefactor. Make
no question as to its severity. But, Your Honors, is justice to be
ever relentless ? Is the fable true, that she is the blind deity, smit-
ing with indiscriminate slaughter, careless of her victims, if but her
gluttony of death be satiated ? No! Your Honors. If she be the
vengeful executioner of guilt, she is, likewise, the strong-armed
savior of innocence. Her watchful eye pierces the murky cloud of
circumstance, searches the mazy web of artful contrivance, until
she grasps the sure and steady arm of her majestic handmaid—
truth. Seek truth, Your Honors. Rest your unwavering justice
upon it, not upon the frail and staggering foundation of misty
doubts and unsteady suspicions.

26. Private character of Colonel North.

And if Your Honors are still unconvinced, regard the spotless
character of the man you judge. It is an unsoiled mantle of purity wrapping its protecting folds around his whole life. An amiable and accomplished gentleman, endeared to his friends; an un-
tarnished merchant and officer, honored by the world; an ardent,
but stainless politician, respected by his adversaries, he appeals to

the congenial instincts of his judges. Had guilt been proven, even his unblemished name would not save him; but, in the sometimes subtle entanglement of malicious circumstance encompassing the good man with shadows, he may confidently and proudly point to his blameless reputation. I repel the idea that there is an atom of proof from which the foulest hate can hatch suspicion. But if there were, I meet it with an invulnerable character and defy its venom. Once, at least, it saves from doubtful circumstance. It can but once; for even defeated accusation leaves its enduring taint. The memory of this trial will cling to Col. North, ever supplying malice with its poison. Your judgment may acquit him, but he has been suspected and accused, and that, with censorious rumor, is guilt.

His fate, Your Honors, is in your hands. All of honor he has won in the past, all of hope he has for the future, awaits your decision. The State whose representative he is, the troops of friends whose devoted faith attests his innocence, loving kindred who lean upon him in gentle affection: all implore you to give him true deliverance. United with their voices, not in supplication but in mandate, Your Honors hear the loud and decisive tones of legal privilege and constitutional immunity. There have been times when all these were unavailing to redeem from the fires of persecution. Their bloody track along the annals of history stands as a warning, not as an example. Succeeding them is traced the magnificent struggle of professional genius with the minions of royal prerogative, and then came the triumph of disenthralled humanity; and, still onward, the growing illumination of American progress has lighted the pathway of civilization. I pray you, let not the record be dishonored by the faltering virtue of our judiciary. It is enough that the bold front of treason defies the Constitution; let it not be defiled in the holy tabernacle of the law.

Here Mr. Beach reviewed the evidence in regard to the defendant Cohn, to show that nothing fraudulent or criminal had been proven against him. After referring to the testimony as to his good character, and analyzing the statements of each of the witnesses against him, he continued:

If Your Honors please, I have thus analyzed the proofs and given them appropriate application. I may have misconceived their character and misjudged their force; but I submit them to the judgment of this Court without apprehension, and to the intelligence of the country without misgiving. Acknowledging, but not

fearing the ability of my learned adversary, without arrogance, but
with boldness, I challenge all dispute of the conclusions I have
established. I demand legal deliberation and logical results, not
the vapid demagogueism and unreasoning prejudice of a political
conclave. My clients are to answer in a court of law for their
proven acts, not to a party caucus for suspected wrong. Your
Honors are judges, not partisans, and I may expect that my learned
friend will demonstrate, not denounce. He is fully able to discuss
this case with the learning and candor of the true lawyer. It will
demand his highest qualities. Although he has not considered it
his duty to yield to my clients a proper acknowledgment of their
innocence, he will, I am persuaded, grant them the fairness of an
honorable debate.

Here Mr. Beach compared the evidence with the charges and specifications,
to show that the evidence was upon authority wholly insufficient to sustain them,
and cited O'Brien on American Military Law, pp. 192, 265, and De Hart on
Courts-martial, p. 298. He then continued:

It is only when Your Honors pass the pitiable insignificance of
the proof, that the real greatness of this issue appears. It is then
you enter the atmosphere of loftiest thought, loaded with the genius
and wisdom of the mighty past, pregnant with the issues of the
mightier future. You tread sanctified ground, and there your
weighty responsibility begins.

27. INTEREST AND IMPORTANCE OF THE ISSUES IN THE CASE.

You see how this case mingles with the great topics of governmental power which have stirred the heart of the world since the
endless struggle began between liberty and oppression. You cannot, if you would, belittle it. It is not alone the fate of these defendants you are to decide. Strange as it may seem, here—even
here, before a military commission, the legal representative of the
government of the United States demands a judgment affirming
the suspension of the Constitution. He seeks the liberty, if not
the lives of these defendants, over the shattered fragments of liberty and law. The issue is sharply made between the government
and the citizen. The learned judge advocate concedes, argument-
atively, that he can reach the accused only through a broken Constitution. Your Honors must approve his amazing doctrines, or
you must acquit. I know not how potentially your decision may
affect the future history of the country; I do know that, whatever
that history may become, you may have the proud satisfaction of

linking your names nobly with the fate of constitutional freedom.
It may be that the forebodings of many good men are but the
childish fears of a timid conservatism. The lessons of the past
may be reversed; triumphant power may surrender its victories
over violated right, and restore a mangled Constitution; but, Your
Honors, it is not for you to speculate upon the desperate venture.
As a court you will administer the supreme law, temporizing with
no considerations of expediency, fearless of all dictation, animated
only by an unswerving love of justice.

It cannot be concealed that this cause derives further interest
from its conflict with the claimed power of the State of New York.
The defendants are her citizens. The law violated, if any has
been violated, is the law of her legislature. The offense, if any, is
against her sovereignty. By taunt and gibe and innuendo, her
executive has been assailed, and the purity of her elective franchise
has been impeached. These have been justified by the revelations
of this trial. The calumnies of a reckless partisanship have been
refuted by the clearest demonstration. They answered their temporary purpose; but their calculating and baseless malice has been
exposed. It remains for this Court to recognize and acknowledge
the jurisdiction of the State of New York over these defendants.
She claims the power to vindicate her own majesty, to avenge her
own laws, and purify her own record. She asks no aid from the
military arm of this government. Competent to punish, if guilty,
and to protect, if innocent, she demands her citizens from the
hands of this Court. Your Honors may heed her not. In the flush
of armed authority, environed by the "pomp and circumstance"
of war, her remonstrating voice may be unheard. She raises above
her persecuted children the double shield of the Constitution and
her own sovereignty. You may suspend the one and deride the
other; but your judgment must meet the review of posterity, if it
shall escape the swift retribution of the present.

And why, Your Honors, deny her claim ? Is the justice of New
York distrusted ? Is her loyalty to our institutions suspected ? Is
she so debauched and impotent that the general government, by
military tribunals, must assume to vindicate her honor ? What
overwhelming State necessity demands a remedy so revolutionary
and perilous ? Is the army endangered ? Is the government
shaken ? Have rebellion and anarchy uprooted the constituted
forms of peaceful society ? Oh no! Your Honors; not in these
must you seek the cause of this unrighteous prosecution. It is

honored by no love of country, dignified by no zealous fear for her security. It is all selfish and malignant. It is the instrumentality of despotism, or it is the refuge for political depravity. It may be both; but whichever it is, it is destined to ignoble failure and per- petual malediction. These defendants may be immolated, but the purpose which sacrifices them shall not be secured. The rebound- ing vigor of the Constitution, the elastic vitality of the law, will ultimately prevail. Patriotism may sleep on in its strange apathy; the delusion of a vicious prosperity may mislead its vigilance; its deathless love for the Union of the fathers may stifle its alarms; but the awakening will surely come. The deadly heresies, infect- ing the political faith of the people, shall be uprooted ; these daring invasions upon republican liberty shall be rebuked ; and then, if not now, my clients shall be vindicated and avenged.

WITHOUT LAW THERE IS NO SECURITY.

JEREMY BENTHAM.

Law, alone, has accomplished what all the natural feelings were not able to do; Law, alone, has been able to create a fixed and durable position, which deserves the name of Property. The law, alone, could accustom men to submit to the yoke of foresight, at first painful to be borne, but, afterwards agreeable and mild ; it alone could encourage them in labor—superfluous at present, and which they are not to enjoy till the future. Economy has as many enemies as there are spendthrifts, or men who would enjoy without taking the trouble to produce. Labor is too painful for idleness ; it is too slow for impatience : Cunning and Injustice underhandedly conspire to appropriate its fruits ; Insolence and Audacity plot to seize them by open force. Hence Society, always tottering, always threatened, never at rest, lives in the midst of snares. It requires, in the legislator, vigilance continually sustained, and power always in action, to defend it against his constantly reviving crowd of adversaries.

The law does not say to a man, " Work, and I will reward you ;" but it says to him, " Work, and by stopping the hand that would take them from you, I will insure to you the fruits of your labor, its natural and sufficient reward, which, without me, you could not preserve." If industry creates, it is the law which preserves; if, at the first moment, we owe everything to labor, at the second, and every succeeding moment, we owe everything to the law.

In order to form a clear idea of the whole extent which ought to be given to the principle of security, it is necessary to consider, that man is not like the brutes, limited to the present time, either in enjoyment or suffering ; but that he is susceptible of pleasure and pain by anticipation, and that it is not enough to guard him against an actual loss, but also to guarantee to him, as much as possible, his possessions against future losses. The idea of his security must be prolonged to him throughout the whole vista that his imagination can measure.

This disposition to look forward, which has so marked an influence upon the condition of man, may be called expectation—expectation of the future. It is by means of this we are enabled to form a general plan of conduct; it is by means of this that the successive moments which compose the duration of life are not like isolated and independent points, but become parts of a continuous whole. Expectation is a chain which unites our present and our future existence, and passes beyond ourselves to the generations which follow us. The sensibility of the individual is prolonged through all the links of this chain. The principle of security comprehends the maintenance of all these hopes ; it directs that events, inasmuch as they are dependent upon the laws, should be conformed to the expectations to which the laws have given birth.—[The Principles of the Civil Code.

ARGUMENT OF JEREMIAH S. BLACK

In Defense of the Right to Trial by Jury.

[*Ex parte* Milligan, 4 Wall. 2.]

IN THE SUPREME COURT OF THE UNITED STATES, DECEMBER TERM, 1866.

CONSTITUTIONAL LAW.—Where the courts are open, and in the proper exercise of their jurisdiction, the right of a citizen to a jury trial, guaranteed by the Constitution, cannot be denied or abridged.

Analysis of Mr. Black's Argument.

Lambdin P. Milligan, W. A. Bowles, and Stephen Horsey, during the war of the rebellion, in October, 1864, were arrested by order of General Alvin P. Hovey, commanding the military district of Indiana, brought before a military commission convened at Indianapolis, tried on certain charges and specifications, found guilty, and sentenced to be hanged. Friday, May 19th, 1865, was the day

fixed for their execution. The charges on which Milligan and his associates were
convicted, were substantially that they had joined and aided a secret society
known as the "Order of American Knights, or Sons of Liberty," for the purpose
of destroying the government, communicating with the enemy, conspiring to
seize munitions of war belonging to the Union forces, and to liberate rebel
prisoners confined within the Federal lines. Nine days prior to the time fixed
for his execution, Milligan applied by petition to the Circuit Court of the United States for his discharge, on the ground that his imprisonment and detention
were unauthorized and illegal. Upon the matters presented by the petition the
court were divided in opinion, and certified the following questions to the
Supreme Court of the United States, based upon all the facts set out in
the record: (1.) Should a writ of *habeas corpus* be issued? (2.) Should Milligan
be discharged as prayed for? (3.) Had the military commission jurisdiction
legally to try and sentence the petitioner? The court held that the writ would
issue, and that Milligan was entitled to his discharge, on the ground that the
military commission was unauthorized and illegal, and acquired no jurisdiction
to try and sentence him. Although the court were unanimous in their judgment
that the relator should be discharged, there seemed to be a difference of opinion
as to the power of Congress to establish military commissions. In view of this
fact, a separate opinion was written by Chief Justice Chase, which was concurred
in by Justices Swayne, Wayne and Miller, declaring that while the particular
commission which sentenced Milligan was not authorized, yet the power of
Congress to authorize trials for crimes against the security and safety of the
national forces may be derived in time of war but not in peace, from its authority to raise and support armies and to declare war, if not from its Constitutional
authority to provide for governing the national forces. Mr. Justice Davis was
the organ of the court, and delivered the opinion of the majority with a power
of convincing logic, which does infinite honor to his name. He fully adopted
the views of the counsel for the relator.

This defense of the right of trial by jury is a marvelous display of Judge
Black's extraordinary power and abilities as a lawyer, and the enduring importance of the subject will render it interesting as long as the individual liberty of
the citizen shall be preserved as part of the frame-work of human government.
It was delivered during a period of great political excitement, before the passions
and prejudices stirred up by the greatest civil war in history had been allayed.
It affected the destiny of one whose crimes were aimed at the destruction of the
government itself, and the public desire to see the sentence of the commission
executed, was very general. Since the anger and excitement of the times have
passed away, and the great questions involved in this case present themselves in
their true aspect and importance, the argument of Judge Black becomes conspicuous as a defense of the dearest rights of the citizen, and stands like a monument
to which the eyes of mankind will turn in the hour when their rights are assailed.
It will be admired by the student as a comprehensive exposition of the fundamental principles upon which the law of civil liberty depends, and the causes
which led to their perfection and adoption under our system. The subject loses
the dry, tedious detail of a legal argument, and becomes animated with the
spirit and genius of the speaker, while presenting a review of the struggle between freedom and arbitrary power which the world has witnessed for centuries.

It will be considered precious by persons in every walk of life, for it defines in a masterly manner the natural rights guaranteed to each individual by the organic law, and its importance in this respect clothes it with the heritage of immortality.

On the part of the relator appeared David Dudley Field, J. E. McDonald, Jeremiah S. Black, and James A. Garfield.   On the part of the government the attorney-general (Mr. Speed) and Mr. Stanberry and Benjamin F. Butler, of counsel.   Mr. Black spoke as follows :

MAY IT PLEASE YOUR HONORS :—I am not afraid that you will underrate the importance of this case.   It concerns the rights of the whole people.   Such questions have generally been settled by arms ; but since the beginning of the world no battle has ever been lost or won upon which the liberties of a nation were so distinctly staked as they are on the result of this argument.   The pen that writes the judgment of the court will be mightier, for good or for evil, than any sword that ever was wielded by mortal arm.

As might be expected from the nature of the subject, it has been a good deal discussed elsewhere, in legislative bodies, in public assemblies, and in the newspaper press of the country.   But there it has been mingled with interests and feelings not very friendly to a correct conclusion.   Here we are in a higher atmosphere, where no passion can disturb the judgment or shake the even balance in which the scales of reason are held.   Here it is purely a judicial question; and I can speak for my colleagues as well as myself, when I say that we have no thought to suggest which we do not suppose to be a fair element in the strictly legal judgment which you are required to make up.

In performing the duty assigned to me in the case, I shall necessarily refer to the mere rudiments of constitutional law; to the most commonplace topics of history, and to those plain rules of justice and right which pervade all our institutions.   I beg your honors to believe that this is not done because I think that the court, or any member of it, is less familiar with these things than I am, or less sensible of their value; but simply and only because, according to my view of the subject, there is absolutely no other way of dealing with it.   If the fundamental principles of American liberty are attacked, and we are driven behind the inner walls of the Constitution to defend them, we can repel the assault only with those same old weapons which our ancestors used a hundred years ago.   You must not think the worse of our armor because it happens to be old-fashioned and looks a little rusty from long disuse.

i. Of the charges against the relator, and the tribunal by which he was convicted.

The case before you presents but a single point, and that an exceedingly plain one. It is not encumbered with any of those vexed
questions that might be expected to arise out of a great war. You
are not called upon to decide what kind of rule a military commander may impose upon the inhabitants of a hostile country
which he occupies as a conqueror, or what punishment he may inflict upon the soldiers of his own army or the followers of his
camp; or yet how he may deal with civilians in a beleaguered city
or other place in a state of actual siege, which he is required to defend against a public enemy. The contest covers no such ground
as that. The men whose acts we complain of erected themselves
into a tribunal for the trial and punishment of citizens who were
connected in no way whatever with the army or navy. And this
they did in the midst of a community whose social and legal organization had never been disturbed by any war or insurrection, where
the courts were wide open, where judicial process was executed
every day without interruption, and where all the civil authorities,
both State and national, were in the full exercise of their functions.

My clients were dragged before this strange tribunal, and after
a proceeding, which it would be mere mockery to call a trial, they
were ordered to be hung. The charge against them was put into
writing and is found on this record, but you will not be able to de-
cipher its meaning. The relators were not accused of treason; for
no act is imputed to them which, if true, would come within the
definition of that crime. It was not conspiracy under the act of
1861; for all concerned in this business must have known that conspiracy was not a capital offense. If the commissioners were able
to read English, they could not help but see that it was made punishable, even by fine and imprisonment, only upon condition that
the parties should first be convicted before a circuit or district
court of the United States. The judge advocate must have meant
to charge them with some offense unknown to the laws, which he
chose to make capital by legislation of his own, and the commissioners were so profoundly ignorant as to think that the legal innocence of the parties made no difference in the case. I do not say
what Sir James Mackintosh said of a similar proceeding: that the
trial was a mere conspiracy to commit willful murder upon three
innocent men. The commissioners are not on trial; they are absent
and undefended; and they are entitled to the benefit of that charity

which presumes them to be wholly unacquainted with the first principles of natural justice, and quite unable to comprehend either the law or the facts of a criminal cause.

2. THE COMMISSION WHICH TRIED THE RELATOR, ILLEGAL AND ITS ENTIRE PROCEEDINGS VOID FOR WANT OF JURISDICTION.

Keeping the character of the charges in mind, let us come at once to the simple question upon which the court below divided in opinion: Had the commissioners jurisdiction—were they invested with legal authority to try the relators and put them to death for the offense of which they were accused? We answer, no; and, therefore, the whole proceeding from beginning to end was utterly null and void. On the other hand, it is absolutely necessary for those who oppose us to assert, and they do assert, that the commissioners had complete legal jurisdiction both of the subject-matter and of the parties, so that their judgment upon the law and the facts is absolutely conclusive and binding, not subject to correction nor open to inquiry in any court whatever. Of these two opposite views, you must adopt one or the other; for there is no middle ground on which you can possibly stand.

I need not say (for it is the law of the horn books) that where a court (whatever may be its power in other respects) presumes to try a man for an offense of which it has no right to take judicial cognizance, all its proceedings in that case are null and void. If the party is acquitted, he cannot plead the acquittal afterwards in bar of another prosecution; if he is found guilty and sentenced, he is entitled to be relieved from the punishment. If a Circuit Court of the United States should undertake to try a party for an offense clearly within the exclusive jurisdiction of the State courts, the judgment could have no effect. If a county court in the interior of a State should arrest an officer of the Federal navy, try him, and order him to be hung for some offense against the law of nations, committed upon the high seas or in a foreign port, nobody would treat such a judgment otherwise than with mere derision. The Federal courts have jurisdiction to try offenses against the laws of the United States, and the authority of the State courts is confined to the punishment of acts which are made penal by State laws. It follows that where the accusation does not amount to an offense against the law of either the State or the Federal government, no court can have jurisdiction to try it. Suppose, for example, that the judges of this court should organize themselves into a tribunal to try a man for witchcraft, or heresy, or treason against the Confederate States of America, would any body say that your judgment had the least validity ?

I care not, therefore, whether the relators were intended to be charged with treason or conspiracy, or with some offense of which the law takes no notice. Either or any way, the men who undertook to try them had no jurisdiction of the *subject-matter*.

Nor had they jurisdiction of the *parties*. It is not pretended that this was a case of impeachment, or a case arising in the land or naval forces. It is either nothing at all or else it is a simple crime against the United States, committed by private individuals not in the public service, civil or military. Persons standing in that relation to the government are answerable for the offenses which they may commit only to the civil courts of the country. So says the Constitution, as we read it ; and the act of Congress of March 3d, 1863, which was passed with express reference to persons precisely in the situation of these men, declares that they shall be delivered up for trial to the proper civil authorities.

3. Duty of the court to discharge the petitióners shown.

There being no jurisdiction of the subject-matter or of the parties, you are bound to relieve the petitioners. It is as much the duty of a judge to protect the innocent as it is to punish the guilty. Suppose that the secretary of some department should take it into his head to establish an ecclesiastical tribunal here in the city of Washington, composed of clergymen " organized to convict" every body who prays after a fashion inconsistent with the supposed safety of the State. If he would select the members with a proper regard to the *odium theologicum*, I think I could insure him a commission that would hang every man and woman who might be brought before it. But would you, the judges of the land, stand by and see their sentences executed ? No ; you would interpose your *writ of prohibition*, your *habeas corpus*, or any other process that might be at your command, between them and their victims. And you would do that for precisely the reason which requires your intervention here—because religious errors, like political errors, are not crimes which any body in this country has jurisdiction to punish, and because ecclesiastical commissions, like military commissions, are not among the judicial institutions of this people. Our fathers long ago cast them both aside among the rubbish of the dark ages; and they intended that we, their children, should know them only that we might blush and shudder at the shameless injustice and the brutal cruelties which they were allowed to perpetrate in other times and other countries.

But our friends on the other side are not at all impressed with these views. Their brief corresponds exactly with the doctrines propounded by the attorney-general, in a very elaborate official paper which he published last July, upon this same subject. He then avowed it to be his settled and deliberate opinion that the military might "*take and kill, try and execute*" (I use his own words) persons who had no sort of connection with the army or navy. And though this be done in the face of the open courts, the judicial authorities, according to him, are utterly powerless to prevent the slaughter which may thus be carried on. That is the thesis which the attorney-general and his assistant counsellors are to maintain this day, if they can maintain it, with all the power of their artful eloquence.

We, on the other hand, submit, that a person not in the military or naval service cannot be punished at all until he has had a fair, open, public trial before an impartial jury, in an ordained and established court, to which the jurisdiction has been given by law to try him for that specific offense. There is our proposition. Between the ground we take and the ground they occupy there is and there can be no compromise. It is one way or the other.

Our proposition ought to be received as true without any argument to support it; because if that, or something precisely equivalent to it, be not a part of our law, this is not what we have always supposed it to be—a free country. Nevertheless, I take upon myself the burden of showing affirmatively not only that it is true, but that it is immovably fixed in the very frame-work of the government, so that it is utterly impossible to detach it without destroying the whole political structure under which we live. By removing it you destroy the life of this nation as completely as you would destroy the life of an individual by cutting the heart out of his body. I proceed to the proof.

4. THE TRIAL AND PUNISHMENT OF AN OFFENSE IS AN EXERCISE OF EXCLUSIVE AUTHORITY, CONFERRED UPON EXPRESS CONDITIONS AND LIMITATIONS.

In the first place, the self-evident truth will not be denied, that the trial and punishment of an offender against the government is the exercise of judicial authority. That is a kind of authority which would be lost by being diffused among the masses of the people. A judge would be no judge if every body else were a judge as well as he. Therefore, in every society, however rude or however perfect its organization, the judicial authority is always committed to the hands of particular persons, who are trusted to use it wisely and well; and their authority is exclusive; they cannot share it with others to whom it has not been committed. Where, then, is the judicial power in this country ? Who are the depositaries of it here? The Federal Constitution answers that question in very plain words, by declaring that "*the judicial power of the United States shall be vested in one Supreme Court, and in such inferior courts as Congress may from time to time ordain and establish.*" Congress *has* from time to time ordained and established certain inferior courts; and in them, together with the one Supreme Court to which they are subordinate, is vested all the judicial power, properly so called, which the United States can lawfully exercise. That was the compact made with the general government at the time it was created. The States and the people agreed to bestow upon that government a certain portion of the judicial power which otherwise would have remained in their own hands, but gave it on a solemn trust, and coupled the grant of it with this express condition : that it should never be used in any way but one; that is, by means of ordained and established courts. Any person, therefore, who undertakes to exercise judicial power in any other way, not only violates the law of the land, but he treacherously tramples upon the most important part of that sacred covenant which holds these States together.

May it please your honors : you know, and I know, and every body else knows, that it was the intention of the men who founded this republic to put the life, liberty and property of every person in it under the protection of a regular and permanent judiciary, separate, apart, distinct from all other branches of the government, whose sole and exclusive business it should be to distribute justice among the people according to the wants and merits of each individual. It was to consist of courts, always open to the complaint of the injured, and always ready to hear criminal accusations when founded upon probable cause ; surrounded with all the machinery necessary for the investigation of truth, and clothed with sufficient power to carry their decrees into execution. In these courts it was expected that judges would sit who would be upright, honest, and sober men, learned in the laws of their country, and lovers of justice from the habitual practice of that virtue; independent because their salaries could not be reduced, and free from party passion because their tenure of office was for life.   Although this would place them above the clamors of the mere mob and beyond the reach of executive influence, it was not intended that they should be wholly irresponsible.   For any willful or corrupt violation of their duty, they are liable to be impeached ; and they cannot escape the control of an enlightened public opinion, for they must sit with open doors, listen to full discussion, and give satisfactory reasons for the judgments they pronounce.   In ordinary tranquil times the citizen might feel himself safe under a judicial system so organized.

But our wise forefathers knew that tranquillity was not to be always anticipated in a republic; the spirit of a free people is often turbulent.   They expected that strife would rise between classes and sections, and even civil war might come, and they supposed that in such times judges themselves might not be safely trusted in criminal cases, especially in prosecutions for political offenses, where the whole power of the executive is arrayed against the accused party.   All history proves that public officers of any government, when they are engaged in a severe struggle to retain their places, become bitter and ferocious, and hate those who oppose them, even in the most legitimate way, with a rancor which they never exhibit towards actual crime.   This kind of malignity vents itself in prosecutions for political offenses, sedition, conspiracy, libel, and treason, and the charges are generally founded upon the information of hireling spies and common delators, who make merchandise of their oaths and trade in the blood of their fellow men.   During the civil commotions in England, which lasted from the beginning of the reign of Charles I to the revolution of 1688, the best men and the purest patriots that ever lived fell by the hand of the public executioner.   Judges were made the instruments for inflicting the most merciless sentences on men, the latchet of whose shoes the ministers that prosecuted them were not worthy to stoop down and unloose.   Let me say here that nothing has occurred in the history of this country to justify the doubt of judicial integrity which our forefathers seem to have felt.   On the contrary, the highest compliment that has ever been paid to the American bench is embodied in this simple fact: that if the executive officers of this government have ever desired to take away the life or the liberty of a citizen contrary to law, they have not come into the courts to get it done; they have gone outside the courts, and stepped over the Constitution, and created their own tribunals, composed of men whose gross ignorance and supple subservience could always be relied on for those base uses to which no judge would ever lend himself. But the framers of the Constitution could act only upon the experience of that country whose history they knew most about, and there they saw the brutal ferocity of Jeffreys and Scroggs, the timidity of Guilford, and the base venality of such men as Saunders and Wright. It seemed necessary, therefore, not only to make the judiciary as perfect as possible, but to give the citizen yet another shield against the wrath and malice of his government. To that end they could think of no better provision than a public trial before an impartial jury.

5. Trial by jury affords the best protection for innocence, and the surest mode of punishing guilt, yet discovered among men.

I do not assert that the jury trial is an infallible mode of ascertaining truth. Like everything human, it has its imperfections. I only say, that it is the best protection for innocence and the surest mode of punishing guilt that has yet been discovered. It has borne the test of a longer experience, and borne it better, than any other legal institution that ever existed among men. England owes more of her freedom, her grandeur, and her prosperity, to that than to all other causes put together. It has had the approbation not only of those who lived under it, but of great thinkers who looked at it calmly from a distance, and judged it impartially. Montesquieu and De Tocqueville speak of it with an admiration as rapturous as Coke and Blackstone. Within the present century, the most enlightened states of continental Europe have transplanted it into their countries; and no people ever adopted it once and were afterwards willing to part with it. It was only in 1830 that an interference with it in Belgium provoked a successful insurrection which permanently divided one kingdom into two. In the same year, the Revolution of the Barricades gave the right of trial by jury to every Frenchman.

Those colonists of this country who came from the British Islands brought this institution with them, and they regarded it as the most precious part of their inheritance. The immigrants from other places where trial by jury did not exist, became equally attached to it as soon as they understood what it was. There was no subject upon which all the inhabitants of the country were more perfectly unanimous than they were in their determination to maintain this great right unimpaired. An attempt was made to set it aside and substitute military trials in its place, by Lord Dunmore, in Virginia, and General Gage, in Massachusetts, accompanied with the excuse which has been repeated so often in late days, namely, that rebellion had made it necessary ; but it excited intense popular anger, and every colony from New Hampshire to Georgia made common cause with the two whose rights had been especially invaded. Subsequently, the Continental Congress thundered it into the ear of the world, as an unendurable outrage, sufficient to justify universal insurrection against the authority of the government which had allowed it to be done.

If the men who fought out our revolutionary contest, when they came to frame a government for themselves and their posterity, had failed to insert a provision making the trial by jury perpetual and universal, they would have covered themselves all over with infamy as with a garment; for they would have proved themselves basely recreant to the principles of that very liberty of which they professed to be the special champions.   But they were guilty of no such treachery.   They not only took care of the trial by jury, but they regulated every step to be taken in a criminal trial.   They knew very well that no people could be free under a government which had the power to punish without restraint.   Hamilton expressed in the Federalist the universal sentiment of his time, when he said that the arbitrary power of conviction and punishment for pretended offenses had been the great engine of despotism in all ages and all countries.   The existence of such power is utterly incompatible with freedom.   The difference between a master and his slave consists only in this : that the master holds the lash in his hands and he may use it without legal restraint, while the naked back of the slave is bound to take whatever is laid on it.

6. Enumeration of the rights for the preservation of individual liberty, which forms part of the organic law.

But our fathers were not absurd enough to put unlimited power in the hands of the ruler and take away the protection of law from the rights of individuals. It was not thus that they meant "to secure the blessings of liberty to themselves and their posterity."

They determined that not one drop of the blood which had been shed on the other side of the Atlantic, during seven centuries of contest with arbitrary power, should sink into the ground ; but the fruits of every popular victory should be garnered up in this new government. Of all the great rights already won, they threw not an atom away. They went over *Magna Charta*, the *Petition of Right*, the *Bill of Rights*, and the rules of the *Common Law*, and whatever was found there to favor individual liberty they carefully inserted in their own system, improved by clearer expression, strengthened by heavier sanctions, and extended by a more universal application. They put all those provisions into the organic law, so that neither tyranny in the executive, nor party rage in the Legislature could change them without destroying the government itself.

Look for a moment at the particulars and see how carefully every thing connected with the administration of punitive justice is guarded.

1. No *ex post facto* law shall be passed. No man shall be answerable criminally for any act which was not defined and made punishable as a crime by some law in force at the time when the act was done.

2. For an act which is criminal he cannot be arrested without a judicial warrant founded on proof of probable cause. He shall not be kidnapped and shut up on the mere report of some base spy who gathers the materials of a false accusation by crawling into his house and listening at the key-hole of his chamber door.

3. He shall not be compelled to testify against himself. He may be examined before he is committed, and tell his own story if he pleases; but the rack shall be put out of sight, and even his conscience shall not be tortured; nor shall his unpublished papers be used against him, as was done most wrongfully in the case of Algernon Sydney.

4. He shall be entitled to a speedy trial; not kept in prison for an indefinite time without the opportunity of vindicating his innocence.

5. He shall be informed of the accusation, its nature and grounds. The public accuser must put the charge into the form of a legal indictment, so that the party can meet it full in the face.

6. Even to the indictment he need not answer unless a grand jury, after hearing the evidence, shall say upon their oaths that they believe it to be true.

7. Then comes the trial, and it must be before a regular court of competent jurisdiction, ordained and established for the State and district in which the crime was committed; and this shall not be evaded by a legislative change in the district after the crime is alleged to be done.

8. His guilt or innocence shall be determined by an impartial jury. These English words are to be understood in their English sense, and they mean that the jurors shall be fairly selected by a sworn officer, from among the peers of the party residing within the local jurisdiction of the court. When they are called into the box, he can purge the panel of all dishonesty, prejudice, personal enmity, and ignorance, by a certain number of peremptory challenges, and as many more challenges as he can sustain by showing reasonable cause.

9. The trial shall be public and open, that no underhand advantage may be taken. The party shall be confronted with the witnesses against him, have compulsory process for his own witnesses, and be entitled to the assistance of counsel in his defense.

10. After the evidence is heard and discussed, unless the jury shall, upon their oaths, *unanimously* agree to surrender him up into the hands of the court as a guilty man, not a hair of his head can be touched by way of punishment.

11. After a verdict of guilty, he is still protected. No cruel or unusual punishment shall be inflicted, nor any punishment at all, except what is annexed by law to his offense. It cannot be doubted for a moment, that if a person convicted of an offense not capital were to be hung on the order of a judge, such judge would be guilty of murder as plainly as if he should come down from the bench, tuck up the sleeves of his gown, and let out the prisoner's blood with his own hand.

12. After all is over, the law continues to spread its guardianship around him. Whether he is acquitted or condemned he shall never again be molested for that offense. No man shall be twice put in jeopardy of life or limb for the same cause.

7. SPECIAL PROVISIONS APPLICABLE TO THE LAW OF TREASON.

These rules apply to all criminal prosecutions. But, in addition to these, certain special regulations were required for *treason*, the one great political charge under which more innocent men have fallen than any other. A tyrannical government calls everybody a traitor who shows the least unwillingness to be a slave. The party in power never fails, when it can, to stretch the law on that subject by construction, so as to cover its honest and conscientious opponents. In the absence of a constitutional provision it was justly feared that statutes might be passed which would put the lives of the most patriotic citizens at the mercy of the basest minions that skulk about under pay of the executive. Therefore a definition of treason was given in the fundamental law, and the legislative authority could not enlarge it to serve the purpose of partisan malice. The nature and amount of evidence required to prove the crime was also prescribed, so that prejudice and enmity might have no share in the conviction. And lastly, the punishment was so limited that the property of the party could not be confiscated and used to reward the agents of his persecutors, or strip his family of their subsistence.

If these provisions exist in full force, unchangeable and irrepealable, then we are not hereditary bondsmen. Every citizen may safely pursue his lawful calling in the open day; and at night, if he is conscious of innocence, he may lie down in security and sleep the sound sleep of the freeman.

I say they are in force, and they will remain in force. We have not surrendered them and we never will. If the worst comes to the worst, we will look to the living God for His help, and defend our rights and the rights of our children to the last extremity. Those men who think we can be subjected and abjected to the condition of mere slaves are wholly mistaken. The great race to which we belong has not degenerated so fatally.

8. HISTORICAL RETROSPECT OF THE PROVISIONS WHICH TO-DAY SECURE THE NATURAL RIGHTS OF MAN.

But how am I to prove the existence of these rights? I do not propose to do it by a long chain of legal argumentation, nor by the production of numerous books with the leaves dog-eared and the pages marked. If it depended upon judicial precedents, I think I could produce as many as might be necessary. If I claimed this freedom, under any kind of prescription, I could prove a good long possession in ourselves and those under whom we claim it. I might begin with Tacitus, and show how the contest arose in the forests of Germany more than two thousand years ago; how the rough virtues and sound common sense of that people established the right of trial by jury, and thus started on a career which has made their posterity the foremost race that ever lived in all the tide of time.

The Saxons carried it to England, and were ever ready to defend it with their blood. It was crushed out by the Danish invasion; and all that they suffered of tyranny and oppression, during the period of their subjugation, resulted from the want of trial by jury. If that had been conceded to them the reaction would not have taken place which drove back the Danes to their frozen homes in the North. But those ruffian sea-kings could not understand that, and the reaction came. Alfred, the greatest of revolutionary heroes and the wisest monarch that ever sat on a throne, made the first use of his power, after the Saxons restored it, to re-establish their ancient laws. He had promised them that he would, and he was true to them because they had been true to him. But it was not easily done; the courts were opposed to it, for it limited their power—a kind of power that every body covets—the power to punish without regard to law. He was obliged to hang forty-four judges in one year for refusing to give his subjects a trial by jury. When the historian says he hung them, it is not meant that he put them to death without a trial. He had them impeached before the grand council of the nation, the Wittenagemote, the parliament of that time. During the subsequent period of Saxon domination no man on English soil was powerful enough to refuse a legal trial to the meanest peasant. If any minister or any king, in war or in peace, had dared to punish a freeman by a tribunal of his own appointment, he would have roused the wrath of the whole population; all orders of society would have resisted it; lord and vassal, knight and squire, priest and penitent, bocman and socman, master and thrall, copyholder and villein, would have risen in one mass and burnt the offender to death in his castle, or followed him in his flight and torn him to atoms. It was again trampled down by the Norman conquerors; but the evils resulting from the want of it united all classes in the effort which compelled King John to restore it by the Great Charter. Everybody is familiar with the struggles which the English people, during many generations, made for their rights with the Plantagenets, the Tudors, and the Stuarts, and which ended finally in the revolution of 1688, when the liberties of England were placed upon an impregnable basis by the Bill of Rights.

Many times the attempt was made to stretch the royal authority far enough to justify military trials; but it never had more than temporary success. Five hundred years ago Edward II closed up a great rebellion by taking the life of its leader, the Earl of Lan-

caster, after trying him before a military court. Eight years later
that same king, together with his lords and commons in parliament
assembled, acknowledged with shame and sorrow that the execution
of Lancaster was a mere murder, because the courts were open and
he might have had a legal trial. Queen Elizabeth, for sundry reasons affecting the safety of the State, ordered that certain offenders not of her army should be tried according to the law martial.
But she heard the storm of popular vengeance rising, and, haughty,
imperious, self-willed as she was, she yielded the point; for she
knew that upon that subject the English people would never
consent to be trifled with. Strafford, as Lord Lieutenant of Ireland, tried the Viscount Stormount before a military commission. When impeached for it, he pleaded in vain that Ireland
was in a state of insurrection, that Stormount was a traitor, and the
army would be undone if it could not defend itself without appealing to the civil courts. The parliament was deaf; the king himself
could not save him; he was condemned to suffer death as a traitor
and a murderer. Charles I issued commissions to divers officers
for the trial of his enemies according to the course of military
law. If rebellion ever was an excuse for such an act, he could
surely have pleaded it; for there was scarcely a spot in his kingdom, from sea to sea, where the royal authority was not disputed
by some body. Yet the parliament demanded in their petition of
right, and the king was obliged to concede, that all his commissions
were illegal. James II claimed the right to suspend the operation
of the penal laws—a power which the courts denied—but the experience of his predecessors taught him that he could not suspend
any man's right to a trial. He could easily have convicted the
Seven Bishops of any offense he saw fit to charge them with, if he
could have selected their judges from among the mercenary creatures to whom he had given commands in his army. But this he
dared not do. He was obliged to send the bishops to a jury, and
endure the mortification of seeing them acquitted. He, too, might
have had rebellion for an excuse, if rebellion be an excuse. The
conspiracy was already ripe, which a few months afterwards made
him an exile and an outcast; he had reason to believe that the
Prince of Orange was making his preparations on the other side of
the channel to invade the kingdom, where thousands burned to join
him; nay, he pronounced the bishops guilty of rebellion by the
very act for which he arrested them. He had raised an army to
meet the rebellion, and he was on Hounslow Heath reviewing the

troops organized for that purpose, when he heard the great shout of joy that went up from Westminster Hall, was echoed back from Temple Bar, spread down the city and over the Thames, and rose from every vessel on the river—the simultaneous shout of two hundred thousand men for the triumph of justice and law.

If it were worth the time I might detain you by showing how this subject was treated by the French Court o Cassation in Geoffroy's case, under the constitution of 1830, when a military judgment was unhesitatingly pronounced to be void, though ordered by the king, after a proclamation declaring Paris in a state of siege. *Fas est ab hoste doceri;* we may lawfully learn something from our enemies—at all events we should blush at the thought of not being equal on such a subject to the courts of Virginia, Georgia, Mississippi, and Texas, whose decisions my colleague, General Garfield, has read and commented on.

9. No military tribunal has power to try a citizen at a place where the courts are open.—The title by which a jury trial is secured.

The truth is, that no authority exists anywhere in the world for the doctrine of the attorney-general. No judge or jurist, no statesman or parliamentary orator, on this or the other side of the water, sustains him. Every elementary writer, from Coke to Wharton, is against him. All military authors who profess to know the duties of their profession, admit themselves to be under, not above, the laws. No book can be found in any library to justify the assertion that military tribunals may try a citizen at a place where the courts are open. When I say no book, I mean, of course, no book of acknowledged authority. I do not deny that hireling clergymen have often been found to disgrace the pulpit by trying to prove the divine right of kings and other rulers to govern as they please. It is true also that court sycophants and party hacks have many times written pamphlets, and perhaps large volumes, to show that those whom they serve should be allowed to work out their bloody will upon the people. No abuse of power is too flagrant to find its defenders among such servile creatures. Those butchers' dogs that feed upon garbage and fatten upon the offal of the shambles are always ready to bark at whatever interferes with the trade of their master. But this case does not depend on authority. It is rather a question of fact than of law.

I prove my right to a trial by jury just as I would prove my

32

title to an estate if I held in my hand a solemn deed conveying it
to me, coupled with undeniable evidence of long and undisturbed
possession under and according to the deed.   There is the charter
by which we claim to hold it.   It is called the Constitution of the
United States.   It is signed by the sacred name of George Washington, and by thirty-nine other names, only less illustrious than his.
They represented every independent State then upon this continent, and each State afterwards ratified their work by a separate
convention of its own people.   Every State that subsequently came
in acknowledged that this was the great standard by which their
rights were to be measured.   Every man that has ever held office
in the country from that time to this, has taken an oath that he
would support and sustain it through good report and through evil.
The attorney-general himself became a party to the instrument
when he laid his hand upon the gospel of God and solemnly swore
that he would give to me and every other citizen the full benefit of
all it contains.   What does it contain ?   This among other things:
" The trial of all crimes, except in cases of impeachment, shall be
by jury."

Again : " No person shall be held to answer for a capital or
otherwise infamous crime unless on a presentment or indictment of
a grand jury, except in cases arising in the land or naval forces, or
in the militia when in actual service in time of war or public danger; nor shall any person be subject for the same offense to be
twice put in jeopardy of life or limb, nor be compelled in any criminal case to be a witness against himself, nor be deprived of life,
liberty, or property, without due process of law; nor shall private
property be taken for public use without just compensation."

This is not all ; another article declares, that "in all criminal
prosecutions the accused shall enjoy the right to a speedy and public trial by an impartial jury of the State and district wherein the
crime shall have been committed, which district shall have been
previously ascertained by law ; and to be informed of the nature
and cause of the accusation ; to be confronted with the witnesses
against him ; to have compulsory process for the witnesses in his
favor, and to have the assistance of counsel for his defense."

Is there any ambiguity there ?   If that does not signify that a
jury trial shall be the exclusive and only means of ascertaining
guilt in criminal cases, then I demand to know what words or what
collocation of words in the English language would have that effect ?   Does this mean that a fair, open, speedy, public trial by an

impartial jury shall be given only to those persons against whom no special grudge is felt by the attorney-general, or the judge advocate, or the head of a department? Shall this inestimable privilege be extended only to men whom the administration does not care to convict? Is it confined to vulgar criminals, who commit ordinary crimes against society, and shall it be denied to men who are accused of such offenses as those for which Sydney and Russell were beheaded, and Alice Lisle was hung, and Elizabeth Gaunt was burnt alive, and John Bunyan was imprisoned fourteen years, and Baxter was whipped at the cart's tail, and Prynn had his ears cut off? No; the words of the Constitution are all-embracing—

"As broad and general as the casing air."

The trial of ALL crimes shall be by jury. ALL persons accused shall enjoy that privilege—and NO person shall be held to answer in any other way.

That would be sufficient without more. But there is another consideration which gives it tenfold power. It is a universal rule of construction that general words in any instrument, though they may be weakened by enumeration, are always strengthened by exceptions. Here is no attempt to enumerate the particular cases in which men charged with criminal offenses shall be entitled to a jury trial. It is simply declared that *all* shall have it. But that is coupled with a statement of two specific exceptions: cases of impeachment; and cases arising in the land or naval forces. These exceptions strengthen the application of the general rule to all other cases. Where the law-giver himself has declared when and in what circumstances you may depart from the general rule, you shall not presume to leave that onward path for other reasons, and make different exceptions. To exceptions, the maxim is always applicable, that *expressio unius est exclusio alterius.*

10. IN TURBULENT TIMES THE RIGHTS OF THE CITIZEN SHOULD BE DOUBLY GUARDED.

But we are answered that the judgment under consideration was pronounced in time of war, and it is therefore, at least, morally excusable. There may or there may not be something in that. I admit that the merits or demerits of any particular act, whether it involve a violation of the Constitution or not, depend upon the motives that prompted it, the time, the occasion, and all the attending circumstances. When the people of this country come to decide upon the acts of their rulers, they will take all these things into consideration. But that presents the political aspect of the case, with which, I trust, we have nothing to do here. I decline to discuss it. I would only say, in order to prevent misapprehension, that I think it is precisely in a time of war and civil commotion that we should double the guards upon the Constitution. If the sanitary regulations which defend the health of a city are ever to be relaxed, it ought certainly not to be done when pestilence is abroad. When the Mississippi shrinks within its natural channel and creeps lazily along the bottom, the inhabitants of the adjoining shore have no need of a dyke to save them from inundation. But when the booming flood comes down from above, and swells into a volume which rises high above the plain on either side, then a crevasse in the levee becomes a most serious thing. So, in peaceable and quiet times, our legal rights are in little danger of being overborne; but when the wave of arbitrary power lashes itself into violence and rage, and goes surging up against the barriers which were made to confine it, then we need the whole strength of an unbroken Constitution to save us from destruction. But this is a question which properly belongs to the jurisdiction of the stump and the newspaper.

II. WHY THE PLEA OF NECESSITY, THE ONLY EXCUSE FOR VIOLATING LAW, HAS NO APPLICATION TO THE CASE.

There is another *quasi* political argument—necessity. If the law was violated because it could not be obeyed, that might be an excuse. But no absolute compulsion is pretended here. These commissioners acted, at most, under what they regarded as a moral necessity. The choice was left them to obey the law or disobey it. The disobedience was only necessary as means to an end which they thought desirable; and now they assert that though these means are unlawful and wrong, they are made right, because without them the object could not be accomplished; in other words, the end justifies the means. There you have a rule of conduct denounced by all law, human and divine, as being pernicious in policy and false in morals. See how it applies to this case. Here were three men whom it was desirable to remove out of this world, but there was no proof on which any court would take their lives; therefore it was necessary, and being necessary it was right and proper, to create an illegal tribunal which would put them to death without proof.   By the same mode of reasoning you can prove it equally right to poison them in their food or stab them in their sleep.   Nothing that the worst men ever propounded has produced so much oppression, misgovernment, and suffering as this pretense of State necessity.   A great authority calls it "the tyrant's devilish plea;" and the common honesty of all mankind has branded it with everlasting infamy.

12. NECESSITY COULD BUT EXCUSE A VIOLATION OF LAW, BUT
CANNOT IMPART VALIDITY TO AN ACT WHICH THE
LAW FORBIDS.

Of course, it is mere absurdity to say that these relators were *necessarily* deprived of their right to a fair and legal trial, for the record shows that a court of competent jurisdiction was sitting at the very time and in the same town, where justice would have been done without sale, denial, or delay.   But concede, for the argument's sake, that a trial by jury was wholly impossible; admit that there was an absolute, overwhelming, imperious necessity operating so as literally to compel every act which the commissioners did, would that give their sentence of death the validity and force of a legal judgment pronounced by an ordained and established court?   The question answers itself.   This trial was a violation of law, and no necessity could be more than a mere *excuse* for those who committed it.   If the commissioners were on trial for murder or conspiracy to murder, they might plead necessity if the fact were true, just as they would plead insanity or anything else to show that their guilt was not willful.   But we are now considering the legal effect of their decision, and that depends on their legal authority to make it.   They had no such authority; they usurped a jurisdiction which the law not only did not give them, but expressly forbade them to exercise, and it follows that their act is void, whatever may have been the real or supposed excuse for it.

If these commissioners, instead of aiming at the life and liberty of the relators, had attempted to deprive them of their property by a sentence of confiscation, would any court in christendom declare that such a sentence divested the title?   Or would a person claiming under the sentence make his right any better by showing that the illegal assumption of jurisdiction was accompanied by some excuse which might save the commissioners from a criminal prosecution?

Let me illustrate still further.   Suppose you, the judges of this court, to be surrounded in the hall where you are sitting by a body of armed insurgents, and compelled by main force to pronounce sentence of death upon the President of the United States, for some act of his upon which you have no legal authority to adjudicate. There would be a valid sentence if necessity alone could create jurisdiction. But could the President be legally executed under it? No; the compulsion under which you acted would be a good defense for you against an impeachment or an indictment for murder, but it would add nothing to the validity of a judgment which the law forbade you to give.

That a necessity for violating the law is nothing more than a mere excuse to the perpetrator, and does not in any legal sense change the quality of the act itself in its operation upon other parties, is a proposition too plain on original principles to need the aid of authority. I do not see how any man of common sense is to stand up and dispute it. But there is decisive authority upon the point. In 1815, at New Orleans, General Jackson took upon himself the command of every person in the city, suspended the functions of all the civil authorities, and made his own will for a time the only rule of conduct. It was believed to be absolutely necessary. Judges, officers of the city corporation, and members of the State Legislature, insisted on it as the only way to save the "booty and beauty" of the place from the unspeakable outrages committed at Badajos and St. Sebastian by the very same troops then marching to the attack. Jackson used the power thus taken by him moderately, sparingly, benignly, and only for the purpose of preventing mutiny in his camp. A single mutineer was restrained by a short confinement, and another was sent four miles up the river. But after he had saved the city, and the danger was all over, he stood before the court to be tried by the law; his conduct was decided to be illegal by the same judge who had declared it to be necessary, and he paid the penalty without a murmur. The Supreme Court of Louisiana, in Johnson v. Duncan, decided that everything done during the siege in pursuance of martial rule, but in conflict with the law of the land, was void and of none effect, without reference to the circumstances which made it necessary. Long afterwards the fine imposed upon Jackson was refunded, because his friends, while they admitted him to have violated the law, insisted that the necessity which drove him to it ought to have saved him from the punishment due only to a willful offender.

The learned counsel on the other side will not assert that there was war at Indianapolis in 1864, for they have read *Coke's Institutes* and Judge Grier's opinion in the *Prize Cases*, and of course they know it to be a settled rule that war cannot be said to exist where the civil courts are open. They will not set up the absurd plea of necessity, for they are well aware that it would not be true in point of fact. They will hardly take the ground that any kind of necessity could give legal validity to that which the law forbids.

This, therefore, must be their position: That although there was no war at the place where this commission sat, and no actual necessity for it, yet if there was a war any where else, to which the United States were a party, the technical effect of such war was to take the jurisdiction away from the civil courts and transfer it to army officers.

GEN. BUTLER. We do not take that position.

MR. BLACK. Then they can take no position at all, for nothing else is left. I do not wonder to see them recoil from their own doctrine when its nakedness is held up to their eyes. But they *must* stand upon that or give up their cause. They may not state their proposition precisely as I state it; that is too plain a way of putting it. But, in substance, it is their doctrine—has been the doctrine of the attorney-general's office ever since the advent of the present incumbent—and is the doctrine of their brief, printed and filed in this case. What else can they say? They will admit that the Constitution is not altogether without a meaning; that at a time of universal peace it imposes some kind of obligation upon those who swear to support it. If no war existed they would not deny the exclusive jurisdiction of the civil courts in criminal cases. How then did the military get jurisdiction in Indiana?

All men who hold the attorney-general's opinion to be true, answer the question I have put by saying that military jurisdiction comes from the mere existence of war; and it comes in Indiana only as the legal result of a war which is going on in Mississippi, Tennessee, or South Carolina. The Constitution is repealed, or its operation suspended in one State because there is war in another. The courts are open, the organization of society is intact, the judges are on the bench, and their process is not impeded; but their jurisdiction is gone. Why? Because, say our opponents, war exists, and the silent, legal, technical operation of that fact is to deprive all American citizens of their right to a fair trial.

13. Results of the doctrine that trial by jury is lost to the citizen during the existence of war.

That class of jurists and statesmen who hold that the trial by jury is lost to the citizen during the existence of war, carry out their doctrine theoretically and practically to its ultimate consequences. The right of trial by jury being gone, all other rights are gone with it; therefore, a man may be arrested without an accusation and kept in prison during the pleasure of his captors; his papers may be searched without a warrant; his property may be confiscated behind his back, and he has no earthly means of redress. Nay, an attempt to get a just remedy is construed as a new crime. He dare not even complain, for the right of free speech is gone with the rest of his rights. If you sanction that doctrine, what is to be the consequence? I do not speak of what is past and gone; but in case of a future war what results will follow from your decision endorsing the attorney-general's views? They are very obvious. At the instant when the war begins, our whole system of legal government will tumble into ruin, and if we are not all robbed, and kidnapped, and hanged, and drawn, and quartered, we will owe our immunity, not to the Constitution and laws, but to the mere mercy or policy of those persons who may then happen to control the organized physical force of the country.

This certainly puts us in a most precarious condition; we must have war about half the time, do what we may to avoid it. The President or Congress can wantonly provoke a war whenever it suits the purpose of either to do so; and they can keep it going as long as they please, even after the actual conflict of arms is over. When peace woos them they can ignore her existence; and thus they can make the war a chronic condition of the country, and the slavery of the people perpetual. Nay, we are at the mercy of any foreign potentate who may envy us the possession of those liberties of which we boast so much; he can shatter our Constitution without striking a single blow, or bringing a gun to bear upon us. A simple declaration of hostilities is more terrible to us than an army with banners.

To me, this seems the wildest delusion that ever took possession of a human brain. If there be one principle of political ethics more universally acknowledged than another, it is that war, and especially civil war, can be justified only when it is undertaken to vindicate and uphold the legal and constitutional rights of the people, not to trample them down.   He who carries on a system of wholesale slaughter for any other purpose, must stand without excuse before God or man.   In a time of war, more than at any other time, public liberty is in the hands of the public officers.   And she is there in double trust: first, as they are citizens, and therefore bound to defend her by the common obligation of all citizens; and next, as they are her special guardians—

> "Who should against her murderers shut the door
> Not bear the knife themselves."

The opposing argument, when turned into plain English, means this, and this only: that when the Constitution is attacked upon one side, its official guardians may assail it upon the other; when rebellion strikes it in the face, they may take advantage of the blindness produced by the blow to sneak behind it and stab it in the back.

14. THE RIGHTS OF THE CIVIL AUTHORITIES HAVE BEEN REGARDED AS SACRED IN THE PAST.

The Convention, when it framed the Constitution, and the people, when they adopted it, could have had no thought like that.   If they had supposed that it would operate only while perfect peace continued, they certainly would have given us some other rule to go by in time of war ; they would not have left us to wander about in a howling wilderness of anarchy, without a lamp to our feet, or a guide to our path.   Another thing proves their actual intent still more strikingly.   They required that every man in any kind of public employment, state or national, civil or military, should swear, without reserve or qualification, that he would support the Constitution.   Surely our ancestors had too much regard for the moral and religious welfare of their posterity to impose upon them an oath like that, if they intended and expected it to be broken half the time.   The oath of an officer to support the Constitution is as simple as that of a witness to tell the truth in a court of justice.   What would you think of a witness who should attempt to justify perjury upon the ground that he had testified when civil war was raging, and he thought that by swearing to a lie he might promote some public or private object connected with the strife ?

No, no, the great men who made this country what it is—the

heroes who won her independence, and the statesmen who settled her institutions—had no such notions in their minds. Washington deserved the lofty praise bestowed upon him by the president of Congress when he resigned his commission—that he had always regarded the rights of the civil authority through all changes and through all disasters. When his duty as President afterwards required him to arm the public force to suppress a rebellion in Western Pennsylvania, he never thought that the Constitution was abolished, by virtue of that fact, in New Jersey, or Maryland, or Virginia. It would have been a dangerous experiment for an adviser of his at that time, or at any time, to propose that he should deny a citizen his right to be tried by a jury, and substitute in place of it a trial before a tribunal composed of men elected by himself from among his own creatures and dependents. You can well imagine how that great heart would have swelled with indignation at the bare thought of such an insulting outrage upon the liberty and law of his country.

In the war of 1812, the man emphatically called the Father of the Constitution was the supreme Executive Magistrate. Talk of perilous times! there was the severest trial this Union ever saw. That was no half-organized rebellion on the one side of the conflict, to be crushed by the hostile millions and unbounded resources of the other. The existence of the nation was threatened by the most formidable military and naval power then upon the face of the earth. Every town upon the northern frontier, upon the Atlantic seaboard, and upon the Gulf coast was in daily and hourly danger. The enemy had penetrated the heart of Ohio. New York, Pennsylvania, and Virginia were all of them threatened from the west as well as from the east. The Capitol was taken, and burned, and pillaged, and every member of the Federal Administration was a fugitive before the invading army. Meanwhile, party spirit was breaking out into actual treason all over New England. Four of those States refused to furnish a man or a dollar even for their own defense. Their public authorities were plotting the dismemberment of the Union, and individuals among them were burning blue lights upon the coast as a signal to the enemy's ships. But in all this storm of disaster, with foreign war in his front and domestic treason on his flank, Madison gave out no sign that he would aid old England and New England to break up this government of laws. On the contrary, he and all his supporters, though compassed round with darkness and with danger, stood faithfully between the Constitution and its enemies

> " To shield it, and save it, or perish there too."

The framers of the Constitution and all their contemporaries died and were buried; their children succeeded them and continued on the stage of public affairs until they, too,

> " Lived out their lease of life, and paid their breath
> To time and mortal custom;"

and a third generation was already far on its way to the grave before this monstrous doctrine was conceived or thought of, that public officers all over the country might disregard their oaths whenever a war or a rebellion was commenced.

15. NEITHER THE LAW OF NATIONS, NOR THE LAWS OF WAR, HAVE ANY BEARING ON THE CASE.

Our friends on the other side are quite conscious that when they deny the binding obligation of the Constitution they must put some other system of law in its place.   Their brief gives us notice that, while the Constitution, and the acts of Congress, and *Magna Charta*, and the common law, and all the rules of natural justice shall remain under foot, they will try American citizens according to *the law of nations !*   But the law of nations takes no notice of the subject.   If that system did contain a special provision that a government might hang one of its own citizens without a judge or jury, it would still be competent for the American people to say, as they have said, that no such thing should ever be done here.   That is my answer to the law of nations.

But then they tell us that the *laws of war* must be treated as paramount.   Here they become mysterious.   Do they mean that code of public law which defines the duties of two belligerent parties to one another, and regulates the intercourse of neutrals with both ?   If yes, then it is simply a recurrence to the law of nations, which has nothing on earth to do with the subject.   Do they mean that portion of our municipal code which defines our duties to the government in war as well as in peace ?   Then they are speaking of the Constitution and laws, which declare in plain words that the government owes every citizen a fair legal trial, as much as the citizen owes obedience to the government.   They are in search of an argument under difficulties.   When they appeal to international law, it is silent ; and when they interrogate the law of the land, the answer is an unequivocal contradiction of their whole theory.

The attorney-general tells us that all persons whom he and his associates choose to denounce for giving aid to the rebellion, are to be treated as being themselves a part of the rebellion ; they are public enemies, and therefore they may be punished without being found guilty by a competent court or a jury. This convenient rule would outlaw every citizen the moment he is charged with a political offense. But political offenders are precisely the class of persons who most need the protection of a court and jury, for the prosecutions against them are most likely to be unfounded, both in fact and in law. Whether innocent or guilty, to accuse is to convict them before the ignorant and bigoted men who generally sit in military courts. But this Court decided, in the *Prize Cases*, that all who live in the enemy's territory are public enemies, without regard to their personal sentiments or conduct ; and the converse of the proposition is equally true, that all who reside inside of our own territory are to be treated as under the protection of the law. If they help the enemy, they are criminals ; but they cannot be punished without legal conviction.

You have heard much (and you will hear more very soon) concerning the natural and inherent right of the government to defend itself without regard to law. This is wholly fallacious. In a despotism the autocrat is unrestricted in the means he may use for the defense of his authority against the opposition of his own subjects or others ; and that is precisely what makes him a despot. But in a limited monarchy the prince must confine himself to a legal defense of his government. If he goes beyond that, and commits aggressions on the rights of the people, he breaks the social compact, releases his subjects from all their obligations to him, renders himself liable to be hurled from his throne, and dragged to the block or driven into exile. This principle was sternly enforced in the cases of Charles I and James II, and we have it announced, on the highest official authority here, that the Queen of England cannot ring a little bell on *her* table and cause a man by her arbitrary order to be arrested under any pretense whatever. If that be true there, how much more true must it be here, where we have no personal sovereign, and where our only government is the Constitution and laws. A violation of law on pretense of saving such a government as ours is not self-preservation, but suicide.

Salus populi suprema lex—observe it is not *salus regis ;* the safety of the *people*, not the safety of the *ruler*, is the supreme law. When those who hold the authority of the government in their hands, behave in such manner as to put the liberties and rights of the people in jeopardy, the people may rise against them and overthrow them without regard to that law which requires obedience to them.   The maxim is revolutionary and expresses simply the right to resist tyranny without regard to prescribed forms.   It can never be used to stretch the powers of government *against* the people.

16. LEGAL MODES POSSESSED BY THE GOVERNMENT FOR PROTECTING ITSELF AGAINST DANGER.

If this government of ours has no power to defend itself without violating its own laws, it carries the seeds of destruction in its own bosom; it is a poor, weak, blind, staggering thing, and the sooner it tumbles over the better.   But it has a most efficient legal mode of protecting itself against all possible danger.   It is clothed from head to foot in a complete panoply of defensive armor. What are the perils which may threaten its existence?   I am not able at this moment to think of more than these which I am about to mention : foreign invasion, domestic insurrection, mutiny in the army and navy, corruption in the civil administration, and last but not least criminal violations of its laws committed by individuals among the body of the people.   Have we not a legal mode of defense against all these?   Yes ; military force repels invasion and suppresses insurrection ; you preserve discipline in the army and navy by means of courts-martial ; you preserve the purity of the civil administration by impeaching dishonest magistrates ; and crimes are prevented and punished by the regular judicial authorities.   You are not merely compelled to use these weapons against your enemies, because they, and they only, are justified by the law; you ought to use them because they are more efficient than any other, and less liable to be abused.

There is another view of the subject which settles all controversy about it.   No human being in this country can exercise any kind of public authority which is not conferred by law ; and under the United States it must be given by express words of a written statute.   Whatever is not so given is withheld, and the exercise of it is positively prohibited.   Courts-martial in the army and navy are authorized ; they are legal institutions ; their jurisdiction is limited, and their whole code of procedure is regulated, by act of Congress.   Upon the civil courts all the jurisdiction they have or can have is bestowed by law, and if one of them goes beyond what is written, its action is *ultra vires* and void.   But a military commission is not a court-martial, and it is not a civil court.   It is not governed by the law which is made for either, and it has no law of its own.   Within the last five years we have seen, for the first time, self-constituted tribunals not only assuming power which the law did not give them, but thrusting aside the regular courts to which the power was exclusively given.

17. A MILITARY COMMISSION AN ANOMALY AUTHORIZED BY NO LAW, AND GOVERNED BY NO LAWS OF ITS OWN.

What is the consequence?   This terrible authority is wholly undefined, and its exercise is without any legal control.   Undelegated power is always unlimited.   The field that lies outside of the Constitution and laws has no boundary.   Thierry, the French historian of England, says, that when the crown and scepter were offered to Cromwell, he hesitated for several days, and answered : "Do not make me a King ; for then my hands will be tied up by the laws which define the duties of that office ; but make me Protector of the Commonwealth, and I can do what I please ; no statute restraining and limiting the royal prerogative will apply to me." So these commissions have no legal origin and no legal name by which they are known among the children of men ; no law applies to them ; and they exercise all power for the paradoxical reason that none belongs to them rightfully.

Ask the attorney-general what rules apply to military commissions in the exercise of their assumed authority over civilians. Come, Mr. Attorney, "gird up thy loins now like a man ; I will demand of thee, and thou shalt declare unto me, if thou hast understanding." How is a military commission organized ?   What shall be the number and rank of its members ?   What offenses come within its jurisdiction ?   What is its code of procedure ?   How shall witnesses be compelled to attend it ?   Is it perjury for a witness to swear falsely ?   What is the function of the judge advocate ?   Does he tell the members how they must find, or does he only persuade them to convict ?   Is he the agent of the government, to command them what evidence they shall admit and what sentence they shall pronounce ? or does he always carry his point, right or wrong, by the mere force of eloquence and ingenuity ? What is the nature of their punishments ?   May they confiscate property and levy fines as well as imprison and kill ?   In addition to strangling their victim, may they also deny him the last consolations of religion, and refuse his family the melancholy privilege of giving him a decent grave?

To none of these questions can the attorney-general make a reply, for there is no law on the subject. He will not attempt to "darken counsel by words without knowledge," and, therefore, like Job, he can only lay his hand upon his mouth and keep silence.

18. MILITARY COMMISSION SYNONYMOUS WITH ARBITRARY POWER.
—REVIEW OF THE VARIOUS MODES IN WHICH IT HAS
BEEN EXERCISED THROUGHOUT THE WORLD.

The power exercised through these military commissions is not only unregulated by law, but it is incapable of being so regulated. What is it that you claim, Mr. Attorney? I will give you a definition, the correctness of which you will not attempt to gainsay. You assert the right of the executive government, without the intervention of the judiciary, to capture, imprison, and kill any person to whom that government or its paid dependents may choose to impute an offense. This, in its very essence, is despotic and lawless. It is never claimed or tolerated except by those governments which deny the restraints of all law. It has been exercised by the great and small oppressors of mankind ever since the days of Nimrod. It operates in different ways; the tools it uses are not always the same; it hides its hideous features under many disguises; it assumes every variety of form;

> "It can change shapes with Proteus for advantages,
> And set the murderous Machiavel to school."

But in all its mutations of outward appearance, it is still identical in principle, object, and origin. It is always the same great engine of despotism which Hamilton described it to be.

Under the old French monarchy the favorite fashion of it was a *lettre de cachet*, signed by the king, and this would consign the party to a loathsome dungeon until he died, forgotten by all the world. An imperial *ukase* will answer the same purpose in Russia. The most faithful subject of that amiable autocracy may lie down in the evening to dream of his future prosperity, and before daybreak he will find himself between two dragoons on his way to the mines of Siberia. In Turkey, the verbal order of the Sultan or any of his powerful favorites will cause a man to be tied up in a sack and cast into the Bosphorus. Nero accused Peter and Paul of spreading a "pestilent superstition," which they called the gospel. He heard their defense in person, and sent them to the cross. Afterwards he tried the whole Christian church in one body, on a charge of setting fire to the city, and he convicted them, though he knew not only that they were innocent, but that he himself had committed the crime. The judgment was followed by instant execution; he let loose the Prætorian guards upon men, women, and children to drown, butcher, and burn them. Herod saw fit, for good political reasons, closely affecting the permanence of his reign in Judea, to punish certain *possible* traitors in Bethlehem by anticipation. This required the death of all the children in that city under two years of age. He issued his "general order," and his provost marshal carried it out with so much alacrity and zeal that in one day the whole land was filled with mourning and lamentation.

Macbeth understood the whole philosophy of the subject. He was an unlimited monarch. His power to punish for any offense or for no offense at all was as broad as that which the attorney-general claims for himself and his brother officers under the United States. But he was more cautious how he used it. He had a dangerous rival, from whom he apprehended the most serious peril to the "life of his government." The necessity to get rid of him was plain enough, but he could not afford to shock the moral sense of the world by pleading political necessity for a murder. He must

> " Mask the business from the common eye."

Accordingly, he sent for two enterprising gentlemen whom he took into his service upon liberal pay—"made love to their assistance," and got them to deal with the accused party. He acted as his own judge advocate. He made a most eloquent and stirring speech to persuade his agents that Banquo was their oppressor, and had "held them so under fortune;" that he ought to die for that alone. When they agreed that he was their enemy, then said the king:

> " So is he mine, and though I *could*
> With *barefaced power* sweep him from my sight,
> And bid my *will* avouch it; yet I *must not,*
> For certain friends, who are both his and mine,
> Whose loves I may not drop."

For these, and "many weighty reasons" besides, he thought it best to *commit* the execution of his design to a subordinate agency.

The commission thus organized in Banquo's case sat upon him that very night at a convenient place beside the road where it was known he would be traveling; and they did precisely what the attorney-general says the military officers may do in this country—they *took* and *killed* him, because their employer at the head of the government wanted it done and paid them for doing it out of the public treasury.

But of all the persons that ever wielded this kind of power, the one who went most directly to the purpose and the object of it, was Lola Montez. She reduced it to the elementary principle. In 1848, when she was minister and mistress to the king of Bavaria, she dictated all the measures of the government. The times were troublesome. All over Germany the spirit of rebellion was rising; everywhere the people wanted to see a first-class revolution, like that which had just exploded in France. Many persons in Bavaria disliked to be governed so absolutely by a lady of the character which Lola Montez bore, and some of them were rash enough to say so. Of course that was treason, and she went about to punish it in the simplest of all possible ways. She bought herself a pack of English bull-dogs, trained to tear the flesh and mangle the limbs, and lap the life-blood; and, with these dogs at her heels, she marched up and down the streets of Munich with a most majestic tread, and with a sense of power which any judge advocate in America might envy. When she saw any body whom she chose to denounce for "thwarting the government," or "using disloyal language," her obedient followers needed but a sign to make them spring at the throat of their victim. It gives me unspeakable pleasure to tell you the sequel. The people rose in their strength, smashed down the whole machinery of oppression, and drove out into uttermost shame king, strumpet, dogs and all. From that time to this neither man, woman, nor beast, has dared to worry or kill the people of Bavaria.

All these are but so many different ways of using the arbitrary power to punish. The variety is merely in the means which a tyrannical government takes to destroy those whom it is bound to protect. Every where it is but another construction, on the same principle, of that remorseless machine by which despotism wreaks its vengeance on those who offend it. In a civilized country it nearly always uses the military force, because that is the sharpest, the surest, as well as the best looking instrument that can be found for such a purpose. But in none of its forms can it be introduced into this country; we have no room for it; the ground here is all preoccupied by legal and free institutions.

Between the officers who have power like this and the people who are liable to become its victims, there can be no relation except that of master and slave. The master may be kind and the slave may be contented in his bondage; but the man who can take your life or restrain your liberty, or despoil you of your property at his discretion, either with his own hands or by means of a hired overseer, owns you and he can force you to serve him. All you are and all you have, including your wives and children, are his property.

If my learned and very good friend, the attorney-general, had this right of domination over me, I should not be very much frightened, for I should expect him to use it as moderately as any man in all the world ; but still I should feel the necessity of being very discreet. He might change in a short time. The thirst for blood is an appetite which grows by what it feeds upon. We cannot know him by present appearances. Robespierre resigned a country judgeship in early life because he was too tender hearted to pronounce sentence of death upon a convicted criminal. Caligula passed for a most amiable young gentleman before he was clothed with the imperial purple, and for about eight months afterwards. It was Trajan, I think, who said that absolute power would convert any man into a wild beast, whatever was the original benevolence of his nature. If you decide that the attorney-general holds in his own hands or shares with others the power of life and death over us all, I mean to be very cautious in my intercourse with him; and I warn you, the judges whom I am now addressing, to do likewise. Trust not to the gentleness and kindness which has always marked his behavior heretofore. Keep your distance ; be careful how you approach him, for you know not at what moment or by what a trifle you may rouse the sleeping tiger. Remember the injunction of scripture, " Go not near to the man who hath power to kill; and if thou come unto him, see that thou make no fault, lest he take away thy life presently; for thou goest among snares and walkest upon the battlements of the city."

The right of the executive government to kill and imprison citizens for political offenses has not been practically claimed in this country, except in cases where commissioned officers of the army were the instruments used ? Why should it be confined to them ? Why should not naval officers be permitted to share in it ? What is the reason that common soldiers and seamen are excluded from all participation in the business? No law has bestowed the right upon army officers more than upon other persons. If men are to be hung up without that legal trial which the Constitution guarantees to them, why not employ commissions of clergymen, merchants, manufacturers, horse-dealers, butchers, or drovers, to do it? It will not be pretended that military men are better qualified to decide questions of fact or law than other classes of people; for it is known on the contrary that they are, as a general rule, least of all fitted to perform the duties that belong to a judge.

The attorney-general thinks that a proceeding which takes away the lives of citizens without a constitutional trial is a most merciful dispensation. His idea of humanity as well as law is embodied in the bureau of military justice, with all its dark and bloody machinery. For that strange opinion he gives this curious reason: that the duty of the commander-in-chief is to kill, and unless he has this bureau and these commissions he must "butcher" indiscriminately without mercy or justice. I admit that if the commander-in-chief or any other officer of the government has the power of an Asiatic king, to butcher the people at pleasure, he ought to have somebody to aid him in selecting his victims, as well as to do the rough work of strangling and shooting. But if my learned friend will only condescend to cast an eye upon the Constitution, he will see at once that all the executive and military officers are completely relieved by the provision that the life of a citizen shall not be taken at all until after legal conviction by a court and jury.

You cannot help but see that military commissions, if suffered to go on, will be used for most pernicious purposes. I have criticised none of their past proceedings, nor made any allusion to their history in the last five years. But what can be the meaning of this effort to maintain them among us? Certainly not to punish actual guilt. All the ends of true justice are attained by the prompt, speedy, impartial trial which the courts are bound to give. Is there any danger that crime will be winked upon by the judges? Does any body pretend that courts and juries have less ability to decide upon facts and law than the men who sit in military tribunals? The counsel in this cause will not insult you by even hinting such an opinion. What righteous or just purpose, then, can they serve? None whatever.

But while they are utterly powerless to do even a shadow of

good, they will be omnipotent to trample upon innocence, to gag the truth, to silence patriotism, and crush the liberties of the country. They will always be organized to convict, and the conviction will follow the accusation as surely as night follows the day. The government, of course, will accuse none before such a commission except those whom it predetermines to ruin and destroy. The accuser can choose the judges, and will certainly select those who are known to be the most ignorant, the most unprincipled, and the most ready to do whatever may please the power which gives them pay, promotion and plunder. The willing witness can be found as easily as the superserviceable judge. The treacherous spy and the base informer—those loathsome wretches who do their lying by the job—will stock such a market with abundant perjury, for the authorities that employ them will be bound to protect as well as reward them. A corrupt and tyrannical government, with such an engine at its command, will shock the world with the enormity of its crimes. Plied as it may be by the arts of a malignant priesthood, and urged on by the madness of a raving crowd, it will be worse than the popish plot, or the French revolution—it will be a combination of both, with Fouquier Tinville on the bench, and Titus Oates in the witness box. You can save us from this horrible fate. You alone can " deliver us from the body of this death." To that fearful extent is the destiny of this nation in your hands.

ARGUMENT OF DAVID DUDLEY FIELD,

On the Constitutionality of the "Enforcement Act."

[U. S. v. Cruikshank, 2 Otto.]

IN THE SUPREME COURT OF THE UNITED STATES, OCTOBER TERM, 1874.

Constitutional Law.—Congress can grant and secure to citizens of the United States, those rights alone, which are, either expressly or by implication, within its jurisdiction. The violation of rights which are within the exclusive protection of the States, are not indictable under an act of Congress.

Analysis of Mr. Field's Argument.

1. The amendments to the Constitution growing out of the war.
2. The legislation to enforce the amendments.
3. The offenses charged in the indictment.
4. Object and design of the war amendments.
5. Theory of the prosecution.
6. Meaning of the term "appropriate legislation."
7. The express and implied prohibitions of power within the Constitution.
8. Limitations upon the mode of enforcing delegated powers.
9. The legislation to enforce the amendments invalid.
10. The tendency towards the centralization of power.
11. Rule of interpretation as to the new amendments.
12. Two propositions which embrace the theory of the defense.
13. Congress has no right to anticipate the action of a State.
14. Failure to provide a remedy not equivalent to the deprivation of a right.
15. A prohibition of the exercise of power, does not confer upon Congress the power prohibited.
16. Mode in which Congress may legally enforce prohibitions upon the States.
17. Constitutional mode of enforcing the amendments.
18. How State laws may be prevented from becoming operative.
19. The legislation assumes that Congress has powers which it does not possess.
20. Second proposition.—Theory and object of government.
21. Practical results of the theory of the prosecution.
22. Rules of interpretation heretofore adopted.

The Greek legends and poetry teach that the golden age is in the past. The wonderful march of improvement which marks the closing century as the most important which has yet occurred; the universal dissemination of knowledge, which has done so much for the welfare of the race ; the remedies which are being contrived, under a progressive civilization, to perfect and protect the recognized rights and liberties of the individual against the encroachments and

[517]

usurpations of arbitrary power; seem to demonstrate that the golden age is in the future. The age in which men are governed least, will be that ideal age. To that we are approaching. Hence the highest and most interesting of secular problems, which has engaged the attention of men, has been to establish a perfect government; and the solution of this question seems to have been reserved for the genius of the American people. It is true that a pure democracy existed at one time in Greece, and republican forms of government have flourished to a certain extent at different periods, but the realization of perfection has never been approached, until the fact of American independence finally led to the establishment of the model government of the world, " an indestructible union of indestructible States." The theory which has prevailed as to the object and nature of government among the splendid empires of the Orient, has been reversed. The old notion, that the king was the source and fountain of all power, has given way entirely to the opposite theory, that all power is in the people, and is delegated under express and clearly defined limitations to be exercised by the ruler. That the right to rule does not descend by divine appointment, but inheres in the people, to be exercised by such servants as they may choose, in such manner as they may ordain.

The union of the States in the American republic, presents an apparently complex, but in reality an exceedingly simple and harmonious system. The powers and workings of this dual government forms the subject of the argument here presented.

When the Union was framed, jealousies arose between the States and the general government, as to the extent of the powers possessed by each, provoking a discussion which finally culminated in a civil war. The results of the conflict are embraced within the three last amendments to the Constitution, forbidding the existence of slavery, and prohibiting the States from interfering with the rights and privileges of citizens of the United States on account of race or color.[1] Out of the legislation to enforce these amendments, the controversy in Cruikshank's case arose, upon the following facts:

William I. Cruikshank and ninety-six others, were indicted in the United States Circuit Court for the District of Louisiana, charged with banding and conspiring together to injure, oppress, threaten and intimidate Levi Nelson and Alexander Tillman, citizens of the United States, of African descent, and persons of color, with the intent thereby to hinder and deprive them in their free enjoyment of certain rights and privileges which, it was claimed, were granted and secured to them, in common with all other good citizens of the United States, by the Constitution and laws of the United States. The indictment contained thirty-two counts, sixteen of which were framed under the sixth, and sixteen under the seventh section of an act of Congress, entitled "An Act to enforce the rights of citizens of the United States," &c., approved May 30, 1870, known as the " Enforcement Act." The present controversy concerns only that portion of the indictment under the sixth section, upon which alone three of the defendants were convicted, the others having been acquitted of all the charges. Of these sixteen counts there were two series, eight charging the defendants with " banding," and eight with "conspiring," to deprive and hinder Nelson and Tillman in the exercise and enjoyment of rights and privileges, substantially as follows : (1) Interfering with their

[1] For text of the amendments, see Appendix, p. 728.

right to assemble with each other and with other good citizens of the United States, for lawful purposes; (2) Interfering with their right to bear arms for lawful purposes; (3) With having taken away their lives and liberty without due process of law; (4) Interfering with their right to the equal protection of the laws secured to white citizens; (5) Interfering with their right to vote at State elections; (6) With having put them in fear and bodily harm, for having voted at State elections; (7) Interfering, on account of their race and color, with their rights and privileges as secured to them, in common with all other citizens, by the laws of the United States and of the State of Louisiana.

Upon these counts, three of the defendants were convicted, and upon the verdict counsel moved an arrest of judgment, upon the ground (1) That the matters charged were not offenses against the laws of the United States, nor within the jurisdiction of the federal courts; but were exclusively within the jurisdiction of the State courts; (2) That the Act of Congress upon which the indictment was framed, was unconstitutional; (3) That the indictment was defective, in that certain of the counts were indefinite, vague and uncertain, charging no particular offense. The court were divided in opinion as to granting the motion, and certified the questions to the Supreme Court.

The issues presented were, whether the people, in amending the Constitution, intended thereby to give power to the general government to enforce rights which had heretofore been wholly enforced and protected by the States? or was the object to prohibit the States from withholding the protection of its laws from any particular class of citizens? Was it intended to give Congress power to enforce the rights, or to prohibit the States from withholding from any citizen the equal protection of its laws? Has any citizen acquired thereby any new rights, or do the amendments simply guarantee existing rights, giving Congress power to enforce the guarantee?

These are the questions discussed by Mr. Field, in his very elaborate and careful argument. He takes the broad ground, that all the rights which it was claimed had been violated and obstructed, were within the exclusive protection of the States, and until a State had, by legislation or otherwise, denied these rights to any citizen or class of citizens, the acts passed by Congress to enforce the war amendments did not become operative; that the failure of a State to provide a remedy for the enforcement of such rights, was not a denial of them within the meaning of the fourteenth amendment, and did not bring it within the prohibition declaring that no State shall make any law which shall abridge the privileges or immunities of citizens of the United States, or deprive any person of life, liberty, or property, without due process of law, or deny to any person within its jurisdiction, the equal protection of the laws; that because a State did not provide a remedy for the violation of rights within its jurisdiction, that fact did not operate to confer upon Congress the power to enforce the rights or provide remedies therefor, and that an indictment under a penal statute, providing for such enforcement, was without authority, illegal and void.

The court held, Chief Justice Waite writing the opinion, that the duties and rights belonging to citizens within the original jurisdiction of the States, still remain there, and the only obligation resting upon the national government, is to see that the States do not deny them. That the right to vote is derived from the State, but the right of exemption from discrimination in the exercise of that right, on account of race or color, is conferred and secured by the fifteenth amendment. The court held, further, that every citizen was entitled to the equal protection of the laws, and this right was also secured by the Constitution, but affirmed the order arresting the judgment and ordering a discharge of the defendants, upon the ground that these offenses were not stated with certainty, but were vague and indefinite, and not sufficient to support the indictment. The case was argued on behalf of the prosecution, by Attorney-General Williams and Mr. Solicitor-General Phillips, and on behalf of the defendants in error, by Mr. Reverdy Johnson, Mr. David Dudley Field, Mr. Philip Phillips, and Mr. R. H. Marr. Mr. Field said :

MAY IT PLEASE THE COURT :—The argument that I shall have the honor to address to the court will be confined to the question of compatibility between the federal Constitution and the legislation of Congress, which is supposed to authorize the present indictment.

It is indeed true, that if the form of the accusation is not conformable to the act of Congress, the defendants are entitled to be presently discharged, but inasmuch as a new indictment might possibly be preferred, supposing the present to fail for defect of form, this question is insignificant compared with the other.

For my part I shall leave the matter of procedure where it now stands upon the argument, and confine myself to the question of conformity or non-conformity of the act of Congress to the Constitution. If the legislation upon which this indictment rests is conformable to the organic law of this country, then it matters little what is or is not decided about the forms of proceeding. The substance of American constitutional government, as received from the Fathers, will have gone, and the forms will not be long in following.

Let us reduce and formulate the question, if we can, so as to separate the incidental from the essential, in order that our attention may be withdrawn from all other considerations than that of the one fundamental and permanent theory, upon which this legislation must stand, if it stand at all.

1. THE AMENDMENTS TO THE CONSTITUTION GROWING OUT OF THE WAR.

The 13th amendment to the Constitution (1865) declares, that neither slavery nor involuntary servitude, except in punishment of crime, shall exist within the United States, and authorizes Congress to enforce the declaration by appropriate legislation.

The 14th amendment (1868), after defining citizenship of the United States, prohibits the States (1) from making or enforcing any law which shall abridge the privileges or immunities of citizens of the United States ; (2) from depriving any person of life, liberty or property, without due process of law ; and (3) from denying to any person within their jurisdiction the equal protection of the laws. And it authorizes Congress to enforce the provisions of the amendment by appropriate legislation.

The 15th amendment (1870) prohibits the States from denying or abridging the rights of citizens of the United States to vote, on account of race, color or previous condition of servitude. This prohibition also Congress is authorized to enforce by appropriate legislation.

2. The legislation to enforce the amendments.

Professing to act under the authority of these amendments, Congress has passed five acts, four only of which were in existence at the time of the indictment now under consideration ; one called the Civil Rights Act, passed April 9, 1866; the second called the Enforcement Act, passed May 31, 1870 ; the third, amending this, passed February 28, 1871, and a fourth act, passed April 20, 1871.

The Civil Rights Act is first in order of time. Section 1, after declaring that all persons born in the United States, and not subject to any foreign power, excluding Indians not taxed, are citizens of the United States, enacts, that "such citizens, of every race and color, without regard to any previous condition of slavery or involuntary servitude, except as a punishment for crime, whereof the party shall have been duly convicted, shall have the same right in every State and Territory of the United States to make and enforce contracts, to sue, be parties, and give evidence, to inherit, purchase, lease, sell, hold and convey real and personal property, and to full and equal benefit of all laws and proceedings for the security of person and property, as is enjoyed by white citizens, and shall be subject to like punishment, pains and penalties, and to none others." Section 2 enacts, that "any person, who, under color of any law, statute, ordinance, regulation or custom," shall cause any inhabitant—the word citizen being dropped—"to be subjected to the deprivation of any right secured or protected by this act," shall be guilty of misdemeanor. Section 3 confers upon the federal courts jurisdiction over infractions of the act. Sections 4 and 5 provide an army of officers to enforce the act. Section 6 enacts penalties for obstructing or resisting the execution of the act. The remaining sections, 7, 8, 9 and 10, are not material to the present inquiry.

The first section of the Enforcement Act declares, that all citizens of the United States, otherwise qualified, shall be allowed to vote at all elections, without distinction of race, color, or previous servitude. Section 2 provides, that if by the law of any State or Territory a prerequisite to voting is necessary, equal opportunity for it shall be given to all, without distinction, &c.; and any person charged with the duty of furnishing the prerequisite, who refuses, or knowingly omits to give full effect to this section, shall be guilty of misdemeanor. Section 3 provides, that an offer of performance, in respect to the prerequisite, when proved by affidavit of the claimant, shall be equivalent to performance; and any judge or inspector of election who refuses to accept it shall be guilty, &c. Section 4 provides, that any person who, by force, bribery, threats, intimidation or other unlawful means, hinders, delays, prevents, or obstructs any citizen from qualifying himself to vote, or combines with others to do so, shall be guilty, &c. Section 5 provides, that any person who prevents, hinders, controls, or intimidates any person from exercising the right of suffrage, to whom it is secured by the 15th amendment, or attempts to do so, by bribery or threats of violence, or deprivation of property or employment, shall be guilty, &c. Section 6 provides, that "if two or more persons shall band or conspire together, * * * with intent to violate any provision of this Act," that is, of either act, "or to injure, oppress, threaten, or intimidate any citizen, with intent to prevent or hinder his free exercise and enjoyment of any right or privilege granted or secured to him by the Constitution or laws of the United States, or because of his having exercised the same, such persons shall be held guilty of felony," &c. Section 7 provides, that if in violating any provision of §§ 5 and 6 any other offense is committed, that shall be visited with such punishments as are prescribed for like offenses by the laws of the State. Sections 8, 9 and 10 give jurisdiction to certain courts, provide commissioners and direct the execution of warrants, &c. Section 11 provides penalties for preventing or obstructing the execution of the act. Section 12 regulates the fees of officers. Section 13 authorizes the President to employ the public forces. Sections 14 and 15 relate to the holding of office by persons disqualified under the 14th amendment. Section 16 enacts, that "All persons within the jurisdiction of the United States shall have the same right in any State and Territory to make and enforce contracts, to sue, be parties, give evidence, and to the full and equal benefit of all laws and proceedings for the security of persons and property as is enjoyed by white citizens, and shall be subject to like punishments, pains, penalties, licenses and exactions of any kind, and none other," &c.; and that no tax or charge shall be imposed upon immigrants from one country not imposed upon immigrants from any other. Section 17 enacts, that any person who, "under color of any law, statute, ordinance, regulation or custom," subjects any inhabitant to the deprivation of any right secured or protected by § 16, or "to different punishment, pains or penalties, on account of such person being an alien, or by reason of his color or race, than is prescribed for the punishment of citizens," shall be guilty, &c. Section 18 re-enacts the Civil Rights Act. The remaining sections, 19, 20, 21, 22, 23, relate to elections, and construct a very large and complicated piece of machinery for their management.

The amendatory Act, passed February 28, 1871, relates chiefly to elections of members of the House of Representatives ; the provisions of which, and of the 4th Act, however extraordinary, are not within the scope of our present inquiry.

3. THE OFFENSES CHARGED IN THE INDICTMENT.

By authority of this legislation, ninety-seven persons were indicted together in the Circuit Court of the United States for the District of Louisiana, and three of them, the present defendants, were found guilty upon the first sixteen counts. The indictment was found under the 6th and 7th sections of the Enforcement Act, sixteen counts being for simple conspiracy under the 6th section, and the other sixteen being for conspiracy, with overt acts resulting in murder.

The first count was for banding together, with intent "unlawfully and feloniously to injure, oppress, threaten and intimidate" two citizens of the United States "of African descent and persons of color," "with the unlawful and felonious intent thereby" them "to hinder and prevent in their respective free exercise and enjoyment of their lawful right and privilege to peaceably assemble together with each other and with other citizens of the said United States for a peaceable and lawful purpose." The second count avers an intent to hinder and prevent the exercise by the same persons of the "right to keep and bear arms for a lawful purpose." The third avers an intent to deprive the same persons "of their respective several lives and liberty of person without due process of law." The fourth avers an intent to deprive the same persons of the "free exercise and enjoyment of the right and privilege to the full and equal benefit of all laws and proceedings for the security of persons and property" enjoyed by white citizens. The fifth avers an intent to hinder and prevent the same persons "in the exercise and enjoyment of the rights, privileges, immunities and protection granted and secured to them respectively as citizens of the said United States, and as citizens of the said State of Louisiana, by reason of and for and on account of the race and color" of the said persons. The sixth avers an intent to hinder and prevent the same persons in "the free exercise and enjoyment of the several and respective right and privilege to vote at any election to be thereafter by law had and held by the people in and of the said State of Louisiana." The seventh avers an intent "to put in great fear of bodily harm, injure and oppress" the same persons "because and for the reason" that, having the right to vote, they had voted. The eighth avers an intent "to prevent and hinder" the same persons "in their several and respective free exercise and enjoyment of every, each, all and singular the several rights and privileges granted and secured" to them "by the Constitution and Laws of the United States." The next eight counts are a repetition of the first eight, except that instead of the words "band together" the words "combine, conspire and confederate together" are used.

This indictment, or that portion of it upon which these defendants have been convicted, is supposed to be justified by the 6th section of the Enforcement Act, and that section is said to rest upon the late amendments. In considering the question, whether it is or is not supported by them, I assume, what cannot be disputed, that before the late amendments this section, and the same may be said of the other sections, would have been beyond the competency of Congress. The point of contention, therefore, is whether the amendments have conferred the power.

4. OBJECT AND DESIGN OF THE WAR AMENDMENTS.

Upon this my first proposition is, that it was not the design of the people, in adopting them, to change the fundamental character of their government, or to alter the relations between the Union and the States. They intended, that the Union should continue to be what it had been before, to use the language slightly changed of the late Chief-Justice, an indestructible union of indestructible States.

The events of the last fifteen years are not secrets. The origin of the war, the war itself, the questions to which, in its varying progress, it gave rise, and its great results, are known of all men. It established the unity of the nation and the freedom of the slaves. Upon the final settlement, while it was not thought necessary to make any constitutional changes in respect to the claim of secession and the relation of the States to the Union, it was thought necessary to provide for the equality of the freedmen.

In doing this, two courses were open ; one was, to place them and all their rights and relations under the cognizance of the federal power, and the other was to leave them as they were, under the cognizance of the States, but to provide that these should make no discrimination to their disadvantage. The latter course was adopted. The articles are congruous and plainly adapted to that end. They all imply that, apart from the prohibitions, the States have plenary power over the subject, and they leave that power as it was, with the single qualification, that it shall treat all alike, the emancipated slaves side by side with their old masters. It was in this respect somewhat like the treaty stipulation that we often make, agreeing that the nation treating with us shall be put on the footing of the most favored nations, which, while it leaves us at full liberty to make what new treaties or enact what new laws we please, obliges us to grant to the one what we grant to the others.

It was the design of the amendments, and their whole design, to raise the freedmen to an equality with their late masters before the law, and to give the blacks all the rights which the whites enjoyed. There was no complaint that the whites were oppressed. There was no mischief in that respect to remedy. They did not need new guarantees, and none were intended for them. The complaint to be relieved, the mischief to be remedied, the guarantee to be provided, had respect to the lately subject race, and to that alone. In saying this, we of course leave out of view the temporary provisions respecting the treatment of the rebels and the rebel debt. So understood, there is symmetry in the whole of the amendments ; they are all conformed to one plan, and carry out one great purpose. Thus the 13th amendment decreed the emancipation of the slaves ; the 14th gave them the privileges of citizens of the United States, and to assure them equality of civil rights and debar forever discriminating legislation to their oppression, forbade the States to deprive any person of the equal protection of the laws, or of life, liberty or property, without due process of law ; and finally, the 15th amendment gave them equality of political rights, to the extent of an equal right to vote.

5. THEORY OF THE PROSECUTION.

The general question now is, what may Congress do to enforce the prohibitions thus directed against the States? The particular question upon which this case depends is, whether, under color of enforcing the prohibitions, and before any State has violated them, Congress can anticipate and prevent their violation by taking into its own hands the regulation of the whole subject.

The penal legislation upon which this indictment is founded, can be defended only on the assumption that Congress has in its keeping the various rights which the legislation aims to protect. The object of punishment is the prevention of crime, and crime is the violation of right. The United States cannot punish the violation of State laws any more than the States can punish the violation of federal laws. When the former assert their competency to punish violations of the right to assemble, the right to bear arms, the right to life, liberty and property, the right to vote, the right to the equal protection of the laws, and the privileges and immunities of citizens of the United States, they assert their competency to enforce each and all of these rights, privileges and immunities, and the competency to enforce includes, of course, the competency to enumerate and define all that are enforced.

Such may be undoubtedly one way of accomplishing the object. You can prevent a thing being done in a manner displeasing to you by doing it yourself. Congress can prevent the States from making a wrong regulation by itself making all the regulations. But is that the fair purport of the authority? Is it the legitimate interpretation of a charter of federal government, by which power is carefully partitioned between the Union and the States, to say that, if the former has authority to prevent the latter from doing a wrong thing, it may prevent their doing anything, by doing everything itself? It seems to me the more natural and convenient way of treating the subject, to discuss, first the general propositions, and then to apply them to the case in hand.

6. MEANING OF THE TERM "APPROPRIATE LEGISLATION."

The prohibitions of these amendments of the last decade are reasonably clear; their general purpose is unmistakable; they are laid upon the States, and Congress has express power to enforce them by appropriate legislation. So much is indisputable. The dispute begins when the word appropriate is to be interpreted. What is, and what is not, appropriate legislation? And who is to judge of the appropriateness? These are the cardinal questions upon which hinges the decision of the present cause, and with it the determination in no small measure of the future of the country.

The first observation to be made is that the amendments being made part of the Constitution are to be construed in connection with the original parts of it, and according to the well-understood and long-established interpretation of that instrument, Congress is within certain limits, the exclusive judge of the appropriateness of its legislation to the end designed; but that there are such limits, and beyond them, Congress may not pass.

The rules of interpretation applicable to the federal Constitution, have not been in any respect changed by the amendments. The question is always, first, what is the natural sense of the language used, and then, if that be doubtful, what was the intention of the law-givers, that is, the people of the United States. In the natural sense is included not only that of the particular provision under consideration, but the other provisions of the same institution. In short, when the question arises, what legislation Congress may adopt to enforce the amendment, the answer that should follow is, that it must be appropriate, and must not be prohibited by other provisions of the Constitution, either expressly or by implication.

7. The express and implied prohibitions of power within the Constitution.

There are certain express prohibitions, which are so many qualifications of the powers granted, and there are also implied prohibitions. For example, Congress could not, under color of preventing a State from doing certain things, destroy the State, or any of its essential attributes. If it were proved, beyond question, that to-morrow the legislature of Massachusetts, if not prevented by Congress, would pass a law denying suffrage to every colored man in the commonwealth, Congress could not, by any legislation whatever, terminate the session of the legislature, or authorize the President to march the garrison of Fort Warren into the State House and turn the members out of doors. Congress could not, I say, do this. I do not confine myself to saying it would not; I say that if it were so minded it could not, and every respectable authority in the land—legislative, executive and judicial—would so pronounce.

Why could not Congress do this? let me ask. The answer is, that the State of Massachusetts is a self-existing and indestructible member of the American Union, and neither Congress nor any other department of the federal government has, expressly or by implication, power to destroy any essential attribute of the sove- reignty of that commonwealth. The word sovereignty I use in its American sense of supreme power, partitioned between the Union and each of the States. Neither the one nor the other is an abso- lute sovereign ; each power is sovereign in its own sphere. The dividing line between them is as marked to the eye of a lawyer as if it were territorial.

Congress, then, is judge of the means to be chosen for attaining a desired end, only in this sense, that it must choose appropriate means, and such as are not expressly or by implication prohibited. Certain means are expressly prohibited, as, for example, the es- tablishment of an order of nobility. Other means are by implica- tion prohibited, as, for example, the destruction of a State. Con- gress is not expressly prohibited from destroying a State ; the im- plied prohibition, however, is not less real and imperative. After eliminating these prohibited means from the category of those which are eligible, there must be a still further elimination of all means which are not appropriate. This word appropriate is one of limitation. Congress is not clothed with power to enforce the prohibition by every kind of legislation, but by appropriate legis- lation. We have, then, in the very body of the Constitution, these limitations upon the choice of means by Congress ; they must not be prohibited, and they must be appropriate.

When, therefore, it is said, as it often is, that Congress is the ex- clusive judge of the means to be chosen for attaining an end, the proposition is to be admitted only with the two qualifications that have been mentioned. So it was said by Madison, Hamilton and Jay, in the *Federalist;* so it was said by Hamilton in his argument for a bank of the United States ; so it was said by Ch. Justice Marshall in McCulloch and Maryland, and so it has been said, scores of times since, by judges of this court and other judges, State and federal.

8. Limitations upon the mode of enforcing delegated powers.

To illustrate the rule that no means can be adopted which con- travene the implied as well as the express limitations of the Constitution, let us suppose a few cases. Congress could not authorize the criminal prosecution of a State legislator who voted for a bill within the prohibition. Why not? Because that would be incompatible with the independence of the State legislatures, an independence essential to the sovereignty, or, if the expression is liked better, the partial independence, or the autonomy, of the States. Congress could not authorize an injunction against a State legislature, forbidding it to pass such a bill, for the like reason. Congress could not subject to criminal process the judges of a State court for deciding against the constitutionality of the enforcement act, and the reason here is the same.

There are many limitations upon the choice of means beyond those which are expressed. They are implied from the nature of the government, the history of the country and the traditions of the people. The right to declare an act invalid, because incompatible with the Constitution, applies with the same effect where the incompatibility relates to the implied, as where it relates to the express limitations of the Constitution.

General language, though in itself unambiguous, is limited by the circumstances in which it is used. Thus, "the United States shall guarantee to every State in this Union a republican form of government." But what sort of a republican government? Is there any express provision of the Constitution which forbids Congress to establish in a State, whose authorities are overthrown, a government like that of Venice, or like that of another of the Italian republics of the middle ages? According to the classification of writers on government, Genoa under its doges, Florence under its dukes, and Poland under its kings, were republics. Why may not Congress take that form of republican government now existing in France, or that lately existing in Spain, or any of the republican forms of past ages, that, for instance, of the Commonwealth of England under Cromwell, or even that of Poland? There is no reason other than this, that there are certain essential, inherent, ineradicable principles of American republican government, to which the framers of the Constitution referred, and by which Congress is bound. And if Congress be thus limited, the courts must say so whenever the question is brought before them. What otherwise could prevent Congress from establishing in a disorganized State, a government of military dukes.

In all that I have said I am justified by recent decisions of this court. Not longer ago than 1868, this court, speaking by its late

34

chief justice, uttered these memorable words, which will live in constitutional history so long as the Constitution lives in its vigor: "Not only, therefore, can there be no loss of separate and independent autonomy to the States through their union under the Constitution, but it may be not unreasonably said, that the preservation of the States, and the maintenance of their governments, are as much within the design and care of the Constitution as the preservation of the Union, and the maintenance of the national government. The Constitution in all its provisions, looks to an indestructible Union, composed of indestructible States."[1] And, in 1870, the court, speaking by Mr. Justice Nelson, used this language: "The general government and the States, although both exist within the same territorial limits, are separate and distinct sovereignties, acting separately and independently of each other, within their respective spheres. The former in its appropriate sphere is supreme, but the States, within the limits of their powers not granted, or, in the language of the tenth amendment, 'reserved,' are as independent of the general government, as that government, within its sphere, is independent of the States."[2] And again : "It," the taxing power, "is therefore one of the sovereign powers vested in the States by their constitutions, which remained unaltered and unimpaired, and in respect to which the State is as independent of the general government, as that government is independent of the States. The supremacy of the general government, therefore, so much relied on in the argument of the counsel for the plaintiff in error, in respect to the question before us, cannot be maintained. The two governments are upon an equality," &c., (p. 126). And again: "In this respect, that is, in respect to the reserved powers, the State is as sovereign and independent as the general government" (p. 127). The case itself is the strongest possible example of an implied limitation upon the powers of Congress. Its power to tax is apparently unlimited, and it had passed an act, by the terms of which the salary of a State judge was liable to taxation, but this court pronounced the act unconstitutional, because, in the exercise of an express power, Congress had transgressed the implied limitations. Other instances of implied limitations will readily suggest themselves; federal judges declining duties not judicial, imposed on them by Congress, and State officers declining federal duties.

[2] Collector v. Day, 11 Wall. 124.   [1] Texas v. White, 7 Wall. 725.

9. THE LEGISLATION TO ENFORCE THE AMENDMENTS INVALID.

The only principle that can justify the legislation now in question, if it be justifiable at all, is this: That, in the choice of means to prevent a State violating the prohibitory clauses of the late amendments, Congress may itself do the things which the State would otherwise have done, in order to make sure that they are not done improperly. The States may, every one of them, do what New York and Massachusetts now do, in securing the right of all citizens to vote, without regard to race, color, or previous condition of servitude; but, for fear that they will not continue to do so, Congress may, it is claimed, register the voters, and receive and count the votes. And if it may do that, it may do any other thing that is to be done by a government in an election; in short, take upon itself to construct and work the whole machinery of elections. And what is true of voting, is, as I shall endeavor to show more fully hereafter, true also of every other subject within the scope of these amendments, and that includes almost every subject of government. For what is there in the world for State legislation but "life, liberty and property," and the "protection of the laws?" If the validity of the present legislation is affirmed, one may affirm the validity of legislation upon any subject concerning life, liberty, property, and protection by the law.

10. THE TENDENCY TOWARDS THE CENTRALIZATION OF POWER.

It is idle to answer that such an attempt will never be made. Who can tell what, in the frenzy of future parties, may not be attempted? Who that has seen the things happening in this generation, can foretell what may not be done or attempted in some of the times to come? One of the most extraordinary phenomena of political history, is the tendency of majorities to oppress minorities, and to trample upon all obstructions standing in the way. It would have been thought probable, that as each person who helps to make the majority is himself but an individual, and may soon be in the minority of individuals, he would be sedulous to guard his own rights, by refusing to join in pressing too heavily upon the rights of others. But the fact is different, though every federal legislator, and every other federal officer does in truth depend for his own protection and that of his family, more upon the State to which he belongs, than upon the federal government which he for the time being serves. Yet this truth is lost sight of in the thoughtlessness and excitement of national discussions. Whoever has carefully watched the political events of the last decade must have seen a constant and constantly accelerated movement toward the organization and cumulation of federal authority. This has been brought about by the action of good men as well as bad, in obliviousness of the truth that every new power added to the nation, is just so much subtracted from the States.

11. RULE OF INTERPRETATION AS TO THE NEW AMENDMENTS.

A political argument addressed to the Supreme Court would, of course, be out of place. Its great but single function is to interpret the law and the Constitution, be the consequences what they may. But it is proper to reflect, that for the true interpretation of language, we may, and should look at the occasion and circumstances in which it was used. This is both natural and philosophical. The imperfection of language leaves room for different interpretations, in the choice of which we put ourselves, so far as may be, in the place of those who used it. see with their eyes, hear with their ears, and imagine ourselves to be aiming at that at which they aimed. We know the history of the federal Constitution; and we know also the history of the late amendments. The matter is too fresh for us to be ignorant of the views and intentions of those who ratified their provisions. We may appeal to the knowledge of men around us, to our fellow-citizens of the whole nation, to bear us out in the assertion, that the people did not suppose they were thereby changing the fundamental theory of their government. If this be assumed, and it be shown, that the legislation in question goes upon a new theory of the government, and of the relation of the States to the Union, then it is shown that the people never contemplated, and much less sanctioned, such an interpretation of their acts. Should this be done, then, in a case where language is susceptible of two interpretations, that one is to be preferred as the true one which conforms to the understanding of the people, whose acts alone these amendments are.

12. TWO PROPOSITIONS WHICH EMBRACE THE THEORY OF THE DEFENSE.

My argument, therefore, will consist of an endeavor to establish the following two propositions:

I. The natural interpretation of the language of the new amendments does not justify the present legislation;

II. If the natural interpretation did justify it, yet, as the language is susceptible of a different one, the latter must be preferred as that alone in which it was understood by the people.

The natural interpretation of the amendments does not justify the legislation. No State, this is the language, shall make or enforce any law which shall abridge the privileges or immunities of citizens of the United States, or deprive any person of life, liberty or property, without due process of law, or deny to any person within its jurisdiction the equal protection of the laws; no State shall deny or abridge the right of citizens of the United States to vote, without regard to race, color, or previous condition of servitude. A State is a corporate body, and can act only by its corporate authorities. Until these corporate authorities have acted, the State has not violated the prohibition. Congress therefore must move after the State, not before it. But as yet no State has moved, so far as we are informed. Not one of them has done anything which a State is, by these amendments, commanded not to do.

13. CONGRESS HAS NO RIGHT TO ANTICIPATE THE ACTION OF A STATE.

The prohibitions being against State action, that action must precede any counter action under act of Congress. This is so obvious, as to amount almost to a truism. Even if Congress should be supposed competent to legislate in anticipation of State action, nothing could be done under the act of Congress until something had been done under the act of the State, contrary to the prohibition.

It follows from the last proposition, as well as from other considerations, that in respect to the mere prohibitions upon the States no action under a law of Congress can be had for the mere inaction of a State. If, for example, a State should wholly fail to provide for certain rights of property, Congress would not thereby become authorized to pass laws for the protection of such rights. There are many rights which courts acting only according to the common law cannot adequately protect. Massachusetts and Pennsylvania were formerly without equitable remedies. If they were so now, no sane man would pretend that therefore Congress would be authorized to establish such remedies for them. So, too, in respect to certain new rights of property, as, for instance, those which arise out of telegraphy, should a State or all the States fail to define and protect them, Congress could not do so.

14. FAILURE TO PROVIDE A REMEDY NOT EQUIVALENT TO THE DEPRIVATION OF A RIGHT.

Failure to provide a remedy for a wrong is not the same thing as depriving of a right. If it were so, then Congress might examine the codes of the States, and, if it found their provisions inadequate, might supplement them. Were a State to repeal a part of its laws for the protection of rights or the punishment of crimes, the national government could not supply the deficiency. Thus, if New York were to repeal all laws for the collection of debts, Congress could not re-enact them. If Massachusetts were to provide no punishment for conspiracy or embezzlement, Congress could not provide it.

It could hardly be claimed that these prohibitions require any more of the State legislatures than would have been required of them if the same had been contained in their own constitutions. Then surely their doing no more and no less cannot give just occasion for federal interposition. State inaction therefore is no cause for federal action. There must be affirmative action by a State tending to deprive a citizen of his rights before Congress can interfere. Should a State legislature attempt to deprive a person of property without due process of law, its action would be a nullity. What, in that event, might Congress do ? Provide legal means for establishing the nullity. What legal means did Congress, long ago, provide for establishing the nullity of an *ex post facto* law, or a law impairing the obligation of contracts, or a bill of attainder ? An appeal to the federal courts. Has not that proved adequate ? The whole question may be stated in these words: How may Congress enforce the nullity of a State law.

15. A PROHIBITION OF THE EXERCISE OF POWER, DOES NOT CONFER UPON CONGRESS THE POWER PROHIBITED.

Guarantee is not the converse of prohibition. The prohibitions do not amount to guarantees. They do not require the States to make sure that no man shall be deprived of life, liberty or property without law. The prohibitory amendments act upon the States and not upon individuals. Because the States are interdicted from certain things, and Congress may enforce the interdict, that does not prove that Congress may do the converse things. Because the States are prohibited, it would be a strange inference that Congress is authorized. When the Constitution says to the States, you shall not, that is not the same thing as saying to Congress, you shall or you may. If it were so, there would be found a strange omission in the Constitution, wide enough to let in many of the mischiefs which the prohibitions were intended to remedy. Congress is not by these amendments prohibited; it is only the States which are. If in consequence of the prohibition upon the States, Congress can exercise plenary power over the subject, it can do some, indeed many, of the very things, which the States were forbidden to do. Congress is not forbidden to pass a law abridging the privileges and immunities of citizens, or denying to certain persons the equal protection of the laws.

16. MODE IN WHICH CONGRESS MAY LEGALLY ENFORCE PROHIBITIONS UPON THE STATES.

But suppose a State, not content with its present laws, to be about to act aggressively, and thus to violate the prohibition, we may speculate upon what Congress could, in that event, enact. The means adopted must be appropriate, and not prohibited. The federal legislature can act only by statute, to be put in execution by the executive and the courts. Could Congress authorize the executive to do anything against the recalcitrant State? It is difficult to see what it could empower the President to do. It must act through the courts. And the only question is, what appropriate action could Congress authorize to be taken in the courts to enforce the prohibition, that is, to prevent or redress the violation. Could it indict and punish the individuals who had taken advantage of the State's violation of the prohibition, or take action against the State authorities, or nullify the acts, which the State ordains or permits? Direct action against the State authorities is out of the question for reasons hereinbefore and hereafter stated. For Congress to punish individuals for violations of State laws is also out of the question. To punish them for obeying the State laws would always be of doubtful expediency, as leading to unnecessary conflict, and would often be unconstitutional. The third remedy is the true if not the only one, to nullify the action which the State should not have ordained or permitted.

We have lived now three-quarters of a century under the Constitution, and it has not been thought necessary to apply to Congress for the punishment of a conspiracy to impair the obligation of a contract, or to pass an *ex post facto* law, or a bill of attainder.

No one seems to have thought that Congress was competent to punish such a conspiracy, or that there was any occasion for such legislation, if it were possible.

17. CONSTITUTIONAL MODE OF ENFORCING THE AMENDMENTS.

Equality before the law is the general aim of the amendments. That is secured by nullifying inequality, that is, for example, by declaring that whatever the State grants to its white citizens, shall for that reason be also the right of the black. This rule would execute itself in most cases. Take that clause of the fourteenth amendment, which forbids a State to make or enforce a law abridging the privileges and immunities of citizens of the United States. The State cannot enforce a law until it is made; if, therefore, it makes no such law, the condition on which alone Congress can act has not arrived. When the State has made such a law then Congress can take steps to enforce the prohibition. What may they be? Not the passing of an Act to declare the State law null; that has already been done by a power higher than act of Congress—that is, the Constitution itself—not by empowering the President to act, for he cannot use force against the State statute, but by protecting the individual aggrieved from the operation of the obnoxious law. How is that to be done? Just as Congress has hitherto protected an individual aggrieved against an *ex post facto* law, or a law impairing the obligation of contracts. It is not necessary to go into details. Various legal processes will readily suggest themselves to a lawyer, the effect of which will be to protect the person from any law aiming to abridge his privileges or immunities as a citizen of the United States, whatever they may be.

Take the next clause, that which forbids a State to deprive any person of life, liberty or property, without due process of law. Upon this the same observations may be made. It is difficult to imagine any proceeding of a State to deprive a person of life, liberty or property, which may not be effectually reached by the means suggested. One of the most powerful instruments for depriving a person of life, liberty or property, is a bill of attainder, or a bill of pains and penalties. This is prohibited by the original Constitution. Is not that prohibition adequately enforced by existing acts of Congress, allowing an appeal to the federal judiciary?

Then take the third clause, that which forbids a State to deny to any person within its jurisdiction the equal protection of the laws. Cannot this be dealt with in the same way? A denial in words only, though in the form of a State statute, would be harm-less. If the denial is followed by acts, the person aggrieved can be defended against them by the same machinery of the courts, which would be sufficient for his defense against a violation of either of the preceding clauses. Indeed, the mode of dealing with the prohibition against bills of attainder is marked out as the true mode of dealing with the other prohibitions. No act of a State could be more violent and aggressive than a bill of attainder, and if the machinery of the twenty-fifth section of the Judiciary Act has hitherto been sufficient to defend the citizen against that, it surely will be sufficient to protect him against whatever is less violent and aggressive.

Will it be said, that life, liberty and property cannot be pro-tected without law; that the equal protection of the laws presup-poses the existence and enforcement of laws, and that if the States do not make the laws, or, being made, do not enforce them, then Congress may interfere? I have already said something on this head, and will add only a few words.

Let the question be put in this form: Suppose a State not to provide adequate remedies for the protection of life, liberty and property, what may Congress do? The answer must be, Congress may do nothing whatever, beyond providing judicial remedies in federal courts for parties aggrieved by deprivation of their rights. Beyond this there is no alternative between doing nothing or doing everything, between leaving the States alone or destroying them al-together. Congress cannot do everything, because that would be the annihilation of the States; therefore it can do nothing, beyond providing the judicial remedies here indicated.

For want of a better expression, I will call affirmative legislation that which declares and enforces substantive law; and by negative legislation, that which operates by way of defense, in giving redress to a party aggrieved. Using the expression in this sense, I should say that affirmative legislation in respect to the prohibitions of the 14th amendment, is not within the competency of Congress. I see no middle ground between giving Congress plenary power over the subject of these fundamental rights, and giving it none. If a State were to abrogate its whole civil and penal code, can Congress make one for it? By neglect of the government of New York, we will suppose A. to be deprived of his property, without due process of law. His remedy is to sue in the State courts. If that remedy is denied he can go into the federal courts by appeal. Should the present process of appeal prove too dilatory or cumbrous, Congress can afford an adequate remedy, by providing a simpler and speedier appeal.

Then let us consider the prohibition of the 15th amendment. "The right of citizens of the United States to vote, shall not be denied or abridged by * * * any State, on account of race, color or previous condition of servitude," and Congress may enforce the provisions of this article. It might seem at first sight, that here is a declaration of the right of citizens of the United States to vote, but that would be an error. No right is guaranteed or asserted. Discrimination only is prohibited. The right or privilege, whichever it may justly be called, of the elective franchise is still where it has always been, under State control, with this single qualification, that in determining it, the State shall make no distinction on account of race, color or previous servitude.

This amendment is nothing but a prohibition, like the first section of the 14th article, and should be dealt with in the same manner. But the right or privilege of voting cannot be exercised without affirmative legislation, it may be said. No more can the right to property be exercised without affirmative legislation. Because a judge of election refuses my right to vote, is that a reason why he should be indicted in the federal courts any more than the judge of a police court, who refuses my claim for redress against a ruffian who has assaulted me in the street? Because individuals, bad men, band together to deprive me of my redress from the police magistrate, is that a constitutional reason why the federal judiciary should be called upon to indict, try and punish them? As individuals they have violated the State laws, and the State must take them in hand; if the State will not, the inhabitants of the State are the sufferers, and in their hands lies the power of redress; let them not call on Congress to help those who can help themselves.

It must never be forgotten that the judges and other officers of all the States, are sworn to support the Constitution. The cases have hitherto proved rare in which they failed justly to interpret, and firmly to enforce the provisions of the Federal Constitution, and there is no reason to suppose that they will be less faithful hereafter. There should seem, therefore, to be no occasion for attempting to bend the Constitution till it snaps asunder.

My proposition, in short, is this: That an act of a State in violation of the prohibitions of the amendments would be a nullity, and that Congress, being authorized to enforce the prohibitions by appropriate legislation, the natural, the true, and the only constitutional mode of enforcement, is by judicial remedies to establish and enforce the nullity.

18. How State laws may be prevented from becoming operative.

The prohibitions of the three amendments present in effect a body of law complete in itself, comprehensive like a law of the twelve tables, and being the only substantive law, in that respect, required or permitted on the part of the United States. All that Congress has to do, by way of legislation, is to provide the means for the courts to enforce the nullity of the prohibited acts, if any such are passed by the States; in other words, to prevent their taking effect. That legislation Congress has, in a great part, supplied, by the act just passed, April 3, 1875, by which a few words have been inserted in the body of that section of the judiciary act of 1789, which conferred jurisdiction upon the Circuit Courts, and giving them hereafter cognizance of suits of a civil nature "arising under the Constitution or laws of the United States, or treaties made or which shall be made under their authority." The questions arising under the prohibitions of these amendments are, like the questions arising under the prohibitions of the original Constitution, judicial in their character. Congress is not competent to decide them, any more than it is competent to decide what are *ex post facto* laws, or what laws impair the obligations of contracts, or what are bills of attainder.

19. The legislation assumes that Congress has powers which it does not possess.

The 6th section of the Enforcement Act assumes that Congress has power to punish a conspiracy to deprive any citizen of the United States of his right to vote; of any right granted or secured by the federal Constitution; of any privilege or immunity of a citizen of the United States; of the right to life, liberty and property, and of the right to the equal protection of the laws.

Let us take one of these, and direct our attention to that; for example, the right of property. The prohibition of the 14th amendment commands a State not to deprive any person of property without due process of law. The State may deprive a person of his property by due process of law, but not without it. To deprive without due process is to proceed, without law, by arbitrary acts of legislation, miscalled law.   The State can act only by its corporate officers, and then only in pursuance of State legislation.   If a State governor despoils a citizen, he is a simple trespasser, unless there be a State law to justify him.   We will suppose then a State law prohibited by this amendment, which law authorizes a certain thing to be done; it is the doing of this thing which Congress may nullify.   Suppose an act declaring that A. shall have a farm belonging to B.   This would be simply void.   If not so declared by the State courts, the federal courts, on appeal, would reverse their decision.   That would be all that need be done.   Suppose that certain tenants in New York conspire to deprive, by force, a citizen of that State of his rights as landlord.   That is a conspiracy to deprive a person of his property without due process of law.   May Congress enact a general law for the punishment of the conspirators by a court of the United States ?

We must discriminate among the prohibitions, between those which aim merely at equality, and those which aim at other rights.   The provision about the right to vote, without disparagement arising from race, confers no right of voting; but simply provides, that if the right be given to whites it shall be given to blacks also.   Had a similar expression been used in respect to the right to hold office, it surely would not have been said that a right to an office was conferred.   So, if the right to education had been mentioned in the same terms, that would not have been construed to confer the right to be educated.

Upon the whole, it is submitted that the amendments, taken in their natural sense, do not justify the legislation now under review.

20. SECOND PROPOSITION.—THEORY AND OBJECT OF GOVERNMENT.

We come now to the second proposition, which is, that if the interpretation contended for were not the more natural one, yet it is at the very least a possible interpretation, and is to be preferred, because it is the only one conformable to the understanding and purpose of the people, by whom the text was adopted.

The general doctrine up to the time of these amendments continued to be, that the States were sovereign over their own State concerns.   This complex government was curiously contrived to give liberty and safety to the people of all the States.   It was fashioned by the people, in the name of the people, and for the people.   Its aim was to keep the peace among the States, and to manage affairs of common concern, while it left the States the entire management of their own affairs. Its founders were wise and practical men. They knew what history had taught from the beginning of Greek civilization, that a number of small republics would perish without federation, and that federation would destroy the small republics without such a barrier as it would be impossible to pass. Liberty and safety were the ends to be won by the double and complex organization; liberty from the States and safety from the Union, and the founders thought that they had contrived a scheme which would make the States and the Union essential parts of a great whole; that they had set bounds to each, which they could not pass; in short, that they had founded "liberty and union, one and inseparable."

No man in his senses could have supposed, at the formation of the Constitution, or can now suppose, that a consolidated government, extending over so much territory and so many people, can last a generation, without the destruction of the States and of republican government with them. History is a fable, and political philosophy a delusion, if any government other than monarchial can stretch itself over fifty degrees of longitude and half as many of latitude with fifty millions of people, where there are no local governments capable of standing by themselves and resisting all attempts to imperil their self-existence or impair their authority. The moment it is conceded that Washington may, at its discretion, regulate all the concerns of New York and California, of Louisiana and Maine ; that the autonomy of the States has no defense stronger than the self-denial of fluctuating congressional majorities ; at that moment the republic of our fathers will have disappeared, and a republic in name, but a despotism in fact, will have taken its place, to give way in another generation to a government with another name, and other attributes.

Observe how far on that road the maintenance of the present legislation will carry us. It has already led to the cases of Kellogg and Warmouth, the United States and Clayton, and Harrison and Hadley, and these cases are but a foretaste of what we may have hereafter. Its essential principle is, that in order to anticipate and prevent a violation of the prohibitions, Congress may establish a system of law for the general regulation of all subjects within the scope of the amendments. The logical and inevitable conclusions from this new theory are, that the prohibition against denying or abridging the right to vote on account of color, race, or previous condition of servitude, may be enforced by framing and working the machinery of elections, no matter what may be the office or the function to be filled by the electors. The prohibition against making or enforcing any law abridging the privileges or immunities of citizens of the United States may be enforced by framing a code of these privileges and immunities, defining the methods of enjoyment, and providing penalties for their violation. And the still more comprehensive prohibitions against depriving any person of life, liberty or property without due process of law, or denying to any person the equal protection of the laws, may be enforced by a more comprehensive code, defining the rights of life, liberty and property, in all their ramifications, the processes of law which are to be deemed due, that protection of the laws which is to be considered equal, and the various modes of enforcing the rights of life, liberty and property by remedies civil and criminal. If these numerous and multiform provisions would not cover the whole ground of law, substantive and remedial, it is not easy to see what would be omitted that is contained in the most comprehensive existing code. The legislation of Congress would, of course, supersede or exclude legislation by the States upon the same subjects; the United States would stand as the universal lawgivers of the country, and the laws of the States would dwindle to the dimensions of corporation ordinances or the regulations of county supervisors.

21. Practical results of the theory of the prosecution.

The argument appears to be unanswerable, that such was not and could not have been the intention of the American people, in sanctioning these amendments, and therefore they should not be thus interpreted, even if the natural significance of their language were, as it is not, favorable to such an interpretation.

To suppose the contrary, is to suppose that the people of this country have forgotten all their history and all their traditions, and have come to regard as evil that which their fathers accounted good, and good evil. If Washington, when he left the chair of the convention and signed his great name to the draft of the Constitution as president and deputy from Virginia; if Franklin, when he uttered there his last words, and looking at a picture of the sun in the horizon, said he had been in doubt whether it was rising or setting, but then, as they had so auspiciously concluded their labors, he knew it was the rising sun; if those patriot fathers had been told that the time would ever come, when the proud commonwealths which they represented would be accounted the vassals of that Union which they were so sedulous to create and so strenuous to defend, they would have turned upon the utterers of such prophesies, as fomentors of discord and enemies of the States.

22. Rules of interpretation heretofore adopted.

If confirmation of these views of the Constitution were needed, it would be found in the interpretation, legislative, executive and judicial, heretofore at all times given. We find that, with few exceptions, the current is all one way. The original instrument contained prohibitions, that "no State shall enter into any treaty, alliance or confederation; grant letters of marque and reprisal; coin money; emit bills of credit; make any thing but gold and silver coin a tender in payment of debts; pass any bill of attainder, *ex post facto* law, or law impairing the obligation of contracts, or grant any title of nobility." These prohibitions have subsisted now for nearly ninety years, but Congress has never attempted to enforce them, except by the 25th section of the Judiciary Act of 1789, which gave an appeal to the Supreme Court from the State courts, upon federal questions, and this action of Congress has proved all sufficient.

As to the executive department, although it is made the duty of the President to recommend to the consideration of Congress "such measures as he shall judge necessary and expedient," there has never been, so far as I am aware, any executive recommendation of further legislation to enforce these prohibitions. As to the judicial department, we have a concurrence and weight of authority, that leaves no room for doubt as to its views of the power of Congress.

Though this court, in every period of its history, has had occasion to interpret the Constitution, and to declare the rules by which it is to be interpreted, we have little occasion to go further back than the last two years, for an exposition of those rules, and their effect, especially upon the last three amendments. In the Slaughter-House cases, the court declared, that any question of doubt concerning the true meaning of the amendments cannot be safely and rationally solved, without a reference to the history of the times, and that

"In any fair and just construction of any section or phrase of these amendments, it is necessary to look to the purpose which * * * was the prevailing spirit of them all, the evil, which they were designed to remedy, and the process of continued addition to the Constitution, until that purpose was supposed to be accomplished, as far as constitutional law can accomplish it.

"It would be the vainest show of learning to attempt to prove, by citations of authority, that up to the adoption of the recent amendments no claim or pretense was set up that those rights depended on the federal government for their existence or protection, beyond the very few express limitations which the federal Constitution imposed upon the States—such, for instance, as the prohibition against *ex post facto* laws, bills of attainder, and laws impairing the obligation of contracts. But, with the exception of these and a few other restrictions, the entire domain of the privileges and immunities of citizens of the States, as above defined, lay within the constitutional and legislative power of the States, and without that of the federal government. Was it the purpose of the fourteenth amendment, by the simple declaration that no State should make or enforce any law which shall abridge the privileges and immunities of citizens of the United States, to transfer the security and protection of all the civil rights which we have mentioned, from the States to the federal government? And where it is declared that Congress shall have the power to enforce that article, was it intended to bring within the power of Congress the entire domain of civil rights heretofore belonging exclusively to the States?

"All this and more must follow, if the proposition of the plaintiffs in error be sound, for not only are these rights subject to the control of Congress, whenever in its discretion any of them are supposed to be abridged by State legislation, but that body may also pass laws in advance, limiting and restricting the exercise of legislative power by the States, in their most ordinary and most useful functions, as in its judgment it may think proper on all such subjects. And still further, such a construction, followed by the reversal of the judgments of the Supreme Court of Louisiana in these cases, would constitute this court a perpetual censor upon all legislation of the States, on the civil rights of their own citizens, with authority to nullify such as it did not approve as consistent with those rights as they existed at the time of the adoption of this amendment.

"The argument, we admit, is not always the most conclusive which is drawn from the consequences urged against the adoption of a particular construction of an instrument. But when, as in the case before us, these consequences are so serious, so far-reaching and pervading, so great a departure from the structure and spirit of our institutions; when the effect is to fetter and degrade the State governments by subjecting them to the control of Congress, in the exercise of powers hereto ore universally conceded to them of the most ordinary and fundamental character; when it fact it radically changes the whole theory of the relations of the State and federal governments to each other, and of both of these governments to the people; the argument has a force that is irresistible, in the absence of language which expresses such a purpose too clearly to admit of doubt.

"We are convinced that no such results were intended by the

Congress which proposed these amendments, nor by the legislatures of the States which ratified them."

* * * * * * * *

" Nor shall any State deny to any person within its jurisdiction the equal protection of the laws."

" In the light of the history of these amendments, and the pervading purpose of them, which we have already discussed, it is not difficult to give a meaning to this clause. The existence of laws in the States where the newly emancipated negroes resided, which discriminated with gross injustice and hardship against them, was the evil to be remedied by this clause as a class, and by it such laws are forbidden.

" If, however, the States did not conform their laws to its requirements, then, by the fifth section of the article of amendment, Congress was authorized to enforce it by suitable legislation. We doubt very much whether any action of a State, not directed by way of discrimination against the negroes as a class, or on account of their race, will ever be held to come within the purview of this provision. It is so clearly a provision for that race and that emergency that a strong case would be necessary for its application to any other. But as it is a State that is to be dealt with, and not alone the validity of its laws, we may safely leave that matter until Congress shall have exercised its power, or some case of State oppression, by denial of equal justice in the courts, shall have claimed a decision at our hands. We find no such case in the one before us, and do not deem it necessary to go over the argument again, as it may have relation to this particular clause of the amendment.

" In the early history of the organization of the government, its statesmen seem to have divided on the line which should separate the powers of the national government from those of the State governments, and though this line has never been very well defined in public opinion, such a division has continued from that day to this.

" The adoption of the first eleven amendments to the Constitution so soon after the original instrument was accepted, shows a prevailing sense of danger at that time from the federal power. And it cannot be denied that such a jealousy continued to exist with many patriotic men until the breaking out of our late civil war. It was then discovered that the true danger to the perpetuity of the Union was in the capacity of the State organizations to combine and concentrate all the powers of the State, and of contiguous States, for the determined resistance to the general government.

" Unquestionably this has given great force to the argument, and added largely to the number of those who believe in the necessity of a strong national government.

" But however pervading this sentiment, and however it may have contributed to the adoption of the amendments we have been considering, we do not see in these amendments any purpose to destroy the main features of the general system. Under the pressure

35

of all the excited feelings growing out of the war, our statesmen
have still believed that the existence of the States with powers for
domestic and local government, including the regulation of civil
rights—the rights of person and of property—was essential to the
perfect working of our complex form of government, though they
have thought proper to impose additional limitations on the States,
and to confer additional power on that of the nation."

These extracts from the opinion of the court, delivered by Mr.
Justice Miller, are given at such length, because they are so important in themselves, and dispose of so many of the questions in the
present case.

Of the three dissenting opinions, two certainly, and perhaps the
third, properly understood, contain nothing in conflict with what is
here stated. The difference of views among the learned judges of
the court was upon the extent of the prohibitions, not upon the
means of enforcing them.

If the thirteenth and fourteenth amendments be understood and
applied, as it is here insisted they should, they will prove most
beneficent in results. The prohibitions upon the States are merely
such as every State Constitution should contain for its own legislature. It is only when the interference of Congress is invoked that
the danger begins, and that will cease so soon as it is understood
that Congress cannot act until the States have legislated in violation
of the prohibition, and then only by way of nullifying their action
through the courts.

I have heard it argued that, as allegiance and protection create
mutual obligations, all who have been made citizens of the United
States by the late amendments are entitled to the protection of the
United States. So they are, but that does not prove the constitutionality of the present legislation, and for two reasons. The first
is, that all the citizens of the States were also citizens of the United
States before the amendments,[1] and the effect of the new definition
was merely to increase the number of citizens, but not their rights.
That protection of the federal government which the whites could
not have claimed before, the blacks cannot claim now. The second
reason is, that the allegiance and protection of the Union are qualified by the allegiance and protection of the States. The same person is a citizen of both, owes allegiance to both, and may claim the
protection of both. Each is his sovereign to a certain extent.
When, therefore, a citizen of the United States claims the protec-

[1] Passenger Cases, 7 How. 492, and Slaughter-House Cases, 16 Wall. 72.

tion of the United States, the first inquiry should be, against what, and in what manner the protection may be given. He cannot be protected against the lawful act of his own State, nor can he be protected against its unlawful act, except in the manner sanctioned by the Constitution of the United States. Who are citizens we learn from one part of that instrument; their rights and duties from another.

I must here close my part of the discussion. The general claim on the part of the federal government is nothing more nor less than this: that Congress is clothed with authority to punish in federal courts any persons for agreeing together in intention to prevent or hinder the free exercise and enjoyment by any citizen of any right or privilege granted or secured to him by the Constitution or laws of the United States, these laws being not only the three statutes just mentioned, but all other existing statutes, revised or not revised, and all statutes which Congress may choose hereafter to pass. And it seems to be assumed, furthermore, that the mere mention in the Constitution of a right is the same thing as granting or securing it, and that whether the mention is made in the old amendments containing prohibitions upon the United States, or in the new containing prohibitions upon the States. This is an assertion of absolutism or legislative omnipotence amazing to contemplate.

The particular claim in the present case is authority to punish an agreement between two or more persons to prevent or hinder the free exercise and enjoyment by any citizen of the right to the equal protection of the laws, the right to life, liberty and property, unless deprived thereof by due process of law, the right to vote, without regard to race, color or previous servitude, the right to meet others in assembly, and the right to keep and bear arms. This is the claim in the present case, reduced to its strictest limit. It includes, of course, as has been already said, the power to define what is the right to the protection of the laws, what is the right to life, liberty and property, what is due process of law, what is the right to vote, what is the right to keep and bear arms, and what is the right of assembly. It would be a logical inconsistency to pretend that a government can clothe its courts with authority to punish for crime without authority to say in what that crime consists. When the Constitution gave Congress power to punish piracies and felonies on the high seas, and offenses against the laws of nations, it gave also the power to define them.

The mere agreement or conspiracy, without any overt act, is the crime, unless the "or" in the second member of the sentence of the 6th section of the Enforcement Act is to be read as if it were "and." It may not be out of place to observe, that an accusation of conspiracy is of all accusations the most dangerous to meet, and the easiest to make men believe, in an excited community. It is the harshest engine of tyranny ever used under the form of law; and its frequent use is the strongest evidence of misgovernment. From the bloody days when the compassing or imagining the death of a king was the miserable pretense upon which tyrants took the lives and confiscated the estates of their victims, to the present hour, no surer proof of good or evil government can be found than the chapter on conspiracies in the statute book of a country. One has but to compare the statutes of well-governed Connecticut with the statutes of misgoverned Ireland to learn what an odious engine of oppression is the law of conspiracy. And what an abundance of materials for the supply of this engine are furnished by these acts of Congress. If two magistrates, being convinced by counsel, decide that some of their provisions are invalid, or if two counsel in consultation come to that conclusion and so advise their clients, do they not put themselves in peril of the penalties denounced by the acts? If two judges of a State court, after painstaking deliberation, decide that a statute of their State, though in conflict with some portions of the Enforcement Act, is nevertheless valid, or even if, without deciding, they agree so to decide, are they not liable to be sent to the penitentiary, under the 6th section? Would not the 6th and 17th sections send to prison the judges of California who decided in favor of sending back the Chinese women?

It is difficult to speak of the pretensions upon which this legislation rests, in guarded language. It is a relief to think that they are here to be tested by the Constitution of the country, without the disturbing influence of party; by that Constitution which is above all parties, and which was made, not for the use of partisans, but for the safety and happiness of the whole people, and not for one, but many generations.

The first two words of the national motto are as much a part of it as the last. They have never been changed since their use began. They have been borne in every battle and on every march, by land or sea, in defeat as in victory. They are still blazoned on our escutcheon, and copied in every seal of office. You will find them on all your commissions. May that motto never be mutilated or disowned. It should be written on the walls of the capitol and of every State house. I would wish it written on the ceiling of this chamber, that, upon every turning of the face upward, the eye might behold it. Its three words contain a faithful history; may they abide for ages, pledges of the future, as they are witnesses of the past.

DECLARATION OF LORD MANSFIELD TO THE MOB, IN THE COURT OF KING'S BENCH.

I will do my duty unawed. What am I to fear? That "*mendax infamia*" [lying scandal] from the press, which daily coins false facts and false motives? The lies of calumny carry no terror to me. I trust that the temper of my mind, and the color and conduct of my life, have given me a suit of armor against these arrows. If during this King's reign I have ever supported his government, and assisted his measures, I have done it without any other reward than the consciousness of doing what I thought right. If I have ever opposed, I have done it upon the points themselves, without mixing in party or faction, and without any collateral views. I honor the King and respect the people; but many things acquired by the favor of either are, in my account, objects not worthy of ambition. I wish popularity, but it is that popularity which follows, not that which is run after. It is that popularity which, sooner or later, never fails to do justice to the pursuit of noble ends by noble means. I will not do that which my conscience tells me is wrong upon this occasion, to gain the huzzas of thousands, or the daily praise of all the papers which come from the press. I will not avoid doing what I think is right, though it should draw on me the whole artillery of libels—all that falsehood and malice can invent, or the credulity of a deluded populace can swallow. I can say with a great magistrate, upon an occasion and under circumstances not unlike, "*Ego hoc animo semper fui, ut invidiam virtute partam, gloriam non invidiam, putarem.*"

The threats go farther than abuse—personal violence is denounced. I do not believe it. It is not the genius of the worst of men of this country, in the worst of times. But I have set my mind at rest. The last end that can happen to any man never comes too soon, if he falls in support of the law and liberty of his country (for liberty is synonymous with law and government). Such a shock, too, might be productive of public good. It might awake the better part of the kingdom out of that lethargy which seems to have benumbed them, and bring the mad part back to their senses, as men intoxicated are sometimes stunned into sobriety.

Once for all, let it be understood, that no endeavors of this kind will influence any man who at present sits here. If they had any effect, it would be contrary to their intent; leaning against their impression might give a bias the other way. But I hope and I know that I have fortitude enough to resist even that weakness. No libels, no threats, nothing that has happened, nothing that can happen, will weigh a feather against allowing the defendant, upon this and every other question, not only the whole advantage he is entitled to from substantial law and justice, but every benefit from the most critical nicety of form which any other defendant could claim under the like objection."—[Lord MANSFIELD, in reversing the Outlawry in Wilkes' Case, June 8, 1768.]

[550]

SPEECH OF THOMAS ERSKINE,

For the Prosecution, in the Proceedings against Thomas Williams, for Publishing Paine's "Age of Reason."

[Howell's St. Tr. vol. 26, p. 653.]

IN THE COURT OF KING'S BENCH, BEFORE LORD KENYON AND A SPECIAL JURY, JUNE 24th, 1797.

ANALYSIS OF MR. ERSKINE'S SPEECH.

1. Attitude of counsel not inconsistent with views formerly expressed.
2. The defense anticipated.
3. Christianity the foundation upon which our system of jurisprudence rests.
4. A free press an inestimable blessing.
5. The principles applicable to the liberty of the press.
6. Distinction between legitimate inquiry and scurrilous abuse.
7. Illustrations of the argument.
8. Mischievous and cruel effects of this illegal publication.
9. The character of the defense an anomaly, and inconsistent with the jurisdiction of the court.
10. Intellectual superiority of Christian believers.—Newton.
11. Boyle, Locke, and Sir Matthew Hale.
12. John Milton's immortal offering.
13. Adherence to doctrines of the New Testament would banish wickedness from the world.
14. Religion and morality alone constitute the safety of the State.
15. Inferior object and capacity of Paine's work.

Thomas Paine, the friend, at one time, of Washington, of Jefferson and Franklin ; who had been honored by the Congress of the United States for his distinguished services during the revolution; whose worth and patriotism were, in like manner, recognized by the great State of New York; Thomas Paine, whose genius contributed so much towards the development and success of the independence of the colonies; who loved freedom for its own sake; who became conspicuous during the French revolution as the "apostle of liberty"—this gifted man, after he had achieved so much for the welfare of his race, chose, unfortunately for himself, to forfeit the respect and esteem of his fellow men, and of posterity, because of his wanton attack upon the Scriptures and the life and character of the Saviour of mankind. In the year 1794, he composed the first part, and in the following year the second part, of an indecent and blasphemous attack upon Christianity, which he entitled the "Age of Reason," being what he was pleased to term an investigation of true and fabulous theology. The work lacks the dignity and candor of respectful inquiry, and is in no way worthy the intellect of Paine. It contains no sublime thought, and presents in support of the theories advanced, no arguments which are at all convincing or satisfactory, or which indicate even a thorough knowledge of the contempo-

raneous history of the Bible. With the great problems of eternity, this defamer
of all theology has no concern, and treats with ridicule, truths which touch the
highest point of human interest and human comprehension.   Instead of meeting
great questions within the domain of reason, he frequently drops into poor attempts at wit, which are painful and disgusting to refined sensibilities, and his
expressions are often tinctured with coarseness and vulgarity. His performance
becomes culpable, in view of the fact that without sufficient reason, and apparently from a desire to indulge his vanity, the author has labored to shake the
faith of those who derive hope and consolation from a book containing higher
thoughts, purer morality, and wiser maxims than has ever been written in any
language or in any age. The promises of an immortal inheritance, the rewards
assured to the Christian, more desirable and enticing than any which have ever
attracted the attention of mortals ; an heirship coeval with the creator of the
world—these are all brushed aside. In their stead, however, the sophistical skeptic
suggests nothing possessing even the merit of novelty or originality. While professing to believe in a God and immortality, Thomas Paine has produced a work,
the tendency of which is to banish from weaker minds than his own, the idea of
the existence of a God and an immortal life; a work which strikes at the very
foundations of society, and assails the moral principles upon which society and
all human obligations must rest.

    Paine, though a man of vigorous mind, was not an accomplished or finished
scholar.   As to acquirements and elegant letters, his warmest admirers would
not venture to compare him with the distinguished jurist, linguist and antiquary,
Sir William Jones; and it is fair to presume, that had he possessed a tithe of that
gentleman's learning, he would, perhaps, never have written the "Age of Reason."   One very singular fact about Paine's production is, that its author fails to
recognize even the literary merit of the book from which, in his early life, he had
often preached. Apart from the inspiration of the sacred volume, he seeks to
deride its sublime eloquence and masterly composition. Sir William Jones,
who was conversant with no less than twenty-seven languages, speaking of its
excellence in this respect, says: "I have carefully and regularly perused these
Holy Scriptures, and am of opinion that the volume, independently of its
divine origin, contains more sublimity, more morality, more important history,
and finer strains of eloquence, than can be collected from any other book, in
whatever language it may have been written."   Upon another occasion the
same author remarks : "The two parts of which the Scriptures consists, are connected by a chain of compositions, which bear no resemblance in form or style to
any that can be produced from the stores of Grecian, Indian, Persian, or even
Arabian learning. The antiquity of those compositions no man doubts, and the
unrestrained application of them to events long subsequent to their publication,
is a solid ground of belief that they are genuine compositions, and consequently
inspired." To demonstrate that these statements are not mere generalities, Mr.
Burgh, an English writer, in his work entitled the "Dignity of Human Nature,"
takes a passage from the beginning of the eighth book of the Iliad, which he
regards as the loftiest strain in the most sublime of all human productions, and
contrasts it with a passage from the Bible. Speaking of this selection from
Homer, quoted below, Mr. Burgh remarks : "There the greatest of all human
imaginations labors to describe, not a hero, but a God ; not an inferior but the

Supreme God ; not to show his superiority over mortals, but to the heavenly powers ; and not to one, but all of them united." The passage is rendered by Mr. Bryant, in his elegant translation, as follows :

> Now morn in saffron robes had spread her light
> O'er all the earth, when Jove, the Thunderer,
> Summoned the gods to council on the heights
> Of many-peaked Olympus.   He addressed
> The assembly, and all listened as he spoke.
> " Hear, all ye gods and all ye goddesses!
> While I declare the thought within my breast,
> Let none of either sex presume to break
> The law I give, but cheerfully obey,
> That my design may sooner be fulfilled.
> Whosoever, stealing from the rest, shall seek,
> To aid the Grecian cause, or that of Troy,
> Back to Olympus, scourged and in disgrace,
> Shall he be brought, or I will seize and hurl
> The offender down to rayless Tartarus ;
> Deep, deep in the great gulf below the earth,
> With iron gates, and threshold forged of brass,—
> As far beneath the shades, as earth from heaven.
> Then shall he learn how greatly I surpass
> All other gods in power.   Try, if ye will,
> Ye gods, that all may know: suspend from heaven
> A golden chain; let all the immortal host
> Cling to it from below ; ye could not draw,
> Strive as ye might, the all-disposing Jove,
> From heaven to earth.   And yet, if I should choose
> To draw it upward to me. I should lift,
> With it and you, the earth itself and sea
> Together, and I then would bind the chain,
> Around the summit of the Olympian mount,
> And they should hang aloft.   So far my power
> Surpasses all the power of gods and men."

" With this most masterly passage," says Mr. Burgh, " of the greatest master of the sublime of all antiquity—the writer who probably had the greatest natural and acquired advantages of any mortal for perfecting a genius—let the following verbal translation of a passage from writings penned by one brought up a shepherd, and in a country where learning was not thought of, be compared, that the difference may appear:

" ' O Lord, my God, thou art very great! thou art clothed with honor and majesty! who coverest thyself with light as with a garment ; who stretchest out the heavens like a canopy ; who layest the beams of his chambers in the waters ; who makest the clouds his chariots ; who walkest upon the wings of the winds ; who makest his angels spirits, his ministers a flame of fire ; who laid the foundation of the earth, that it should not be moved forever.   Thou coverest it with the deep, as with a garment—the waters that stood above the mountains.   At thy rebuke they fled; at the voice of thy thunder they hasted away.   They go up by the mountains ; they go down by the valleys, unto the place thou hast founded for them.   Thou hast set a bound, that they may not pass over ; that they may turn not again to cover the earth.

" ' O Lord, how manifold are thy works!   In wisdom hast thou made them all.   The earth is full of thy riches.   So is the great and wide sea, wherein are creatures innumerable, both small and great.   There go the ships ; there is that leviathan, which thou hast made to play therein.   These all wait upon thee, that thou mayest give them their food in due season.   That thou givest them they gather.   Thou openest thy hand, they are filled with good ; thou hidest thy face

they are troubled ; they die and return to their dust. Thou sendest forth thy
spirit, they are created; and thou renewest the face of the earth. The glory of
the Lord shall endure forever. The Lord shall rejoice in his works. He looketh on the earth, and it trembleth. He toucheth the hills, and they smoke. I
will sing unto the Lord as long as I live. I will sing praises unto my God, while
I have my being.' "

This single illustration shows the sophistry of Paine's criticism on the grandest
and most dignified literary production in the world. The "Age of Reason," however, produced pernicious effects among the middle and lower classes in Corn-
wall, Nottingham, Leeds, and many other places in England, and even in Scotland, where the work had been circulated. Its influence was regarded as dangerous, affecting the happiness and welfare of the uneducated or ignorant classes,
who could not readily answer its plausible utterances, and the " Society for the
Prevention of Vice " decided to attempt its suppression. An indictment was accordingly preferred against Thomas Williams, of the parish of St. Giles, in the
county of Middlesex, for a blasphemous libel in publishing Paine's work. The
legal theory of this indictment was, that every publication which has a direct
tendency to debauch the morals of the people, is punishable as a libel ; that
blasphemy is an offense, not only against God and religion, but a crime against
the laws, the State and the government ; for to say that Christianity is a cheat
is to dissolve all those obligations whereby civil societies are preserved. (Taylor's Case, 1 Ventris, 293; s. c. 3 Keble, 607 ; Rex v. Curl, Strange, 789; Rex v.
Woolston, Fitzgibbon, 64 ; Strange, 834 ; Blackstone's Com. vol. 4, pp. 43, 59.)

The prosecution was conducted by Thomas Erskine, the first and greatest
of English advocates, who, five years before, at the expense of his office of attorney-general, defended Paine on an indictment for libel for publishing the second
part of the " Rights of Man." The Prince of Wales, as a reward for his brave
and honest defense of his client, disgraced himself by removing Erskine from
office. In his opening to the jury in that case, Mr. Erskine made the noble declaration : " I will forever—at all hazards—assert the dignity, independence and
integrity of the English bar, without which impartial justice, the most valuable
part of the English Constitution, can have no existence."

With Mr. Erskine, in the case of Williams, were associated William Gar-
row and John Bayley. The defendant was represented by Stewart Kyd. Mr.
Erskine opened the case for the prosecution as follows :

GENTLEMEN OF THE JURY:—The charge of blasphemy, which
is put upon the record against the printer of this publication, is
not an accusation of the servants of the Crown, but comes before
you sanctioned by the oaths of a grand jury of the country. It
stood for trial upon a former day ; but it happening, as it frequently does, without any imputation on the gentlemen named in the
panel, that a sufficient number did not appear to constitute a full
special jury, I thought it my duty to withdraw the cause from trial
till I could have the opportunity, which is now open to me, of addressing myself to you, who were originally appointed to try it. I
pursued this course, however, from no jealousy of the common

juries appointed by the laws for the ordinary service of the court, since my whole life has been one continued experience of their virtues, but because I thought it of great importance that those who were to decide upon a cause so very momentous to the public, should have the highest possible qualifications for the decision. That they should not only be men capable, from their education, of forming an enlightened judgment, but that their situations should be such as to bring them within the full view of their enlightened country, to which, in character and in estimation, they were in their own turns to be responsible.

1. Attitude of counsel not inconsistent with views formerly expressed.

Not having the honor, gentlemen, to be sworn for the king, as one of his counsel, it has fallen much oftener to my lot to defend indictments for libels, than to assist in the prosecution of them. But I feel no embarrassment from that recollection, since I shall not be found to-day to express a sentiment or to utter an expression inconsistent with those invaluable principles for which I have uniformly contended in the defense of others. Nothing that I have ever said, either professionally or personally, for the liberty of the press, do I mean to deny, to contradict, or counteract. On the contrary, I desire to preface the discourse I have to make to you, with reminding you that it is your most solemn duty to take care it suffers no injury in your hands. A free and unlicensed press, in the just and legal sense of the expression, has led to all the blessings, both of religion and government, which Great Britain, or any part of the world, at this moment enjoys, and is calculated still further to advance mankind to higher degrees of civilization and happiness. But this freedom, like every other, must be limited to be enjoyed, and, like every human advantage, may be defeated by its abuse.

2. The defense anticipated

Gentlemen, the defendant stands indicted for having published this book, which I have only read from the obligations of professional duty, and which I rose from the reading of with astonishment and disgust. Standing here with all the privileges belonging to the highest counsel for the Crown, I shall be entitled to reply to any defense that shall be made for the publication. I shall wait with patience till I hear it. Indeed, if I were to anticipate the defense which I hear and read of, it would be defaming, by anticipation, the learned counsel who is to make it. For if I am to collect it, even from a formal notice given to the prosecutors in the course of the proceedings, I have to expect that, instead of a defense conducted according to the rules and principles of English law and justice, the foundation of all our laws, and the sanctions of all our justice, are to be struck at and insulted.

3. CHRISTIANITY THE FOUNDATION UPON WHICH OUR SYSTEM OF JURISPRUDENCE RESTS.

What is the force of that jurisdiction which enables the court to sit in judgment ? What but the oath which his lordship as well as yourselves have sworn upon the Gospel to fulfill. Yet in the King's Court, where his majesty is himself also sworn to administer the justice of England in the King's Court, who receives his high authority under a solemn oath to maintain the Christian religion, as it is promulgated by God in the Holy Scriptures, I am nevertheless called upon, as counsel for the prosecution, to produce a certian book described in the indictment to be the Holy Bible. No man deserves to be upon the rolls of the court who dares, as an attorney, to put his name to such a notice. It is an insult to the authority and dignity of the court of which he is an officer ; since it seems to call in question the very foundations of its jurisdiction. If this is to be the spirit and temper of the defense ; if, as I collect from that array of books which are spread upon the benches behind me, this publication is to be vindicated by an attack on all the truths which the Christian religion promulgates to mankind, let it be remembered that such an argument was neither suggested nor justified by anything said by me on the part of the prosecution. In this stage of the proceedings, I shall call for reverence to the sacred Scriptures, not from their merits unbounded as they are, but from their authority in a Christian country ; not from the obligations of conscience, but from the rules of law. For my own part, gentlemen, I have been ever deeply devoted to the truths of Christianity, and my firm belief in the Holy Gospel is by no means owing to the prejudices of education, though I was religiously educated by the best of parents, but arises from the fullest and most continued reflections of my riper years and understanding. It forms at this moment the great consolation of a life which, as a shadow, must pass away ; and without it, indeed, I should consider my long course of health and prosperity, perhaps too long and uninterrupted to be good for any man, only as the dust which the wind scatters, and rather as a snare than as a blessing. Much, however, as I wish to support the authority of the Scriptures, from a reasoned consideration of them, I shall repress that subject for the present. But if the defense shall be as I have suspected, to bring them at all into argument or question, I shall then fulfill a duty which I owe, not only to the court, as counsel for the prosecution, but to the public, to state what I feel and know concerning the evidences of that religion which is reviled without being examined, and denied without being understood.

4. A FREE PRESS AN INESTIMABLE BLESSING.

I am well aware, that by the communications of a free press, all the errors of mankind, from age to age, have been dissipated and dispelled ; and I recollect that the world, under the banners of reformed Christianity, has struggled through persecution to the noble eminence on which it stands at this moment shedding the blessings of humanity and science upon the nations of the earth. It may be asked, by what means the Reformation would have been effected if the books of the reformers had been suppressed, and the errors of condemned and exploded superstitions had been supported as unquestionable by the State, founded upon those very superstitions formerly, as it is at present upon the doctrines of the Established Church ? or how, upon such principles, any reformation, civil or religious, can in future be effected ? The solution is easy. Let us examine what are the genuine principles of the liberty of the press, as they regard writings upon general subjects, unconnected with the personal reputations of private men, which are wholly foreign to the present inquiry. They are full of simplicity, and are brought as near perfection by the law of England as, perhaps, is consistent with any of the frail institutions of mankind.

5. THE PRINCIPLES APPLICABLE TO THE LIBERTY OF THE PRESS.

Although every community must establish supreme authorities, founded upon fixed principles, and must give high powers to magistrates to administer laws for the preservation of the government itself, and for the security of those who are to be protected by it ; yet, as infallibility and perfection belong neither to human establishments nor to human individuals, it ought to be the policy of all free establishments, as it is most peculiarly the principle of our own Constitution, to permit the most unbounded freedom of discussion, even by detecting errors in the Constitution or administration of the very government itself, so as that decorum is observed which every State must exact from its subjects, and which imposes no restraint upon any intellectual composition, fairly, honestly, and decently addressed to the consciences and understandings of men. Upon this principle I have an unquestionable right—a right which the best subjects have exercised—to examine the principles and structure of the Constitution, and by fair, manly reasoning, to question the practice of its administrators. I have a right to consider and to point out errors in the one or in the other; and not merely to reason upon their existence, but to consider the means of their reformation.

By such free, well-intentioned, modest, and dignified communication of sentiments and opinions, all nations have been gradually improved, and milder laws and purer religions have been established. The same principles which vindicate civil contentions, honestly directed, extend their protection to the sharpest controversies on religious faiths. This rational and legal course of improvement was recognized and ratified by Lord Kenyon as the law of England, in a late trial at Guildhall, when he looked back with gratitude to the labors of the reformers, as the fountains of our religious emancipation, and of the civil blessings that followed in their train. The English Constitution, indeed, does not stop short in the toleration of religious opinions, but liberally extends it to practice. It permits every man, even publicly, to worship God according to his own conscience, though in marked dissent from the national establishment, so as he professes the general faith, which is the sanction of all our moral duties, and the only pledge of our submission to the system which constitutes a State. Is not this system of freedom of controversy and freedom of worship, sufficient for all the purposes of human happiness and improvement? and will it be necessary for either that the law should hold out indemnity to those who wholly abjure and revile the government of their country, or the religion on which it rests for its foundation?

6. DISTINCTION BETWEEN LEGITIMATE INQUIRY AND SCURRILOUS ABUSE.

I expect to hear, in answer to what I am now saying, much that will offend me. My learned friend, from the difficulties of his situation—which I know, from experience, how to feel for very sincerely—may be driven to advance propositions which it may be my duty, with much freedom, to reply to ; and the law will sanction that freedom. But will not the ends of justice be completely answered by the right to point out the errors of his discourse in terms that are decent and calculated to expose its defects ? or will any argument suffer, or will public justice be impeded, because neither private honor and justice, nor public decorum, would endure my telling my very learned friend that he was a fool, a liar, and a scoundrel, in the face of the court, because I differed from him in argument or opinion ? This is just the distinction between a book of free legal controversy and the book which I am arraigning before you. Every man has a legal right to investigate, with modesty and decency, controversial points of the Christian religion; but no man, consistently with a law which only exists under its sanctions, has a right not only broadly to deny its very existence, but to pour forth a shocking and insulting invective, which the lowest establishments in the gradations of civil authority ought not to be permitted to suffer, and which soon would be borne down by insolence and disobedience, if they did.

7. ILLUSTRATIONS OF THE ARGUMENT.

The same principle pervades the whole system of the law, not merely in its abstract theory, but in its daily and most applauded practice. The intercourse between the sexes, and which, properly regulated, not only continues, but humanizes and adorns our natures, is the foundation of all the thousand romances, plays, and novels which are in the hands of every body. Some of them lead to the confirmation of every virtuous principle; others, though with the same profession, address the imagination in a manner to lead the passions into dangerous excesses. But though the law does not nicely discriminate the various shades which distinguish these works from one another, so as that it suffers many to pass, through its liberal spirit, that upon principle might be suppressed, would it or does it tolerate, or does any decent man contend that it ought to pass by unpunished, libels of the most shameless obscenity, manifestly pointed to debauch innocence, and to blast and poison the morals of the rising generation? This is only another illustration to demonstrate the obvious distinction between the works of an author who fairly exercises the powers of his mind in investigating doctrinal points in the religion of any country, and him who attacks the rational existence of every religion, and brands with absurdity and folly the State which sanctions, and the obedient tools who cherish, the delusion.

8. Mischievous and cruel effects of this illegal publication.

But this publication appears to me to be as mischievous and cruel in its probable effects, as it is manifestly illegal in its principles; because it strikes at the best, sometime, alas, the only refuge and consolation amid the distresses and afflictions of the world. The poor and humble, whom it affects to pity, may be stabbed to the heart by it. They have more occasion for firm hopes beyond the grave than those who have greater comforts to render life delightful. I can conceive a distressed, but virtuous man, surrounded by children, looking up to him for bread when he has none to give them, sinking under the last day's labor, and unequal to the next, yet still looking up with confidence to the hour when all tears shall be wiped from the eyes of affliction, bearing the burden laid upon him by a mysterious Providence which he adores, and looking forward with exultation to the revealed promises of his Creator, when he shall be greater than the greatest, and happier than the happiest of mankind. What a change in such a mind might be wrought by such a merciless publication?

Gentlemen, whether these remarks are the overcharged declamations of an accusing counsel, or the just reflections of a man anxious for the public freedom, which is best secured by the morals of a nation, will be best settled by an appeal to the passages in the work, that are selected in the indictment for your consideration and judgment. You are at liberty to connect them with every ·context and sequel, and to bestow upon them the mildest interpretation.

Here Mr. Erskine read and commented upon several of the selected passages. He continued:

9. The character of the defense an anomaly, and inconsistent with the jurisdiction of the court.

Gentlemen, it would be useless and disgusting to enumerate the other passages within the scope of the indictment. How any man can rationally vindicate the publication of such a book, in a country where the Christian religion is the very foundation of the law of the land, I am totally at a loss to conceive, and have no wish to discuss. How is a tribunal, whose whole jurisdiction is founded upon the solemn belief and practice of what is denied as falsehood, and reprobated as impiety, to deal with such an anomalous defense? Upon what principle is it even offered to the court, whose authority is contemned and mocked at? If the religion proposed to be called in question is not previously adopted in belief, and solemnly acted upon, what authority has the court to pass any judgment at all of acquittal or condemnation? Why am I now, or upon any other occasion, to submit to your lordship's authority? Why am I now, or at any time, to address twelve of my equals, as I am now addressing you, with reverence and submission? Under what sanction are the witnesses to give their evidence, without which there can be no trial? Under what obligations can I call upon you, the jury, representing your country, to administer justice? Surely upon no other than that you are sworn to administer it under the oaths you have taken. The whole judicial fabric, from the king's sovereign authority to the lowest office of magistracy, has no other foundation. The whole is built, both in form and substance, upon the same oath of every one of its ministers, to do justice, "as God shall help them hereafter." What God? and what hereafter? That God, undoubtedly, who has commanded kings to rule, and judges to decree with justice; who has said to witnesses, not by the voice of nature, but in revealed commandments, "thou shalt not bear false witness against thy neighbor;" and who has enforced obedience to them by the revelation of the unutterable blessings which shall attend their observances, and the awful punishments which shall await upon their transgressions.

10. INTELLECTUAL SUPERIORITY OF CHRISTIAN BELIEVERS.— NEWTON.

But it seems this course of reason, and the time and the person are at last arrived, that are to dissipate the errors which have overspread the past generations of ignorance! The believers in Christianity are many, but it belongs to the few that are wise to correct their credulity! Belief is an act of reason; and superior reason may, therefore, dictate to the weak. In running the mind along the numerous list of sincere and devout Christians, I cannot help lamenting that Newton had not lived to this day, to have had his shallowness filled up with this new flood of light. But the subject is too awful for irony. I will speak plainly and directly. Newton was a Christian! Newton, whose mind burst forth from the fetters cast by nature upon our finite conceptions; Newton, whose science was truth, and the foundation of whose knowledge of it was philos-

36

ophy. Not those visionary and arrogant assumptions which too often usurp its name, but philosophy resting upon the basis of mathematics, which, like figures, cannot lie. Newton, who carried the line and rule to the utmost barriers of creation, and explored the principles by which, no doubt, all created matter is held together and exists. But this extraordinary man, in the mighty reach of his mind, overlooked, perhaps, the errors which a minuter investigation of the created things on this earth might have taught him of the essence of his Creator.

II. BOYLE, LOCKE, AND SIR MATTHEW HALE.

What shall then be said of the great Mr. Boyle, who looked into the organic structure of all matter, even to the brute inanimate substances which the foot treads on. Such a man may be supposed to have been equally qualified with Mr. Paine, to "look through nature, up to nature's God." Yet the result of all his contemplation was the most confirmed and devout belief in all which the other holds in contempt as despicable and driveling superstition. But this error might, perhaps, arise from a want of due attention to the foundations of human judgment, and the structure of that understanding which God has given us for the investigation of truth. Let that question be answered by Mr. Locke, who was to the highest pitch of devotion and adoration a Christian. Mr. Locke, whose office was to detect the errors of thinking, by going up to the fountains of thought, and to direct into the proper track of reasoning the devious mind of man, by showing him its whole process, from the first perceptions of sense to the last conclusions of ratiocination; putting a rein, besides, upon false opinion, by practical rules for the conduct of human judgment.

But these men were only deep thinkers, and lived in their closets, unaccustomed to the traffic of the world, and to the laws which practically regulate mankind. Gentlemen, in the place where you now sit to administer the justice of this great country, above a century ago the never-to-be-forgotten Sir Matthew Hale presided, whose faith in Christianity is an exalted commentary upon its truth and reason, and whose life was a glorious example of its fruits in man; administering human justice with a wisdom and purity drawn from the pure fountain of the Christian dispensation, which has been, and will be, in all ages, a subject of the highest reverence and admiration.

12. John Milton's immortal offering.

But it is said by Mr. Paine, that the Christian fable is but the tale of the more ancient superstitions of the world, and may be easily detected by a proper understanding of the mythologies of the heathens. Did Milton understand those mythologies? Was he less versed than Mr. Paine in the superstitions of the world? No; they were the subject of his immortal song; and though shut out from all recurrence to them, he poured them forth from the stores of a memory rich with all that man ever knew, and laid them in their order as the illustration of that real and exalted faith, the unquestionable source of that fervid genius, which cast a sort of shade upon all the other works of man:

> He pass'd the bounds of flaming space,
> Where angels tremble while they gaze;
> He saw, ti!], blasted with excess of light,
> He clos'd his eyes in endless night![1]

But it was the light of the body only that was extinguished; "the celestial light shone inward," and enabled him to "justify the ways of God to man." The result of his thinking was, nevertheless, not the same as Mr. Paine's. The mysterious incarnation of our blessed Saviour, which the "Age of Reason" blasphemes in words so wholly unfit for the mouth of a Christian, or for the ear of a court of justice, that I dare not and will not give them utterance, Milton made the grand conclusion of "Paradise Lost," the rest of his finished labors, and the ultimate hope, expectation, and glory of the world:

> A Virgin is his mother, but his sire
> The power of the Most High; he shall ascend
> The throne hereditary, and bound his reign
> With earth's wide bounds, his glory with the heavens.

The immortal poet having thus put into the mouth of the angel the prophecy of man's redemption, follows it with that solemn and beautiful admonition, addressed in the poem to our great First Parent, but intended as an address to his posterity through all generations:

> This having learned, thou hast attained the sum
> Of wisdom: hope no higher, though all the stars
> Thou knew'st by name, and all th' ethereal powers,

[1] Grey's Ode on the Progress of Poetry.

All secrets of the deep, all Nature's works,
Or works of God in heaven, air, earth, or sea,
And all the riches of this world enjoy'st,
And all the rule one empire; only add
Deeds to thy knowledge answerable, add faith,
Add virtue, patience, temperance; add love,
By name to come call'd Charity, the soul
Of all the rest: then wilt thou not be loth
To leave this Paradise, but shalt possess
A paradise within thee, happier far.

Thus you find all that is great, or wise, or splendid, or illustrious among created beings—all the minds gifted beyond ordinary
nature, if not inspired by their universal Author for the advancement and dignity of the world, though divided by distant ages, and
by the clashing opinions distinguishing them from one another, yet
joining, as it were, in one sublime chorus to celebrate the truths of
Christianity, and laying upon its holy altars the never-fading offer-
ings of their immortal wisdom.

13. ADHERENCE TO DOCTRINES OF THE NEW TESTAMENT WOULD
    BANISH WICKEDNESS FROM THE WORLD.

Against all this concurring testimony, we find suddenly, from
Mr. Paine, that the Bible teaches nothing but "lies, obscenity,
cruelty, and injustice." Did the author or publisher ever read the
sermon of "Christ upon the Mount," in which the great principles
of our faith and duty are summed up? Let us all but read and
practice it, and lies, obscenity, cruelty, and injustice, and all human
wickedness, would be banished from the world.

14. RELIGION AND MORALITY ALONE CONSTITUTE THE SAFETY
    OF THE STATE.

Gentlemen, there is but one consideration more, which I cannot
possibly omit, because, I confess, it affects me very deeply. Mr.
Paine has written largely on public liberty and government; and
this last performance has, on that account, been more widely circulated, and principally among those who attached themselves from
principle to his former works. This circumstance renders a public
attack upon all revealed religion, from such a writer, infinitely more
dangerous. The religious and moral sense of the people of Great
Britain is the great anchor which alone can hold the vessel of the
State amid the storms which agitate the world. If I could believe,
for a moment, that the mass of the people were to be debauched

from the principles of religion, which form the true basis of that humanity, charity, and benevolence that has been so long the national characteristic, instead of mixing myself, as I sometimes have done, in political reformations, I would rather retire to the uttermost corners of the earth to avoid their agitation; and would bear, not only the imperfections and abuses complained of in our own wise establishment, but even the worst government that ever existed in the world, rather than go to the work of reformation with a multitude set free from all the charities of Christianity, who had no sense of God's existence but from Mr. Paine's observation of nature, which the mass of mankind have no leisure to contemplate; nor any belief of future rewards and punishments to animate the good in the glorious pursuit of human happiness, nor to deter the wicked from destroying it even in its birth. But I know the people of England better. They are a religious people; and, with the blessing of God, as far as it is in my power, I will lend my aid to keep them so. I have no objection to the freest and most extended discussions upon doctrinal points of the Christian religion; and, though the law of England does not permit it, I do not dread the reasoned arguments of Deists against the existence of Christianity itself, because, as was said by its divine author, if it is of God it will stand.

15. INFERIOR OBJECT AND CAPACITY OF PAINE'S WORK.

An intellectual book, however erroneous, addressed to the intellectual world upon so profound and complicated a subject, can never work the mischief which this indictment is calculated to repress. Such works will only employ the minds of men enlightened by study in a deeper investigation of a subject well worthy of their profound and continued contemplation. The powers of the mind are given for human improvement in the progress of human existence. The changes produced by such reciprocations of lights and intelligences are certain in their progressions, and make their way imperceptibly, as conviction comes upon the world, by the final and irresistible power of truth. If Christianity be founded in falsehood, let us become Deists in this manner, and I am contented. But this book hath no such object and no such capacity; it presents no arguments to the wise and enlightened. On the contrary, it treats the faith and opinions of the wisest with the most shocking contempt, and stirs up men without the advantages of learning or sober thinking to a total disbelief of everything hitherto held sacred, and, consequently, to a rejection of all the laws and ordinances of the State, which stand only upon the assumption of their truth.

Gentlemen, I cannot conclude without expressing the deepest regret at all attacks upon the Christian religion by authors who profess to promote the civil liberties of the world. For under what other auspices than Christianity have the lost and subverted liberties of mankind in former ages been reasserted? By what zeal, but the warm zeal of devout Christians, have English liberties been redeemed and consecrated? Under what other sanctions, even in our own days, have liberty and happiness been extending and spreading to the uttermost corners of the earth? What work of civilization, what commonwealth of greatness has the bald religion of nature ever established? We see, on the contrary, the nations that have no other light than that of nature to direct them, sunk in barbarism, or slaves to arbitrary governments; while, since the Christian era, the great career of the world has been slowly, but clearly, advancing lighter at every step, from the awful prophecies of the Gospel, and leading, I trust, in the end, to universal and eternal happiness. Each generation of mankind can see but a few revolving links of this mighty and mysterious chain; but, by doing our several duties in our allotted stations, we are sure that we are fulfilling the purposes of our existence. You, I trust, will fulfill yours this day!

The evidence was very brief. The sale of the book by the prisoner was shown, the notice by the defense to produce the Bible in evidence was read, and the prosecution rested. Mr. Kyd then delivered an address to the jury, to which Mr. Erskine replied. He closed his speech as follows: " I have only, therefore, to remind you, gentlemen, that this indictment was not preferred from any idea that the Christian religion could be affected, in its character or irresistible progress, by this disgusting and contemptible work; but to prevent its circulation amongst the industrious poor, too much engaged in the support of their families by their labor, and too uninformed to be secure against artful wickedness. Of all human beings they stand most in need of the consolations of religion, and the country has the deepest stake in their enjoying it, not only from the protection which it owes them, but because no man can be expected to be faithful to the authority of man who revolts against the government of God." The jury found a verdict of Guilty, without retiring from their seats.

SPEECH OF SIR JAMES MACKINTOSH

In Behalf of Jean Peltier, Indicted for a Libel against Napoleon Bonaparte.

[Howell's St. Tr. vol. 28, p. 566.]

IN THE COURT OF KING'S BENCH. MICHAELMAS TERM, 43d GEORGE III, FEB. 21, 1803.

POLITICAL LIBEL.—Every publication which has a tendency to promote public mischief by defaming the persons and characters of magistrates, and others in high and eminent situations of power and dignity in other countries, inconsistent with amity and friendship, expressed in such terms and such a manner as to interrupt the amity and friendship between the two countries, is in law a libel.—[Lord Ellenborough's charge in Rex *v.* Peltier.]

ANALYSIS OF MR. MACKINTOSH'S SPEECH.

1. The nominal parties to the record, not the real parties to the issue.
2. The real issue—a conflict between the greatest power in the world, and the only free press in Europe.
3. Reason for the temporary toleration of a free press in the minor European States.
4. How the liberty of the continental press perished, while the press of England alone remained free.
5. Distinction between libel and history.—Philosophy of the law of libel.
6. The Maintenance of justice on the continent essential to the security of Great Britain.
7. War never beneficial to a commercial nation.
8. The freedom of the press cannot be impaired without danger to the State.
9. Malice the essence of the crime of libel.—The privilege of the historian.
10. A satire not a libel.
11. Defendant had a legal right to satirize Jacobinism.
12. The spirit of Jacobinism not extinguished.
13. A picture of the French Jacobins.
14. Republicans and Jacobins distinguished.
15. The publication cannot represent the opinions of the defendant, who is a royalist.
16. Observations upon the ode.
17. The verses contain no exhortation to assassinate Napoleon.
18. Free discussion the most important interest of mankind. — The reign of Elizabeth.
19. Power and importance of the press in preserving the liberties of Englishmen.
20. Louis XIV.—His arraignment by French refugees no libel.
21. The invasion of Holland an avowed attack upon the liberty of the press.
22. William of Orange saves England from the power of Louis XIV.
23. Animadversion of the English press on the projects of Louis XIV.
24. Influence of newspapers on domestic and foreign politics.
25. Arraignment by the press of the crime against Poland.
26. The invasion of Switzerland.—England an asylum for its oppressed heroes.
27. The reign of Robespierre.—Illustrations to show the fallacy of the theory of the prosecution.

[567]

On the 21st of February, 1803, Jean Peltier was brought up for trial, charged with having published a wicked and malicious libel against Napoleon Bonaparte (at that time First Consul and Chief Magistrate of France), with the intent and purpose of bringing him into hatred and contempt at home and abroad; to incite his subjects to rebel against him; and, further, for the purpose of exhorting his assassination.

Mr. Peltier was a French royalist, who, in the memorable autumn of 1792, fled from his country on account of political persecution. In 1802, he commenced the publication of a French journal in the city of London, entitled *L'Ambigu, ou Variétés atroces et amusantes.* On the title page was the representation of a Sphynx, with a head representing Bonaparte, wearing a crown. A number of hieroglyphics were engraven on the pedestal on which it rested, indicative of mystery. The columns of *L'Ambigu* were devoted to an exposure of the conduct, designs and ambitions of Napoleon. The publication irritated the First Consul to such a degree that he demanded of the English authorities that Peltier be sent out of the country, but his solicitations were refused. He then insisted that as France was at peace with England, the king should proceed against Peltier for a libel on a friendly government, which was, by the laws of England, a crime to which severe penalties attached.

There appeared in the first number of *L'Ambigu* an ode, attributed to Chenier (a Jacobin, and a man of distinguished talents), which hinted at the assassination of Bonaparte. It also contained some verses of the same character, entitled, " The Wish of a Dutch Patriot."[1] The third number contained a parody on the harangue of Lepidus to Sylla, which pointed at Bonaparte as having assumed the dictatorship. These three articles were set out in the indictment, and embraced the charge on which Peltier was arraigned.

He was defended by Sir James Mackintosh. The time when the trial occurred, and the peculiar circumstances under which it took place, afforded Mr. Mackintosh an opportunity to display the abilities with which he was so liberally endowed. Such was the nature and importance of the affair, that, during the week preceding the trial, it was believed in commercial circles that the acquittal of Peltier would be considered in France as tantamount to a declaration of war against the First Consul: and such was the feverish and uncertain tenure of the peace between the two countries, that war was actually declared before the prisoner (who was convicted) was brought up for sentence.

Mr. Mackintosh's defense of Peltier must always rank as a model of chaste and manly eloquence, which, as a display of intellectual power, has not been surpassed in ancient or modern times. The vigor of thought and the wonderful exhibition of memory which characterize this great speech, demonstrate that Lord Macaulay did not place too high an estimate on the abilities of this eminent Scotchman when he said : " His mind was a vast magazine, admirably arranged. Everything was there, and everything was in its place. His judgments on men, on sects, on books, had been often carefully tested and weighed, and had then been committed, each to his proper receptacle, in the most capacious and admirably constructed memory that any human being ever possessed. While speaking, he seemed to be recollecting, not creating. You never saw his opinions in the making, still rude, still inconsistent, and requiring to be fashioned by thought

[1] For the Ode and Verses, see Appendix, pp. 730, 731.

and discussion. They came forth like the pillars of that temple, in which no sound of axes or hammers was heard, finished, rounded, and exactly suited to their places." Lord Erskine, who was present during Mr. Mackintosh's address, wrote to him that, while he approved the verdict, he should always consider the manner in which it was opposed as one of the most splendid monuments of genius, literature and eloquence; and Robert Hall, in acknowledging the receipt of a copy of it from Mr. Mackintosh, remarked that it was "the most extraordinary ssemblage of whatever is most refined in address, profound in political and moral speculation, and masterly in eloquence in the language." Madame de Staël was charmed with its fine passages, which she said seemed to touch her very soul. She translated it into French, and it became widely known on the continent.

The attorney-general (Mr. Percival, afterwards Prime Minister) opened the case to the jury. No evidence was offered by the prisoner. When the testimony for the crown closed, Mr. Mackintosh said :

GENTLEMEN OF THE JURY :—The time is now come for me to address you in behalf of the unfortunate gentleman who is the defendant on this record.

I must begin with observing, that though I know myself too well to ascribe to anything but to the kindness and good nature of my learned friend, the attorney-general, the unmerited praises which he has been pleased to bestow on me, yet, I will venture to say, he has done me no more than justice in supposing that in this place, and on this occasion, where I exercise the functions of an inferior minister of justice, an inferior minister, indeed, but a minister of justice still, I am incapable of lending myself to the passions of any client, and that I will not make the proceedings of this court subservient to any political purpose.

Whatever is respected by the laws and government of my country shall, in this place, be respected by me. In considering matters that deeply interest the quiet, the safety, and the liberty of all mankind, it is impossible for me not to feel warmly and strongly ; but I shall make an effort to control my feelings, however painful that effort may be ; and, where I cannot speak out, but at the risk of offending either sincerity or prudence, I shall labor to contain myself and be silent.

I cannot but feel, gentlemen, how much I stand in need of your favorable attention and indulgence. The charge which I have to defend is surrounded with the most invidious topics of discussion ; but, they are not of my seeking. The case and the topics which are inseparable from it are brought here by the prosecutor. Here I find them, and here it is my duty to deal with them, as the interests of Mr. Peltier seem to me to require. He, by his choice and confidence, has cast on me a very arduous duty, which I could not decline, and which I can still less betray. He has a right to expect from me a faithful, a zealous, and a fearless defense ; and this, his just expectation, according to the measure of my humble abilities, shall be fulfilled.

I have said a fearless defense. Perhaps that word was unnecessary in the place where I now stand. Intrepidity in the discharge of professional duty is so common a quality at the English bar, that it has, thank God, long ceased to be a matter of boast or praise. If it had been otherwise, gentlemen, if the bar could have been silenced or overawed by power, I may presume to say that an English jury would not this day have been met to administer justice. Perhaps I need scarce say that my defense *shall* be fearless, in a place where fear never entered any heart but that of a criminal. But you will pardon me for having said so much when you consider who the real parties before you are.

I. THE NOMINAL PARTIES TO THE RECORD, NOT THE REAL
PARTIES TO THE ISSUE.

Gentlemen, the real prosecutor is the master of the greatest empire the world ever saw. The defendant is a defenseless, proscribed exile. He is a French royalist, who fled from his country in the autumn of 1792, at the period of that memorable and awful emigration, when all the proprietors and magistrates of the greatest civilized country of Europe were driven from their homes by the daggers of assassins; when our shores were covered, as with the wreck of a great tempest, with old men, and women, and children, and ministers of religion, who fled from the ferocity of their countrymen as before an army of invading barbarians.

The greatest part of these unfortunate exiles, of those, I mean, who have been spared by the sword, who have survived the effect of pestilential climates or broken hearts, have been since permitted to revisit their country. Though despoiled of their all, they have eagerly embraced even the sad privilege of being suffered to die in their native land.

Even this miserable indulgence was to be purchased by compliances, by declarations of allegiance to the new government, which some of these suffering Royalists deemed incompatible with their consciences, with their dearest attachments, and their most sacred duties. Among these last is Mr. Peltier. I do not presume to blame those who submitted, and I trust you will not judge harshly of those who refused. You will not think unfavorably of a man who stands before you as the voluntary victim of his loyalty and honor. If a revolution (which God avert) were to drive us into exile, and to cast us on a foreign shore, we should expect, at least, to be pardoned by generous men, for stubborn loyalty, and unseasonable fidelity to the laws and government of our fathers.

This unfortunate gentleman had devoted a great part of his life to literature. It was the amusement and ornament of his better days. Since his own ruin and the desolation of his country, he has been compelled to employ it as a means of support. For the last ten years he has been engaged in a variety of publications of considerable importance; but since the peace, he has desisted from serious political discussion, and confined himself to the obscure journal which is now before you; the least calculated, surely, of any publication that ever issued from the press, to rouse the alarms of the most jealous government; which will not be read in England, because it is not written in our language; which cannot be read in France, because its entry into that country is prohibited by a power whose mandates are not very supinely enforced, nor often evaded with impunity; which can have no other object than that of amusing the companions of the author's principles and misfortunes, by pleasantries and sarcasms on their victorious enemies. There is, indeed, gentlemen, one remarkable circumstance in this unfortunate publication; it is the only, or almost the only journal which still dares to espouse the cause of that royal and illustrious family, which, but fourteen years ago, was flattered by every press and guarded by every tribunal in Europe. Even the court in which we are met affords an example of the vicissitudes of their fortune. My learned friend has reminded you that the last prosecution [1] tried in this place, at the instance of a French government, was for a libel on that magnanimous princess, who has since been butchered in sight of her palace.

I do not make these observations with any purpose of questioning the general principles which have been laid down by my learned friend. I must admit his right to bring before you those who libel any government recognized by his Majesty, and at peace with the British empire. I admit that, whether such a government be of yesterday, or a thousand years old; whether it be a crude and bloody usurpation, or the most ancient, just, and paternal authority upon earth, we are *here* equally bound, by his Majesty's recognition, to protect it against libelous attacks.

[1] The prosecution of Lord George Gordon.

I admit that if, during our usurpation, Lord Clarendon had published his history at Paris, or the Marquess of Montrose his verses on the murder of his sovereign, or Mr. Cowley his Discourse on Cromwell's Government, and if the English embassador had complained, the President de Molí, or any other of the great magistrates who then adorned the Parliament of Paris, however reluctantly, painfully, and indignantly, might have been compelled to have condemned these illustrious men to the punishment of libelers.

I say this only for the sake of bespeaking a favorable attention from your generosity, and compassion to what will be feebly urged in behalf of my unfortunate client, who has sacrificed his fortune, his hopes, his connections, his country, to his conscience; who seems marked out for destruction in this his last asylum.

That he still enjoys the security of this asylum, that he has not been sacrificed to the resentment of his powerful enemies, is perhaps owing to the firmness of the king's government. If that be the fact, gentlemen; if his Majesty's ministers have resisted applications to expel this unfortunate gentleman from England, I should publicly thank them for their firmness, if it were not unseemly and improper to suppose that they could have acted otherwise—to thank an English government for not violating the most sacred duties of hospitality; for not bringing indelible disgrace on their country.

But be that as it may, gentlemen, he now comes before you perfectly satisfied that an English jury is the most refreshing prospect that the eye of accused innocence ever met in a human tribunal; and he feels with me the most fervent gratitude to the Protector of empires that, surrounded as we are with the ruins of principalities and powers, we still continue to meet together, after the manner of our fathers, to administer justice in this her ancient sanctuary.

2. THE REAL ISSUE—A CONFLICT BETWEEN THE GREATEST POWER IN THE WORLD, AND THE ONLY FREE PRESS IN EUROPE.

There is another point of view in which this case seems to me to merit your most serious attention. I consider it as the first of a long series of conflicts between the greatest power in the world, and the only free press remaining in Europe.

No man living is more thoroughly convinced than I am that my learned friend, Mr. Attorney General, will never degrade his excellent character; that he will never disgrace his high magistracy by mean compliances; by an immoderate and unconscientious exercise of power; yet I am convinced, by circumstances which I shall now abstain from discussing, that I am to consider this as the first of a long series of conflicts between the greatest power in the world and the only free press now remaining in Europe.

Gentlemen, this distinction of the English press is new; it is a proud and melancholy distinction. Before the great earthquake of the French Revolution had swallowed up all the asylums of free discussion on the Continent, we enjoyed that privilege, indeed, more fully than others; but we did not enjoy it exclusively. In great monarchies, the press has always been considered as too formidable an engine to be intrusted to unlicensed individuals. But, in other continental countries, either by the laws of the State, or by long habits of liberality and toleration in magistrates, a liberty of discussion has been enjoyed, perhaps sufficient enough for most useful purposes. It existed, in fact, where it was not protected by law; and the wise and generous connivance of governments was daily more and more secured by the growing civilization of their subjects. In Holland, in Switzerland, in the imperial towns of Germany, the press was either legally or practically free. Holland and Switzerland are no more; and, since the commencement of this prosecution, fifty imperial towns have been erased from the list of independent States by one dash of the pen. Three or four still preserve a precarious and trembling existence. I will not say by what compliances they must purchase its continuance. I will not insult the feebleness of States, whose unmerited fall I do most bitterly deplore.

3. REASONS FOR THE TEMPORARY TOLERATION OF A FREE PRESS IN THE MINOR EUROPEAN STATES.

These governments were, in many respects, one of the most interesting parts of the ancient system of Europe. Unfortunately for the repose of mankind, great States are compelled, by regard to their own safety, to consider the military spirit and martial habits of their people as one of the main objects of their policy. Frequent hostilities seem almost the necessary condition of their greatness; and, without being great, they cannot long remain safe. Smaller States exempted from this cruel necessity—a hard condition of greatness, a bitter satire on human nature—devoted themselves to the arts of peace, to the cultivation of literature, and the improvement of reason. They became places of refuge for free and fearless discussion; they were the impartial spectators and judges of the various contests of ambition which, from time to time, disturbed the quiet of the world. They thus became peculiarly qualified to be the organs of that public opinion which converted Europe into a great republic, with laws which mitigated, though they could not extinguish ambition; and with moral tribunals to which even the most despotic sovereigns were amenable. If wars of aggrandizement were undertaken, their authors were arraigned in the face of Europe. If acts of internal tyranny were perpetrated, they resounded from a thousand presses throughout all civilized countries. Princes on whose will there were no legal checks, thus found a moral restraint which the most powerful of them could not brave with absolute impunity. They acted before a vast audience, to whose applause or condemnation they could not be utterly indifferent. The very constitution of human nature, the unalterable laws of the mind of man, against which all rebellion is fruitless, subjected the proudest tyrants to this control. No elevation of power, no depravity, however consummate, no innocence, however spotless, can render man wholly independent of the praise or blame of his fellow-men.

These governments were, in other respects, one of the most beautiful and interesting parts of our ancient system. The perfect security of such inconsiderable and feeble States, their undisturbed tranquillity amid the wars and conquests that surrounded them, attested, beyond any other part of the European system, the moderation, the justice, the civilization to which Christian Europe had reached in modern times. Their weakness was protected only by the habitual reverence for justice, which, during a long series of ages, had grown up in Christendom. This was the only fortification which defended them against those mighty monarchs to whom they offered so easy a prey. And till the French Revolution, this was sufficient. Consider, for instance, the situation of the republic of Geneva. Think of her defenseless position, in the very jaws of France; but think also of her undisturbed security, of her profound quiet, of the brilliant success with which she applied to industry and literature, while Louis XIV was pouring his myriads into Italy before her gates. Call to mind, if ages crowded into years have not effaced them from your memory, that happy period, when we scarcely dreamed of the subjugation of the feeblest republic of Europe than of the conquest of her mightiest empire;

and tell me, if you can imagine a spectacle more beautiful to the moral eye, or a more striking proof of progress in the noblest principles of true civilization.

4. HOW THE LIBERTY OF THE CONTINENTAL PRESS PERISHED, WHILE THE PRESS OF ENGLAND ALONE REMAINED FREE.

These feeble States—these monuments of the justice of Europe —the asylum of peace, of industry, and of literature—the organs of public reason—the refuge of oppressed innocence and persecuted truth, have perished with those ancient principles which were their sole guardians and protectors. They have been swallowed up by that fearful convulsion which has shaken the uttermost corners of the earth. They are destroyed and gone forever.

One asylum of free discussion is still inviolate. There is still one spot in Europe where man can freely exercise his reason on the most important concerns of society; where he can boldly publish his judgment on the acts of the proudest and most powerful tyrants. The press of England is still free. It is guarded by the free Constitution of our forefathers. It is guarded by the hearts and arms of Englishmen, and, I trust I may venture to say, that if it be to fall, it will fall only under the ruins of the British empire.

It is an awful consideration, gentlemen. Every other monument of European liberty has perished. That ancient fabric which has been gradually reared by the wisdom and virtue of our fathers still stands. It stands, thanks be to God! solid and entire; but it stands alone, and it stands amid ruins.

In these extraordinary circumstances, I repeat that I must consider this as the first of a long series of conflicts between the greatest power in the world and the only free press remaining in Europe. And, I trust, that you will consider yourselves as the advance guards of liberty, as having this day to fight the first battle of free discussion against the most formidable enemy that it ever encountered. You will, therefore, excuse me if, on so important an occasion, I remind you, at more length than is usual, of those general principles and law of policy on this subject which have been handed down to us by our ancestors.

5. THE DISTINCTION BETWEEN LIBEL, AND HISTORY OR DISCUSSION. PHILOSOPHY OF THE LAW OF LIBEL.

Those who slowly built up the fabric of our laws never attempted anything so absurd as to define, by any precise rule, the obscure

and shifting boundaries which divide libel from history or discussion. It is a subject which, from its nature, admits neither rules
nor definitions. The same words may be perfectly innocent in
one case, and most mischievous and libelous in another. A change
of circumstances, often apparently slight, is sufficient to make the
whole difference. These changes, which may be as numerous as
the variety of human intentions and conditions, can never be foreseen nor comprehended under any legal definitions, and the framers
of our law have never attempted to subject them to such definitions.
They left such ridiculous attempts to those who call themselves
philosophers, but who have, in fact, proved themselves most grossly
and stupidly ignorant of that philosophy which is conversant with
human affairs.

The principles of the law of England on the subject of political
libel are few and simple, and they are necessarily so broad, that,
without an habitually mild administration of justice, they might encroach materially on the liberty of political discussion. Every
publication which is intended to vilify either our own government
or the government of any foreign State in amity with this kingdom,
is, by the law of England, a libel. To protect political discussion
from the danger to which it would be exposed by these wide principles, if they were severely and literally enforced, our ancestors
trusted to various securities—some growing out of the law and
Constitution, and others arising from the characters of those public
officers whom the Constitution had formed, and to whom its administration is committed. They trusted, in the first place, to the
moderation of the legal officers of the Crown, educated in the maxims and imbued with the spirit of a free government; controlled
by the superintending power of Parliament, and peculiarly watched
in all political prosecutions by the reasonable and wholesome jealousy of their fellow subjects. And, I am bound to admit, that,
since the glorious era of the Revolution [1688], making due allowance for the frailties, the faults, and the occasional vices of men,
they have, upon the whole, not been disappointed. I know that,
in the hands of my learned friend, that trust will never be abused.
But, above all, they confided in the moderation and good sense of
all juries, popular in their origin, popular in their feelings, popular
in their very prejudices, taken from the mass of the people, and
immediately returning to that mass again. By these checks and
temperaments they hoped that they should sufficiently repress
malignant libels, without endangering that freedom of inquiry

which is the first security of a free State. They knew that the offense of a political libel is of a very peculiar nature, and differing in the most important particulars from all other crimes. In all other cases, the most severe execution of law can only spread terror among the guilty; but, in political libels, it inspires even the innocent with fear. This striking peculiarity arises from the same circumstances which make it impossible to define the limits of libel and innocent discussion; which make it impossible for a man of the purest and most honorable mind to be always perfectly certain whether he be within the territory of fair argument and honest narrative, or whether he may not have unwittingly overstepped the faint and varying line which bounds them. But, gentlemen, I will go further. This is the only offense where severe and frequent punishments not only intimidate the innocent, but deter men from the most meritorious acts, and from rendering the most important services to their country. They indispose and disqualify men for the discharge of the most sacred duties which they owe to mankind. To inform the public on the conduct of those who administer public affairs, requires courage and conscious security. It is always an invidious and obnoxious office; but it is often the most necessary of all public duties. If it is not done boldly, it cannot be done effectually, and it is not from writers trembling under the uplifted scourge that we are to hope for it.

6. THE MAINTENANCE OF JUSTICE ON THE CONTINENT ESSENTIAL TO THE SECURITY OF GREAT BRITAIN.

There are other matters, gentlemen, to which I am desirous of particularly calling your attention. These are the circumstances in the condition of this country which have induced our ancestors, at all times, to handle with more than ordinary tenderness that branch of the liberty of discussion which is applied to the conduct of foreign states. The relation of this kingdom to the commonwealth of Europe is so peculiar, that no history, I think, furnishes a parallel to it. From the moment in which we abandoned all projects of continental aggrandizement, we could have no interest respecting the state of the Continent but the interests of national safety and of commercial prosperity. The paramount interest of every state—that which comprehends every other—is security. And the security of Great Britain requires nothing on the Continent but the uniform observance of justice. It requires

37

nothing but the inviolability of ancient boundaries and the sacredness of ancient possessions, which, on these subjects, is but another form of words for justice. A nation which is herself shut
out from the possibility of continental aggrandizement can have no
interest but that of preventing such aggrandizement in others. We
can have no interest of safety but the preventing of those encroachments which, by their immediate effects, or by their example, may
be dangerous to ourselves. We can have no interest of ambition
respecting the Continent. So that neither our real, nor even our
apparent interests, can ever be at variance with justice.

7. War never beneficial to a commercial nation.

As to commercial prosperity, it is, indeed, a secondary, but it is
still a very important branch of our national interests, and it requires nothing on the continent of Europe but the maintenance of
peace, as far as the paramount interest of security will allow.

Whatever ignorant or prejudiced men may affirm, no war was
ever gainful to a commercial nation. Losses may be less in some,
and incidental profits may arise in others. But no such profits
ever formed an adequate compensation for the waste of capital and
industry which all wars must produce. Next to peace, our commercial greatness depends chiefly on the affluence and prosperity
of our neighbors. A commercial nation has, indeed, the same interest in the wealth of her neighbors that a tradesman has in the
wealth of his customers. The prosperity of England has been
chiefly owing to the general progress of civilized nations in the
arts and improvements of social life. Not an acre of land has
been brought into cultivation in the wilds of Siberia or on the
shores of the Mississippi which has not widened the market for
English industry. It is nourished by the progressive prosperity of
the world, and it amply repays all that it has received. It can
only be employed in spreading civilization and enjoyment over the
earth ; and by the unchangeable laws of nature, in spite of the
impotent tricks of government, it is now partly applied to revive
the industry of those very nations who are the loudest in their
senseless clamors against its pretended mischiefs. If the blind and
barbarous project of destroying English prosperity could be accomplished, it could have no other effect than that of completely beg-
garing the very countries who now stupidly ascribe their own poverty to our wealth.

8. THE FREEDOM OF THE PRESS CAN NOT BE IMPAIRED WITHOUT DANGER TO THE STATE.

Under these circumstances, gentlemen, it became the obvious policy of the kingdom, a policy in unison with the maxims of a free government, to consider with great indulgence even the boldest animadversions of our political writers on the ambitious projects of foreign states.

Bold, and sometimes indiscreet as these animadversions might be, they had, at least, the effect of warning the people of their danger, and of rousing the national indignation against those encroachments which England has almost always been compelled in the end to resist by arms. Seldom, indeed, has she been allowed to wait till a provident regard to her own safety should compel her to take up arms in defense of others. For as it was said by a great orator of antiquity that no man ever was the enemy of the republic who had not first declared war against him, so I may say, with truth, that no man ever meditated the subjugation of Europe who did not consider the destruction or the corruption of England as the first condition of his success. If you examine history, you will find that no such project was ever formed in which it was not deemed a necessary preliminary, either to detach England from the common cause or to destroy her. It seems as if all the conspirators against the independence of nations might have sufficiently taught other states that England is their natural guardian and protector ; that she alone has no interest but their preservation ; that her safety is interwoven with their own. When vast projects of aggrandizement are manifested, when schemes of criminal ambition are carried into effect, the day of battle is fast approaching for England. Her free government cannot engage in dangerous wars without the hearty and affectionate support of her people. A state thus situated, can not without the utmost peril, silence those public discussions which are to point the popular indignation against those who must soon be enemies. In domestic dissensions, it may sometimes be the supposed interest of government to overawe the press. But it never can be even their apparent interest when the danger is purely foreign. A King of England who, in such circumstances, should conspire against the free press of this country, would undermine the foundations of his own throne ; he would silence the trumpet which is to call his people round his standard.

Our ancestors never thought it their policy to avert the resentment of foreign tyrants by enjoining English writers to contain and repress their just abhorrence of the criminal enterprises of ambition. This great and gallant nation, which has fought in the front of every battle against the oppressors of Europe, has sometimes inspired fear, but, thank God, she has never felt it. We know that they are our real, and must soon become our declared foes. We know that there can be no cordial amity between the natural enemies and the independence of nations. We have never adopted the cowardly and short-sighted policy of silencing our press, of breaking the spirit and palsying the hearts of our people for the sake of a hollow and precarious truce. We have never been base enough to purchase a short respite from hostilities by sacrificing the first means of defense ; the means of rousing the public spirit of the people, and directing it against the enemies of their country and of Europe.

Gentlemen, the public spirit of a people, by which I mean the whole body of those affections which unites men's hearts to the commonwealth, is in various countries composed of various elements, and depends on a great variety of causes. In this country, I may venture to say that it mainly depends on the vigor of the popular parts and principles of our government, and that the spirit of liberty is one of its most important elements. Perhaps it may depend less on those advantages of a free government, which are most highly estimated by calm reason, than upon those parts of it which delight the imagination, and flatter the just and natural pride of mankind. Among these we are certainly not to forget the political rights which are not uniformly withheld from the lowest classes, and the continual appeal made to them in public discussion, upon the greatest interests of the state. These are undoubtedly among the circumstances which endear to Englishmen their government and their country, and animate their zeal for that glorious institution which confers on the meanest of them a sort of distinction and nobility unknown to the most illustrious slaves, who tremble at the frown of a tyrant. Whoever were unwarily and rashly to abolish or narrow these privileges, which it must be owned are liable to great abuse, and to very specious objections, might perhaps discover too late that he had been dismantling his country. Of whatever elements public spirit is composed, it is always and everywhere the chief defensive principle of a state. It is perfectly distinct from courage. Perhaps no nation, certainly

no European nation, ever perished from an inferiority of courage.
And undoubtedly no considerable nation was ever subdued in
which the public affections were sound and vigorous.

It is public spirit which binds together the dispersed courage
of individuals and fastens it to the commonwealth. It is, therefore, as I have said, the chief defensive principle of every country.
Of all the stimulants which arouse it into action, the most powerful among us is certainly the press ; and it cannot be restrained or
weakened without imminent danger that the national spirit may
languish, and that the people may act with less zeal and affection
for their country in the hour of its danger.

These principles, gentlemen, are not new—they are genuine old
English principles. And though, in our days, they have been disgraced and abused by ruffians and fanatics, they are, in themselves,
as just and sound as they are liberal; and they are the only principles on which a free State can be safely governed. These principles
I have adopted since I first learned the use of reason, and I think I
shall abandon them only with life. On these principles I am now
to call your attention to the libel with which this unfortunate gentleman is charged.

9 MALICE THE ESSENCE OF THE CRIME OF LIBEL.—THE PRIV-
ILEGE OF THE HISTORIAN.

I heartily rejoice that I concur with the greatest part of what has
been said by my learned friend, Mr. Attorney General, who has done
honor even to his character by the generous and liberal principles
which he has laid down. He has told you that he does not mean to
attack historical narrative. He has told you that he does not mean
to attack political discussion. He has told you, also, that he does
not consider every intemperate word into which a writer, fairly
engaged in narration or reasoning, might be betrayed, as a fit subject for prosecution.

The essence of the crime of libel consists in the malignant mind
which the publication proves, and from which it flows. A jury
must be convinced, before they find a man guilty of libel, that his
intention was to libel, not to state facts which he believed to be
true, or reasonings which he thought just. My learned friend has
told you that the liberty of history includes the right of publishing
those observations which occur to intelligent men when they consider the affairs of the world; and, I think, he will not deny that it

includes also the right of expressing those sentiments which all good men feel on the contemplation of extraordinary examples of depravity or excellence.

One more privilege of the historian, which the attorney-general has not named, but to which his principles extend, it is now my duty to claim on behalf of my client; I mean the right of *republishing, historically*, those documents, whatever their original malignity may be, which display the character and unfold the intentions of governments, or factions, or individuals. I think my learned friend will not deny that a historical compiler may innocently republish in England the most insolent and outrageous declaration of war ever published against his Majesty by a foreign government. The intention of the original author was to vilify and degrade his Majesty's government; but the intention of the compiler is only to gratify curiosity, or, perhaps, to rouse just indignation against the calumniator whose production he republishes. His intention is not libelous—his republication is, therefore, not a libel. Suppose this to be the case with Mr. Peltier. Suppose him to have republished libels with a merely historical intention. In that case it cannot be pretended that he is more a libeler than my learned friend, Mr. Abbott,[1] who read these supposed libels to you when he opened the pleadings. Mr. Abbott republished them to you, that you might know and judge of them—Mr. Peltier, on the supposition I have made, also republished them, that the public might know and judge of them.

You already know that the general plan of Mr. Peltier's publication was to give a picture of the cabals and intrigues, of the hopes and projects of French factions. It is undoubtedly a natural and necessary part of this plan to republish all the serious and ludicrous pieces which these factions circulate against each other. The ode ascribed to Chenier or Ginguené I do really believe to have been written at Paris, to have been circulated there, to have been there attributed to some one of these writers, to have been sent to England as their work, and as such, to have been republished by Mr. Peltier. But I am not sure that I have evidence to convince you of the truth of this. Suppose that I have not, will my learned friend say that my client must necessarily be convicted? I, on the contrary, contend that it is for my learned friend to show that it is not a historical republication. Such it professes to be, and that profession it is for him to disprove. The profes-

[1] Junior counsel for the Crown, afterward Lord Tenterden.

sion may indeed be "a mask;" but it is for my friend to pluck off the mask, and expose the libeler, before he calls upon you for a verdict of guilty.

If the general lawfulness of such republications be denied, then I must ask Mr. Attorney-General to account for the long impunity which English newspapers have enjoyed. I must request him to tell you why they have been suffered to republish all the atrocious, official and unofficial libels which have been published against his Majesty for the last ten years, by the Brissots, the Marats, the Dantons, the Robespierres, the Barrères, the Talliens, the Reubells, the Merlins, the Barrases, and all that long line of bloody tyrants who oppressed their own country and insulted every other which they had not the power to rob. What must be the answer? That the English publishers were either innocent, if their motive was to gratify curiosity, or praiseworthy, if their intention was to rouse indignation against the calumniators of their country. If any other answer be made, I must remind my friend of a most sacred part of his duty—the duty of protecting the honest fame of those who are absent in the service of their country. Within these few days we have seen, in every newspaper in England, a publication, called the Report of Colonel Sebastiani, in which a gallant British officer [General Stuart] is charged with writing letters to procure assassination. The publishers of that infamous report are not, and will not be prosecuted, because their intention is not to libel General Stuart. On any other principle, why have all our newspapers been suffered to circulate that most atrocious of all libels against the king and people of England, which purports to be translated from the *Moniteur* of the ninth of August, 1802—a libel against a prince who has passed through a factious and stormy reign of forty-three years, without a single imputation on his personal character; against a people who have passed through the severest trials of national virtue with unimpaired glory —who alone in the world can boast of mutinies without murder; of triumphant mobs, without massacre; of bloodless revolutions, and of civil wars unstained by a single assassination. That most impudent and malignant libel which charges such a king of such a people, not only with having hired assassins, but with being so shameless, so lost to all sense of character, as to have bestowed on these assassins, if their murderous projects had succeeded, the highest badges of public honor, the rewards reserved for statesmen and heroes—the order of the garter—the order which was founded by

the heroes of Cressy and Poitiers—the garter which was worn by
Henry the Great and by Gustavus Adolphus, which might now be
worn by the hero who, on the shores of Syria [Sir Sydney Smith]
—the ancient theater of English chivalry—has revived the renown
of English valor and of English humanity—that unsullied garter
which a detestable libeler dares to say is to be paid as the price of
murder.

If I had now to defend an English publisher for the republication of that abominable libel, what must I have said in his defense?
I must have told you that it was originally published by the French
government in their official gazette; that it was republished by the
English editor to gratify the natural curiosity, perhaps to rouse the
just resentment of his English readers. I should have contended,
and, I trust, with success, that his republication of a libel was not
libelous; that it was lawful, that it was laudable. All that would
be important, at least all that would be essential in such a defense,
I now state to you on behalf of Mr. Peltier; and, if an English newspaper may safely republish the libels of the French government
against his Majesty, I shall leave you to judge whether Mr. Peltier,
in similar circumstances, may not, with equal safety, republish the
libels of Chenier against the First Consul. On the one hand, you
have the assurances of Mr. Peltier in the context that this ode is
merely a republication—you have also the general plan of his work,
with which such a republication is perfectly consistent. On the
other hand, you have only the suspicions of Mr. Attorney-General
that this ode is an original production of the defendant.

10. A SATIRE NOT A LIBEL.

But supposing that you should think it his production, and that
you should also think it a libel, even in that event, which I cannot
anticipate, I am not left without a defense. The question will still
be open, " Is it a libel on Bonaparte, or is it a libel on Chenier or
Ginguené ?" This is not an information for a libel on Chenier, and
if you should think that this ode was produced by Mr. Peltier, and
ascribed by him to Chenier, for the sake of covering that writer
with the odium of Jacobinism, the defendant is entitled to your verdict of not guilty. Or, if you should believe that it is ascribed to
Jacobinical writers, for the sake of satirizing a French Jacobinical
faction, you must also, in that case, acquit him. Butler puts sedi-
tious and immoral language into the mouth of rebels and fanatics;

but Hudibras is not, for that reason, a libel on morality or government. Swift, in the most exquisite piece of irony in the world (his argument against the abolition of Christianity), uses the language of those shallow, atheistical coxcombs whom his satire was intended to scourge. The scheme of his irony required some levity and even some profaneness of language. But nobody was ever so dull as to doubt whether Swift meant to satirize atheism or religion. In the same manner Mr. Peltier, when he wrote a satire on French Jacobinism, was compelled to ascribe to Jacobins a Jacobinical hatred of government. He was obliged, by dramatic propriety, to put into their mouths those anarchical maxims which are complained of in his ode. But, it will be said, these incitements to insurrection are here directed against the authority of Bonaparte. This proves nothing, because they must have been so directed, if the ode were a satire on Jacobinism. French Jacobins must inveigh against Bonaparte, because he exercises the powers of government. The satirist who attacks them must transcribe their sentiments and adopt their language.

I do not mean to say, gentlemen, that Mr. Peltier feels any affection, or professes any allegiance to Bonaparte. If I were to say so, he would disown me. He would disdain to purchase an acquittal by the profession of sentiments which he disclaims and abhors. Not to love Bonaparte is no crime. The question is not whether Mr. Peltier loves or hates the First Consul, but whether he has put revolutionary language into the mouth of Jacobins with a view to paint their incorrigible turbulence, and to exhibit the fruits of Jacobinical revolutions to the detestation of mankind.

:1. DEFENDANT HAD A LEGAL RIGHT TO SATIRIZE JACOBINISM.

Now, gentlemen, we cannot give a probable answer to this question without previously examining two or three questions, on which the answer to the first must very much depend. Is there a faction in France which breathes the spirit, and is likely to employ the language of this ode? Does it perfectly accord with their character and views? Is it utterly irreconcilable with the feelings, opinions, and wishes of Mr. Peltier? If these questions can be answered in the affirmative, then, I think, you must agree with me that Mr. Peltier does not, in this ode, speak his own sentiments; that he does not here vent his own resentment against Bonaparte; but that he personates a Jacobin, and adopts his language for the sake of satirizing his principles.

These questions, gentlemen, lead me to those political discussions which, generally speaking, are in a court of justice odious and disgusting. Here, however, they are necessary, and I shall consider them only as far as the necessities of this cause require.

12. THE SPIRIT OF JACOBINISM NOT EXTINGUISHED.

Gentlemen, the French Revolution—I must pause after I have uttered words which present such an overwhelming idea. But I have not now to engage in an enterprise so far beyond my force as that of examining and judging that tremendous Revolution. I have only to consider the character of the factions which it must have left behind it.

The French Revolution began with great and fatal errors. These errors produced atrocious crimes. A mild and feeble monarchy was succeeded by bloody anarchy, which, very shortly, gave birth to military despotism. France, in a few years, described the whole circle of human society.

All this was in the order of nature. When every principle of authority and civil discipline, when every principle which enables some men to command, and disposes others to obey, was extirpated from the mind by atrocious theories, and still more atrocious examples; when every old institution was trampled down with contumely, and every new institution covered in its cradle with blood; when the principle of property itself, the sheet-anchor of society, was annihilated; when in the persons of the new possessors, whom the poverty of language obliges us to call proprietors, it was contaminated in its source by robbery and murder, and it became separated from that education and those manners, from that general presumption of superior knowledge and more scrupulous probity which form its only liberal titles to respect; when the people were taught to despise everything old, and compelled to detest everything new, there remained only one principle strong enough to hold society together, a principle utterly incompatible, indeed, with liberty, and unfriendly to civilization itself, a tyrannical and barbarous principle; but, in that miserable condition of human affairs, a refuge from still more intolerable evils. I mean the principle of military power which gains strength from that confusion and bloodshed in which all the other elements of society are dissolved, and which, in these terrible extremities, is the cement that preserves it from total destruction.

Under such circumstances Bonaparte usurped the supreme

power in France. I say *usurped,* because an illegal assumption of power is a usurpation. But usurpation, in its strongest moral sense, is scarcely applicable to a period of lawless and savage anarchy.

The guilt of military usurpation, in truth, belongs to the author of those confusions which, sooner or later, give birth to such a usurpation.

Thus, to use the words of the historian, "by recent as well as ancient example, it became evident that illegal violence, with whatever pretenses it may be covered, and whatever object it may pursue, must inevitably end at last in the arbitrary and despotic government of a single person." [1] But though the government of Bonaparte has silenced the revolutionary factions, it has not and it cannot have extinguished them. No human power could reimpress upon the minds of men all those sentiments and opinions which the sophistry and anarchy of fourteen years had obliterated. A faction must exist which breathes the spirit of the ode now before you.

It is, I know, not the spirit of the quiet and submissive majority of the French people. They have always rather suffered than acted in the revolution. Completely exhausted by the calamities through which they have passed, they yield to any power which gives them repose. There is, indeed, a degree of oppression which rouses men to resistance; but there is another and a greater, which wholly subdues and unmans them. It is remarkable that Robespierre himself was safe till he attacked his own accomplices. The spirit of men of virtue was broken, and there was no vigor of character left to destroy him but in those daring ruffians who were the sharers of his tyranny.

As for the wretched populace who were made the blind and senseless instrument of so many crimes, whose frenzy can now be reviewed by a good mind with scarce any moral sentiment but that of compassion; that miserable multitude of beings, scarcely human, have already fallen into a brutish forgetfulness of the very atrocities which they themselves perpetrated. They have already forgotten all the acts of their drunken fury. If you ask one of them, who destroyed that magnificent monument of religion and art? or who perpetrated that massacre? they stupidly answer, the Jacobins! though he who gives the answer was probably one of those Jacobins himself; so that a traveler, ignorant of French history, might suppose the name of Jacobins to be the name of some Tartar horde,

[1] Hume Hist. of England, v. 7, p. 220.

who, after laying waste France for ten years, were, at last, expelled by
the native inhabitants. They have passed from senseless rage to
stupid quiet. Their delirium is followed by lethargy.

13. A PICTURE OF THE FRENCH JACOBINS.

In a word, gentlemen, the great body of the people of France
have been severely trained in those convulsions and proscriptions
which are the school of slavery. They are capable of no mutinous,
and even no bold and manly political sentiments. And if this ode
professed to paint their opinions, it would be a most unfaithful
picture. But it is otherwise with those who have been the actors
and leaders in the scene of blood. It is otherwise with the numerous agents of the most indefatigable, searching, multiform, and
omnipresent tyranny that ever existed, which pervaded every class
of society which had ministers and victims in every village in
France.

Some of them, indeed, the basest of the race, the sophists, the
rhetors, the poet-laureates of murder, who were cruel only from cowardice and calculating selfishness, are perfectly willing to transfer
their venal pens to any government that does not disdain their infamous support. These men, republicans from servility, who published rhetorical panegyrics on massacre, and who reduce plunder
to a system of ethics, are as ready to preach slavery as anarchy.
But the more daring, I had almost said, the more respectable ruffians, cannot so easily bend their heads under the yoke. These
fierce spirits have not lost

" That unconquerable will,
And study of revenge, immortal hate."

They leave the luxuries of servitude to the mean and dastardly
hypocrites, to the Belials and Mammons of the infernal faction.
They persue their old end of tyranny under their old pretext of
liberty. The recollection of their unbounded power renders every
inferior condition irksome and vapid; and their former atrocities
form, if I may so speak, a sort of moral destiny which irresistibly
impels them to the perpetration of new crimes. They have no
place left for penitence on earth. They labor under the most
awful proscription of opinion that ever was pronounced against
human beings. They have cut down every bridge by which they
could retreat into the society of men. Awakened from their dreams

of democracy, the noise subsided that deafened their ears to the voice of humanity; the film fallen from their eyes which hid from them the blackness of their own deeds; haunted by the memory of their inexpiable guilt; condemned daily to look on the faces of those whom their hands made widows and orphans, they are goaded and scourged by these *real* furies, and hurried into the tumult of new crimes, which will drown the cries of remorse; or, if they be too depraved for remorse, will silence the curses of mankind. Tyrannical power is their only refuge from the just vengeance of their fellow-creatures. Murder is their only means of usurping power. They have no taste, no occupation, no pursuit but power and blood. If their hands are tied, they must at least have the luxury of murderous projects. They have drunk too deeply of human blood ever to relinquish their cannibal appetite.

Such a faction exists in France. It is numerous, it is powerful, and it has a principle of fidelity stronger than any that ever held together a society. *They are banded together, by despair of forgiveness, by the unanimous detestation of mankind.* They are now contained by a severe and stern government. But they still meditate the renewal of insurrection and massacre; and they are prepared to renew the worst and most atrocious of their crimes, that crime against posterity and against human nature itself, that crime of which the latest generations of mankind may feel the fatal conse- quences—the crime of degrading and prostituting the sacred name of liberty.

I must own, that however paradoxical it may appear, I should almost think not worse, but more meanly of them if it were otherwise. I must then think them destitute of that which I will not call courage, because that is the name of a virtue ; but of that ferocious energy which alone rescues ruffians from contempt. If they were destitute of that which is the heroism of murderers, they would be the lowest as well as the most abominable of beings.

It is impossible to conceive anything more despicable than wretches who, after hectoring and bullying over their meek and blameless sovereign and his defenseless family, whom they kept so long in a dungeon trembling for their existence—whom they put to death by a slow torture of three years, after playing the Republican and the tyrannicide to women and children, become the supple and fawning slaves of the first government that knows how to wield the scourge with a firm hand.

14. Republicans and Jacobins distinguished.

I have used the word Republican because it is the name by which this atrocious faction describes itself. The assumption of that name is one of their crimes. They are no more Republicans than Royalists. They are the common enemies of all human society. God forbid that by the use of that word I should be supposed to reflect on the members of those respectable Republican communities which did exist in Europe before the French Revolution. That Revolution has spared many monarchies, but it has spared no republic within the sphere of its destructive energy. One republic only now exists in the world—a republic of English blood, which was originally composed of Republican societies, under the protection of a monarchy, which had, therefore, no great and perilous change in their internal constitution to effect ; and of which, I speak it with pleasure and pride, the inhabitants, even in the convulsions of a most deplorable separation, displayed the humanity as well as valor which, I trust I may say, they inherited from their forefathers.

Nor do I mean by the use of the word "Republican" to confound this execrable faction with all those who, in the liberty of private speculation, may prefer a Republican form of government. I own that, after much reflection, I am not able to conceive an error more gross than that of those who believe in the possibility of erecting a republic in any of the old monarchical countries of Europe, who believe that in such countries an elective supreme magistracy can produce anything but a succession of stern tyrannies and bloody civil wars. It is a supposition which is belied by all experience, and which betrays the greatest ignorance of the first principles of the constitution of society. It is an error which has a false appearance of superiority over vulgar prejudice ; it is, therefore, too apt to be attended with the most criminal rashness and presumption, and too easy to be inflamed into the most immoral and anti-social fanaticism. But as long as it remains a mere quiescent error, it is not the proper subject of moral disapprobation.

If, then, gentlemen, such a faction, falsely calling itself republican, exists in France, let us consider whether this ode speaks their sentiments, describes their character, agrees with their views. Trying it by the principle I have stated, I think you will have no difficulty in concluding that it is agreeable to the general plan of this publication to give a historical and satirical view of the Brutuses and brutes of the republic—of those who assumed and disgraced the name of Brutus, and who, under that name, sat as judges in their mock tribunals, with pistols in their girdles, to anticipate the office of the executioner on those unfortunate men whom they treated as rebels, for resistance to Robespierre and Couthon.

15. THE PUBLICATION CANNOT REPRESENT THE OPINIONS OF THE DEFENDANT, WHO IS A ROYALIST.

I come now to show you that this ode[1] cannot represent the opinions of Mr. Peltier. He is a French royalist. He has devoted his talents to the cause of his king. For that cause he has sacrificed his fortune and hazarded his life. For that cause he is proscribed and exiled from his country. I could easily conceive powerful topics of royalist invective against Bonaparte; and, if Mr. Peltier had called upon Frenchmen by the memory of St. Louis and Henry the Great, by the memory of that illustrious family which reigned over them for seven centuries, and with whom all their martial renown and literary glory are so closely connected; if he had adjured them by the spotless name of that Louis XVI, the martyr of his love for his people, which scarce a man in France can now pronounce but in the tone of pity and veneration; if he had *thus* called upon them to change their useless regret and their barren pity into generous and active indignation; if he had reproached the conquerors of Europe with the disgrace of being the slaves of an upstart stranger; if he had brought before their minds the contrast between their country under her ancient monarch—the source and model of refinement in manners and taste—and since their expulsion, the scourge and the opprobrium of humanity; if he had exhorted them to drive out their ignoble tyrants and to restore their native sovereign, I should then have recognized the voice of a royalist. I should have recognized language that must have flowed from the heart of Mr. Peltier, and I should have been compelled to acknowledge that it was pointed against Bonaparte.

Here Mr. Mackintosh showed that the ode expressed the sentiments of a Jacobin, not of a royalist. That it could not have been written by a royalist who assumed a Jacobin disguise to serve a royalist purpose, for it would then have to be considered an address to Jacobins, and the fact that the name of the defendant, who was an avowed enemy of Jacobinism, was prefixed to it, was wholly inconsistent with such a theory. He continued:

[1] For the Ode, see Appendix, p. 730.

16. Observations upon the Ode.

I can not conceive it to be necessary that I should minutely examine this poem to confirm my construction. There are one or two passages on which I shall make a few observations. The first is the contrast between the state of England and that of France, of which an ingenious friend[1] has favored me with a translation, which I shall take the liberty of reading to you.

> Her glorious fabric England rears
>   On law's fixed base alone;
> Law's guardian pow'r while each reveres,
> England! thy people's freedom fears
>   No danger from the Throne.
>
> For there, before the almighty Law,
> High birth, high place, with pious awe,
>   In reverend homage bend:
> There man's free spirit, unconstrain'd
> Exults, in man's best rights maintain'd.
> Rights, which by ancient valor gain'd,
>   From age to age descend.
>
> Britons, by no base fear dismay'd,
>   May power's worst acts arraign:
> Does tyrant force their rights invade?
> They call on Law's impartial aid,
>   Nor call that aid in vain.
>
> Hence, of her sacred charter proud,
> With every earthly good endow'd,
>   O'er subject seas unfurl'd,
> Britannia waves her standard wide,
> Hence, sees her freighted navies ride
> Up wealthy Thames' majestic tide,
>   The wonder of the world.[2]

Here, at first sight, you may perhaps think that the consistency of the Jacobin character is not supported, that the Republican disguise is thrown off, that the Royalist stands unmasked before you; but, on more consideration, you will find that such an inference would be too hasty. The leaders of the Revolution are now reduced to envy that British Constitution which, in the infatuation of their presumptuous ignorance, they once rejected with scorn. They are now slaves, as they themselves confess, because twelve

---

[1] Mr. Canning.

[2] It seems that the entire ode was not set out in the indictment, and these particular verses do not appear. For the benefit of the reader, we give them in the appendix, p. 734.

years ago they did not believe Englishmen to be free. They can not but see that England is the only popular government in Europe, and they are compelled to pay a reluctant homage to the justice of English principles. The praise of England is too striking a satire on their own government to escape them ; and I may accordingly venture to appeal to all those who know anything of the political circles of Paris, whether such contrasts between France and England as that which I have read to you be not the most favorite topics of the opponents of Bonaparte. But in the very next stanza,

> Cependant, encore affligée
> Par l'odieuse hérédité,
> Londres de titres surchargée,
> Londres n'a pas *l'Egalité.*

You see, that though they are forced to surrender an unwilling tribute to our liberty, they can not yet renounce all their fantastic and deplorable chimeras. They endeavor to make a compromise between the experience on which they can not shut their eyes, and the wretched systems to which they still cling. Fanaticism is the most incurable of all mental diseases ; because in all its forms, religious, philosophical, or political, it is distinguished by a sort of mad contempt for experience, which alone can correct the errors of practical judgment. And these democratical fanatics still speak of the odious principle of " hereditary government." They still complain that we have not " equality." They know not that this odious principle of inheritance is our bulwark against tyranny ; that if we had their pretended equality, we should soon cease to be the objects of their envy. These are the sentiments which you would naturally expect from half-cured lunatics. But once more I ask you, whether they can be the sentiments of Mr. Peltier? Would he complain that we have too much monarchy, or too much of what they call aristocracy? If he has any prejudices against the English government, must they not be of an entirely opposite kind?

Here Mr. Mackintosh showed that there was nothing in the ode which could be construed as an exhortation to assassinate Napoleon. He continued :

17. THE VERSES CONTAIN NO EXHORTATION TO ASSASSINATE NAPOLEON.

Having said so much on the first of these supposed libels, I shall be very short on the two that remain—the verses ascribed to

38

a Dutch patriot, and the parody of the speech of Lepidus.　In the first of these, the piercing eye of Mr. Attorney General has again discovered an incitement to assassinate—the most learned incitement to assassinate that ever was addressed to such ignorant ruffians as are most likely to be employed for such nefarious purposes ! An obscure allusion to an obscure and perhaps fabulous part of Roman history, to the supposed murder of Romulus, about which none of us know anything, and of which the Jacobins of Paris and Amsterdam probably never heard.　But the apotheosis ! Here my learned friend has a little forgotten himself.　He seems to argue as if apotheosis always presupposed death.　But he must know that Augustus, and even Tiberius and Nero, were deified during their lives, and he can not have forgotten the terms in which one of the court poets of Augustus speaks of his master's divinity :

> ——Præsens divus habebitur
> Augustus adjectis Britannis
> Imperio.

If any modern rival of Augustus should choose that path to Olympus, I think he will find it more steep and rugged than that by which Pollux and Hercules climbed to the ethereal towers, and that he must be content with purpling his lips with Burgundy on earth, as he has very little chance of purpling them with nectar among the gods.

The utmost that can seriously be made of this passage is, that it is a wish for a man's death.　I repeat that I do not contend for the decency of publicly declaring such wishes, or even for the propriety of entertaining them ; but the distance between such a wish and a persuasive to murder is immense.　Such a wish for a man's death is very often little more than a strong, though, I admit, not a very decent way of expressing detestation for his character.

But without pursuing this argument any further, I think myself entitled to apply to these verses the same reasoning which I have already applied to the first supposed libel on Bonaparte.　If they be the real composition of a pretended Dutch patriot, Mr. Peltier may republish them innocently.　If they be a satire on such pretended Dutch patriots, they are not a libel on Bonaparte.　Granting, for the sake of argument, that they did entertain a serious exhortation to assassinate, is there anything in such an exhortation inconsistent with the character of these pretended patriots ?

They who were disaffected to the mild and tolerant government of their flourishing country, because it did not exactly square with all their theoretical whimsies; they who revolted from that administration as tyrannical, which made Holland one of the wonders of the world for protected industry, for liberty of action and opinion, and for a prosperity which I may venture to call the greatest victory of man over hostile elements; they who called in the aid of the fiercest tyrants that Europe ever saw, who served in the armies of Robespierre, under the impudent pretext of giving liberty to their country, and who have finally buried in the same grave its liberty, its independence, and perhaps its national existence, they are not men entitled to much tenderness from a political satirist, and he will scarcely violate dramatic propriety if he impute to them any language, however criminal and detestable. They who could not brook the authority of their old, lazy, good-natured government, are not likely to endure with patience the yoke of that stern domination which they have brought upon themselves, and which, as far as relates to them, is only the just punishment of their crimes. They who call in tyrants to establish liberty, who sacrifice the independence of their country under pretense of reforming its internal constitution, are capable of everything.

I know nothing more odious than their character, unless it be that of those who invoked the aid of the oppressors of Switzerland to be the deliverers of Ireland! Their guilt has, indeed, peculiar aggravations. In the name of liberty, they were willing to surrender their country into the hands of tyrants, the most lawless, faithless, and merciless that ever scourged Europe; who, at the very moment of their negotiation, were covered with the blood of the unhappy Swiss, the martyrs of real independence and of real liberty. Their success would have been the destruction of the only free community remaining in Europe—of England, the only bulwark of the remains of European independence. Their means were the passions of an ignorant and barbarous peasantry, and a civil war, which could not fail to produce all the horrible crimes and horrible retaliations of the last calamity that can befall society—a servile revolt. They sought the worst of ends by the most abominable of means. They labored for the subjugation of the world at the expense of crimes and miseries which men of humanity and conscience would have thought too great a price for the deliverance of mankind.

Here Mr. Mackintosh referred to the third and last publication set out in the indictment, the parody on the speech of Lepidus, and claimed that it could only be reasonably construed as a libel on M. Fouché, having no reference to Bonaparte. He continued:

18. Free discussion the most important interest of mankind.—The reign of Elizabeth.

Believing, as I do, that we are on the eve of a great struggle; that this is only the first battle between reason and power; that you have now in your hands, committed to your trust, the only remains of free discussion in Europe, now confined to this kingdom —addressing you, therefore, as the guardians of the most important interests of mankind; convinced that the unfettered exercise of reason depends more on your present verdict than on any other that was ever delivered by a jury, I cannot conclude without bringing before you the sentiments and examples of our ancestors in some of these awful and perilous situations by which Divine Providence has, in former ages, tried the virtue of the English nation. We are fallen upon times in which it behooves us to strengthen our spirits by the contemplation of great examples of constancy. Let us seek for them in the annals of our forefathers.

The reign of Queen Elizabeth may be considered as the opening of the modern history of England, especially in its connection with the modern system of Europe, which began about that time to assume the form that it preserved till the French Revolution. It was a very memorable period, of which the maxims ought to be engraven on the head and heart of every Englishman. Philip II, at the head of the greatest empire then in the world, was openly aiming at universal domination, and his project was so far from being thought chimerical by the wisest of his contemporaries, that, in the opinion of the great Duke of Sully, he must have been successful, " if, by a most singular combination of circumstances, he had not at the same time been resisted by two such strong heads as those of Henry IV and Queen Elizabeth." To the most extensive and opulent dominions, the most numerous and disciplined armies, the most renowned captains, the greatest revenue, he added also the most formidable power over opinion. He was the chief of a religious faction, animated by the most atrocious fanaticism, prepared to second his ambition by rebellion, anarchy and regicide in every protestant State. Elizabeth was among the first objects of his hostility. That wise and magnanimous princess placed herself in the front of the battle for the liberties of Europe. Though she had to contend at home with his fanatical faction, which almost occupied Ireland, which divided Scotland, and was not of contemptible strength in England, she aided the oppressed inhabitants of the Netherlands in their just and glorious resistance to his tyranny; she aided Henry the

Great in suppressing the abominable rebellion which anarchical principles had excited and Spanish arms had supported in France, and after a long reign of various fortune, in which she preserved her unconquered spirit through great calamities and still greater dangers, she at length broke the strength of the enemy, and reduced his power within such limits as to be compatible with the safety of England and of all Europe. Her only effectual ally was the spirit of her people, and her policy flowed from that magnanimous nature which, in the hour of peril, teaches better lessons than those of cold reason. Her great heart inspired her with a higher and nobler wisdom—which disdained to appeal to the low and sordid passions of her people even for the protection of their low and sordid interests, because she knew, or, rather, she felt, that these are effeminate, creeping, cowardly, short-sighted passions, which shrink from conflict even in defense of their own mean objects. In a righteous cause she roused those generous affections of her people which alone teach boldness, constancy and foresight, and which are, therefore, the only safe guardians of the lowest as well as the highest interests of a nation. In her memorable address to her army, when the invasion of the kingdom was threatened by Spain, this woman of heroic spirit disdained to speak to them of their ease and their commerce, and their wealth and their safety. No! She touched another chord—she spoke of their national honor, of their dignity as Englishmen, of " the foul scorn that Parma or Spain *should dare* to invade the borders of her realms." She breathed into them those grand and powerful sentiments which exalt vulgar men into heroes, which led them into the battle of their country, armed with holy and irresistible enthusiasm; which even cover with their shield all the ignoble interests that base calculation and cowardly selfishness tremble to hazard, but shrink from defending.

19. POWER AND IMPORTANCE OF THE PRESS IN PRESERVING THE LIBERTIES OF ENGLISHMEN.

A sort of prophetic instinct, if I may so speak, seems to have revealed to her the importance of that great instrument for rousing and guiding the minds of men, of the effects of which she had no experience, which, since her time, has changed the condition of the world, but which few modern statesmen have thoroughly understood or wisely employed; which is, no doubt, connected with many ridiculous and degrading details, which has produced, and which may again produce, terrible mischiefs, but of which the influence must, after all, be considered as the most certain effect and the most efficacious cause of civilization, and which, whether it be a blessing or a curse, is the most powerful engine that a politician can move—I mean the press. It is a curious fact that, in the year of the Armada, Queen Elizabeth caused to be printed the first gazettes that ever appeared in England; and I own, when I consider that this mode of rousing a national spirit was then absolutely unexampled, that she could have no assurance of its efficacy from the precedents of former times, I am disposed to regard her having recourse to it as one of the most sagacious experiments, one of the greatest discoveries of political genius, one of the most striking anticipations of future experience that we find in history. I mention it to you to justify the opinion that I have ventured to state of the close connection of our national spirit with our press, even our periodical press.

I cannot quit the reign of Elizabeth without laying before you the maxims of her policy, in the language of the greatest and wisest of men. Lord Bacon, in one part of his discourse on her reign, speaks thus of her support of Holland : "But let me rest upon the honorable and continual aid and relief she hath given to the distressed and desolate people of the Low Countries—a people recommended unto her by ancient confederacy and daily intercourse, by their cause so innocent and their fortune so lamentable !" In another passage of the same discourse, he thus speaks of the general system of her foreign policy as the protector of Europe, in words too remarkable to require any commentary. " Then it is her government, and her government alone, that hath been the sconce and fort of all Europe, which hath let this proud nation from overrunning all. If any state be yet free from his factions erected in the bowels thereof ; if there be any state wherein this faction is erected that is not yet fired with civil troubles ; if there be any state under his protection that enjoyeth moderate liberty, upon whom he tyrannizeth not, it is the mercy of this renowned Queen that standeth between them and their misfortunes !"

20. LOUIS XIV.—HIS ARRAIGNMENT BY FRENCH REFUGEES
NO LIBEL.

The next great conspirator against the rights of men and of nations, against the security and independence of all European states, against every kind and degree of civil and religious liberty, was Louis XIV. In his time the character of the English nation was the more remarkably displayed, because it was counteracted by an apostate and perfidious government. During great part of his reign, you know that the throne of England was filled by princes who deserted the cause of their country and of Europe, who were the accomplices and the tools of the oppressor of the world, who were even so unmanly, so unprincely, so base, as to have sold themselves to his ambition ; who were content that he should enslave the continent, if he enabled them to enslave Great Britain. These princes, traitors to their own royal dignity and to the feelings of the generous people whom they ruled, preferred the condition of the first slave of Louis XIV to the dignity of the first freemen of England ; yet even under these princes, the feelings of the people of this kingdom were displayed, on a most memorable occasion, toward foreign sufferers and foreign oppressors. The revocation of the Edict of Nantes threw fifty thousand French Protestants on our shores. They were received as I trust the victims of tyranny ever will be in this land, which seems chosen by Providence to be the home of the exile, the refuge of the oppressed. They were welcomed by a people high-spirited as well as humane, who did not insult them by clandestine charity ; who did not give alms in secret lest their charity should be detected by their neighboring tyrants ! No ! They were publicly and nationally welcomed and relieved. They were bid to raise their voice against their oppressor, and to proclaim their wrongs to all mankind. They did. so. They were joined in the cry of just indignation by every Englishman worthy of the name. It was a fruitful indignation, which soon produced the successful resistance of Europe to the common enemy. Even then, when Jeffreys disgraced the bench which his lordship (Lord Ellenborough) now adorns, no refugee was deterred by prosecution for libel from giving vent to his feelings, from arraigning the oppressor in the face of all Europe.

21. THE INVASION OF HOLLAND AN AVOWED ATTACK UPON THE LIBERTY OF THE PRESS.

During this ignominious period of our history, a war arose on the continent, which cannot but present itself to the mind on such an occasion as this ; the only war that was ever made on the avowed ground of attacking a free press. I speak of the invasion of Holland by Louis XIV. The liberties which the Dutch gazettes had taken in discussing his conduct were the sole cause of this very extraordinary and memorable war, which was of short duration, unprecedented in its avowed principle, and most glorious in its event for the liberties of mankind. That republic, at all times so interesting to Englishmen—in the worst times of both countries our brave enemies ; in their best times our most faithful and valuable friends—was then charged with the defense of a free press against the oppressor of Europe, as a sacred trust for the benefit of all generations. They felt the sacredness of the deposit; they felt the dignity of the station in which they were placed, and though deserted by the un-English government of England, they asserted their own ancient character, and drove out the great armies and great captains of the oppressor with defeat and disgrace. Such was the result of the only war hitherto avowedly undertaken to oppress a free country because she allowed the free and public exercise of reason. And may the God of justice and liberty grant that such may ever be the result of wars made by tyrants against the rights of mankind, especially against that right which is the guardian of every other.

22. WILLIAM OF ORANGE SAVES ENGLAND FROM THE POWER OF LOUIS XIV.

This war, gentlemen, had the effect of raising up from obscurity the great Prince of Orange, afterward King William III, the deliverer of Holland, the deliverer of England, the deliverer of Europe ; the only hero who was distinguished by such a happy union of fortune and virtue that the objects of his ambition were always the same with the interests of humanity ; perhaps the only man who devoted the whole of his life exclusively to the service of mankind. This most illustrious benefactor of Europe, this " hero without vanity or passion," as he has been justly and beautifully called by a venerable prelate (Dr. Shipley, Bishop of St. Asaph), who never made a step toward greatness without securing or advancing liberty, who had been made Stadtholder of Holland for the salvation of his own country, was soon after made King of England for the deliverance of ours. When the people of Great Britain had once more a government worthy of them, they returned to the feelings and principles of their ancestors, and resumed their former station and their former duties as protectors of the independence of nations. The people of England, delivered from a government which disgraced, oppressed, and betrayed them, fought under William as their forefathers had fought under Elizabeth, and after an almost uninterrupted struggle of more than twenty years, in which they were often abandoned by fortune, but never by their own constancy and magnanimity, they at length once more defeated those projects of guilty ambition, boundless aggrandizement, and universal domination, which had a second time threatened to overwhelm the whole civilized world. They rescued Europe from being swallowed up in the gulf of extensive empire, which the experience of all times points out as the grave of civilization ; where men are driven by violent conquest and military oppression into lethargy and slavishness of heart ; where, after their arts have perished with the mental vigor from which they spring, they are plunged by the combined power of effeminacy and ferocity into irreclaimable and hopeless barbarism. Our ancestors established the safety of their own country by providing for that of others, and rebuilt the European system upon such firm foundations that nothing less than the tempest of the French Revolution could have shaken it.

23. ANIMADVERSION OF THE ENGLISH PRESS ON THE PROJECTS OF LOUIS XIV.

This arduous struggle was suspended for a short time by the peace of Ryswick. The interval between that treaty and the war of the succession enables us to judge how our ancestors acted in a very peculiar situation, which requires maxims of policy very different from those which usually govern states. The treaty which they had concluded was in truth and substance only a truce. The ambition and the power of the enemy were such as to render real peace impossible. And it was perfectly obvious that the disputed succession of the Spanish Monarch would soon render it no longer practicable to preserve even the appearance of amity. It was desirable, however, not to provoke the enemy by unseasonable hostility ; but it was still more desirable, it was absolutely necessary, to keep up the national jealousy and indignation against him who was soon to be their open enemy. It might naturally have been apprehended that the press might have driven into premature war a Prince who, not long before, had been violently exasperated by the press of another free country. I have looked over the political publications of that time with some care, and I can venture to say that at no period were the system and projects of Louis

XIV animadverted on with more freedom and boldness than during that interval. Our ancestors and the heroic Prince who governed them did not deem it wise policy to disarm the national mind
for the sake of prolonging a truce. They were both too proud
and too wise to pay so great a price for so small a benefit.

24. INFLUENCE OF NEWSPAPERS ON DOMESTIC AND FOREIGN POLITICS.

In the course of the eighteenth century, a great change took
place in the state of political discussion in this country. I speak
of the multiplication of newspapers. I know that newspapers are
not very popular in this place, which is, indeed, not very surprising, because they are known here only by their faults. Their publishers come here only to receive the chastisement due to their
offenses. With all their faults, I own I cannot help feeling some
respect for whatever is a proof of the increased curiosity and increased knowledge of mankind; and I cannot help thinking that if
somewhat more indulgence and consideration were shown for the
difficulties of their situation, it might prove one of the best cor-
rectives of their faults, by teaching them that self-respect which is
the best security for liberal conduct toward others. But however
that may be, it is very certain that the multiplication of these
channels of popular information has produced a great change in
the state of our domestic and foreign politics. At home, it has,
in truth, produced a gradual revolution in our government. By
increasing the number of those who exercise some sort of judgment on public affairs, it has created a substantial democracy, infinitely more important than those democratical forms which have
been the subject of so much contest. So that I may venture to
say, England has not only in its forms the most democratical government that ever existed in a great country, but in substance has
the most democratical government that ever existed in any country:
if the most substantial democracy be that state in which the greatest number of men feel an interest and express an opinion upon
political questions, and in which the greatest number of judgments
and wills concur in influencing public measures.

The same circumstances gave great additional importance to
our discussion of continental politics. That discussion was no
longer, as in the preceding century, confined to a few pamphlets,
written and read only by men of education and rank, which
reached the multitude very slowly and rarely. In newspapers an

almost daily appeal was made, directly or indirectly, to the judgment and passions of almost every individual in the kingdom, upon the measures and principles not only of his own country, but of every state in Europe. Under such circumstances, the tone of these publications, in speaking of foreign governments, became a matter of importance. You will excuse me, therefore, if, before I conclude, I remind you of the general nature of their language on one or two very remarkable occasions, and of the boldness with which they arraigned the crimes of powerful sovereigns, without any check from the laws and magistrates of their own country. This toleration, or rather this protection, was too long and uniform to be accidental. I am, indeed, very much mistaken, if it be not founded upon a policy which this country cannot abandon without sacrificing her liberty and endangering her national existence.

25. Arraignment by the press of the crime against Poland.

The first remarkable instance which I shall choose to state of the unpunished and protected boldness of the English press, of the freedom with which they animadverted on the policy of powerful sovereigns, is the partition of Poland in 1772; an act not, perhaps, so horrible in its means, nor so deplorable in its immediate effects, as some other atrocious invasions of national independence which have followed it ; but the most abominable in its general tendency and ultimate consequences of any political crime recorded in history; because it was the first practical breach in the system of Europe, the first example of atrocious robbery perpetrated on unoffending countries which have been since so liberally followed, and which has broken down all the barriers of habit and principle which guarded defenseless states. The perpetrators of this atrocious crime were the most powerful sovereigns of the continent, whose hostility it certainly was not the interest of Great Britain wantonly to incur. They were the most illustrious princes of their age, and some of them were, doubtless, entitled to the highest praise for their domestic administration, as well as for the brilliant qualities which distinguished their characters. But none of these circumstances, no dread of their resentment, no admiration of their talents, no consideration for their rank, silenced the animadversion of the English press. Some of you remember, all of you know, that a loud and unanimous cry of reprobation and execration broke out against them from every part of this kingdom. It was perfectly uninfluenced by any considerations of our own mere national interest, which might perhaps be supposed to be rather favorably affected by that partition. It was not, as in some other countries, the indignation of rival robbers, who were excluded from their share of the prey. It was the moral anger of disinterested spectators against atrocious crimes, the gravest and the most dignified moral principle which the God of justice has implanted in the human heart; that of which the dread is the only restraint on the actious of powerful criminals, and of which the promulgation is the only punishment that can be inflicted on them. It is a restraint which ought not to be weakened. It is a punishment which no good man can desire to mitigate.

That great crime was spoken of as it deserved in England. Robbery was not described by any courtly circumlocutions. Rapine was not called policy; nor was the oppression of an innocent people termed a mediation in their domestic differences. No prosecutions, no criminal informations followed the liberty and the boldness of the language then employed. No complaints ever appear to have been made from abroad, much less any insolent menaces against the free constitution which protected the English press. The people of England were too long known throughout Europe for the proudest potentate to expect to silence our press by such means.

I pass over the second partition of Poland in 1792. You all remember what passed on that occasion, the universal abhorrence expressed by every man and every writer of every party, the succors that were publicly preparing by large bodies of individuals of all parties for the oppressed Poles.

I hasten to the final dismemberment of that unhappy kingdom, which seems to me the most striking example in our history of the habitual, principled, and deeply rooted forbearance of those who administer the law toward political writers. We were engaged in the most extensive, bloody, and dangerous war that this country ever knew ; and the parties to the dismemberment of Poland were our allies, and our only powerful and effective allies. We had every motive of policy to court their friendship. Every reason of state seemed to require that we should not permit them to be abused and viilified by English writers. What was the fact ? Did any Englishman consider himself at liberty, on account of temporary interests, however urgent, to silence those feelings of humanity and justice which guard the certain and permanent interests of all countries ? You all remember that every voice, and every pen, and every press in England were unceasingly employed to brand that abominable robbery. You remember that this was not confined to private writers, but that the same abhorrence was expressed by every member of both Houses of Parliament who was not under the restraints of ministerial reserve. No minister dared even to blame the language of honest indignation which might be very inconvenient to his most important political projects; and I hope I may venture to say that no English assembly would have endured such a sacrifice of eternal justice to any miserable interest of an hour. Did the law officers of the Crown venture to come into a court of justice to complain of the boldest of the publications of that time? They did not. I do not say that they felt any disposition to do so. I believe that they could not. But I do say that if they had; if they had spoken of the necessity of confining our political writers to cold narrative and unfeeling argument; if they had informed the jury that they did not prosecute history, but invective; that if private writers be allowed at all to blame great princes, it must be with moderation and decorum; the sound heads and honest hearts of an English jury would have confounded such sophistry, and declared by their verdict that moderation of language is a relative term, which varies with the subject to which it is applied; that atrocious crimes are not to be related as calmly and coolly as indifferent or trifling events; that if there be a decorum due to exalted rank and authority, there is also a much more sacred decorum due to virtue and to human nature, which would be outraged and trampled under foot by speaking of guilt in a lukewarm language, falsely called moderate.

26. THE INVASION OF SWITZERLAND;—ENGLAND AN ASYLUM FOR ITS OPPRESSED HEROES.

Soon after, gentlemen, there followed an act, in comparison with which all the deeds of rapine and blood perpetrated in the world are innocence itself—the invasion and destruction of Switzerland, that unparalleled scene of guilt and enormity; that unprovoked aggression against an innocent country, which had been the sanctuary of peace and liberty for three centuries; respected as a sort of sacred territory by the fiercest ambition; raised, like its own mountains, beyond the region of the storms which raged around on every side; the only warlike people that never sent forth armies to disturb their neighbors; the only government that ever accumulated treasures without imposing taxes, an innocent treasure, unstained by the tears of the poor, the inviolate patrimony of the commonwealth, which attested the virtue of a long series of magistrates, but which at length caught the eye of the spoiler, and became the fatal occasion of their ruin.

Gentlemen, the destruction of such a country,[1] "its cause so innocent and its fortune so lamentable !" made a deep impression on the people of England. I will ask my learned friend if we had then been at peace with the French republic, whether we must have been silent spectators of the foulest crimes that ever blotted the name of humanity! whether we must, like cowards and slaves, have repressed the compassion and indignation with which that horrible scene of tyranny had filled our hearts ? Let me suppose, gentlemen, that Aloys Reding, who has displayed in our times the simplicity, magnanimity, and piety of ancient heroes, had, after his glorious struggle, honored this kingdom by choosing it as his refuge; that after performing prodigies of valor at the head of his handful of heroic peasants on the field of Morgarten, where his ancestor, the Landmann Reding, had, five hundred years before, defeated the first oppressors of Switzerland, he had selected this country to be his residence, as the chosen abode of liberty, as the ancient and inviolable asylum of the oppressed, would my learned friend have had the boldness to have said to this hero "that he must hide his tears" (the tears shed by a hero over the ruins of his country!) "lest they might provoke the resentment of Reubell or Rapinat ! that he must smother the sorrow and the anger with which his heart was loaded; that he must breathe his murmurs low, lest they might be overheard by the oppressor!" Would this have been the language of my learned friend ? I know that it would not. I know that by such a supposition I have done wrong to his honorable feelings, to his honest English heart. I am sure that he knows, as well as I do, that a nation which should *thus* receive the oppressed of other countries would be preparing its own neck for the yoke. He knows the slavery which such a nation would deserve, and must speedily incur. He knows that sympathy with the unmerited sufferings of others, and disinterested anger against their oppressors, are, if I may so speak, the masters which are appointed by Providence to teach us fortitude in the defense of our own rights; that selfishness is a dastardly principle, which betrays its charge and flies from its post; and that those only can defend themselves with valor who are animated by the moral approbation with which

[1] Switzerland.

they can survey their sentiments towards others, who are ennobled in their own eyes by a consciousness that they are fighting for justice as well as interest; a consciousness which none can feel but those who have felt for the wrongs of their brethren. These are the sentiments which my learned friend would have felt. He would have told the hero: "Your confidence is not deceived; this is still that England, of which the history may, perhaps, have contributed to fill your heart with the heroism of liberty. Every other country of Europe is crouching under the bloody tyrants who destroyed your country. *We* are unchanged; we are still the same people which received, with open arms, the victims of the tyranny of Philip II and Louis XIV. We shall not exercise a cowardly and clandestine humanity! Here we are not so dastardly as to rob you of your greatest consolation. Here, protected by a free, brave and high-minded people, you may give vent to your indignation; you may proclaim the crimes of your tyrants, you may devote them to the execration of mankind; there is still one spot upon earth in which they are abhorred, without being dreaded!"

27. THE REIGN OF ROBESPIERRE.—ILLUSTRATIONS TO SHOW THE FALLACY OF THE THEORY OF THE PROSECUTION.

I am aware, gentlemen, that I have already abused your indulgence, but I must entreat you to bear with me for a short time longer, to allow me to suppose a case which might have occurred, in which you will see the horrible consequences of enforcing rigorously principles of law, which I cannot counteract, against political writers. We might have been at peace with France during the whole of that terrible period which elapsed between August, 1792 and 1794, which has been usually called the reign of Robespierre! The only series of crimes, perhaps, in history which, in spite of the common disposition to exaggerate extraordinary facts, has been beyond measure underrated in public opinion. I say this, gentlemen, after an investigation which, I think, entitles me to affirm it with confidence. Men's minds were oppressed by atrocity and the multitude of crimes; their humanity and their indolence took refuge in skepticism from such an overwhelming mass of guilt; and the consequence was, that all these unparalleled enormities, though proved not only with the fullest historical but with the strictest judicial evidence, were at the time only half believed and are now scarcely half remembered. When these atrocities were daily perpetrating, of which the greatest part are as little known to the public in general as the campaigns of Genghis Khan, but are still protected from the scrutiny of men by the immensity of those voluminous records of guilt in which they are related, and under the mass of which they will be buried till some historian be found with patience and courage enough to drag them forth into light, for the shame indeed, but for the instruction of mankind— when these crimes were perpetrating, which had the peculiar malignity, from the pretexts with which they were covered, of making the noblest objects of human pursuit seem odious and detestable ; which has almost made the names of liberty, reformation, and humanity synonymous with anarchy, robbery, and murder ; which thus threatened not to extinguish every principle of improvement, to arrest the progress of civilized society, and to disinherit future generations of that rich succession, which they were entitled to expect from the knowledge and wisdom of the present, but to destroy the civilization of Europe, which never gave such a proof of its vigor and robustness as in being able to resist their destructive power—when all these horrors were acting in the greatest empire of the continent, I will ask my learned friend, if we had then been at peace with France, how English writers were to relate them so as to escape the charge of libeling a friendly government ?

When Robespierre, in the debates in the National Convention on the mode of murdering their blameless sovereign, objected to the formal and tedious mode of murder called a trial, and proposed to put him immediately to death, " on the principles of insurrection," because to doubt the guilt of the king would be to doubt of the innocence of the convention; and, if the king were not a traitor, the convention must be rebels, would my learned friend have had an English writer state all this with "*decorum and moderation ?*" Would he have had an English writer state that though this reasoning was not perfectly agreeable to our national laws, or, perhaps, to our national prejudices, yet it was not for him to make any observations on the judicial proceedings of foreign States ?

When Marat, in the same convention, called for two hundred and seventy thousand heads, must our English writers have said that the remedy did, indeed, seem to their weak judgment rather severe; but that it was not for them to judge the conduct of so illustrious an assembly as the National Convention, or the suggestions of so enlightened a statesman as M. Marat ?

When that convention resounded with applause at the news of

several hundred aged priests being thrown into the Loire, and particularly at the exclamation of Carrier, who communicated the intelligence, "What a revolutionary torrent is the Loire"—when these suggestions and narrations of murder, which have hitherto been only hinted and whispered in the most secret cabals, in the darkest caverns of banditti, were triumphantly uttered, patiently endured, and even loudly applauded by an assembly of seven hundred men, acting in the sight of all Europe, would my learned friend have wished that there had been found in England a single writer so base as to deliberate upon the most safe, decorous, and polite manner of relating all these things to his countrymen?

When Carrier ordered five hundred children under fourteen years of age to be shot, the greater part of whom escaped the fire from their size; when the poor victims ran for protection to the soldiers, and were bayoneted clinging around their knees! *would my friend*—but I cannot pursue the strain of interrogation. It is too much. It would be a violence which I cannot practice on my own feelings. It would be an outrage to my friend. It would be an insult to humanity. No! Better, ten thousand times better, would it be that every press in the world were burned; that the very use of letters were abolished; that we were returned to the honest ignorance of the rudest times, than that the results of civilization should be made subservient to the purposes of barbarism; than that literature should be employed to teach a toleration for cruelty, to weaken moral hatred for guilt, to deprave and brutalize the human mind. I know that I speak my friend's feelings as well as my own, when I say God forbid that the dread of any punishment should ever make any Englishman an accomplice in so corrupting his countrymen, a public teacher of depravity and barbarity!

Mortifying and horrible as the idea is, I must remind you, gentlemen, that even at that time, even under the reign of Robespierre, my learned friend, if he had then been attorney-general, might have been compelled, by some most deplorable necessity, to have come into this court to ask your verdict against the libelers of Barrère and Collot d'Herbois. Mr. Peltier then employed his talents against the enemies of the human race, as he has uniformly and bravely done. I do not believe that any peace, any political considerations, any fear of punishment would have silenced him. He has shown too much honor, and constancy, and intrepidity, to be shaken by such circumstances as these.

39

My learned friend might then have been compelled to have filed a criminal information against Mr. Peltier, for " wickedly and maliciously intending to vilify and degrade Maximilian Robespierre, President of the Committee of Public Safety of the French Republic." He might have been reduced to the sad necessity of appearing before you to belie his own better feelings, to prosecute Mr. Peltier for publishing those sentiments which my friend himself had a thousand times felt, and a thousand times expressed. He might have been obliged even to call for punishment upon Mr. Peltier for language which he and all mankind would forever despise Mr. Peltier if he were not to employ. Then, indeed, gentlemen, we should have seen the last humiliation fall on England; the tribunals, the spotless and venerable tribunals of this free country reduced to be the ministers of the vengeance of Robespierre! What could have rescued us from this last disgrace ? *The honesty and courage of a jury.* They would have delivered the judges of this country from the dire necessity of inflicting punishment on a brave and virtuous man, because he spoke truth of a monster. They would have despised the threats of a foreign tyrant, as their ancestors braved the power of oppression at home.

In the court where we are now met, Cromwell twice sent a satirist on his tyranny to be convicted and punished as a libeler; and in this court, almost in sight of the scaffold streaming with the blood of his sovereign, within hearing of the clash of his bayonets which drove out Parliament with contumely, two successive juries rescued the intrepid satirist [Lilburne] from his fangs, and sent out with defeat and disgrace the usurper's attorney-general from what he had the insolence to call *his* court! Even then, gentlemen, when all law and liberty were trampled under the feet of a military banditti; when those great crimes were perpetrated on a high place and with a high hand against those who were the objects of public veneration, which, more than anything else, break their spirits and confound their moral sentiments, obliterate the distinctions between right and wrong in their understanding, and teach the multitude to feel no longer any reverence for that justice which they thus see triumphantly dragged at the chariot-wheels of a tyrant; even then, when this unhappy country, triumphant, indeed, abroad, but enslaved at home, had no prospect but that of a long succession of tyrants wading through slaughter to a throne—*even then, I say, when all seemed lost, the unconquerable spirit of English liberty survived in the hearts of English jurors.* That spirit is, I trust in God, not extinct; and, if any modern tyrant were, in the drunkenness of his insolence, to hope to overawe an English jury, I trust and I believe that they would tell him: "Our ancestors braved the bayonets of Cromwell; we bid defiance to yours. *Contempsi Catiline gladios—non pertimescam tuos!*" [1]

What could be such a tyrant's means of overawing a jury? As long as their country exists, they are girt round with impenetrable armor. Till the destruction of their country, no danger can fall upon them for the performance of their duty, and I do trust that there is no Englishman so unworthy of life as to desire to outlive England. But, if any of us are condemned to the cruel punishment of surviving our country—if, in the inscrutable counsels of Providence, this favored seat of justice and liberty, this noblest work of human wisdom and virtue, be destined to destruction, which I shall not be charged with national prejudice for saying, would be the most dangerous wound ever inflicted on civilization; at least let us carry with us into our sad exile the consolation that we ourselves have not violated the rights of hospitality to exiles—that we have not torn from the altar the suppliant who claimed protection as the voluntary victim of loyalty and conscience.

Gentlemen, I now leave this unfortunate gentleman in your hands. His character and his situation might interest your humanity; but, on his behalf, I only ask justice from you. I only ask a favorable construction of what cannot be said to be more than ambiguous language, and this you will soon be told, from the highest authority, is a part of justice.

The attorney-general then closed the case for the Crown. He began by referring to the speech of the opposing counsel. He said: "In rising, gentlemen, "to address myself to you, on the part of the prosecution, after your attention "has been so long rivetted to one of the most splendid displays of eloquence I "ever had occasion to hear; after your understandings have been so long daz-"zled by the contemplation of that most splendid exhibition, I cannot but fear "that, whatever the feeble light of such understandings as mine present to you, I "can scarcely feel a hope of making any impression on your senses. And if I "felt, on this occasion, that there was any necessity to answer much of my "learned friend's speech, I should feel myself embarked in an undertaking in "which it was absolutely necessary I should fail." When he had finished

---

[1] "Defendi rempublicam adolescens; non deseram senex: contempsi Catilinæ gladios; non pertimescam tuos."—I defended the republic in my youth, I will not desert her in my age; I have despised the daggers of Catiline, and I shall not fear yours.—[Cicero to Anthony, at the close of his second oration against him.]

his address, Lord Ellenborough charged the jury strongly against the prisoner. He took occasion to say: " Gentlemen, I trust your verdict will strengthen the " relations by which the interests of this country are connected with those of " France, and that it will illustrate and justify, in every quarter of the world, the " conviction that has been long and universally entertained of the unsullied " purity of British judicature, and the impartiality by which their decisions are " uniformly governed." The jury, without retiring from the box, immediately returned a verdict of guilty.

SPEECH OF WILLIAM C. PLUNKET.

OPENING FOR THE CROWN IN REX v. FORBES AND OTHERS.—
CONSPIRACY AND RIOT.

IN THE COURT OF KING'S BENCH, DUBLIN, HILARY TERM,
3D GEORGE IV, FEBRUARY 3d, 1823.

ANALYSIS OF MR. PLUNKET'S SPEECH.

1. Nature of the offense charged.—Object of the prosecution.
2. Motive of the Attorney-General in filing an *ex officio* information.
3. The legality of the proceeding.
4. Statement of the case relied upon as a precedent.
5. The charges not intended as a protest against the Society of Orangemen.
6. Panegyric on William of Orange.
7. Political events in which the conspiracy had its origin.
8. William's campaign in Ireland conferred upon its people blessings in disguise.
9. The visit of George IV to Ireland.
10. Lord Wellesley commended.—Defense of his character.
11. The object of Lord Wellesley in preventing the decoration of King William's statue.
12. Legal methods resorted to as the only means of preventing it.
13. Narration of the facts constituting the charges against the defendants.
14. The action of the attorney-general an exercise of wise discretion.

About no figure in history have clustered such bitter memories and deadly feuds, as are associated with Macaulay's favorite hero, the Prince of Orange, afterwards William the Third. As no man has ever won more genuine and profound admiration and reverence, so none has ever occasioned more deep-seated and lasting animosities. The recollections of his campaign in Ireland are the fruitful theme of religious strife, which has been kept alive till our own time. No battle has ever been fought, the anniversary of which has been so enthusiastically observed, as the battle of the Boyne. It is celebrated in song as well as in story, and the stirring music is invariably the signal for violence and bloodshed. As often as the anniversary recurs, the calendars of criminal courts, not only in Ireland, but elsewhere, exhibit, as a legitimate sequel, numerous informations and indictments for murder and assault, and the unfortunate sufferers, go to swell the long list of killed and wounded, who have, from time to time, revived the memory of this famous engagement. And this spectacle, strange as it may seem, is frequently repeated on the 12th of July, in our country and in our own age.

It is also true that the political results of the battle of the Boyne are still felt in Ireland. Penal laws against Catholics have disgraced the English statute book for more than a century. Consequently Irish politics became, in one sense, narrowed to an issue between Catholics and Anti-Catholics; the friends of the

former, among whom were very many staunch Protestants, advocated the re-
moval of political disabilities from their oppressed countrymen, and demanded
the complete restoration of their civil and constitutional rights.

William Conyngham Plunket, the son of a Presbyterian minister, became
attached to the liberal party, and labored consistently throughout his long and
honorable career for Catholic emancipation. When George the Fourth came to
the throne, he paid a friendly visit to Ireland, and was received everywhere with
the most profound reverence and enthusiasm by men of all parties and sects.
He sent Lord Wellesley to Ireland, as Lord Lieutenant, and that minister determined to treat all men alike, without respect to creed or opinion. He desired, if possible, to break the ascendency of the Orange society, because he
believed that its custom of celebrating the achievements of King William tended
to keep fresh the bitterness of religious feuds.

In a public square in the city of Dublin, known as College Green, stands a
statue of William the Third. For years it had been the custom of the Orangemen to show their respect for the memory of the illustrious monarch by decorating this image on the 4th of November, in honor of his birth, and the 12th
of July, in honor of his victory at the Boyne. Lord Wellesley determined to
abolish these ceremonies, and finally resorted to legal methods to accomplish his
purpose. This course aroused the hatred and indignation of a certain element
of the Protestant community. In order to show their contempt for the Lord
Lieutenant, a number of Orangemen arranged to insult him publicly. They
seized the opportunity of his visit to the theatre. On the evening of December
14th, 1822, they early assembled in the galleries, and began to hiss and hoot as
soon as the Lord Lieutenant entered; and after he had taken his seat in the box,
hurled at him all sorts of missiles. One of the party threw an empty whisky
bottle, which struck the chair on which Lord Wellesley sat, and glanced off on
to the stage. From this circumstance the affair was known as the "bottle riot."
The parties were arrested, but such was the state of public feeling that the grand
jury threw out the indictments and refused to find a true bill against them.

Notwithstanding the popular sentiment, Mr. Plunket determined to sustain
the dignity of his friend, the Lord Lieutenant, and resolutely assumed the responsibility of filing, in his official capacity as attorney-general, an *ex officio*
information against the accused, under which they were brought to trial on the
3d of February, 1824, in the Court of King's Bench, in the city of Dublin.[1]

Lord Plunket, as a lawyer, was considered the leader of the Dublin bar at
its golden age; as an advocate he was comparable only with Erskine; as a statesman he ranked among the foremost of his age; as an orator he has not been surpassed by any of its contemporaries. " His oratory," says a writer in the *Edin-
burgh Review*, "was of a very high kind; in perfect mastery of the topics it
touched; in fullness and accuracy of information; in reasoning, not rapid and
vehement, but earnest, vigorous and sustained; in the dignity and propriety of
its diction, and in the occasional beauty of its illustrations—it has not been excelled in the British Senate." As a chancery lawyer he was unrivaled, and Sheil
has remarked, that his arguments in important equity causes were most extraordi-

---

[1] For a statement of the details of the charge, names of the prisoners, the
counsel, and the justices who presided, see *post*, pp. 641, 642.

nary exhibitions of human intellect. Through the tedious mazes of purely legal discussion, his poetical fancy never forsakes him, but enriches his speech, like exquisite gilding. The following, from one of his arguments, illustrates his delicate fancy. Referring to the wisdom of the rule that long possession raises a legal presumption as to the validity of the title, he said: " Time is the great destroyer of evidence, but he is also the great protector of titles. If he comes with a scythe in one hand to mow down the muniments of our possessions, he holds an hourglass in the other from which he incessantly metes out the portions of duration that are to render those muniments no longer necessary."

His speech on the present occasion contains many beautiful and striking illustrations, and displays his wonderful skill and ability as an advocate. In order not to make his remarks odious to the majority, he abstains from fierce denunciation against the Orange societies, and pays a tribute to the memory of King William, which, for graceful and elegant expression, is worthy of his great powers as an advocate and orator. This case is rendered more interesting from the fact that his conduct in presenting the *ex officio* information against the accused, after the grand jury had refused to find a bill, was made the subject of a motion for a vote of censure in the House of Commons, and Plunket's vindication on that occasion was complete and overwhelming. He literally carried everything before him, and his address in his own defense has been regarded as one of the most impassioned specimens of eloquence ever delivered in Parliament. He closed with these simple words: " My public conduct and private character have been alike assailed. I will retire, so that the House may more freely and unrestrainedly consider the question. My public conduct I consign to the justice of this House; my private character I leave to its honor." In opening for the Crown, Mr. Plunket said :

My Lords, and Gentlemen of the Jury:—It becomes now my duty to lay before you the case on behalf of the Crown, and to put you in possession of the grounds on which the present prosecution has been instituted, and of the evidence by which it is intended to be supported. It has often been my lot, in the eventful history of this country, to appear in the character of a public prosecutor, and still more frequently to be a witness of the course and conduct of public prosecutions. But certainly never in my life have I approached a court of justice with sensations of more deep anxiety, or with a more intense feeling of the importance of the subject to be decided on, than I feel at the present moment. It is a case, my Lords and gentlemen, not touching the life of the parties; the offense as laid amounting only to a misdemeanor. It is undoubtedly, however, to them a case of no small importance; involving them, if the facts charged be proved, in very heavy penal consequences. But with respect to the public at large, it is a case of as deep and vital importance, as for the last fifty years has been brought under the consideration of a court and of a jury. It is a great satisfaction to me, and a great part of my object has been achieved in knowing that this case is now ready to be brought fully before an intelligent court and jury; and that, whatever its merits may be, it is impossible they can be stifled or extinguished, but must be fairly brought under the consideration of the court, the jury, and the public.

I. Nature of the offense charged.—Object of the prosecution.

The charge is one of no light or ordinary character. You are already, my Lords, probably apprized of it from public rumor; the nature of it has been more particularly stated by my learned friend who has opened the informations. It imports no less a crime than having assaulted the person of the king's representative in this country; of having committed a riot in his presence for the purpose of insulting him; and of having done so in pursuance of a deliberate conspiracy previously entered into for the purpose.

This is a charge which ought not lightly to be made; and one, gentlemen, on which you ought not to act, unless fully and distinctly proved. But I should consider it as an insult to your character and understandings, to urge any argument to establish the enormity of the crime, if fully ascertained to have been committed. I should blush for our country, were it necessary to state in a court of justice, that a deliberate insult of the king's representative, in a public theatre, the result of a previous conspiracy, is no light or trivial or ordinary offense. In the mind of every man who has not banished the feelings of a gentleman, and who is not lost to every public and private consideration, there can be but one sentiment— a deep sense of indignity at the outrage, and an entire conviction of the necessity of vindicating the national character and the dignity of the laws, by affixing punishment, if deserved.

But, my Lords, daring and unexampled as is the crime, I hesitate not to say, that the enormity of the act is lost in the boldness and description of the motives. I fairly tell you that I come not here on the part of Lord Wellesley, to ask for personal redress, or even to call for public justice so far as he is personally concerned; not even on the part of the Lord Lieutenant of Ireland, to seek atonement for the outrage committed against the king's representative; but on behalf of the country and its laws; on behalf of its hopes of peace and safety; to claim your aid, backed by all the authority of opinion, in putting down a desperate and insolent attempt to overawe the king's government in Ireland; and to compel his representative, by the arm of personal violence and by the demonstration of a force above the law, to change the measures of his government. I call on you to put down a base conspiracy of a contemptible gang, who have associated to put down the laws and to overbear the king's representative, because he has presumed to execute the king's commands. I think I know the feelings of the illustrious personage against whom this villainy has been directed; with respect to his own personal safety, much as it has been endangered, the attack was fitted only to rouse his gallant mettle; indignant as he must have felt to be "hawked at" by such "mousing" owls as these, their base attempt excited no terror, it left no resentment. That there should have been in this land hearts capable of conceiving, and hands capable of executing, such an outrage against their countryman, must have excited sensations of regret and pain; but in this respect the national character has been redeemed by the universal expression of indignation which has issued from the hearts of the Irish people.

But, beyond all this, much remains to be done: it is necessary to put down the daring pretensions of those who have associated themselves for the purpose of defying the king and the law, and setting up an authority superior to them both. They and all others who announce such projects, must be taught that their plans are vain and hopeless, as they are insolent.

This I freely avow as my object. I trust that no unworthy prejudices, that no angry feeling, that no sentiment other than that which belongs to the conscientious discharge of public duty, has been suffered to mingle itself in the course of public justice. I shall go away from this court, humiliated and under the heavy sentence of self-reproach, if, after the evidence in this case shall have been disclosed, any honest or impartial man shall censure me for instituting this prosecution; or shall hesitate to think that it would have been a mean abandonment of duty to have shrunk from it.

2. MOTIVE OF THE ATTORNEY-GENERAL IN FILING AN EX OFFICIO INFORMATION.

You are apprized, my Lords, that this is an *ex officio* information filed by his majesty's attorney-general upon his own authority; you are also probably aware, that this *ex officio* information has been filed after bills had been preferred against the same persons for the same offense, and had been ignored by a grand jury of the

country. Before I proceed to trouble your lordships with any observation upon the exact nature and on the legality of this proceeding, I wish to disembarrass the case of a few topics which may attach to it. In the proceeding which I have thought it my duty to
institute, though I have been governed by my strong impression
that public justice had not been effected, I do not involve in this
conclusion any imputation on the sheriff who returned the grand
jury, still less on the grand jury themselves who have acted on their
oaths in throwing out those bills. For the purposes of the present
trial, whatever opinions I may entertain on that subject, I have no
right to advert to them. The sheriff who returned that grand jury
is not on his trial, and it would be gross injustice to arraign his
conduct when he cannot defend it. The grand jury are not on
their trials, and it would be injustice equally gross to make a charge
against them where they can have no opportunity of vindicating
themselves. A time may come and an occasion may arise in which
these considerations may be proper and necessary; and most certainly I will not, in that event, be found wanting to the discharge
of any duty, however painful, which may devolve on me. But in
the meantime, and with reference to the present proceeding, I wish
distinctly to be understood as disclaiming all imputations upon
either. I am ready to suppose, for the purposes of this trial, that
if the parties and the cause were the exact reverse of what they now
are; that if it had been the pleasure of the government to direct
that the statue of King William should be dressed on the 4th of
November, and a body of Roman Catholics, feeling themselves insulted, had risen against the law and the magistracy, and had flung
a bottle or other missile at the Lord Lieutenant's head, and these
facts had been before the grand jury, they would have ignored the
bills; as, so help me God, I would, under the same circumstances,
had I remained the king's attorney-general, have filed my information *ex officio*. I claim only for myself equal credit for the purity
of my motives and the fair discharge of my sworn duty.

3. THE LEGALITY OF THE PROCEEDING.

I am told that it has been alleged that this proceeding on the
part of the attorney-general, by an *ex officio* information, is illegal.
I do not know whether what has been said in this respect has been
rightly reported; or whether it is meant that the proceeding is in
point of law invalid, or that the resorting to it, though a legal right,
is not a fair exercise of discretion. I am led naturally, without

going out of the pleadings, to make a few observations upon this part of the subject; for although all the traversers have put in pleas amounting to not guilty, yet two of them have thought proper to put upon the record what cannot properly belong to that plea—a sort of preamble or inducement, in which they state that those informations have been filed against them after a grand jury had ignored bills for the same charge. My learned friends, who framed those defenses, knew perfectly well that on that allegation no issue could be joined, either of law or of fact. It amounts, therefore, to nothing else than a plea of not guilty. But I presume they thought it might be made use of (though scarcely to your lordships or the jury whom I address) to swell the cry which amongst the vulgar of the public has been raised against the legality of this proceeding.

I think that on that subject I need occupy but little time in addressing the court before which I have now the honor to appear. What I am about to say is rather with a view to set right the public mind, and that it should be known that I have stated, in the presence of this enlightened court, what is the law upon this subject. I assert, then, that the ignoring of a bill by a grand jury is, according to the known and established principles of our law, no bar to any subsequent legal proceeding against the same individual for the same offense. It is competent to the Crown or the prosecutor to send up another bill to the same or any other grand jury; and the same power belongs to that public authority in which is vested the right of filing an information. A party who has been already tried may protect himself against a subsequent prosecution for the same offense. He may do so by plea. It is a principle of our law that no man shall be twice tried for the same offense. If he has been already acquitted, there is a known legal form of pleading as old as the law itself, by which he can defend himself. But it is settled by authorities coeval with the law itself, that the plea of *autrefois acquit* is not supported by evidence that a bill of indictment for the same offense has been preferred to a grand jury, and ignored. It must be an acquittal by a petit jury. Your lordships would consider it a waste of time to refer to authorities in support of such a position. It is laid down by Lord Hale, Lord Coke, and every writer on the subject of Crown law. I shall not consume time by adverting to cases for recognition of known principles. The thing can only be doubted by those who are ignorant of our laws and Constitution. That another indictment could be sent up is clear; and I think I go a good way to show its legality by calling upon those who deny it, to show me any form of pleading by which it can be resisted. There is no legal right belonging to any subject of this realm, which the law has not afforded him a mode of setting forth; and, therefore, if there be no form of pleading (and if there were such, my learned friends, in whose hands the interests of the traversers are so effectually secured, would have discovered it) by which the throwing out of a bill by a grand jury may be set up as a bar to a subsequent information, that is in itself a full proof of the legality of such a proceeding. They have, indeed, distinctly admitted it by putting in pleas not denying the competence of the attorney-general to file, or of the court to entertain, the present information, but asserting their innocence of the charge imputed to them. In an ordinary case, not affecting the rights of the Crown, this court is in the habit of granting criminal informations. The right formerly exercised by the master in the Crown office has been narrowed by statute, and is now subject to the discretion of the court. Has it ever been heard of that the Court of King's Bench would refuse an information because a grand jury had ignored the bill ?

So much trash has been circulated, and the public mind so much abused upon this subject, that I hope your lordships will excuse my calling your attention to it. So far from its being considered an objection that a grand jury has ignored the bill, it is often a reason why the Court of King's Bench grants an information. I have often applied for liberty to file an information, when I had the honor of practicing in this court; and the court has asked me whether I had tried a grand jury, saying, that if they refused to find a bill, they would then entertain the application. The Court of King's Bench in England, in the last term, granted an information in a case where bills had been twice ignored by a grand jury, and because they had been ignored. So far, therefore, is that circumstance from being considered an objection to putting a party on his trial, that it is frequently insisted upon as a requisite condition. Thus it is where application is made to the Court of King's Bench. This is an information filed by the sworn officer of the Crown, in whom the law has vested that privilege. Were I to come in as attorney-general, and apply for liberty to file an information against these parties, what would be your lordships' answer ? The same as was given by my Lord Mansfield to De Grey, and I think to Sir Fletcher Norton, namely: "We will not file an information at your suit; the law has made you the sole judge of its propriety; if you think it proper, you have a right to file it; if not, why should we do so ?" I am

not now applying myself to the soundness of this exercise of discretion, but to the new-fangled notion of the illegality of this information. It is the privilege of the lowest subject in the realm,
if by the error or impropriety of a grand jury he do not obtain
justice, to apply to the Court of King's Bench for a criminal information; but the king, it is said, is to be in a totally different
situation; and though for an offense indictable the court would
grant an information because a grand jury has ignored the bill, the
sovereign himself shall not have that redress which is open to the
meanest of his subjects. A proposition, this, too monstrous to bear
debate. I am asked for an authority; permit me to say, this is not
quite a fair requisition. Where a circumstance is totally immaterial, it is not to be expected that it should be the subject of notice; and therefore we are not to be surprised, if in the greater
number of reported cases of informations it should not appear
whether a grand jury had previously thrown out bills or not. Such
a fact would be totally immaterial. It cannot be stated in a plea;
it could not be proved in evidence, and therefore it would be too
much to say, that, because it is not mentioned, the case had not existed.

4. STATEMENT OF THE CASE RELIED UPON AS A PRECEDENT.

It has been my principle to hold in utter contempt the vile and
scurrilous publications which have been circulated through the
city, in order to prejudge the matters to be tried and affect the
characters of the persons employed as public functionaries. But
I have, by the generosity of some of their authors, been furnished
with a case directly in point, in which, by accident, the fact of bills
having been ignored by the grand jury before the information filed
does distinctly appear.

I shall detail the facts as they appear in the Commons' Journals.
In the latter end of the reign of Queen Anne, in the year 1713, on
King William's birth-day, the play of Tamerlane was to be represented. King Wiliiam, as your lordships are aware, was compared
to Tamerlane, and very deservedly so, if the possession of every
virtue that could ennoble a monarch entitled him to the distinction.
The name of Tamerlane had been connected with his. A prologue
to the play, written by Doctor Garth, was very generally repeated
at the time. The Doctor, it seems, was more happy as a poet than
as a courtier, and his reverence for King William led him to compliment that monarch in terms not sufficiently guarded to avoid

giving offense to Queen Anne. The government, therefore, thought it right that the prologue should not be repeated. When the play, therefore, came on for representation, the actor omitted to repeat it, and by so doing gave great offense to the audience. They were full of respect for the memory of William, and did not wish that attention to Queen Anne should break in on the ancient practice. Mr. Dudley Moore, a zealous Protestant, who was in the house, leaped upon the stage and repeated the prologue. This gave rise to something like a riot. The government indicted Mr. Moore for the riot. The bills were sent up to a grand jury, who returned a true bill, and were then dismissed. In about half an hour after, the foreman came into court and made an affidavit that *billa vera* was a mistake, and that they meant to return *ignoramus.* The court refused to receive his affidavit; but then came in the three and twenty, and swore positively to the same fact to which their foreman had deposed. The party was, notwithstanding this, in my opinion very unwisely, put to plead to the indictment. But the attorney-general, thinking it would be hard to compel him to plead when the bill had been in fact ignored, moved to quash the indictment, which was done.

Do I overstate the matter when I say, that things were then in the same situation as if the bill had been ignored by the grand jury? And yet, under these circumstances, the attorney-general thought himself at liberty to file an *ex officio* information against the same person for the same offense. Sir Constantine Phipps, who was then Lord Chancellor, and one of the Lords Justices, was considered by many as a great Tory and Jacobite, and as an enemy to the Protestant interest. History has done more justice to him in that respect than in the heat of party he received from his contemporaries. He interfered with the prosecution; he sent for the Lord Mayor and lectured him as to the mode in which he was to conduct himself. He was even supposed to have interfered with the return of the jury. The whole matter was brought before the House of Commons, who addressed the throne to remove Sir Constantine Phipps for intermeddling in the trial. No fault was found with the information though directly before them, but the trial was treated as legally depending, and a petition presented against the Chancellor for interfering with that trial. Do I not here show a case in which an *ex officio* information had been filed after a bill had been thrown out, and where though the zeal of a party generated an anxiety to lay hold of anything that could warrant an imputation on the proceeding? as the information filed was never questioned, but the Chancellor and Chief Governor petitioned against for interfering with the proceeding.

5. THE CHARGES NOT INTENDED AS A PROTEST AGAINST THE SOCIETY OF ORANGEMEN.

I shall not trouble your lordships farther upon the legality of this proceeding. With respect to the soundness of the exercise of my discretion under the circumstances, in resorting to the prerogative right, I shall reserve myself until I shall have laid before the court and the jury the facts which will be proved in the case. I have already said, that I will prove that an attempt has been made by a gang in this city for the purpose of controlling the law and putting down the authority of the king's lieutenant. It is unfortunately necessary to show, that the individuals concerned in this outrage are persons belonging to a society known by the name of the Orange Society. But it is particularly necessary, gentlemen of the jury, that you and the court, and the public, should understand what was formerly uttered by me, and what I now repeat. I am desirous of expressly stating, that with the general nature of the Orange societies in relation to the laws, the interests and happiness of the country, I have on this trial nothing to do. Upon this subject I have my opinions, which at a proper place and season I shall not shrink from avowing. But with the present investigation they have no concern. I do believe in my conscience, that the greater proportion of the persons associated in that society feel as strong and lofty a contempt for those concerned in this disgraceful attack as I do, and are as incapable of participating, authorizing, vindicating, or palliating it. Every public man must expect to be the subject of no very candid criticism. I wish distinctly to have it understood, that this is no after-thought of mine, for the purpose of qualifying expressions either inadvertently or too strongly used. Had I applied these expressions indiscriminately to the Orangemen of Ireland, I should have violated my duty and stepped beyond that line of conducting this prosecution which was distinctly agreed upon between me and the eminent and respectable persons by whom I have been advised. I am glad to take this opportunity once for all, of returning my thanks to my learned colleague, by whose high talents, enlightened information and extensive knowledge I have been assisted in every stage of this proceeding, and to whose cordial zeal and co-operation no terms can be too strong to render justice and express my gratitude.

6. Panegyric on William of Orange.

My Lords, I am anxious to proceed to an immediate statement of the facts in this case, and to disperse that mass of scurrility and falsehood which for some weeks past has disgraced this city. I must, however, first trespass on your time with some preliminary observations.

It is impossible to lay this case truly before the public without briefly reverting to the political events in which the conspiracy originated. The foundations of it were laid so long back as the period when his majesty was pleased to honor this country with his presence.

It is not, my Lords, my intention to occupy your time by attempting a description of what took place on that occasion. From the minds of those who witnessed the transaction, the splendor and glory of that day never can be effaced. To those who have not, no powers of mine can give an adequate description. It falls to me to have the less pleasing task of remarking, that even then some indications were to be found that his majesty's gracious dispositions were not likely to be met with that degree of gratitude and respect to which they were entitled; and that, even before he left the Irish shore, the elements of mischief were at work. It was understood that the king, before he honored the Mansion House with his presence, had signified his desire that the glorious memory should not be given as a toast. I must entreat your excuse, my Lords (it connects itself intimately with the matter of this trial), if I advert more particularly to this topic, and endeavor to disabuse the public mind upon the subject.

Perhaps, my Lords, there is not to be found in the annals of history a character more truly great than that of William the Third. Perhaps no person has ever appeared on the theatre of the world, who has conferred more essential or more lasting benefits on mankind; on these countries certainly none. When I look at the abstract merits of his character, I contemplate him with admiration and reverence. Lord of a petty principality; destitute of all resources but those with which nature had endowed him; regarded with jealousy and envy by those whose battles he fought; thwarted in all his counsels; embarrassed in all his movements; deserted in his most critical enterprise; he continued to mould all those discordant materials, to govern all these warring interests, and merely by the force of his genius, the ascendancy of his integrity, and the unmovable firmness and constancy of his nature, to combine them into an indissoluble alliance against the schemes of despotism and universal domination of the most powerful monarch in Europe, seconded by the ablest generals, at the head of the bravest and best disciplined armies in the world, and wielding, without check or control, the unlimited resources of his empire. He was not a consummate general; military men will point out his errors; in that respect fortune did not favor him, save by throwing the lustre of adversity over all his virtues. He sustained defeat after defeat, but always rose *adversa rerum immersabilis unda.* Looking merely at his shining qualities and achievements, I admire him as I do a Scipio, a Regulus, a Fabius; a model of tranquil courage, undeviating probity, and armed with a resoluteness and constancy in the cause of truth and freedom, which rendered him superior to the accidents that control the fate of ordinary men.

7. Political events in which the conspiracy had its origin.

But this is not all. I feel that to him, under God, I am at this moment indebted for the enjoyment of the rights which I possess as a subject of these free countries. To him I owe the blessings of civil and religious liberty, and I venerate his memory with a fervor of devotion suited to his illustrious qualities and to his godlike acts.

Did our gracious sovereign come here to trample on the memory of the most illustrious of his predecessors? No, my Lords; the high errand on which he landed on our shores was worthy of him, and bespoke a kindred mind to that of the immortal personage whose name and character he vindicated. He knew that the whole life of King William was a continued struggle against intolerance; that the policy of his reign was opposed, and his most favorite objects for the peace and happiness of his people were baffled by the folly and bigotry of those who surrounded him; and that the career of his glorious life was obstructed, as the lustre of his glorious memory has been tarnished, by the absurd and intolerant dogmatism of those who were rescued by his exertions from that yoke which they sought, in opposition to his eager wishes, to impose on others. It was the unhappy but inevitable result of the circumstances in which the people of this unfortunate country were placed, that they had to meet that great man, not as subjects but as enemies.

The peculiar good fortune of the British people was, that every feeling of religion corresponded with their innate love of freedom to alienate them from the cause of the exiled monarch. His designs, his determinations against their civil and religious liberties, were notorious and unalterable. An inflexible bigot and despot, he was too intense in both characters to endure the appearance of a compromise with toleration or with freedom. Yet every man knows through what difficulties and dangers they had to struggle before the house of Brunswick was firmly seated on the throne. Even with the full tide of religion running in their favor, the principle of loyalty to an hereditary succession was so indigenous to British character, that it was not until after the lapse of nearly a century that the principles of Jacobitism were finally subdued.

8. William's campaign in Ireland conferred upon its people blessings in disguise.

But in unhappy Ireland the exiled king was the professor and patron of the religion to which they were enthusiastically devoted. He must be a preposterous critic who will impute as a crime to that unhappy people, that they did not rebel against their lawful king, because he was of their own religion, even if they had been so fully admitted to the blessings of the British Constitution as to render them equally alive to the value of freedom. They seem, therefore, by the nature of things, almost necessarily thrown into a state of resistance. Nothing could have saved them from it but so strong a love of abstract freedom as might subdue the principles of loyalty and the feelings of religion. No candid man can lay so heavily on poor human nature, nor fairly say that he thinks worse of the Roman Catholic for having on that day abided by his lawful sovereign and his ancient faith. What was the result? They were conquered; conquered into freedom and happiness—a freedom and happiness to which the successful result of their ill-fated struggles would have been destructive. There is no rational Roman Catholic in Ireland who does not feel this to be the fact. Even the name of the exiled family is now unknown; the throne rests on the firm basis of the unanimous recognition of the entire people. The memory of their unfortunate struggles is lost in the conviction of the reality of those blessings which have been derived from their results equally to the conqueror and to the conquered. What wise or good man can feel a pleasure in recalling to the minds of a people so circumstanced the fact that they have been conquered? What but the spirit of folly and of mischief can take a satisfaction in interrupting them in the enjoyment of the blessings of their defeat, by taunting them with the recollection that they were defeated? Why is conquest desirable to any one but the Trooper? Because it opens the way to peace and harmony; but to those I have now to deal with, the fruits of the conquest are valueless, without the perpetuation of the triumph.

He is a mischievous man who desires to remind the people of this country that they are a conquered people. He is a mischievous man who, for the gratification of his own whim, desires to celebrate, in the midst of that people, the anniversary of their conquest. Never was there a subject more loudly calling for and justifying the gracious and saving interposition of the royal wisdom.

9. THE VISIT OF GEORGE IV TO IRELAND.

In the history of royal lives, there seldom has occurred an instance affording a more gratifying subject for the historian to dwell on, than the royal visit to Ireland. The statement of splendid victories, the development of profound schemes of policy, the application of able counsels and of powerful resources, the defense of the liberties of the world—all these are the subjects of historic detail, and may be the fair subjects of political controversy. But here, by the mere impulse of his own feelings, the heartiness of his nature, a moment was created in which, without calling on any of the common places of royalty, without the aid of force, or fear, or flattery; without arms, or power, or patronage; by the mere indulgence of his kind and generous nature, he gained to himself the most exalted privileges which a human being can exercise—that of bestowing happiness on, and sharing it with, millions of his fellow-creatures. The promptness with which this moment was seized; the gracious and condescending manner by which it was improved; the thousand and ten thousand blessings which are derived from it —all these may be subjects of just applause and of sober criticism. But here the true value of the act is its simplicity. To enter into the hearts and become master of the enthusiastic affections of an entire people, merely by showing himself the friend and father of them all, was a felicity to him and them unparalleled in the eventful history of this nation. It was worthy of a successor of the great monarch whose talents and virtues he emulated, and whose memory he rescued from the disgraceful orgies by which it had been tarnished. Equal in the motive and the feeling—happier in this that the hard fortune of William the Third compelled him to visit this country as a conqueror; but it was reserved for the peculiar felicity of George the Fourth, that he was the first British king who ever placed a friendly footstep upon the Irish soil.

I have already had occasion to remark, that the intimation of his majesty's pleasure on the subject of public concord was not perfectly agreeable to a certain portion of his subjects. Some little clouds were seen flitting along the horizon, which indicated the probability of a future storm. How far the government of the country were enabled to act on the personal recommendation and parting injunction of the king—what were the difficulties the Irish government had to encounter; what were the means they used to surmount them—these are matters which do not belong to the present subject.

10. Lord Wellesley commended.—Defense of his character.

I pass to the period of Lord Wellesley's arrival in this country. He found a great portion of the South of Ireland in a state of licentiousness, surpassing the worst excesses of former unhappy times. He had to deal with dangerous and secret conspiracies in other parts of the country. In what manner the Lord Lieutenant applied the powerful energies of his great mind to meet these complicated difficulties does not fall within the compass or limit of this trial. It would ill suit with my notions of what is due to the Marquis Wellesley, and of his temper and character, to offer up the suspicious praises which an Irish attorney-general is supposed bound to tender to the Lord Lieutenant. I am too sensible of the well-formed taste of this illustrious person, not to be convinced that he would reject with disdain the vulgar incense of official adulation, if I could stoop to offer it. No, my Lords, it would be an unsuited return for the kindness, the confidence, I will presume to say the friendship with which he has honored me; I know too well his lofty feelings and noble nature, *cui male si palpere, recalcitrat undique tutus;* but I will not be deterred by the apprehension of a suspicion which I disdain, and to which I trust the character of my life renders me superior, from expressing my sentiments of that exalted personage when he has become the object of vulgar scurrility, and when an open and desperate attack is made upon his person and his government. I will not be deterred from saying, that, had our gracious sovereign surveyed the extent of his dominions in search of one fitted to execute the magnificent purposes of benevolence to his people with which his royal breast was filled, he could not have found a person whom the gifts of nature, improved by every noble art, and mellowed by a long and arduous experience in the most difficult exigencies of this great empire, so eminently qualified for the task; or one whose heart so entirely and cordially vibrated in unison with the gracious and paternal interest which was felt for the welfare of his native land. That noble peer entered on the government of this country under this royal instruction; he had to explore a very difficult and dangerous and untried path, but he had the parting admonition and the renewed injunctions of his sovereign for his pole star. He entered on that government, carefully distinguishing his opinions and duties as a politician and a legislator, from those which necessarily involved the system of government of the country committed to him. Never abandoning, but carefully distinguishing his individual opinion from his official duties, he applied himself strictly and exclusively to effectuate the orders of the king, by the equal administration of the existing laws, and by the promotion of peace, happiness and concord among all the various classes of his subjects. I defy the malignity of criticism to point out a false move in the government of that noble person; one instance in which he departed from the spirit of that mission of conciliation which was confided to him; an act or an expression calculated to excite offense or disapprobation in the mind of any honest man or lover of his country, be his sect or his party what it may. Pursuing his clear and undeviating course, raised above all party, the laws for his guide, and the public happiness for his object, his fame is independent of the praise of his friends and above the malice of his enemies; it is our business, my Lords, to guard his person and his government against their secret machinations and their open violence.

The discontinuance of the public insults to which I have already alluded, and which had been so highly disapproved of by the king, necessarily had a place in the system of the Lord Lieutenant. The offensive toast which had been renewed in the presence of the late Lord Lieutenant was withheld in the presence of Lord Wellesley. I grieve to say that a spirit of mutiny and dissatisfaction on this subject was giddily and rashly encouraged by many who knew and ought to have reverenced the king's commands. The Lord

Lieutenant, however highly he disapproved the giving the toast on public occasions, did not think it became him to take any further step, having taken care that the king's authority should not, in his presence, be insulted by it. Another subject, or rather another part of the same subject, called his attention.

11. The object of Lord Wellesley in preventing the decoration of King William's statue.

The statue of King William, you all know, has been, for some years back, bedaubed with ridiculous painting and tawdry orange colors—a ludicrous specimen of bad taste, with which, however, his excellency did not feel himself called on to intermeddle. But, beyond this, a set of low persons, whose names were not avowed, had been for some years back in the habit of mounting the statue in the night of the 3d of November and of the 11th of July, and putting on it a fantastic drapery of orange scarfs, in themselves ridiculous, if they had not been meant as a mark of triumph over a certain portion of their fellow-subjects. This being done by a party of sworn Orangemen, and for the avowed purpose of insult, had been resented by the Roman Catholics whom it was intended to insult; and on the 12th of July last a serious riot had occurred, the insulted party conceiving that they had as good a right to un-dress, as the other had to dress, the statue of King William. In the course of this affray lives had been endangered, the peaceable inhabitants of College Green seriously alarmed, the tranquillity of the metropolis disturbed, and evil passions of the most furious kind engendered in the minds of the parties. It is obvious that one of these three courses was to be pursued. Either the dressers of the statue were to be protected by public force and the constituted au-thorities; or they were to be forbidden and prevented; or the par-ties were to be left to fight it out, till outrage, riot and bloodshed arrived at such a height that the civil power must act against both. I have never heard it distinctly stated, or that it was distinctly stated by any person, that either the first or the last of these courses ought to have been proved; either that the public authori-ties should have been called to assist the nightly party in making the toilet of King William, and to apprehend any person who should presume to interrupt them; or that the streets of the capital should be disgraced by the continuance of these senseless brawls. The first question on which his Excellency had to satisfy his mind was, whether the continuance of the practice of dressing the statue might, under such circumstances, be legally prevented.

He was advised that it clearly might; that these mummers had no right to lay their hands on this public ornament, whether for the purpose of decoration or dedecoration. Gentlemen, I remember that, on one occasion, a set of ruffians mounted this statue and daubed it over with lampblack. Neither they nor any other persons had a right to meddle with the public ornaments, either to adorn or to disgrace them. But, independently of this, his Excellency was advised that this being proposed to be done, not in discharge of any acknowledged duty, or in the prosecution of any known business, or in the exercise of any right of property or franchise, either by grant or usage, and being found by experience to have a tendency to produce, and to have actually produced, a breach of the peace, and it being proved on oath that it had done so, and that its continuance excited well-grounded apprehensions for the safety of their persons in the minds of the king's subjects residing in the neighborhood, several of whom, persons of known respectability, and Protestants too, had made affidavit to that effect, his Excellency was advised that he would be well warranted in using the civil force to prevent the dressing of the statue.

I am ashamed to think that it should be necessary to say, in a court of justice, that they were Protestants. I say this, because there are persons weak enough to imagine that the oath of a Catholic is not to be attended to on this subject, and because it has been untruly stated that these were affidavits of Catholics of the lower order. I owe an apology to the good sense and feeling of the court and the jury, for stating what their religion was; it is a disgrace to our country that such topics should be adverted to. Gentlemen, I have been public prosecutor in this country, at a period when the passions of men were most alive; and never in the course of my official experience have I given any other advice to the solicitor for the crown, than to select honest and fair men, without reference to their religious opinions, and I have never felt myself disappointed in the result; and therefore you will not suppose that the circumstance of these persons being Protestants was necessary to prop their credit in my estimation.

I am glad to have this opportunity of stating, that being called on in the discharge of my sworn duty for my opinion, I gave it as I have stated, and I challenge any man who respects his character as a constitutional lawyer to correct its soundness. It is no light matter to charge the executive government with acting contrary to law against any portion of the people; it begets in their minds the notion that, in resisting the civil authorities, they are resisting not law but power. Such a course is calculated to bring the government of the country into contempt; and when the acts so spoken of have been done in pursuance of the king's instructions, it is a violation of the personal respect which is due to him, independently of its tendency, to weaken the authority of his government in this country.

His Excellency was, independently of any respect which his kindness might dispose him to attach to the opinion of his law adviser, perfectly satisfied of the illegality of the practice in question; and I am authorized to take this public opportunity of stating, that having communicated on the subject with the king's government in England, he was sanctioned by their unanimous opinion in using the civil power for the prevention of these illegal practices. I am further authorized to state, that since his Excellency adopted the measures which are so publicly known for the carrying that opinion into effect, his conduct has received the unanimous approbation of the entire British cabinet, and has, above all, been crowned by the highest reward which a subject can receive for the faithful discharge of his duty, the personal approbation of his sovereign, whose commands he executed and whose government he sustained.

12. Legal methods resorted to as the only means of preventing it.

Before his Excellency resorted to any public means for the suppression of this practice, he tried every expedient, by persuasion and remonstrance, to obviate the necessity of public interference. It is but justice to say, that many, very many of the principal persons who were supposed to have an influence over the Orange associations did exert their authority for the purpose; but whatever were their exertions, they were unavailing; they found they could not govern the party with whom they had associated themselves. So must it ever be when rank and station and education condescend to combine in a secret bond with the vulgar and the ignorant. They must not expect to govern them; so long as they run in the same course of party and opinion, they may be suffered to lead; but in vain will they endeavor to alter the direction or moderate the violence. When the evil spirit is unchained and let loose, the spell that raised it will be unavailing to allay it—for the pur-

poses of a greater excitement they may be powerful and dangerous; for those of repression and restraint altogether impotent. The
lower classes of these persons declared they would disobey the
Lord Mayor's proclamation, and resist the magistrates. Furious
and absurd speeches were made at public meetings, filled with
vulgar invectives against the constituted authorities; and preparations were made for resistance to the law. The dressing of the
statue on the night of the third and day of the fourth of November was prevented; but on subsequent nights, particularly on the
night of the sixth of November, several of the party assembled for
the purpose, and were not dispersed without considerable disturbance
and difficulty. On this occasion the traverser Henry Handwich
was particularly active; he headed a party who arrayed themselves
against the magistracy for the purpose of dressing the statue. He
was, it seems, the regular manteau-maker to King William. He collected subscriptions on the night between the fifth and sixth of
November; he mounted on the statue, and nailed upon it the
tawdry ornaments with which he was furnished. With some difficulty he and his party were suppressed; they were dispersed before
morning. Two or three similar attempts were afterwards made,
but the firmness of the magistrates was sufficient to put them down.

In this situation of affairs, the Lord Lieutenant availed himself
of the first opportunity which the various claims of public care allowed him, to announce his intention of honoring the Theater
Royal with his presence. A play was accordingly announced, and
notice given.

13. Narration of the facts constituting the charges against the defendants.

I shall now state the facts of this case, which will be so clearly
proved, and placed so far beyond all doubt, that no gentleman
whom I have the honor of seeing in that jury box, can leave it
with a doubt upon his mind as to the real nature of the transaction.
Certain persons met together, and conceived that this would be a
good opportunity of marking their public indignation against the
Marquis Wellesley, for presuming to enforce the king's command in
forbidding the dressing of the statue. One of those persons, gentlemen (melancholy, if this be so, is the situation of the Lord
Lieutenant), holds high situations under the king's government, a
place in the post office, and another in the customs, producing
nearly £800 a year. I allude to a man named William Heron.

This person, and another of the name of M'Culloch, who holds a situation in the Meath hospital; a man named Atkinson, holding a situation in the Custom House, and others, on the night of Wednesday or the morning of the Thursday before the play, consulted as to the best means of dealing with the subject. The result they came to was, that this would be a proper opportunity for acting in the theater in such a manner as to evince the unpopularity of the Lord Lieutenant and his government, and make it necessary for him to leave the house, and eventually to leave the country. It was determined that a subscription should be raised to purchase tickets. Well knowing that the true expression of the public sentiment would be strong in favor of his Excellency, they resolved, in order to thwart it, to collect a party and pack the theater. They thought the persons who were associated would of themselves be sufficient for the pit and the middle gallery; but that, for the inferior orders, seats must be purchased. Accordingly a subscription of £2 was collected by Heron and sent by him to Atkinson. This was to be communicated to an Orange lodge, assembled at the house of one Daly, in Werburgh street, in what is called the Purple Order of the lodge. That, gentlemen, is not conferred upon any person until he has been for a certain time a member of the general institution. This subscription was given to the parties present at the lodge, and an additional subscription was raised by them. Two of those lodges were concerned. The traverser, James Forbes, is a member of the lodge 1660. He is deputy master of that lodge. William Graham is secretary of the same. Henry Handwich and Matthew Handwich are members of the lodge 780, of which Henry is deputy master; and William Brownlow is a member of 1612. Although it is necessarily my duty to show who and what these persons are, I do not meddle with the general character of Orange lodges in Ireland, the merits of which are for another place. I am well satisfied that the great body of Orangemen feel as much abhorrence at this crime as any individual can do. With this subscription a number of pit tickets were purchased on Saturday morning from the book-keeper at the play house. This was for the purpose of filling the upper gallery. It was thought that the members who were able to purchase tickets for themselves would be sufficient for the pit and middle gallery. One pit ticket was to be given to every three. Forbes was present when this subscription was raised. On the Saturday morning, Forbes, M'Culloch and Atkinson went together to the theater and purchased the tickets. They regularly proceeded to fashion the conspiracy in all its parts. It was determined that an inferior Orange lodge, to which Handwich belonged, and which met at Mrs. Daly's, in Ship street, should be ready to go to the theater to execute the plan. Application was made in the morning to Matthew Handwich at his work, and he was desired to communicate with his brother Henry. Accordingly, about four o'clock in the evening of Saturday, the parties met—Forbes, Atkinson, the Handwiches, and others. They were first supplied with drink. They came armed with sticks. Handwich had been asked if he could furnish sixty men. He said he could. He had not quite so many at first, but the number was completed in the passage to the theater. They were dispatched from the place of meeting in parties of three, each with a pit ticket. The number was at first sixty, but afterwards increased to near an hundred. They were armed with bludgeons. The residue of the whisky they had been drinking they put into a bottle and carried to the theater. The last words of Handwich, on leaving the place of meeting, were, "Boys, be wicked." It was settled that the duty of lodge 1612 should be to go to the pit door and beset it before it was open, and to rush in in a body and occupy that part of the pit next to his Excellency's box. Their directions were, that as soon as "God save the King" was played, the "Boyne Water" should be called for, and if it were refused, that the play should be stopped, and that a system of hissing, groaning and violence should commence. One of the party had a large rattle in his hand, for the purpose of riot.

I should tell you, that at the meeting held of the Purple Order, on Friday evening, and at which Forbes was present, the plan was fully announced of compelling the Lord Lieutenant to leave the theater, and, if possible, the country. One of the party even offered to lay a wager, that before March he would be out of the country. Finding that these conspirators entertained such serious views; that their object was to make such a demonstration of hostility as to compel his Excellency to quit the country, and that this was to be effected by resistance, by riot, and even by personal violence, one of the parties engaged took the alarm. He was shocked at the extent to which their fury might go. At one time he had formed the resolution of going to the Lord Lieutenant and apprising him of the truth and the danger to which he was exposed. He went to the park; a sentinel at the gate of the Viceregal lodge asked him his business; his mind was in that situation in which a trivial circumstance makes an alteration—he hesitated and returned, and the disclosure was not made.

Gentlemen, the party (1612), which had been arranged for the purpose, rushed into the pit and occupied that part of it which was nearest the viceregal box. The upper gallery party, to the number of sixty, went there with the pit tickets. They had fixed upon a watch-word: "Look Out." They seated themselves on the left-hand side of the gallery, where the violence was carried on during the night. Forbes placed them at their posts in the upper gallery, armed with bludgeons. The police occupied the opposite side of the house, and, like faithful watchmen, fell asleep on their posts. No interruption was given to the merriment or to the mischief of the party. To show the deliberation of their plans, I should mention that, previously to the play, handbills were struck off, containing expressions insulting to the Lord Lieutenant, such as, "Down with the Popish government," &c., and other expressions insignificant and contemptible, except as evincing deliberation and concert. These handbills were brought to the theater, and disposed of by the members of the conspiracy. Several were thrown by M'Culloch, from the lattices over the Lord Lieutenant's box, and others from various parts of the house. It will be proved that, from the opening of the theater, the grossest system of insulting and offensive expressions was commenced; groans were raised for "The Popish Lord Lieutenant," and cries of "No Popish government." There were also groans for the house of Wellesley. They did not confine themselves to the noble lord at the head of the government; they extended to the duke of Wellington, and the other branches of his illustrious family. Not satisfied with that, these advocates of religion gave "a clap for the calf's head," an allusion to a monstrous outrage committed, in or near Ardee, by some ruffians who profaned a Roman Catholic place of worship by placing such a thing upon the altar. They applauded also Sheriff Thorpe, with the calf's head. There was "a groan for the bloody Popish Lord Lieutenant." I cannot remember all the terms of outrage which were used. Some persons, not connected with the gang, cried out: "Shame, shame." Of these some were severely beaten, and one man had a narrow escape by getting down from the upper into the middle gallery; several were alarmed and left the house. When the Lord Lieutenant came in, there was a general expression of approbation from the audience, which, for some time, bore down the hisses of the conspirators. But when an opportunity arose, a violent hissing and groaning were set up. These things went on till "God save the King" was played; at that period a bottle was thrown from the upper gallery, which hit the stage curtain. The fact will be proved by a variety of witnesses, who will leave no doubt upon it in your minds. It was flung from the gallery by Henry Handwich. He will appear to have been a leader of the party. You will have the testimony of several distinct and independent witnesses, who can have no other object than to tell the truth. Several persons saw the bottle in its progress. Amongst the idle reports which have been circulated as to this transaction, it has been said, that this came from the carpenters' gallery, and from the pit; but, gentlemen, we shall put the fact beyond all controversy. As to the precise point where it hit the curtain, there is a diversity of opinion; but that it hit somewhere nearer to the Lord Lieutenant than to the center, all the accounts concur. Some of the witnesses say, it struck within four feet of the side next the Lord Lieutenant, and within four feet of the stage. Another says, that it was the breadth of the festoon. But all concur in this, that it was thrown, and that their impression was that it was directed against the Lord Lieutenant. It was thrown from the same side on which his Excellency sat. You will ask why did they get to that side. The right-hand side had been early occupied by other persons; and the conspirators, feeling it necessary to be in a body, were obliged to go to the left. The precise situation in which Handwich was placed when he threw the bottle, will be proved to you. He threw it under him, or by a side motion, and not over him. Any person who will attend to the position in which he was, as well as to that of the Lord Lieutenant, will easily account for the aberration of the instrument. All the witnesses agree in stating it to be their impression that the bottle was directed against his Excellency. Besides the general proof to show that the bottle came from the upper gallery, there are three witnesses who distinctly saw Henry Handwich throw it. One, whose arrival we hourly expect, had his attention excited by some expression of Handwich, and immediately marked him. He swears positively to his having thrown the bottle.

George Graham was one of the principal rioters. He had a large rattle which he used at first for the purpose of making a noise; and when it had performed its services in that department, he converted it into an instrument of personal attack. He broke it into two pieces, and it will be distinctly proved that he came forward and took deliberate aim at the Lord Lieutenant's head; so good an aim that it struck the cushion of the next box, and with such force that it cut the cushion and rebounded on the stage. If it had taken effect, in all probability it would have put an end to his life.

When I state that a bottle was thrown at the king's representative, and that implements of violence were flung at his person, such is the state of the public mind, that it is listened to as if it were a mere bagatelle, a *jeu d'esprit*, a trifle of which the Lord Lieutenant need not take any notice, and which is below the attention of the government and the law officers. Why, gentlemen of the jury, are we awake? Can we be insensible to the effect of such occurrences upon the honor and safety of the country? Can we reflect, without indignation, that such an outrage should be committed in a civilized country against the person of his majesty's representative, because he had the presumption, in opposition to a desperate gang, to execute the parting injunctions of the king in a manner not calculated to give offense or excite animosity? The sentiments of the audience were roused; some rushed up to the gallery. Graham first flung the heavy part of the rattle, and then the light. It will be produced to you. Forbes, as I have already stated, was a party to the entire system of the party, and was present at the sending the men from Daly's to the gallery with bludgeons. He stationed them in the upper gallery at their post. After the bottle and rattle had been thrown, he was observed in the lattices or pigeon holes, immediately adjoining the left side of the upper gallery, in which he had previously stationed the party; he was separated from them only by the spikes dividing those two parts of the house. He was seen actively encouraging the rioters; he held in his hand a whistle with which he sounded the alarm, and gave a signal which was answered through the whole house. He was asked by a magistrate why he used the whistle, to which he replied, "for fun." He was then arrested, but liberated on promise to give bail.

Here Mr. Plunkett briefly referred to conversations of some of the traversers, after the affair at the theatre, to show that they boasted of what they had done. He then continued:

14. THE ACTION OF THE ATTORNEY-GENERAL AN EXERCISE OF WISE DISCRETION.

Am I now to justify myself in your opinion, and in that of the public, for the exercise of my discretion in this *ex officio* information, by which I have been enabled for the first time to bring these facts before the public? I ask any man who has a principle of candor or honesty in his composition, whether he is not bound to acquit me, and whether I should not have basely betrayed the king whom I serve, and the office with which he has honored me, if I suffered public justice to be stifled and obstructed? When these transactions were brought under the consideration of the government, the law officers were consulted by the magistrates. We bestowed the most patient attention and laborious investigation on the case; for five or six days we were occupied at this business. Every day some new light was thrown upon it, until it at length assumed an aspect so formidable as to lead us to the apprehension that his Excellency's life had been directly aimed at. When we learned that Forbes had avowed his approbation of the act; when, after the conspiracy had shown itself in its most desperate effects, he expressed his regret at its failure, and his determination to make another attempt more effectual; we felt, when called upon for our advice upon his application to be discharged, that we could not justify it to our conscience and our sworn duty, or to the respect due to the high personage and illustrious character who had been offered at, if we had suffered him to go at large till we knew the whole of the transaction. There was at that time evidence, not only sufficient to warrant a grand jury for finding a bill for conspiracy to murder, but even for a petty jury to found a verdict for conviction. It was one thing to consider the proper species of committal, and another in what way we should ultimately proceed. When that point came to be finally decided on, and we had reason to believe that the whole of the evidence was before us, our determination was not to proceed on the capital charge. It was infinitely better we should be censured for the tameness of our proceeding, than that we should be arraigned for its rigor. We felt that before we sent up an indictment containing a capital charge, we should be clearly satisfied that the primary object of the conspiracy was to take away the life of the Lord Lieutenant, and that, if any doubt rested on the case, it would be better to be blamed for the timidity and forbearance of the prosecution than exposed to the heavy charge of exerting a rigor beyond the law. We were glad to show in the instance of the most illustrious personage of the realm a strict observance of the law. What satisfied my mind against sending up a bill of indictment on a capital charge was this, that the object of driving the Lord Lieutenant by violence from the theater, and from the country, though it involved the imminent hazard of the life of the Lord Lieutenant, was distinct from the notion of a conspiracy to murder him. When it clearly appeared that the object was to put down the Lord Lieutenant's government and force him from the country, although this plot involved in it an outrage on his person, I did not think that in a capital case a jury could be called upon to say that murder was the aim of the conspiracy. Under these circumstances, therefore, we thought it right to send up the indictments for the misdemeanors which the grand jury have thrown out.

The nature of these informations has already been laid before you. There are two distinct informations; one is for a riot and the other for a conspiracy to riot. The counts vary; but in each there is alleged, first, a conspiracy to riot, and then a conspiracy to hoot, groan, hiss and assault the Lord Lieutenant. In point of law, either or any part of these charges, if proved, will justify a verdict. I have no doubt of being able to prove the whole. I have stated this case without exaggeration against the traversers at the bar. I have no feelings in the discharge of my duty, except the desire faithfully to acquit myself of what I owe to my country and to my sovereign. I may have expressed myself with warmth, I hope not with intemperance. But after I have disabused your minds of the ten thousand falsehoods which have been circulated on this subject, I feel it would be trifling with public justice to say, that this was the act of a few misguided ruffians, growing out of any sudden impulse. It is a proceeding originating with a gang within the limits of this city, associated for the purpose of putting down the king's government, of driving the Lord Lieutenant from this country, and of showing that he has not the power, against their wishes and their authority, to discharge the duties belonging to his exalted station.

SPEECH OF JOHN HENRY NORTH.

Opening for the Defense in Rex v. Forbes and Others.—
Conspiracy and Riot.

IN THE COURT OF KING'S BENCH, DUBLIN, HILARY TERM,
3D GEORGE IV, FEBRUARY 5th, 1823.

Analysis of Mr. North's Speech.

1. A proceeding based upon an *ex officio* information, illegal and without precedent.
2. The charges and the evidence.
3. Loyalty the chief characteristic of Orangemen.
4. Propriety of decorating King William's statue discussed. — Scene when the ceremony was forbidden.
5. The attorney-general's tribute to the memory of King William.—Right of defendants to respect his memory.
6. The real object of the Lord Lieutenant's visit to the theater.
7. A protest against unmerited applause no crime.
8. The defendants never contemplated personal violence.
9. The testimony of the Atkinson brothers discredited.
10. Sketch of Michael Farrell, and review of his testimony.
11. Arraignment of Proctor M'Namara, who saw the bottle " in transit."
12. The conduct of defendants not criminal.— Supposed dialogue between Addison and Lord Somers.
13. References to Bolingbroke, the Duke of Rutland, and Queen Elizabeth.
14. Political aspect of a verdict considered.

The defendants embraced in the information in this remarkable trial were James Forbes, George Graham, William Graham, Henry Handwich, otherwise called Henry Handbridge, Matthew Handwich, otherwise called Matthew Handbridge, Robert Fletcher the younger, Thomas Kelly, William Brownlow, Richard McIntosh, William McCullogh, and William Heron, and divers other persons to the attorney-general unknown. There were two informations. The first charged a conspiracy, confederation and agreement to hiss, groan, insult and assault the Lord Lieutenant while he should be present in the theater, and to procure the same to be done. The second charged that the defendants did, with force and arms, unlawfully make a great noise, riot and disturbance in the theater, the Lord Lieutenant then and there being present, and did then and there, with force and arms, publicly and openly hiss, hoot, groan, insult and assault the Lord Lieutenant, and with force and arms throw, fling and cast at the Lord Lieutenant, with intent to strike and hit the Lord Lieutenant, " divers pieces of wood and copper, and divers glass bottles, in contempt of our lord the king and his laws, to the evil example of all others in like cases offending, and against the peace of our said lord the king, his crown and dignity." The counsel engaged in the cause were numerous. For the crown appeared the Attorney-General (Mr. Plunket), the Solicitor-General (Mr. Joy), Sergeant Lefroy, Sergeant Torrens, Mr. Townsend, and Mr. Greene; Agent, Mr. Kemmis. For the prisoner James Forbes appeared Mr. Johnstone, Mr. Blackburne, Mr. Speer, Mr. Rolleston, Mr. Hamilton, Mr. Perrin, and Mr. Law; Agent, Mr. Chambers. For Matthew Handwich and George Graham appeared Mr. Driscoll, Mr. Scriven, Mr. Speer and Mr. Hamilton. Mr. North appeared for Henry Handwich and George Graham. For William Brownlow Mr. Scriven appeared; Agent, Mr. Fearon. Upon the bench were the Lord Chief Justice (Charles Kendal Bushe) and Mr. Justice Jebb, Mr. Justice Burton and Mr. Justice Vandeuleur, associates.

When the crown rested, Mr. Driscoll opened for the defense. Mr. North then delivered the following address, after which Mr. Johnstone spoke to the jury. The case was summed up by the Solicitor-General (Mr. Joy). The Chief Justice and Mr. Justice Jebb charged the jury. The trial commenced on Monday morning, February 3d, and was closed late on Friday the 7th. The following day, the jury, having been unable to agree except as to the defendant Brownlow who was acquitted, was discharged.

John Henry North died in September, 1831, at the early age of forty-two, without having gained the distinctions to which his abilities entitled him. He was a man of first-rate talents. His university career was one of the most brilliant ever attained, and no student within a century was graduated from Trinity College, Dublin, with greater honors. He had conferred upon him an *optime*, a mark of distinction seldom obtained, and only given as a recognition of the highest merit in every department of learning. When called to the bar it was fondly predicted that his career would form a new and splendid era in the annals of Irish oratory, but this expectation, for some reason, was not fulfilled. Speaking of his power as an advocate, Sheil says: "One qualification of a speaker he possessed in an extraordinary degree. For extemporaneous correctness and copiousness of phrase, I would place him in the very highest rank. All that he utters, wherever the occasion justifies the excitement of his faculties, might be safely printed without revision. Period after period rolls on, stately, measured and complete. There is a paternal solicitude—perhaps a slight tinge of aristocratic pride, in his determination that the children of his fancy should appear abroad in no vulgar garb. He is not like O'Connell, who, with the improvidence of his country, has no compunction in flinging a brood of robust young thoughts upon the world without a rag to cover them."

His speech to the jury in the present case, though it cannot be regarded as a specimen of the first order of excellence, is an able address. His plea was rather ingenious. He advanced the theory that the real object of the Lord Lieutenant's presence at the theater was to test the popularity of his administration, and therefore the marks of approval or disapproval were not only justified, but were called forth by Lord Wellesley himself, and were the legitimate result of his visit. His tribute to the accomplishments of Lord Plunket as an orator, in connection with the latter's panegyric on King William, is one of the most finished passages in the speech. Mr. North spoke as follows:

GENTLEMEN OF THE JURY:—I rise to address you on behalf of Henry Handwich and William Graham. When these men ap-

peared to these informations, on the first day of the term, I confess
I was most anxious to obtain a postponement of their trial.   I was
apprehensive that in the unexampled ferment of the public mind it
would have been impossible to procure for them a fair and impartial hearing.   What corner is there of the land; what shore so
lonely and remote; what glen or valley so silent and sequestered,
that has not been disturbed by the din of this extraordinary proceeding?   The innumerable addresses pouring in day after day and
hour after hour, from almost every county, from every corporation—
the church, the university, the capital—collectively in an aggregate
meeting, distributively in parish meetings, taking guilt for granted,
anticipating conviction, and imploring punishment upon these yet
untried individuals; while the answers of the Lord Lieutenant to
those addresses, by their rich, ever-varying, and, let me add, most
agitating eloquence, kept alive and fanned the popular flame until
it had become a consuming fire.   At one period, I am convinced,
all hope of a fair investigation would have been utterly vain, and
these men must have come before the tribunals of justice like victims bound and bleeding at the foot of the altar, and ready for immolation.   Thank God, however, that dreadful interval is past.
The first gleam of safety and deliverance broke from the darkest
quarter of the heavens, and, through the merciful interposition of
providence, was at length afforded by the extravagance and exaggeration of our enemies.   The most violent were startled into reflection; the most intemperate were stunned into sobriety, by the
monstrous and incredible charge of assassination and murder; yet
the sea still rolls and heaves though the storm has subsided, and I
am well warranted even now in demanding from you, on the
ground of the public agitation alone, a more than ordinary vigilance and attention.

But there is yet another circumstance which characterizes this
case, and entitles me to call for the most scrutinizing jealousy, and,
gentlemen, it is this: that there exists in this case an inauspicious
and unnatural alliance between the natural favorites of the people
and the official servants of the crown—an alliance at all times most
dangerous to the rights and privileges of the subject.   Never are
they in such imminent hazard as when the resentment of the court
and the rage of the people—the *vultus instantis tyranni* and the
civium ardor prava jubentium—unite in one common object and
concur in the same design.   When those two antagonist forces,
popularity and power, conspire in the same direction, their strength

is irresistible; the floodgates of oppression are thrown wide open, and our liberties and laws are borne down by an overwhelming torrent. I am fully convinced—I do most sincerely, and from my heart, believe, it was no consciousness of the support to be derived from this alliance, but a sense of duty, which, however, I must consider a mistaken one, that induced the attorney-general to adopt this strange and hitherto unheard-of proceeding.

I. A PROCEEDING BASED UPON AN EX OFFICIO INFORMATION, ILLEGAL AND WITHOUT PRECEDENT.

It is, I believe, as yet unknown in the annals of our jurisprudence, that the self-same charge which has been dismissed by the verdict of a grand jury should be brought forward again by an attorney-general, upon an appeal to his own private judgment. Gentlemen of the jury, this is new; and I expected therefore, when this case was opened, that some precedent, some authority, some dictum at least, would have been cited in support of it. For see to what it leads: if this course of proceeding is to be sanctioned, the authority of a grand jury is annihilated, and the institution itself becomes a mere formal nullity. They are intrusted with just power enough to forward the objects of the crown by finding bills according to its wishes; but if they presume to ignore them, their judgment is set aside as a matter of course by the attorney-general, who files his *ex officio* information. Preferring bills to a grand jury under circumstances like these, seems to me a circuitous and unnecessary proceeding. It would surely be better and more seemly that the affront thus given to them should be dispensed with, and that the attorney-general should file his information at once.

But, it is said, an authority is to be found for this singular mode of proceeding, which has been hunted out of the Commons journals of Ireland. The attorney-general mentioned this case, by a piece of admirable forensic address, to evade the force of it; because, as far as it is any authority at all, it is decidedly against him. Bills, it appears, had been sent up to the grand jury, and returned by mistake indorsed as true. The foreman, and afterwards the other members of the jury, made affidavits that they had intended to ignore the bills. On the motion of the attorney-general, the indictments were then quashed, and he filed an *ex officio* information. But what was the consequence? The matter attracted the immediate attention of the House of Commons. They entered warmly into the subject, appointed a committee to search for precedents, and having inquired from the members of the House who belonged to the legal profession, whether any existed, were by them informed that such a proceeding was without example. An *ex officio* information, even in those circumstances under which it is ordinarily filed, is, to say the least of it, a severe exercise of the prerogative; but an information of this nature, after bills had been ignored by a grand jury, is without example; at least I have not been able to discover one, and my search has been laborious, since the institution of grand juries itself has been transmitted to us from our Saxon ancestors. What says Sir Matthew Hale, that great model of Christian piety, political integrity, and legal wisdom? "In all criminal cases, the safest mode of proceeding, and the most consonant to the statutes of Magna Charta, is by presentment or indictment of twelve sworn men." What says Mr. Fox, who brought to the study of the Constitution the knowledge of a statesman as well as of a lawyer? "There are," he observes, "two great mainsprings in the Constitution, which, if preserved in unimpaired vigor, the other parts may be occasionally repaired; but if these be suffered to decay, the whole system will fall into confusion; and these two mainsprings," says he, "are the representation of the people in the Commons House of Parliament, and the juridical power of the people through the medium of the grand and petty jury." I have dwelt upon this topic, because I feel its importance. They are not obviously violent or arbitrary measures that we have reason to apprehend, so much as those silent encroachments upon the Constitution, which are the more dangerous, because they are the less glaringly perceptible. A precedent of this kind, my Lords, is always fruitful, and the progeny is ever more mischievous than the parent. It is against such attempts that we are warned by a celebrated writer, who has become a classic in our language. "One precedent," says he, "creates another. They soon accumulate and constitute law. What yesterday was fact, to-day is doctrine. Examples are supposed to justify the most dangerous measures, and when they do not suit exactly, the defect is supplied by analogy." Therefore, although it would be in me an indecorous presumption, before their lordships have intimated an opinion, to pronounce this proceeding absolutely illegal; yet here, in the presence of this high court, before that learned bar, and in the face of the whole country, I do arraign it as discountenanced by all great authority, as without the warrant of any sound precedent, as alien to the mild spirit of the British law, and practically and essentially unconstitutional.

2. The charges and the evidence.

Gentlemen, having made these observations on the nature of the proceeding, let me now examine the charge contained in the informations, and the evidence adduced in support of it. The offense charged is a conspiracy to insult and assault the Lord Lieutenant in the public theater. I shall not examine the information as a special pleader. I do not condescend to legal subtleties. I say, that is the charge *bona fide* and substantially; and the attorney-general is of a character far too sincere and manly to pretend that there is any other. I say it in his hearing, and without fear of contradiction, that the benches of the pit might have been torn up, the panels of the boxes broken in, and every luster in the house demolished, before he would have filed an *ex officio* information, if the Lord Lieutenant had not been in the theater. There are circumstances in this case ridiculous enough; but the great absurdity does not attach to it, of our being assembled here, day after day, in the middle of term, before the whole court, upon a solemn trial at bar, to ascertain whether or not there has been a riot in the upper gallery. No, gentlemen; this is emphatically a State trial, for State purposes; and the question which is now before you and before the country, the issue which you have to try, is whether these men conspired together personally to insult or assault his Excellency the Lord Lieutenant.

3. Loyalty the chief characteristic of Orangemen.

The first circumstance which the attorney-general has brought forward (for I must take the liberty of following him through a part of his statement), as giving color to the accusation, is, that the defendants belong to the society of Orangemen. They do so; it is the fact; they do not disguise it; they glory in it; it is their boast that they are Orangemen. Gentlemen, I do not stand here to give my applause to that institution. Perhaps my private opinion may be that it is not calculated to accomplish the ends it was originally instituted to attain. Perhaps it may be my private opinion that it is not likely to advance public prosperity, or to promote national security, happiness or peace. But what of that? I have the misfortune on this subject to differ from some of the greatest, wisest, and most experienced men in the country. But whether they or I be right in this respect, is not the question. The question is this:

Whatever men of this description have been charged with, whether
illiberality of sentiment, mistaken opinions—a wrong political bias
—have they ever been accused of disloyalty? Has that ever been
one of the crimes imputed to them? Have they ever been reproached with want of loyalty to their king, or disloyal disrespect
for the king's representative? Why, gentlemen; the loyalty of these
men is the bond which unites them. It is an inborn, inbred quality
of their nature, growing with their growth, and strengthening with
their strength—part of their bone and their flesh. Theirs is not
the loyalty which is assumed for a purpose; which comes in and
goes out with an occasion; which compounds for factious insolence
to-day, by cringing adulation to-morrow. It is a steady, permanent,
unfailing principle of action. More than a principle—it is a passion. Their enemies say, it is a prejudice. Perhaps it is all three,
and has the strength of all three united. I do not hesitate, therefore, to say, that a charge of disloyalty, or of anything approaching
to disloyalty, made against such men, is *prima facie*, and upon the
first opening of it, glaringly improbable.

4. PROPRIETY OF DECORATING KING WILLIAM'S STATUE DIS-
CUSSED.—SCENE WHEN THE CEREMONY WAS
FORBIDDEN.

But the attorney-general has adverted to certain circumstances
in the history of this country, which, he presumes, may take off in
your estimation this first apparent improbability. For this purpose
he has called your attention to that State measure of his majesty's
government as he has now instructed us it was; but it is a fact of
which the public, or at least I may say myself, had not been previously apprised—I mean the interruption to the dressing of the
statue of King William. Upon that subject, gentlemen, I may
venture to give my opinion, because I am not restrained, as the
attorney-general is, by the reserve which belongs to a high official
situation. I say, therefore, it is my sincere opinion, that that idle
ceremony ought to be discontinued. I have felt all my life, that
everything in the slightest degree offensive to my Roman Catholic
fellow-subjects ought to be studiously and anxiously avoided.
There does not live a man more desirous than myself that they
should be admitted to the fullest privileges of the British Constitution, and maintained in the secure enjoyment of every advantage,
honor, and distinction, which may be the acquisition of industry,
the prize of talents, or the reward of virtue. These are the senti-

ments which I have always avowed, in private and in public, in pe-
titions to the legislature, in requisitions to the magistrates to assemble meetings for the purpose of petitioning, and in canvassing
for a seat in the House of Commons amongst electors exclusively
Protestant. Gentlemen, notwithstanding these impressions, and
notwithstanding my opinions on the particular subject itself of un
dressing the statue, and which opinions I had expressed somewhat
strongly and, perhaps, imprudently, I will frankly own to you, that,
when the thing itself occurred, I was taken by surprise. Never
shall I forget the emotions which I felt when, on the 4th of November, I walked down to College Green and beheld the scene which
was there exhibited. When I saw the statue of that illustrious
monarch, which, though I had not been so much accustomed to
reverence it, was so dear to my fathers and my kinsmen, stripped,
for the first time, of its accustomed honors, deprived of those annual decorations which had been the old man's pleasure and the
poor man's pride, surrounded by armed horsemen with drawn
swords, hemming in and closing on the captive hero; it seemed to
me, for a moment, as if a successful invasion had been effected on
our shores, as if military occupation had been taken of the capital,
and some Scythian barbarian, from the Tanais or the Volga, was
heading the licentious troop, triumphing in the heart of the city,
and with his flickering sabre, menacing and insulting the venerable
monument of our laws, our liberties, and our religion.

5. The attorney-general's tribute to the memory of King
William.—Right of defendants to respect
his memory.

Gentlemen of the jury: When such were my feelings, thinking
as I do, and with the political sentiments which I entertain, and
having my views upon the great subject of Catholic claims, what,
I leave you to suppose, were the feelings of men who thought differently from me, who believed that Protestant rights and Protestant privileges, and all that is meant by Protestant ascendancy, were
main props and pillars of the British Constitution, and that, without them, there was no security for Protestant property or peace?
What, I ask you, were likely to be their feelings? The attorney-
general has done justice to them; he has portrayed the character
and sketched the history of King William. I shall not attempt to
follow him there; I shall not enter into any such vain and foolish
emulation; I might as well think to shoot arrows at the sun. Gen-

tlemen, you have heard that fine description. The attorney-general
has laid his offering on the altar of King William; an offering of
his own workmanship, fresh from the mint of his transcendent
genius, and glowing with all those divine attributes and godlike
qualities which the powers of a sublime eloquence enabled him to
stamp upon it. But let him not, therefore, sneer at the poorer offering of humbler men to the same object of their worship; his
gift was one every way worthy of him, suited to his extraordinary
talents, his refined taste and superior education; but we are taught
to believe that the rude wonder of the shepherds was as acceptable
as the gold, frankincense and myrrh of the eastern kings. The
attorney-general has taunted these poor men with their want of
taste; the sashes and scarfs with which they decorated the statue
were tawdry and vulgar, it seems, and the mantua-maker of King
William, as he termed him, did not adjust his millinery as well as
he might. But, gentlemen, this is not a point of taste; it is a matter of feeling. The soldier, in the field of battle, clings with as
much devotion and fidelity to his tattered colors as if they displayed
the painting of Rubens or the designs of Raphael. I, therefore,
claim for these men what the attorney-general has demanded for
himself; I claim for them the right to express, in their own homely
dialect and after their own vulgar and tasteless manner, if you will
have it so, their respect for the memory of King William, and their
gratitude for the benefits which he has conferred upon them and
on their country.

But such sentiments or such expression of them, you may tell
me, are not justified by philosophy and reason; and if you will
argue the point with me like metaphysicians or professors, perhaps I shall be compelled to admit that they are not; but be it that
they are not reason, I tell you they are nature. There is a principle implanted in the human breast for the highest and the noblest
purposes, that, by attractions which we cannot always explain, but
which we never can resist, draws us together into bands and companies of kindred feeling. Sometimes it is the recollection that we
are sprung from the same endeared and consecrated soil; sometimes
the spirit-stirring thought that we have drawn our loyal swords in
defense of the same sovereign and the same law, or, perhaps, the
touching remembrance that we have bowed together before the altar
of a common faith. Whatever they may be, they are the links that
join heart to heart; the fine chords that bind man to man, that are
as sensitive as they are strong, and never yet were broken with im-

punity. If the attorney-general had consulted the illustrious person at the head of his majesty's government in this country, he
would have told him that even the feeble pliant Hindoo who bows
his neck beneath the yoke of every conqueror, Christian and Ma-
hometan, Tartar and European, will not permit one darling rite,
one ancient usage, one cherished prejudice to be touched, revolted
or disturbed. Not Tamerlane nor Zingis, not Clive nor Wellesley,
in the plenitude of their power, ever dared to assail him in the
sanctuary of his feelings; and shall Irishmen endure in tame and
uncomplaining submission, what would not be borne by the feeble
and enslaved Hindoo?

6. The real object of the Lord Lieutenant's visit to the theater.

I am so far from wishing to conceal, then, that the discontinuance of the annual commemoration of King William's birth-day
gave dissatisfaction to a certain class of his majesty's subjects, that
I freely admit it. I admit also that to this class the defendants belonged. Let us now inquire how far, and to what extent, their dis-
pleasure carried them. Apply yourselves with diligence to this
inquiry, for it is the issue you are to try. When the Lord Mayor
published his proclamation to prohibit the decoration of the statue,
a considerable degree of irritation was produced. It was not confined to the defendants; it was felt by their fellow-citizens of a
higher order, and expressed in resolutions of the common council
and, I believe, some of the guilds. In this state of the public
mind, and while men were under the influence of these feelings, the
Lord Lieutenant, who had now been nearly a year at the head of
the government, announces his intention of publicly visiting the
theater for the first time. Pause, gentlemen, and ask yourselves for
what purpose a Lord Lieutenant visits the theater. Let no man
deceive you into a notion that he goes there for the sole object of
witnessing the spectacle. There is another and principal purpose
to which this is collateral and subordinate—the purpose, namely, of
receiving the applauses of the people and publicly manifesting the
popularity of his administration. If he should be fortunate enough
to receive these testimonies of public approbation, the fact is immediately signified to the government in England. It appears in the
official papers, and is understood to bestow lustre, if it does not
confer strength, on the ministers of the crown.

7. A PROTEST AGAINST UNMERITED APPLAUSE NO CRIME.

Now, gentlemen, it so happens that I feel, or that Graham feels,
or that Handwich feels, that the Lord Lieutenant does not deserve
this popularity which he thus publicly looks for.   We are unwilling
that our sentiments should be misunderstood, as they would be if
the Lord Lieutenant were received with universal and unanimous
applause.   I protest I have yet to learn that there is anything criminal in going to the theater to oppose the tide of that popularity
which I think unmerited, or in refusing to join in those plaudits by
which it is evinced.   And yet has any other offense been proved
against these men?   We were told, and the nation actually believed
it, that an attempt had been made to assassinate the Lord Lieutenant.   But what are the facts disclosed by the witnesses?   That
a number of persons of the purest and most untainted loyalty,
meeting in their Orange lodges, agree together to assemble on the
night of the Lord Lieutenant's going to the theater—in the upper
gallery—why be it so; but what to do there? to perpetrate what?
deadly treason?   Why, after "God save the King" had been played,
to call for the "Boyne Water," to let the Lord Lieutenant know
what, perhaps, had been concealed from him by his confidential ad-
visers, that there were men of too humble a rank to approach his
person and attend his levees, yeomen, and artificers, who still loved
the old favorite and once national air of the "Boyne Water," who
felt their blood warmed and their hearts cheered by its notes, and
kindling within them the spirit of their conquering ancestors.
Gentlemen, they assembled for that purpose, and for that purpose
only.   I beg pardon—there might have been another.   I will not
say it was no part of their intention to show signs of disapprobation on the appearance of the Lord Mayor.   But I have yet to
learn that that worshipful person comes within the statutes of treason, or that, in the dignity of Lord Mayor, there is anything *ex vi
termini*, to speak with the grammarians, or *ex officio*, to speak with
the attorney-general, which gives him the protection of prerogative.
I never heard that he could touch for the king's evil, or that royal
virtue emanated from the white wand and gold chain.   The Lord
Mayor is, I dare say, a very excellent man and a very worthy magistrate, and, like his predecessor in the Commons' journals, he may
yet be knighted for his political merits; but it is no misprision of
treason to hiss him in the theater.

8. THE DEFENDANTS NEVER CONTEMPLATED PERSONAL
VIOLENCE.

To call for the "Boyne Water" then, and possibly to hiss the
Lord Mayor, these men assembled. But take this with you, that
when they made these determinations, it was no part of the agreement; nay, it was expressly guarded against by the agreement, that
any personal violence should be offered, or any personal insult or
offense given to the Lord Lieutenant. We have that upon the evidence of George Atkinson. We have, further, that when they were
collected at Ship street, one of them seeing his companions with
sticks, advised that they should be left behind, lest by any accident
they might lead to mischief. Nor would the witness swear that
this advice was not taken by many. Others, indeed, thought that
they were sufficiently masters of themselves, not to be exposed to
this danger; and others, again, no doubt, believed them requisite to
their safety. It was amusing enough to hear the terms in which
these sticks were described. One witness told us, very significant-
ly, they were short sticks, and another disclosed the prodigious
fact that they had knobs at the end of them; but that any improper
use was made of them, of this there was no evidence at all.

Any one who knows the powers of the attorney-general, must
be perfectly aware that it is with him a matter of the greatest facility to represent the plainest and simplest facts in such a manner as
to make them appear strange, startling and extraordinary. Never
have I seen him exert this wonderful talent to the same degree as
on the present occasion. I know not whether you have yet recovered from the emotions which his speech excited. But the
moment that George Atkinson was examined, no man, with the
slightest experience in courts of justice, but must have perceived
that the fabric which he had so artfully built up in the statement
was crumbling and dilapidating before the evidence. Admitting
every word spoken by George Atkinson to be true, is there any
other conspiracy proved than a conspiracy to call for the "Boyne
Water" after "God save the King," and to show the Lord Lieutenant, by the expression of their feelings, that with them at least
he was unpopular.

But they had a further object, it is said—to drive the Lord
Lieutenant from the theater, and eventually from the country.
Here is one of the ingenious but cruel artifices I complain of. See
the turn that is given to the evidence. It was said, proposed,

agreed, that they should go together to the theater and call for the "Boyne Water;" "he will then see," says some one, "that he is not liked, and perhaps in disgust, for he is a sensitive man, he may leave the theater;" "and perhaps," says another, yet more sanguine, "perhaps, with the blessing of God, he may leave the country, too." Something of that sort was probably said. But will you believe that it was part of the original design, one of the direct objects then in contemplation, to drive the Lord Lieutenant that night from the theater and afterwards from the country? Drive him from the theater! How? Where were the means? Exquisite absurdity! What were the arms they had collected for this great undertaking? What were the weapons, swords, guns, pistols, pikes, to be used for his expulsion?

I think I see these dreadful conspirators in close divan seated round a table in full council: "We'll have him off, that's poz; but, brother, what will you arm yourself with?" "I'll arm myself with a whistle; I'll whistle him off." "Ah," says the musician, "there's nothing like the Boyne Water." If there was a tailor amongst them, an assassinating tailor, he, to be sure, would "his quietus make with a bare bodkin." The majority, however, are for a bottle and rattle, and with these *armamentaria belli* they repair to the scene of action, the upper gallery. And now observe how they conduct their operations. In the first place, it would be prudent one would think, if one meant to assassinate another, to get as near to him as possible; but our wise conspirators take another view of the case, and the Lord Lieutenant being close to the stage, they file off to the upper gallery. Again, the Lord Lieutenant sitting on the left hand of the house, and the object, as asserted, being to launch some missile from their infernal machine which should reach his person, they take their station in the extreme left of the gallery, where they could not possibly see his figure, and whence, from the construction of the house, the most dexterous hand could send nothing that would strike him. Nay, what is more extraordinary, if you believe George Atkinson, they occupied at first the right-hand seats, where they had a full view of his Excellency, and might take a just aim; yet this advantage they immediately resign, and of their own accord quit that position and move off to the left. All this is surprising, and leaves to the charge not a shadow of probability. Were ever such means employed for such ends? Or did ever men possessing the use of their natural faculties, having such designs, take such measures to effect them?

9. THE TESTIMONY OF THE ATKINSON BROTHERS DISCREDITED.

But on whose evidence does this whole representation rest, even such as it is? Upon the testimony of two brothers, so help me— the greatest villains I ever saw produced in a court of justice. The old friends, as they described themselves, the sworn associates and companions, the ancient allies of my clients—they steal into their confidence, they get possession of their secrets and their hearts, join with them in all their plans, concur in everything, go hand in hand with them to the accomplishment of their common purposes, and then they turn round—the Judases, the Arch-traitors—they turn round upon their long endeared friends and sworn brother Orangemen, and betray them to their bitterest enemies. Is it part of an Orangeman's oath not to reveal the secrets of his lodge? I know not whether it be so or not, but it is a matter of no consequence; the violation of an oath could add nothing to their guilt; the bond of an oath is as nothing compared with the bond of an association like theirs; linked together by the same political feelings, by the bands of ancient friendship, by the ties of convivial fellowship and social intercourse, by all that men hold most dear and respected—they come forward to depose against their old associates, to blast their fair fame and reputation, and expose them to the full weight of that dire persecution with which the government of the country has determined to bear them down. What was their temptation? Is it lucre? That seems hardly a sufficient motive for such complicated iniquity; yet I cannot perceive any other. There was no hate, no jealousy to gratify, no deadly revenge to be satiated. When this trial is over, let them receive their reward. It is quite right and proper. They have well deserved it. Verily, verily, they should have their reward; but I trust it will be in hard cash. I hope they will not be remunerated with a place in any department—customs, excise, police, any department, however inferior or subordinate; if they should, they will pollute it; they will carry into it infection, contagion, and corruption; they will dissolve the ties that hold man to man, and spread through the community an epidemic treason.

If there were no other evidence than that of these men, would you convict any human being upon it? Would you take a single limb from the spider that crawls upon the wall, upon the testimony of men like these? The grave solicitor-general, however, may tell me bye-and-bye, that they may yet regard one solitary virtue, though they have ceased to reverence the rest, and may tell truth, though they have broken confidence. Gentlemen, one falsehood George Atkinson has unquestionably told you. I am not a living man this moment, if every word he swore as to his going to the park was not a willful fabrication? What! He tells you, that resolved to confederate with these men, for purposes which he would represent as of the blackest nature, and concurring with them up to the very day of their execution, he is at length struck with remorse, that he yields to it; but instead of giving notice of the plot at the police offices, or in any of the hundred ways that were open to him, he takes the extraordinary course of walking out forthwith to the vice-regal lodge, to intimate the fact personally to the Lord Lieutenant. At the gate he is stopped by the sentinel, who asks him what business he had there, and upon this interruption, without one further effort to obtain admission, without the slightest importunity, without a word of remonstrance or expostulation, or the least hint of the nature or importance of his business, he turns round upon his heel and goes straight back to Dublin, repairs to Ship street where his associates were assembled, becomes the most active amongst them, furnishes the whistles, stations the party in the upper gallery, and takes the most conspicuous part in all the proceedings of the night; and after all, when the worst had happened, repairs to Flanagan's, sits down to supper with the rest, and joins in the toasts and conversation. Do you believe him, gentlemen? Do you, sir? Or you, or you? No; no man can believe that he went that morning to the park. Why, gentlemen, see what they might have done. The crown lawyers might have produced the sentinel. They could ascertain who was the sentinel that day, and procure his attendance here with as much ease as I could take a tent of ink from that ink-stand. Why is not the sentinel forthcoming? Be he what he may, Englishman, Irishman or Scotchman, Roman Catholic, Protestant or Presbyterian, I am not a living man, as I said before, if he would not give the lie to George Atkinson, and therefore it is that he is not produced, and that he cannot be produced. No intelligent man, whatever may be his wishes or opinions, can believe this part of George Atkinson's evidence, and discrediting him in that main fact, you are bound to disbelieve him in every other. Great latitude is given to a jury, but it does not extend to this that they may believe a witness to have sworn deliberately false in one part of his evidence, and yet found a verdict upon the remainder. If you disbelieve him in this part of his narrative, I tell you, in the hearing of those learned judges, who will hereafter direct you in point of law, that you must expunge the evidence of George Atkinson from your notes. We have had enough of him.

I shall not long detain you with his brother. They were indeed *par nobile fratrum.* I wonder why the father was not produced. He was waiting here at the door to see that his sons did their duty; to see whether they would flinch; whether they would dare to look Forbes and Graham in the face; whether their tongues would not cleave to the roof of their mouths, while they were fabricating this story against their old friends and companions. They maintained their resolution, though it cost them a pang. Did you observe the first of them? Did you see the terrors of his conscience working within him—issuing from his pores and steaming from his forehead —a natural embarrassment of utterance, aggravated and increased by his guilty confusion; and his shame and terror giving obscurity to his expressions, so that he reminded me of Dr. Johnson's remark upon the language which Shakespeare has put into the mouth of Caliban, that "it is clouded by the gloominess of his temper and the malignity of his purposes." Every answer he gave was at the first unintelligible. He was always obliged to explain; and when the most obvious questions were put to him, as: "Why he did not endeavor to dissuade his companions?" "Why he did not remonstrate with the sentinel?"—he had no other reply than it did not occur. "It did not occur!" *Non mi ricordo* was nothing to him; and if his "did not occur" had the singularity of an Italian phrase to give it currency, it would spread like the other, and be the ready reproach for every shuffling, stammering and guilty witness.

It is not easy to distinguish between the evidence of the two brothers; yet, perhaps, there are shades in their guilt. I think, of the two, George is the worst. John, to be sure, was as willing to betray his companions; but he did not resort to the miserable hypocrisy of affecting a compunction which he never felt. When he had stated all for which he was produced, he reserved a kind of *locus penitentiæ,* made a compromise with his conscience, and tried to lay up a store of merit by telling a little truth. On his cross-examination, he admitted the important fact that Mr. Forbes had said, "he could be no true Orangemen who threw the bottle." The attorney-general attempted to destroy the effect of this admission, by calling on the judges to refer to their notes for the words used, and by observing that they went no further than his belief, and were elicited by a leading question. Be it so. Who doubts that Mr. Forbes used the expression? If he had not, would John Atkinson have dared to admit it? I am glad he gave it the little tack of his belief. It cannot impair the value of the evidence; it adds to it, because it shows that it was wrung from an unwilling and reluctant witness.

Here Mr. North reviewed the evidence briefly to show that nothing had been proven against William Graham. He then referred to the testimony affecting Henry Handwich, the person charged with having flung the bottle, as follows:

10. Sketch of Michael Farrell, and review of his testimony.

Dismissing William Graham, therefore, I come to Henry Handwich. He, to be sure, is made a prominent figure in the piece— the assassination part has been attributed to him, and the public ear yet vibrates with the charge that he flung a bottle at the Lord Lieutenant from the upper gallery of the theater. The great improbability of the fact I have already endeavored to show from the general plan and construction of the house, and from the relative situation of all the parties. To descend a little more into detail. By the evidence of all the witnesses it appears that Handwich was in the third row of the gallery. I don't know, gentlemen, whether any of you have been there. If you have, you must have found in that third row a number of wooden pillars, or supports, bearing up what is called the dip of the gallery, and which I suppose to be the general cornice of the house. This dip, or cornice, is no more than five feet from the floor; and under this, from the third row, in a crowded gallery, "cribbed, cabined and confined," it is alleged that Handwich flung the bottle which was exhibited on the stage.

Who are the persons who attest this extraordinary statement? The first is Mr. Michael Farrell, the jeweller, from Dame court. Unfortunately we know of Mr. Michael Farrell no more than he has been pleased to communicate himself. When an infant, he tells us, he was taken to London and did not return to this city till about four years ago. O, I do wish that the venue in this case had been laid in Covent Garden. We should then, I shrewdly suspect, have had no difficulty in dealing with Mr. Michael Farrell. I'll venture to say, his *ore rotundo*, his broad O and his long E are as familiar in the strand as any London cry. If these poor fellows were rich enough for such a prosecution as this; if their last shil-

42

ling had not been drained from them, we might have got some information in London relative to Mr. Farrell; at present all we know is, that having gone there in his earliest years, and spent there the greatest part of his life, he leaves, for what reason he has not informed us, that great mart of wealth and commerce, where no man ever took root and wished to be transplanted thence, and sets up for a working jeweller in Dame court. A more pragmatical gentleman I never beheld. He seemed disposed to lecture us all, with such rhetorical flourishes, and such a volume of voice, that I actually trembled for the windows. He put me in mind of the famous Mr. Birkbeck, who went some time since to the banks of the Mississippi, and I have no doubt we shall, very shortly, have his letters from Dame court, with remarks on the capabilities of Dublin, the facilities of emigration to Ireland, and notices of the manners and customs of its savage inhabitants. His evidence is, that Henry Handwich was the last person upon the left, and that behind him there was a large empty space—an empty space! Do you believe that on your oaths? Was there as much free space as there is now next to me? Have you a doubt that the upper gallery was not packed as close as close could be; that the people were not wedged together, with their elbows pinned to their sides? What was Tiernan's evidence? Tiernan, a plain, ready, unsophisticated, natural Irishman, free and frank; he spoke fast, and he spoke out; he wrote a running hand that had nothing stiff or cramped in it, and he told you what it is easy to believe: "We were packed as close as we could be; there was no room to budge; never was such a crush, both to the sides and to the back." Which will you believe—the natural Irishman or the Anglo-Hibernian? There is not to be found a more odious production of perverted nature than an Irish seedling grafted upon an English stock; it makes the worst and sourest crab; it is a mixture that combines all that is bad in each; with the dogged pertinacity, which is the worst part of the English character, it wants the honest sincerity that redeems it. Yes! Tiernan may be trusted. If I were to cross a lonely heath at night, Tiernan should be my man. I'd not ask Farrell to go along with me.

11. Arraignment of Proctor M'Namara, who saw the bottle "in transit."

But we have another witness, it seems, the far-famed Doctor M'Namara, fresh from the pound of Ballinakill. Gentlemen, you

saw the peaceable Doctor, you marked his comportment and demeanor. "Up I came," says the Doctor, "from Ballinakill, went to
the middle gallery, and took my seat in the center. There I was
disporting myself, when suddenly I heard a cry of 'boys, mind your
fire.'" Oh, how fortunate it is that a man never comes to fabricate
a story, that he does not, by a sure infatuation, insert some little
circumstance that serves to betray him. If the Doctor had said
he heard the words "look out," he would have been corroborated;
but now he is contradicted by every witness. This cry, he says,
attracted his attention; he looked up and saw Handwich in the
third row. The Doctor, in the middle gallery, sees Handwich in
the third row of the upper one, though between them there were
two benches covered with people, and the boarded parapet in front
of the upper gallery besides! Through all these obstacles he sees
him in that dark corner of the gallery where he represents him to
be placed; sees him fling the bottle, and is now able, at this distance of time, to identify his person. ✓ The bottle itself he saw in
what he learnedly calls its *transit*. A word or two on that same
transit. I hold it physically impossible that a bottle could have
taken the course described by Farrell and M'Namara, from the upper gallery to the stage, without being observed by four or five
hundred spectators. Just think what the theater is: a wide, illumi-
nated area, whose bounding surfaces are studded with eyes as
numerous as those of Argus. Not a square inch in that field of
view which was not painted on the retina of some one eye or other
in that vast assembly. Consider, too, the time—the interval between
the play and farce—when the attention of the audience was not
fixed upon the stage, when people were all looking about them, recognizing and greeting their friends and acquaintances. Was there
no one to mark this bottle but Farrell, M'Namara, and the young
medical student? What, not one giggling girl in the boxes, glanc-
ing round for admiration! not an opera glass pointed! no fortunate
observer of the transit but the astronomer from Ballinakill! Is all
this credible? But this is not all—voonders upon voonders, as the
Dutchman said when he got to London—the greatest miracle is to
come. Down comes the bottle, thundering from the upper gallery
to the stage, and falls unbroken! If they had candidly produced
it, I am instructed, it would appear to be one of those starred sandy
bottles that fly in pieces on the slightest collision. I don't know,
gentlemen, whether you are aware that glass is one of the most
elastic substances with which we are acquainted, far more elastic

than ivory, which, you know, is used for billiard balls on account of its great elasticity. This is the property which makes glass ring, and it would be much more familiar to us if it were not counteracted by the great fragility of the material. If the bottle, therefore, did not break, it must have rebounded to the center, if not to the back of the pit, supposing it to have been thrown from the upper gallery; but it rolls gently along the stage and is taken up from behind the foot-lights. You all remember the prodigious efforts made by counsel for the prosecution to establish from the evidence that the bottle fell towards the left of the stage, and near the Lord Lieutenant's box; but the fact and the intended inference are at an end when it is recollected that Mr. Barton, from the center of the orchestra, is the person who takes up the bottle, and who does so without rising from his seat. Who, after this, will presume to tell us that it was intended for one side more than the other? The truth seems to be, it was designed for the stage, and in all probability came from the pit or from the lattices, after receiving a very slight and, perhaps, an accidental impulse. Ah, gentlemen, we have not been fairly dealt with; indeed we have not. Why is not the bottle forthcoming? Why is not Mr. Barton produced? You know the insinuation that this bottle was taken from Ship street, and was the same which contained the whisky. Surely you might judge of its contents if it were now produced, and we should not be left to criticisms on the testimony of Mr. Cahill; you would then be able to perceive whether it had been filled with porter or with spirits. These are facts perhaps of small moment; but the case for the prosecution is sought to be made out by circumstantial evidence, and the counsel for the crown were bound to have furnished you with all imaginable means of arriving at a just conclusion.

Here Mr. North referred to the testimony as to what Mr. Forbes had said when he was arrested, when he declared that he was an Orangeman, and would perhaps be sent to Botany Bay for it. He contended it was said without consciousness of guilt, openly, and evinced no criminality. He then continued:

12. THE CONDUCT OF DEFENDANTS NOT CRIMINAL.—SUPPOSED DIALOGUE BETWEEN ADDISON AND LORD SOMERS.

And now, gentlemen, having closed my observations on the evidence and given you the means, I hope, to take the sting out of this charge, allow me to inquire into the nature of the offense imputed, if offense it should be. Gentlemen, I have been accustomed all my life long to believe it to be a privilege possessed by the people of Great Britain and Ireland, to give free expression in places of public and general resort to a popular and political feeling. We are not, indeed, to speak or to act to the terror of his majesty's subjects, but short of that, I have always deemed it to be the privilege of every Englishman or Irishman to give expression in places of public resort, such as a theater, to his public and political sentiments. If I am to lose this privilege, I will not part with it without a struggle. The attorney-general has set up for a theatrical reformer. I think he will find it a troublesome task, but I trust he will not expose himself to the same censure with the parliamentary reformers who have been so often reproached with not furnishing a specific and detailed plan of their projected improvements. If our ancient privilege is to be curtailed, at least, I hope he will point out the exact limits within which we are to enjoy it: whether it be conceded to the boxes, although refused to the gallery; and whether, though suspended during the play, it may not revive in the entertainment; or whether it be only when the Lord Lieutenant is at the theater, that the silence of La Trappe is to prevail there. But I trust it is not the presence of the Lord Lieutenant, no; nor of the king himself, deeply as I reverence him, that shall ever frown a British audience into Eastern sycophancy or silence. The privilege I contend for is not a new one; it has been recognized in all periods of our history.

I do not know what the attorney-general would say to the trunk-maker, described by Addison, who used to signify his approbation at the theater by beating the benches with an oaken plank, and the critical correctness of whose strokes was the joy of the actors and the delight of the house. The *Spectator* is not as much read now as it used to be, and as it ought to be; but, gentlemen, if you have not read that inimitable paper, do so by all means when you go home. According to the new *ex officio* law, however, the poor trunk-maker would have been made the subject of a State prosecution; he would have been tried at bar. I can suppose Bishop Hurd, who possessed a charming talent for writing dialogues, imagining a conversation between Lord Somers and Addison, after the appearance of that paper: we may conceive Addison dropping in at the breakfast table of Lord Somers, where the paper is lying: "Well, my Lord, how were you amused with my last night's lucubrations?" "I was, indeed, charmed and delighted, Addison; but are you aware that your trunk-maker has violated the law of the land, and that the attorney-general may file an *ex officio* information against him?" And then imagine Addison, smiling, with that inimitable grace which we may suppose to have belonged to him, and replying: "Yes, my Lord, the attorney-general may file his *ex officio* information, but there is a fund of good sense and natural equity in a British jury which will ever make the trunk-maker too strong for the attorney-general." It is somewhat in this manner, perhaps, that Hurd would have treated the subject.

13. REFERENCES TO BOLINGBROKE, THE DUKE OF RUTLAND, AND QUEEN ELIZABETH.

As I have fallen into the vein of story-telling, gentlemen, you will allow me to relate another, which belongs to the same times, and of which they have reminded me. There was a great man in those days, Lord Bolingbroke. Lord Wellesley resembles him in some of the noblest parts of his character: his high spirit, his inimitable style, his rich and flowing eloquence. In the other and defective parts of Bolingbroke's character I believe there is no resemblance. He came into power during the four last years of Queen Anne's reign, that period to which the attorney-general is so fond of adverting, when a plan was formed for defeating the succession in the House of Hanover, and bringing back the pretender. He and Harley, who were suspected of entertaining these designs (at that time only surmised), became justly unpopular with the nation. It was in this crisis of public feeling that Addison wrote his celebrated tragedy of Cato, almost every line of which was intended as a reflection upon Bolingbroke and his administration. Bolingbroke was aware of this, and determined to be present at the performance. With admirable address, he took a conspicuous box and seated himself in the full view of the whole house. As the play proceeded, the pit grew clamorous in their applause, pointing the application of every stinging antithesis or swelling sentiment to the unpopular minister. Was Bolingbroke offended? No; he returned the angry gaze of the people with a countenance beaming with smiles, seemed to go along with the general current, was loudest in his applause, and when the representation was over, sent for Booth, who had performed the part of Cato, to his box and, in the presence of the whole audience, presented him with a purse of sixty guineas for having defended the cause of liberty so well against a perpetual dictator. There was an example, gentlemen—it might be disrespectful to say for whom.

But there are instances nearer home. I am not old enough to remember the brilliant times of the Duke of Rutland, but I have heard of them. Chivalrous and gallant, generous and gay, he had the faults of a man of pleasure and dissipation, and accordingly he never went into the theater that he was not assailed with some coarse and offensive allusion to the supposed scandals of his private life. We all know the story of Peg Plunket and Manners. But yet I have never heard that the Duke of Rutland instituted a prosecution. We are told, indeed, that on some of those occasions he had the grace to blush; but it is added that he always had the good humor to smile. The privilege, I insist on, has not only been conceded by ministers and lord lieutenants, it has been allowed by kings. Even in the most arbitrary period of our history, we find the British sovereigns freely presenting themselves to their people, and admitting the right to censure or applaud them. Even the Tudors, in that critical interval when the prerogative stood highest, after the ancient aristocracy was dissolved and before the Commons had emerged to wealth and importance, never disputed this well established privilege. Elizabeth herself, in the full maturity of her greatness, when she had trampled on the necks of all her competitors, broken the power of Spain and scattered the invincible armada, even she did not dispute it. When, in a fatal hour of pride and irritation, she had consigned the gallant Essex, the favorite of the nation, to his untimely destiny; as she rode through the streets of her capital to assemble her parliament, a murmur of disapprobation rose around her loud and strong. All-unused to such sounds, and spoiled, as she might well be supposed to be, by the prosperity of forty years, she did not dare to complain: yet she possessed a court of star-chamber, she had a privy council that assumed a criminal jurisdiction, she had an attorney-general ready at her slightest beck to file his *ex officio* information. But she resorted to none of these. She was too magnanimous a princess; she had too much of an English heart. No; she retired to her chamber, wrung her hands in agony, smote her breast, and recognized within the justice of the people's censure.

I shall not tarnish the luster of examples like these, or diminish their effect, by reminding you of the well-known interruption given to the performances of Covent Garden theater, which continued for sixty-six nights and has been called the O. P. war. *There*, indeed, was a riot, something different from the "Boyne Water;" and yet, when the subject came into a court of justice, an English jury—I don't say whether properly or improperly, right or wrong—but an English jury found a verdict for the audience against the manager; and when the Chief Justice, Sir James Mansfield, asked the foreman his reasons for the verdict, he informed him that the jury did not think it consistent with the rights of Englishmen to punish a British subject for distributing placards or wearing the letters O. P. in his hat. Gentlemen, I am not holding this example up for your imitation. Do not suppose me capable of so gross and palpable an artifice. You will find your verdict according to the evidence and the law as it applies to it. But I do mention it for the purpose of showing you what the notions and the feelings of the British people are upon the rights and privileges of a British audience; and we may affect what prudery or delicacy we please upon these subjects, I tell you it is that sturdy English feeling, that sound sense, and *crassa* Minerva, not to be duped by any sophistry, legal, political or religious, which has made England the nation she is. This is the true source of her splendor, the real foundation of her greatness.

—— Sic fortis Etruria crevit
Scilicet et rerum facta est pulcherrima Roma.

May you ever partake of that feeling! May you ever guard and cherish it! May you ever look with jealousy on any attempt on the part of your rulers to take from you the right of pronouncing on the merits of their government, and of determining without appeal, whether they are popular or unpopular. Preserve it as you would the apple of your eye or the life-blood of your heart! It is better, it is of more value than all your other privileges together. Without it they are paralyzed and lifeless. This is the soul and spirit which gives strength and animation to them all.

14. POLITICAL ASPECT OF A VERDICT CONSIDERED.

Only one topic more, gentlemen. The attorney-general would fain represent to you that your verdict may forward the great cause of national conciliation. Oh, gentlemen of the jury, consider well before you suffer your minds to be entranced and your judgments led along by so captivating an argument as this. I have heard of various nostrums and specifics for the cure of all Irish diseases. There is not a Right Hon. Secretary, or a Right Rev. Bishop, who comes here from England, that does not bring with him some infallible receipt of this description—some cordial or another—some Dr. Solomon's balm of Gilead, that is to take the vertigo from our

heads and the acid from our stomachs, and to restore us to political sanity and vigor. It was only the other day that the philanthro-
pist Mr. Owen—indeed, I believe he is still in the kingdom, and a
most excellent and benevolent man he is—proposed to set everything to rights by cutting up the country into small square pieces,
and raising our population from seven millions to seven and twenty.
Then all was to be harmony and conciliation. But of all the extravagant projects I have yet heard of, surely the most desperate
and hopeless seems to be this of conciliating us all by an *ex officio*
information. Every man, to be sure, has a natural attachment to
his own profession. I would have given something to have been
present at the grand consultation when this expedient was agreed
on. "What shall we do," says the president of the council, "to
allay the differences of this unhappy people?" "Call out the artillery," says the commander of the forces, "erect barriers on the
bridges." "Put them down with the police," say Mr. Graves and
Mr. Tudor. "Shuffle them well together," says the Lord Mayor.
"No," says the attorney-general, "believe me, there is nothing like
an *ex officio* information."

> " The currier wiser than all put together."

But I will not sport any longer with the subject; it is too grave,
it is too serious, it is too affecting. Conciliation! Conciliation!—
magical, mysterious word! How often misapplied and misunderstood! Like the happiness described by the poet:

> That still so near us, yet beyond us lies,
> O'erlook'd, seen double, by the fool and wise.
> Plant of celestial seed, if dropp'd below,
> Say in what mortal soil thou deign'st to glow.

Alas, gentlemen of the jury, it is not within the precincts of a
court of justice we shall find it to flourish. Prosecutions and convictions, the halter and the prison-bar, are but coarse instruments
of conciliation. It is with this as with the other virtues of the
same family: friendship and affection, reciprocal esteem and mutual forbearance. It possesses that attribute which Shakespeare
has ascribed to the quality of mercy: "It is not strained." It will
not be commanded. A king may place his throne upon the sands,
and tell the stormy wave to roll back at his bidding; but whether
it be the swelling tide of popular emotion, or the bursting billows
of the tempestuous sea, they will equally teach him the littleness

of all mortal power, and the impassable limits which nature has prescribed to the authority of man. Do not for a moment suppose that I mean any bold and disrespectful allusion to the parting injunctions of his majesty. I remember too well—who amongst us does not remember—that great and ever-memorable day when the king made his triumphal entry into this city, when the hearts of this mighty population beat together in loyal unison as if it had been the heart of one individual man, and the monarch was received among his people like a father into the bosom of his family.

> As a fair morning of the blessed spring,
>   After a tedious, stormy night;
> Such was the glorious entry of our king!
>   Enriching moisture dropp'd on everything.
> Plenty he sow'd below, and cast around him light.

To what enchanting prospects did we then surrender our delighted imaginations! Why have these blissful hopes been thus severely disappointed? It is not because the great absurdity has been attempted of conciliating men by force—of producing, by constraint and violence, that which is the natural offspring of persuasion? Hence what we have seen; hence unfounded committals upon capital charges, refusal of bail and mainprise, the solemn verdicts of grand juries slighted, scorned and set at defiance; hence *ex officio* informations. Do not be persuaded, therefore, gentlemen of the jury, that any verdict which you can pronounce will advance the cause of conciliation; believe it not. You can find no conciliatory verdict, but you may find a righteous one. The Lord Lieutenant has been deceived and abused; your verdict may undeceive and disabuse him. His noble mind has been practiced upon: he has been taught to believe that he is surrounded by conspirators and traitors; that weapons are raised against his life; he has been induced to bare his manly breast and to desire "the assassin, if not yet disarmed, to strike now." Tell him by your verdict, gentlemen, that he has no conspirators to fear; that he has no assassins to dread; that there is no dagger aimed at his life, but the "air-drawn dagger" of his own imagination. Such a verdict as this may not be conciliatory, but in my heart I believe it will be just; it will be one that to the latest hour of your lives will receive the approbation of your own consciences; it is one already anticipated by every thinking and reflecting man in the community; and at no distant period it will be hailed by the whole country.

SPEECH OF BARTHOLOMEW HOAR.

OPENING FOR PLAINTIFF IN MASSY V. THE MARQUIS OF HEAD-
FORT.—DAMAGES FOR CRIMINAL CONVERSATION.

AT ENNIS ASSIZES, COUNTY CLARE, BEFORE BARON SMITH
AND A SPECIAL JURY, FRIDAY, JULY 27th, 1804.

Damages claimed, £40,000.   Amount recovered, £10,000.

ANALYSIS OF MR. HOAR'S SPEECH.

1. The narration.—Facts and circumstances
   of the case.
2. How plaintiff's suspicions were aroused.
3. Mrs. Massy's exemplary behavior quiets
   his fears.—Circumstances of the ab-
   duction.
4. Defendant's crime compared to the
   treachery of pirate wreckers.—A
   striking simile.
5. Grounds of the defense anticipated and
   discussed.
6. The rule of damages.

The famous case of Massy *v.* The Marquis of Headfort, tried at the Ennis
Assizes, County Clare, Ireland, Friday, July 27th, 1804, was brought to recover
damages alleged to have been sustained by the plaintiff in consequence of the defendant seducing and taking away his wife. The amount claimed was £40,000.
The case was rendered interesting on account of the rank and station of the
parties. The complainant was a clergyman of the Church of England; the defendant, a peer of the realm and an officer in the British army. He was the son
of the Earl of Bective, and had been created, by the royal favor, a Baronet, a
Baron, a Viscount, an Earl, and finally a Marquis, and was possessed of an income of £40,000 a year. The "lady in the case" was remarkable for grace,
beauty and accomplishments. The Rev. Charles Massy was the second son of a
gentleman of rank and distinction in the County of Clare. In March, 1796, he
married, contrary to his father's wishes, Mary Ann Rosslewin, a belle of eighteen,
of great personal attractions. The father's principal objection to the match was
based upon the fact that the lady was without fortune. He desired his son to
marry a person of wealth, and offered, in case of his compliance, to settle upon
him £11,000 a year in landed property. The son, however, sacrificed this ample
provision, and wedded the lady of his choice. For eight years their domestic
happiness was unbroken. At the time of the plaintiff's misfortune, he lived at
Summer Hill, near Limerick. While the defendant was stationed at the latter
place Mr. Massy made his acquaintance. At one time the plaintiff had a living
in the County of Meath, where Lady Bective, the Mother of the Marquis, was
one of his parishoners. Mr. Massy now extended to the son of his former parishoner, who was then over fifty years of age, every hospitality, as a mark of respect
to the Lady Bective, whose memory he cherished and esteemed. Under such
circumstances, by taking advantage of the confidence of his host, the defendant

consummated his diabolical crime. On Sunday, while the plaintiff was administering the functions of his sacred office, the defendant eloped with Mrs. Massy, and took her with him to London.

The trial occasioned great excitement, and the small town of Ennis was crowded with persons from all parts of the country. It is said that ten guineas were paid for a bed the night before the trial, and large sums were offered for a place in court to witness the proceedings. A stenographer, all the way from London, was present to report the trial. A large array of counsel appeared. For the plaintiff: John Philpot Curran, Bartholomew Hoar, Henry Dean Grady, Thomas Casey, John White, Amory Hawksworth, William O. Regan, Thomas Lloyd, William McMahon and George Bennett, Esqs.; agent, Anthony Hogan, Esq. For the defendant: Hon. George Ponsonby, Thomas Quin, Thomas Goold, John Franks, Charles Burton and Richard Pinnefather, Esqs.; agent, James Sims, Esq.

It is, indeed, seldom we find at *nisi prius*, a controversy depending almost entirely upon the forensic abilities of the advocate, where the measure of success may be a farthing or a fortune, which can compare, for the skillful manner in which it was conducted by all parties concerned, with this famous case. There was no dispute about the fact that the defendant had eloped with the plaintiff's wife. Indeed, it seemed, from the manner of the occurrence, as if the defendant regarded his crime as an achievement which he desired to render conspicuous, rather than a disgrace which he wished to conceal. It was insisted, however, that the plaintiff was at least guilty of a moral delinquency or constructive connivance in permitting his wife to associate with the Marquis, after knowledge of the latter's loose character, and that, therefore, he could claim no compensation on the theory that his own acts tended to contribute to his misfortune.[1] The issue, therefore, was narrowed mainly to the question of pounds, shillings and pence. Mr. Bartholomew Hoar opened for the plaintiff; and Mr. Thomas Quin for the defendant; Hon. George Ponsonby summed up on the same side, and the case was closed for plaintiff by John Philpot Curran. All the speaking was of a high order, entirely free from coarse expressions or offensive matter. The arguments partake rather of the nature of essays on moral ethics than speeches to a jury at *nisi prius*. We have, therefore, concluded to give them in full, and also Baron Smith's able and instructive charge to the jury. Mr. Hoar's opening is certainly an able effort. His statement is clear, his language choice, his style compact. The striking parallel of the defendant's conduct with the treachery of the Cornish pirates, who burn false lights on the rocky coast in order to lure the gallant ship to destruction, presents a graphic picture. Mr. Hoar spoke as follows:

MAY IT PLEASE THE COURT,—*Gentlemen of the Jury:*—This is the first action of the kind a jury of this county has ever been impanelled to try; and, as it is the first, so I hope in Heaven it may be the last. Many idle reports have been circulated, and the subject of this trial has engaged much of public attention; but it is your duty, as I am sure it is your wish, to discharge your minds

---

[1] For a synopsis of the testimony, see *post*, page 677.

from every idle rumor, to stand indifferent between the parties, and relying upon the evidence, and collecting information from the witnesses on their oaths, who will be produced before you, to found your verdict upon facts well attested, and of which you only are the constitutional judges.

1. THE NARRATION.—FACTS AND CIRCUMSTANCES OF THE CASE.

The plaintiff, the Rev. Charles Massy, is the second son of a gentleman of high distinction in this county, who has been more than once called to the representation of it by a free and honorable election, and not only so descended, but is a person of liberal education; a member of one of the learned professions in the prime of manhood; a man, not only of inoffensive manners and of innocent life, but a man whose virtues correspond with his situation in society and adorn the profession he has adopted. In 1796 Mr. Massy became attached to Miss Rosslewin. Mr. Massy, being a second son, and not independent of the bounty of his father, possessed then a living of but £300 a year. Sir Hugh Massy, his father, disapproved a match "which had not fortune to support the claim of beauty," and had, therefore, proposed one with a young lady of a neighboring county, which he conceived, in point of fortune and of connection, far more eligible, and on that occasion had offered to settle on his son, the plaintiff, £1,100 a year in landed property, together with the young lady's fortune; but, declining the hand of an amiable and accomplished lady, refusing an ample and independent establishment, with the additional enjoyment of parental bounty and approbation, and foregoing all these advantages, Mr. Massy proved the sincerity and purity of his attachment by a generous sacrifice of fortune to affection, and married Miss Rosslewin in March, 1796. The happiness of the young couple during eight succeeding years, not only seemed to be but really was unmixed and unabated; he loving with constant and manly ardor; she with chaste and equal affection; and, during that interval, Heaven had blessed their union with a boy, the bond and cement of their present happiness, the pledge and promise of future multiplied felicities. Then Mr. and Mrs Massy exhibited such an example of domestic contentment and satisfaction to their neighbors, their relatives and their friends, as to convince them that the sacrifices he had made were not too great; that her grateful and affectionate returns to a conduct so nobly liberal and disinterestedly affectionate, were not too little; guilt and treachery had not yet made their way into the abode of peace and innocence; all was quiet, tranquil and happy till, to the misfortune of this county and couple, the Marquis of Headfort made his appearance at Limerick.

Mr. Massy happened to have had, some years since, a living in the county of Meath, where Lady Bective, the mother of the Marquis of Headfort, was a principal parishoner, and from whom, during his residence in the parish, Mr. Massy received much polite and hospitable attention. From this circumstance of his acquaintance with her, Mr. Massy waited on her son on his arrival at Limerick, invited him to the house, and strained his narrow means to give the son of Lady Bective every proof of his sense of her former attentions and politeness; but, while indulging the hospitable spirit of our county, little did Mr. Massy think he was introducing into his house the man who could conceive the blackest and basest designs against his peace and honor; that this stranger, so hospitably received and so affectionately cherished, was to pour poison into his peace and make him a wretch; for no reasonable man could suppose that Lord Headfort, *at his time*, ever could disturb the peace of any family, his age (for he is above fifty), his figure, his face, made such a supposition not only improbable, but almost ridiculous; yet so it happened that this "hoary veteran," in whom, like Ætna, the snow above did not quench the flames below, looked at Mrs. Massy and marked her for ruin. And nothing more beautiful could he behold, and nothing upon whom it was more unlikely that such a *venerable* personage as his Lordship could have made an improper impression.

2. How plaintiff's suspicions were aroused.

Lord Headfort spent four days at Summer Hill, on his first visit, and was introduced by Mr. Massy to the gentlemen of the first rank and consideration in the county, the Bishop of Limerick, brother-in-law of Mr. Massy, and every other gentleman and nobleman in the neighborhood. I need not, in this most hospitable part of Ireland, mention to you the consequence. Lord Headfort was received, entertained, and cherished by the friends and relatives of Mr. Massy. Whilst Mr. Massy was endeavoring, by every polite and hospitable attention in his power, to render his temporary stay in this county not unpleasant to him, some anonymous letters first created in the breast of the plaintiff—not suspicion; but conveyed an intimation "that the Marquis of Headfort was too attentive to

Mrs. Massy." Too confident in the virtue of his wife, too generous to credit information so conveyed, and yet too prudent wholly to overlook or disregard it, Mr. Massy prohibited his wife's visits to Limerick, and this was followed up by intimating to Lord Headfort that his Lordship's visits would be dispensed with at Summer Hill, his (Mr. Massy's) place of residence. Lord Headfort's visits were discontinued. His Lordship promised not to repeat them.

3. Mrs. Massy's exemplary behavior quiets his fears. —Circumstances of the abduction.

And yet, though Mr. Massy took these precautions, he still had the utmost confidence in the virtue of his wife, and not without apparent reason, for she still preserved the appearance of the most affectionate attachment to him, and acquiesced without a murmur in what his prudence prescribed. Her correct manners, her strict attention to her religious duties, might have imposed upon a keener penetration than her husband's. She regularly attended divine service, took the sacrament, and has been heard to reprove her brother and brother-in-law for want of attention to these duties; and in conversation, turning on the indiscretions of other women, was often heard to declare: "that if affection for her husband so well merited, or for her child, were not sufficient checks to keep her steady to her virtue, her sense of religious obligations would alone have that effect." The unaffected liveliness and simplicity of her manners, the decency of her deportment, her endearing attentions to him and her child, left not the shadow of suspicion on the mind of Mr. Massy, that she could, in anywise, forget her sex, her situation, or her duty, much less that she could run into the coarse toils spread for her by Lord Headfort. It will shock and appal you, gentlemen, to hear the time and occasion which Lord Headfort selected for the final accomplishment of his designs upon the honor of this unfortunate woman, and the happiness of his host and his friend. The day was Sunday; the hour, the time of divine service. Yes, gentlemen, on that day and on that hour set apart for the service of our Creator, whilst the reverend rector was bending before the altar of his God, invoking blessings, not only on his flock there assembled, but on the head of the unfeeling and profligate destroyer of his comfort and honor. On such a day, at such an hour, upon such an occasion, did the *noble* Lord think proper to commit this *honorable* breach of hospitable faith; this highminded violation of the little laws of your diminutive county; this contempt

—I would almost call it, this defiance of the Almighty himself. And will not you, gentlemen, the sworn arbitrators of this profanation, the guardians of our laws and our religion, the conscientious ministers of divine and human justice, reward the *noble* delinquent accordingly? I know you will; and to your just estimate of such an act I commit this *noble* act and its *most noble* actor.

I have to state what will be proved, that on a Sunday, at such an hour, Lord Headfort took off Mrs. Massy from her husband's house at Summer Hill; they crossed the Shannon in a boat, got into a chaise in waiting for them on the road, and from thence posted to Pallas, eighteen or nineteen miles only from Summer Hill. There he and Mrs. Massy, heedless of the misery and distraction of her unhappy husband, remained in the same room the whole of Sunday night. The noble peer did not fly. No; he made short and easy stages—not fearful of pursuit, not as a criminal endeavoring to effect his escape, but as a conqueror, parading slowly through the country, and quietly enjoying the glory and honor of his triumph! What was his triumph? The distraction of the friend he maddened with agony! the pollution of a, till then, spotless and innocent woman! From Pallas his Lordship pursued his route to Clonmel, and there rested a night; from thence to Waterford, then to England, where, I trust, he will ever remain, because I am satisfied that no advantage to be derived to the country, from the most ample fortune expended here, could countervail the mischiefs that must flow from the application of enormous wealth to extravagant vices, and the example of such prodigal profligacy amongst us. I fear I detain you too long, yet it is necessary to detail the enormity of this foul transaction, "in itself most foul." To you, then, I will leave it to mark, by the verdict you will give, your approbation or disapprobation of the conduct of this *nobleman.* He was not young. If young, the ardor and inexperience of youth might have been some extenuation of this enormity; but many years has elapsed since the *venerable* Peer could have insisted upon such a plea. The noble Lord is, I am instructed, between fifty and sixty years of age, and from the life he has led and the pursuits he has been engaged in, we must conclude his constitution not to be that of a very green old age. At this advanced period of life, the slightest check of principle must rein in and restrain the passions.

But if a sickly appetite cannot be controlled, and must be fed with perpetual supplies of dearly purchased variety, let the wealth he commands and abuses procure it, without breaking in upon the peace and honor of respectable families. The noble Lord proceeded to the completion of his diabolical project, not with the rash precipitancy of youth, but with the cool and deliberate consideration of age.

4. DEFENDANT'S CRIME COMPARED TO THE TREACHERY OF PIRATE WRECKERS.—A STRIKING SIMILE.

The Cornish plunderer, intent on the spoil, callous to every touch of humanity, shrouded in darkness, holds out false lights to the tempest-tost vessel, and lures her and her pilot to that shore upon which she must be lost forever—the rock unseen, the ruffian invisible, and nothing apparent but the treacherous signal of security and repose. So, this prop of the throne, this pillar of the State, this stay of religion, the ornament of the Peerage, this common protector of the people's privileges and of the crown's prerogatives, descends from these high grounds of character to muffle himself in the gloom of his own base and dark designs; to play before the eyes of the deluded wife and the deceived husband the falsest lights of love to the one, and of friendly and hospitable regards to the other, until she is at length dashed upon that hard bosom where her honor and happiness are wrecked and lost forever. The agonized husband beholds the ruin with those sensations of horror which you can better feel than I can describe. Her upon whom he had embarked all his hopes and all his happiness in this life, the treasure of all his earthly felicities, the rich fund of all his hoarded joys, sunk before his eyes into an abyss of infamy, or if any fragment escape, escaping to solace, to gratify, and to enrich her vile destroyer. Such, gentlemen, is the act upon which you are to pass your judgment; such is the injury upon which you are to set a price, and I lament that the moderation of the pleader has circumscribed within such narrow limits the discretion you are to exercise upon the damages. You cannot exceed the damages laid in the declaration. I lament, and so I hope do you, that you cannot, for the damages laid do not exceed one year's income of the noble Lord's estates. The life of the adulterer is in some degree in the power of the injured husband. If the husband kill the adulterer caught in the act, the killing is not murder: what, according to the noble Lord's own estimate, would be the value of the noble Lord's life? In mine, and perhaps in your estimation, the value of the noble Lord's life would not be very high; but take it according to his own, and it is invaluable. The ransom of his life ought to be

43

the measure of your damages. What can he plead? Is it that he
too has a wife and children? Is it that as a double adulterer he
comes into this court of justice and interposes the innocence of his
family between his crime and your justice? Are his *titles* and
honors, as they are vulgarly called, to dazzle your eyes and blind
you to the demerits of his conduct? No, no. What are titles con·
ferred by kings if the souls of those who wear them be not ennobled
by the king of kings. These badges of distinction, these splendid
emblems of shining merit; these rewards conferred by grateful
sovereigns on eminent attainments in science, or achievements in
war, may be well allowed to adorn wisdom and virtue, but cannot
make the fool wise, the coward brave, or the knave honest.

5. Grounds of the defense anticipated and discussed.

There are two grounds of defense upon which I hear that the
noble Lord means to submit his case to the jury. The connivance
of the husband, the notorious general misconduct of the wife;
both, if I am rightly instructed, unfounded in fact and not to be
supported by any credible testimony. Witnesses to these, or to
any other facts, may be procured, but the jury is to determine on
their credit. But who is the man who will have the hardihood to
come forward and tell you that Mr. Massy, or any gentleman of his
family, rank, character, education or profession, could stoop to a
conduct so uniformly mean, so scandalously dishonorable; and if
such a witness can be found, who is the juror will believe him?
Can any *gentleman* believe that a *gentleman* could be willfully in-
strumental to his own disgrace, the promoter of his own dishonor,
a pander to the prostitution of an adored wife, the stigmatizer of
his idolized offspring? Such a tale (let the relator be who he may)
is in itself utterly improbable. The proud mind of my client cannot condescend to contradict it; but let the tenor of his whole life,
his character yet unaspersed and unblemished, his generous sacrifices to this very woman before her honor became his honor, and
her character the object of his protection, his exemplary conduct
as an husband, a father, a pastor of our church, a member of society, give the lie to a story which cannot be told by any man of
honor, or be believed by any man of sense. It is not impossible,
however, gentlemen, that the Marquis of Headfort may attempt to
cover his retreat from the pursuit of justice by some contrivance
of this kind, nor is it quite impossible, however improbable, that
he may find some plausible instrument, hard of forehead and flip-

pant of tongue, ready from the motives which generally actuate such instruments, to devote himself to the perilous service. If such a witness should appear before you, I will give you a clue to his character, I will describe to you what he is, and I much mistake if by these marks and tokens you can fail to know him if he shall appear. He is not like those whom I have the honor to address, a gentleman who has a character to stake upon the testimony he will give. He is not a gentleman whose intercourse with the world has fashioned him to courtesy without wearing out and defacing those sharp, prominent features of oldfashioned probity, undeceiving truth, and unbending pride, which characterize the Irish gentleman.

Let me now touch the second ground of what I understand is to be the noble Lord's defense, the general misconduct of Mrs. Massy before her elopement with him. It well becomes the Marquis of Headfort to cover with additional disgraces the unfortunate victim of his delusions. Is it that in the struggle between his avarice and his vanity the former has conquered, or is it so ordered by the wise and just dispensations of Providence that the best boons successful vice bestows upon subdued chastity are private contempt and public infamy? But though the noble Marquis may not hesitate to sink still lower and lower the degraded object of his guilty passion, yet there are other considerations which might hold back from such an attempt, a man not inaccessible to the feelings of humanity. Mr. Massy has a son still living. Why should this innocent be more involved than he already is in his mother's dishonor? Why should this half-orphaned child, robbed of one parent by the *noble* Marquis, become, by the deliberate act of his and his family's enemy, the sad remembrancer of the other, of a father's doubt and a mother's dishonor? Is this additional pang to be inflicted on the lacerated bosom? Is this new wound to be opened in a bleeding and exhausted heart? Why will the *noble* Marquis endeavor to infuse this horrid suspicion into Mr. Massy's mind that the offspring of his marriage bed is spurious; that though the father of a living son, he is perhaps childless, his affections lavished upon, his name borne by, his fortune destined for, perhaps an impostor? This attempt the noble Marquis will make, I am told, to mitigate the injury and diminish the damages. If such an endeavor be made, you, gentlemen, will appreciate such an attempt according to its real worth and true value. This attempt can only be supported by such a witness as I have already described to you, and from whom your honorable hearts will recoil with scorn and abhorrence. We are

prepared to show you, by the testimony of most respectable person-
ages, that the fame of this now unhappy woman had never been
sullied by the slightest imputation until her connection with the
Marquis of Headfort.

6. THE RULE OF DAMAGES.

I feel, gentlemen, I have been honored with your attention too
long. I shall detain it but a very little longer. In this action the
plaintiff is entitled either to the largest or the smallest damages. If
connivance be proved to your satisfaction, a single shilling would be
too much; if not, I know not what measure of damages, under all
the circumstances of the case, would be too large. It will be proved
to you how he received the first news of her flight. The first intimation was like the stroke of death. His portion for several weeks
after, agony and distraction. Happy would it have been for him
if death had followed the shock, or madness relieved him from
misery. It now rests with you to compensate the sufferings of this
deeply injured individual. It is with you to determine whether the
penalty you inflict on lawless lust shall operate as a protection to
legitimate happiness; whether your ample verdict shall not, like a
shield, cover domestic peace and social order from brutal insult
and dishonest violation. If the "compunctious visitings" of conscience and duty cannot dissuade the black adulterer from his designs upon the quiet of others, let the example you make drive him
from your doors, and deter him from the spoil of your dearest and
most invaluable possessions, your happiness and your honor. And
may that God, under whose eye and in whose presence we act,
when his hand shall hold the balance of divine justice, when those
transgressions from which the errors and infirmities of our nature
exempt no human creature, shall be put into one scale, may the
weighty and exemplary verdict of this day accompany your merits
into the other, and make it preponderate.

SPEECH OF THOMAS QUIN

OPENING FOR DEFENDANT IN MASSY v. THE MARQUIS OF HEAD-
FORT.—DAMAGES FOR CRIMINAL CONVERSATION.

AT ENNIS ASSIZES, COUNTY CLARE, BEFORE BARON SMITH
AND A SPECIAL JURY, FRIDAY, JULY 27th, 1804.

Damages claimed, £40,000.—Amount recovered, £10,000.

ANALYSIS OF MR. QUIN'S SPEECH.

1. The rule of law in relation to the injury and claim in this class of actions.
2. The defense of connivance goes to the foundation of the action.—Connivance may be actual or constructive.
3. Character and conduct of Mrs. Massy.
4. The verdict must not be the result of vengeance, but of reason and justice
5. A good wife likened to a jewel, to be worn next the heart.

In view of the fact that the speeches on both sides are published, we shall give a synopsis of the evidence in the case, which was very brief.[1] But six witnesses were called, four for plaintiff, two for defendant. The Rev. Dr. Parker proved the marriage; Mr. Stackpole stated, that if plaintiff had married according to the wishes of his father, he would have received a large fortune. His cross-examination elicited the fact that plaintiff's brother had separated from his wife, and was living with a Mrs. Harvey; the defendant's object being to show that plaintiff, by allowing his wife to visit at his brother's, was careless of her moral character. Patrick Dunn proved the elopement, and Jane Apjohn, a chamber-maid, swore that defendant and Mrs. Massy occupied the same room that night at the inn where she was employed. Colonel Pepper was called by the defendant, and testified that he had often seen the Marquis pay marked attention to Mrs. Massy, who seemed flattered thereby. He was corroborated by George E. Bruce, who testified also that he had seen defendant at the races with Mrs. Massy; that about six weeks before the elopement, he noticed she was extravagantly dressed, and wore expensive jewelry and ornaments; that on one occasion, defendant accompanied her from Limerick to Summer Hill in his carriage *tête-à-tête*. On his cross-examination he testified that Mrs. Harvey, the lady who lived with plaintiff's brother, was a gentlewoman of refined manners, and very fond of children. Mr. Curran, who cross-examined, put the following question to the witness: "Do you believe on your oath, as a man of honor, and in the presence of your country and your God, that plaintiff connived at the conduct of his wife?" He answered: "I believe not. I am sure he was incapable of it. His fault was more of the head than of the heart."

Mr. Quin's opening was very adroit. He pursued the same line of argument afterwards taken by his associate, Mr. Ponsonby, and without attempting

[1] For a statement of the facts in the case, see *ante*, pages 667, 669.

to justify defendant's conduct, claimed that the burden was on the husband to show that his conduct was exemplary in all respects, and that if he was guilty of any moral delinquency, it was *pro tanto*, in proportion to its flagrancy, a bar to his recovery. He said:

MAY IT PLEASE THE COURT,—*Gentlemen of the Jury:*—It is the particular duty of my situation to lay before you the circumstances of the defendant's case; submitting it on his behalf to your investigation, with a perfect confidence of your discharging the important duty devolved upon you with all that justice and fidelity which may be expected from the goodness of your understandings and the integrity of your hearts.

I. THE RULE OF LAW IN RELATION TO THE INJURY AND CLAIM IN THIS CLASS OF ACTIONS.

Cases of this sort impose painful tasks upon the counsel for the respective parties. They will not bear much ceremony, no polite forbearance, no punctilious restraint can reasonably be expected; of this you have had tolerable evidence already. The husband who brings his action as such, to recover compensation for an injury offered to the most sacred relation in society, does thereby put his character and conduct, as a husband, directly at issue, and if he expects to succeed, must show that he fulfilled and discharged the duties springing from that relation, because it is the violation of it which constitutes at once the injury and the claim. We cannot differ as to the principle and foundation of this action; it arises out of the necessary politic provisions of society. It is bottomed on the finest and purest affections of the human heart. What man is there possessed of rationality and feeling, what husband who deserves the name, that can resist to sympathize with, and is not impatient to redress the sufferings of a person deprived, without default of his, of that most inestimable of all human treasures, an amiable and virtuous wife? Here we agree; but in proportion as such feelings impel us to remunerate *such* an injury, and vindicate the wrongs of *such* a sufferer, so do we turn with disgust and reprobation from an attempt to pervert the sacred nature of this remedy from its just and honest purpose, from the assistance of the pure, genuine and legitimate objects of its care, to lavish its redress upon factitious injury, and make that jury who should be the instruments of its salutary efficacy subservient to the scheme of hypocrisy and imposition. If the husband, who by his deportment is entitled to the name, meets such an injury, and sustains such a loss, compensate him (if he can be compensated) to the utmost limit which the case may bear. You, at the same time, requite the most poignant abuse which man can suffer, and give a wholesome lesson to society. But if all who call themselves husbands shall appeal successfully to this tribunal, and under pretense of injury shall clamor for money, to assuage their feelings by supplying their wants, you, in defiance of reason and of feelings, confound all claimants, you confer what should remunerate the injured on him who has received no injury, and equalize those persons who should stand, in your estimation, as separate as innocence and guilt; you sanction, nay, encourage an adulterous traffic : the matrimonial bond will become assailed by the most licentious, dissolute, and sordid motives; lust, avarice and indigence will institute treaties on the subject : husbands will take their wives to market, and instead of restraining, you will promote the vice.

2. The defense of connivance goes to the foundation of the action.—Connivance may be actual or constructive.

The case of the defendant is not, because it cannot be, a case of justification. The fact stands admitted, and however it may be accounted for, it cannot be morally defended under any circumstances. The advocates of the defendant would not outrage moral decency, or affront the feelings and understanding of a jury. But the principle of the action should be exactly understood. The defendant is not here upon his trial for the commission of an offense against society ; you are not placed there on this occasion as moral censors of the actions of men ; public duties should not be confounded ; the defendant is not the subject of criminal prosecution ; but the plaintiff seeks compensation for a specific injury, and must show he has sustained it. He says he has lost, by means of the defendant, the comforts and enjoyments of conjugal domestic life. The law upon the subject is simple and well settled. If the husband, in the emphatical language of the law, connives at his own dishonor (which I would not be understood to say he has done in the present case), it goes to the foundation of the action, and he is not entitled to a verdict. That must, of course, be collected from the circumstances. Neglect and inattention may be so gross as to amount to satisfactory evidence of connivance, or may disclose such demerits on the plaintiff's part as should mitigate the damages to nothing.

3. CHARACTER AND CONDUCT OF MRS. MASSY.

The case before you is of the latter class, and as such we put it to you. Let me advert to the circumstances under which the plaintiff married Miss Rosslewin. She was young, volatile and giddy, beautiful and vain, of an uncommon levity (the witness called it *gayety*) of disposition, and fond of dress beyond even the ordinary passion of her sex. His manly advantages and liberal education enabled him, and the prudential duties of his station enjoined him, to observe and guide her. Lest uncontrolled by the presence and unassisted by the instruction of a husband, unrestrained by a marital admonition, unattended, unadvised, unchecked and unreproved by him who was the natural guardian of her morals and his own honor, indulged in profusion to which his income was inadequate, she engaged in a career of dissipation, and plunged into that vicious vortex which hurried her to the depth of her own infamy and his disgrace. Her life was passed and occupied ; the plaintiff suffered it to pass amidst those scenes of fashionable enjoyment wherein women, unfortified by principle and unaided by advice, become exposed to the most dangerous impressions ; her improving beauty solicited and provoked the admiration of our sex, and her situation encouraged their approaches. Devoted to his own amusements, her natural protector wandered from her and left "her fair side all unguarded ;" she received and permitted, with undisguised delight, assiduities too observable to pass unnoticed, or escape the effect of public observation. Her dress became magnificent and costly. She passed months at the houses of single gentlemen, unaccompanied or unattended, save occasionally by the plaintiff ; and, at Galway in particular, where she went on an excursion, the attentions of a military man of rank became so remarkable, and her encouragement so glaring, that her own connections found it necessary to snatch her from the spot, as from impending infamy, and hurried her to Limerick.

Thus it will appear that this unfortunate young lady, who has been poetically represented by the plaintiff's counsel as a paragon of domestic fidelity and female purity until the spoiler came, and whose *piety* has composed one topic of the panegyric, had never beheld the defendant, or he her, until the breath of public remark had tainted, if not blasted, her reputation. Such as I have described her, so did the defendant find her : engaged in public fashionable life, immersed in pleasures, and practiced in those arts which too often render a lovely married woman more *seducer* than *seduced*. He met her first at the races of Limerick, then at the races of Mallow, unattended by the plaintiff at either place. The attentions of a man of such superior rank were too flattering to be declined; they passed under public observation at all places of public or private fashionable resort; the eyes of all companies were fixed upon them, and her reception of them, being too obvious to pass unmarked, became the subject of general conversation. She avowed to her relations her attachment to the defendant, and her determination to go off with him. Are you to presume that all this took place unknown to her husband? Was he, though on the spot, alone deceived? It is said the defendant's propensity to gallantry is notorious; was that unknown to the plaintiff? It would be monstrous indeed, under such circumstances, to presume him ignorant; but he should have known her conduct, because it was his duty to observe and govern it. That such was her demeanor will appear in proof. We have heard and read of various husbands—the tender, the careless, the mysterious, the suspicious—but the plaintiff adds a new one to the drama, and gives the *unsuspecting* or the *sightless* husband! Here was no breach of friendship, no confidence abused; the intercourse went on in public, and it was not until after a familiar acquaintance with the wife, well known to the plaintiff, that he and the defendant became known to each other.

4. The verdict must not be the result of vengeance, but of reason and justice.

While these proceedings were in progress to their consummation, the plaintiff, who had resigned Mrs. Massy to her own good guidance, passed his time at the house of his brother, enjoying the highly moral intercourse of him and Mrs. Harvey. What! Gentlemen of the Jury! the man who claims £40,000 against another for a breach of the most sacred moral relations in society—himself of a sacred and highly moral function—associates with the mistress of his brother; sanctions, by his presence, the expulsion of an amiable and deserving woman, cast into exile from that mansion which she could adorn, and witnesses her rights supplanted and her place usurped by the dominion of a concubine! And if these be the plaintiff's claims to your regard, indulge him to the extent of his demand; but before you do so, you will expect that he shall show himself entitled from his own deportment, for your verdict will be the result of reason and of justice, and not, as has been said, of vengeance. What will you be disposed to feel when you shall hear that she dined repeatedly at the house of the defendant, alone, unaccompanied and uncountenanced by any other female, and surrounded by his officers? To what can you ascribe such an unblushing breach of delicacy? What inference do you draw from that? Why, that her principles were sapped before, and that it is as idle, as unjust to charge the defendant with her ruin! What will you think when I inform you that after, in consequence of such misconduct, her relations shut their doors against her, the husband opened his? She returned from Limerick to Summer Hill, the plaintiff's house, accompanied by the defendant, and no other person, in the defendant's carriage, and was received by her *unsuspecting* husband. What did he do? Did he express a natural indignation? Did he remonstrate? Did he reprove? No, gentlemen of the jury! He retired to Dian's temple at Donass, and, the key of the cellar being left behind, nothing remained to impede the indulgences of love and wine; from thence till he went off the defendant passed whole days at Summer Hill, uninterrupted by the plaintiff. Allow me to ask, where was Mr. Massy, and how was he occupied while his wife was so conducting herself? Was he engaged away in the service of his king and country? Was he laudably employed in the industrious task of furnishing the comforts and elegancies of life for the partner of his heart and the dear pledges of their love? No.

5. A GOOD WIFE LIKENED TO A JEWEL, TO BE WORN NEXT THE HEART.

The man possessing a jewel of inestimable worth, who wished, in truth, to guard its value and preserve its lustre, would wear it next the heart; but the plaintiff threw this *gaudy, worthless trinket* here and there, to be picked up by every casual finder, or let it hang so loosely from his person as to invite and, ready as it were, to bless the silly hand which, tempted by its glitter, might feel disposed to rid him of the contemptible embarrassment, and snip it from his side. It has been lost, and you are called upon to estimate the injury and to reprize the loss. You will reflect how far it was worth the keeping; you will consider what pains he took to guard it; you will appreciate the value of the article, and then determine upon what grounds, and to what extent, the plaintiff merits the interposition of a jury.

SPEECH OF Rt. Hon. GEORGE PONSONBY.

Closing for Defendant in Massy v. The Marquis of Headfort.—Damages for Criminal Conversation.

AT ENNIS ASSIZES, COUNTY CLARE, BEFORE BARON SMITH AND A SPECIAL JURY, FRIDAY, JULY 27th, 1804.

Damages claimed, £40,000.—Amount recovered, £10,000.

Analysis of Mr. Ponsonby's Speech.

1. Duty of the jury.—Varied character and nature of the defenses to the action.
2. Observations as to the plaintiff's deportment, and its influence upon the wife.
3. If plaintiff's conduct contributed to his misfortune, he cannot be rewarded for it.
4. Vindictive damages not recoverable.— The damages must be proportionate to the injury and the conduct of the parties.
5. While the defendant's acts cannot be justified, the plaintiff's conduct is not free from blame.

The Right Honorable George Ponsonby, at the time this speech was delivered, stood at the head of his profession in Ireland, and it is said that he derived from his practice an income of £6,000 a year. He possessed landed estates, was knight of the shire of Wicklow, and allied to several noble families both in England and Ireland. He succeeded Lord Redesdale, in 1806, to the office of Chancellor, and received the unanimous congratulation of the Bar on his appointment to the seals. Upon his retirement from office, his merits were recognized, and the high appreciation in which his integrity, diligence and talents were held, and the deep regret felt on the occasion, were expressed at the time by Mr. Plunket, in an address in behalf of his professional brethren. In the debate in the Commons, regarding his pension, Lord Howick remarked, that a more upright and efficient judge never graced the Chancery bench. He earned a reputation as an honest, upright official, and no incumbent rendered more general satisfaction.

His address on the present occasion is characteristic of the man. It contains no attempt at ornament. No effort is made to justify his client's crime. It is a frank, calm statement, containing many shrewd and practical observations, bearing directly upon the legal aspect of the case, based upon the fixed and settled principles of the law. Through it all there is a vein of candor, which always goes far towards allaying the prejudices, which conduct like that of the defendant invariably excites. If it is said that, notwithstanding this effort, the damages were great, it should be remembered that the defense was mainly technical, and the jury might have given four times as much. At the close of the testimony Mr. Ponsonby said :

MAY IT PLEASE THE COURT :—It is my duty, gentlemen of the jury, as counsel for the defendant, to trouble you with a few observations on the whole of the evidence that has been laid before you.[1] You will please to observe, that this action is brought to recover compensation, in money, for the injury sustained by the plaintiff. That injury, only, is the foundation of this action ; and, therefore, what you have heard of juries giving damages by way of example, in order to deter others from the commission of a like offense, of setting themselves up as censors, is perfectly irrelevant to the case before you. It is the usual practice of counsel to have recourse to this artifice, because they know well, should they succeed in imposing such a principle on a jury, there is no redress for the defendant if the damages should be excessive. In other cases such excess may be rectified, but in this never can ; and therefore, from the consequence of inflamed passions, there is no relief to be had, and this should be a peculiar reason with a jury to reflect most maturely in apportioning damages, because should they happen to be mistaken, their mistakes can never be rectified.

I. DUTY OF THE JURY.—VARIED CHARACTER AND NATURE OF THE DEFENSES TO THE ACTION.

In this action the law is plain and simple. The plaintiff in it complains that the defendant deprived him of the comfort and society of his wife, and the business for a jury is, on their oaths, to inquire what comfort has been lost, or injuries sustained by the plaintiff, and whether such have been brought on by his own misconduct. This must be the rule to regulate the jury.

The degrees of defense to the action are various. A defendant may show the plaintiff is not entitled to any damages, because, if any injury has been sustained, it was occasioned by his default, in conniving at his own disgrace. If such a defense should be proved, the plaintiff must fail altogether; but that is not the defense meant to be set up here. There are other degrees of defense: the husband is, not only in fact, but is considered by the law, the guardian and protector of his wife; but if, instead of so protecting her, he puts her in a situation to provoke temptation, he is not entitled to such damages as he might otherwise have been. The defense I am instructed to insist upon goes not to the right of

---

[1] For the facts of the case, and the evidence, see pages 667, 677, 679.

the action, but is irresistible in mitigation of the damages. I do not accuse plaintiff of connivance at the misconduct of his wife, but I do insist, it must be inferred from the evidence that he is not entitled to damages so great as his counsel would seem to require. If a woman has long lived with her husband in affection, and discharging, as became her, the duties of her situation, and is seduced, the jury ought to compensate him most amply. If a long supposed friendship is perverted to the seduction of such a wife, the seducer ought to be punished—the jury ought to be liberal in compensation. It would be well if society were so perfect that there could be no danger of such an offense. The truth is, men are more in fault than women. Women are, in all countries, regulated by the conduct of men, and if men will talk with levity; if they will talk lightly of women who have been guilty; if those who are guilty are received into society; it is but natural their own wives should be induced to act the same part those guilty women have acted. It is the husband's own conduct with regard to other women ; his conduct in society in general, in deportment, in conversation, that can entitle him to damages in an action of this sort. It is painful to an advocate to speak of a man in the same society with himself with severity, but it is often his duty to do so.

2. OBSERVATIONS AS TO THE PLAINTIFF'S DEPORTMENT, AND ITS INFLUENCE UPON THE WIFE.

What has been the conduct of this plaintiff's family ? To be sure it has been endeavored to prove, that the lady was very religious; that she remonstrated at the conduct of her brother-in-law; that she was fond of Sunday devotion; but was there not in such devotion as much affectation as there was religion ! There was in the plaintiff's brother so much of immorality, that even the plaintiff was prevailed upon to remonstrate with him. What time more fit for such remonstrance than his dinner visits ! No doubt, the way of life of his brother was extremely disagreeable to the plaintiff, and therefore he frequently visited him for the purpose of affecting a reform in his religious principles and habits. But, admitting the fact to be so, if the plaintiff's wife saw the frequency of those visits, she might reasonably enough consider it strange in him to visit a house whose legitimate owner was expelled, in order to make way for a woman, a kept mistress of her husband, and, therefore, the plaintiff's wife might consider it venial in herself to indulge a little in the same guilt. Will you then say, gentlemen of the jury, that the plaintiff has not been at least indiscreet to a very great degree; and that connubial honor and domestic peace were not so highly valued by him as his counsel would fain persuade you they were.

You will consider, gentlemen, whether, as a minister of religion, he should not have forborne to associate with a relative who had thus set at defiance every moral and social duty, and by the severity of his censure prove he could not pardon such an offense. But, instead of that, has he not sanctioned by his conduct the acts of another man, and now complains of the very same when done by the Marquis of Headfort?

Is has been said that the defendant was a man of very notorious gallantry, regardless of the ties which bind society, and trampling under foot those bonds that secure the happiness and comfort of families. How often he has sinned in this respect I know not; but I would venture to say, this is the *first* action of this sort that ever was brought against him. But even admitting the fact to be as charged against the defendant, was it not notice to the husband to regard, with a more watchful eye, the connection he saw increasing between his wife and Lord Headfort? Why did he allow any intimacy at all to subsist under such circumstances? Why allow his wife to dine with him? Why allow her to visit him, when his actions were so pointed? Was it not the height of indiscretion in plaintiff to allow his wife to continue this intimacy—an intimacy that could not proceed from any friendship between the plaintiff and defendant, for none such subsisted? To what account, then, was he to place those attentions to his wife? Was it not the defendant's regard for *her*, and not for plaintiff? The history of the world unfortunately affords many instances of the violation of friendships the most sacred, and of their perversion to purposes the most abominable. But here no previous friendship existed. Sufficient occurred to awaken the attention of plaintiff when those unusual tendernesses were shown by the defendant to his wife.

It has been said, to be sure, that his confidence in her honor and principles were even so great as not to allow him to suspect her. Why, it reminds me of one of the plays of Congreve, where a lady laments the violence of her passion to her confidant. The confidant says : "Ah, you will never yield ; your honor, your integrity will support you." The lady replies: "Ah, me, what is *integrity* to *opportunity;*" and, therefore, if a husband allows a partiality for his wife to continue without interruption, he contributes to his own misfortune; most particularly if the suitor be a man of the character and conduct this defendant has been said to be. What can it be but the grossest folly in the husband not to discountenance his advances altogether? If anything detrimental to him follows from such neglect, who has he to blame but himself? Is he equally entitled to damages with the husband who would, instead of winking at the imprudencies of his wife, have removed her altogether from the neighborhood of her gallant, or at least have forbidden her a longer continuance of his acquaintance? To talk, therefore, of the kindness of this husband; of his unwillingness to open his eyes to the conduct of his wife, is but idle declamation; he has nobody to blame but himself.

3. IF PLAINTIFF'S CONDUCT CONTRIBUTED TO HIS MISFORTUNE, HE CANNOT BE REWARDED FOR IT.

There are other considerations, gentlemen of the jury, of great moment, necessary for your deliberation. I mean the actual loss the husband has sustained independent of what is called the loss of honor. Was not her conduct such as ought to make every prudent husband watchful? Was she not the subject of public animadversion? And, if he has not discharged his duty, ought he to get the compensation of a husband the most virtuous? He comes for compensation for the loss he has sustained in the society of his wife; but if she would make the same mistake with any other person, this defendant ought not to be punished beyond the proportion of his offense. There is no man so rude or dull as not to understand, that if the approaches of a stranger be well received by a married woman the husband cannot lose much by the loss of her society. The plaintiff here lays his damages at £40,000—a sum never heard of even in the days of Lord Kenyon, a judge remarkable for the severity of his principles. The truth is, gentlemen of the jury, no woman capable of conduct such as plaintiff's wife has been guilty of, could be worth £40,000. So strange was her conduct, and so negligent was her husband, that one would think it would be almost reasonable to expect he should have told the defendant that he valued his wife at £40,000. One begins to think it was not fair in the plaintiff to allow the address of my Lord Headfort to his wife, without giving him some notice that he valued her so high. Had he done so, are you sure, gentlemen, that the defendant would not have withdrawn his assiduities? And this is the only want of candor I impute to the plaintiff. Admitting that defendant's object was the reputation of gallantry, and that plaintiff knew that was the fact, and encouraged it, and wished to make the defendant pay for it, he ought, at least, to have told the defendant he expected £40,000 for his indulgence of him. What, gentlemen of the jury, £40,000 for the seduction of a woman only four months known to the defendant, previously too successfully assailed by others, and plaintiff the claimant for such a sum, who has been, himself, guilty of great moral delinquency! I am no advocate for gallantry of this kind, but I would ask you, has there been in this case a long train of seduction, a long friendship violated, or a confiding husband betrayed? If such be the case, punish the defendant; punish him amply. But, on the contrary, if that be not the fact, and the evidence laid before you shows it was not the fact; if plaintiff's own conduct has contributed to his own misfortune, you are not to reward him for it. What is it to the plaintiff that Lord Headfort is a married man? Is his injury the greater? You have nothing to do with the marriage of the defendant. It can make no difference in point of loss whether he was so or not. His being separate from his wife is a reason, a strong reason, why the plaintiff should not allow his wife to associate with him.

4. VINDICTIVE DAMAGES NOT RECOVERABLE.—THE DAMAGES MUST BE PROPORTIONATE TO THE INJURY AND THE CONDUCT OF THE PARTIES.

The plaintiff's counsel have talked of vindictive damages; it is an expression unintelligible to me. They have said he should be made an example for all other adulterers. But your duty is to give damages proportionate to the injuries sustained, and the conduct of the parties, otherwise you may as well give damages because others have committed the same offense, so as to prevent the repetition of it. If one man had assaulted another so grievously as to put out his eyes, it seems to me it would be equally right in you to give vindictive damages to prevent the repetition of it, as it would be to do so in the present case. But the fact is, each case must rest on its own merits. You will ask yourselves these questions: Did the plaintiff see his wife dressed in ornaments beyond her means, and which he never supplied? Had he such warning as ought to have been sufficient to put him on his guard? If he had discharged his duty, could he have occasion for bringing this action? The evidence laid before you has given an answer to these questions, and ought to be the rule by which your verdict should

be regulated.   The liberty happily allowed to women in these
countries will often subject the best of husbands to deception ; but
it is better, allow it, than to have recourse to the horrible and abominable coercions practiced in other countries.   Here, women are
their own mistresses, and men are not their masters.   If husbands,
acting under the generous feelings that are encouraged in these
countries, are deceived, and if foul advantages are taken of them,
it is hard to consider any compensation too great for the injury
they sustain ; but if the husband not only neglects, but almost in-
vites addresses to his wife, he shall not be compensated.   What is
the law in other cases?   Is not the neglect or want of vigilance of
one's property considered by the law as not entitled to redress?   Is
not an estate often lost because the claim has not been made in a
reasonable time?   And why should it be otherwise in an action
like this?   Was the plaintiff's own conduct prudent and discreet?
It has been said he ordered separate beds for himself and his wife ;
that he had forbid her for three weeks to visit Limerick? and yet,
strange to tell, the defendant during that time was received at his
house.   But suppose the defendant was not received there—supposing the worst that can be said for my client—could not the
plaintiff have denied him admittance?   Could not he have removed
for a time to the country with his wife?   The conduct of the
plaintiff and his relations was far different.   No indignation was
expressed among them at the defendant's conduct.   He dined
often after at plaintiff's brother's house.   Could the rigid injunction
of plaintiff on his wife, not to visit Limerick or receive the defendant, be considered serious?   Was he not induced to think, when
he was received at plaintiff's house after such an injunction, that
the whole proceeding was a mockery?   The witness said it was the
fault of the head and not of the heart of the plaintiff that occasioned this neglect of his wife.   Admitted.   It was still weakness
in the extreme not to discountenance the defendant altogether.   If
a man is told in words his advances are not welcome, and yet the
manner and actions contradict these words, which is to be believed?   The defendant knew that plaintiff lived in habits of intimacy with his brother, frequented that brother's house, dined
with him, when he well knew that the wife of that brother was banished from her home, and, in her place, was substituted the mistress
of the brother, who sat at the head of his table and discharged all
the other duties of the legitimate wife.   The plaintiff left his wife
alone, spent days and dined in company with Mrs. Harvey.   The
44

plaintiff being a clergyman has nothing to do with this action. He is no more entitled to damages for that reason than any other man. It makes it only the more incumbent on him to attend to the morals and conduct of his wife.

5. WHILE THE DEFENDANT'S ACTS CANNOT BE JUSTIFIED, THE PLAINTIFF'S CONDUCT IS NOT FREE FROM BLAME.

I do not justify the defendant; I do not accuse the plaintiff of connivance; but I do insist that his own conduct, his own way of life, has occasioned whatever misfortune he has suffered. That this unhappy woman has yielded to the addresses of four months cannot be disputed. What was the occasion of it? Was it the prospect of marriage? Was it love? No. Twenty-five does not love fifty. Her husband was but twenty-eight. She could not leave

"That fair and fertile plain to batten on that moor."

Love might be a strong excuse for such conduct, because it is often too strong for law, virtue, or morality; it becomes entitled, therefore, to human commiseration. But how is it possible to conceive that a woman of twenty-five could, after an acquaintance of four months, be induced by a violence of love to throw herself into the arms of a man of fifty? If this husband's conduct was virtuous and vigilant; if his wife's conduct was moral and domestic; and if *not*, notwithstanding she was seduced from him; if the plaintiff was everything that was right, and the defendant everything that was abominable, why, then, give damages? But do not say that because defendant is rich; because he is a man of intrigue; because he is a man of gallantry; therefore give vindictive damages. If the breath of slander had never reached this lady previous to her acquaintance with the defendant, punish the defendant for his seduction; but, on the contrary, if the defendant has been deceived by the husband and seduced by the wife, as men of sense consider whether he ought, therefore, to be punished by vindictive damages.

SPEECH OF JOHN PHILPOT CURRAN.

Closing for Plaintiff in Massy v. The Marquis of Headfort.—Damages for Criminal Conversation.

AT ENNIS ASSIZES, COUNTY CLARE, BEFORE BARON SMITH AND A SPECIAL JURY, FRIDAY, JULY 27th, 1804.

Damages claimed, £40,000.   Amount recovered, £10,000.

Analysis of Mr. Curran's Speech.

1. Theory of damages in this class of actions.—Why the verdict cannot be set aside for excess.
2. Statement of the questions to be considered by the jury.
3. The charge of connivance a false and impudent defense.—Plaintiff's indiscretion no crime.
4. Supposed remonstrance with the defendant, when about to commit the offense.
5. Shameful experience resulting from a previous elopement of which the defendant had been guilty.
6. Disgraceful conduct of the defendant in the present case.
7. The character of the defense an aggravation of the crime, and an insult to the jury.
8. Reasons why liberal damages should be awarded.
9. Sketch of the trial and nature of the verdict anticipated by the defendant.
10. Exemplary damages should be given for a breach of plaintiff's hospitality.—The husband's sufferings depicted.

Mr. Curran has been considered by competent critics the most complete example of the Irish school of eloquence, and his effort on the present occasion is generally regarded as one of his best. "His speeches" says a learned British reviewer, "combine the most prominent beauties and defects ; those beauties frequently overshadowed, as it were, by their neighboring deformities ; and those very deformities sometimes consecrated by their adjoining beauties. Tried within the jurisdiction of severe taste, the style would be condemned as too florid and Asiatic. We are grieved at this unrestrained appetite for decoration. We look in vain for those under-parts in rhetoric which ought to be occasionally interposed as resting places to relieve the mind in its efforts to follow him. Every topic, whether primary or subordinate, is dressed in the same gorgeous trappings ; more ambitious of starting and surprising than of fixing a steady and gradual conviction in the understanding, he misses the object which ought to be the exclusive aim of the orator. He deserts the high road to the human heart by perpetual deviations after the flowers that grow by the wayside. The unintermitted play of metaphor dazzles and fatigues us. In the perusal of his speeches we are indulged to satiety with a gaudy succession of images, scattered about by a fancy perpetually at work, but not unfrequently offending us by that which is fatal to an image, the want of congruity in fitness. The reason and judgment reject the unsubstantial and airy creations of an unfettered imagination. They demand that chaste, though not unadorned diction in which the cause itself may be said to speak, and the pleader is comparatively silent." [1]

If, however, Mr. Curran is to be considered as the most shining example of the Irish school, to what class must we assign Burke and Flood, Grattan, Sheridan and Plunket? Theirs was not the exuberant and florid style of Mr. Curran, but it will not be denied that their more restrained and elegant diction belongs to the highest order of intellect, and that their work is immortal. They were Irishmen, but they belonged to no school. One proof of genuine eloquence is, that independent of local or historical associations, there is nothing, in the mannerism of the speaker, to indicate to what age or country he belonged.

Notwithstanding his alleged imperfections, Mr. Curran was a great advocate, and his power over juries was wonderful. Those things which the precise scholiast may characterize as faults of style, were the very elements of his success. His ability to paint the misfortunes of his client in vivid colors, to awaken sympathy and allay prejudices, brought him large verdicts. He cared not how his speech looked in print. He was not talking to posterity, nor to please the schoolmen. All his powers were concentrated to sway the passions of the heart ; and if the result elicited the applause of the multitude, or created an irresistible desire to carry him in triumph through the streets; if his advocacy effected the release of the accused, or gained liberal verdicts, his success was genuine and his reward instant. One secret of Mr. Curran's power was that he appealed to the heart rather than to the intellect.

In pleading the cause of Mr. Massy, Mr. Curran was in a position to appreciate keenly his client's situation, since he had himself previously suffered the same injury, under the same circumstances. He presented the plaintiff's case as follows :

MAY IT PLEASE THE COURT,—*Gentlemen of the Jury :*—Never, so clearly as in the present instance, have I observed that safeguard of justice which Providence has placed in the nature of man. Such is the imperious dominion with which truth and reason wave their scepter over the human intellect, that no solicitation, however artful, no talent, however commanding, can reduce it from its allegiance. In proportion to the humility of our submission to its rule, do we rise into some faint emulation of that ineffable and presiding divinity whose characteristic attribute it is to be coerced and bound by the inexorable laws of its own nature, so as to be *all-wise* and *all-just* from necessity rather than election. You have seen it, in the learned advocate who has preceded me, most peculiarly and strikingly illustrated. You have seen even his great talents, perhaps the first in any country, languishing under a cause too weak to carry him, and too heavy to be carried by him. He was forced to dismiss his natural candor and sincerity, and, having

[1] Monthly Review, vol. 90, page 337.

no merits in his case, to substitute the dignity of his own manner, the resources of his own ingenuity, over the overwhelming difficulties with which he was surrounded. Wretched client! unhappy advocate! What a combination do you form! But such is the condition of guilt—its commission mean and tremulous; its defense artificial and insincere; its prosecution candid and simple; its condemnation dignified and austere. Such has been the defendant's guilt; such his defense; such shall be my address, and such, I trust, your verdict.

1. Theory of damages in this class of actions.—Why the verdict cannot be set aside for excess.

The learned counsel has told you that this unfortunate woman is not to be estimated at forty thousand pounds. Fatal and unquestionable is the truth of this assertion. Alas! gentlemen, she is no longer worth anything; faded, fallen, degraded and disgraced, she is worth less than nothing. But it is for the honor, the hope, the expectation, the tenderness and the comforts that have been blasted by the defendant, and have fled forever, that you are to remunerate the plaintiff by the punishment of the defendant. It is not her present value which you are to weigh; but it is her value at that time when she sat basking in a husband's love, with the blessing of Heaven on her head, and its purity in her heart; when she sat among her family and administered the morality of the parental board; estimate that past value, compare it with its present deplorable diminution, and it may lead you to form some judgment of the severity of the injury and the extent of the compensation.

The learned counsel has told you you ought to be cautious, because your verdict cannot be set aside for excess. The assertion is just; but has he treated you fairly by its application? His cause would not allow him to be fair, for why is the rule adopted in this single action? Because, this being peculiarly an injury to the most susceptible of all human feelings, it leaves the injury of the husband to be ascertained by the sensibility of the jury, and does not presume to measure the justice of their determination by the cold and chilly exercise of its own discretion. In any other action it is easy to calculate. If a tradesman's arm is cut off, you can measure the loss which he has sustained; but the wound of feeling and the agony of the heart cannot be judged by any standard with which I am acquainted. You are, therefore, unfairly dealt with when you are called on to appreciate the present suffering of the husband by the present guilt, delinquency and degradation of his wife. As well might you, if called on to give compensation to a man for the murder of his dearest friend, to find the measure of his injury by weighing the ashes of the dead. But it is not, gentlemen of the jury, by weighing the ashes of the dead that you would estimate the loss of the survivor.

The learned counsel has referred you to other cases and other countries for instances of moderate verdicts. I can refer you to some authentic instances of just ones. In the next county, £15,000 against a subaltern officer. In Travers and M'Carthy, £5,000 against a servant. In Tighe against Jones, £10,000 against a man not worth a shilling. What, then, ought to be the rule where rank and power, and wealth and station have combined to render the example of his crime more dangerous; to make his guilt more odious; to make the injury to the plaintiff more grievous, because more conspicuous? I affect no leveling familiarity when I speak of persons in the higher ranks of society. Distinctions of orders are necessary, and I always feel disposed to treat them with respect. But when it is my duty to speak of the crimes by which they are degraded, I am not so fastidious as to shrink from their contact when to touch them is essential to their dissection. In this action, the condition, the conduct and circumstances of the party are justly and peculiarly the objects of your consideration. Who are the parties? The plaintiff, young, amiable, of family and education. Of the generous disinterestedness of his heart you can form an opinion, even from the evidence of the defendant, that he declined an alliance which would have added to his fortune and consideration, and which he rejected for an unportioned union with his present wife. She, too, at that time young, beautiful and accomplished; and feeling her affection for her husband increase in proportion as she remembered the ardor of his love and the sincerity of his sacrifice. Look now to the defendant! I blush to name him! I blush to name a rank which he has tarnished, and a patent that he has worse than cancelled. High in the army; high in the State; the hereditary counsellor of the king; of wealth incalculable, and to this last I advert with an indignant and contemptuous satisfaction, because, as the only instrument of his guilt and shame, it will be the means of his punishment and the source of compensation for his guilt.

2. STATEMENT OF THE QUESTIONS TO BE CONSIDERED BY THE JURY.

But let me call your attention distinctly to the questions you have to consider. The first is the fact of guilt. Is this noble Lord guilty? His counsel knew too well how they would have mortified his vanity, had they given the smallest reason to doubt the splendor of his achievement. Against any such humiliating suspicion, he had taken the most studious precaution by the publicity of the exploit. And here in this court, and before you, and in the face of the country, has he the unparalleled effrontery of disdaining to resort even to a *confession of innocence.* His guilt established, your next question is the damages you should give. You have been told that the amount of the damages should depend on circumstances. You will consider these circumstances, whether of aggravation or mitigation. His learned counsel contend that the plaintiff has been the author of his own suffering, and ought to receive no compensation for the ill consequences of his own conduct. In what part of the evidence do you find any foundation for that assertion? He indulged her, it seems, in dress. Generous and attached, he probably indulged her in that point beyond his means; and the defendant now impudently calls on you to find an excuse for the adulterer in the fondness and liberality of the husband.

But you have been told that the husband *connived.* Odious and impudent aggravation of injury, to add calumny to insult, and outrage to dishonor. From whom but a man hackneyed in the paths of shame and vice; from whom but from a man having no compunctions in his own breast to restrain him, could you expect such brutal disregard for the feelings of others? From whom but the cold-blooded, veteran seducer; from what but from the exhausted mind, the habitual community with shame; from what but the habitual contempt of virtue and of man, could you have expected the arrogance, the barbarity and folly of so foul, because so false, an imputation? He should have reflected and have blushed before he suffered so vile a topic of defense to have passed his lips. But, ere you condemn, let him have the benefit of the excuse, if the excuse be true. You must have observed how his counsel fluttered and vibrated between what they called connivance and injudicious confidence; and how, in affecting to distinguish, they have confounded them both together. If the plaintiff has connived, I freely say to you, do not reward the wretch who has prostituted his wife and surrendered his own honor; do not compensate the pander of his own shame, and the willing instrument of his own infamy. But as there is no sum so low to which such a defense, if true, ought not to reduce your verdict, so neither is any so high to which such a charge ought not to inflame it, if such a charge be false.

3. THE CHARGE OF CONNIVANCE A FALSE AND IMPUDENT DEFENSE.—PLAINTIFF'S INDISCRETION NO CRIME.

Where is the single fact in this case on which the remotest suspicion of connivance can be hung? Odiously has the defendant endeavored to make the softest and most amiable feelings of the heart the pretext of his slanderous imputations. An ancient and respectable prelate, the husband of his wife's sister, was chained down to the bed of sickness, perhaps to the bed of death. In that distressing situation, my client suffered that wife to be the bearer of consolation to the bosom of her sister; he had not the heart to refuse her, and the softness of his nature is now charged on him as a crime! He is now insolently told that he connived at his dishonor, and that he ought to have foreseen that the mansion of sickness and of sorrow would have been made the scene of assignation and of guilt. On this charge of connivance I will not further weary you, or exhaust myself; I will add nothing more than that it is as false as it is impudent; that, in the evidence, it has not a color of support; and that, by your verdict, you should mark it with reprobation. The other subject, namely, that he was indiscreet in his confidence, does, I think, call for some discussion; for I trust you see that I affect not any address to your passions by which you may be led away from the subject. I presume merely to separate the parts of this affecting case, and to lay them, item by item, before you, with the coldness of detail, and not with any coloring or display of fiction or of fancy. Honorable to himself was his unsuspecting confidence; fatal must we admit it to have been, when we look to the abuse committed upon it; but where was the *guilt* of this indiscretion? He did admit this noble Lord to pass his threshold as his guest. Now the charge which this noble Lord builds on this indiscretion, is: "Thou fool! thou hast confidence in my honor, and that was a guilty indiscretion; thou simpleton, thou thoughtest that an admitted and cherished guest would have respected the laws of honor and hospitality, and thy indiscretion was guilt. Thou thoughtest that he would have shrunk from the meanness and barbarity of requiting kindness with treachery, and thy indiscretion was guilt."

Gentlemen, what horrid alternative in the treatment of wives would such reasoning recommend? Are they to be immured by worse than Eastern barbarity? Are their principles to be depraved, their passions sublimated, every finer motive of action extinguished by the inevitable consequences of thus treating them like slaves? Or is a liberal and generous confidence in them to be the passport of the adulterer, and the justification of his crime?

Honorably but fatally for his own repose, he was neither jealous, suspicious, nor cruel. He treated the defendant with the confidence of a friend, and his wife with the tenderness of a husband. He did leave to the noble Marquis the physical possibility of committing against him the greatest crime which can be perpetrated against a being of an amiable heart and refined education. In the middle of the day, at the moment of divine worship, when the miserable husband was on his knees, directing the prayers and thanksgiving of his congregation to their God, that moment did the remorseless adulterer choose to carry off the deluded victim from her husband, from her child, from her character, from her happiness, as if not content to leave his crime confined to its miserable aggravations, unless he also gave it a cast and color of factitious sacrilege and impiety.

4. SUPPOSED REMONSTRANCE WITH THE DEFENDANT, WHEN ABOUT
TO COMMIT THE OFFENSE.

Oh! how happy had it been when he arrived at the bank of the river with the ill-faded fugitive, ere yet he had committed her to that boat, of which, like the fabled bark of Styx, the exile was eternal; how happy at that moment, so teeming with misery and with shame, if you, my Lord, had met him, and could have accosted him in the character of that good genius which had abandoned him. How impressively might you have pleaded the cause of the father, of the child, of the mother, and even of the worthless defendant himself. You would have said: "Is this the requittal that you are about to make for the respect, and kindness and confidence in your honor? Can you deliberately expose this young man in bloom of life, with all his hopes yet before him? Can you expose him, a wretched outcast from society, to the scorn of a merciless world? Can you set him adrift upon the tempestuous ocean of his own passions, at this early season when they are most headstrong;

and can you cut him out from the moorings of those domestic obligations by whose cable he might ride at safety from their turbulence ?   Think, if you can conceive it, what a powerful influence
arises from the sense of home, from the sacred religion of the heart
in quelling the passions, in reclaiming the wanderings, in correcting
the disorders of the human heart.   Do not cruelly take from him
the protection of these attachments.   But if you have no pity for
the father, have mercy, at least, upon his innocent and helpless
child.   Do not condemn him to an education scandalous or neglected.   Do not strike him into that most dreadful of all human
conditions, the orphanage that springs not from the grave, that falls
not from the hand of Providence or the stroke of death ; but comes
before its time, anticipated and inflicted by the remorseless cruelty
of parental guilt."   For the poor victim herself, not yet immolated,
while yet balancing upon the pivot of her destiny, your heart could
not be cold, nor your tongue be wordless.   You would have said to
him : " Pause, my Lord, while there is yet a moment for reflection.
What are your motives, what your views, what your prospects, from
what you are about to do ?   You are a married man, the husband
of the most amiable and respectable of women ; you cannot look
to the chance of marrying this wretched fugitive.   Between you
and such an event there are two sepulchers to pass.   What are your
inducements ?   Is it love, think you ?   No.   Do not give that name
to any attraction you can find in the faded refuse of a violated bed.
Love is a noble and generous passion ; it can be founded only on
a pure and ardent friendship, on an exalted respect, on an implicit
confidence in its object.   Search your heart ; examine your judgment.   Do you find the semblance of any one of these sentiments
to bind you to her ?   What could degrade a mind to which nature
or education had given port or stature; or character, into a friendship for her ?   Could you repose upon her faith ?   Look in her face,
my Lord ; she is at this moment giving you the violation of the
most sacred of human obligations as the pledge of her fidelity.   She
is giving you the most irrefragable proof that as she is deserting her
husband for you, so she would without scruple abandon you for
another.   Do you anticipate any pleasure you might feel in the possible event of your becoming the parents of a common child ?   She
is at this moment proving to you that she is as dead to the sense of
parental as of conjugal obligation, and that she would abandon
your offspring to-morrow with the same facility with which she now
deserts her own.   Look, then, at her conduct as it is, as the world

must behold it, blackened by every aggravation that can make it either odious or contemptible, and unrelieved by a single circumstance of mitigation that could palliate its guilt or retrieve it from abhorrence.

"Mean, however, and degraded as this woman must be, she will still (if you take her with you) have strong and heavy claims upon you. The force of such claims does certainly depend upon circumstances. Before, therefore, you expose her fate to the dreadful risk of your caprice or ingratitude, in mercy to her weigh well the confidence she can place in your future justice and honor. At that future time, much nearer than you think, by what topics can her cause be pleaded to a sated appetite, to a heart that repels her, to a just judgment in which she never could have been valued or respected? Here is not the case of an unmarried woman, with whom a pure and generous friendship may insensibly have ripened into a more serious attachment, until at last her heart became too deeply pledged to be reassumed. If so circumstanced, without any husband to betray, or child to desert, or motive to restrain, except what related solely to herself, her anxiety for your happiness made her overlook every other consideration, and commit her destiny to your honor; in such a case (the strongest and the highest that man's imagination can suppose), in which you, at least, could see nothing but the most noble and disinterested sacrifice; in which you could find nothing but what claimed from you the most kind and exalted sentiment of tenderness and devotion and respect, and in which the most fastidious rigor would find so much more subject for sympathy than blame; let me ask you, could you, even in that case, answer for your own justice and gratitude? I do not allude to the long and pitiful catalogue of paltry adventures in which, it seems, your time has been employed: the coarse and vulgar succession of casual connections, joyless, loveless, and unendeared. But do you not find upon your memory some trace of an engagement of the character I have sketched?"

5. SHAMEFUL EXPERIENCE RESULTING FROM A PREVIOUS ELOPEMENT OF WHICH THE DEFENDANT HAD BEEN GUILTY.

"Has not your sense of what you would owe in such a case, and to such a woman, been at least once put to the test of experiment? Has it not once, at least, happened that such a woman, with all the resolution of strong faith, flung her youth, her hope, her beauty, her talent, upon your bosom, weighed you against the world, which

she found but a feather in the scale, and took you as an equivalent?
How did you then acquit yourself? Did you prove yourself worthy
of the sacred trust reposed in you? Did your spirit so associate
with hers as to leave her no room to regret the splendid and disinterested sacrifice she had made? Did her soul find a pillow in the
tenderness of yours, and a support in its firmness? Did you preserve her high in her own consciousness, proud in your admiration
and friendship, and happy in your affection? You might have so
acted (and the man that was worthy of her would have perished
rather than not so act) as to make her delighted with having confided so sacred a trust to his honor. Did you so act? Did she
feel that, however precious to your heart, she was still more exalted
and honored in your reference and respect? Or did she find you
coarse and paltry, fluttering and unpurposed, unfeeling and ungrateful? You found her a fair and blushing flower, its beauty
and its fragrance bathed in the dews of Heaven. Did you so tenderly transplant it as to preserve that beauty and fragrance unimpaired? Or did you so rudely cut it as to interrupt its nutriment,
to waste its sweetness, to blast its beauty, to bow down its faded
and sickly head? And did you at last fling it, like 'a loathsome
weed, away?' If, then, to such a woman, so clothed with every
title that could ennoble and exalt, and endear her to the heart of
man, you could be cruelly and capriciously deficient, how can a
wretched fugitive like this, in every point her contrast, hope to find
you just? Send her, then, away. Send her back to her home, to
her child, to her husband, to herself."

6. Disgraceful conduct of the defendant in the present case.

Alas, there was none to hold such language to this noble defendant; he did not hold it to himself. But he paraded his despicable prize in his own carriage, with his own retinue, his own servants. This veteran Paris hawked his enamored Helen from this
western quarter of the island to a seaport in the eastern, crowned
with the acclamations of a senseless and grinning rabble, glorying
and delighted, no doubt, in the leering and scoffing admiration of
grooms and hostlers and waiters, as he passed. In this odious
contempt of every personal feeling, of public opinion, of common
humanity, did he parade this woman to the seaport, whence he
transported his precious cargo to a country where her example may
be less mischievous than in her own; where, I agree with my

learned colleague in heartily wishing, he may remain with her forever. We are too poor, too simple, too unadvanced a country for
the example of such achievements. When the relaxation of morals
is the natural growth and consequence of the great progress of arts
and wealth, it is accomplished by a refinement that makes it less
gross and shocking. But for such palliations we are at least a century too young. I advise you, therefore, most earnestly to rebuke
this budding mischief, by letting the wholesome vigor and chastisement of a liberal verdict speak what you think of its enormity.
In every point of view in which I can look at the subject, I see
you are called upon to give a verdict of bold and just and indignant
and exemplary compensation. The injury of the plaintiff demands
it from your justice. The delinquency of the defendant provokes
it by its enormity. The rank on which he has relied for impunity
calls upon you to tell him that crime does not ascend to the rank
of the perpetrator, but the perpetrator sinks from his rank and
descends to the level of his delinquency.

7. THE CHARACTER OF THE DEFENSE AN AGGRAVATION OF THE
CRIME, AND AN INSULT TO THE JURY.

The style and mode of his defense is a gross aggravation of his
conduct, and a gross insult upon you. Look upon the different
subjects of his defense as you ought, and let him profit by them as
he deserves. Vainly presumptuous upon his rank, he wishes to
overawe you by the despicable consideration. He next resorts to
a cruel aspersion upon the character of the unhappy plaintiff whom
he had already wounded beyond the possibility of reparation. He
has ventured to charge him with connivance. As to that, I will
only say, gentlemen of the jury, do not give this vain boaster a pretext for saying, that if the husband connived in the offense the jury
also connived in the reparation.

But he has pressed another curious topic upon you. After the
plaintiff had cause to suspect his designs, and the likelihood of their
being fatally successful, he did not then act precisely as he ought.
Gracious God, what an argument for him to dare to advance! It
is saying thus to him: "I abused your confidence, your hospitality;
I laid a base plan for the seduction of the wife of your bosom; I
succeeded at last, so as to throw in upon you that most dreadful of
all suspicions to a man fondly attached, proud of his wife's honor,
and tremblingly alive to his own; that you were possibly a dupe
to the confidence in the wife as much as in the guest. In this so

him from pursuits in which, though he may be insensible of shame, he will not be regardless of expense. You will do more, you will not only punish him in his tender point, but you will weaken him in his strong one—his money. We have heard much of this noble Lord's wealth, and much of his exploits, but not much of his accomplishments or his wit. I know not that his verses have soared even to the poet's corner. I have heard it said that an ass laden with gold could find his way through the gate of the strongest city. But, gentlemen, lighten the load upon his back, and you will completely curtail the mischievous faculty of a grave animal, whose momentum lies not in his agility, but his weight ; not in the quantity of motion, but the quantity of his matter.

There is another ground on which you are called upon to give most liberal damages, and that has been laid by the unfeeling vanity of the defendant. This business has been marked by the most elaborate publicity. It is very clear that he has been allured by the glory of the chase, and not the value of the game. The poor object of his pursuit could be of no value to him, or he could not have so wantonly and cruelly and unnecessarily abused her. He might easily have kept this unhappy intercourse an unsuspected secret. Even if he wished for her elopement, he might easily have so contrived it that the place of her retreat would be profoundly undiscoverable. Yet, though even the expense (a point so tender to his delicate sensibility) of concealing could not be a one-fortieth of the cost of publishing her, his vanity decided him in favor of glory and publicity. By that election he has in fact put forward the Irish nation and its character, so often and so variously calumniated, upon its trial before the tribunal of the empire ; and your verdict will this day decide whether an Irish jury can feel with justice and spirit upon a subject that involves conjugal affection and comfort, domestic honor and repose, the certainty of issue, the weight of public opinion, the gilded and presumptuous criminality of overweening rank and station.

9. SKETCH OF THE TRIAL AND NATURE OF THE VERDICT ANTIC-
IPATED BY THE DEFENDANT.

I doubt not but he is at this moment reclined on a silken sofa, anticipating that submissive and modest verdict by which you will lean gently on his errors ; and expecting from your patriotism, no doubt, that you will think again and again before you condemn any great portion of the immense revenue of a great absentee to be detained in the nation that produced it, instead of being transmitted, as it ought, to be expended in the splendor of another country. He is now probably waiting for the arrival of the report of this day, which I understand a famous note-taker has been sent hither to collect. (Let not the gentleman be disturbed.) Gentlemen, let me assure you it is more, much more the trial of you than of the noble Marquis, of which this imported recorder is at this moment collecting the materials. His noble employer is now expecting a report to the following effect: "Such a day came on to be tried at Ennis, by a special jury, the cause of Charles Massy against the most noble the Marquis of Headfort. It appeared that the plaintiff's wife was young, beautiful and captivating. The plaintiff himself a person fond of this beautiful creature to distraction, and both doting on their child; but the noble Marquis approached her; the plume of glory nodded on his head. Not the Goddess Minerva, but the Goddess Venus had lighted upon his casque, 'the fire that never tires, such as many a lady gay had been dazzled with before.' At the first advance she trembled, at the second she struck to the redoubted son of Mars and pupil of Venus. The jury saw it was not his fault (it was an Irish jury); they felt compassion for the tenderness of the mother's heart, and for the warmth of the lover's passion. The jury saw on the one side a young, entertaining gallant, on the other a beauteous creature of charms irresistible. They recollected that Jupiter had been always successful in his amours, although Vulcan had not always escaped some awkward accidents. The jury was composed of fathers, brothers, husbands, but they had not the vulgar jealousy that views little things of that sort with rigor; and wishing to assimilate their country in every respect to England, now that they are united to it, they, like English gentlemen, returned to their box with a verdict of sixpence damages and sixpence costs." Let this be sent to England. I promise you your odious secret will not be kept better than that of the wretched Mrs. Massy. There is not a bawdy chronicle in London in which the epitaph which you would have written on yourselves will not be published, and our enemies will delight in the spectacle of our precocious depravity, in seeing that we can be rotten before we are ripe. I do not suppose it, I do not, cannot, will not, believe it. I will not harrow up myself with the anticipated apprehension.

45

10. Exemplary damages should be given for a breach of
plaintiff's hospitality.—The husband's
sufferings depicted.

There is another consideration, gentlemen, which, I think, most
imperiously demands even a vindictive award of exemplary damages, and that is the breach of hospitality.   To us peculiarly does
it belong to avenge the violation of its altar.   The hospitality of
other countries is a matter of necessity or convention ; in savage
nations of the first, in polished of the latter ; but the hospitality of
an *Irishman* is not the running account of posted and legered
courtesies, as in other countries ; it springs, like all his qualities,
his faults, his virtues, directly from his heart.   The heart of an
Irishman is by nature bold, and he confides : it is tender, and he
loves; it is generous, and he gives; it is social, and he is hospitable.
This sacrilegious intruder has profaned the religion of that sacred
altar so elevated in our worship, so precious to our devotion ; and
it is our privilege to avenge the crime.   You must either pull down
the altar and abolish the worship, or you must preserve its sanctity
undebased.   There is no alternative between the universal exclusion of all mankind from your threshold, and the most rigorous
punishment of him who is admitted and betrays.   This defendant
has been so trusted, has so betrayed, and you ought to make him a
most signal example.

Gentlemen, I am the more disposed to feel the strongest indignation and abhorrence of this odious conduct of the defendant,
when I consider the deplorable condition to which he has reduced
the plaintiff, and perhaps the still more deplorable one that he has
in prospect before him.   What a progress has he to travel through
before he can attain the peace and tranquillity which he has lost?
How like the wounds of the body are those of the mind !   How
burning the fever !   How painful the suppuration !   How slow,
how hesitating, how relapsing the process to convalescence !
Through what a variety of suffering, what new scenes and changes,
must my unhappy client pass ere he can re-attain, should he ever
re-attain, that health of soul of which he has been despoiled by the
cold and deliberate machinations of this practiced and gilded seducer ?   If, instead of drawing upon his incalculable wealth for a
scanty retribution, you were to stop the progress of his despicable
achievements by reducing him to actual poverty, you could not
even so punish him beyond the scope of his offense, nor reprize the

plaintiff beyond the measure of his suffering.   Let me remind you,
that in this action the law not only empowers you, but that its
policy commands you to consider the public example, as well as the
individual injury, when you adjust the amount of your verdict.   I
confess I am most anxious that you should acquit yourself worthily
upon this important occasion.   I am addressing you as fathers,
husbands, brothers.   I am anxious that a feeling of those high relations should enter into and give dignity to your verdict.   But I
confess it, I feel a tenfold solicitude when I remember that I am
addressing you as my countrymen, as Irishmen, whose characters
as jurors, as gentlemen, must find either honor or degradation in
the result of your decision.   Small as must be the distributive
share of that national estimation that can belong to so unimportant
an individual as myself, yet do I own I am tremblingly solicitous
for its fate.   Perhaps it appears of more value to me, because it is
embarked on the same bottom with yours ; perhaps the community
of peril, of common safety or common wreck, gives a consequence
to my share of the risk which I could not be vain enough to give
it, if it were not raised to it by that mutuality.   But why stoop to
think at all of myself, when I know that you, gentlemen of the jury,
when I know that our country itself are my clients on this day, and
must abide the alternative of honor or of infamy, as you shall decide.   But I will not despond ; I will not dare to despond.   I have
every trust and hope and confidence in you.   And to that hope I
will add my most fervent prayer to the God of all truth and justice,
so to raise and enlighten and fortify your minds, that you may so
decide as to preserve to yourselves while you live, the most delightful of all recollections, that of acting justly, and to transmit to your
children the most precious of all inheritances, the memory of your
virtue.

Baron SMITH'S CHARGE TO THE JURY,

In the Case of Massy v. The Marquis of Headfort.—Damages for Criminal Conversation.

AT ENNIS ASSIZES, COUNTY CLARE, IRELAND, FRIDAY, JULY 27th, 1804.

Damages claimed, £40,000.—Amount recovered, £10,000.

Analysis of the Charge.

1. The rules of law governing this class of actions illustrated and explained.
2. The nature of the injury.—What circumstances must be considered in fixing the amount of damages, and the reasons therefor.
3. Why connivance destroys the right of action.—Distinction between errors of the head and heart.
4. When the husband's conduct will not defeat his right to recover.
5. Moral considerations bearing upon the question of damages.

Mr. Curran did not finish his remarks until near midnight, but as soon as he sat down, notwithstanding the lateness of the hour, Baron Smith proceeded to charge the jury. His observations will be found to contain a philosophical and comprehensive statement of the legal principles governing actions for criminal conversation, expressed in elegant language, and with a degree of clearness and force indicative of his learning and ability as a jurist. The reasons why certain facts and circumstances must be considered by the jury, and the bearing they should have on the result of their deliberations, are stated so that all can understand them. In this view his charge is rendered generally instructive and interesting, because the legal principles here enunciated are law to-day on this side of the Atlantic. It will be valuable to the profession, and especially to students, since it embraces, in a remarkably brief space, a thorough abridgment of the law on the subject. Although it can be regarded neither as a speech nor an argument, it may perhaps be considered as an instructive specimen of legal eloquence. The Court said:

Gentlemen of the Jury:—After the long and serious demands which this trial has already made on your attention, rendered the less irksome by the brilliant displays of eloquence which we have witnessed, I am sorry it has fallen to my lot to trespass farther on your patience ; nor shall I do so in any greater degree than is prescribed to me by the duties of my situation, considering the importance of the question which you are to decide, and the large amount of the damages which the plaintiff claims.

I shall set out by informing you, to the best of my knowledge, of the legal doctrines which are applicable to actions of the description of this which is on trial, and shall then proceed to sum up the evidence which has been given, without feeling it necessary to interrupt the recapitulation by any general remarks. In short, I shall leave to you to apply to the facts of the case (of which you are the proper judges), those preliminary statements of the law which I shall have made.

1. The rules of law governing this class of actions illustrated and explained.

In the first place, I feel myself not only warranted, but bound to apprise you of a principle which I find laid down in books of high authority and modern law. The principle is, that this sort of action partakes of the nature of a penal prosecution, and that large and exemplary damages are usually awarded. The rigor of the above doctrine, it must however be observed, is regulated and restrained by a variety of qualifications, and appears to be so diluted and softened that it amounts at last to little more than this, that where the plaintiff's right of action is indisputable, and the injury he hath sustained is manifestly great, and where (as it must always be the case) it is impossible to calculate, with exact precision, the amount in pounds, shillings, and pence, of the value of those comforts of which he has been deprived ; there juries should not be parsimonious in the damages which they award, but, on the contrary, should be liberal, to a degree bordering on prodigality and profusion, for the benefit of public example and the protection of public morals. This part of the question may, perhaps, be illustrated by a familiar usage in the case of assaults. An assault is at once a civil injury for which the sufferer has a right to be retributed in damages, and it is an offense for which the aggressor is liable to punishment. If he be convicted on an indictment for the misdemeanor, the practice is for the Crown Judge to ascertain whether the prosecutor intends to bring an action. If not, a punishment is inflicted commensurate to the crime. Otherwise, a lenient and inadequate sentence is pronounced. In this latter case, the verdict of a record jury is, in some measure, substituted for the judgment of a criminal court.   To apply this, adultery is a crime, not indeed of temporal cognizance, but punishable by the spiritual law, which is part of the law of the land. But, proceedings of such a nature in the spiritual courts, having become so unusual as to be nearly obsolete, perhaps we may, by a fair analogy, consider the transaction as indirectly subject to the animadversion of the jury which tries the civil action.

We must not, however, carry this principle too far. We must not forget, first, that ours is a mere civil tribunal; or, secondly, that adultery is no crime of temporal cognizance. If it were, that would not be law which we know is law. The law is, that if the jury be convinced, from the conduct of the plaintiff, that he was consenting to the infamy of his wife, they are bound, in such circumstances, to find a verdict for the defendant. Now this could never be the case, if their province were to punish adultery as a crime, since it is plain that the guilt of the defendant would not be diminished by the plaintiff's having been accessory to his offense. Thus, the position to which I have adverted can only admit of the interpretation which I have given it, viz., that where it is (as in every such action it must be) difficult to make the value of the plaintiff's loss a subject of pecuniary calculation, there it shall be competent to the jury to take the advancement of public morality into their consideration. But they must make it a matter of collateral and subordinate consideration ; they must recollect that they are not sitting on the Crown side, but that their main, or rather their only province is, to decide on a violation of the private rights of parties.

2. THE NATURE OF THE INJURY.—WHAT CIRCUMSTANCES MUST
BE CONSIDERED IN FIXING THE AMOUNT OF DAMAGES,
AND THE REASONS THEREFOR.

The civil injury for which the plaintiff is entitled to compensation, is the wound given to his feelings and happiness as a husband, and, therefore, the damages should be proportioned to its poignancy and extent. Accordingly, these are susceptible of aggravation or mitigation, on various grounds, which are all, in fact, merely detailed applications of the principle which I have mentioned last, namely, that the degree of the injury sustained is the proper standard for measuring the amount of the compensation.

The first ground which I shall notice, as one upon which the jury may compute and justify the quantum of damages which they award, is the rank and situation of the plaintiff. Nor does this rule trench on the impartial character of our law, or hold out different measures of justice to the rich and to the poor. It merely provides that the severer the injury is, the greater shall be the retribution. Virtue is far from being peculiar to the higher ranks ; but there is, perhaps, a delicacy of sentiment and punctilio of honor engendered by the refined habits which belong to opulence and distinction, and which sharpen the sting of such an injury as this. Besides, the more exalted is the sphere, the more are those who move in it exposed to observation, and consequently the more must such be injured by an aggression which subjects the sufferer to scorn.

The fortune of the defendant supplies another consideration, by which, estimating damages, a jury might be guided. Not that they ought to more than compensate a plaintiff, merely because the defendant happened to be rich. This would be to violate the maxim which we have laid down : that the damages awarded should bear a proportion to the injury sustained. But a jury, in the case of an indigent defendant, may be disposed to give a plaintiff less than the value of what he has lost, rather than, by awarding adequate compensation, doom him who is to make it to imprisonment for life. Where the aggressor is in affluent circumstances, they will be relieved from such humane difficulties, and may find damages commensurate to the injury which has been sustained.

It is also the duty of a jury to inquire whether the criminal intercourse has, or has not, been the consequence of a preceding seduction of the wife. As evidence of this, they should examine her previous character and conduct, and may found their estimate of damages on such investigation. They may also take into account the connection which subsisted between the parties, and ascertain how far it involved those rights of hospitality or friendship which might justify the plaintiff in being less circumspect and suspicious, and reposing the greater confidence in the person who betrayed it. To the same head I would refer the age of the defendant, and the circumstance of his being married. It would be injurious to morals to discourage that greater reliance which it is natural to place on an aged and married, than on a younger and a single man. The duties and attachments which may be supposed to belong to the married state, and the bodily infirmities, the extinguished passions, and confirmed and settled morality which should belong to age, are so many securities for the honor of a husband, and justify the confidence which they inspire. If, however, these securities should appear in proof to have been lessened by the gallantries of a defendant, by his reputation in this respect, and by the footing on which he lived with his own wife ; a jury would be bound to throw these latter considerations into the opposite scale.

The injured husband's obligation, by settlement or otherwise, to provide for the issue of that marriage whose rights have been encroached on, is also a fit object of inquiry for the jury. Neither, indeed, can I conceive a more malignant source of agony to a feeling heart ; a greater exasperation of the pain of that wound to whose poignancy the compensation should be proportioned, than must arise from the perplexing doubt in a supposed father's mind, whether the child who shares his caresses ; who is to inherit his possessions ; for whom he is bound to provide ; to whose advancement he has devoted his industry and his talents, has any natural and just claim to this parental care ; whether it be a pledge of his wife's past affection for himself, or the offspring and memorial of her infidelity and his own disgrace.

If the complainant has had criminal connections with other women, his damages shall be curtailed on this account : both because these connections negative the existence of a high degree of matrimonial comfort, and because such dissipation and neglect is calculated to set an ill example to the woman : it tends to sap her morals, to estrange her affections, and facilitate her seduction. Therefore, though he have not actually been unfaithful, yet, by associating with women of forfeited and sullied honor, he may diminish his claim to damages, if this association has fallen under the eye of his wife, and has arisen, not from peculiarity of circumstance, but from laxity of principle.

Again, in ascertaining the damages to which such a plaintiff is entitled, his having treated his wife with tenderness or harshness, their having lived on terms of harmony or discord (let the fault have lain where it may), are proper subjects of attention from a jury ; for the gist of this action is the husband's loss of the comfort and society of his wife, and this comfort must be in proportion to their mutual cordiality and attachment. Indeed, where this affection appears by the evidence to have amounted to that engrossing and subjugating sentiment called love, the keenness of the wound is infinitely augmented, and the amount of the compensation should be proportionably increased.

3. WHY CONNIVANCE DESTROYS THE RIGHT OF ACTION.—DISTINCTION BETWEEN ERRORS OF THE HEAD AND HEART.

We have already seen, that where a husband connives at the infidelity of his wife, the effect shall be, not only to diminish his compensation, but to destroy his right of action altogether, and disentitle him to any verdict whatsoever; and this on one or both of the following grounds : First, that *volenti non fit injuria;* secondly, that a profligate accomplice in his wife's dishonor forfeits his right to the protection of the court. But there may be a levity in the husband's behavior, and a culpable inattention to the conduct of his wife, which, not amounting to a consent of her infamy, shall not, indeed, disentitle him to a verdict, but which, having probably contributed to her seduction, shall mitigate the damages which are awarded to him.

It has been urged in the present case, that if any such negligence existed, it arose (to adopt the language of one of the witnesses) "not from the fault of the heart, but of the head." This excuse is founded in misapprehension. If the inattention arose from the fault of the heart, it would amount to connivance and destroy the plaintiff's right of action altogether. When the neglect arises only from an error of the head, it leaves him a right of action; but it is evidence admissible in mitigation of damages. Otherwise, a snare would be laid for the defendant, who, judging of the plaintiff's motive by his conduct, might suppose that he intended to connive, and was an accommodating husband, not from inadvertence, but design.

4. WHEN THE HUSBAND'S CONDUCT WILL NOT DEFEAT HIS RIGHT TO RECOVER.

At the same time, towards entitling a plaintiff to recover largely, we must not require that he should have been a Spanish or an Oriental husband. We must recollect the freedom which our customs allow to females, and not lay down a rule so rigorous as this : that the rights of every married man may be invaded whose conduct is not a system of suspicion and control, exposing the jealous spy to public derision, and degrading the woman who is the object of his distrust, offending her pride, and alienating her affections.

It should suffice that he does not negligently overlook behavior, which ought to excite the vigilance of a man duly attentive to his wife's honor. The law invests every husband with certain privileges and authorities ; and if he will not use them for his own protection, he must forfeit a part of his claim to damages, as the reasonable consequence of his default. It is the vigilant, not the indolent, whom the law assists.

5. MORAL CONSIDERATIONS BEARING UPON THE QUESTION OF DAMAGES.

There are but two observations more which I have to make : First, that if, in measuring the damages, public morals and example should be at all taken into the question, we must remember that plaintiffs as well as defendants are subject to the infirmities and depravities of our imperfect nature. We must therefore take care how, by awarding damages to an enormous amount, we hold out a temptation to the unprincipled husband, dissembling his own connivance, to wink however at his wife's dishonor, when he finds that her infamy will bring so high a price.

The second and last remark which I have to trouble you with, is this, that you will be the more scrupulous in measuring the compensation which you award ; because, if you grant too much, it is improbable that your error can ever be corrected, it being the established practice, if it be not the undoubted law, that in actions of this nature, however high the damages which are found may be, the verdict cannot be set aside on the mere ground of their being excessive.

The Court then proceeded to recapitulate the evidence as it appeared upon his notes, without any further observations on the law.

N. B.—At 12 o'clock the same night, the jury, having been out only a short time, returned a verdict for plaintiff for £10,000 damages, and costs. The sequel only proves the truth of the old maxim in regard to the way of the transgressor. It seems, when the Marquis returned to London with Mrs. Massy, he settled upon her an annuity of £1,000 a year. As Mr. Ponsonby sagely remarked, however, *twenty-five* does not love *fifty*. It was the old story of January and May. Notwithstanding the wealth and luxury with which she was surrounded, after living about six weeks with the Marquis, Mrs. Massy left him, and went off with a young officer of the guards.

APPENDIX.

DIAGRAM PREPARED BY DR. THOMAS SPENCER, ONE OF THE EXPERTS FOR THE STATE, AND REFERRED TO BY MR. SEWARD IN HIS ADDRESS TO THE JURY.

[See text, p. 184.]

THREE CLASSES—THIRTY-SIX FACULTIES.

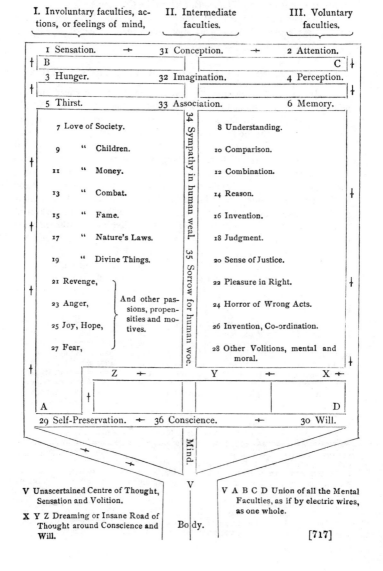

I. Involuntary faculties, actions, or feelings of mind,

II. Intermediate faculties.

III. Voluntary faculties.

1 Sensation.   31 Conception.   2 Attention.

B   C

3 Hunger.   32 Imagination.   4 Perception.

5 Thirst.   33 Association.   6 Memory.

7 Love of Society.   34 Sympathy in human weal.   8 Understanding.

9 " Children.   10 Comparison.

11 " Money.   12 Combination.

13 " Combat.   14 Reason.

15 " Fame.   16 Invention.

17 " Nature's Laws.   18 Judgment.

19 " Divine Things.   20 Sense of Justice.

21 Revenge,   35 Sorrow for human woe.   22 Pleasure in Right.

23 Anger,   And other passions, propensities and motives.   24 Horror of Wrong Acts.

25 Joy, Hope,   26 Invention, Co-ordination.

27 Fear,   28 Other Volitions, mental and moral.

Z   Y   X

A   D

29 Self-Preservation.   36 Conscience.   30 Will.

Mind.

V

V Unascertained Centre of Thought, Sensation and Volition.

X Y Z Dreaming or Insane Road of Thought around Conscience and Will.

Body.

V A B C D Union of all the Mental Faculties, as if by electric wires, as one whole.

[717]

REQUESTS TO CHARGE AND RULINGS THEREON, IN THE SICKLES' CASE.

[See text, p. 327.]

At the trial of Hon. Daniel E. Sickles the Court was requested to instruct the jury as to the law governing the case. The following are the
instructions presented by counsel, upon which the arguments were based,
and the rulings made by the Court.

INSTRUCTIONS SUBMITTED FOR THE PROSECUTION.

I.—If the jury believe, from the evidence in this whole cause, that the
prisoner, on the day named in the indictment, and in the county of Washington aforesaid, killed the said Philip Barton Key, by discharging at,
against, and into the body of him, the said Philip Barton Key, a pistol or
pistols loaded with gunpowder and ball, thereby giving him a mortal
wound or wounds, and that such killing was the willful and intentional
act of the prisoner, and was induced by the belief that the said deceased
had seduced his (the prisoner's) wife, and on some day or days, or for any
period definite or indefinite, prior to the day of such killing, had adulterous intercourse with the said wife, and that the prisoner was not provoked
to such killing by any assault or offer of violence then used and there made
by the deceased upon or against him, then such willful and intentional
killing, if found by the jury upon the facts and circumstances given in evidence, is murder. But such killing cannot be found to have been willful
and intentional in the sense of this instruction if it shall have been proven
to the satisfaction of the jury upon the whole evidence aforesaid that the
prisoner was in fact insane at the time of such killing.

RULING.—The first instruction ask for by the United States embodies the
law of this case on the particular branch of it to which it relates, and is granted
with some explanatory remarks as to insanity, with a reference to which the
prayer closes. A great English judge has said on the trial of Oxford, who shot
at the Queen of England, 9 Carrington and Paine's Reports. p. 533, "That if
the prisoner was laboring under some controlling disease, which was in truth the
acting power within him, which he could not resist, then he will not be responsible." And again: " The question is whether he was laboring under that species
of insanity which satisfies you that he was quite unaware of the nature, character
and consequences of the act he was committing, or in other words, whether he
was under the influence of a diseased mind and was really unconscious at the time
he was committing the act that it was a crime. A man is not to be excused from
responsibility if he has capacity and reason sufficient to enable him to distinguish
between right and wrong as to the particular act he is doing, a knowledge and
consciousness that the act he is doing is wrong and criminal and will subject him
to punishment. In order to be responsible, he must have sufficient power of
memory to recollect the relation in which he stands to others, and in which others
stand to him ; that the act he is doing is contrary to the plain dictates of justice and right, injurious to others, and a violation of the dictates of duty. On
the contrary, although he may be laboring under a partial insanity, if he still understands the nature and character of his act and its consequences ; if he has a
knowledge that it is wrong and criminal, and a mental power sufficient to apply

that knowledge to his own case, and to know that if he does the act, he will do wrong and receive punishment, such partial insanity is not sufficient to exempt him from responsibility for criminal acts. 7 Metcalfe's Reports, pp. 500–503.

II.—If the jury believe, from the evidence, that the deceased was killed by the prisoner by means of a leaden bullet discharged from a pistol, such killing implies malice in law, and is murder.

III.—That the burden of rebutting the presumption of malice by showing circumstances of alleviation, excuse or justification, rests on the prisoner, and it is incumbent on him to make out such circumstances to the satisfaction of the jury, unless they arise out of the evidence produced against him.

RULING.—The second and third instructions asked for by the United States are granted.

IV.—That every person is presumed to be of sound mind until the contrary is proved, and the burden of rebutting this presumption rests on the prisoner, with the addition of the matters set forth in the next instruction (No. V).

RULING.—The fourth instruction asked for by the United States is answered by prayer eleven of the defense.

V.—If the jury believe, from the evidence, that the deceased, previous to the day of his death, had adulterous intercourse with the wife of the prisoner; and further, that the deceased, on the day of his death, shortly before the prisoner left his house, made signals, inviting to a further act or acts of adultery, which said signals, or a portion of them, were seen by the prisoner; and, that, influenced by such provocation, the prisoner took the life of the deceased, such provocation does not justify the act or reduce such killing from murder to manslaughter.

RULING.—The fifth instruction asked for by the United States, the Court thinks, is the law and grants the instruction.

INSTRUCTIONS SUBMITTED FOR THE PRISONER.

I.—There is no presumption of malice in this case, if any proof of " alleviation, excuse, or justification," arise out of the evidence for the prosecution. (State *v.* John, 3 Jones, p. 366; McDaniel *v.* State, 8 Smead's and Marshall's, p. 401; Day's Case, p. 17 of pamphlet.)

RULING.—There is, gentlemen, a legal presumption of malice in every deliberate killing, and the burden of repelling it is on the slayer, unless evidence of alleviation, mitigation, excuse or justification, arise out of the evidence adduced against him. The alleviation, mitigation, excuse or justification must be such as the law prescribes, and within the limits already laid down in the instructions given to you.

II.—The existence of malice is not presumable in this case, if on any rational theory consistent with all the evidence the homicide was either justifiable or excusable, or an act of manslaughter. (Same cases as above cited; United States *v.* Mingo, 2 Curtis C. C. R. p. 1; Commonwealth *v.* York, 2 Bennett & Heard Leading Criminal Cases, p. 505.)

RULING.—In regard to the second instruction asked for by the defense, I would say: The answer to the first prayer will be taken in connection with his response to prayer number two: "If upon any course of reasoning consistent with all the evidence," and the law as laid down to you by the Court, and the rules by which it is ascertained what is legal provocation, what is justification or excuse, you should come to the conclusion that there was such justification or excuse, or that the homicide was manslaughter, then the presumption of malice which every killing of a human being involves, is met. You will recollect that manslaughter is the killing of a man without malice.

III —If, on the whole evidence presented by the prosecution, there is any rational hypothesis consistent with the conclusion that the homicide was justifiable or excusable, the defendant cannot be convicted.

RULING.—The third prayer on the part of the defense is answered in the same manner as prayer number two.

IV.—If the jury believe that Mr. Sickles, when the homicide occurred, intended to kill Mr. Key, he cannot be convicted of manslaughter.

RULING.—The fourth prayer the Court declines to grant; manslaughter may exist, and most frequently does where the slayer intended to destroy life, but under circumstances which reduce the offense.

V.—It is for the jury to determine, under all the circumstances of the case, whether the act charged upon Mr. Sickles is murder or justifiable homicide. (Ryan's Case, 2 Wheeler's Criminal Cases, p. 54.)

RULING.—The fifth prayer cannot be granted, as to the jury belongs the decision of matters of fact, and to the Court the decision of matters of law, which it is the duty of the jury to receive from the Court; and from the evidence and the law applied to the facts, it is the province and legal right of the jury to return a verdict of guilty or not guilty of murder or manslaughter.

VI.—If the jury find that Mr. Sickles killed Mr. Key while the latter was in criminal intercourse with the wife of the former, Mr. Sickles cannot be convicted of either murder or manslaughter.

RULING.—In regard to the sixth instruction for the defense, I would remark: If this prayer refers to actual (existing at the moment) adulterous intercourse with the wife of the prisoner, the slaying of the deceased would be manslaughter. And by existing adultery, I do not mean that the prisoner stood by and witnessed the fact of adultery progressing, for it is easy to suppose the actual fact to be established simultaneously with the killing by other evidence, and perfectly consistent with the law; if, for instance, the husband saw the adulterer leave the bed of the wife, or shot him while trying to escape from his chamber. If, however, a day or half a day intervene between the conviction of the husband of the guilt of his wife and the deceased, and after the lapse of such time the husband take tce life of the deceased, the law considers that it was done deliberately, and dehares that it was murder. (Jarboe's Case.)

VII.—If, from the whole evidence, the jury believe that Mr. Sickles committed the act, but at the time of doing so was under the influence of a diseased mind, and was really unconscious that he was committing a crime, he is not in law guilty of murder. (Day's Case, p. 9 of pamphlet.)

VIII.—If the jury believe that from any predisposing cause the prisoner's mind was impaired, and at the time of killing Mr. Key he became or was mentally incapable of governing himself in reference to Mr. Key, as the debauchee of his wife, and at the time of his committing said act, was, by reason of such cause, unconscious that he was committing a crime as to said Mr. Key, he is not guilty of any offense whatever. (Day's Case, p. 17 of pamphlet.)

RULING.—The seventh and eighth instructions can be answered together. They are granted.

IX.—It is for the jury to say what was the state of the prisoner's mind as to the capacity to decide upon the criminality of the particular act in question—the homicide—at the moment it occurred, and what was the condition of the parties respectively as to being armed or not at the same moment. These are open questions for the jury, as are any other questions which may arise upon the consideration of the evidence, the whole of which is to be taken into view by the jury. (Jarboe's Case, p. 20 of pamphlet.)

RULING.—In reply to the ninth instruction the Court responds thus : " It is for the jury to say what was the state of Mr. Sickles' mind as to the capacity to decide upon the criminality of the homicide, receiving the law as given to them in relation to the degree of insanity, whether it will, or will not, excuse, they (the jury) finding the fact of the existence or non-existence of such degree of insanity." The gist of this prayer is, " what was the condition of the parties respectively as to being armed or not at the same moment." So much of the instructions I have now read, I grant without qualification.

X.—The law does not require that the insanity, which absolves from crime, should exist for any definite period, but only that it exists at the moment when the act occurred with which the accused stands charged.

RULING.—The tenth instruction is granted. The time when the insanity is to operate is the moment when the crime charged upon the party was committed, if committed at all.

XI.—If the jury have any doubt as to the case, either in reference to the homicide or the question of sanity, Mr. Sickles should be acquitted.

RULING.—This instruction, as I mentioned in referring to prayer four of the United States, will be answered in conjunction with it.

It does not appear to be questioned that if a doubt is entertained by the jury the prisoner is to have the benefit of it. As to the sanity or insanity of the prisoner at the moment of committing the act charged, it is argued by the United States that every man being presumed to be sane, the presumption must be overcome by evidence satisfactory to the jury, that he was insane when the deed was done.

This is not the first time this inquiry has engaged my attention. The point was made and decided at the June Term, 1858. In the case of the United States v. Devlins, when the Court gave the following opinion, which I read from my notes of the trial. This prayer is based on the idea that the jury must be satisfied, beyond all reasonable doubt, of the insanity of the party for whom the

46

defense is set up. Precisely as the United States are bound to prove the guilt of a defendant to warrant a conviction. I am well aware, and it has appeared on this argument, that it has been held by a Court of high rank and reputation, that there must be a preponderance of evidence in favor of the defense of insanity to overcome the presumption of law that every killing is murder; and that the same Court has said that if there is an equilibrium, including, I suppose, the presumption mentioned as to evidence, the presumption of the defendant's innocence makes the preponderance in his favor.

Whether a man is insane or not is a matter of fact; what degree of insanity will relieve him from responsibility is a matter of law, the jury finding the fact of the degree, too. Under the instruction of the Court, murder can be committed only by a sane man. Everybody is presumed to be sane who is charged with a crime, but when evidence is adduced that a prisoner is insane, and conflicting testimony makes a question for the jury, they are to decide it like every other matter of fact, and if they should say or conclude that there is uncertainty, that they cannot determine whether the defendant was or is not so insane as to protect him, how can they render a verdict that a sane man perpetrated the crime, and that no other can?

Nor is this plain view of the question unsupported by authority. In the case of the Queen v. Ley, in 1840, Lewins C. C. p. 239, on a preliminary trial to ascertain whether a defendant was sufficiently sane to go before a petit jury on an indictment, Hullock, B., said to the jury: "If there be a doubt as to the prisoner's sanity, and the surgeon says it is doubtful, you cannot say he is in a fit state to be put on trial." This opinion was approved in the People v. Freeman, 4 Denio's Reports, p. 9. This is a strong case, for the witness did not say the prisoner was insane, but only that it was doubtful whether he was so or not. The humane, and, I will add, just doctrine, that a reasonable doubt should avail a prisoner, belongs to a defense of insanity, as much, in my opinion, as to any other matter of fact. I believe, gentlemen, that that answers all the questions.

REFERENCES IN THE CASE OF THE "SAVANNAH PRIVATEERS."

LETTER OF MARQUE ISSUED BY JEFFERSON DAVIS TO CAPTAIN BAKER OF THE PRIVATEER "SAVANNAH."

[See text, p. 354.]

"JEFFERSON DAVIS,

"PRESIDENT OF THE CONFEDERATE STATES OF AMERICA.

" *To all who shall see these presents, greeting :*—Know ye, that by virtue of the power vested in me by law, I have commissioned, and do hereby commission, have authorized, and do hereby authorize, the schooner or vessel called the Savannah (more particularly described in the schedule hereunto annexed), whereof T. Harrison Baker is commander, to act as a private armed vessel in the service of the Confederate States, on the high seas, against the United States of America, their ships, vessels, goods, and effects, and those of her citizens, during the pendency of the war now existing between the said Confederate States and the said United States.

" This commission to continue in force until revoked by the President of the Confederate States for the time being.

" Schedule of description of the vessel:—Name, Schooner Savannah; tonnage, 53⁴⁴⁄₉₉ tons; armament, one large pivot gun and small arms; number of crew, thirty.

" Given under my hand and the seal of the Confederate States, at Montgomery, this 18th day of May, 1861,

" JEFFERSON DAVIS.

" By the President—R. TOOMBS, Secretary of State."

GARIBALDI'S LETTER, REFERRED TO BY MR. BRADY
AND MR. EVARTS.

[See text, pp. 358, 419.]

" CAPRERA, *Sept.* 10.

" *Dear Sir :* I saw Mr. Sandford, and regret to be obliged to announce to you that I shall not be able to go to the United States at present. I do not doubt of the triumph of the cause of the Union, and that shortly; but, if the war should unfortunately continue in your beautiful country, I shall overcome the obstacles which detain me and hasten to the defense of a people who are dear to me. G. GARIBALDI."

CITATIONS, FROM VATTEL'S LAW OF NATURE AND NATIONS,
BY MR. JAMES T. BRADY.

[See text, p. 365.]

" *Sec.* 287. It is a question very much debated whether a sovereign is bound to observe the common laws of war towards rebellious subjects who have openly taken up arms against him. A flatterer, or a Prince of cruel and arbitrary disposition, will immediately pronounce that the laws of war were not made for rebels, for whom no punishment can be too severe. Let us proceed more soberly, and reason from the incontestible principles above laid down."

" *Sec.* 292. When a party is formed in a State who no longer obey the sovereign, and are possessed of sufficient strength to oppose him; or when, in a Republic, the nation is divided into two opposite factions, and both sides take up arms, this is called a civil war. Some writers confine this term to a just insurrection of the subjects against their sovereign to distinguish that lawful resistance from rebellion, which is an open and unjust resistance. But what application will they give to a war which arises in a Republic, torn by two factions, or, in a Monarchy, between two competitors for the Crown ? Custom appropriates the term of civil war to every war between the members of one and the same political society. If it be between part of the citizens on the one side, and the sovereign with those who continue in obedience to him on the other, provided the malcontents have any reason for taking up arms, nothing further is required to entitle such disturbance to the name of civil war, and not that of rebellion. This latter term is applied only to such an insurrection against lawful authority as is void of all appearance of justice. The sovereign, indeed, never fails to bestow the application of rebels on all such of his subjects as openly resist him; but when the latter have acquired sufficient strength to give him effectual opposition, and to oblige him to carry on the war against them according to the established rules, he must necessarily submit to the use of the term civil war.

" *Sec.* 293. It is foreign to our purpose, in this place, to weigh the reasons which may authorize and justify a civil war; we have elsewhere treated of the cases wherein subjects may resist the sovereign. (Book 1, cap. 4.) Setting, therefore, the justice of the cause wholly out of the question, it only remains for us to consider the maxims which ought to be observed in a civil war, and to examine whether the sovereign, in particular, is on such an occasion bound to conform to the established laws of war.

" A civil war breaks the bonds of society and Government, or at least suspends their force and effect; it produces in the nation two independent parties, who consider each other as enemies, and acknowledge no common judge. Those two parties, therefore, must necessarily be considered as thenceforward constituting, at least for a time, two separate bodies—two distinct societies. Though one of the parties may have been to blame in breaking the unity of the State, and resisting the lawful authority, they are not the less divided in fact. Besides, who shall judge them ? Who should pronounce on which side the right or the wrong lies ? On each they have no common superior. They stand, therefore, in precisely the same predicament as two nations who engage in a contest, and, being unable to come to an agreement, have recourse to arms.

" This being the case, it is very evident that the common laws of war —those maxims of humanity, moderation and honor, which we have already detailed in the course of this work—ought to be observed by both parties in every civil war. For the same reasons which render the observance of those maxims a matter of obligation between State and State, it becomes equally and even more necessary in the unhappy circumstances of two incensed parties lacerating their common country. Should the sovereign conceive he has a right to hang up his prisoners as rebels, the opposite party will make reprisals; if he does not religiously observe the capitulations, and all other conventions made with his enemies, they will no longer rely on his word ; should he burn and ravage, they will follow his example; the war will become cruel, horrible, and every day more destructive to the nation."

After noticing the cases of the Duc de Montpensier and Baron des Adrets, he continues :

" At length it became necessary to relinquish those pretensions to iudicial authority over men who proved themselves capable of supporting their cause by force of arms, and to treat them not as criminals, but as enemies. Even the troops have often refused to serve in a war wherein the Prince exposed them to cruel reprisals. Officers who had the highest sense of honor, though ready to shed their blood on the field of battle for his service, have not thought it any part of their duty to run the hazard or an ignominious death. Whenever, therefore, a numerous body of men think they have a right to resist the sovereign, and feel themselves in a condition to appeal to the sword, the war ought to be carried on by the contending parties in the same manner as by two different nations, and they ought to leave open the same means for preventing its being carried into outrageous extremities and for the restoration of peace."

ABSTRACT OF DOCUMENTARY EVIDENCE OFFERED BY DEFENDANTS IN THE CASE OF THE "SAVANNAH PRIVATEERS."

[See text, p. 367.]

MR. BRADY, for the defense, put in evidence the following documents:

1. Preliminary Chart of Part of the sea-coast of Virginia, and Entrance to Chesapeake Bay.—Coast Survey Work, dated 1855.

2. The Constitution of Virginia, adopted June 29, 1776. It refers only to the western and northern boundaries of Virginia—Art. 21—but recognizes the Charter of 1609. That charter (Hemmings' Statutes, 1st vol. p. 88) gives to Virginia jurisdiction over all havens and ports, and all islands lying within 100 miles of the shores.

3. The Act to Ratify the Compact between Maryland and Virginia, passed January 3, 1786—to be found in the Revised Code of Virginia, page 53. It makes Chesapeake Bay, from the capes, entirely in Virginia.

MR. SULLIVAN also put in evidence, from Putnam's Rebellion Record, the following documents:

1. Proclamation of the President of the United States, of 15th April, 1861.

2. Proclamation of the President, of 19th April, 1861, declaring a blockade.

3. Proclamation of 27th April, 1861, extending the blockade to the coasts of Virginia and North Carolina.

4. Proclamation of May 3d, for an additional military force of 42,034 men, and the increase of the regular army and navy.

5. The Secession Ordinance of South Carolina, dated Dec. 20, 1860.

MR. SULLIVAN read in evidence from page 10 of Putnam's Rebellion Record:

Letter from Secretary of War, John B. Floyd, to President Buchanan, dated December 29, 1860.

President Buchanan's reply, dated December 29, 1860.

Also, from page 11 of Rebellion Record:

The Correspondence between the South Carolina Commissioners and the President of the United States.

Also referred to page 19 of Rebellion Record, for the Correspondence between Major Anderson and Governor Pickens, with reference to firing on the Star of the West.

Read Major Anderson's first letter (without date), copied from Charleston Courier, of Jan. 10, 1861.

Governor Pickens' reply, and second communication from Major Anderson.

Also, from page 29 of Rebellion Record, containing the sections of the Constitution of the Confederate States which differ from the Constitution of the United States.

Also, from page 31 of Rebellion Record: Inaugural of Jefferson Davis, as President of the Confederate States.

Also, page 36 of Rebellion Record: Inaugural of Abraham Lincoln, President of the United States.

Also, page 61 of Rebellion Record: The President's Speech to the Virginia Commissioners.

Also, page 71 of Rebellion Record: Proclamation of Jefferson Davis, with reference to the letters of marque, dated 17th April, 1861.

Also, page 195 of Rebellion Record: An Act recognizing a state of war, by the Confederate Congress,—published May 6, 1861.

MR. LORD read from pages 17, 19, and 20 of Diary of Rebellion Record, to give the date of certain events:

1861, February 8. The Constitution of the Confederate States adopted.
       "   18. Jefferson Davis inaugurated President.
       "   21. The President of the Southern Confederacy nominates members of his Cabinet.
       "   21. Congress at Montgomery passed an Act declaring the establishment of free navigation of the Mississippi.
     March 19. Confederates passed an Act for organizing the Confederate States.
      April 8. South Carolina Convention ratified the Constitution of the Confederate States by a vote of 119 to 16.

CITATIONS ON MILITARY LAW BY MR. WILLIAM A. BEACH.

[See text, p. 455.]

A MILITARY CRIME MUST BE IMPUTED IN THE CHARGES AND SPECIFICATIONS.

" The jurisdiction of court-martial is special and limited, arising from the cognizance of crimes as committed by individuals, that is, by individuals subject to military law; and the crimes or acts are such as are repugnant to military discipline, and are pointed out by law, by the general regulations for the army, and by the custom of war.

"Those acts defined by law are sufficiently distinct for the observation of members of military courts, whereby they may regulate their proceedings, and no embarrassment can arise in regard to making them the subject of military investigation.

"The general regulations for the army are a permanent body of rules for the better ordering and methodical arrangement of subjects of military concernment, and have a view to establish uniformity of the affairs of the army by determining, to a greater or less degree, the requisite minutiæ and detail. Their character, while mandatory, is also ministerial, and, proceeding from the President of the United States, the highest military authority, claims the utmost respect, observance and obedience. It is true, they are not in the nature of a subordinate legislation to determine or to define offenses and affix penalties, for that belongs to Congress only, and such as are set forth in the rules and articles of war; but they are of the nature and character of orders, pertaining to the executive and administrative branches of the service; and although they denounce no punishment in terms, yet the neglect or positive breaches of their requirements are immediately referable to the established laws for the enforcement of discipline, to which they appeal for an appropriate sanction.

"The custom of war is the unwritten or common law of the army. In order to apply it to any particular case, it must be certain and well defined, and clearly not opposed to any law or regulation. The custom of war is rather sought for as explanatory of some doubtful question in which, without its aid, a decision might become certain, then as a source of authority by itself. It must be understood, too, that a custom to have any validity, besides having the quotations above mentioned, must also be a custom of the army for the government of which it is intended to be applied. To resort to a foreign military service, and draw thence customs of war which are genuine and acknowledged in such service, might be very illegal when introduced into our own, as the circumstances or conditions which called them into existence, and continued them in being, in the one might be entirely wanting in the other. It is an authority which ought to be well scrutinized before allowed to have a determining influence. The customs and usages of an army are, when considered in contradistinction to the positive laws and regulations for the same, generally pretty well understood, and when adduced, as illustrative of the forms adhered to, or the interpretation of acts, should have the certainty of established fact.

"In concluding this chapter, it is proper to observe, that it is a principle by which the power and jurisdiction of courts-martial are restrained, that they cannot take cognizance of any acts or offenses which are not conceded by statute, or the custom of war, as specific crimes against the military State, or as disorders and neglects tending to the prejudice of discipline and good order."—*De Hart on Courts-martial*, pp. 298, 299.

The Specifications must embrace the Charge and sustain the Offense.

[See text, p. 456.]

" The fact or facts ought to be very distinctly specified or alleged, in such manner that neither the prisoner or court can have any difficulty in knowing what is the precise object of investigation. Facts distinct in their nature are not to be included in the same specifications. Every fact in the specification should be such as, if proved, would convict the prisoner of the charge, or at least might convict him of it. Any allegation in the specification which, if proved, could not convict the prisoner of any degree of the crime charged, is irrelevant and should be rejected. Its retention will not vitiate the charge, but it is surplusage, and no evidence should be received thereon. It is always better to reject such matter at first. This rule is applicable, though the facts irrelevant to the particular charge do themselves amount to a distinct crime.

"If all the facts stated in the specification would not, if proved, amount to the crime stated in the charge, both charge and specification must be rejected; for the court is to pronounce only in the crime named in the charge, and no other.

"From the preceding it results that the court-martial may and ought to refuse to try on accusations,—4th, when the specification alleges only certain acts, either not at all criminal, or not constituting any degree of the crime stated in the charge."—*O'Brien on American Military Law*, pp. 234, 235.

THE WAR AMENDMENTS TO THE CONSTITUTION.

[See text, p. 518.]

ARTICLE XIII.

SEC. 1. Neither slavery nor involuntary servitude, except as a punishment for crime, whereof the party shall have been duly convicted, shall exist within the United States, or any place subject to their jurisdiction.

SEC. 2. Congress shall have power to enforce this article by appropriate legislation.

ARTICLE XIV.

SEC. 1. All persons born or naturalized in the United States, and subject to the jurisdiction thereof, are citizens of the United States, and of the State wherein they reside. No State shall make or enforce any law which shall abridge the privileges or immunities of citizens of the United States; nor shall any State deprive any person of life, liberty, or property, without due process of law, nor deny to any person within its jurisdiction, the equal protection of the laws.

SEC. 2. Representatives shall be apportioned among the several States according to their respective numbers, counting the whole number of persons in each State, excluding Indians not taxed. But when the right to vote at any election for choice of electors for president and vice-president of the United States, representatives in congress, the executive and judicial officers of a State, or the members of the legislature thereof, is denied to any of the male inhabitants of such State being twenty-one years of age, and citizens of the United States, or in any way abridged, except for participation in rebellion or other crime, the basis of representation therein shall be reduced in the proportion which the number of such male citizens shall bear to the whole number of male citizens twenty-one years of age in such State.

SEC. 3. No person shall be a senator, or representative in congress, or elector of president and vice-president, or hold any office, civil or military, under the United States, or under any State, who, having previously taken an oath as a member of congress, or as an officer of the United States, or as a member of any State legislature, or as an executive or judicial officer of any State, to support the Constitution of the United States, shall have engaged in insurrection or rebellion against the same, or given aid and comfort to the enemies thereof; but congress may, by a vote of two-thirds of each house, remove such disability.

SEC. 4. The validity of the public debt of the United States authorized by law, including debts incurred for payment of pensions and bounties for services in suppressing insurrection or rebellion, shall not be questioned. But neither the United States nor any State shall assume or pay any debt or obligation incurred in aid of insurrection or rebellion against the United States, or any claim for the loss or emancipation of any slave; but all such debts, obligations, and claims, shall be held illegal and void.

SEC. 5. The congress shall have power to enforce, by appropriate legisation, the provisions of this article.

ARTICLE XV.

SEC. 1. The right of citizens of the United States to vote shall not be denied or abridged by the United States or by any State on account of race, color, or previous condition of servitude.

SEC. 2. The congress shall have power to enforce this article by appropriate legislation.

ODE AND VERSES REFERRED TO BY MR. MACKIN-TOSH IN HIS DEFENSE OF PELTIER.

[See text, pp. 568, 591, 592.]

That the reader may thoroughly comprehend the argument of Mr. Mackintosh, we present the portions of the first two publications set out in the pleadings, for the Crown, and the translation as they appear upon the record, in the language of the indictment. The allegation is that the defendant, on the 16th of August, 1802, " within the liberty of Westminster, in the county of Middlesex, unlawfully and maliciously did print and publish, and cause and procure to be printed and published, a most slandalous and malicious libel, in the French language, of and concerning the said Napoleon Buonaparté, that is to say, one part thereof to the tenor following, to wit:

"LE 18 BRUMAIRE AN VIII.

"*Ode attribuée à* Chénier.

" Quelles tempêtes effroyables
Grondent sur les flots déchaînés
Dieux! quels torrents épouvantables
Roulent ces rocs déracinés ?
Les fleuves n'ont plus de rivages
Couvert d'écume et de naufrages
L'océan mugit dans les airs
Sur ses fondements ébranlée
La terre va-t-elle écroulée
Se détacher de l'univers ?

" Ah plutôt pour se faire absoudre !
D'une trop longue impunité
Les cieux peut-être avec la foudre
Vont protéger la Liberté
Dieux du peuple que l'on opprime
Vengez cette auguste victime
De l'audacieux attentat
Qu'aux jours malheureux de Brumaire
Les lois ont dans leur sanctuaire
Vu consommer par un soldat

" Trop vain espoir de la vengeance !
Peuples livrés aux oppresseurs
N'auriez vous dans votre souffrance
Que vos bras pour libérateurs ?
Le ciel est aveugle au barbare
Et lorsque sa foudre s'égare
Portée au hasard sur les vents
Qu'elle dévaste les campagnes
Ou frappe d'arides montagnes
Elle respecte les tirans

" Jouets des flots et des orages
Voyez ces utiles vaisseaux
De leurs débris couvrir vos plages

Ou s'abymer au fond des eaux
Tandis que la nef criminelle
Qui porte ce Corse rebelle
Déserteur des champs Africains
Tranquillement vogue sur l'onde
Et de César annonce au monde
Et la fortune et les desseins

"De la France, ô honte éternelle
César au bord du Rubicon
A contre lui dans sa querelle
Le Sénat Pompée et Caton
Et dans les plaines de Pharsale
Si la fortune est inégale
S'il te faut céder aux destins
Rome dans ce revers funeste
Pour te venger au moins il reste
Un poignard aux derniers Romains

"Mais sous quelles viles entraves
A succombé notre vertu!
Quoi! l'univers nous voit esclaves
Sans que nous ayons combattu!
Au sein d'un sénat parricide
La noire trahison préside
Fiere encore de nos revers
Le pouvoir sans appui sans force
Tombe à sa voix et c'est d'un Corse
Que le Français reçoit des fers?

"And in another part thereof to the tenor following, that is to say:

"Déjà dans sa rage insolente
Le despote ose menacer . . . . .
Tel des flots la vague écumante
Se brise contre le rocher
Est-ce pour vous donner un maître
Est-ce pour couronner un traître
Que la France a puni ses rois?
Non non l'ambition coupable
Saura qu'il n'est d'inviolable
Que les droits du peuple et ses lois.

And in another part thereof to the tenor following, that is to say:

"*Vœu d'un bon Patriote au* 14 *Juillet*, 1802.

"Quel fortune a fait le fils de Létitie!
Corse il devient Français Sa nouvelle partie
L'adopte le nourrit au rang de ses enfants
Et déjà lui promet les destins les plus grands!
Un orage survient sous l'effort des tempêtes
L'état est renversé les plus augustes têtes
Tombent tout est brisé le Français malheureux
Regrette en soupirant son erreur et ses vœux!
Napoléon paraît! de victoire en victoire
Il atteint *en volant* au faîte de la gloire!

L'Orient, l'Occident témoins de ses exploits
Par lui sont terrassés et reçoivent ses loix !
Le Nil avait frémi mais le sort qui l'entraine
Rappelle son vainqueur aux rives de la Seine
Cinq chefs ou cinq tyrans partageaient le pouvoir
Il arrache à leur mains le sceptre et l'encensoir
Le voilà donc assis où s'élevait le trône !
Que faut-il à ses vœux ? un sceptre ? une couronne ?
Consul il regle tout il fait defait des rois
Peu soigneux d'être aimé la terreur fait ses droits !
Sur un peuple avili jusqu'au rang des esclaves
Il regne-il est despote on baise ses entraves
Qu'a-t-il à redouter ?   Il a dicté la paix
Des rois sont à ses pieds, mendiant ses bienfaits ?
D'assurer en ses mains l'autorité suprème
On lui porte les vœux !   Les Français des rois même
A le féliciter's'empressent humblement
Et voudraient en sujets lui prêter le serment . . .
Il est proclamé chef et consul pour la vie . . .
       Pour moi loin qu'à son sort je porte quelqu'envie
Qu'il nomme j'y consens son digne *successeur*
Sur le pavois porté qu'on l'élise *empereur*
Enfin et Romulus nous rappelle la chose
Je fais vœu . . . . dès demain qu'il ait l'apothéose !   AMEN.

"Which said scandalous and malicious words in the French language, first above-mentioned and set forth, being translated into the English language, were and are of the same signification and meaning as these English words following, that is to say :

"What frightful tempests growl on the unchained waves ? Gods, what dreadful torrents roll these uprooted rocks ? The rivers have no longer any banks. The ocean, covered with foam and shipwrecks, bellows in the air. Shaken at its foundation, is the earth fallen—going to detach itself from the universe ! Ah ! rather to obtain their acquittal for too long impunity, the heavens, perhaps, are going to protect liberty with the thunder. Gods of an oppressed people ! Avenge this august victim of the audacious attempt which on the unhappy days of Brumaire, the laws, in their sanctuary, saw completed by a soldier ! (meaning the said Napoleon Buonaparté). Too vain hope of vengeance ! Nations given up to oppressors, have you in your sufferings only your arms for deliverers ? The heaven is blind or cruel, and when its thunder flies, carried by chance upon the winds, whether it lays waste the plains or strike the arid mountains, it respects tyrants. Behold those useful vessels, the sport of the waves and storms, cover your coasts with their wrecks or sink to the bottom of the waters, while the guilty ship that carries that rebel Corsican (meaning the said Napoleon Buonaparté) deserter of the plains of Africa, sails tranquilly on the wave, and announces to the world the fortune and the designs of Cæsar. Oh, eternal disgrace of France ! Cæsar, on the bank of the Rubicon, has against him in his quarrel the senate, Pompey and Cato, and in the plains of Pharsalia, if fortune is unequal, if you must yield to the destinies of Rome, in this sad reverse, at least, there remains to avenge you, a poignard among the last Romans. But, under what vile fetters has our valour fallen ! What ! the universe beholds us slaves without our having combatted ! In the bosom of a parricide senate black treason presides, still fierce at our misfortunes; power without support and without force falls at its voice, and it is from a Corsican (meaning the said Napoleon Buonaparté) that the Frenchman receives his chains.

"And which said scandalous and malicious words, in the French language, secondly above-mentioned and set forth, being translated into the English language, were and are of the same signification and meaning as these English words following, that is to say:

"Already, in his insolent rage, the despot (meaning the said Napoleon Buonaparté) dares to menace; but the foaming wave of the sea breaks itself against the rock. Is it to give you a master—is it to crown a traitor (meaning the said Napoleon Buonaparté (that France has punished her kings? No, no; guilty ambition shall know that there is nothing inviolable but the rights of the people and their laws.

"And which said scandalous and malicious matters in the French language last above-mentioned and set forth, being translated into English, are as follows, that is to say:

"*Wish of a good patriot on the fourteenth day of July, in the year of our Lord one thousand eight hundred and two.*

"What fortune has the son of Lætitia (meaning the said Napoleon Buonaparté) arrived at! A Corsican, he becomes a Frenchman. His new country adopts him, nourishes him in the rank of its children, and already promises him the greatest destinies. A storm arises. By the force of the tempests the State is overturned; the most noble persons fall; everything is broken. The unhappy Frenchman regrets with sighs his error and his wishes. Napoleon appears, flying from victory to victory. He reaches the summit of glory. The east, the west, witnesses of his exploits are vanquished by him and receive his laws. The Nile had shuddered, but the lot that forces him on recalls his vanquisher to the banks of the Seine. Five chiefs or five tyrants shared the power. He forces from their hands the sceptre and the censer. Behold him, then, seated where the throne was raised. What is wanting to its wishes? A sceptre? a crown? Consul, he governs all; he makes and unmakes kings. Little careful to be beloved, terror establishes his rights over a people degraded even to the rank of slaves. He reigns; he is despotic; they kiss their chains. What has he to dread? He has dictated peace. Kings are at his feet begging his favors. He is desired to secure the supreme authority in his hands! The French, nay, kings themselves, hasten to congratulate him, and would take the oath to him like subjects. He is proclaimed chief and consul for life. As for me, far from envying his lot, let him name, I consent to it, his worthy successor. Carried on the shield, let him be elected emperor! Finally (and Romulus recalls the thing to mind), I wish that on the morrow he may have his apotheosis. Amen.

"To the great scandal, disgrace and danger of the said Napoleon Buonaparté, to the great danger of creating discord between our said lord the king and his subjects and the said Napoleon Buonaparté, the French republic and the citizens of the said republic, in contempt of our said lord the king and his law, to the evil example of all others in the like case offending, and against the peace of our said lord the king, his crown and dignity."

PASSAGES OF THE ODE TRANSLATED IN VERSE, AND CITED, BY MR. MACKINTOSH.

[See Text p. 592.]

C'est par les lois que l'Angleterre
Affermit sa prospérité :
Là, sous leur abri tutélaire,
On peut braver la royauté ;
Là, devant leur toute puissance,
Et le pouvoir et la naissance
Baissent un front religieux ;
Là, l'homme pense sans contrainte,
Et, satisfait, jouit sans crainte
Des memes droits que ses ayeux.

Du pouvoir censeur nécessaire,
L'Anglais n'en peut craindre les coups ;
Des lois jamais sur l'arbitraire
Il n'invoque en vain le courroux.
Fiere de sa charte sacrée,
De gloire et de biens entourée,
Albion regne sur les mers ;
Elle chérit sa destinée,
Et la Tamise fortunée
Fixe les yeux de l'univers.

Cependant encore affligée
Par l'odieuse hérédité,
Londres, de titres surchargée,
Londres n'a pas l'égalité ;
Mais son rempart impénétrable,
Est dans le pouvoir responsable
De la volonté de ses Rois :
Tandis que la main despotique
Qui conduit notre République
Est plus puissante que les lois.

INDEX.

INDEX.

A

Addison, supposed dialogue between Lord Somers and, 660.

Advocate, duties of, require high moral courage, 371.

Æneas, reference to, by Mr. Wirt, 65; Dido's entreaty with, 291.

Age of Reason, the, mischievous effects of, 560; intellectual inferiority of the work, 565.

Alexander the Great, debts of Thessalians remitted by, 5, 33.

Amendments, text of war amendments, 728. (See, also, Constitution.)

America, greatness of as a nation, 8; period of her independence, 12; necessities which compelled her revolt, 13; struggles of, 15; right of, to be considered a nation, 20; result had she been conquered, 21; condition of, in 1812, 201.

Americans, what things distinguished for, 348.

Animus furandi, legal definition of, 349; must depend on something more than presumption, 352.

"Appropriate Legislation," meaning of the term, 526.

Armstrong, Brig-of-war, Gen., case of, 191; circumstances of her destruction, 192; story of her loss, 202; circumstances under which she fired the first gun, 225.

Askin, Francis, circumstances of his death, 127.

B

Bacon, Lord, law of necessity, p. 125, cited, 134, 135; extract from his discourse on the reign of Elizabeth, 598.

Baker, Thomas Harrison, captain of the "Savannah," trial of, 343.

Baldwin, Hon. Henry, his charge in United States v. Holmes, 147.

Bankrupt Laws, right of Congress to establish, exclusive, 69; object of prohibiting the States from passing, 83.

BEACH, WILLIAM A., his defense of Col. North, 449; his argument before the Commission in case of, 451–480; observations as to crime, and punishment, 453; defines consequences of usurping unlawful authority, 459; shows that constitutional rights can not be suspended, 464; nor the Constitution suspended, 466; defines limitations of constitutional authority, 467; defines origin of legal tribunals, 471.

Belligerents, rights of, in neutral territory, 204; status of, defined, 389; condition of, no protection to citizens, 390.

Bentham Jeremy, observations of, as as to the security afforded by law, 480.

Bible, views of Sir William Jones concerning, 552; literary merit of, 552; doctrines of, would banish wickedness, 564.

BLACK, JEREMIAH S., his defense of Milligan, 482; his argument before the U. S. Supreme Court, 483, 516; his review of the charges against Milligan, 484; of the tribunal in which he was tried, 484; of the jurisdiction of the Commission, 485; enumerates the safeguards to protect from illegal punishment, 492; sketches the history of jury trials, 494; proves title to right to jury trial, 497; disposes of the plea of necessity, 500; historical review of exercise of illegal authority throughout the world, 511.

Blasphemy, prosecution of Williams on charge of, 554.

Blockade defined, 396.

Bolingbroke, reference to, by Mr. North, 662.

Bonaparte. (See Napoleon Bonaparte.)

"Bottle Riot" case, 613; speech of Mr. Plunket, 615–640; speech of Mr. North, 642–666; nature of the offense charged, object of the prosecution, 616; political events in which conspiracy had its origin, 625; narration of the facts constituting charge against the defendants, 633; conduct

47

Overt acts, when evidence, 40.

Orange, Prince of. (See William III.)

Orangemen, charges in "Bottle Riot Case" not intended as protest against, 623; loyalty chief characteristic of, 646.

P

Paine, Thomas, his "Age of Reason," 551; publication of held blasphemous, 566; defended by Erskine, for publishing "Rights of Man," 554; inferiority of his work, 565.

Paley, William, observations of, concerning uncertainty of the law, 84.

Paper money, compelled by necessity, 18; effect of payment of in war time, 26.

Pardoning power, wisdom and justice of, 379.

Parent and child, sacred relationship between, 330.

Patent Laws, nature and character of, 59.

Peltier Jean, his libel against Napoleon Bonaparte, 568; argument in his defense by Sir James Mackintosh, 569-612; sketch of his misfortunes, 570; the real issue, 572; his right to satirize Jacobinism, 585; the ode cannot represent his opinions, 591; observations on the ode by Mr. Mackintosh, 592; text of the ode, 730; extract from indictment against, 730.

Pinkney, William, argument of U. S. v. Hodges, 35-46; conduct at Bladensburg, 35; his strictures on Justice Duvall; regards the jury judges of the law and the facts, 37; remarks on criminal intent, 38; defines the law of treason, 42; arraigns the doctrine of constructive treason, 44; views of on perfection of the Union, 411.

Piracy, nature and character of crime, 344, 346; under the law of nations, and under the acts of Congress, 347; proof required to convict, 349; letter of marque, a defense against, 354; crime of, 369; elements of, 380; false views of property rights, no defense of, 381; what sufficient evidence to constitute element of force, 382; treason no defense, 397; good faith no defense, 417.

Plunkett, William Conyngham, his conduct of the prosecution in Rex v. Forbes, 613; his abilities as a lawyer, 614; his oratory, 614; his defense

for filing the information in Rex v. Forbes, 615, 638; his speech to the jury in, 615-640; motive of in filing an ex-officio information, 617; legality of the proceeding, 618; his panegyric on William of Orange, 624; his defense of Lord Wellesley, 628; narration of the facts in case of Rex v. Forbes, 633.

Poland, crime against, and dismemberment of, 603.

Police and quarantine, regulations distinguished, 61; how far controlled by Congress, 63.

Ponsonby, Rt. Hon. George, his character as a lawyer, 683; his conduct of the defense of the Marquis of Headford, 683; his speech to the jury, 684-690; remark as to duty of the jury, 684; observations as to plaintiff's deportment, and its influence upon the wife, 685; states the rule of damages, 687.

Porter, John K., argument of on the constitutionality of the legal tender acts, 423-448; his definition of the Constitution, 423; its object, 424; the powers delegated to give it effect, 425; defines the necessity for pledging the public credit, 425; sketches history of legal tenders in colonial times, 428; reviews the events of the rebellion, 431; defines the subject of legal tender, 443.

Portugal, liability incurred at Battle of Fayal, 202; bound to prevent hostilities, 206; when liability became extinguished, 227.

Powers, exclusive and concurrent, distinguished, 51, 59; of a State may be taken away by implication, 53; repugnancy of conflicting, 53; what exclusive, 55.

Power, synonymous with right, 362; power and right distinguished, 416.

Powers, express and implied prohibitions of in the Constitution, 527; limitation on mode of enforcing delegated powers, 528. (See, also, Constitution.)

Prentiss, Sergeant S, style of his eloquence, 86; his defense of Judge Wilkinson, 86; his speech to the jury, 87; his arraignment of the witness Oldham, 109; of other conspirators, 111; his arraignment of Redding, 121.

Press, freedom of an inestimable blessing, 557; principles applicable to

tween rebellion and civil war, 365; cited for the prosecution in Savannah case, 398.

Vallandingham, case of, distinguished, 468 ; extract from Judge Leavitt's opinion in, 468.

Van Dyck *ads.* Metropolitan Bank, 421; Judge Porter's argument in, 423.

Vindictive damages, in cases of crim. con., 688, 693.

Virgil, cited by Mr. Wirt, 65.

W

Waite, Hon. Morrison R., reference to opinion of, in U. S. *v.* Cruikshank, 519.

War Amendments. (See Constitution.)

War distinguished from revolution, 15 ; levying of, defined, 39; combatants in civil war entitled to rights of, 368; privateering under laws of, 385; rights of neutrals with respect to privateers in time of, 387 ; status of belligerents, 389; actual existence of, when no defense to piracy, 394; definition of war, 395; when plea of, a confession of treason, 396; political results of, 407; power to wage, vested in Congress, 430; events of the war of the rebellion, 431 ; right to jury trials during, 504; reference to laws of, 507 ; war of 1812, reference to State of country during, 506; war never beneficial to a commercial nation, 578.

Washington, reference to character of, 505.

Webster, Daniel, argument of, in Ogden *v.* Saunders, 67, 83; defines power of Congress to pass bankrupt laws, 69; meaning of term obligation of contracts, remarks on duty of performing contracts, 71; State bankrupt laws impair, 72; existing law forms no part of contract, 73; considers constitutional grants and prohibitions, 79; letter to, in case of brig Gen. Armstrong, 232 ; submits

the Armstrong case to Napoleon, 222; reference to his eulogy on Washington, 419.

Wellesley, Lord, defense of his character by Lord Plunket, 628 ; his object in preventing the decoration of King William's statue, 630; real object of his visit to the theater, 650.

Wharton, Francis, definition of homicide, 325.

Wife, sacred relationship between husband and, 329; consent of wife no qualification of adulterer's guilt, 337; cannot shield him, 339.

Wilkes' outlawry case, observations of Lord Mansfield in passing judgment in, 550.

Wilkinson, Edward C., circumstances of his arrest and trial, 85; defense of, by Seargent S. Prentiss, 87.

William III, Prince of Orange, comparison of, to Tamerlane. 621 ; panegyric on, by Lord Plunket, 624; his campaign in Ireland a blessing in disguise, 626; Lord Wellesley's object in preventing decoration of statue of, 630; propriety of such decoration discussed by Mr. North, 647; scene in Dublin when the ceremony was forbidden, 647; Mr. North's reference to Mr. Plunket's panegyric on, 648; panegyric on, by Sir James Mackintosh, 600.

Williams, Thomas, indictment of, for blasphemy, 551; speech of Thomas Erskine for the prosecution, 554–566; his defense an anomaly in the law, 560.

Wirt, William, argument of, in Gibbons *v.* Ogden, 47–66; letter to Judge Carr, 49 ; reply to Emmett, 65 ; defines rules of constitutional construction, 50 ; distinguishes exclusive and concurrent powers, 51; defines nature and character of patent laws, 59; distinguishes quarantine and police regulations, 61; his reply to Emmett, 65.

Witness, inferences from refusal of, to answer under privilege, 278.